ISBN 978-0-428-09514-7
PIBN 11244836

1 MONTH OF
FREE
READING

at

www.ForgottenBooks.com

By purchasing this book you are eligible for one month membership to ForgottenBooks.com, giving you unlimited access to our entire collection of over 1,000,000 titles via our web site and mobile apps.

To claim your free month visit:
www.forgottenbooks.com/free1244836

English
Français
Deutsche
Italiano
Español
Português

www.forgottenbooks.com

Mythology Photography **Fiction**
Fishing Christianity **Art** Cooking
Essays Buddhism Freemasonry
Medicine **Biology** Music **Ancient
Egypt** Evolution Carpentry Physics
Dance Geology **Mathematics** Fitness
Shakespeare **Folklore** Yoga Marketing
Confidence Immortality Biographies
Poetry **Psychology** Witchcraft
Electronics Chemistry History **Law**
Accounting **Philosophy** Anthropology
Alchemy Drama Quantum Mechanics
Atheism Sexual Health **Ancient History**
Entrepreneurship Languages Sport
Paleontology Needlework Islam
Metaphysics Investment Archaeology
Parenting Statistics Criminology
Motivational

CATALOGUE

OF

LOMBARD COLLEGE,

GALESBURG, ILLINOIS,

FOR THE YEAR ENDING JUNE 7, 1900.

GALESBURG, ILL.:

THE WAGONER PRINTING CO.

1900.

College Calendar.

1900.
MARCH 6—Tuesday ....Third Term begins.
MARCH 6—Tuesday, 8 a. m...Registration.
MAY 19—Saturday...Senior Vacation begins.
MAY 31, JUNE 1—Thursday, Friday...................................Examinations.
JUNE 3—Sunday...Baccalaureate Sermon.
JUNE 4—Monday... Field Day.
JUNE 4—Monday...................................... Gymnasium Exhibition.
JUNE 4—Monday.......................Townsend Prize Contest in Declamation.
JUNE 5—Tuesday...Class Day.
JUNE 5—Tuesday...................Annual Meeting of Association of Graduates.
JUNE 5—Tuesday, Evening...............Exhibition of Department of Elocution.
JUNE 6—Wednesday...........................Meeting of the Board of Trustees.
JUNE 6—Wednesday, Evening...........................Commencement Concert.
JUNE 7—Thursday....................   ....Commencement Day.

Summer Vacation.

SEP. 3—Monday..Entrance Examinations.
SEP. 4—Tuesday................................. Beginning of the College Year.
SEP. 4—Tuesday ....First Term begins.
SEP. 4—Tuesday, 8 a. m..Registration.
NOV. 26, 27—Monday, Tuesday....................................Examinations.
NOV. 27—Tuesday..First Term Ends.

Thanksgiving Vacation.

DEC. 4—Tuesday......: ....Second Term begins.
DEC. 4—Tuesday, 8 a. m...Registration.
DEC. 21—Friday...........,.Last Day of Recitations preceding Christmas Recess.

Christmas Recess.

1901.
JAN. 2—Wednesday...........................Recitations of Second Term resumed.
JAN. 25—Friday, Evening..........................Swan Prize Contest in Oratory.
FEB. 12—Tuesday.....................................Holiday, Lincoln's Birthday.
FEB. 22—Friday..................................Holiday, Washington's Birthday.
MARCH 6, 7—Wednesday, Thursday................................Examinations
MARCH 7—Thursday..Second Term ends.

Spring Vacation.

MARCH 12—Tuesday..Third Term begins.
MARCH 12—Tuesday, 8 a. m............................ ....Registration.
MAY 30, 31—Thursday, Friday.....................................Examinations.
JUNE 2—Sunday...Baccalaureate Sermon.
JUNE 3—Monday .... Field Day.
JUNE 3—Monday..,. Gymnasium Exhibition.
JUNE 3—Monday, Evening.............Townsend Prize Contest in Declamation.
JUNE 4—Tuesday.................................... ....Class Day.
JUNE 4—Tuesday..............Annual Meeting of the Association of Graduates.
JUNE 4—Tuesday, afternoon.....................Annual Recital of Music Pupils.
JUNE 4—Tuesday, Evening...............Exhibition of Department of Elocution.
JUNE 5—Wednesday...........................Meeting of the Board of Trustees.
JUNE 5—Wednesday, Evening...........................Commencement Concert.
JUNE 6—Thursday..Commencement Day.

Board of Trustees.

CHARLES ELLWOOD NASH, D. D., EX-OFFICIO.

TERM EXPIRES.

*GEORGE TAPPER, *Riverside* ....1900.
ROBERT CHAPPELL, *Galesburg* ....1900.
HOWARD KNOWLES, *Galesburg.* ....1900.
LAKE W. SANBORN, *Galesburg* ....1900.
REV. JOHN HUGHES, *Table Grove* ....1900.
ALBERT WEBSTER, *Galesburg* ....1901.
W. W. WASHBURN, *Galesburg* ....1901.
HON. SAMUEL KERR, *189 La Salle St., Chicago* ....1901.
HON. J. B. HARSH, *Creston, Iowa* ....1901.
†REV. AMOS CRUM, D. D., *Webster City, Iowa* ....1901.
REV. GEO. B. STOCKING, D. D., *Galesburg* ....1902.
MRS. MARY CLAYCOMB GRUBB, *Galesburg.* ....1902.
ALMON KIDDER, *Monmouth* ....1902.
REV. M. D. SHUTTER, D. D., *Minneapolis, Minn.* ....1902.
C. A. WEBSTER, *Galesburg* ....1902.
JAMES L. LOMBARD, *Kansas City, Mo* ....1903.
THOMAS LOWRY, *Minneapolis, Minn* ....1903.
CHARLES STYER, *1511 Park Ave., Indianapolis, Ind* ....1903.
A. B. TOMPKINS, *Avon* ....1903.
J. D. WELSH, *Galesburg* ....1903.
HON. HAMILTON L. KARR, *Osceola, Iowa* ....1904.
J. N. CONGER, *Galesburg* ....1904.
REV. A. J. CANFIELD, D. D., PH. D., *Brooklyn, N. Y.* ....1904.
MRS. E. P. TOWNSEND, *Sycamore* ....1904.
HON. LYMAN McCARL, *Quincy* ....1904.

*Deceased, Jan. 9, 1900.
†Deceased, Jan. 30, 1900.

Officers of the Board.

HON. SAMUEL KERR, CHICAGO,
PRESIDENT.

CHARLES A. WEBSTER, GALESBURG,
TREASURER.

PHILIP G. WRIGHT, GALESBURG,
SECRETARY.

W. F. CADWELL, GALESBURG,
AUDITOR.

Executive Committee.

HOWARD KNOWLES, CHAIRMAN,

W. W. WASHBURN, SECRETARY,

CHARLES ELLWOOD NASH, D. D.,

ROBERT CHAPPELL.   CHARLES A. WEBSTER.

Board of Visitors.

Each Universalist State Convention, which adopts Lombard College as its Institution of Learning, is entitled to send two visitors, whose duty it is to examine into the condition of the College and to assist in the choice of Trustees.

GENERAL STATEMENT.

LOCATION.

LOMBARD COLLEGE is located in Galesburg, Knox County, Illinois, a healthful and beautiful city of 20,000 inhabitants, noted for its public buildings, its elegant churches, and the good order, intelligence, thrift, and refinement of its people.

Galesburg is easily accessible by railroad from all parts of the West; being the center of the great Burlington R. R. system, leading to Chicago, Burlington, Quincy, Peoria, Rock Island, St. Louis, Kansas City, Omaha, Denver, and Minneapolis; and also the terminus of the Fulton County Narrow Gauge R. R., connecting with the great Wabash system. It is on the main line of the Santa Fe system.

THE COLLEGE CAMPUS.

The College Campus is situated in the southeastern part of the city and may readily be reached by the electric cars. It is thirteen acres in extent, and affords ample space for base ball, foot ball, tennis, and other athletic sports. A large part is planted with trees, which have been growing many years and have attained noble size and graceful forms. Among them are pines, larches, hemlocks, cedars, maples, elms, ash-trees, tulip-trees, and others, embracing about forty species. The trees and lawns are well kept and cared for, and the beauty of the surroundings thus created is a pleasing and attractive feature of the College.

HISTORY.

The Illinois Liberal Institute was chartered in 1851, opened for students in the autumn of 1852, invested with College powers in 1853, and took the name of Lombard University (in honor of Mr. Benjamin Lombard, at that time the largest donor to its properties) in 1855. It was one of the first Colleges in the country to admit women as students on the same terms with men, allowing them to graduate in the same class and with the same honors. The first class was graduated in 1856. The Ryder Divinity School was opened September 5, 1881.

THE ELECTIVE SYSTEM.

Experience has demonstrated the soundness of the educational principle that the selection of studies, in some degree, at least, should be adapted to the needs, tastes, and talents of the student. At Lombard this principle is fully recognized, and the greatest liberty is given to students in the choice of their studies. At the same time the fact is recognized that there is a distinct educational gain to a student in pursuing a well matured and logically developed course of study. The method by which it is sought to reconcile these important principles of education at Lombard is fully explained on page 28.

THE COLLEGE YEAR.

The College year begins early in September and closes early in June. It is divided into three terms of approximately equal length. (See Calendar, page 2.)

Students should, if possible, enter at the beginning of the College year, since much of the work is arranged progressively from that date. They will, however, be allowed to enter at any time when there seems a prospect of their being able to do so profitably.

Commencement day occurs the first Thursday in June.

APPORTIONMENT OF TIME.

The regular sessions of the College are held on Monday, Tuesday, Wednesday, Thursday, and Friday.

From the courses of study offered, each student is expected to elect work to an amount sufficient to keep him profitably employed. In all full courses each recitation occupies one hour. Absence from a recitation will forfeit the mark in that study for the day.

GRADES OF SCHOLARSHIP.

At the end of every term the standing of a student in each of his courses will be expressed, according to his proficiency, by one of four grades, designated respectively by the letters A, B, C, D.

The grade is determined by term work estimated on the basis of attendance, quality of recitations or laboratory work, occasional tests, written exercises, etc., and by final examinations at the end of the term, the term grade and the final examination being valued in the ratio of two to one.

Grade C is the lowest which will be accepted in any study as counting towards the fulfillment of the requirements of graduation.

Students who receive grade D in any study shall not elect more than three courses for the succeeding term.

Students whose lowest grade is C in one or more studies, shall not elect more than three and one-half courses for the succeeding term.

Students whose lowest grade is B in two or more studies, shall not elect more than four courses for the succeeding term.

Students whose lowest grade is B in one course, shall not elect more than four and one-half courses for the succeeding term.

CHAPEL EXERCISES.

Religious exercises, at which attendance is required, are conducted daily in the college chapel.

With the view of imparting additional interest and value to these exercises, relieving them of mere formality, brief addresses by members of the faculty or by invited speakers upon practical life questions or upon topics of the day, will be given from time to time. At intervals, also, special musical numbers will be introduced by the Director of the Musical Department.

APPARATUS.

The department of Physics is well equipped with apparatus for experimentation. Students have an opportunity to obtain a practical acquaintance with the principles of Physics through a series of Laboratory experiments, which they perform for themselves under the direction of the instructor.

LABORATORY.

The extended courses in Chemistry, described elsewhere in this Catalogue, require a large amount of practical work on the part of the student. Each student in Chemistry has a desk provided with gas, water, re-agents, and all necessary conveniences. The Laboratory is thoroughly equipped for work in General Chemistry, and in Qualitative and Quantitative Analysis.

MUSEUM.

The Museum contains valuable collections duly classified and arranged, and available for purposes of instruction. The collection of corals is especially fine. A fine collection of minerals, birds and ethnological specimens, the loan of A. B. Cowan, Esq., a former citizen of Galesburg, is known and designated as the Cowan collection.

LIBRARY.

The Library of the College contains about seven thousand volumes. It is located in the College building and is open daily. The books are systematically arranged and easy of access. They may be taken out by the students upon application to the Librarian.

READING ROOM.

A Reading Room under the auspices of a Reading Room Association is supported by the voluntary efforts and contributions of the students, faculty and friends. The leading newspapers and periodicals are kept on file. The Reading Room is open daily, except Sundays, for the use of the students, from 8:00 a. m. until 6:00 p. m.

GYMNASIUM.

The Gymnasium is a building 50 x 80 feet on the ground. On the ground floor, besides the Gymnasium proper, there is a large room, at present used as a recitation room, which can be thrown into the main room by withdrawing the movable partitions. There is also a stage, equipped with an adequate outfit of scenery, for the special use of the Department of Elocution. A gallery runs around the building, affording a suitable running track for indoor practice. The basement contains bathrooms and lockers, and other conveniences.

Regular exercise in the Gymasium will be required of all students for two years of their college course. The exercise will consist of class drill, under the charge of a director, or of special work on the apparatus in accordance with the prescription of the medical examiner. It is intended that the instruction shall be thoroughly scientific, aiming not so much at special muscular or athletic development, as at a sound physical culture, which is the true basis of health and so of energy and endurance.

ATHLETICS.

The Athletic interests of the college are in charge of a Board of Management consisting of three members chosen from the student body, two from the faculty, and four from the alumni. The Campus affords opportunity for foot ball, base ball, and track and field events. During the past year a quarter mile track has been laid out and bleachers erected. During the winter basket ball is played in the Gymnasium. The foot ball team receives regular training from a competent coach.

THE LADIES' HALL.

The new Ladies' Hall, finished and first opened for use in the Fall of 1896, is a thoroughly modern building and complete in all its appointments. It is heated by steam, lighted by gas, fitted with sanitary plumbing, including porcelain baths, closets, lavatories, etc., and supplied with every convenience of a well equipped home. The Hall will accommodate forty young ladies; and all non-resident lady students, unless permission is obtained from the President to live elsewhere, are expected to make their home in this building.

Each room is finished with hard wood floor and furnished with bedstead, springs, mattress, chairs, desk, dresser, and rugs. The occupants are expected to furnish bedding, pillows, towels, napkins, to pay for washing of said articles, and to keep their own rooms in order.

The charge for board is $36 per term for each person, payable in advance. This does not include the Christmas recess. The charge for room rent is from $6 to $15 per term, according to location of room, payable to the registrar in advance. Where one person occupies a double room from choice an extra charge of 50 cents a week will be made; but the privilege of assigning two persons to such room, is reserved.

Board will be furnished to women students of the College who do not have rooms in the Hall for $2.75 a week, payable in advance.

Applications for rooms in the hall should be made during the summer vacation to the Treasurer, Charles A. Webster, Galesburg; at other times to the lady in charge, Mrs. Emily A. Hadley.

THE LOMBARD REVIEW.

A College paper, called *The Lombard Review*, is published monthly by the students. It makes a record of College events, and serves as a medium of communication with the friends and Alumni of the College. Subscription price $1.00.

THE LOMBARD LETTER

is a small publication issued every month by the college administration as a medium of announcements and appeals. Subscription 25 cents. Sample copies sent on application.

SOCIETIES.

The Erosophian.

The Erosophian Society was organized January 29, 1860. Any gentleman connected with the College or Divinity School is eligible to membership, and is entitled to all the benefits of the, society. Its regular meetings are held on Friday evening of each week. The literary exercises consist of orations, debates, and essays.

The Zetecalian.

This Society was organized in 1863, by the ladies of the University. Its exercises consist of debates, essays, historical narrations, and general discussions. Regular meetings are held on Wednesday afternoon of each week. The officers are elected quarterly.

PRIZES.

1. The Swan Prizes.

Two prizes for excellence in Oratory are offered annually by Mrs. J. H. Swan, of Chicago. They are of the value of fifteen dollars and ten dollars, respectively. The contest for these prizes is held in January.

2. The Townsend Prizes.

Two prizes for excellence in Declamation are offered annually by Mrs. E. P. Townsend, of Sycamore. They are of the value of fifteen dollars and ten dollars, respectively. The contest for these prizes is held during Commencement week.

3. Faculty Prize.

A prize of twenty dollars, donated by the faculty, will be given for original work upon an assigned subject. The subject for 1900-1901 will be "A Scheme for the Organization of Public Charities in Galesburg."

EXPENSES.

Boarding.

Good board, including furnished room, fuel, and light, may be obtained at $2.50 per week and upwards.

Not infrequently students board themselves. This method of boarding is especially adapted to students living near Galesburg and coming from the same family or neighborhood. Unfurnished rooms may be hired at $1.00 per month and upwards. The whole cost of living in this way need not exceed $1.50 per week.

The yearly expenses, exclusive of tuition, may be set down as follows:

To those who board themselves—

Room-rent, boarding, fuel and light, at $1.50 per week	$57 00
Charges for incidentals, per annum	12 00
Washing, estimated for the year	15 00
Books	15 00
Total	$99 00

To those who pay the medium rates in private families, the cost will be $3.25 per week for board, room, fuel, and light, making an addition to the foregoing estimate of $66 per annum.

A faculty committee will assist students in securing comfortable, home-like accommodations.

The charge for board in the Ladies' Hall is $36 per term, for each person, payable in advance. This does not include the

Christmas recess. The charge for room rent is from $6 to $15 per term, according to location of room, payable to the registrar in advance. Where one person occupies a double room from choice an extra charge of 50 cents per week will be made, but the privilege of assigning two persons to such room is reserved. Board will be furnished to women students of the College who do not have rooms in the Hall at the rate of $2.75 per week, payable in advance.

Tuition and Incidentals.

In the College of Liberal Arts and in the Preparatory School the student will pay a tuition fee for each study pursued. The charge, except in theoretical music, is $3.50 per term for each full course; a course being a study taken for one term and counting as one credit toward graduation. The rate for each fractional course is in proportion to the credit allowed for such fractional course toward graduation. Thus, a half course is half rate; a third course, third rate, etc.

Students in Chemistry are required to deposit with the Registrar a sum sufficient to cover laboratory bills. Students in General Chemistry will deposit two dollars, students in Analytical Chemistry, five dollars, and students in Mineralogy, three dollars, each. At the close of the term there will be returned the balance remaining after deducting cost of chemicals and broken apparatus.

The charge for incidentals, to be paid by all students of the College, is $4.00 per term.

No student will be enrolled in any class until he presents the Registrar's receipt for the payment of Tuition and Incidentals. The registration fee is twenty-five cents. The payment of this fee will be remitted to all who register on the first day of the term.

Tuition and Incidentals will not be refunded. In case a student is absent a half term or more from sickness or other adequate cause a certificate for a half term's tuition and incidentals will be given the student (at his request), said certificate good "to order" for its face value at any succeeding term.

Art and Music.

For information as to charges in Art and Music, see under these Departments later in this Catalogue.

AID TO WORTHY STUDENTS.

Free tuition will be given to the student who graduates with

highest rank from an approved high school.   Students receiving
this concession may be called upon for some College service.

Through the generosity of its friends the College is enabled to offer assistance to worthy students desiring to secure
an education.   The income of endowed scholarships is applied
toward paying the tuition of a limited number.

Perpetual Scholarships.

Sixteen Perpetual Scholarships of $1,000 each have been
founded by the following named persons.

The F. R. E. Cornell Scholarship, by Mrs. E. O. Cornell.
The George B. Wright Scholarship, by Mrs. C. A. Wright.
The George Power Scholarship, by George and James E. Power.
The Mrs. Emma Mulliken Scholarship, by Mrs. Emma Mulliken.
The Clement F. LeFevre Scholarship, by William LeFevre and Mrs. Ellen
R. Coleman.
The Samuel Bowles Scholarship, by Samuel Bowles.
The Dollie B. Lewis Scholarship, by Mrs. Dollie B. Lewis.
The O. B. Ayres Scholarship, by O. B. Ayres.
The C. A. Newcomb Scholarship, by C. A. Newcomb.
The Mary Chapin Perry Scholarship, by T. T. Perry.
The Mary W. Conger Scholarship, by the children of Mrs. Mary W. Conger.
The Hattie A. Drowne Scholarship, by Rev. E. L. Conger, D. D.
The A. R. Wolcott Scholarship, by A. R. Wolcott.
The Woman's Association Scholarship, by the U. W. A. of Illinois.
The Calista Waldron Slade Scholarship, by E. D. Waldron and sisters.
The Mary L. Pingrey Scholarship, by Mrs. Mary L. Pingrey.

BEQUESTS.

For the convenience of those who may wish to secure, by bequest, to the University, any given sum for a specific purpose,
the accompanying form is here given:

I hereby give and bequeath to The Lombard College.........
for ....(state the object).......and direct that my
executor pay said bequest to the Treasurer of said College
within...........after my death.

(Signed)...................... ....

Dated....... ... .

CATALOGUES.

Former students of the College, whether graduates or not,
are requested to inform the President of any change of residence, in order that the publications of the college may be sent
to them.   Catalogues and Circulars of information will be sent
to all that apply for them.

MORALE AND SOCIAL POLICY.

Aside from a few obvious regulations designed to secure punctuality and regularity in attendance on college exercises, and to protect students and teachers from disturbance while at work, no formal rules are imposed upon the students.

It is expected that, as young men and women of somewhat mature years, they will observe the usual forms of good breeding, and enjoy the ordinary privileges of good society in so far as the latter do not conflict with the best interests of the institution or with their own health and intellectual advancement.

Should any student show a disposition to engage in conduct detrimental to his own best interests, or to those of his fellow students or of the college, the faculty will deal with the case in such manner as will protect the common welfare of all.

OFFICERS OF THE COLLEGE.

CHARLES ELLWOOD NASH, A. M., S. T. D., PRESIDENT,

*Hall Professor of Intellectual and Moral Philosophy.

A. B., Lombard University, 1875; B. D., Tufts College, 1878; A. M., Lombard University, 1878; S. T. D.,Tufts College, 1891; President Lombard College, 1895—.

ISAAC AUGUSTUS PARKER, A. M., PH. D.,

†Williamson Professor of the Greek Language and Literature.

A. B., Dartmouth College, 1853; A. M., ibid, 1856; Ph. D., Buchtel College, 1892; Principal Orleans Liberal Institute, Glover, Vt., 1853-58; Professor of Ancient Languages, Lombard University, 1858-68; Professor of Greek Language and Literature, Lombard College, 1868—.

NEHEMIAH WHITE, A. M., PH. D., S. T. D.,

In charge of the Ryder Divinity School, Professor of Biblical Languages and Exegesis.

A. B., Middlebury College, 1857; A. M., ibid, 1860; Ph. D., St. Lawrence University, 1876; S. T. D., Tufts College,1889; Associate Principal Green Mt. Perkins Institute, 1857-58; Principal Clinton Liberal Institute, 1859-60; Principal Pulaski Academy, 1865; Professor Mathematics and Natural Science, St. Lawrence University, 1865-71; Professor Ancient Languages, Buchtel College, 1872-75; President Lombard University, 1875-92; In charge of the Ryder Divinity School, and Professor of Biblical Languages and Exegesis, 1892—.

JON WATSON GRUBB, M. S.,

Professor of Latin and Instructor in charge of the Preparatory School.

B. S., Lombard University, 1879; M. S., Lombard University, 1882; Adjunct Professor of Mathematics, Lombard University, 1882-94; Registrar, Lombard University, 1893—; Professor of Latin, Lombard College, 1894—.

FREDERICK WILLIAM RICH, B. S.,

‡Conger Professor of Natural Science.

B. S., Cornell University, 1881; Graduate Student, Cornell University, 1881; Instructor in Analytical Chemistry, Cornell University, 1882-84; Professor Natural Science, Lombard College, 1884—.

PHILIP GREEN WRIGHT, A. M.,

Professor of Mathematics, Astronomy, and Economics.

A. M. B., Tufts College, 1884; A. M., Harvard University, 1887; Teacher of Mathematics and Science, Goddard Seminary, Vt., 1883; Adjunct Professor of Mathematics, Buchtel College, 1884-86; Professor of Mathematics Lombard College, 1892—.

---

*In honor of the late E. G. Hall of Chicago.
†In honor of the late I. D Williamson, D. D., of Cincinnati.
‡In honor of the late L. E. Conger, of Dexter, Iowa.

FRANK HAMILTON FOWLER, Ph. D.,

Professor of English Literature and Rhetoric.

A. B., Lombard University, 1890; Ph. D., The University of Chicago, 1896; Graduate Student, Johns Hopkins University, 1890-91; Principal Peaster Academy, 1891-92; Fellow in the University of Chicago, 1892-96; Professor of English Literature, Lombard College, 1897—.

RALPH GRIERSON KIMBLE,

Professor of Sociology.

A. B., Lombard University, 1896; University Scholar University of Chicago, 1896-97; Fellow, ibid, 1897-1900; Professor of Sociology, Lombard College, 1900—.

KARL JAKOB RUDOLPH LUNDBERG,

Director of Music Department, and Instructor in Voice, Piano, Organ and Theory.

Graduate Royal Musical Academy of Stockholm, Sweden, in voice, piano, organ and theory 1892; studied voice with Prof. Ivar Hallstrom, 1893; organist and choirmaster in Lindesberg, Sweden, 1894-1897; Musical Director, Burlington Institute College, Burlington, Iowa, 1897-1899; Director of Music Department, Lombard College, 1899—.

EMMA B. WAIT,

Professor of French and German.

Principal of Schools, Los Angeles, California, 1881-83; Student, École Sévigné, Sévres, 1891, Université de Génève, 1896-98, The University of Chicago, 1899; Professor of French and German, Lombard College, 1899—.

MAUD AUGUSTA MINER,

Instructor in Elocution and Dramatic Art, and Instructor for Women in Physical Culture.

Graduated from Chicago Conservatory, 1895; studied with Prof. S. H. Clark, University of Chicago; Holman-Dickerman School, Chicago, 1895-96; Private studio, 1896-98; Instructor in Elocution, Dramatic Art, and Physical Culture, Lombard College, 1898—.

M. ISABELLE BLOOD,

Instructor in Drawing and Painting.

Studied with Dean Fletcher, N. Y.; William Bertram, Chicago; at the Art Institute and with Nellie Davis, St. Louis; Instructor in Drawing and Painting, Lombard College, 1889—.

FAY ALEXANDER BULLUCK,

Assistant in Gymnasium.

EMILY AUGUSTA HADLEY,

Principal in charge of the Ladies' Hall.

Dr. GUY A. LONGBRAKE and Dr. DELIA M. RICE,

Medical Examiners.

NON-RESIDENT LECTURER.

MARION D. SHUTTER, D. D.

FRANK HAMILTON FOWLER, PH. D.,
Librarian.

DONALD McALPINE,
Assistant Librarian.

JON WATSON GRUBB, M. S.,
Registrar.

FREDERICK WILLIAM RICH, B. S.,
Curator of the Museum.

PHILIP G. WRIGHT, A. M.,
Director of the Gymnasium.

ALLEN HARSHBARGER,
Janitor.

STANDING FACULTY COMMITTEES.

ADVISORY—
PROFESSORS WRIGHT AND FOWLER.

CREDITS—
PROFESSORS PARKER AND RICH.

HOMES FOR NEW STUDENTS—
PROFESSOR FOWLER.

CATALOGUE—
PROFESSORS WRIGHT AND FOWLER.

HIGHER DEGREES—
PRESIDENT NASH AND PROFESSOR PARKER.

LIBRARY—
PROFESSORS WHITE AND WAIT.

CHAPEL EXCUSES—
PROFESSORS RICH AND GRUBB.

CHAPEL EXERCISES—
PRES. NASH, PROFS. WAIT AND LUNDBERG.

ATHLETICS—
PROFESSORS WRIGHT AND MINER.

ORDER AND DISCIPLINE—
PRESIDENT NASH, PROFS. RICH AND PARKER.

ORGANIZATION.

The College embraces four distinct Departments of Instruction:

   I. THE COLLEGE OF LIBERAL·ARTS.

  II. THE PREPARATORY SCHOOL.

 III. THE RYDER DIVINITY SCHOOL.

 IV. THE SCHOOL OF MUSIC AND ART.

College of
of
Liberal
Arts

Faculty of Liberal Arts.

CHARLES ELLWOOD NASH, A. M., S. T. D., PRESIDENT,

NEHEMIAH WHITE, A. M., PH. D., S. T. D.,
*Hall Professor of Intellectual and Moral Philosophy.

ISAAC AUGUSTUS PARKER, A. M., PH. D.,
†Williamson Professor of the Greek Language and Literature.

RALPH GRIERSON KIMBLE,
Professor of Sociology.

JON WATSON GRUBB, M. S.
Professor of Latin.

FREDERICK WILLIAM RICH, B. S.,
‡Conger Professor of Natural Science.

EMMA B. WAIT,
Professor of French and German.

PHILIP GREEN WRIGHT, A. M.,
Professor of Mathematics, Astronomy, and Economics.

FRANK HAMILTON FOWLER, PH. D.,
Professor of English Literature and Rhetoric.

KARL JAKOB RUDOLPH LUNDBERG,
Professor of Musical Theory.

MAUD AUGUSTA MINER,
Instructor in Elocution and Physical Culture.

---

*In honor of the late E. G. Hall, of Chicago.
†In honor of the late I. D. Williamson, D. D., of Cincinnati.
‡In honor of the late L. E. Conger, of Dexter, Iowa.

Degrees Conferred in 1899.

MASTER OF ARTS.

John Wesley Hanson, Jr., (causa honoris)..............*Chicago.*

BACHELOR OF ARTS.

Christen Martin Alsager................................. ....*Lee.*
Ella Berry Boston............................ ....*Galesburg.*
Henry William Dubee......................*Grand Haven, Mich.*
Howard Everett Foster............................. *Galesburg.*
Homer Edwin Garvin...... ....*Quincy.*
Fannie Pauline Gingrich....... .. ..*Galesburg.*
George Runyan Longbrake..........................*Galesburg.*
Helen Jessie MacKay.... ....*Galesburg.*
Nellie Stuart Russell .... *Woodhull.*
Benjamin Franklin Stacey............... ....*Chicago.*
Lora Adelle Townsend............................ ...*Galesburg.*

Candidates for Degrees in 1900.

CANDIDATE FOR THE DEGREE OF MASTER OF ARTS.

Claude Bryant Warner........... ....*Avon.*

CANDIDATES FOR THE DEGREE OF BACHELOR OF ARTS.

Martha Belle Arnold.................................*Galesburg.*
Fay Alexander Bulluck..............................*Galesburg.*
Gertrude Grace Kidder..............................*Galesburg.*
Edwin Julius McCullough.................... *La Prairie Center.*
Carrie Ruth Nash..... ... .*Galesburg.*
Charles Wait Orton....... ....*Mt. Pleasant, Ia.*
Burt G. Shields........ ....*Galesburg.*
Iva May Steckel..*Macomb.*
Earle Walcott Watson....................................*Barry.*
Harry William Weeks................................*Galesburg.*

Students in the College of Liberal Arts. ✓

Charlotte Alspaugh.................... ....*Washington, Kan.*
John Andrew, Jr....................................*New Salem.*
Martha Belle Arnold................................*Galesburg.*
John Donington Bartlett.... .... *Galesburg.*
Pearle Bigger...*Galesburg.*
George Melvin Boyer................................*Altamont.*
Bertha Pamele Bradford................................*Quincy.*
Athol Ray Brown............................*North Henderson.*
Murray Truman Bruner...................... ....*Gerlaw.*
Nannie Mer Buck............................ ....*Le Roy.*
Fay Alexander Bulluck...............................*Galesburg.*
Jessie Evelyn Collins..................... .... *Stoughton, Wis.*
Sarah Lucy Cook.......................................*Le Roy.*
Edna May Cranston............................. ....-*Galesburg.*
Charles Julius Efner...............................*Galesburg.*
Edna Ethel Epperson....................................*Rio.*
Henry Ericson........ ....*Galesburg.*
Mae Victoria Fifield.................................. *Buda.*
Dudley Claude Fosher...............................*Galesburg.*
Anna Moore Gillis......................*Mt. Pleasant, Ia.*
Lillian Charles Harris..... ....*Galesburg.*
Claude Webster Hartgrove......................... *Galesburg.*
Gertrude West Hartgrove..................... ....*Galesburg.*
Virginia C. Henney..............................*Mitchellville, Ia.*
Augusta Eaton Hitchcock...................... . ....*Osage, Ia.*
Eugene Mark Holroyd............................... *Chicago.*
Major Clifford Holroyd..............................*Chicago.*
Harrie Albin Jansen...... ....*Woodhull.*
Gertrude Grace Kidder........................ ....*Galesburg.*
Florence Pearl King............................. .... *Waukegan.*
Donald McAlpine................................*Charlotte, Mich.*
Edwin Julius McCullough.....................*La Prairie Center.*
Jennie Eliza Marriott..............................*La Moille.*
Helen Augusta Miles................................ *Galesburg.*
Robert Todd Miller..............................*Monmouth.*
Mabel Louise Mills.................................*Ossian, Ia.*
Carrie Ruth Nash..................................*Galesburg.*
Charles Wait Orton............................*Mt. Pleasant, Ia.*

Grace Olive Pingrey....................... ....*Coon Rapids, Ia.*
Frederick Preston......... ....*Boston, Mass.*
Jenkins Bennett Rees................................*Galesburg.*
Grace Schnur...*Adams.*
Burt G. Shields................................ *Galesburg.*
Edwin Milton Smith ....*Edinburg.*
Iva May Steckel......................................*Macomb.*
Herbert Leonard Stoughton...........................*Osage, Ia.*
Nellie Clanton Turner........................ ...*Unionville, Mo.*
Mary Warner......................................*Table Grove.*
Earle Walcott Watson ....*Barry.*
Harry William Weeks................................*Galesburg.*

The following students have each twenty-one or more preparatory credits, but lack one or more of the credits in specific
studies requisite to full college standing: (See p. 25.)

James Earl Bowles......................................*Astoria.*
Kate Clark................................ ....*Maquon.*
Inez May De Voll.................................*Stoughton, Wis.*
Frederick Dickinson ....*Chicago.*
Earl Eppsteiner....... ....*Galesburg.*
Emma Flinn...................................... ......*Galesburg.*
Rob Roy Grubb................................ ....*Galesburg.*
Spencer Pritchard Howell........... .... *Woodhull.*
Harrison Burton Linderholm..........................*Altona.*
Edith Louise Miller...................................*Monmouth.*
Floyd Selby....................... ....*Maquon.*
Clifford Hoxey Wolcott................. ... .*Hillsdale, Mich.*

SPECIAL STUDENTS.

Ella Berry Boston............................. ....*Galesburg.*
Emma Hutchings Browning....................... *Galesburg.*
Annie Coleman........................ ....*Dallas, Tex.*
Mamie Ferris...*Galesburg.*

Admission and Graduation.

REQUIREMENTS FOR ADMISSION.

The number of credits required for admission to the College of Liberal Arts is twenty-one. These twenty-one credits must include three in Mathematics, three in English, six in some language other than English, three in History, and three in Natural Science. The following list includes the subjects most frequently presented by students applying for admission, together with the credit allowed for each. Any excess of credits presented upon entering will count on requirements for graduation.

SUBJECTS.	CREDITS.
English (usual High School course)	3
German (one year's High School work or equivalent)	2
French " " " " " " "	2
Harkness' Latin Grammar and Reader	2
Cæsar's Commentaries, four to six books	2
Cicero, six to eight orations	2
Virgil, four books.	2
Greek Grammar and Lessons	2
Xenophon's Anabasis, two to four books	2
Homer's Iliad, three books	1
Elementary Algebra	2
Plane Geometry	1
Solid Geometry	1
Descriptive Astronomy	1
Physics: Carhart and Chute's Elements of Physics, or an equivalent	1
Chemistry: Remsen's Elements of Chemistry, or an equivalent	1
Physical Geography: Tarr's Elements, or an equivalent	1
Botany: Gray's, or an equivalent	1
Physiology: Martin's Human Body, or an equivalent	1
Grecian and Roman History (elementary)	1
History of the United States	1
History of England	1
Civil Government	1

The work expected in the above studies may be seen from the detailed descriptions in the body of this catalogue.

In estimating credits the unit is the value of one term's work in this institution. The value of grades brought from other schools will be estimated by a comparison with this unit. Our experience has shown that this unit is practically equivalent in general to a half year's work in the best high schools.

Students may meet the above requirements by examination, by promotion from the Preparatory School, or by certificate (without examination) from certain approved schools.

In the last case the candidate, applying for admission, will be furnished with blank forms, upon which the subjects pursued in the school, the number of weeks, and the number of hours per week devoted to each, the text-book used, and the grade attained, are to be explicitly stated. These certificates, when endorsed by the principal of the school, or other responsible officer, will be received in lieu of an examination, and credits will be given to such an extent as the work done seems fairly to warrant, the above table being the basis of estimate. Students so received, however, are understood to be admitted to classes on probation; and if, after a week's trial, it is found that their previous training is insufficient to render it advisable for them to continue in these classes, they will be assigned work elsewhere.

ADMISSION TO ADVANCED STANDING.

Students from other institutions, who present letters of honorable dismissal, may be admitted to such standing and upon such terms as the Faculty may deem equitable. Every such student is required to present, along with the catalogue of the institution in which he has studied, a full statement, duly certified, of the studies he has completed, including preparatory studies. Candidates for advanced standing who wish to receive credit for work accomplished in private study, are permitted to take examinations in such subjects upon payment of the regular term fee for the course in which the examination is taken. A minimum residence of the two terms next preceding the completion of the requirements for graduation, and a minimum of eight courses taken in this College, are required of all applicants for a baccalaureate degree.

ADMISSION AS SPECIAL STUDENTS.

Persons who are not candidates for a degree may be admitted as special students to such courses as they are qualified to pursue. They will be required to maintain a standing in all respects satisfactory to the instructor in charge of each study chosen.

NON-RESIDENT STUDENTS.

Non-resident students who pursue any course of study taken by a class in the College, may be examined with the class in that course and receive a certificate for successful work, upon payment of the usual tuition fee for the course.

GRADUATION.

The degree of Bachelor of Arts will be conferred upon any candidate who has satisfactorily completed the aggregate of forty courses, elected from the studies offered in the College of Liberal Arts, in addition to the twenty-one courses required for admission. The forty credits must include a major course in Mathematics, English, Ancient or Modern Language, Natural Science, or Philosophy, as approved by the candidate's official adviser or by the advisory committee.

Every student who is a candidate for a degree, or a diploma, is required to present a graduation thesis upon some subject in which he, or she, has prosecuted original research or special study.

The subject selected for treatment must be approved by the President within four weeks after the opening of the Fall term.

A syllabus of the thesis must be handed to the President at least six weeks before the close of the Winter term.

The completed thesis is limited to fifteen hundred words, and must be handed in for criticism at least ten weeks before Commencement.

In lieu of a thesis, original work, performed under the direction of some member of the Faculty, may be accepted.

Five members from the graduating class, (three from the College of Liberal Arts, and two from the Divinity School,) will be selected by the Faculty to represent the class as speakers on Commencement Day. The basis of selection will be excellence in scholarship (two points); excellence of thesis (one point); and excellence of delivery of thesis (one point).

Degrees will be conferred only on the annual Commencement Day.

ADVANCED DEGREES.

The Master's degree will be conferred upon graduates of this College, or of other institutions of equal rank, on the satisfactory completion of ten courses, pursued in actual study at this College, beyond the requirements for the baccalaureate degree. The candidate must present a thesis showing original research in the special line of study pursued.

Departments and Courses of Instruction.

ENTRANCE CREDITS.

All candidates for admission to the College who expect to receive credit for work done in other schools, should, if possible, submit their certificates, properly filled out, before applying for admission. To facilitate this process, blank forms of such certificates are kept on file in many of the leading high schools of the State, and the same will be promptly sent to any person applying for them.

Hereafter no candidate will be admitted to classes without examination who has not presented his certificate, and even in cases where certificates are presented, the student is understood to be admitted to a class on probation. If, after a week's trial, it is found that his previous training is insufficient to justify his continuing in that class, he will be assigned work elsewhere.

INDIVIDUALIZATION.

An effort is made at Lombard to deal with each student according to his individual needs. The candidate is first required to confer with the Advisory Committee. Then, his previous course of study and his present state of mental discipline having been ascertained as accurately as possible, he will choose, subject to the advice of this committee, such a course of study as shall seem best adapted to meet his requirements. Some member of the Faculty is then appointed the student's official adviser, who shall have supervision of his work during his entire college course.

RECITATIONS AND CREDITS.

The following studies are classed as full courses or fractional courses, according to the estimated amount of work in each, and its value in fulfilling the requirements for graduation. Unless otherwise stated, a course in any study consists of five hours of recitations or lectures, per week, for one term. Certain courses, however, are given in three hours per week recitations. Laboratory courses require ten hours of work per week in the Laboratory, in addition to a considerable amount of study outside. Certain other studies, as indicated in each case, count only as half courses, or less.

ENGLISH.

[For courses 1 to 4 inclusive see Preparatory Department.]

5. The Forms of Discourse.

Baldwin's Specimens of Prose Description and Baker's Specimens of Argumentation will be used as texts. Weekly themes will be required. Tuesday, Wednesday, Thursday, and Friday. Fall term.   Professor FOWLER.

Open to students who have completed English 4.

6. The Forms of Discourse. (Continued.)

Brewster's Specimens of Narration and Lamont's Specimens of Exposition will be used as texts. Weekly Themes will be required. Tuesday, Wednesday, Thursday, and Friday. Winter term.   Professor FOWLER.

Open to students who have completed English 4.

7. Daily Themes. (Half Course.)

The object of this course is the attainment of rapidity and skill in composition. Each student will be required to hand in a short theme daily for one term. Class meets for conference and criticism every Friday. Winter term.

Professor WRIGHT.

Open to students who have completed English 5.

8. Daily Themes. (Half Course.)

This course is similar to English 7. Tuesday. Spring term.

Professor FOWLER.

Open to students who have completed English 5.

9. English Lyric Poetry.

Wordsworth, Tennyson, Browning. Fall term.

Professor FOWLER.

Open to students who have completed English 4.

10. English Prose.

Caxton, Addison, Macaulay. Fall term.

Professor FOWLER.

Open to students who have completed English 4.

[English 10 will not be given in 1900.]

11. Old English.

An introduction to the older language. Cook's first book in

Old English will be used as a text. The relations between Old and Modern English will be studied. Winter term.

Professor FOWLER.

Open to students who have completed English 4.

12. History of the English Language and Literature.

Lectures and text-book recitations. Taine's History of English Literature and Emerson's History of the English Language will be used as texts. Winter term.   Professor FOWLER.

Open to students who have completed English 4.

[English 12 will not be given in 1900-01.]

13. The English Drama.

Shakespeare will form the center of the work. Two or three plays will be studied critically and the class will read a number of plays by different authors. Spring term.

Professor FOWLER.

Open to students who have completed English 4.

14. Epic Poetry.

Milton. Spring term.   Professor FOWLER.

Open to students who have completed English 4.

[English 14 will not be given in 1901.]

FRENCH.

1. Elementary Course.

Pronunciation, grammar, conversation, and composition. Edgren's Grammar, Part I. Fall term.   Miss WAIT.

Open to all students of the College of Liberal Arts.

2. Elementary Course.

Grammar, composition, conversation, dictation. Van Daell's Introduction to French Authors. Halévy, L'Abbé Constantin. Winter term.   Miss WAIT.

Open to students who have completed French 1.

3. Elementary Course.

Grammar. Grandgent, French composition. George Sand, La Mare au Diable. Labiche et Martin, Le Voyage de M. Perrichon. Spring term.   Miss WAIT.

Open to students who have completed French 2.

4. Advanced Course.

Syntax, Composition. Molière, L' Avare, Le Bourgeois Gentilhomme; Hugo, Quatrevingt-treize. Fall term.

Miss WAIT.

Open to students who have completed French 3.

[French 4 will not be given in 1900].

5. Advanced Course in French Conversation.

Syntax, composition. Marchand's Method of French Conversation. Fall term. Miss WAIT.

Open to students who have completed French 3.

6. Advanced Course.

Syntax, composition. Prose, fiction, and drama of the 19th century. Chateaubriand. Sandeau, Hugo, Daudet. Winter term. Miss WAIT.

Open to students who have completed French 4 or 5.

[French 6 will not be given in 1900-01.]

7. Advanced Course.

French Literature in the Nineteenth Century, the Romantic movement, collateral reading, composition. Winter term.
Miss WAIT.

Open to students who have completed French 4 or 5.

8. Advanced Course.

General History of French Literature. Gazier, Histoire de la Litterature Française. Corneille, LeCid. Racine, Les Plaideurs. Voltaire, prose extracts. Hugo, Hernani. Composition. Spring term. Miss WAIT.

Open to students who have completed French 6 or 7.

[French 8 will not be given in 1901.]

9. Advanced Course.

Sources and Development of French Comedy. De Juleville, Le Théatre en France, Les Comédiens en France. Composition. Spring term. Miss WAIT.

Open to students who have completed French 6 or 7.

GERMAN.

1. Elementary Course.

Grammar, composition, conversation, reading. Eysenbach-Collar's Grammar. Fall term. Miss WAIT.

Open to all students of the College of Liberal Arts.

2. Elementary Course.

Grammar, composition, translation. Thomas's Grammar. Harris's German Composition. Super's German Reader. Winter term. Miss WAIT.

Open to students who have completed German 1.

3. Elementary Course.

Grammar, composition, translation. Storm's Immensee. Heine's Harzreise. Zschokke's Das Abenteur der Neujahrsnacht. Spring term. 　　　　　　　　　　　Miss Wait.

Open to students who have completed German 2.

4. Advanced Course.

Conversation, composition, translation. Schiller's Der Neffe als Onkel. Selections from Heyse, Auerbach, etc. Fall term.

　　　　　　　　　　　　　　　　　　Miss Wait.

Open to students who have completed German 3.

[German 4 will not be given in 1900.]

5. Advanced Course.

Composition, conversation. Lessing's Nathan der Weise. Schiller's Wilhelm Tell. Fall term. 　　　　Miss Wait.

Open to students who have completed German 3.

6. Advanced Course.

Goethe's Götz von Berlichingen. Lessing's Minna von Barnhelm. Freytag, Aus dem Jahrhundert des grossen Krieges. Composition. Winter term. 　　　　　　　　Miss Wait.

Open to students who have completed German 4 or 5.

[German 6 will not be given in 1900–01.]

7. Advanced Course.

Sheffel's Der Trompeter von Säkkingen. Freytag, Bilder aus der deutschen Vergangenheit. History of German Civilization. Composition, essays. Winter term. 　　　　Miss Wait.

Open to students who have completed German 4 or 5.

8. Advanced Course.

The History of German Literature, Scherer's History of German Literature. Readings from Miller's German Classics. Composition. Spring term. 　　　　　　　　Miss Wait.

Open to students who have completed German 6 or 7.

[German 8 will not be given in 1901.]

9. Advanced Course.

Goethe's life and works, with particular study of his lyrics; Werther's Leiden, Goethe's Egmont, Dichtung und Wahrheit; etc. Composition, essays, conversation. Spring term.

　　　　　　　　　　　　　　　　　　Miss Wait.

Open to students who have completed German 6 or 7.

LATIN.

1. Latin Lessons.

Tuell and Fowler's First Book in Latin. Fall term.

Professor GRUBB.

Open to Preparatory and College students.

2. Latin Lessons. (Continued.)

Winter term. Professor GRUBB.

Open to students who have completed Latin 1.

3. Caesar.

Texts, Rolfe and Dennison's Junior Latin Book and Daniell's Latin Prose Composition. Spring term.

Professor GRUBB.

Open to students who have completed Latin 2.

4. Caesar. (Continued.)

Fall term. Professor GRUBB.

Open to students who have completed Latin 3.

5. Cicero.

Kelsey's Cicero's Orations and Daniell's Latin Prose Composition. Winter term. Professor GRUBB.

Open to students who have completed Latin 4.

6. Cicero. (Continued.)

Spring term. Professor GRUBB.

Open to students who have completed Latin 5.

7. Virgil.

Greenough's Virgil's Aeneid. Fall term.

Professor PARKER.

Open to students who have completed Latin 6.

8. Virgil. (Continued.)

Winter term. Professor PARKER.

Open to students who have completed Latin 7.

9. Horace, Odes and Epodes.

Chase and Stuart's edition. Spring term of 1902, and the spring term of every alternate year thereafter.

Professor PARKER.

Open to students who have completed Latin 8.

10. Horace (Satires and Epistles), or Ovid.

Given in the Spring term of 1901, and in the Spring term of every alternate year thereafter. Professor PARKER.

Open to students who have completed Latin 8.

11. Livy, First Book.

Chase and Stuart's Edition. Fall term of 1900, and the Fall term of every alternate year thereafter.

Professor PARKER.

Open to students who have completed Latin 8.

12. Livy, Twenty-first Book.

Given in Fall term of 1901 and in the Fall term of every alternate year thereafter.   Professor PARKER.

Open to students who have completed Latin 8.

13. Cicero's De Senectute and De Amicitia.

Chase and Stuart's Edition. Winter term of 1901-1902, and the Winter term of every alternate year thereafter.

Professor PARKER.

Open to students who have completed Latin 8.

14. Curtius Rufus's Life of Alexander.

Crosby's Edition. Winter term of 1900-1901 and the Winter term of every alternate year thereafter.

Professor PARKER.

Open to students who have completed Latin 8 or 10.

15. Tacitus's Germania and Agricola.

Chase and Stuart's Edition. Spring term of 1902, and the Spring term of every alternate year thereafter.

Professor PARKER.

Open to students who have completed Latin 8.

16. Juvenal.

Anthon's Edition. Spring term of 1901, and the Spring term of every alternate year thereafter.   Professor PARKER.

Open to students who have completed Latin 8.

Latin Composition may be given in connection with Latin courses 9, 10, 11, 12, 13, and 14.

BOOKS OF REFERENCE.

The following books are recommended for reference to students pursuing the study of Latin:

Harper's Latin Lexicon; White's Junior Student's Latin Lexicon; Doederlein's Latin Synonyms; Liddell's History of Rome; Long's, or Ginn & Co.'s Classical Atlas; Anthon's or Smith's Classical Dictionary; Harper's Dictionary of Classical Literature and Antiquities; Harkness's and Bennett's Latin Grammar.

GREEK.

1. Grammar and Lessons.

Boise and Pattengill's Greek Lessons. Goodwin's Greek Grammar. Fall term. Professor PARKER.

Open to all students in the College.

2. Grammar and Lessons. (Continued.)

Winter term. Professor PARKER.

Open to students who have completed Greek 1.

3. Anabasis.

Goodwin's Xenophon's Anabasis, Collar and Daniell's Greek Composition. Spring term. Professor PARKER.

Open to students who have completed Greek 2.

4. Anabasis. (Continued.)

Collar and Daniell's Greek Composition. Fall term.
Professor PARKER.

Open to students who have completed Greek 3.

5. Orations of Lysias.

Stevens' Edition. Winter term. Professor PARKER.

Open to students who have completed Greek 4.

6. Iliad.

Keep's Homer's Iliad. Spring term. Professor PARKER.

Open to students who have completed Greek 5.

7. Odyssey.

Merry's Homer's Odyssey. Fall term. Professor PARKER.

Open to students who have completed Greek 6.

8. Plato's Apology of Socrates.

Dyer's Edition. Winter term of 1900-01 and the Winter term of every alternate year thereafter. Professor PARKER.

Open to students who have completed Greek 5.

9. Plato's Gorgias.

Lodge's Edition. Winter term of 1901-02 and the Winter term of every alternate year thereafter. Professor PARKER.

Open to students who have completed Greek 5.

10. Herodotus.

Fernald's Selections. Spring term of 1902, and the spring term of every alternate year thereafter. Professor PARKER.

Open to students who have completed Greek 8 or 9.

11. Prometheus of Aeschylus, or Medea of Euripides.

Wecklein's Prometheus, Allen's Medea. Spring term of 1901, and the Spring term of every alternate year thereafter.

Professor PARKER.

Open to students who have completed Greek 8 or 9.

12, 13, 14, 15, 16. Greek New Testament.

These classes, while primarily intended for theological students, are open also to college students who have the requisite preparation. A full description is given in the Divinity School courses.

BOOKS OF REFERENCE.

The following books are recommended for reference to those pursuing the study of Greek.

Liddell and Scott's Greek Lexicon; Autenrieth's Homeric Dictionary; Long's or Ginn & Co.'s Classical Atlas; Anthon's, or Smith's Classical Dictionary; Harper's Dictionary of Classical Literature and Antiquities; Smith's History of Greece; Goodwin's Greek Grammar; Goodwin's Greek Modes and Tenses.

HEBREW.

1, 2, 3. Grammar and Old Testament.

These are primarily courses in the Divinity School, but may be elected by students in the College of Liberal Arts whenever they are offered. Classes will be formed each year if a sufficient number of students apply.

It is the aim to give the student such a knowledge of the forms and structure of the Hebrew language as shall enable him to use it efficiently in the criticism and literary analysis of the Old Testament Scriptures. The text-books used are H. G. Mitchell's Hebrew Lessons and the Hebrew Old Testament. Three terms—Fall, Winter and Spring—each term counting as a course.   Dr. WHITE.

Open (under conditions as described above) to students who, in the judgment of the Instructor, are qualified by previous training to take the course.

MATHEMATICS.

The primary aim of this department is to cultivate habits of precision in thought, and power of abstract reasoning. It is believed that these qualities of mind can nowhere better be acquired than in mathematical study. In addition, mathematical facts and formulæ are learned, and practice is given in the solution of practical problems.

[For courses 1 to 4 inclusive, see Preparatory Department.]

5. Elementary Algebra.

This course embraces the Theory of Exponents, the solution of Quadratic, Simultaneous, and Indeterminate Equations, Ratio and Proportion, and Arithmetical and Geometrical Progressions. Wells's College Algebra is used. Fall term.

Professor WRIGHT.

Open to all students who have completed Mathematics 4.

6. Plane Geometry.

This course is designed to give students thorough drill in the first principles of Geometry. Each proposition is carefully analyzed, and particular attention is given to correct reasoning and precise expression. Phillips and Fisher's Elements of Geometry is used. Winter term. Professor WRIGHT.

Open to students who have completed Mathematics 5.

7. Plane and Solid Geometry.

A continuation of Mathematics 6. It is the design in these two courses to take up all the matter contained in the text-book. This includes the fundamental propositions of Plane Geometry, the circle, the polyhedron, the cylinder, the cone, and the sphere. Spring term. Professor WRIGHT.

Open to students who have completed Mathematics 6.

8. Higher Algebra.

This course assumes a thorough knowledge on the part of the student of Mathematics 5, and also some knowledge of Plane Geometry. It embraces the study of Series, Undetermined Coefficients, the Binomial Theorem, Logarithms, Permutations and Combinations, Probability, and the Theory of Equations. Fall term. Professor WRIGHT.

Open to students who have completed Mathematics 6.

9. Plane and Spherical Trigonometry.

This course includes the solution of trigonometrical equations, the solution of plane and spherical triangles, and problems involving an application of Trigonometry to Mensuration, Surveying, and Astronomy. Crockett's Plane and Spherical Trigonometry is used as a text-book. Winter term.

Professor WRIGHT.

Open to students who have completed Mathematics 8.

10. Analytic Geometry.

This course treats of the straight line, the conic sections, and higher plane curves. Hardy's Analytic Geometry is used. Mondays, Wednesdays, and Fridays. Spring term.

Professor WRIGHT.

Open to students who have completed Mathematics 9.

11. Surveying and Leveling.

Field work and problems. Field work on Saturdays at the option of the instructor. Spring term. Professor WRIGHT.

Open to students who have completed Mathematics 9.

12. Differential Calculus.

Osborne's Differential and Integral Calculus is used. Mondays, Wednesdays, and Fridays. Fall term.

Professor WRIGHT.

Open to students who have completed Mathematics 10.

13. Integral Calculus.

Mondays, Wednesdays, and Fridays. Winter term.

Professor WRIGHT.

Open to students who have completed Mathematics 12.

14. Descriptive Geometry.

This course embraces orthographic projection, shades and shadows, and perspective. Church's Descriptive Geometry is used. Mondays, Wednesdays, and Fridays. Fall term.

Professor WRIGHT.

Open to students who have completed Mathematics 9.

15. Strength of Structures.

This course takes up the computation of the strains in bridge and roof trusses, by graphical and analytical methods. Shreve's Strength of Bridges and Roofs is used as a text-book. Mondays, Wednesdays, and Fridays. Winter term.

Professor WRIGHT.

Open to students who have completed Mathematics 13.

[Mathematics 12 and 13 will be given in 1900-01, but will not be given in 1901-02, alternating with Mathematics 14 and 15.]

16. Quaternions.

A class will be formed for the study of Quaternions when a sufficient number of advanced students apply. The class will meet once a week for a year at such hour as the instructor may appoint. Professor WRIGHT.

ASTRONOMY.

1. General Astronomy.

This course is largely descriptive in character, though some of the simpler mathematical problems connected with Astronomy are solved. It embraces a study of the imaginary lines into which the heavens are divided; latitude, longitude, time; the sun, moon, and planets; comets, meteors, and the stars. Some attention is given to the constellations and the myths connected with them. The Nebular Hypothesis is presented and discussed. Young's Lessons in Astronomy is used. Fall term.

Professor WRIGHT.

Open to students who have completed Mathematics 9.

2. Mathematical Astronomy.

This course will have to do with the solution of various Astronomical problems. Computations in latitude, longitude, and time, eclipses, orbits, etc., will be among the subjects considered. Three hours a week. Winter term.

Professor WRIGHT.

Open to students who have completed Mathematics 13 and Astronomy 1.

PHYSICS.

The work in Physics consists of a careful consideration of the various phenomena treated under mechanics, acoustics, heat, light, electricity, and magnetism. The student is led to note the general principles of mechanics that apply throughout, and the application of modern theories. The courses in Physics consist of recitations, lectures, with demonstrations, and laboratory work.

1. Mechanics, Hydrostatics, Pneumatics.

Fall Term. Professor RICH.

Open to students who have completed Mathematics 9.

2. Acoustics, Optics, Heat.

Winter term. Musical students, taking the work in Acoustics, will be counted a half credit. Professor RICH.

Open to students who have completed Mathematics 9.

3. Electricity, Magnetism.

Spring term.   Professor RICH.

Open to students who have completed Physics 2.

CHEMISTRY.

The aim of the course is: first, a general knowledge of chemical phenomena; second, a thorough knowledge of Theoretical Chemistry and Stoichiometry; third, a careful study of the elements and their more important compounds; fourth, methods and work in Analysis, Qualitative and Quantitative.

1. Inorganic Chemistry.

This work consists of four hours per week of recitations or lectures, and two hours per week of experimental work. Remsen's Inorganic Chemistry, or an equivalent, is used as the basis of courses 1 and 2. Fall term.   Professor RICH.

Open to all students.

2. Inorganic Chemistry.

This is a continuation of Chemistry 1, and consists of four hours per week of recitations or lectures, and of two hours per week of experimental work. The course consists chiefly of Theoretical Chemistry, Stoichiometry, and a study of metals. Winter term.   Professor RICH.

Open to students who have completed Chemistry 1, or its equivalent.

3. Organic Chemistry.

This course consists of recitations, lectures, with experimental demonstrations, and laboratory work. The lectures treat chiefly of new methods and of food-stuffs, their composition and adulteration. Remsen's Organic Chemistry is used. Spring term.

Professor RICH.

Open to students who have completed Chemistry 2.

In each of the courses 1, 2, and 3' the work is profusely illustrated by experiments, and the laboratory gives opportunity for individual work on the principles discussed.

4. Analytical Chemistry.

Laboratory work. Fall term.   Professor RICH.

Open to students who have completed Chemistry 2.

5. Analytical Chemistry.

Laboratory work. Winter term.   Professor RICH.

Open to students who have completed Chemistry 4.

6. Analytical Chemistry.

Laboratory work. Spring term. Professor RICH.

Open to students who have completed Chemistry 5.

Chemistry 4, 5, and 6, form progressive courses in Qualitative and Quantitative Analysis. General Qualitative and Quantitative methods are studied, and analysis is made of such compounds as ores, soils, fertilizers, milk, butter, water, soaps, gas, drugs, etc.

For the present, no student is allowed to register for more than fifteen hours per week in laboratory courses.

BIOLOGY.

The work in Biology is given chiefly by text-book recitations, supplemented by lectures and numerous experimental demonstrations. The attention of the students is called to the structural and physiological relations of the various organs of plants and animals. Charts and the projecting lantern are used in illustrating different parts of the work.

1. Physiology.

The course in Human Physiology consists of topical recitations, and lectures, with demonstrations. The microscope furnishes valuable aid in the study of tissues. Hygiene is made a large element of the work. Text-book, Martin's Human Body, Advanced Course, or an equivalent. Fall term.

Professor RICH.

Open to students who have completed Chemistry 1.

2. Zoology.

Packard's Zoology is made the basis of the work in this course. Lectures are also given and typical forms dissected. The valuable collection of the University is made use of for purposes of illustration and study. Winter term.

Professor RICH.

Open to students who have completed Chemistry 1.

3. Botany.

The course in Botany consists of recitations, lectures, and laboratory work. Each student is required to make for himself a herbarium. The aim of the course is to give instruction in the anatomy and physiology of plants, and in the methods of analysis, and of the preservation of specimens. Text-book, Gray's Lessons. Spring term. Professor RICH.

Open to students who have completed Chemistry 1.

GEOLOGY AND MINERALOGY.

1. Geology.

The work in Geology is given by text-book recitations, supplemented by lectures, and excursions for field work. The University has a valuable collection of minerals, which serves for purposes of illustration and study. Dana's work is used. Spring term.   Professor RICH.

Open to students who have completed Chemistry 1, Biology 2 and Biology 3.

2. Mineralogy.

This course consists of a qualitative determination of minerals by means of the blow pipe. Winter term.

Professor RICH.

Open to students who have completed Chemistry 2.

HISTORY.

[For History 1 to 4 inclusive, see courses in Preparatory School.]

5. History of the Christian Church.

A. The Ancient and Mediæval Eras (1-1517).

This course in Church History is primarily intended for the members of the Divinity School, but is now open to College students. It will require the investigation of the early organization and extension of Christianity, and the successive periods of the Church down to the time of Charlemagne; followed by a careful inquiry into the causes of the rise of the Papacy, of the political relations of the Church, and of the Crusades. Fisher's History of the Church will be used as a hand book and topics will be assigned to each member of the class for special investigation and reports. Fall term.   Dr. WHITE.

Open to students who have completed History 1 and 2.

6. History of the Christian Church.

B. The Modern Era (1517-1900).

This course will begin with the study of the Reformation, and trace the history of the Church down to the present time. It will include the history of Christian missions, revivals, social reforms and philanthropy. The same text-book will be used as in History 5. Spring term.   Dr. WHITE.

Open to students who, in the judgment of the instructor, are qualified by previous training to take the course.

ECONOMICS.

1. Science of Government.

This course is designed to give students some insight into the nature and theory of government, especially of the National, State, and Municipal governments of the United States. It also deals briefly with the rights of citizens and the elements of common law. Texts, Fiske's Civil Government and Andrews's Constitution of the United States. Spring term.

Professor GRUBB.

Open to Preparatory and College Students.

2. Political Economy.

The standard economic theories of production, exchange, and distribution are developed before the class; and the bearing of these theories on vital economic questions of the day is frankly and freely discussed. Students are encouraged to write essays on economic topics, and to read them for discussion. In preparing these essays, students will receive the personal aid of the instructor in directing their reading. A good reference library for this purpose is at the disposal of the class. Bullock's Introduction to the Study of Economics is used. Spring term.

Professor WRIGHT.

Open to all College students.

3. Financial History of the United States.

This course embraces the finances of the Revolution; the financial administrations of Morris, Hamilton, and Gallatin; the bank struggle, tariff legislation, and the financial measures of the civil war and reconstruction period. This course will be conducted by lectures and frequent reviews. Fall term.

Professor WRIGHT.

Open to students who have completed Economics 2.

JURISPRUDENCE.

1. International Law.

The general principles which govern the relation of states, as historically developed in express agreements and by usage, are elucidated, and these principles are discussed from the standpoints of reason and justice. Special study is made of current international problems and theses on these subjects are required. Particular attention is paid to terminology. Lawrence's International Law is used as a text book. Frequent reference is made to the works on International Law by Woolsey, Wheaton, Glenn, etc. Professor FOWLER.

Open to students who, in the judgment of the instructor, are qualified by previous training to take the course.

SOCIOLOGY.

1. An Introduction to the Study of Sociology.

The purpose of this course is to afford an opportunity for the student to gain a knowledge of the characteristic conceptions and main trend of modern sociological thought. Constant reference to the works of the more important modern sociologists is required. The preparation and presentation of frequent and substantial papers by the student is an integral part of the work of the course. Professor KIMBLE.

Open to those students who, in the judgment of the instructor, are fitted for the work.

2. An introduction to the Study of Society.

The purpose here is to gain a familiarity with the process of learning about society from society itself. This is virtually a laboratory course. The work will consist largely of investigations carried on by the students. Frequent papers will be required. Professor KIMBLE.

Open to students who have completed Sociology 1.

3. The Family.

An outline study of the origin, development, and present significance of the human Family. Professor KIMBLE.

Open to students who have completed Sociology 1 and 2.

4. Anthropo-Geography.

A study of the influence of the non-human environment upon the development of human association. Professor KIMBLE.

Open to students who have completed Sociology 1 and 2.

5. Social Pathology.

An investigation of certain of the pathological elements of society. Special emphasis is laid upon modern charities methods. Papers. Primarily for the Divinity School.
Professor KIMBLE.

Open to students who have completed Sociology 1 and 2.

6. A Study of certain of the phenomena of Religion from the standpoint of Sociology.

The work of this course will center about the development of the function of the minister. Its purpose will be to enable the student to gain a more adequate idea of the social significance of the religious factor of society. Primarily for the Divinity

School. Members of the course will meet at times to be determined upon. A large amount of investigatory work will be required.

Professor KIMBLE.

Open to students who have completed Sociology 1 and 2.

PHILOSOPHY.

1. (a) Psychology.

After a somewhat detailed inquiry into the general relations of mind and body, followed by a close examination of the phenomena of perception, the more complex mental processes, as memory, association, apperception, hallucination, imagination, impulse, habit, volition, are taken up for careful study. Special emphasis is laid upon self-observation, and the indications for self-culture are attentively marked. Stress is also laid upon the definition and use of technical terms. Baldwin's Elements are used for text; Halleck, Lindner, and Ladd for reference.

Dr. WHITE.

Open to students who, in the judgment of the instructor, are qualified by previous training to take the course.

1. (b). Psychology.

A second term in Psychology, using Ladd's Physiological Psychology, has been given in 1899–1900.   Dr. WHITE.

2. Metaphysic.

This is primarily a course in the Divinity School, but it may be elected by students in the College of Liberal Arts whenever it is offered. Classes will be formed whenever a sufficient number of students apply. Lotze's Outlines of Metaphysic is used as a text-book. Fall term.   Dr. WHITE.

Open to students who, in the judgment of the instructor, are qualified by previous training to take the course.

3. Logic.

Having first obtained a thorough grounding in the principles and methods of correct reasoning, both deductive and inductive, at least one-half of the term is given to the detection and discrimination of fallacies in actual examples. Such examples the class is required to search out in current literature and bring in for discussion. Davis's Elements of Deductive Logic, and Davis's Elements of Inductive Logic are used. Winter term.

Professor FOWLER.

Open to students who, in the judgment of the instructor, are qualified by previous training to take the course.

4. Ethics.[1]

Ethics is treated from the standpoint of Philosophy, and the different systems are discussed. The nature and grounds of obligation are investigated and applied to the practical affairs of life. Spring term.   Professor KIMBLE.

Open to students who, in the judgment of the instructor, are qualified by previous training to take the course.

5. Philosophy of Religion.

Caird's Introduction to the Philosophy of Religion is the textbook. Lotze, Sabatier, and Martineau are used as works of reference. The aim of the instructor is to acquaint the student with the proper office of reason in the effort to find argumentative grounds for religious ideas. Most of the modern theories respecting the nature and scope of the religious feeling pass under review; and in such discussions free questioning on the part of the student is encouraged. Winter term.   Dr. WHITE.

Open to students who, in the judgment of the instructor, are qualified by previous training to take the course.

6. Ethical Theories.

Martineau's Types of Ethical Theory is used as a text-book with frequent references to the works of Sidgwick, Green, Smyth, and others. Much attention is paid to the elucidation and criticism of the modern ethical theories. Spring term.
                                        Dr. WHITE.

Open to students who, in the judgment of the instructor, are qualified by previous training to take the course.

FINE ARTS.

1. History of Art.

This course gives a brief survey of the progress of Art from the earliest to the present time. The course will consist of lectures, recitations, and frequent reviews. Students will study under direction of the instructor from numerous works of reference in the college and public libraries. The course is copiously illustrated with photographs and engravings of the masterpieces of painting and sculpture. Two hours a week. Fall term.
                                        Miss BLOOD.

Open only to advanced students.

2, 3, 4. Drawing.

This course includes perspective, drawing from casts in charcoal and crayon, still life studies in crayon, etc. It will count as one credit for the entire year.   Miss BLOOD.

Open to all students in the University.

MUSIC.

1, 2, 3. Harmony.

Class-room work, lectures, recitations, and written exercises, covering theory of the elements of music, triads, chords of the seventh, augmented chords, chords of the ninth and eleventh, modulation, suspension, and harmonizing of melodies. Text-books, Emery, Richter, and Jadassohn. Three hours a week for one year. Professor LUNDBERG.

Open to all students in the University.

4, 5, 6. Simple and Double Counterpoint.

Lectures, recitations, and daily written exercises, based on the text-books of Richter, Haupt, and others. Three hours a week for one year. Professor LUNDBERG.

Open to students who have completed Music 3.

7, 8, 9. Fugue, Canon, Musical Form, and the elements of Orchestration.

Lectures, recitations and written exercises. Text-books, Prout, Cherubini, Rieman, Berlioz. Three hours a week for one year. Professor LUNDBERG.

Open to students who have completed Music 6.

10. History of Music. [Half Course.]

Introductory course on the lives of the great composers. Two hours a week. Fall term. Professor LUNDBERG.

Open to students who, in the judgment of the instructor, are qualified by previous training to take the course.

11. History of Music. [Half Course.]

Advanced course on the development of music from the earliest times until to-day, with special reference to critical analysis of the works of the greatest masters. Text-books, Naumann, Langhans, Rieman. Two hours a week. Winter term.

Professor LUNDBERG.

Open to students who have completed Music 10.

ELOCUTION.

[Not more than four credits can be counted in this department towards the degree of A. B.]

1. Elocution. [Half Course.]

The aim of this course is to rid the voice of all impurities, secure correct placing of the voice, proper breathing, and beauty of tone for conversational purposes. Notes will be given upon the anatomy of the vocal organs and the care of the voice. Physical exercises will be introduced as a means of securing grace and becoming deportment. Recitations Mondays, Wednesdays, and Fridays. Fall term. Miss MINER.

Open to all students of the University.

2. Elocution. [Half Course.]

In this course attention will be given to the adaptation of the conversational voice to the requirements of platform speaking. Continued work in bodily expression and deportment. Each pupil will be required to deliver three selections before the class for criticism. In the preparation of these selections at least one private rehearsal will be given by the instructor. Recitations Mondays, Wednesdays, and Fridays. Winter term.

Miss MINER.

Open to students who have completed Elocution 1.

3. Elocution. [Half Course.]

This course will consist of a continuation of the work outlined in Elocution 2. Three selections will be required from each pupil and individual drill continued. Recitations Mondays, Wednesdays, and Fridays. Spring term. Miss MINER.

Open to students who have completed Elocution 2.

4. Elocution. [Half Course.]

The study of the emotions with illustrative readings will be begun in this course. Pantomime will be made a chief feature— a series of pantomimic studies being given for the highest expression of thought and feeling through the medium of a cultivated body. Recitations Mondays and Thursdays. Fall term.

Miss MINER.

Open to students who have completed Elocution 3.

5. Elocution. [Half Course.]

The work in this course will be a continuation of that begun in Elocution 4, together with personations. Pantomimic studies continued. Recitations Mondays and Thursdays. Winter term.

Miss MINER.

Open to students who have completed Elocution 4.

6. Elocution. [Half Course.]

This course will consist of a continuation of Elocution 5. Recitations Mondays and Thursdays. Spring term.

Miss MINER.

Open to students who have completed Elocution 5.

7. Oratory. [Half Course.]

The direct aim of this course will be the study of the great orators. Each student will be required to deliver before the class for criticism a certain number of selections chosen from the orators studied. Extemporaneous talks will also be a feature of this work. Recitations Mondays and Thursdays. Fall term   Miss MINER.

<small>Open to students who have completed Elocution 3.</small>

8. Oratory. [Half Course.]

. A continuation of extemporaneous speaking will be given in this course with criticism. Two orations will be required from each member of the class. Recitations Mondays and Thursdays. Winter term.   Miss MINER.

<small>Open to students who have completed Elocution 7.</small>

9. Dramatic Expression. [Half Course.]

This course consists of the study of one and two act comedies for character interpretation and elements of stage business. Recitations Tuesdays and Thursdays. Fall term.

Miss MINER.

<small>Open to students who have completed Elocution 6.</small>

10, 11. Dramatic Expression. [Half Courses.]

These courses will be a continuation of Elocution 9, taking up longer plays. Recitations Tuesdays and Thursdays. Winter and Spring terms.   Miss MINER.

<small>Open to students who have completed Elocution 9.</small>

RECITALS.

Recitals will be given during the year to show the proficiency of pupils, and to give them assistance in acquiring confidence, ease, and self control.

GYMNASIUM WORK.

Regular class work in the Gynasium is required of all students in the institution during two years of their college course. This work will embrace Swedish Gymnastics; Marching; Wand, Dumb-bell, and Indian Club drills. Instruction is also given in the use of the Apparatus and in Heavy Gymnastics. Especial attention is given to correct posture of the body and good form in walking and standing. Each student is given a thorough physical examination by the medical examiner, and private work is prescribed to him in accordance with his individual needs. All students will provide themselves with regular gynasium uniforms. The price of the uniform is about $2.75 for the men and $6.50 for the women.

TABULAR VIEW FOR THE YEAR 1900-1901.

Courses are given in 5 hours a week recitations unless otherwise stated.

HOUR.	FALL TERM.	WINTER TERM.	SPRING TERM.
8:00	Economics 3. English 9. *English 10. History 5. Homiletics 1. (3 h) Latin 4. Latin 7. Music 1. (3 h) Music 4. (3 h) Physics 1.	Astronomy 2. English 11. *English 12. History 1. History 6. Homiletics 2. (1 h) Latin 5. Latin 8. Music 2. (3 h) Music 5. (3 h) Physics 2.	English 13. *English 14. *Greek 12. Greek 13. Homiletics 6. (1 h) Latin 6. *Latin 9. Latin 10. Music 3 (3 h) Music 6 (3 h) Physical Geography. Physics 3.
9:30	Chemistry 1. Elocution 7. (2 h) *German 4. German 5. Greek 7. Homiletics 4. Mathematics 1. Mathematics 8. Music 10. (2 h) Philosophy 1.	Chemistry 2. Elocution 8. (2 h) *German 6. German 7. Greek 8. *Greek 9. *Greek 14. Greek 15. Homiletics 5. (3 h) Mathematics 2. Mathematics 9. Music 11. (2 h) Pastoral Theology. Philosophy 3.	Chemistry 3. Economics 1. *German 8. German 9. *Greek 10. Greek 11. Homiletics 3. Jurisprudence 1. Mathematics 10. (3 h) Philosophy 4. Theo. of Universalism.
10:30	Astronomy 1. Biology 1. English 5. French 1. Greek 4. History 2. Philosophy 2. Sociology 4.	Biology 2. Dogmatic Theology. English 6. English 7. French 2. Greek 5. History 3. Sociology 5.	Biology 3. Economics 2. French 3. Greek 6. History 4. Sociology 6.
11:30	Apologetics. Elocution 4. (2 h) English 2. (4 h) Fine Arts 1. (3 h) German 1. Greek 1. Mathematics 5. Sociology I.	Elocution 5. (2 h) English 3. (4 h) German 2. Greek 2. Mathematics 3. Mathematics 6. Philosophy 5. Sociology 2.	Elocution 6. (2 h) English 4. (4 h) Philosophy 6. Geology 1. German 3. Greek 3. Mathematics 4. Mathematics 7. Sociology 3.
2:00	Chemistry 4. Elocution 1. (3 h) Elocution 9. (2 h) English Bible. (1 h) *French 4. (3 h) French 5. (3 h) Latin 1. Latin 11. *Latin 12. Mathematics 12.(3 h) *Mathematics 14.(3 h) *N. T. Introduction. O. T. Introduction.	Chemistry 5. Elocution 2. (3 h) Elocution 10. (2 h) English Bible. (1 h) *French 6. French 7. Geology 2. Latin 2. *Latin 13. Latin 14. Mathematics 13. (3 h) *Mathematics 15. (3 h)	Chemistry 6. Comparative Religions Elocution 3. (3 h) Elocution 11. (2 h) English Bible. (1 h) English 8. (1 h) *French 8. French 9. Latin 3. *Latin 15. Latin 16. Mathematics 11.
3:00	Chemistry 4. Fine Arts 2.	Chemistry 5. Fine Arts 3. Geology 2.	Chemistry 6. Fine Arts 4.

*Not given in 1900-01.

Preparatory School

Preparatory School.

DEPARTMENT OF ELEMENTARY INSTRUCTION, INTRO-DUCTORY TO THE COLLEGE COURSES.

The primary object of this Department is to prepare students thoroughly for admission to College, but it also affords special advantages to those students who wish to become teachers or to fit themselves tor active business, and who are unable to pursue a complete course.

Thorough preparation is the price of sure success both in and out of College.

Students may enter this department with the full assurance that they will receive thorough instruction in those subjects and principles which contribute to sound scholarship and success.

SUPERVISION.

The Preparatory School is under the general superintendence of the President and Faculty, and its students are under the same regulations as those of the College. Instruction is given by the regular College Professors, as well as by the Department Instructors.

ADVANTAGES.

All the advantages of the College, such as libraries, museums, lectures, and instruction in elocution, are open to all.

One hour is devoted to every recitation, and, as the number in each class is not large, each student recites and receives individual drill every day. Contrast such opportunities with the disadvantages of membership in crowded classes and note the gain to the student here.

ATTENDANCE.

To secure the full benefit of all the opportunities here afforded, it is necessary for the student to enter at the beginning of the College year and remain until its close.

ABSENCE.

The vacations are so long and so arranged that it is unnecessary for students to visit their friends during term time, except for the most urgent reasons. The student's absence, even for a few days, entails upon him much greater injury than is commonly supposed. Parents are earnestly requested to cooperate with the Faculty in securing continuous attendance.

Faculty.

CHARLES ELLWOOD NASH, A. M., S. T. D., President.
JON WATSON GRUBB, M. S.
ISAAC AUGUSTUS PARKER, A. M., Ph. D.
FREDERICK WILLIAM RICH, B. S.
PHILIP GREEN WRIGHT, A. M.
FRANK HAMILTON FOWLER, Ph. D.

Students in the Preparatory School.

Will McCall Baird.................................*Biggsville.*
Charles Peter Boeck..... ....*Chicago.*
Paul Claflin Brigham................................*Chicago.*
Fannie Estelle Churchill......... ....*Avon.*
John Lewson Clay ....*Galesburg.*
Walter Timothy Clay........... ....*Galesburg.*
Henry Mack Cooper............................. ....*Oquawka.*
Rauseldon Cooper, Jr......... ....*Oquawka.*
Nellie Ewart....................................... ...*Greenup.*
Cora Margaret Fosher..............................*Galesburg.*
Clyde Percy Gingrich..............................*Galesburg.*
George Roscoe Grubb............................. ....*Liberty.*
Mary Arrah Hart...............................*Eureka, Kan.*
Harley Lucius Kennedy............................*Galesburg.*
Anna Pearl Koons................................*Knoxville.*
Luther Landon......................................*Rio.*
Whittier Kerle Lothian..............................*Chicago.*
Pearl Luckhurst........ ....*Clark, S. D.*
Faith Tenney Nash................................*Galesburg.*
Clarence LeRoy Perrine.......................*Burlington, Ia.*
Lydia Ringenberg......... ....*Lombardville.*
Claude Robinson....................................*Elmwood.*
Harvey Parker Robinson.......................*Rich Hill, Mo.*
Frances Lunettee Ross..................... ....*Avon.*

Charles Clinton Rogers................. ....*Galesburg.*
Charles August Sandberg................ ....*Galesburg.*
Milo A. Stevens......................................*Galesburg.*
Frank Roy Strubinger............................. ....*El Dara.*
Joseph Boniface Sutter...........................*Burlington, Ia.*
Levi James Thompson ....*Stony Point, Mich.*
Luke Tinker............... ....*Oquawka.*
Raymond E. Van Camp..... ....*Otranto, Ia.*
Ethel Van Cise..... ....*Deadwood, S. D.*
Leura Willis ....*Table Grove.*

Courses of Study.

The following courses of study are open to students in the Preparatory School. A student will be admitted to the College of Liberal Arts upon the successful completion of twenty-one of these courses. In arranging these courses he will consult with the Advisory Committee. (See pp. 17 and 28.)

ENGLISH.

2. Studies in English Literature and Composition.

Macaulay's Essays on Milton and Addison will be studied with care, and the class will be required to read specimens of the writings of Addison and of Lowell. It is expected that more than half the student's time will be given to work in Composition. Four hours a week. Fall term.   Professor FOWLER.

Open to all Preparatory students.

3. Studies in English Literature and Composition. (Continued.)

Work for careful study will be Burke's Speech on Conciliation with America. The class will read carefully Pope's Translation of the Iliad (books I, VI, XXII, and XXIV), Goldsmith's Vicar of Wakefield, Coleridge's Ancient Mariner, and Cooper's Last of the Mohicans. Four hours a week. Winter term.

Professor FOWLER.

Open to students who have completed English 2.

4. Studies in English Literature and Composition. (Continued.)

Shakespeare's Macbeth and Milton's L'Allegro, Il Penseroso, Comus, and Lycidas will be carefully studied; and the class will read Shakespeare's Merchant of Venice, George Eliot's Silas Marner, Tennyson's Princess, and Scott's Ivanhoe. Four hours a week. Spring term.   Professor FOWLER.

Open to students who have completed English 3.

ELOCUTION.

1, 2, 3. Elementary Courses. (Half Courses.)

These three courses are continuous through the year, each term counting as one-half a course. (See page 47.)

Miss MINER.

Open to all students.

LATIN.

1. Latin Lessons.

Tuell and Fowler's First Book in Latin. Fall term.

Professor GRUBB.

Open to Preparatory and College students.

2. Latin Lessons. (Continued.)

Winter term. Professor GRUBB.

Open to students who have completed Latin 1.

3. Caesar.

Texts, Rolfe and Dennison's Junior Latin Book and Daniell's Latin Prose Composition. Spring term.

Professor GRUBB.

Open to students who have completed Latin 2.

4. Caesar. (Continued.)

Fall term. Professor GRUBB.

Open to students who have completed Latin 3.

5. Cicero.

Kelsey's Cicero's Orations and Daniell's Latin Prose Composition. Winter term. Professor GRUBB.

Open to students who have completed Latin 4.

6. Cicero. (Continued.)

Spring term. Professor GRUBB.

Open to students who have completed Latin 5.

7. Virgil.

Greenough's Virgil's Aeneid. Fall term.

Professor PARKER.

Open to students who have completed Latin 6.

8. Virgil. (Continued.)

Winter term. Professor PARKER.

Open to students who have completed Latin 7.

GREEK.

1. Grammar and Lessons.

Boise and Pattengill's Greek Lessons. Goodwin's Greek Grammar. Fall term. Professor PARKER.

Open to all students in the College.

2. Grammar and Lessons. (Continued.)

Winter term.   Professor PARKER.

Open to students who have completed Greek 1.

3. Anabasis.

Goodwin's Xenophon's Anabasis.   Collar and Daniell's Greek
Composition.   Spring term.   Professor PARKER.

Open to students who have completed Greek 2.

4. Anabasis. (Continued.)

Collar and Daniell's Greek Composition.   Fall term.
                                   Professor PARKER.

Open to students who have completed Greek 3.

5. Orations of Lysias.

Stevens' Edition.   Winter term.   Professor PARKER.

Open to students who have completed Greek 4.

6. Iliad.

Keep's Homer's Iliad.   Spring term.   Professor PARKER.

Open to students who have completed Greek 5.

MATHEMATICS.

1. Arithmetic.

Robinson's Higher Arithmetic.   Study of the subject matter
of the text to Interest.   This course includes thorough work in
analysis and mental arithmetic.   Fall term.

                                   Professor GRUBB.

Open to Preparatory students.

2. Arithmetic. (Continued.)

Interest and its applications, Alligation, Extraction of Roots,
Mensuration, including the Metric System.   This course is supplemented by seven hundred practical problems in mensuration
from Mechanic's Arithmetic.   Winter term.

                                   Professor GRUBB.

Open to Preparatory students who have completed Mathematics 1.

(Mathematics 1 and 2 do not count as credits for admission to
the College of Liberal Arts.)

3. Elementary Algebra.

Wells's Academic Algebra is used.   Winter term.

                                   Professor GRUBB.

Open to Preparatory students.

4. Elementary Algebra. (Continued.)

Spring term. Professor GRUBB.

Open to Preparatory students who have completed Mathematics 3.

Mathematics 3 and 4 are continuous through the winter and spring terms and include everything in the text-book preceding quadratic equations.

5. Elementary Algebra.

This course embraces the Theory of Exponents, the solution of Quadratic, Simultaneous, and Indeterminate Equations, Ratio and Proportion, and Arithmetical and Geometrical Progressions. Wells's College Algebra is used. Fall term.

Professor WRIGHT.

Open to all students who have completed Mathematics 4.

6. Plane Geometry.

This course is designed to give students thorough drill in the first principles of Geometry. Each proposition is carefully analyzed, and particular attention is given to correct reasoning and precise expression. Phillips and Fisher's Elements of Geometry is used. Winter term. Professor WRIGHT.

Open to students who have completed Mathematics 5.

7. Plane and Solid Geometry.

A continuation of Mathematics 6. It is the design in these two courses to take up all the matter contained in the text-book. This includes the fundamental propositions of Plane Geometry, the circle, the polyhedro' the cylinder, the cone, and the sphere. Spring term. Professor WRIGHT.

Open to students who have completed Mathematics 6.

PHYSICAL GEOGRAPHY.

1. Physical Geography.

Text-book, Tarr's Elementary Physical Geography. Spring term.

Open to all students of the Preparatory School.

CHEMISTRY.

1. Inorganic Chemistry.

The work consists of four hours per week of recitations or lectures and two hours of experimental work. Remsen's Inorganic Chemistry. Fall term. Professor RICH.

Open to all students.

HISTORY.

1. American.

History of the United States. Text-book, Channing's Student's History of the United States, with Scudder and Fiske for reference. Winter term.

Open to all students of the Preparatory School.

2. Greece.

History of Greece. Text-book, Smith's History of Greece. Fall term.   Professor GRUBB.

Open to all students of the Preparatory School.

3. Rome.

History of Rome. Text-book, Liddell's History of Rome. Winter term.   Professor GRUBB.

Open to all students of the Preparatory School.

4. England.

History of England. Text-book, Montgomery's Leading Facts of English History. Spring term.   Professor GRUBB.

Open to all students of the Preparatory School.

ECONOMICS.

1. Science of Government.

Text-books, Fiske's Civil Government in the United States, and Andrew's Manual of the Constitution. Spring term.

Professor GRUBB.

Open to all students.

Ryder Divinity School

Ryder Divinity School.

The Divinity School of Lombard College was opened for the admission of students on the 5th of September, 1881. The first class was graduated in 1885.

At the annual meeting of the Board of Trustees in 1890, it was voted to name the theological department of the College the RYDER DIVINITY SCHOOL, in honor of the late William Henry Ryder, D. D., whose munificent bequests to the College exceed fifty thousand dollars.

The largest benefaction to the Divinity School from any other source was received from the late Hon. A. G. Throop, founder of the Throop Polytechnic Institute at Pasadena, California. In 1890, Mr. Throop gave twenty thousand dollars towards the endowment of the Divinity School.

ADMISSION.

Applicants unknown to the faculty must bring satisfactory evidences of good moral and religious character. They should also bring certificates of their church membership.

Candidates for admission to the Divinity School must be prepared to sustain examination in the following subjects.

I. ENGLISH.

(a) Grammar and Analysis.

Reed and Kellogg's Higher Lessons in English, or an equivalent.

(b) Composition.

An extemporaneous composition on an assigned subject, correct as to paragraphing, grammar, and rhetorical form.

(c) Literature.

An equivalent of English 2, 3, and 4 as described on page 54 of this catalogue.

II. HISTORY.

(a) Bible History.

A general knowledge of the leading characters, events, and localities in the Bible record.

(b) General History.

Swinton's General History or an equivalent.

III. MATHEMATICS.

(*a*) **Arithmetic.**

Higher Arithmetic, including percentage, alligation, extraction of roots, mensuration and the metric system.

(*b*) **Elementary Algebra.**

Wells's Academic Algebra, or an equivalent.

IV. GEOGRAPHY.

Tarr's Elementary Geography, or an equivalent.

V. SCIENCE.

(*a*) **Physical Geography.**

Tarr's Elementary Physical Geography, or an equivalent.

(*b*) **Elementary Physics.**

Carhart and Chute's Elements of Physics, or an equivalent.

ADMISSION BY CERTIFICATE.

Satisfactory grades from approved schools will be accepted in lieu of examination. Students thus admitted by certificate will be regarded as on probation during the first term of their course.

ADMISSION TO ADVANCED STANDING.

Students who bring satisfactory evidence of work done beyond the requirements of admission will be given credit for the same on the regular course, so far as the faculty may deem consistent with the special aims of that course.

The members of the Divinity School are admitted to the advantages presented by the other Departments of the College.

EXPENSES.

Tuition is free to all regular members of the Divinity School who are candidates for the ministry.

The charge for incidentals is the same as in the College of Liberal Arts, $4 per term.

Board in good families can be secured for from $2.50 to $3.25 per week. Students may greatly reduce their expenses by forming clubs, or boarding themselves.

PECUNIARY AID.

Students who are candidates for the ministry of the Universalist church, may, upon complying with the prescribed conditions and receiving the recommendation of the faculty, obtain assistance from the Universalist General Convention in the form of a gratuity, to an amount not exceeding $125 per year. Applications will be granted only when entirely satisfactory. The first installment of this gift will not be issued until January, the second will be issued in May. Students should therefore come with resources of their own sufficient to pay their expenses for at least one term.

Those who have not a definite purpose of entering the Universalist ministry are not eligible to the Convention gift.

During the two last years of their regular course, students who show due proficiency are permitted to secure appointments to preach, and thus to add to their pecuniary resources.

All who intend to enter the Divinity School the coming year, are advised to correspond immediately with the president.

Courses of Instruction.

1. Regular Course.

The full course of study occupies four years of three terms each, as exhibited in the schedule on page 65. Those who complete this course will be entitled to the degree of Bachelor of Divinity.

2. Special Work.

(a) Candidates for the ministry who can not take the Regular Course, will be permitted to elect special studies, so far as their preparation warrants. Pastors already engaged in ministerial work, who can spare a period for further study, are particularly invited to avail themselves of this opportunity.

(b) The School is also open to persons who do not intend to enter the ministry. The pursuit of studies of a theological or religious character is an interesting and helpful means of personal culture. Such a course is especially recommended to those who desire to become better fitted for service in the Sunday school, the church, the Young People's Christian Union and similar societies, or for charitable and philanthropic work.

Upon those who come with these purposes, no denominational test will be imposed. Students of all denominations and beliefs will be welcome to the advantages of study and training in the Divinity School, as in other departments of the College.

Faculty of the Divinity School.

CHARLES ELLWOOD NASH, A. M., S. T. D., PRESIDENT,

NEHEMIAH WHITE, A. M., PH. D., S. T. D.,
*Hall Professor of Intellectual and Moral Philosophy.
In charge of the Ryder Divinity School, Professor of Biblical
Languages and Exegesis.

†Hull Professor of Biblical Geography and Archæology.

ISAAC AUGUSTUS PARKER, A. M., PH. D.,
Professor of Greek.

FRANK HAMILTON FOWLER, PH. D.,
Professor of English Literature.

RALPH GRIERSON KIMBLE,
Professor of Sociology.

MAUD AUGUSTA MINER,
Instructor in Elocution.

NON-RESIDENT LECTURER.
MARION D. SHUTTER, D. D.

* In honor of the late E. G. HALL, of Chicago.
† In honor of the REV. STEPHEN HULL, of Kansas City, Mo.

Degrees Conferred in 1899.

Lloyd Champlain.............................. .....*Deadwood, S. D.*

Students in the Divinity School.

FOURTH YEAR.

William David Buchanan.......... ....*Coon Rapids, Ia.*

THIRD YEAR.

Francis Britton Bishop.........................*New London, Ia.*
George Francis Thompson....................*Stony Point, Mich.*

SECOND YEAR.

George Melvin Boyer................................*Altamont.*
Kiyoshi Satoh............. .... *Miyagiken, Japan.*
Ward Watson Stratton...............................*Galesburg.*

FIRST YEAR.

George R. Longbrake.... ....*Galesburg.*

Course of Study

LEADING TO THE DEGREE OF BACHELOR OF DIVINITY.

FIRST YEAR.

FALL TERM.	WINTER TERM.	SPRING TERM.
Chemistry 1.	Chemistry 2.	Chemistry 3.
English 5.	English 6.	English 8.
Greek 1.	Greek 2.	Greek 3.
Elocution 1.	Elocution 2.	Elocution 3.
English Bible.	English Bible.	English Bible.

SECOND YEAR.

Philosophy 1.	Philosophy 3.	Philosophy 4.
Greek 4.	Greek 5.	Greek 12, 13.
Elocution 4.	Elocution 5.	Elocution 6.
History 5.	History 6.	Elective.

THIRD YEAR.

Homiletics 1.	Homiletics 2.	Homiletics 3.
Sociology 1.	Sociology 2.	Sociology 3.
Philosophy 2.	Dogmatic Theology.	Comparative Religions.
O. T. Introduction.	Greek 14, 15.	Greek 12, 13.

FOURTH YEAR.

Homiletics 4.	Homiletics 5.	Homiletics 6.
Sociology 4.	Sociology 5.	Sociology 6.
Apologetics.	Philosophy of Religion.	Ethical Theories.
N. T. Introduction.	Pastoral Care.	Theology of Universalism.
	Greek 14, 15.	

Description of Studies.

HEBREW.

1, 2, 3.   Grammar and Old Testament.

These are primarily courses in the Divinity School, but may be elected by students in the College of Liberal Arts whenever they are offered.   Classes will be formed each year if a sufficient number of students apply.

It is the aim to give the student such a knowledge of the forms and structure of the Hebrew language as shall enable him to use it efficiently in the criticism and literary analysis of the Old Testament Scriptures.   The text-books used are H. G. Mitchell's Hebrew Lessons and the Hebrew Old Testament. Three terms—Fall, Winter and Spring—each term counting as a course.   Dr. WHITE.

Open (under conditions as described above) to students who, in the judgment of the Instructor, are qualified by previous training to take the course.

BIBLE STUDY.

1.   English Bible.   (One-third course for each term.)

A general view of Biblical Literature and a more careful study of selected portions, with reference both to form and to content.   One hour a week throughout the year.

Professor FOWLER.

2.   Biblical Criticism.

Driver's Introduction to the Old Testament is used as a text-book, with references to Fripp, Ryle, Bacon, Robertson, and other works.   A course of lectures is given on the Science of Documentary Analysis, the Principles and Methods of Historical Criticism, and the Religious Aspects of the Higher Criticism. Winter term.   Dr. WHITE.

PREPARATORY GREEK.

(For Greek 1, 2, 3, 4, 5, see page 35.)

THE GREEK NEW TESTAMENT.

(The courses are numbered continuously with the Greek courses of the College of Liberal Arts.)

12.   Exegesis of the Synoptic Gospels.

Critical rendering of selections from the Synoptic Gospels. Exegesis of Mark's Gospel; Origin and peculiar characteristics of the Gospel, and its relation to the other Synoptists—their harmonies, divergencies, and interdependence. Date of Synoptic Gospels; their genuineness and authenticity. Theology and Christology of the Synoptic Gospels. Spring term.

Dr. White.

13. The Acts of the Apostles.

Critical rendering of the Greek text of the Acts of the Apostles, their genuineness and authenticity, date of the work, sources of the narrative. Exegesis of the Acts. Spring term.

Dr. White.

14. Thessalonians and Galatians.

Critical rendering of the Greek text of the epistles to the Thessalonians. Exegesis of the Epistles. Eschatology of the epistles. Primitive Paulinism. Critical rendering of the Greek text of the Epistle to the Galatians. Winter term.

Dr. White.

15. Corinthians, Romans, and Apocalypse.

Selections from the first and the second Epistle to the Corinthians. Critical rendering of the Greek text of the Epistle to the Romans. Examination of the nature of Pauline Theology and Christology. Development of the doctrine of Paul. Character of later Paulinism. Critical rendering of the Greek text of the Apocalypse. Examination of the resemblances and differences in the style and language of the Apocalypse and of the fourth gospel. Winter term.

Dr. White

THEOLOGY.

1. Apologetics.

Bruce's Apologetics is the text-book used. Considerable collateral reading is required of the student. Comparison is instituted between modern methods in Apologetics and the methods of Primitive Christianity. Fall term.

Dr. White.

2. Dogmatic Theology.

Martensen's Christian Dogmatics is used as a text-book. A thorough investigation is made of the several Christian doctrines, with an extended examination of associated questions and controversies. The widest liberty is given for questions and discussions on the various topics presented. Winter term.

Dr. White.

3. Theology of Universalism.

The Scriptural and rational bases of Universalism will be examined. Instruction will be given for the most part by lectures. Frequent reference will be made to such well known Universalist works as Manuals of Faith and Duty, Allin's Universalism Asserted, Thayer's Theology of Universalism, and Dr. Dodge's Purpose of God. Spring term.   Dr. WHITE.

4. Comparative Religions.

The work of the students consists in the examination and comparison of the authorities upon the great Non-Christian religions. Special topics are investigated and reports made by each member of the class. Spring term.   Dr. WHITE.

APPLIED CHRISTIANITY.

The demand for a more thorough investigation of the bearings of Christian Doctrine upon the social, political, and industrial organisms, coupled with the demand for a more diversified and scientific administration of religion through the churches, is met at Lombard College by the establishment of a chair of Applied Christianity and Pastoral Theology. The course of study provided for will occupy seven terms, six terms being devoted to Sociology, and one term to Pastoral Care.

A. SOCIOLOGY.

1. An Introduction to the Study of Sociology.

The purpose of this course is to afford an opportunity for the student to gain a knowledge of the characteristic conceptions and main trend of modern sociological thought. Constant reference to the works of the more important modern sociologists is required. The preparation and presentation of frequent and substantial papers by the student is an integral part of the work of the course.   Professor KIMBLE.

Open to those students who, in the judgment of the instructor, are fitted for the work.

2. An introduction to the Study of Society.

The purpose here is to gain a familiarity with the process of learning about society from society itself. This is virtually a laboratory course. The work will consist largely of investigations carried on by the students. Frequent papers will be required.   Professor KIMBLE.

Open to students who have completed Sociology 1.

3. The Family.

An outline study of the origin, development, and present significance of the human Family.   Professor KIMBLE.

Open to students who have completed Sociology 1 and 2.

4. Anthropo-Geography.

A study of the influence of the non-human environment upon the development of human association.   Professor KIMBLE.

Open to students who have completed Sociology 1 and 2.

5. Social Pathology.

An investigation of certain of the pathological elements of society. Special emphasis is laid upon modern charities methods. Papers. Primarily for the Divinity School.

Professor KIMBLE.

Open to students who have completed Sociology 1 and 2.

6. A Study of certain of the phenomena of Religion from the standpoint of Sociology.

The work of this course will center about the development of the function of the minister. Its purpose will be to enable the student to gain a more adequate idea of the social significance of the religious factor of society. Primarily for the Divinity School. Members of the course will meet at times to be determined upon. A large amount of investigatory work will be required.

Professor KIMBLE.

Open to students who have completed Sociology 1 and 2.

B. PASTORAL CARE.

The pastoral office will be specially studied. The spiritual, mental, and social qualifications of the minister for his work will be noted, and his administration of the special services of the church—baptism, confirmation, the Lord's Supper, marriage, and the burial of the dead. A liberal portion of the term will be devoted to an examination of various methods of church organization, for the purpose of giving the minister facility in adapting himself to parish needs, especially to those peculiar to the locality in which he may be settled. Winter term.

President NASH.

PHILOSOPHY.

1. (a) Psychology.

After a somewhat detailed inquiry into the general relations of mind and body, followed by a close examination of the phenomena of perception, the more complex mental processes, as memory, association, apperception, hallucination, imagination, impulse, habit, volition, are taken up for careful study. Special emphasis is laid upon self-observation, and the indications for self-culture are attentively marked. Stress is also laid upon the definition and use of technical terms. Baldwin's Elements are used for text; Halleck, Lindner, and Ladd for reference.

Dr. WHITE.

Open to students who, in the judgment of the instructor, are qualified by previous training to take the course.

1. (*b*). Psychology.

A second term in Psychology, using Ladd's Physiological Psychology, has been given in 1899–1900. Dr. WHITE.

2. Metaphysic.

This is primarily a course in the Divinity School, but it may be elected by students in the College of Liberal Arts whenever it is offered. Classes will be formed whenever a sufficient number of students apply. Lotze's Outlines of Metaphysic is used as a text-book. Fall term. Dr. WHITE.

Open to students who, in the judgment of the instructor, are qualified by previous training to take the course.

3. Logic.

Having first obtained a thorough grounding in the principles and methods of correct reasoning, both deductive and inductive, at least one-half of the term is given to the detection and discrimination of fallacies in actual examples. Such examples the class is required to search out in current literature and bring in for discussion. Davis's Elements of Deductive Logic, and Davis's Elements of Inductive Logic are used. Winter term.

Professor FOWLER.

Open to students who, in the judgment of the instructor, are qualified by previous training to take the course.

4. Ethics.

Ethics is treated from the standpoint of Philosophy, and the different systems are discussed. The nature and grounds of obligation are investigated and applied to the practical affairs of life. Spring term. Professor KIMBLE.

Open to students who, in the judgment of the instructor, are qualified by previous training to take the course.

5. Philosophy of Religion.

Caird's Introduction to the Philosophy of Religion is the text-book. Lotze, Sabatier, and Martineau are used as works of reference. The aim of the instructor is to acquaint the student with the proper office of reason in the effort to find argumentative grounds for religious ideas. Most of the modern theories respecting the nature and scope of the religious feeling pass under review; and in such discussions free questioning on the part of the student is encouraged. Winter term. Dr. WHITE.

Open to students who, in the judgment of the instructor, are qualified by previous training to take the course.

6. Ethical Theories.

Martineau's Types of Ethical Theory is used as a text-book with frequent references to the works of Sidgwick, Green, Smythe, and others. Much attention is paid to the elucidation and criticism of the modern ethical theories. Spring term.

Dr. WHITE.

Open to students who, in the judgment of the instructor, are qualified by previous training to take the course.

CHURCH HISTORY.

(The courses in Church History are numbered continuously with the courses in History in the Preparatory School. See page 58.)

5. History of the Christian Church.

A. *The Ancient and Mediæval Eras (1-1517).*

This course in Church History is primarily intended for the members of the Divinity School, but is now open to College students. It will require the investigation of the early organization and extension of Christianity, and the successive periods of the Church down to the time of Charlemagne; followed by a careful inquiry into the causes of the rise of the Papacy, of the political relations of the Church, and of the Crusades. Fisher's History of the Church will be used as a hand book and topics will be assigned to each member of the class for special investigation and reports. Fall term. Dr. WHITE.

Open to students who have completed History 1 and 2.

6. History of the Christian Church.

B. *The Modern Era (1517-1900).*

This course will begin with the study of the Reformation, and trace the history of the Church down to the present time. It will include the history of Christian missions, revivals, social reforms, and philanthropy. The same text-book will be used as in History 5. Spring term. Dr. WHITE.

Open to students who, in the judgment of the instructor, are qualified by previous training to take the course.

HOMILETICS.

The course in Homiletics covers the third and fourth years. The primary aim is practical. Upon a general but adequate groundwork of theory and history of preaching the effort is made to construct an art of effective pulpit oratory. Elaborate and exacting drill in the logical conception and construction of the sermon plan, with constant application of rhetorical principles, occupies the major part of the first year. Inspiration and direction are sought in the frequent analysis of the discourses of great preachers of all styles, and in the study of their sources of power. Individuality and originality are emphasized as desiderata. In the second year the stress is laid upon flexibility and adaptability, upon invention, upon the rationale of interesting preaching, and upon the acquisition of freedom in extempore address. Throughout the course the preparation and criticism of sermons by the class continues uninterruptedly.

ELOCUTION.

In view of the fact that a good delivery is of inestimable advantage to the preacher, the students in the Divinity School are offered an extended course in Elocution and Physical Culture.

The students are not only admitted to all Elocution classes in the College, but also receive a large amount of individual training.

Courses 1, 2, 3, 4, 5, 6, as outlined on pp. 47 and 48 of this catalogue are required.

ENGLISH.

For English 5, 6, 8, which courses are required in the Divinity School, see p. 29 of this catalogue.

8. Daily Themes.

This course will be made a full course for students in the Divinity School. Besides the daily themes, fortnightly themes will be required. Spring term.   Professor FOWLER.

COLLEGE STUDIES.

Divinity students are permitted, with the consent of the Faculty, to pursue studies in the College of Liberal Arts. Graduates of the Divinity School may receive the additional degree of Bachelor of Arts, upon the satisfactory completion of an aggregate of twenty full courses taken in the classes of the College of Liberal Arts, beyond the full requirements of the Divinity School for the degree of Bachelor of Divinity.

In addition to the above twenty credits, the candidate must furnish the full quota of twenty-one credits required for admission to the College of Liberal Arts. Of these twenty-one credits, the courses required for admission to the Divinity School (see p. 60) will count ten.

Department of Music

Department of Music.

Instruction is provided in the various branches of Theoretical, Vocal, and Instrumental Music. These courses are distinct from the work in the other departments of the college, and unless otherwise specified do not count toward a college degree. Students are classed and registered as private pupils of the several instructors, with whom arrangements may be made in regard to lessons. Instruction is given either at the college, or at the instruction-rooms of the teachers, as preferred.

Faculty.

KARL JAKOB RUDOLPH LUNDBERG,
Director and Instructor in Voice, Piano, Organ, and Theory.

W. H. CHEESMAN,
Instructor in Violin.

Students in the Department of Music.

HARMONY.

Nellie Ewart..*Greenup.*
Mae Victoria Fifield......................................*Buda.*
Mary Arrah Hart ....*Eureka, Kan.*
Virginia C. Henney.....................*Mitchellville, Ia.*
Augusta Eaton Hitchcock..................... . ....*Osage, Ia.*
Leura Willis................................. .....*Table Grove.*

INSTRUMENTAL MUSIC.

Lilian Bäckman....... ....*Galesburg.*
Nannie Mer Buck.............. ,....................*Le Roy.*
Ruth Chamberlain.... ....*Galesburg.*
Walter Timothy Clay........... ....*Galesburg.*
Sarah Lucy Cook........ ....*Le Roy.*
Nellie Ewart........... ....*Greenup.*
Mae Victoria Fifield......... ....*Buda.*

Lelia Harner...*Sangemon.*
Ethyline Hastings....................... ..... *Owatonna, Minn.*
Mary Arrah Hart...................................*Eureka, Kan.*
Virginia C. Henney............... ....*Mitchellville, Ia.*
Augusta Eaton Hitchcock...........................*Osage, Ia.*
Pauline Marsh......... ....*Galesburg.*
Mrs. H. Martin...................................*East Galesburg.*
Pearl Maxwell.......................................*Burlington, Ia.*
Helen Augusta Miles...................................*Galesburg.*
Mabel Louise Mills..................................*Ossian, Ia.*
Faith Tenney Nash...................................*Galesburg.*
Lydia Ringenberg.............................*Lombardville.*
Gertrude Rich...*Galesburg.*
Willis Rich................. ....*Galesburg.*
Carrie Schroeder..................... ....*Galesburg.*
Mrs. E. S. Scott..................................*Galesburg.*
Tommye Slaid. ....*Owatonna, Minn.*
Elsie Sommers....................................*Burlington, Ia.*
L. A. Sward...................................*Galesburg.*
Hannah Swanson.....................................*Galesburg.*
Lora Adelle Townsend....................... ....*Galesburg.*
Ethel Van Cise...............................*Deadwood, S. D.*
Cyrenia Weir............... ....*Galesburg.*
Leura Willis.....................................*Table Grove.*

VOCAL MUSIC.

Nannie Mer Buck..*LeRoy.*
Fay Alexander Bulluck...............................*Galesburg.*
Fannie Estelle Churchill................................*Avon.*
May Victoria Fifield........ ....*Buda.*
Emma Flinn.............................. ......*Galesburg.*
Ethyline Hastings...........................*Owatonna, Minn.*
Frank Johnson. ....*Galesburg.*
Jennie Eliza Marriott.......................*La Moille.*
Mrs. H. Martin ....*East Galesburg.*
Clara Matson....................................*Lake Geneva, Wis.*
Faith Tenney Nash......................... ......*Galesburg.*
Tommye Slaid............................. *Owatonna, Minn.*
L. A. Sward. ....*Galesburg.*
Ethel Van Cise..... ....*Deadwood, S. D.*

A. THEORETICAL COURSES.

Professor Lundberg.

1. **Harmony.** (Music 1, 2, 3.)

Class-room work, lectures, recitations, and written exercises, covering theory of the elements of music, triads, chords of the seventh, augmented chords, chords of the ninth and eleventh, modulation, suspension, and harmonizing of melodies. Text-books, Emery, Richter, and Jadassohn. Three hours a week for one year.   Professor LUNDBERG.

Open to all students in the University.

2. Simple and Double Counterpoint. (Music 4, 5, 6.)

Lectures, recitations, and daily written exercises, based on the text-books of Richter, Haupt, and others. Three hours a week for one year.   Professor LUNDBERG.

Open to students who have completed Music 3.

3. Fugue, Canon, Musical Form, and the elements of Orchestration. (Music 7, 8, 9.)

Lectures, recitations and written exercises. Text-books, Prout, Cherubini, Rieman, Berlioz. Three hours a week for one year.   Professor LUNDBERG.

Open to students who have completed Music 6.

4. History of Music. (Music 10.) [Half Course.]

Introductory course on the lives of the great composers. Two hours a week. Fall term.   Professor LUNDBERG.

Open to students who, in the judgment of the instructor, are qualified by previous training to take the course.

5. History of Music. (Music 11.) [Half Course.]

Advanced course on the development of music from the earliest times until to-day, with special reference to critical analysis of the works of the greatest masters. Text-books, Naumann, Langhans, Rieman. Two hours a week. Winter term.

Professor LUNDBERG.

Open to students who have completed Music 10.

6. Acoustics.

Theory of sound in its connection with Music and musical instruments. Open to students who have finished Course 1. Text-books, Helmholtz, Tyndall.

Music 1 to 9 count each as a credit towards a degree in the College of Liberal Arts, Music 10, 11, and the course in Acoustics, each as a half credit.

B. PIANOFORTE COURSES.

Professor Lundberg.

1. Preparatory Year.

Five-finger exercises; scales in major and minor; triads; selected studies by Czerney, Vol. 1 (Germer Edition.)

2. First Grade.

Finger exercises; scales; Czerney's studies, Vol. 1 and 2; (Germer edition;) Sonatinen by Dussek, Clementi, Diabelli, Kuhlau, Reinecke. Memorizing.

3. Second Grade.

Finger exercises; scales; arpeggios; Czerney's studies, Vol. 3; (Germer edition); Sonatinas by Clementi, Kuhlau, Dussek, Haydn, Mozart, Beethoven. Pieces by American and foreign composers.

4. Third Grade.

Finger exercises with modulation to different keys. Scales in fourths, sixths, and thirds. Czerney's studies, Vol. 4; Bach's Inventions for two and three voices. Pieces by different composers.

5. Fourth Grade.

Finger exercises in different keys. Scales; études by Cramer; preludes and fugues by Bach. Easier sonatas by Haydn, Clementi, Mozart and Beethoven. Memorizing; pieces by different composers.

6. Fifth Grade.

Finger exercises in different keys; scales. Clementi's Gradus ad Parnassum. Etudes by Moscheles, Chopin, etc. Sonatas by Bach, Mozart, Beethoven and Hummel. Memorizing. Pieces by different composers.

VOICE CULTURE.

Professor Lundberg.

1. First Grade.

Exercises in breathing, tone placing, sustained tones, etc. Voice training exercises by Emil Behnke and C. W. Pearce. 50 vocalises by Concone. Easy songs.

2. Second Grade.

Masset's exercises; 30 exercises by Concone; 25 and 15 vocalises by Concone. Songs by American and foreign composers.

3. Third Grade.

Vocalises by Reber, Panofka, and Masset. Songs, and oratorios. Recitatives. Practicing of duets, trios and quartets.

C. PIPE ORGAN COURSES.

Professor Lundberg.

Students who wish to begin the study of the Organ should have completed the Second Grade of the Piano Course.

The chief aim of this department is the thorough preparation of church organists. Organ students should also make a conscientious study of Solo and Chorus Singing, with a view of becoming efficient chorus-masters and directors of church music.

The study of Harmony, Counterpoint, and History of Music is absolutely necessary to an intelligent study of the instrument.

1. First Grade.

Exercises in pedal playing, Ritter's Organ School, hymns, construction of interludes, Modulation, Transposing, and Elementary Registration.

2. Second Grade.

Studies in Pedal Phrasing by Buck, Volkmar, and Schneider. Polyphonic compositions by Rink, Bach, Fisher. Easy pieces by Merkel, Dubois, Guilmant, Mendelssohn, and others. Registration, Structure of the Organ, Choir Accompaniment.

3. Third Grade.

Study of Sonatas and Fugues by Bach, Mendelssohn, Rheinberger, and others. Modern compositions of German, English and French masters. Choir accompaniment.

D. VIOLIN COURSES.

Professor Cheesman.

1. Preparatory Grade.

Elementary exercises in position, bowing, etc. Easy exercises in major and minor keys in the first book from Wichtl's Violin School. Pleyel's Duets, and twelve studies by H. E. Kayser, op. 20. Memorizing.

2. Intermediate Grade.

Studies by Kayer and Wohlfahrt. Systematic progress through the various positions, beginning with the second book of F. Hermann. Studies from Schradieck for the development of technic and pure tone qualities. Selections from compositions by Dancla, Mazas, Weiss, DeBeriot: also solos and fantasias based upon operatic themes.

3. Advanced Grade.

Technical studies from the works of Kruetzer, Fiorillo, Rode, together with duets, trios and quartets, arranged for strings; overtures; sight-reading. Sonatas and concertos by Bach, Haydn, Spohr, Beethoven, Mendelssohn, DeBeriot, Wieniawsky, Grieg, and others.

E. MANDOLIN AND GUITAR COURSES.

The study of these popular instruments has become a favorite recreation with those students of our colleges who may not have the time or inclination to pursue the study of music in its more serious forms.

At the conclusion of the first term of lessons (twelve weeks), a "Lombard Mandolin Club" will be organized, with rehearsals one evening a week. The Italian method is used entirely in the study of these instruments, thereby establishing the very best method of picking the strings and fingering, with special attention to the tone quality of the "tremolo," which relieves the mandolin of much of its so-called monotony. Solos, duets, and quartets will also be prepared in addition to the regular club work, with special numbers to be given by the lady members of the club.

G. SIGHT SINGING AND CHORUS CLASSES.

Professor Lundberg.

1. Elementary Sight Singing Class.

The rudiments of Music, the intervals of the Major Scale, exercises in one and two parts, and easy songs. Ear-training. One college term.

2. Advanced Class.

Solfeggios in major and minor keys, three and four part songs. One college term.

3. Chorus Class.

Four part compositions, glees, sacred and secular choruses from our best classic and modern composers. Oratorios.

Only those students who have finished the work done in the Advanced Sight-Singing Class will be admitted into the Chorus Class.

Requirements for Graduation.

A diploma will be conferred upon any student who shall satisfactorily complete any of the following courses in instrumental or vocal music. In addition to the requirements enumerated below, the candidate will prepare a thesis, present an original musical composition, or perform other original work satisfactory to the instructor, and also appear in public at a graduating recital.

A. THE PIANOFORTE.

Musical Requirements.

Five grades of the Piano Courses, Nos. 1, 2, 3, 4, 5, 6, 10, and 11 of the Theoretical Courses; Acoustics; and one year's membership in the Chorus Class.

Literary Requirements.

English Grammar, English Composition, Rhetoric, English and American Literature, one year of French or German.

If the candidate upon entering brings satisfactory proof of proficiency in any of these courses, he is advised to take one study each term from such electives in the College of Liberal Arts as the Director may recommend.

B. THE PIPE ORGAN.

Musical Requirements.

The full Organ Course, Nos. 1, 2, 3, 4, 5, 6, 10, and 11 of the Theoretical Courses; and Acoustics.

Literary Requirements.

The same as for Piano students.

C. THE VOICE.

Musical Requirements.

All the prescribed studies for Voice Culture; grade 2 of the Piano Courses, with special view to accompaniments; and Nos. 1, 2, 3, 10, 11, of the Theoretical Courses.

Literary Requirements.

The same as for Piano students, except that Italian may be substituted for French or German.

TUITION.

The following prices are for a term of twelve weeks:

THEORETICAL COURSES—
Music 1 to 9, each, $5.00.
Music 10 and 11, each, $3.00.

PIANOFORTE—
Private Lessons—one hour per week, $18.00.
Private Lessons—two half hours per week, $18.00.
Private Lessons—one half hour per week, $10.00.
Private Lessons—one 45-minute lesson per week, $14.00.

Class Lessons, one hour per week, each—
     In classes of two, $10.00.
     In classes of three, $7.00.

VOICE CULTURE—
Charges same as for piano forte.

RENT OF PIANO—1 hour per day, per term, $2.75.
2 hours per day, per term, $5.00.
3 hours per day, per term, $6.75.
4 hours per day, per term, $8.00.

PIPE ORGAN—
Private Lessons—one hour per week, $24.00.
In classes of two, one hour per week, each person, $13.00.

VIOLIN—
Private Lessons—one hour per week, $15.00.
Private Lessons—two half hours per week, $15.00.
Private Lessons—one 45-minute lesson per week, $12.00.

CLASS LESSONS, one hour per week, each—
In classes of two, $8.00.
In classes of three, $6.00.

MANDOLIN AND GUITAR—
Private Lessons—one hour per week, $12.00.
Private Lessons—two half hours per week, $12.00.

Class Lessons—charges will be given on application to teacher.
(A weekly rehearsal for club practice without extra charge).
SIGHT SINGING CLASSES—
Each, $1.00.

CHORUS CLASS—
A charge of $1.00 per term each will be made for the use of music to be supplied by the department.

The privilege of joining the Lombard Mandolin and Guitar Club, or the Lombard String Orchestra is extended to any student outside of the private pupils of the instructor, by the payment of $1.25 per term of twelve weeks. Rehearsals one evening each week.

General Remarks:

Tuition and other charges must be paid before lessons are assigned.

In case of protracted sickness only, will a proportionate deduction be made from term charges.

No visitors are allowed in practice rooms during practice hours.

All concerts and recitals given by the school of music or its faculty are free to music students.

A course of free lectures on musical culture will be given each year by the Director.

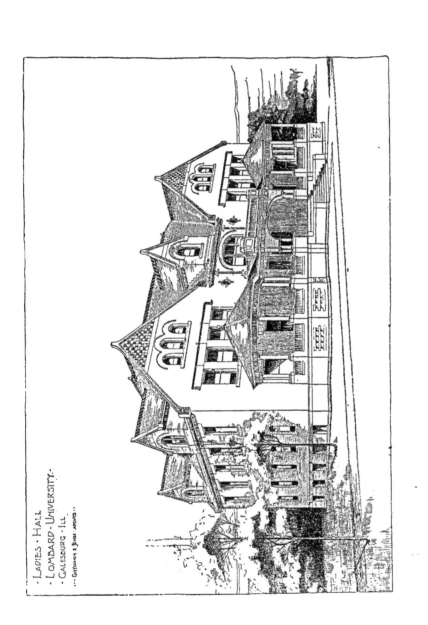

· LADIES · HALL
· LOMBARD · UNIVERSITY ·
· GALESBURG · ILL ·
··· GOTTSCHALK & BEACH · ARCH'TS ···

Department of Art

Department of Art.

Instructor.

M. ISABELLE BLOOD.

Students in the Department of Art.

Maude Andrew...*New Salem.*
Roland Buckley...*Knoxville.*
Jessie Evelyn Collins...............................*Stoughton, Wis.*
Inez May De Voll....................................*Stoughton, Wis.*
Josephine Ericson...................................*Galesburg.*
Howard Foster.......................................*Galesburg.*
Jennie A. Fowler....................................*Galesburg.*
Bessie Fuller.......................................*Galesburg.*
Ora Head..*Galesburg.*
Ida Hopkins...*Galesburg.*
Florence Pearl King.................................*Waukegan.*
Pearl Luster..*Galesburg.*
Helen Manny...*Galesburg.*
Mabel Mills...*Ossian, Ia.*
Mabel Munson ....*Galesburg.*
Ada Peterson..*Galesburg.*
Grace Olive Pingrey.................................*Coon Rapids, Ia.*
Lulu Ramp...*Knoxville.*
Lydia Ringenberg....................................*Lombardville.*
Lora Adelle Townsend................................*Galesburg.*
Frances Cora White..................................*Galesburg.*
Bessie Yetter.......................................*Galesburg.*

Course in Art.

The Art Department affords a practical course in Drawing and Painting to those who wish to become teachers, designers, illustrators, or portrait artists. Regular students in this department who wish to take the entire course in Art will be given careful training in the following branches: Perspective drawing; drawing from casts in charcoal and crayon; still life studies in crayon, oil, water color, and pastel; landscape from nature; and copying from good studies.

The entire course will occupy from two to three years, according to the ability of the student and the amount of time given to the work. A thorough knowledge of the elements of drawing being necessary to independent work, at least one year's work will be required in drawing in black and white from models of simple form, casts, still life, and those studies which will best prepare the student for the special line of work preferred.

Students may enter the Art Department at any time; and though they are advised to take a full course in order to obtain the best results, arrangements can be made for lessons in any line desired.

While portrait work, pen and ink drawing, and china painting are not required in the regular course, credit will be given for good work in any of these branches if it is desired to substitute them in part for oil, water color, or pastel.

A course of study in the History of Art and a thesis upon some subject approved by the instructor will also be required of students wishing to graduate from this department.

Those who complete the work as outlined above will be entitled to a Diploma.

For description of courses in the History of Art, and in Free Hand Drawing, and for credit allowed for these courses in the College of Liberal Arts, see p. 46.

TUITION.

The tuition fees will be as follows:

Drawing or Sketching—3-hour lesson, 35 cents.
Painting in Water Colors—3-hour lesson, 50 cents.
Oil Painting—3-hour lesson, 50 cents.
Portrait and China Painting—3-hour lesson, 50 cents.

For those who work six hours per week for the entire year, a rebate will be made at the end of the Spring term, so that the lessons in drawing will be less than 35 cents.

If pupils in Art desire four or more lessons per week, special rates are made.

THE GYMNASIUM.

Department of Elocution and Dramatic Expression

Department of Elocution and Dramatic Expression.

The object of the work in this department is to acquire a knowledge of the Art of Expression by means of the cultivated voice and educated body. A complete and thorough course is offered in its various branches, affording a theoretical and practical training in all the principles upon which the art is based. The aim is to study the individual needs of the student mentally, vocally, and pictorially, and to found upon this study a discipline which shall develop the powers of expression through intelligent grasp of thought and trained aesthetic conception. Three years are necessary for the fulfillment of all requirements in this department. Instruction is given in the class room or the auditorium of the gymnasium building, which is provided with a stage well equipped with curtain, scenery, appliances, etc., affording ample opportunity of obtaining facility in voice and action.

Recitals will be made a prominent feature during the year, to show the proficiency of pupils and to afford them assistance in acquiring confidence, ease, and self-control. These recitals are to be considered, not as an end in themselves, but as an auxiliary to the course of the work.

Instructor.

MAUD AUGUSTA MINER.

PRIVATE PUPILS IN ELOCUTION AND DRAMATIC EXPRESSION.

Charles Peter Boeck...... .... *Chicago.*
Ella Berry Boston................. .... *Galesburg.*
W. D. Buchanan............................... *Coon Rapids, Ia.*
Kate Clark................................,............ *Maquon.*
Inez May De Voll............................... *Stoughton, Wis.*
Cora Fosher............................. .... *Galesburg.*
Myrtle Hall.. *Galesburg.*
Lelia Harner... *Sangamon.*
Helen Augusta Miles................................ *Galesburg.*
Mabel Louise Mills.................................. *Ossian, Ia.*

PUPILS IN PHYSICAL CULTURE.

Ethel Chamberlain.............................. ....*Galesburg.*
Marie Seacord......................................*Galesburg.*
Lucy Terry....... ....*Galesburg.*

[The names of other pupils doing class work in Elocution and Dramatic Expression are included in the lists of students in the College of Liberal Arts and in the Preparatory and Divinity Schools.]

DESCRIPTION OF STUDIES.

1. Elocution. [Half Course.]

The aim of this course is to rid the voice of all impurities, secure correct placing of the voice, proper breathing, and beauty of tone for conversational purposes. Notes will be given upon the anatomy of the vocal organs and the care of the voice. Physical exercises will be introduced as a means of securing grace and becoming deportment. Recitations Mondays, Wednesdays, and Fridays. Fall term. Miss MINER.

Open to all students of the College.

2. Elocution. [Half Course.]

In this course attention will be given to the adaptation of the conversational voice to the requirements of platform speaking. Continued work in bodily expression and deportment. Each pupil will be required to deliver three selections before the class for criticism. In the preparation of these selections at least one private rehearsal will be given by the instructor. Recitations Mondays, Wednesdays, and Fridays. Winter term.

Miss MINER.

Open to students who have completed Elocution 1.

3. Elocution. [Half Course.]

This course will consist of a continuation of the work outlined in Elocution 2. Three selections will be required from each pupil and individual drill continued. Recitations Mondays, Wednesdays, and Fridays. Spring term. Miss MINER.

Open to students who have completed Elocution 2.

4. Elocution. [Half Course.]

The study of the emotions with illustrative readings will be begun in this course. Pantomime will be made a chief feature— a series of pantomimic studies being given for the highest expression of thought and feeling through the medium of a cultivated body.　Recitations Mondays and Thursdays.　Fall term.

Miss Miner.

Open to students who have completed Elocution 3.

5. Elocution. [Half Course.]

The work in this course will be a continuation of that begun in Elocution 4, together with personations.　Pantomimic studies continued.　Recitations Mondays and Thursdays.　Winter term.

Miss Miner.

Open to students who have completed Elocution 4.

6. Elocution. [Half Course.]

This course will consist of a continuation of Elocution 5. Recitations Mondays and Thursdays.　Spring term.

Miss Miner.

Open to students who have completed Elocution 5.

7. Oratory. [Half Course.]

The direct aim of this course will be the study of the great orators.　Each student will be required to deliver before the class for criticism a certain number of selections chosen from the orators studied.　Extemporaneous talks will also be a feature of this work.　Recitations Mondays and Thursdays.　Fall term.　　　　　　　　　　　　　　　　　　　Miss Miner.

Open to students who have completed Elocution 3.

8. Oratory. [Half Course.]

A continuation of extemporaneous speaking will be given in this course with criticism.　Two orations will be required from each member of the class.　Recitations Mondays and Thursdays. Winter term.　　　　　　　　　　　　　　　　Miss Miner.

Open to students who have completed Elocution 7.

9. Dramatic Expression. [Half Course.]

This course consists of the study of one and two act comedies for character interpretation and elements of stage business. Recitations Tuesdays and Thursdays.　Fall term.

Miss Miner.

Open to students who have completed Elocution 6.

10, 11. Dramatic Expression. [Half Courses.]

These courses will be a continuation of Elocution 9, taking up longer plays.　Recitations Tuesdays and Thursdays.　Winter and Spring terms.　　　　　　　　　　　　　　Miss Miner.

Open to students who have completed Elocution 9.

REQUIREMENTS FOR GRADUATION IN ELOCUTION.

Elocution courses 1, 2, 3, 4, 5, 6; Oratory 7, 8; Dramatic Art 9, 10, 11. One private lesson a week for two years.

Literary Requirements.

English Grammar; English and American Literature; one year of French; one year of German; one year of Music; Roman and Grecian History.

A thesis upon some subject approved by the instructor.

TERMS.

Class Lessons—
Regular charge in class per term, besides incidentals.....................$1.75

Private Lessons—
One half hour a week, per term...$ 6.00
Two half hour a week, per term.... .... 10.00

General Summary.

COLLEGE OF LIBERAL ARTS.

Candidates for degrees in 1900.

Master of Arts.................................... 1
Bachelor of Arts.....................................10
                — 11
Students in the College of Liberal Arts................ ... 66

PREPARATORY SCHOOL.

Students in the Preparatory School......................... 34

RYDER DIVINITY SCHOOL.

Candidates for degrees in 1899.

Bachelor of Divinity................................... 1

Students in the Divinity School.

Fourth Year.. 1
Third Year... 2
Second Year.. 3
First Year... 1
                — 7

MUSIC.

Students in Harmony and Musical Composition.......... .. 6
Students in Instrumental Music.......................31
Students in Vocal Culture 14
                — 51

ART.

Students in Art...................................22

ELOCUTION AND DRAMATIC EXPRESSION.

Private Pupils in Elocution and Dramatic Expression..... 10
Special Pupils in Physical Culture....................... 3
               ——
               205
Names entered twice.................................. 58
               ——
Total 147

Association of Graduates.

1899-1900.

OFFICERS.

PRESIDENT,

REV. EBEN H. CHAPIN, ROCKLAND, ME.

VICE PRESIDENT,

ALVA T. WING, KNOXVILLE.

SECRETARY,

NINA ALTA HARRIS, GALESBURG.

TREASURER,

JON W. GRUBB, GALESBURG.

HISTORIAN,

WILLARD J. WHITE, M. D., LONGMONT, COLO.

BOARD OF DIRECTORS.

E. H. CHAPIN.	MRS. JENNIE T. WEBSTER.
J. D. WELSH.	C. ELLWOOD NASH.
J. J. WELSH.	ALVA T. WING.
R. D. BOWER.	H. M. CHASE.

NINA ALTA HARRIS.

Graduates.

The degree of A. M. or M. S. placed immediately after a name, implies that the corresponding Bachelor's degree (A. B. or B. S.) was received on graduation.

The person to whose name a star is attached is deceased. The date following designates the year of his death.

1856.

William Worth Burson, A. M..........Manufacturer, 322 Racine Ave., Chicago.
William Ramey Cole, A. M......................Clergyman, Mt. Pleasant, Iowa.
Hon. Thompson W. McNeeley, A. M.............Ex-M. C., Attorney, Petersburg.
Hon. Lewis Alden Simmons, A. M., *1889....................Wellington, Kansas.
Addie Hurd, A. M., (Mrs. Wm. VanHorn).....917 Sherbrooke St., Montreal, Can.
Jennie Miles, A. M., *1859...Decatur.

1857.

Fielding B. Bond, A. B., *1862...Greenbush.
Floyd G. Brown, A. B., *1868......................................Mankato, Minn.
James Henry Chapin, A. M., Ph. D., *1892......................Meriden, Conn.
Hon. Edward D. Laning, A. B.............................Attorney, Petersburg.
Hon. Scott Wike, B. S..............Ex-Asst. Sec. U. S. Treas., Attorney, Barry.

1858.

Anson L. Clark, A. M., M. D., President Bennett Eclectic Medical College,
Chicago...Elgin.
Thomas Gorman, A. B., *1891...Columbus, O.

1859.

Hon. George W. Elwell, B. S., *1869...............................Chillicothe, Mo
Eugene Beauharnais Hill, B. S....................Manufacturer, Ottumwa, Iowa.
Almon Kidder, A. M...Attorney, Monmouth.
Mary Jane Fuller, B. S.......................................Tarpon Springs, Fla.
Ruth Waldron Miller, M. S., (Mrs. Brower) *1892.........................Chicago.

1860.

Jonathan Eden Brown, A. B............................Farmer, Peabody, Kan.
Arick Burr, B. S., *1860..Charleston.
Hon. William Judah Frisbee, A. M............................Druggist, Bushnell.
James Scott Lindsay, A. B., *1860......................................Onarga.
Albert Sidney Slater, M. S., M. D.......................................Wataga.

1861.

Hon. Franklin Fayette Bower, A. M., *1869 ....Ottawa.
Everett Lorentus Conger, A. M., D. D.................Clergyman, Pasadena, Cal.
Henry George Pollock, A. M.......................Clergyman, Shelbyville, Ind.
Mary Stewart Miller, A. B., (Mrs. Catlin) *1867.......................Vinton, Ia.

1862.

Hon. Edward Hurd Conger, A. M........U. S. Minister to China, Peking, China.
Samuel Alvus Dow, A. M., M. D.........Wyalong, New South Wales, Australia.
William Sampson Dow, B. S., *1863.......................................Galesburg.
Hon. Charles Allen Holmes, A. M.........................Attorney, Victor, Colo.
Hamilton Lafayette Karr, A. M...........................Attorney, Osceola, Ia.
Frederick Warren Livingston, M. S.....................Teacher, San Diego, Cal.
Harvey Rowell, A. B.......................Solicitor of Patents, Columbus, Wis.
Hon. John Crocker Sherwin, M. S., Ex-M. C., Attorney,
1234 Columbus St., Denver, Colo.
Alfred Henry Trego, A. M..............................Manufacturer, Hoopeston.
George John Turner, A. M., M. D., *1899...............................Oskaloosa, Ia.
Eugenia Adaline Fuller, B. S., (Mrs. J. W. Ranstead)......................Elgin.

1863.

Samuel Addison Calhoun, A. B.....Adv. Solicitor "German Demokrat," Peoria.
Hon. John W. Ranstead, B. S..Attorney, Elgin.
Hannah Jane Biddlecome, M. S..Bookkeeper Glendale Furnace Co.,Columbus, O.
Oricy Villa Crocker, L. A., (Mrs. Nead) *1880............................Galesburg.
Sarah Jane Miles, A. M., (Mrs. Bullman)................................Galesburg.
Mary Addie Moore, M. S., (Mrs. Sumner Ellis).........2734 Prairie Ave., Chicago.
Sarah Jane Pike, L. A., (Mrs. E. H. Conger)......................Peking, China.

1864.

Elmore Chase, B. S......................................Teacher, Fair Oaks, Cal.
Leslie Greenwood, A. M......With Farmers' Loan and Trust Co., Sioux City, Ia.
Laura Lavinia Pike, A. M., (Mrs. J. S. McConnell)......4359 Lake Ave., Chicago.
Josephine Raymond, A. M., (Antioch College), (Mrs. Maxwell).......Champaign.
Sallie Raymond, L. A., (Mrs. J. B. Green)...............................Ramsey.

1865.

Elmore Chase, B. S., A. M...............................Teacher, Fair Oaks, Cal.
John Henry McCormick, B. S...Caledonia, Mo.
Alice Caroline Chapin, B. S.,Teacher, 222 West 3d South St., Salt Lake City, Utah

1866.

Hon. Elwin Wallace Claycomb, A. M......................Farmer, Eureka, Kan.
Hon. Geo. R. Shook, B. S....................Teacher and Surveyor, Fruita, Colo.
James Smith McConnell, B. S.............Attorney, 84 Washington St., Chicago.
Emma N. H. Conger, A. M., (Mrs. S. W. Conger).................Villa Park, Cal.

1867.

William Bryan Carlock, B. S..........................Attorney, Bloomington.
William Harvey Woods, B. S...................................Farmer, Mendota.
Helen Maria Bingham, L. A., M. D...............1623 Gaylord St., Denver, Colo.

1868.

Henry Moses Chase, A. B., *1870.......................................Concord, Vt.
Hon. James O'Donnell, B. S..............................Attorney, Cherokee, Ia.
Wellington Smith, B. S., *1870...Annawan.
Edward Keys Walbridge, B. S........Loan and Real Estate Agent, Girard, Kan.
Mary J. Claycomb, A. M., (Mrs. J. W. Grubb).........................Galesburg.
Josephine Merrian Kirk, A. M., (Mrs. Kerr) *1879......................Chicago.

Almeda Beals, L. A., (Mrs. Chas. Wickwire).........................Farmington.
Sarah Elvira Edwards, L. A., (Mrs. Otis Jones), *1899.........Los Angeles, Cal.
Grace Greenwood, L. A., (Mrs. E. E. Holroyd), *1898......................Chicago.
Emeline Elizabeth Kirk, L. A., *1881...Rockford.
Frances Elizabeth Pike, L. A., (Mrs. J. Kirke Keller,)
                         Artist, 243 Bd. Rospail, Paris, France.
Mary Ann Sparks, L. A., (Mrs. Milnor)................................Litchfield.
Florence Adeline Tenny, L. A., (Mrs. Edwards,) *1871...............Omaha, Neb.
Mary Emeline Weston, L. A.,(Mrs. Woodman,) *1888...............Portland, Me.

1869.

Rauseldon Cooper, B. S..Attorney, Oquawka.
Hon. Samuel Kerr, A. M.......................Attorney, 189 LaSalle St., Chicago.
Hon. Michael F. Knappenberger, B. S...............Attorney, Jewel City, Kan.
Howard Knowles, B. S..Galesburg.
Patrick Talent, B. S......................................Attorney, Butte City, Mont.
John Ewalt Wiley, B. S...Farmer, Elmwood.
Mary Emily Dunton, A. M., (Mrs. Sam'l Kerr)..1323 Washington Blvd., Chicago.
Ella May Greenwood, L. A., (Mrs. S. O. Snyder).687 3rd St., Salt Lake City, Utah.
Mary Hartman, L. A., A. M., 1888. ....Teacher in State Normal Univ., Normal.

1870.

Jared Perkins Blood, A. B............................Attorney, Sioux City, Iowa.
Hon. Abraham Miller Brown, A. M..........................Attorney, Galesburg.
Nathaniel Ray Chase, A. M., M. D................................Newport, R. I.
Matthias Crum, M. S...Banker, Farmer City.
Hon. Charles Electus Hasbrook, A. M., LL. B. (Chicago University),
             Business Manager Denver Republican, Denver, Colo.
Elmer Clifford Johnson, B. S........Manufacturer, 36 Main St., Evansville, Ind.
Otis Jones, B. S..............................Real Estate dealer, San Antonio, Cal.
Israel Cyrus Stockton, M. S......Clerk, Interior Department, Washington, D. C.
Hon. John Hill Walbridge, B. S.......................Farmer, West Concord, Vt.
Mary Ann Chapin, L. A., (Mrs. T. T. Perry) *1883...................Girard, Kan.
Flora Amanda Edwards, L. A., (Mrs. J. F. Fargo)..............San Antonio, Cal.

1871.

Hon. Martin Ireneus Brower, A. M....................Attorney, Fullerton, Neb.
Hon. Willis Hardin Fuson, A. M., *1884..........................Wa Keeney, Kan.
Frank Tenney Greenwood, A. B......................... Druggist, Seneca, Kan.
Hon. Madison Reynolds Harris, A. B. Att'y, 148 W. Madison St., Rm. 30, Chicago.
Hon. Samuel Parsons McConnell, A. B.,
            Ex-Circuit Judge, Attorney, Home Insurance Building, Chicago.
John DeBolt Stephenson, B. S., *1872...................................Dexter, Ind.
Ida Bullock, L. A., (Mrs. Thatcher) *1894.......................Attleboro, Mass.
Hanna Laura Haight, B. S......................................Teacher, Mendota.
Ada May Hasbrook, A. M., (Mrs. Hale)...........87 Warren Ave., Boston, Mass.
Mary Knowles, L. A., (Mrs. J. S. Alspaugh)...................Washington, Kan.
Flora Adaline Prindle, L. A., (Mrs. A. G. Dow)......................Galesburg.

1872.

Albert Elmore Chase, B. S........Deputy U. S. Mining Surveyor, Boulder, Colo.
Joseph Albert Gates, A. B......... ....
Alice M. Bingham, L. A., (Mrs. Copeland).........School Trustee, Monroe, Wis.
Mattie Wilburn Burford, L. A., (Mrs. Bates)...........Merchant, Wichita, Kan.

1873.

Theodore C. Stevens, A. M., *1892..Lincoln, Neb.
Ada D. Bingham, L. A., M. D......................1623 Gaylord St., Denver, Colo.
Ella M. Brown. L. A., (Mrs. Salley), *1883...........................Monroe, Wis.
Anna L. Nelson, L. A., (Mrs. Fuson)................................Emporia, Kan.
Clara Richardson, L. A., (Mrs. G. F. Claycomb).....................Farragut, Ia.
Sarah A. Richardson, A. M..Lawrence, Kan.
Mary M. Stevens, A. M...............................871 East St., Lincoln, Neb.

1874.

William Albrecht, B. S., *1878...Tiskilwa.
Eugene E. Brunson, B. S., M. D...................................Ganges, Mich.
Daniel Clingingsmith, B. S...Newton, Kan.
William E. Day, B. S................Teacher, 198 Oakwood Boulevard, Chicago.
Morris W. Fletcher, B. S., M. D...............................Collierville, Tenn.
Irene A. Conger, L. A., (Mrs. Courtney), *1891...........................Chicago.
Belle Sherman, B. S...Teacher, Ithaca, N. Y.

1875.

Charles A. Buck, L. A..Merchant, LeRoy.
Lucien J. Dinsmore, B. S., A M. 1886........Clergyman, 1389 Perry St., Chicago.
Charles Ellwood Nash, A. M., S. T. D., (Tufts),
                            President Lombard College, Galesburg.
Carrie Brainard, A. M., B. D., (St. Lawrence).....Clergyman, Little Hocking, O.
Emma S. Collins, L. A., (Mrs. J. E. Buchanan)...................Teacher, Elgin.
Lillie E. Conger, L. A., *1877...Oneida.
Genie R. Edwards, L. A., (Mrs. Noteware), *1888..............Minneapolis, Minn
Jennie C. Nelson, L. A., (Mrs. Nichols).... ....St. Charles
Josie M. Pryne, L. A..........................113 Hanover St., Mankato, Minn
Luella R. Warner, L. A., (Mrs. Frank Hitchcock),
                            Teacher of Painting, Mosca. Colo.

1876.

Hon. Jay L. Hastings, B. S., *1894.......................................Galesburg.
Charlotte Fuller, M. S., (Mrs. S. M. Risley).........................Harvard, Neb.
Stella Hale, L. A...Galesburg.
Lottie E. Leighton, B. S., Mrs. L. J. Dinsmore)...........1389 Perry St., Chicago.
Izah T. Parker, A. M., *1891...Banning, Cal.

1877.

George F. S. Baker, A. M., *1891.......................................Goodenow.
Charles C. Maynard, A. M...................Dentist, 97 S. 1st St., San Jose, Cal.
Clara Z. Edwards, L. A., (Mrs. J. F. Calhoun),
                            2121 Bryant Ave., South, Minneapolis, Minn.
Emily L. Fuller, A. M.............................. ....Teacher, Galesburg.
Eugenia Fuller, A. M.....................Principal High School, Riverside, Cal.
Lottie J. Humphrey, B. S., *1879...Tipton, Ia.
Ella McCullough, L. A., (Mrs. J. D. Welsh)......................... Galesburg.

1878.

Ozro P. Bostwick, A. B............................Supt. City Schools, Clinton, Ia.
Eben H. Chapin, A. M., B. D., (Tufts)...............Clergyman, Rockland, Me.
Shirley C. Ransom, B. S., A. M. 1892..Agent Prudential Insurance Co., Kewanee.
Adah M. Mariner, M. S...Walnut Grove.

1879.

Jon. W. Grubb, M. S......................Professor Lombard College, Galesburg.
Charles P. Hale, A. M..............................Bank Cashier, Pittsburg, Kan.
Douglas A. Myers, B. S....................................Real Estate Agent, Peoria.
Chas. A. Webster, B. S..................Treasurer Lombard College, Galesburg.
J. Edwin Webster, B. S...Merchant, Galesburg.

1880.

Henry S. Livingston, A. M., *1895...Galesburg.
William H. Livingston, A. B., Auditor Mercantile Mutual Building and Loan
　　　　　　　　　Association, 716 Delaware St., Kansas City, Mo.
William A. Parker, A. M...........Civil Engineer, U. P. R. R., Kansas City, Mo.
Otto H. Swigart, B. S........................Farmer and Stockman, Champaign.
Mollie B. Devendorf, B. S..............Stenographer, 689 W. Adams St., Chicago.
Jennie B. Townsend, B. S., (Mrs. C. A. Webster).......................Galesburg.

1881.

George F. Hughes, A. B......................................Attorney, Yates City.
Milo C. Summers, M. S., War Department Clerk, Surgeon General's office,
　　　　　　　314 Seventh Street, Northeast, Washington, D. C.
Lura D. Bailey, A. B., (Mrs. G. F. Hughes)..............................Yates City.

1882.

Reuben D. Bower, B. S....................................Clerk, Galesburg.
Henry M. Chase, A. M................. Loan and Real Estate Agent, Galesburg.
Lafayette Swart, B. S.....................Farmer, Dike, Hifchcock Co., Neb.
Elmer H. West, M. S., *1894..Yates City.

1883.

Chas. E. Brewster, A. B., Loan and Real Estate Agent,
　　　　　　　1770 Emerson Avenue, South, Minneapolis, Minn.
James Weston Carney, B. S., B. D. (Tufts)..................Attorney, Galesburg.
Lloyd Z. Jones, B. S.........................County Surveyor and Farmer, Galva.
John H. Miles, B. S...Farmer, Bushnell.
Fannie M. Edwards, A. B., (Mrs. C. E. Brewster)
　　　　　　　1770 Emerson Ave., South, Minneapolis, Minn.
Lizzie E. Furniss, B. S., (Mrs. W. J. Moring)
　　　　　　　Teacher, 2200 Logan Ave., Denver, Colo.
Emma J. Livingston, L. A., (Mrs. A. T. Wing)......................Knoxville.
Elma E. Williams, A. M......................Student Univ. of Chicago, Chicago.

1884.

Anna M. Brewster, M. S., (Mrs. E. H. West).. ....Yates City.
Gay M. Brunson, B. S., M. D., D. D. S..............................Dentist, Joliet.
Lulu M. Burt, B. S., (Mrs. W. B. Cravens)......2401 E. 11th St., Kansas City, Mo.
Charles L. Edwards, B. S., Ph. D. (Leipsic), Professor of Biology,
　　　　　　　Cincinnati University, Loraine Avenue, Clifton, O.
Jay C. Edwards, M. S...Teacher, Union Hill.
Frank R. Jones, B. S....................Cashier American Well Works, Aurora·

1885.

Jennie B. Conger, A. M., (Mrs. Conger)..217 N. Los Angeles St., Los Angeles, Cal.
Eugene F. Carney, B. S., *1887...Galesburg.
Alma J. Devore, B. S., (Mrs. J. H. Miles)................................Bushnell.

Lizzie B. Hughes, B. L., (Mrs. D. Perry)............................Table Grove.
Ella Suiter, B. S., (Mrs. Geo. Pittard), *1894.................................Alexis.
Hon. Lyman McCarl, M. S....................Attorney, 304 N. Sixth St., Quincy.
J. Douglas Welsh, B. S.......................................Attorney, Galesburg.
George Crum, B. D..............................Clergyman, Owatonna, Minn.
Wallace F. Small, B. D...Everett, Wash.

1886.

Rainie Adamson, M. S., (Mrs. W. F. Small).............Teacher, Everett, Wash.
L. Ward Brigham, M. S., M. D., B. D. (Canton)....Clergyman, Rochester, Minn.
John M. Davies, M. S...........................Teacher, 285 Ontario St., Chicago.
Anna H. Ebberd, B. S., (Mrs. Cyrus Hannum).....................Campbell, Neb.
Alice L. Roberts, B. S., (Mrs. J. L. Andrew)...................National City, Cal.
Rachel A. Watkins, M. S., (Mrs. Billings), B. D. 1894.................Hico, Texas.
August Dejlgren, B. D............................Clergyman, Minneapolis, Minn.
Hiram J. Orelup, B. D..............................Clergyman, Whitesville, N. Y.

1887.

Ella M. Grubb, A. M...........................Student Univ. of Chicago, Chicago.
Hon. Henry C. Morris, A. M...Attorney, 100 Washington St., Suite 510, Chicago.
Jay W. Crane, B. S.....Attorney, 908 Guarantee Loan Bldg., Minneapolis, Minn.
Perry B. Fuller, B. S ....Clerk, Elgin.
Jay Welsh, M. S. ....Teacher, Williamsfield.
Alva T. Wing, B. S................................Merchant, Knoxville.
John R. Carpenter, B. D................................Clergyman, Rockland, O.
Osgood G. Colegrove, B. D..............................Clergyman, Woodstock, O.
Mary Garard, B. D., (Mrs. I. Rollin Andrews)......3221 Pacific St., Omaha, Neb.

1888.

Peter T. Hawley, B. S.......................................Merchant, Ralston, Ia.
Harry H. Jones, M. S...........Manager American Well Works, Dallas, Texas.
Allen W. Lapham, M. S., M. D., *1894................................Victoria.
Elmer E. Taylor, B. S.........................Clergyman, Wellsville, Mo.
Elfreda L. Shaffer, B. D., (Mrs. Newport)..............Clergyman, Wauponsee.

1889.

Elmer E. Taylor, B. S., A. B..........................Clergyman, Wellsville, Mo.
George E. Dutton, M. S.......Assistant Cashier First National Bank, Sycamore.
Frank H. Fowler, B. S., Ph. D. (The Univ. of Chicago),
                          Professor Lombard College, Galesburg.
Edward P. McConnell, M. S., Manager United Telegraph, Telephone,
                          and Electric Co., 4705 Cottage Grove Ave., Chicago.
Allen F. Moore, B. S..............................Merchant, Monticello.
William T. Smith, M. S..................................Attorney, Galesburg.
Vanna R. Williams, B. L., (Mrs. W. W. Slaughter)...............Brookston, Ind.
Charles A. C. Garst, B. D., *1896.....................................Riverside, Cal.
Carrie A. Rice, B. D......................Clergyman, 6019 Prairie Ave., Chicago.

1890.

Frank H. Fowler, B. S., A. B., Ph. D. (The Univ. of Chicago),
                          Professor Lombard College, Galesburg.
Claude N. Anderson, B. S...................Teacher, Tecumseh, Neb.
Bert H. Brigham, M. S.........................Attorney, 803 Perry St., Chicago.
Elizabeth Gaile Durston, M. S., (Mrs. H. F. Simmons),
          B. O. (Columbia School of Oratory), Woodhull.

Fred Farlow, B. S.....................................Stock Dealer, Camp Point.
Samuel D. Harsh, B. S., *1893...Creston, Iowa.
Anna E. Ross, M. S., (Mrs. A. Lapham), M. D.......   ....Chicago
Richard L. Slater, B. S., *1894..Wataga.
Loring Trott, M. S..Junction City, Kan.
James J. Welsh, B. S..Attorney, Galesburg.
Lizzie Wigle, B. S., (Mrs. C. N. Anderson).........................Tecumseh, Neb.
Burtrust T. Wilson, M. S..........Professor Guadalupe College, Seguin, Texas.
Lilian J. Wiswell, B. L., (Mrs. E. P. McConnell).......4359 Lake Ave., Chicago.
Thomas Dotter, B. D...Clergyman, Sullivan, Mo.

1891.

Willard J. White, A. M., M. D......................................Longmont, Colo.
M. McClelland Case, M. S.................................Teacher, Williamsfield.
Villa A. Cole, B. S., (Mrs. M. M. Case),..............................Williamsfield.
S. Taylor Donohoe, M. S............................ United States Gauger, Pekin.
Jennie A. Grubb, B. S., (Mrs. F. H. Fowler)...........................Galesburg.
Robert D. Hill, M. S..Attorney, Lewistown.
Della M. Rogers, B. L., (Mrs. Chas. Garber) ....Reardan, Wash.
William Franklin Smith, B. D., *1897..........................Whitewater, Wis.

1892.

Frank N. Allen, B. S.......................Bookkeeper, 442 E. 45th St., Chicago.
Curtis P. Beale, M. S...........Agent New York Life Insurance Co., Yates City.
Harry A. Blount, B. S..Merchant, Macomb.
Ben F. Brady, B. S...Attorney, Ottawa.
Alice C. Durston, A. M...New Windsor.
Chas. W. Elliott, M. S.................................Jeweler, Williamsfield
Grace S. Harsh, B. S...Creston, Ia.
Lissie Seeley, B. S., (Mrs. Leonard Crew)...............................Salem, Ia.
Daniel P. Wild, M. S.....................................Bank Clerk, Sycamore.
Luther E. Wyman, B. S...................Broker, Board of Trade, Chicago.
Benjamin W. Jones, Jr., B. D., *1898......................................Barre, Vt.
Effie K. (McCollum) Jones, B. D., (Mrs. B. W. Jones)......Clergyman, Barre, Vt.
George W. Skilling, B. D...............................Clergyman, Iowa Falls, Ia.

1893.

Robert F. Anderson, A. B....................Principal City Schools, Princeville.
Carl C. Countryman, A. M....................Impersonator and Author, Chicago.
Ethel M. Tompkins, A. M., (Mrs. W. S. Clayberg)..........................Avon.
F. Louise Bradford, B. S...Teacher, Quincy.
Richard Brown, M. S....................................Attorney, Creston, Ia.
Kate A. Carlton, B. S., (Mrs. F. W. Smith)...........................DeLand, Fla.
J. Newton Conger, Jr., M. S..........................Attorney, Galesburg.
States Dickson, B. S.....................................Attorney, Kewanee.
S. Hepsey Fuller, M. S., (Mrs. J. M. Earhart)...........................Wyoming.
Daisy D. Wiswell, M. S., (Mrs. G. A. Franklin)................Carpentaria, Cal.
Guy A. Longbrake, B. L., M. D..Galesburg.
Charles E. Varney, B. D...............................Clergyman, Monroe, Wis.

1894.

William Richard Tapper, A. B................Attorney, 157 E. 47th St., Chicago.
Guy Henry Bernard, B. S....................................Teacher, Delphos, Kan.
Lucy Minerva Conger, B. S..Teacher New England Conservatory, Boston, Mass.
Joseph Amos Crum, B. S.. M. D...Oshkosh, Wis. .

Maude Alice Crum, B. S..Boone, Ia.
Adelphia Gould Durston, B. S.............................Teacher, New Windsor.
Albert Prentice Smith, B. S..............................Merchant, Denver, Colo.
Lucy Titus, B. S., (Mrs. R. F. Anderson)..............................Princeville.
Eliza M. Drake Curtis, B. D., (Mrs. J. L. Everton)...........Clergyman, Osage,Ia.
Rachel C. Watkins Dellgren, B. D., (Mrs. Billings).................Hico, Texas.
Jasper Leroy Everton, B. D...............................Clergyman, Osage, Ia.
Martha Dandridge Garner, B. D., (Mrs. L. P. Jones)........Clergyman, Macomb.
Henry LaFayette Gillespie, B. D.....................Clergyman, Clarinda, Ia.
Elijah Emmet Hamand, B. D.......................Clergyman, Kansas City, Mo.
Rett E. Olmstead, B. D................................Clergyman, Storm Lake, Ia.
Margaret Titus, B. D., (Mrs. R. E. Olmstead).....Clergyman, Albert Lea, Minn.
Albert Ernest Menke, Ph. D...........................Chemist, Fayetteville, Ark.
Hans Schuler, Ph. D.......................................Teacher, Flushing, N. Y.

1895.

John McDuffie, Ph. D...............................Teacher, Springfield, Mass.
Lucile Bragg, A. B..Clerk, Humboldt, Kan.
William Robert Chapin, B. S............................Bank Cashier, Kirkwood.
Frank Loren Conger, A. B................................Bank Clerk, Galesburg.
Grace Winifred Conley, A. B..........................Postal Clerk, Galesburg.
Mabel Dow, A. B., (Mrs. F. L. Conger)....................................Galesburg.
Robert Pinckney Higgins, B. S.Attorney, 4444 Cote Brilliante Ave., St. Louis, Mo.
John Richard Stanley, A. B.......Agricultural Implement Dealer, Stronghurst.
Nellie Christine Tompkins, A. B......................................Avon.
Albert Orin Wakefield, A. B...........................Attorney, Sioux City, Ia.
Frances Elizabeth Cheney, B. D.............................Clergyman, Greenup.
Orrin Carleton Evans, B. D.............................Clergyman, Marseilles.
Charles Robert Jones, B. D........................Clergyman, Nettleton, Mo.
Thomas Francis Rayon, B. D.,.....................Clergyman, Bellaire, Mich.

1896.

Jessie Beatrice Brown, A. B., (Mrs. E. H. Mitchell)..................Galesburg.
Fred Leo Camp, A. B...Druggist, Galesburg.
Bertha Alice Cook, A. B., (Mrs. O. C. Evans)...........................Marseilles.
Almira Lowrey Cheney, A. B..Saybrook.
Elice Crissey, A. B...Teacher, Avon.
Homer Franklin Harsh, A. B.,..........................Stockman, Lowell, Neb.
Hamilton Lafayette Karr, Jr., A. B...................Attorney, Osceola, Ia.
Marion Alice Kendall, A. B...................................Brockton, Mass.
Harry Magee Lessig, A. B...Knoxville.
Ralph Grierson Kimble, A. B...........Professor Lombard College, Galesburg.
Iva Della Myers. A. B.............................. ...Bookkeeper, Galesburg.
Edward Leroy Shinn, A. B., Sec. and Treas. Atlantic Fuel Co.,
                    918 Stephen Girard Building, Philadelphia, Pa.
Emma Genevra Van Liew, A. M., (Mrs. Guy Tuttle)..................Galesburg.
Jean Gillette White, A. B., (Mrs. A. B. McGill)............................Peoria.
James Alvin Clark, B. D.................................Clergyman, Neenah, Wis.
Charles William Edward Gossow, B. D.....................Clergyman, Clinton.
Maurice Gilbert Linton, B. D.........................Clergyman, Blanchester, O.
Eugene Southwick, B. D...............................Clergyman, Corfu, N. Y.

Georgia Stanley, Diploma in Art, (Mrs. C. H. Wickham)...Teacher, Stronghurst.

1897.

Frank Pierce Anderson, A. B.............................Teacher, Yates City.
Loetta Frances Boyd, A. B.......................................Teacher, Plano.

Flora May Cutter, A. B...Camp Point.
Benjamin Downs. A. B.....................................Clerk, Winslow, Ariz.
Nina Alta Harris, A. B...Teacher, Galesburg.
Fred Louis Holcomb, A. B............ ....Medical Student, Keokuk, Ia.
Theodore Lindquist, A. B., Instructor Kansas State Agricultural
					College, Manhattan, Kan.
Carrie Alice Stickney, A. B...Student New England Conservatory, Boston, Mass.
Elmer Joseph Tapper, A. B.......................Insurance Solicitor, Riverside.
Claude Bryant Warner, A. B...Dentist, Avon.
Guy Henry Weeks, A. B.......................................Teacher, Galesburg.
Frances Cora White, A. B...Galesburg.
Fred Minosuke Yamaguchi, A. B...Student Yale University, New Haven, Conn.
George Hilary Ashworth, B. D...........................Clergyman, Mt. Gilead, O.
Edward Milton Minor, B. D..............................Clergyman, Mt. Vernon.
George Burr Rogers, B. D.............................Clergyman, Decatur, Mich.
William Willis Slaughter, B. D....................................Clergyman, Texas.
Simeon Lafayette Taylor, B. D...........................Clergyman, Plainfield.

1898.

Mervin Wallace Allen, A. B........Agent Metropolitan Life Ins. Co., Galesburg.
Alice Helen Bartlett, A. B...Galesburg.
Charles Reid Brown, A. B.................Student Kent College of Law, Chicago.
Joshua Jay Bullman, A. B.................... ....Farmer, Galesburg.
Ida Galbreath, A. B.......................................Teacher, Galveston, Ind.
Charles Edward Piper, A. B.:..Student Yale Divinity School, New Haven, Conn.
Simeon Lafayette Taylor, B. D., A. B......................Clergyman, Plainfield.
Edna Madison McDonald, B. D...............................Clergyman, Urbana.
John Willis Slaughter, B. D..... .Student Univ. of Michigan, Ann Arbor, Mich.
Benjamin Franklin Stacey.....................Fellow Univ. of Chicago, Chicago.
Oluf Tandberg, B. D ....Clergyman, Augusta, Wis.

Isal Caldwell, Diploma in Vocal Music. (Mrs. Lewis)...................Knoxville.

1899.

Christen Martin Alsager, A. B..................Principal City Schools, Fairdale.
Ella Berry Boston, A. B...Galesburg.
Henry William Dubee, A. B......Student Harvard University, Cambridge, Mass.
Howard Everett Foster, A. B...........................Photographer, Galesburg.
Homer Edwin Garvin, A. B..........................Traveling Salesman, Quincy.
Fannie Pauline Gingrich, A. B....................................Clerk, Galesburg.
George Runyan Longbrake, A. B., Student Ryder Divinity School,
					Lombard College, Galesburg.
Nellie Stuart Russell, A. B..Teacher, Woodhull.
Lora Adelle Townsend, A. B...:...............................Teacher, Galesburg.
Lloyd Champlain, B. D.......................................Clergyman, Galesburg.

Edith C. Crissey, Diploma in Instrumental Music.................Teacher, Avon.
Jennie Holmes, Diploma in Art............... :...................North Henderson.

Honorary Degrees.

The degree placed immediately after the name is the honorary degree conferred by Lombard University.

An additional degree, followed by a date only, is one conferred by Lombard University.

An additional degree, without date, is one conferred by another institution, the name of which is given, if known.

1858. *Rev. Otis A. Skinner, D. D............Ex-President Lombard University.
1859. Rev. George S. Weaver, A. M.................................Canton, N. Y.
1860. *Ansel Streeter, A. M.......................................Weston, Mo.
1862. *Rev. Ebenezer Fisher, D. D., Principal Theological School, Canton, N. Y.
1862. Rev. Joseph Selmon Dennis, A. M...................................Chicago.
1863. *Rev. William Henry Ryder, D. D.; A. M. (Harvard).............Chicago.
1864. *Rev. Holden R. Nye, A. M................................Philadelphia, Pa.
1864. *Rev. Charles Woodhouse, A. M.; M. D....... ....Rutland, Vt.
1865. Rev. A. G. Hibbard, A. M...Wheaton.
1865. *Rev. J. G. H. Hartzell, A. M.; D. D. (St. Lawrence)..........Detroit, Mich.
1867. *Rev. William Ethan Manley, A. M.......................... Denver, Colo.
1867. Rev. Thomas E. St. John, A. M.......................................
1868. *Rev. Clement G. Lefevre, D. D............................Milwaukee, Wis.
1868. William B. Powell, A. M...................................Washington, D. C.
1868. Rev. James Harvey Tuttle, A. M.; D. D...............Minneapolis, Minn.
1869. Rev. John Wesley Hanson, A. M.; D. D. (Buchtel)..........Pasadena, Cal.
1869. Rev. William Wallace Curry, A. M.....................Washington, D. C.
1869. *Rev. Daniel Parker Livermore, A. M.. ....Melrose, Mass.
1869. Rev. Augusta J. Chapin, A. M..............................Mt. Vernon, N. Y.
1870. Rev. John S. Cantwell, A. M......................................Chicago.
1870. Daniel Lovejoy Hurd, A. M.; M. D....................................
1870. *Rev. George Truesdale Flanders, D. D................Rockport, Mass.
1870. *Rev. Alfred Constantine Barry, D. D..........................Lodi, Mass.
1872. *Rev. William Ethan Manley, D. D.; A. M. 1867............. Denver, Colo.
1872. Rev. R. H. Pullman, A. M..................................Baltimore, Md.
1872. *Rev. Gamaliel Collins, A. M.....................U. S. A., Chatham, Mass.
1872. *Rev. B. F. Rogers, A. M................................Fort Atkinson, Wis.
1875. *Rev. J. H. Chapin, Ph. D.; A. B. 1857; A. M. 1860..........Meriden, Conn.
1876. Rev. George S. Weaver, D. D.; A. M. 1859.....:..............Canton, N. Y.
1876. Rev. John S. Cantwell, D. D.; A. M. 1870...........................Chicago.
1877. Rev. O. Cone; D. D...Canton, N. Y.
1879. Elias Fraunfelter, Ph. D....................................Akron, O.
1879. Milton L. Comstock, Ph. D............Professor Knox College, Galesburg.
1882. Rev. Charles W. Tomlinson, D. D..........................Taunton, Mass.
1883. *Rev. Amos Crum, A. M...................................Webster City, Ia.
1884. Matthew Andrews, A. M..Monmouth.
1886. Rev. L. A. Dinsmore, A. M.; B. S. 1875............................Chicago.
1887. *Rev. Holden R. Nye, D. D.; A. M. 1864...... ....Towanda, Pa.
1887. Rev. Charles Fluhrer, D. D................................Albion, N. Y.

*Deceased.

1887. Hon. Lewis E. Payson, LL. D..Pontiac.
1887. Hon. George W. Wakefield, A.'M............................Sioux City, Ia.
1888. Rev. George H. Deere, D. D..............................Riverside, Cal.
1888. Homer M. Thomas, A. M.; M. D..................................Chicago.
1888. Rev. Charles A. Conklin, A. M...........................Springfield, Mass.
1888. Mary Hartman, A. M.; L. A. 1859...................................Normal.
1890. Rev. Jacob Straub, D. D...Chicago.
1890. George B. Harrington, A. M......................................Princeton.
1890. Carl F. Kolbe, Ph. D..Akron, O.
1891. Rev. A. G. Gaines, LL. D.; D. D.,
                     Ex-President St. Lawrence University, Canton, N. Y.
1892. Rev. George Thompson Knight, D. D.,
           `   Professor Divinity School, Tufts College, Mass.
1892. Charles Kelsey Gaines, Ph. D.,
                     Professor St. Lawrence University, Canton, N. Y.
1892. Shirley C. Ransom, A. M.; B. S. 1878.............................Kewanee.
1893. Rev. Augusta J. Chapin, D. D.; A. M. 1869..............Mt. Vernon, N. Y.
1893. *Rev. Amos Crum, D. D.; A. M. 1885.....................Webster City, Ia.
1895. John Huston Finley, Ph. D..................................New York City.
1893. Charles Loring Hutchinson, A. M....................................Chicago.
1894. Rev. Royal Henry Pullman, D. D.; A. M. 1872...............Baltimore, Md.
1894. Rev. George B. Stocking, D. D....................................Galesburg.
1895. Rev. Aaron Aldrich Thayer, D. D................................California.
1895. Rev. Andrew Jackson Canfield, Ph. D.; D. D....'...........Brooklyn, N. Y.
1897. Rev. Daniel Bragg Clayton, D. D.............................Columbia, S. C.
1897. Rev. Thomas Sander Guthrie, D. D.....................,.Logansport, Ind.
1898. Rev. Rodney F. Johonnot, D. D....................................Oak Park.
1898. Henry Priest, Ph. D., Professor St. Lawrence University....Canton, N. Y.
1899. John Wesley Hanson, Jr., A. M..................................Chicago.

_____

*Deceased.

Acknowledgement of Donations for 1899-1900.

SCIENTIFIC BOOKS AND APPARATUS.

A. C. Grier.

COLLECTION OF BIRDS' EGGS.

C. W. Orton.

ADDENDA.

NON-RESIDENT LECTURER.

(Add to page 16.)

A course of lectures on Preacher and Pastor, by the
Rev. Geo. L. Perin, D. D.

PORTRAITS.

(Add to page 105.)

Of James H. Swan, by Mrs. Jas. H. Swan.
Of Amos G. Throop, by Mrs. J. C. Vaughan.
Of Rev. Stephen Hull, by Mrs. Stephen Hull.

HARVARD UNIVERSITY SCHOLARSHIP.

By request of the Harvard Club of Chicago we publish the following notice:
At the annual meeting of the Harvard Club of Chicago December 14, 1897, an
amendment to the constitution of the Club was adopted, establishing on a permanent basis a scholarship at Harvard University of the minimum annual value
of three hundred dollars. This scholarship is open to the graduates of the universities and colleges of Illinois who wish to follow a graduate course of study
at Harvard University. Applications must be made before May 1st in each
year, but senior students about to finish their undergraduate course are eligible
as candidates. Communications may be addressed to Murry Nelson, Jr.,
Chairman, 99 Randolph street, Chicago.

1887. Hon. Lewis E. Payson, LL. D...Pontiac.
1887. Hon. George W. Wakefield, A.'M............................ Sioux City, Ia.
1888. Rev. George H. Deere, D. D..................................Riverside, Cal.
1888. Homer M. Thomas, A. M.; M. D...................................Chicago.
1888. Rev. Charles A. Conklin, A. M...........................Springfield, Mass.
1888. Mary Hartman, A. M.; L. A. 1859..................................Normal.
1890. Rev. Jacob Straub, D. D..Chicago.
1890. George B. Harrington, A. M......................................Princeton.
1890. Carl F. Kolbe, Ph. D..Akron, O.
1891. Rev. A. G. Gaines, LL. D.; D. D.,
                    Ex-President St. Lawrence University, Canton, N. Y.
1892. Rev. George Thompson Knight, D. D.,
                    Professor Divinity School, Tufts College, Mass.
1892. Charles Kelsey Gaines, Ph. D.,
                    Professor St. Lawrence University, Canton, N. Y.
1892. Shirley C. Ransom, A. M.; B. S. 1878..............................Kewanee.
1893. Rev. Augusta J. Chapin, D. D.; A. M. 1869.............Mt. Vernon, N. Y.
1893. *Rev. Amos Crum, D. D.; A. M. 1885.....................Webster City, Ia.
1895. John Huston Finley, Ph. D..................................New York City.
1893. Charles Loring Hutchinson, A. M................................Chicago.

Acknowledgement of Donations for 1899-1900.

SCIENTIFIC BOOKS AND APPARATUS.

A. C. Grier.

COLLECTION OF BIRDS' EGGS.

C. W. Orton.

ENDOWMENT FUND.

Mrs. M. L. Pingrey, Estate of Mrs. Gennett Baker, Mrs. E. Forbes, Mrs. A. J. Hodges, Geo. L. Perrin, Jas. Houghton, Benj. Downs.

EXTENSION AND IMPROVEMENT FUND.

Robert Allerton, George H. Brown, Crocker & Robbins, Mrs. E. F. Dutton, Mrs. Sarah E. Evans, Mrs. Emeline Forbes. D. A. Hulett, H. L. Hier, L. J. Itish, A. C. Kohrt, L. Lord, M. C. Larson, Henry C. Lytton, Will Luce, Cora M. Lane, Mrs. A. T. Lane, H. B. Laflin, Henry H. Massey, J. E. Sanford, F. A. Schumacher, F. A. Smith, E. L. Spicer, Miss Mary D. Torrance, Wm. Torrance, Eleanor P. Townsend, Parry L. Wright, A. F. Walbridge,

In addition to the above, we acknowledge the receipt of the second and third installment on pledges to this fund from donors whose names have appeared in preceding catalogues.

HARVARD UNIVERSITY SCHOLARSHIP.

By request of the Harvard Club of Chicago we publish the following notice:

At the annual meeting of the Harvard Club of Chicago December 14, 1897, an amendment to the constitution of the Club was adopted, establishing on a permanent basis a scholarship at Harvard University of the minimum annual value of three hundred dollars. This scholarship is open to the graduates of the universities and colleges of Illinois who wish to follow a graduate course of study at Harvard University. Applications must be made before May 1st in each year, but senior students about to finish their undergraduate course are eligible as candidates. Communications may be addressed to Murry Nelson, Jr., Chairman, 99 Randolph street, Chicago.

INDEX.

OMBARD COLLEGE

CATALOGUE

1899 ✦ 1900

CATALOGUE

OF

LOMBARD COLLEGE,

GALESBURG, ILLINOIS.

FOR THE YEAR ENDING JUNE 6, 1901.

GALESBURG, ILL.:
REPUBLICAN-REGISTER PRINT.
1901.

College Calendar.

1901.

MARCH 12—Tuesday..Third Term Begins.
MARCH 12—Tuesday, 8 a. m..Registration.
MAY 30, 31—Thursday, Friday......................................Examinations.
JUNE 2—Sunday....................................Baccalaureate Sermon.
JUNE 3—Monday..Field Day.
JUNE 3—Monday................................Gymnasium Exhibition.
JUNE 3—Monday, Evening..............Townsend Prize Contest in Declamation.
JUNE 4—Tuesday..Class Day.
JUNE 4—Tuesday.............Annual Meeting of the Association of Graduates.
JUNE 4—Tuesday, Afternoon.....................Annual Recital of Music Pupils.
JUNE 4—Tuesday, Evening................Exhibition of Department of Elocution.
JUNE 5—Wednesday.........................Meeting of the Board of Trustees.
JUNE 5—Wednesday, Evening.........................Commencement Rally.
JUNE 6—Thursday....................................Commencement Day.

Summer Vacation.

SEP. 2—Monday...............................Entrance Examinations.
SEP. 3—Tuesday.......................Beginning of the College Year.
SEP. 3—Tuesday......................................First Term Begins.
SEP. 3—Tuesday, 8 a. m.....................................Registration.
NOV. 25, 26—Monday, Tuesday......................................Examinations.
NOV. 26—Tuesday...First Term Ends.

Thanksgiving Vacation.

DEC. 3—Tuesday.....................................Second Term Begins.
DEC. 3—Tuesday, 8 a. m...Registration.
DEC. 20—Friday.............Last Day of Recitations preceding Christmas Recess.

1902.

Christmas Recess.

JAN. 3—Friday...................Recitations of Second Term Resumed.
JAN. 24—Friday, Evening.........................Swan Prize Contest in Oratory.
FEB. 12—Wednesday....................................Holiday, Lincoln's Birthday.
MARCH 5, 6—Wednesday, Thursday................................Examinations.
MARCH 6—Thursday...Second Term Ends.

Spring Vacation.

MARCH 4—Tuesday...Third Term Begins.
MARCH 4—Tuesday, 8 a. m..Registration.
MAY 17—Saturday..Senior Vacation Begins.
MAY 29, 30—Thursday, Friday..................................Examinations.
JUNE 1—Sunday..Baccalaureate Sermon.
JUNE 2—Monday..Field Day.
JUNE 2—Monday......................................Gymnasium Exhibition.
JUNE 2—Monday..............Townsend Prize Contest in Declamation.
JUNE 3—Tuesday..Class Day.
JUNE 3—Tuesday.............Annual Meeting of Association of Graduates.
JUNE 3—Tuesday, Evening...............Exhibition of Department of Elocution.
JUNE 4—Wednesday...........................Meeting of the Board of Trustees.
JUNE 4—Wednesday, Evening..........................Commencement Concert.
JUNE 5—Thursday....................................Commencement Day.

Officers of the Board.

Hon. SAMUEL KERR, CHICAGO,

PRESIDENT.

CHARLES A. WEBSTER, GALESBURG,

TREASURER.

PHILIP G. WRIGHT, GALESBURG,

SECRETARY.

W. F. CADWELL, GALESBURG,

AUDITOR.

Executive Committee.

HOWARD KNOWLES, CHAIRMAN,

*W. W. WASHBURN, SECRETARY.

CHARLES ELLWOOD NASH, D. D.,

ROBERT CHAPPELL,   CHARLES A. WEBSTER.

*Deceased Feb. 8, 1901.

Board of Visitors.

Each Universalist State Convention, which adopts Lombard College as its institution of Learning, is entitled to send two visitors, whose duty it is to examine into the condition of the College and to assist in the choice of Trustees.

GENERAL STATEMENT.

LOCATION.

LOMBARD COLLEGE is located in Galesburg, Knox County, Illinois, a healthful and beautiful city of 20,000 inhabitants, noted for its public buildings, its elegant churches, and the good order, intelligence, thrift and refinement of its people.

Galesburg is easily accessible by railroad from all parts of the West; being the center of the great Burlington R. R. system, leading to Chicago, Burlington, Quincy, Peoria, Rock Island, St. Louis, Kansas City, Omaha, Denver, and Minneapolis; and also the terminus of the Fulton County Narrow Gauge R. R., connecting with the great Wabash system. It is on the main line of the Santa Fe system.

THE COLLEGE CAMPUS.

The College Campus is situated in the southeastern part of the city and may readily be reached by the electric cars. It is thirteen acres in extent and affords ample space for base ball, foot ball, tennis and other athletic sports. A large part is planted with trees, which have been growing many years and have attained noble size and graceful forms. Among them are pines, larches, hemlocks, cedars, maples, elms, ash-trees, tulip-trees, and others, embracing about forty species. The trees and lawns are well kept and cared for, and the beauty of the surroundings thus created is a pleasing and attractive feature of the College.

HISTORY.

The Illinois Liberal Institute was chartered in 1851, opened for students in the autumn of 1852, invested with College powers in 1853, and took the name of Lombard University (in honor of Mr. Benjamin Lombard, at that time the largest donor to its properties,) in 1855. It was one of the first Colleges in the country to admit women as students on the same terms with men, allowing them to graduate in the same class and with the same honors. The first class was graduated in 1856. The Ryder Divinity School was opened September 5, 1881.

THE ELECTIVE SYSTEM.

Experience has demonstrated the soundness of the educational principle that the selection of studies, in some degree, at least, should be adapted to the needs, tastes, and talents of the student. At Lombard this principle is fully recognized, and the greatest liberty is given to students in the choice of their studies. At the same time the fact is recognized that there is a distinct educational gain to a student in pursuing a well matured and logically developed course of study. The method by which it is sought to reconcile these important principles of education at Lombard is fully explained on page 28.

THE COLLEGE YEAR.

The College year begins early in September and closes early in June. It is divided into three terms of approximately equal length. (See Calendar, page 4.)

Students should, if possible, enter at the beginning of the College year, since much of the work is arranged progressively from that date. They will, however, be allowed to enter at any time when there seems a prospect of their being able to do so profitably.

Commencement day occurs the first Thursday in June.

APPORTIONMENT OF TIME.

The regular sessions of the College are held on Monday, Tuesday, Wednesday, Thursday, and Friday.

From the courses of study offered, each student is expected to elect work to an amount sufficient to keep him profitably employed. In all full courses each recitation occupies one hour. Absence from a recitation will forfeit the mark in that study for the day.

GRADES OF SCHOLARSHIP.

At the end of every term the standing of a student in each of his courses will be expressed, according to his proficiency, by one of four grades, designated respectively by the letters A, B, C, D.

The grade is determined by term work estimated on the basis of attendance, quality of recitations or laboratory work, occasional tests, written exercises, etc., and by final examinations at the end of the term, the term grade and the final examination being valued in the ratio of two to one.

Grade C is the lowest which will be accepted in any study as counting towards the fulfillment of the requirements of graduation.

Students who receive grade D in any study shall not elect more than three courses for the succeeding term.

Students whose lowest grade is C in one or more studies, shall not elect more than three and one-half courses for the succeeding term.

Students whose lowest grade is B in two or more studies, shall not elect more than four courses for the succeeding term.

Students whose lowest grade is B in one course, shall not elect more than four and one-half courses for the succeeding term.

CHAPEL EXERCISES.

Religious exercises, at which attendance is required, are conducted daily in the college chapel.

With the view of imparting additional interest and value to these exercises, relieving them of mere formality, brief addresses by members of the faculty or by invited speakers upon practical life questions or upon topics of the day, will be given from time to time. At intervals, also, special musical numbers will be introduced by the Director of the Musical Department.

APPARATUS.

The department of Physics is well equipped with apparatus for experimentation. Students have an opportunity to obtain a practical acquaintance with the principles of Physics through a series of Laboratory experiments, which they perform for themselves under the direction of the instructor.

LABORATORY.

The extended courses in Chemistry, described elsewhere in this Catalogue, require a large amount of practical work on the part of the student. Each student in Chemistry has a desk provided with gas, water, re-agents and all necessary conveniences. The Laboratory is thoroughly equipped for work in General Chemistry, and in Qualitative and Quantitative Analysis.

MUSEUM.

The Museum contains valuable collections duly classified and arranged, and available for purposes of instruction. The collection of corals is especially fine. A fine collection of minerals, birds and ethnological specimens, the loan of A. B. Cowan, Esq., a former citizen of Galesburg, is known and designated as the Cowan collection.

LIBRARY.

The Library of the College contains about seven thousand volumes. It is located in the College building and is open daily. The books are systematically arranged and easy of access. They may be taken out by the students upon application to the Librarian.

READING ROOM.

A Reading Room under the auspices of a Reading Room Association is supported by the voluntary efforts and contributions of the students, faculty and friends. The leading newspapers and periodicals are kept on file. The Reading Room is open daily, except Sundays, for the use of the students, from 8:00 a. m. until 6:00 p. m.

GYMNASIUM.

The Gymnasium is a building 50 x 80 feet on the ground. On the ground floor, besides the Gymnasium proper, there is a large room, at present used as a recitation room, which can be thrown into the main room by withdrawing the movable partitions. There is also a stage, equipped with an adequate outfit of scenery, for the special use of the Department of Elocution. A gallery runs around the building, affording a suitable running track for indoor practice. The basement contains bathrooms and lockers and other conveniences.

Regular exercise in the Gymnasium will be required of all students for two years of their college course. The exercise will consist of class drill, under the charge of a director, or of special work on the apparatus in accordance with the prescription of the medical examiner. It is intended that the instruction shall be thoroughly scientific, aiming not so much at special muscular or athletic development, as at a sound physical culture, which is the true basis of health and so of energy and endurance.

ATHLETICS.

The Athletic interests of the College are in charge of a Board of Management consisting of two members chosen from the student body, one from the faculty and two from the alumni. The Campus affords opportunity for foot ball, base ball, and track and field events. During the winter basket ball is played in the Gymnasium. The foot ball team receives regular training from a competent coach.

THE LADIES' HALL.

The new Ladies' Hall, finished and first opened for use in the Fall of 1896, is a thoroughly modern building and complete in all its appointments. It is heated by steam, lighted by gas, fitted with sanitary plumbing, including porcelain baths, closets, lavatories, etc., and supplied with every convenience of a well equipped home. The Hall will accommodate forty young ladies; and all non-resident lady students, unless permission is obtained from the President to live elsewhere, are expected to make their home in this building.

Each room is finished with hard wood floor and furnished with bed-stead, springs, mattress, chairs, desk, dresser and rugs. The occupants are expected to furnish bedding, pillows, towels, napkins, to pay for washing said articles, and to keep their own rooms in order.

The charge for board is $36 per term for each person, payable in advance. This does not include the Christmas recess. The charge for room rent is from $6 to $15 per term, according to the location of the room, payable to the Registrar in advance. Where one person occupies a double room from choice an extra charge of 50 cents a week will be made; but the privilege of assigning two persons to such room, is re-served.

Board will be furnished to women students of the College who do not have rooms in the Hall for $2.75 a week, payable in advance.

Applications for rooms in the Hall should be made during the sum-mer vacation to President C. Ellwood Nash; at other times to Prof. J. W. Grubb, 1427 East Knox Street.

THE LOMBARD REVIEW.

A College paper, called *The Lombard Review*, is published monthly by the students. It makes a record of College events, and serves as a medium of communication with the friends and Alumni of the College. Subscription price $1.00.

SOCIETIES.

The Erosophian.

The Erosophian Society was organized January 29, 1860. Any gentleman connected with the College or Divinity School is eligible to membership, and is entitled to all the benefits of the society. Its regu-lar meetings are held on Thursday evening of each week. The literary exercises consist of orations, debates and essays.

The Zetecalian.

This Society was organized in 1863 by the ladies of the University. Its exercises consist of debates, essays, historical narrations and general discussions. Regular meetings are held on Wednesday afternoon of each week. The officers are elected quarterly.

PRIZES.

1. The Swan Prizes.

Two prizes for excellence in Oratory are offered annually by Mrs. J. H. Swan, of Chicago. They are of the value of fifteen dollars and ten dollars, respectively. The contest for these prizes is held in January.

2. The Townsend Prizes.

Two prizes for excellence in Declamation are offered annually by Mrs. E. P. Townsend, of Sycamore.   They are of the value of fifteen dollars and ten dollars, respectively.   The contest for these prizes is held during Commencement week.

3. Faculty Prize.

A prize of twenty dollars, donated by the faculty, will be given for original work upon an assigned subject.   The subject for 1901-1902 will be "A Scheme for the Organization of Public Charities in Galesburg."

EXPENSES.

Boarding.

At the beginning of the Fall term, 1900, College Commons were opened furnishing board at the following rates:

Board, 37 weeks; Tuition, one year (without restriction of number of studies); incidentals, one year; payable annually or semi-annually in advance.......$105.00

Board, one term; Tuition, one term (without restriction of number of studies); Incidentals, one term; payable in advance,................................ 36.00

Board per week, payable in advance,.. 1.75

Single meal tickets, 8 tickets.. 1.00

The College Commons were opened on the south side of the basement of the main College building, which was deepened, cemented and thoroughly prepared for this purpose during the summer. The room is now well lighted, airy, and spacious, and will accommodate about one hundred students. The quality of the board furnished is not indicated by the price. Owing to the facts that provisions can be obtained at wholesale rates, that service at the table is co-operative, several students paying in part for their board in this manner, and that it is the purpose of the management to make no profit out of this department above actual operating expenses, the board is certainly equal in quality to that furnished in private families for $2.75 per week.

The yearly expenses may be estimated as follows:

Board at Commons, Tuition, Incidentals,............................... $105.00

Room rent,.. 22.50

Washing,.. 15.00

Books,.. 15.00

                                                                     $157.50

The record of the Commons during the past year has been one of steadily increasing popularity. Students, however, are not required to board at the Commons; some board themselves, and some board in private families. Students who board themselves may possibly cut their expenses a trifle below the above rates. In private families rates of from $2.75 per week for board, and upwards, may be obtained.

A faculty committee will assist students in securing comfortable, home-like accommodations.

The charge for board in the Ladies' Hall is $36 per term, for each person, payable in advance. This does not include the Christmas recess. The charge for room rent is from $6 to $15 per term, according to location of room, payable to the Registrar in advance. Where one person occupies a double room from choice, an extra charge of 50 cents per week will be made, but the privilege of assigning two persons to such room is reserved. Board will be furnished to women students of the College who do not have rooms in the Hall at the rate of $2.75 per week, payable in advance.

Tuition and Incidentals.

In the College of Liberal Arts and in the Preparatory School the student will pay a tuition fee for each study pursued. The charge, except in theoretical music, is $3.50 per term for each full course, a course being a study taken for one term and counting as one credit toward graduation. The rate for each fractional course is in proportion to the credit allowed for such fractional course toward graduation. Thus, a half course is half rate; a third course, third rate, etc.

Students in Chemistry, Mineralogy and Biology are required to deposit with the Registrar a sum sufficient to cover laboratory bills. Students in General Chemistry will deposit two dollars; students in Analytical Chemistry, five dollars; students in Mineralogy, three dollars; and students in Biology, three dollars, each. At the close of the term there will be returned the balance remaining after deducting cost of chemicals and broken apparatus.

The charge for incidentals, to be paid by all students of the College, is $5.00 per term.

No student will be enrolled in any class until he presents the Registrar's receipt for the payment of tuition and incidentals. The registration fee is twenty-five cents. The payment of this fee will be remitted to all who register on the first day of the term.

Tuition and incidentals will not be refunded. In case a student is absent a half term or more from sickness or other adequate cause a certificate for a half term's tuition and incidentals will be given the student (at his request), said certificate good "to order" for its face value at any succeeding term.

Art and Music.

For information as to charges in Art and Music, see under these departments later in this Catalogue.

AID TO WORTHY STUDENTS.

Free tuition will be given to the student who graduates with highest rank from an approved high school. Students receiving this concession may be called upon for some College service.

Through the generosity of its friends the College is enabled to offer assistance to worthy students desiring to secure an education. The income of endowed scholarships is applied toward paying the tuition of a limited number.

Perpetual Scholarships.

Sixteen Perpetual Scholarships of $1,000 each have been founded by the following named persons.

The F. R. E. Cornell Scholarship, by Mrs E. O. Cornell.
The George B. Wright Scholarship, by Mrs. C. A. Wright.
The George Power Scholarship, by George and James E. Power.
The Mrs. Emma Mulliken Scholarship, by Mrs. Emma Mulliken.
The Clement F. LeFevre Scholarship, by William LeFevre and Mrs. Ellen R. Coleman.
The Samuel Bowles Scholarship, by Samuel Bowles.
The Dollie B. Lewis Scholarship, by Mrs. Dollie B. Lewis.
The O. B. Ayers Scholarship, by O. B. Ayers.
The C. A. Newcomb Scholarship, by C. A. Newcomb.
The Mary Chapin Perry Scholarship, by T. T. Perry.
The Mary W. Conger Scholarship, by the children of Mrs. Mary W. Conger.
The Hattie A. Drowne Scholarship, by Rev. E. L. Conger, D. D.
The A. R. Wolcott Scholarship, by A. R. Wolcott.
The Woman's Association Scholarship, by the U. W. A. of Illinois.
The Calista Waldron Slade Scholarship, by E. D. Waldron and sisters.
The Mary L. Pingrey Scholarship, by Mrs. Mary L. Pingrey.

BEQUESTS.

For the convenience of those who may wish to secure, by bequest, to the College, any given sum for a specific purpose, the accompanying form is here given:

I hereby give and bequeath to The Lombard College.............

for..............(state the object)..............and direct that my executor pay said bequest to the Treasurer of said College within ....after my death.

(Signed).................................

Dated................................

CATALOGUES

Former students of the College, whether graduates or not, are requested to inform the President of any change of residence, in order that the publications of the College may be sent to them. Catalogues and circulars of information will be sent to all that apply for them.

MORALE AND SOCIAL POLICY.

Aside from a few obvious regulations designed to secure punctuality and regularity in attendance on college exercises, and to protect students and teachers from disturbance while at work, no formal rules are imposed upon the students.

It is expected that, as young men and women of somewhat mature years, they will observe the usual forms of good breeding, and enjoy the ordinary privileges of good society in so far as the latter do not conflict with the best interests of the institution or with their own health and intellectual advancement.

Should any student show a disposition to engage in conduct detrimental to his own best interests, or to those of his fellow students or of the college, the faculty will deal with the case in such manner as will protect the common welfare of all.

OFFICERS OF THE COLLEGE.

CHARLES ELLWOOD NASH, A. M., S. T. D., President,

A. B., Lombard University, 1875; B. D., Tufts College, 1878; A. M., Lombard University, 1878; S. T. D., Tufts College, 1891; President Lombard College. 1895—.

ISAAC AUGUSTUS PARKER, A. M., Ph. D.,

†Williamson Professor of the Greek Language and Literature.

A. B., Dartmouth College, 1853; A. M., ibid, 1856; Ph. D., Buchtel College, 1892; Principal Orleans Liberal Institute, Glover, Vt., 1853-58; Professor of Ancient Languages, Lombard University, 1858-68; Professor of Greek Language and Literature, Lombard College, 1868—.

NEHEMIAH WHITE, A. M., Ph. D., S. T. D.,

*Hall Professor of Intellectual and Moral Philosophy.

In charge of the Ryder Divinity School, Professor of Biblical Languages and Exegesis.

A. B., Middlebury College, 1857; A. M., ibid, 1860; Ph. D., St. Lawrence University, 1876; S. T. D., Tufts College, 1889; Associate Principal Green Mt. Perkins Institute, 1857-58; Principal Clinton Liberal Institute, 1859-60; Principal Pulaski Academy, 1865; Professor Mathematics and Natural Science, St. Lawrence University, 1865-71; Professor Ancient Languages, Buchtel College, 1872-75; President Lombard University, 1875-92; In charge of the Ryder Divinity School, and Professor of Biblical Languages and Exegesis, 1892—.

EVERETT LORENTUS CONGER, A. M., D. D.,

Professor of Homiletics and Pastoral Care.

A. B., Lombard University, 1861; B. D., St. Lawrence University, N. Y., 1863; A. M., Lombard University, 1864; D. D., Buchtel College, Ohio, 1890; Vice-President Throop Polytechnic Institute, Pasadena, Cal., 1891-99; Professor Homiletics and Pastoral Care, Lombard College, 1900—.

JON WATSON GRUBB, M. S.,

Professor of Latin and Instructor in charge of the Preparatory School.

B. S., Lombard University, 1879; M. S., Lombard University, 1882; Adjunct Professor of Mathematics, Lombard University, 1882-94; Registrar, Lombard College 1893—; Professor of Latin, Lombard College, 1894—.

FREDERICK WILLIAM RICH, B. S.,

‡Conger Professor of Natural Science.

B. S., Cornell University, 1881; Graduate Student, Cornell University, 1881; Instructor in Analytical Chemistry, Cornell University, 1882-84; Professor of Natural Science, Lombard College, 1884—.

---

*In honor of the late E. G. Hall, of Chicago.
†In honor of the late I. D. Williamson, D. D. of Cincinnati.
‡In honor of the late L. E. Conger, of Dexter, Iowa.

PHILIP GREEN WRIGHT, A. M.,
Professor of Mathematics, Astronomy and Economics.

A. M. B., Tufts College, 1884; A. M., Harvard University. 1887; Teacher of Mathematics and Science, Goddard Seminary, Vt., 1883; Adjunct Professor of Mathematics, Buchtel College, 1884-86; Professor of Mathematics, Lombard College, 1892—.

FRANK HAMILTON FOWLER, PH. D.,
Professor of English Literature and Rhetoric.

A. B., Lombard University, 1890; Ph. D., The University of Chicago, 1896; Graduate Student, John Hopkins University, 1890-91; Principal Peaster Academy, 1891-92; Fellow in the University of Chicago, 1892-96; Professor of English Literature, Lombard College, 1897—.

RALPH GRIERSON KIMBLE,
Professor of Sociology.

A. B., Lombard University, 1896; University Scholar University of Chicago, 1896-97; Fellow, ibid, 1897-1900; Professor of Sociology, Lombard College, 1900—.

THADDEUS CAREY KIMBLE, M. D.
Instructor in Biology.

M. D., St. Louis College of Physicians and Surgeons, 1898; Supt. A., T. & S. F. R. R. Hospital, Ottawa, Ks., 1898-99; Instructor in Biology, Lombard College, 1900—.

CHARLES E. VARNEY,
Instructor in Biblical History and Archæology.

B. D., Lombard University, 1893; Instructor in Biblical History and Archæology, Lombard College, 1901—.

KARL JAKOB RUDOLPH LUNDBERG,
Director of Music Department and Instructor in Voice, Piano, Organ and Theory.

Graduate Royal Musical Academy of Stockholm, Sweden, in voice, piano, organ and theory, 1892; studied voice with Prof. Ivar Hallstrom. 1893; organist and choir-master in Lindesberg, Sweden, 1894-97; Musical Director Burlington Institute College, Burlington, Iowa, 1897-99; Director Musical Department, Lombard College, 1899—.

EMMA B. WAIT,
Professor of French and German.

Principal of School, Los Angeles, Cal., 1881-83; Student, École Sévigné, Sévres, 1891, Université de Généve, 1896-98, The University of Chicago, 1899; Professor of French and German, Lombard College, 1899—.

M. AGNES HATHAWAY,
Dean of Women and Instructor in Preparatory School.

Graduated from Genesee Wesleyan Seminary, Lima, New York, 1888; Student at National Normal University, Lebanon, Ohio. 1895-96; Teacher in Public Schools of New York and Illinois; Dean of Women and Instructor in Preparatory School, Lombard College, 1900—.

MAUD AUGUSTA MINER,
Instructor in Elocution and Physical Culture, Fall Term.

AMANDA KIDDER,
Instructor in Elocution and Physical Culture, Winter and Spring Terms.

Graduated from the Detroit Training School of Elocution and English Literature, 1890; Post-Graduate course, 1897; Darling College, Minn., 1891; Academy of Our Lady of Lourds, 1892-94; Private Studio, LaCrosse, Wis., 1895-1900; Instructor in Elocution and Physical Culture, Lombard College, 1900—.

M. ISABELLE BLOOD,
Instructor in Drawing and Painting.

Studied with Dean Fletcher, N. Y.; William Bertram, Chicago; at the Art Institute and with Nellie Davis, St. Louis; Instructor in Drawing and Painting, Lombard College, 1889—.

MARY C. BARTLETT,
Matron Ladies' Hall, Fall Term.

ADA M. H. HALE,
Matron Ladies' Hall, Winter and Spring Terms.

DR. GUY A. LONGBRAKE AND DR. DELIA M. RICE.
Medical Examiners.

NON-RESIDENT LECTURERS.

MARION D. SHUTTER, D. D.

REV. ALAN RAY TILLINGHAST.

REV. GEORGE A. SAHLIN.

FRANK HAMILTON FOWLER, PH. D.,
Librarian.

DONALD P. McALPINE,
Assistant Librarian.

JON WATSON GRUBB, M. S.,
Registrar.

FREDERICK WILLIAM RICH, B. S.,
Curator of the Museum.

PHILIP G. WRIGHT, A. M.,
Director of the Gymnasium.

DUDLEY CLAUDE FOSHER, FREDERICK DICKENSON,
Assistants in Gymnasium.

ALLEN HARSHBARGER,
Janitor.

Standing Faculty Committees.

ADVISORY—

PROFESSORS WRIGHT AND FOWLER.

CREDITS—

PROFESSORS PARKER AND RICH.

HOMES FOR NEW STUDENTS—

PROFESSOR FOWLER.

CATALOGUE—

PROFESSORS WRIGHT AND FOWLER.

HIGHER DEGREES—

PRESIDENT NASH AND PROFESSOR PARKER.

LIBRARY—

PROFESSORS WHITE AND WAIT.

CHAPEL EXCUSES—

PROFESSORS RICH AND GRUBB.

CHAPEL EXERCISES—

PRES. NASH, PROFS. WAIT AND LUNDBERG.

ATHLETICS—

PROFESSORS WRIGHT AND KIDDER.

ORDER AND DISCIPLINE—

PRES. NASH, PROFS. RICH AND PARKER.

COLLEGE OF LIBERAL ARTS.

Faculty of Liberal Arts.

CHARLES ELLWOOD NASH, A. M., S. T. D., PRESIDENT.

NEHEMIAH WHITE, A. M., PH. D., S. T. D.,
*Hall Professor of Intellectual and Moral Philosophy.

ISAAC AUGUSTUS PARKER, A. M., PH. D.,
†Williamson Professor of the Greek Language and Literature.

RALPH GRIERSON KIMBLE,
Professor of Sociology.

JON WATSON GRUBB, M. S.,
Professor of Latin.

FREDERICK WILLIAM RICH, B. S.,
‡Conger Professor of Natural Science.

EMMA B. WAIT,
Professor of French and German.

PHILIP GREEN WRIGHT, A. M.,
Professor of Mathematics, Astronomy and Economics.

FRANK HAMILTON FOWLER, PH. D.,
Professor of English Literature and Rhetoric.

THADDEUS CAREY KIMBLE, M. D.,
Instructor in Biology.

KARL JAKOB RUDOLPH LUNDBERG,
Professor of Musical Theory.

MAUD AUGUSTA MINER,
Instructor in Elocution and Physical Culture, Fall Term.

AMANDA KIDDER,
Instructor in Elocution and Physical Culture, Winter and Spring Terms.

---

*In honor of the late E. G. Hall, of Chicago.
†In honor of the late I. D. Williamson, D. D., of Cincinnati.
‡In honor of the late L. E. Conger, of Dexter, Iowa.

Degrees Conferred in 1900.

DOCTOR OF DIVINITY.

Alfred Howitzer Laing, (causa honoris,)......................*Joliet.*

MASTER OF ARTS.

Claude Bryant Warner.. ....*Avon.*

BACHELOR OF ARTS.

Martha Belle Arnold.....................................*Galesburg.*
Fay Alexander Bulluck..................................*Galesburg.*
Gertrude Grace Kidder..................................*Galesburg.*
Edwin Julius McCullough.......................*La Prairie Center.*
Carrie Ruth Nash..*Galesburg.*
Charles Wait Orton............................*Mt. Pleasant, Ia.*
Iva May Steckel...*Macomb.*
Earle Wolcott Watson.......................................*Barry.*
Harry William Weeks...................................*Galesburg.*

BACHELOR OF SCIENCE.

Burt G. Shields...*Galesburg.*

Candidates for Degrees in 1901.

CANDIDATES FOR THE DEGREE OF MASTER OF ARTS.

Martha Belle Arnold....................................*Galesburg.*
Carrie Ruth Nash.......................................*Galesburg.*

CANDIDATES FOR THE DEGREE OF BACHELOR OF ARTS.

John Donington Bartlett................................*Galesburg.*
Nannie Mer Buck...*Le Roy.*
Gertrude West Hartgrove..............................*Galesburg.*
Julia Evelyn Lombard........................*East Orange, N. J.*
Jennie Eliza Marriott...................................*La Moille.*
Donald P. McAlpine............................*Charlotte, Mich.*
William J. Orton.............................*Mt. Pleasant, Ia.*
Grace Olive Pingrey..........................*Coon Rapids, Ia.*
Frederick Preston...... ....*Boston, Mass.*
Grace Schnur.......................... ....*Adams.*

Students in the College of Liberal Arts.

GRADUATE STUDENTS.

Martha Belle Arnold..................................*Galesburg.*
Carrie Ruth Nash....................................*Galesburg.*

UNDERGRADUATES.

Blanche Clarinda Mary Allen........................*Galesburg.*
Charlotte Alspaugh............................*Washington, Kan.*
John Andrew, Jr ....*New Salem.*
Mary Maud Andrew.................................*New Salem.*
John Donington Bartlett.............................*Galesburg.*
John Edward Bellot......................................*Odell.*
James Earle Bowles....................................*Astoria.*
Athol Ray Brown............................*North Henderson.*
Nannie Mer Buck.......................................*Le Roy.*
Kate Clark...*Maquon.*
Sarah Lucy Cook.......................................*Le Roy.*
Edna Mae Cranston....................................*Hermon.*
Frederick Dickinson...................................*Chicago.*
Charles Julius Efner..................................*Galesburg.*
Edna Ethel Epperson..*Rio.*
Earl Harold Eppsteiner...............................*Galesburg.*
Henry Ericson..*Galesburg.*
Dudley Claude Fosher.................................*Galesburg.*
John Kendall Gibson ....*Kirkwood.*
Anna Moore Gillis...............................*Mt. Pleasant, Ia.*
Hudson McBain Gillis............................*Mt. Pleasant, Ia.*
Clyde Percy Gingrich.................................*Galesburg.*
Cora Margaret Hanna...........................*Roachdale, Ind.*
Lillian Harris.......................................*Galesburg.*
Alta Ellen Harsh ....*Baxter, Ia.*
Claude Webster Hartgrove.............................*Galesburg.*
Gertrude West Hartgrove.............................*Galesburg.*
Virginia C. Henney.............................*Mitchellville, Ia.*
Augusta Eaton Hitchcock..............................*Osage, Ia.*

Roy Victor Hopkins.................................*Princeville.*
Harry Albin Jansen.....................................*Woodhull.*
Olïn Arvin Kimble................................*Carbondale, Kan.*
Thaddeus Carey Kimble, M. D....................*Carbondale, Kan.*
Florence Leclerc Kober..................................*Macomb.*
Harrison Burton Linderholm..............................*Altona.*
Julia Evelyn Lombard...........................*East Orange, N. J.*
Jennie Eliza Marriott........................　...........*La Moille.*
Ruth Ellen McAchran............................*Bloomfield, Ia.*
Donald P. McAlpine...................　...........*Charlotte, Mich.*
Albert Graham McCoy ....　..........*Monmouth.*
Ralph Todd Miller....................................*Monmouth.*
Emma Annette Muffler..................................*Serena.*
Faith Tenney Nash..................................*Galesburg.*
Nellie Jeannette Needham.................................*Racine.*
William ɪ. Orton...............................*Mt. Pleasant, Ia.*
Mila Parke.............................　...................*Sycamore.*
Ruth Parke...*Sycamore.*
Elizabeth Freeman Philbrook................... ....*Racine, Wis.*
Grace Olive Pingrey............................*Coon Rapids, Ia.*
Frederick Preston..................................*Boston, Mass.*
Rosa Rains........................... ....*Hutsonville.*
Frances Lunette Ross.....................................*Avon.*
Grace Schnur.........................ː.....................*Adams.*
Edward Milton Smith...........................ː....*Edinburg.*
Alice Stokes...*Galesburg.*
Herbert Leonard Stoughton................. ....*Osage, Ia.*
Charles E. Varney, B. D............................*Galesburg.*
Franklin Gardiner Varney.............................*Galesburg.*
Albert Sanger Webster...............................*Galesburg.*

The following students have each twenty-one or more preparatory credits, but lack one or more of the credits in specific studies requisite to full college standing.

Roy Swan Belcher....................................*Galesburg.*
Henry Mac Cooper.........　........................*Oquawka.*
Cora Margaret Fosher.................................*Galesburg.*
Mary Elizabeth Gosselin...................　 ....*Fort Atkinson, Wis.*
Ethelwyn Sophia Grier..................... ....*Racine, Wis.*
Rob Roy Grubb..*Galesburg.*
Jay Clinton Hurd.......................................*Maquon.*
Mary Markmann.....................................*Muscatine, Ia.*

Levi Berl McDaniel..*Barry.*
Harold Metcalf.....................................*Blandinsville.*
Maud Alvira Oldfield..............................*Mitchellville, 'Ia.*
Hubert Elbridge Perrine..................................*Bushnell.*
Charles August Sandburg..............................*Galesburg.*
Lewis Owen Schoettler.................................*Galesburg.*
William Floyd Selby......................................*Maquon.*
Melvina Stapp...*Colchester.*
Mary Elizabeth Stockton..............................*Monmouth.*
Ralph Darrell Tinkham.................................*Kirkwood.*
Raymond E. Van Camp.................... ....*Otranto, Ia.*
Vina May Ward.......,...........................*Superior, Neb.*
Clifford Hoxey Wolcott............................*Hillsdale, Mich.*
Ellamae Wright.......................................*Port Byron.*

SPECIAL STUDENTS.

Emma Hutchins Browning.............................*Galesburg.*
Catherine Maria Osborn........................ .....*Tokio, Japan.*
Clyde Peck...*Galesburg.*
Ada Peterson........ ....*Galesburg.*
Lucia Louise Pettee....................................*Galesburg.*
Cyrena Baldwin Wier............................ ...*Galesburg.*
Jesse Edward Williams................................ *Galesburg.*
Anne Marion Wrigley...*Chicago.*

Admission and Graduation.

REQUIREMENTS FOR ADMISSION.

The number of credits required for admission to the College of Liberal Arts is twenty-one. These twenty-one credits must include three in Mathematics, three in English, six in some language other than English, three in History, and three in Natural Science. The following list includes the subjects most frequently presented by students applying for admission, together with the credit allowed for each. Any excess of credits presented upon entering will count on requirements for graduation.

SUBJECTS.	CREDITS.
English (usual High School Course)	3
German (one year's High School work or equivalent)	2
French " " " " " "	2
Harkness' Latin Grammar and Reader	2
Cæsar's Commentaries, four to six books	2
Cicero, six to eight orations	2
Virgil, four books	2
Greek Grammar and Lessons	2
Xenophon's Anabasis, two to four books	2
Homer's Iliad, three books	1
Elementary Algebra	2
Plane Geometry	1
Solid Geometry	1
Descriptive Astronomy	1
Physics: Carhart and Chute's Elements of Physics, or an equivalent	1
Chemistry: Remsen's Elements of Chemistry, or an equivalent	1
Physical Geography: Tarr's Elements, or an equivalent	1
Botany: Gray's, or an equivalent	1
Physiology: Martin's Human Body, or an equivalent	1
Grecian and Roman History (elementary)	1
History of the United States	1
History of England	1
Civil Government	1

The work expected in the above studies may be seen from the detailed description in the body of this catalogue.

In estimating the credits the unit is the value of one term's work in this institution. The value of grades brought from other schools will be estimated by a comparison with this unit. Our experience has shown that this unit is practically equivalent in general to a half year's work in the best high schools.

Students may meet the above requirements by examination, by promotion from the Preparatory School, or by certificate (without examination) from certain approved schools.

In the last case the candidate, applying for admission, will be furnished with blank forms, upon which the subjects pursued in the school, the number of weeks, and the number of hours per week devoted to each, the text-book used, and the grade attained, are to be explicitly stated. These certificates, when endorsed by the principal of the school, or other responsible officer, will be received in lieu of an examination, and credits will be given to such an extent as the work done seems fairly to warrant, the above table being the basis of estimate. Students so received, however, are understood to be admitted to classes on probation; and if, after a week's trial, it is found that their previous training is insufficient to render it advisable for them to continue in these classes, they will be assigned work elsewhere.

ADMISSION TO ADVANCED STANDING.

Students from other institutions, who present letters of honorable dismissal, may be admitted to such standing and upon such terms as the Faculty may deem equitable. Every such student is required to present, along with the catalogue of the institution in which he has studied, a full statement, duly certified, of the studies he has completed, including preparatory studies. Candidates for advanced standing who wish to receive credit for work accomplished in private study, are permitted to take examinations in such subjects upon payment of the regular term fee for the course in which the examination is taken. A minimum residence of the two terms next preceeding the completion of the requirements for graduation, and a minimum of eight courses taken in this College, are required of all applicants for a baccalaureate degree.

ADMISSION AS SPECIAL STUDENTS.

Persons who are not candidates for a degree may be admitted as special students to such courses as they are qualified to pursue. They will be required to maintain a standing in all respects satisfactory to the instructor in charge of each study chosen.

NON-RESIDENT STUDENTS.

Non-resident students who pursue any course of study taken by a class in the College, may be examined with the class in that course and receive a certificate for successful work, upon payment of the usual tuition fee for the course.

GRADUATION.

The degree of Bachelor of Arts will be conferred upon any candidate who has satisfactorily completed the aggregate of forty courses, elected from the studies offered in the College of Liberal Arts, in addition to the twenty-one courses required for admission. The forty credits must include a major course in Mathematics, English, Ancient or Modern Language, Natural Science, or Philosophy, as approved by the candidate's official adviser or by the advisory committee.

Every student who is a candidate for a degree, or a diploma, is required to present a graduation thesis upon some subject in which he, or she, has prosecuted original research or special study.

The subject selected for treatment must be approved by the President within four weeks after the opening of the Fall term.

A syllabus of the thesis must be handed to the President at least six weeks before the close of the Winter term.

The completed thesis is limited to fifteen hundred words, and must be handed in for criticism at least ten weeks before Commencement.

In lieu of a thesis, original work, performed under the direction of some member of the Faculty, may be accepted.

Five members from the graduating class, (three from the College of Liberal Arts, and two from the Divinity School,) will be selected by the Faculty to represent the class as speakers on Commencement Day. The basis of selection will be excellence in scholarship (two points); excellence of thesis (one point); and excellence of delivery of thesis (one point).

Degrees will be conferred only on the annual Commencement Day.

ADVANCED DEGREES.

The Master's degree will be conferred upon graduates of this College, or of other institutions of equal rank, on the satisfactory completion of ten courses, pursued in actual study at this College, beyond the requirements for the baccalaureate degree. The candidate must present a thesis showing original research in the special line of study pursued.

Departments and Courses of Instruction.

ENTRANCE CREDITS.

All candidates for admission to the College who expect to receive credit for work done in other schools, should, if possible, submit their certificates, properly filled out, before applying for admission. To facilitate this process, blank forms of such certificates are kept on file in many of the leading high schools of the State, and the same will be promptly sent to any person applying for them.

Hereafter no candidate will be admitted to classes without examination who has not presented his certificate, and even in cases where certificates are presented, the student is understood to be admitted to a class on probation. If, after a week's trial, it is found that his previous training is insufficient to justify his continuing in that class, he will be assigned work elsewhere.

INDIVIDUALIZATION.

An effort is made at Lombard to deal with each student according to his individual needs. The candidate is first required to confer with the Advisory Committee. Then, his previous course of study and his present state of mental discipline having been ascertained as accurately as possible, he will choose, subject to the advice of this committee, such a course of study as shall seem best adapted to meet his requirements. Some member of the Faculty is then appointed the student's official adviser, who shall have supervision of his work during his entire college course.

RECITATIONS AND CREDITS.

The following studies are classed as full courses or fractional courses, according to the estimated amount of work in each, and its value in fulfilling the requirements for graduation. Unless otherwise stated, a course in any study consists of five hours of recitations or lectures, per week, for one term. Certain courses, however, are given in three hours per week recitations. Laboratory courses require ten hours of work per week in the Laboratory, in addition to a considerable amount of study outside. Certain other studies, as indicated in each case, count only as half courses, or less.

ENGLISH.

[For courses 1 to 4 inclusive see Preparatory Department.]

5. The Forms of Discourse.

Baldwin's Specimens of Prose Description and Baker's Specimens of Argumentation will be used as texts. Weekly themes will be required. Tuesday, Wednesday, Thursday and Friday. Fall term.

Professor FOWLER.

Open to students who have completed English 4.

6. The Forms of Discourse. (Continued.)

Brewster's Specimens of Narration and Lamont's Specimens of Exposition will be used as texts. Weekly themes will be required. Tuesday, Wednesday, Thursday and Friday. Winter Term.

Professor FOWLER.

Open to students who have completed English 4.

7. Daily Themes. (Half Course.)

The object of this course is the attainment of rapidity and skill in composition. Each student will be required to hand in a short theme daily for one term. Class meets for conference and criticism every Friday. Winter term.

Professor WRIGHT.

Open to students who have completed English 5.

8. Daily Themes. (Half Course.)

This course is similar to English 7. Tuesday. Spring term.

Professor FOWLER.

Open to students who have completed English 5.

9. English Lyric Poetry.

Wordsworth, Tennyson, Browning. Fall term.

Professor FOWLER.

Open to students who have completed English 4.

[English 9 will not be given in 1901.]

10. English Prose.

A study of English prose writers. Fall term.

Professor FOWLER.

Open to students who have completed English 4.

11. Old English.

An introduction to the older language. The relations between Old and Modern English will be studied. Winter term.

Professor FOWLER.

Open to students who have completed English 4.

[English 11 will not be given in 1901-02.]

12. History of the English Language and Literature.

Lectures and text-book recitations.. Winter term.

Professor FOWLER.

Open to students who have completed English 4.

13. The English Drama.

Shakespeare will form the center of the work. Two or three plays will be studied critically and the class will read a number of plays by different authors. Spring term.   Professor FOWLER.

Open to students who have completed English 4.

[English 13 will not be given in 1902.]

14. Epic Poetry.

Milton. 'Spring term.   Professor FOWLER.

Open to students who have completed English 4.

15. Oratory.

The preparation and delivery of six original orations. Fall term.

Professor FOWLER.

Miss KIDDER.

Open to students who have completed English 5 and Elocution 3.

FRENCH.

1. Elementary Course.

Pronunciation, grammar, conversation, and composition. Edgren's Grammar, Part I. Fall term.   Miss WAIT.

Open to all students of the College of Liberal Arts.

2. Elementary Course.

Grammar, composition, conversation, dictation. Van Daell's Introduction to French Authors. Halévy, L'Abbé Constantin. Winter term.

Miss WAIT.

Open to students who have completed French 1.

3. Elementary Course.

Grammar. Grandgent, French composition. George Sand, La Mare au Diable. Labiche et Martin, Le Voyage de M. Perrichon. Spring term. Miss WAIT.

Open to students who have completed French 2.

4. Advanced Course.

Syntax, Composition. Molière, L'Avare, Le Bourgeois Gentil-homme ; Hugo, Quatrevingt-treize. Fall term. Miss WAIT.

Open to students who have completed French 3.

5. Advanced Course in French Conversation.

Syntax, composition. Marchand's Method of French Conversation. Fall term. Miss WAIT.

Open to students who have completed French 3.

[French 5 will not be given in 1901.]

6. Advanced Course.

Syntax, composition. Prose, fiction, and drama of the 19th century. Chateaubriand. Sandeau, Hugo, Daudet. Winter term.

Miss WAIT.

Open to students who have completed French 4 or 5.

7. Advanced Course.

French Literature in the Nineteenth Century, the Romantic move-ment, collateral reading, composition. Winter term. Miss WAIT.

Open to students who have completed French 4 or 5.

[French 7 will not be given in 1901-02.]

8. Advanced Course.

General History of French Literature. Gazier, Histoire de la Lit-terature Française. Corneille, LeCid. Racine, Les Plaideurs. Vol-taire, prose extracts. Hugo, Hernani. Composition. Spring term.

Miss WAIT.

Open to students who have completed French 6 or 7.

9. Advanced Course.

Sources and Development of French Comedy. De Juleville, Le Théatre en France, Les Comédiens en France. Composition. Spring term. Miss WAIT.

Open to students who have completed French 6 or 7.

[French 9 will not be given in 1902.]

GERMAN.

1. Elementary Course.

Grammar, composition, conversation, reading.   Eysenbach-Collar's
Grammar.   Fall term.   Miss WAIT.
Open to all students of the College of Liberal Arts.

2. Elementary Course.

Grammar, composition, translation.· Thomas's Grammar.   Harris's
German Composition.   Super's German Reader.   Winter term.
                                                Miss WAIT.
Open to students who have completed German 1.

3. Elementary Course.

Grammar, composition, translation.   Storm's Immensee.   Heine's
Haizreise.   Zschokke's Das Abenteur der Neujahrsnacht.   Spring term.
                                                Miss WAIT.
Open to students who have completed German 2.

4. Advanced Course.

Conversation, composition, translation.   Schiller's Der Neffee als
Onkel.   Selections from Heyse, Auerbach, etc.   Fall term.
                                                Miss WAIT.
Open to students who have completed German 3.

5. Advanced Course.

Composition, conversation.   Lessing's Nathan Der Weise.   Schiller's
William Tell.   Fall term.   Miss WAIT.
Open to students who have completed German 3.

[German 5 will not be given in 1901.]

6. Advanced Course.

Goethe's Götz von Berlichingen.   Lessing's Minna von Barnhelm.
Freytag, Aus dem Jahrhundert des grossen Krieges.   Composition.
Winter term.   Miss WAIT.
Open to students who have completed German 4 or 5.

7. Advanced Course.

Sheffel's Der Trompeter von Säkkingen.   Freytag, Bilder aus der
deutschen Vergangenheit.   History of German civilization.   Composition, essays.   Winter term.   Miss WAIT.
Open to students who have completed German 4 or 5.

[German 7 will not be given in 1901-02.]

8. Advanced Course.

The History of German Literature. Scherer's History of German Literature. Readings from Miller's German Classics. Composition. Spring term.   Miss WAIT.

Open to students who have completed German 6 or 7.

9. Advanced Course.

Goethe's life and works, with particular study of his lyrics; Werther's Leiden, Goethe's Egmont, Dichtung und Wahrheit; etc. Composition, essays, conversation. Spring term.   Miss WAIT.

Open to students who have completed German 6 or 7.

[German 9 will not be given in 1902.]

LATIN.

1. Latin Lessons.

Tuell and Fowler's First Book in Latin.   Fall term.

Professor GRUBB.

Open to Preparatory and College students.

2. Latin Lessons.   (Continued.)

Winter term.   Professor GRUBB.

Open to students who have completed Latin 1.

3. Caesar.

Texts, Rolfe and Dennison's Junior Latin Book and Daniell's Latin Prose Composition.   Spring term.   Professor GRUBB.

Open to students who have completed Latin 2.

4. Caesar.   (Continued.)

Fall term.   Professor GRUBB.

Open to students who have completed Latin 3.

5. Cicero.

Kelsey's Cicero's Orations and Daniell's Latin Prose Composition. Winter term.   Professor GRUBB.

Open to students who have completed Latin 4.

6. Cicero.   (Continued.)

Spring term.   Professor GRUBB.

Open to students who have completed Latin 5.

7. Virgil.

Greenough's Virgil's Aeneid. Fall term.   Professor PARKER.
Open to students who have completed Latin 6.

8. Virgil. (Continued.)

Winter term.   Professor PARKER.
Open to students who have completed Latin 7.

9 Horace, Odes and Epodes.

Chase and Stuart's edition. Spring term of 1902, and the spring term of every alternate year thereafter.   Professor PARKER.
Open to students who have completed Latin 8.

10. Horace (Satires and Epistles), or Ovid.

Given in the Spring term of 1901, and in the Spring term of every alternate year thereafter.   Professor PARKER.
Open to students who have completed Latin 8.

11. Livy, First Book.

Chase and Stuart's Edition. Fall term of 1902, and the Fall term of every alternate year thereafter.   Professor PARKER.
Open to students who have completed Latin 8.

12 Livy, Twenty-first Book.

Given in Fall term of 1901 and in the Fall term of every alternate year thereafter.   Professor PARKER.
Open to students who have completed Latin 8.

13. Cicero's DeSenectute and De Amicitia.

Chase and Stuart's Edition. Winter term of 1901-1902, and the Winter term of every alternate year thereafter. Professor PARKER.
Open to students who have completed Latin 8.

14. Curtius Rufus's Life of Alexander.

Crosby's Edition. Winter term of 1902-1903 and the Winter term of every alternate year thereafter.   Professor PARKER.
Open to students who have completed Latin 8 or 10.

15. Tacitus's Germania and Agricola.

Chase and Stuart's Edition. Spring term of 1902 and the Spring term of every alternate year thereafter.   Professor PARKER.
Open to students who have completed Latin 8.

16. Juvenal.

Anthon's Edition.   Spring term of 1901, and the Spring term of every alternate year thereafter.   Professor PARKER.

Open to students who have completed Latin 8.

Latin Composition may be given in connection with Latin courses 9, 10, 11, 12, 13 and 14.

BOOKS OF REFERENCE.

The following books are recommended for reference to students pursuing the study of Latin:

Harper's Latin Lexicon; White's Junior Student's Latin Lexicon; Doederlein's Latin Synonyms; Liddell's History of Rome; Long's, or Ginn & Co.'s Classical Atlas; Anthon's or Smith's Classical Dictionary; Harper's Dictionary of Classical Literature and Antiquities; Harkness's and Bennett's Latin Grammar.

GREEK.

1. Grammar and Lessons.

Boise and Pattengill's Greek Lessons.   Goodwin's Greek Grammar. Fall term.   Professor PARKER.

Open to all students in the College.

2. Grammar and Lessons.   (Continued.)

Winter term.   Professor PARKER.

Open to students who have completed Greek 1.

3. Anabasis.

Goodwin's Xenophon's Anabasis.   Collar and Daniell's Greek Composition.   Spring term.   Professor PARKER.

Open to students who have completed Greek 2.

4. Anabasis.   (Continued.)

Collar and Daniell's Greek Composition.   Fall term.

Professor PARKER.

Open to students who have completed Greek 3.

5. Orations of Lysias.

Stevens' Edition.   Winter term.   Professor PARKER.

Open to students who have completed Greek 4.

6. Iliad.

Keep's Homer's Iliad.   Spring term.   Professor PARKER.
Open to students who have completed Greek 5.

7. Odyssey.

Merry's Homer's Odyssey.   Fall term.   Professor PARKER.
Open to students who have completed Greek 6.

8. Plato's Apology of Socrates.

Dyer's Edition.   Winter term of 1902-03 and the Winter term of
every alternate year thereafter.   Professor PARKER.
Open to students who have completed Greek 5.

9. Plato's Gorgias.

Lodge's Edition.   Winter term of 1901-02 and the Winter term of
every alternate year thereafter.   Professor PARKER.
Open to students who have completed Greek 5.

10. Herodotus.

Fernald's Selections.   Spring term of 1902 and the Spring term of
every alternate year thereafter.   Professor PARKER.
Open to students who have completed Greek 8 or 9.

11. Prometheus of Aeschylus, or Medea of Euripides.

Wecklein's Prometheus, Allen's Medea.   Spring term of 1901, and
the Spring term of every alternate year thereafter.

                                            Professor PARKER.
Open to students who have completed Greek 8 or 9.

12, 13, 14, 15.   Greek New Testament.

These classes, while primarily intended for theological students, are
open also to College students who have the requisite preparation.   A full
description is given in the Divinity School courses.

BOOKS OF REFERENCE.

The following books are recommended for reference to those pursuing the study of Greek.

Liddell and Scott's Greek Lexicon; Autenrieth's Homeric Diction-
ary; Long's, or Ginn & Co.'s Classical Atlas; Anthon's, or Smith's
Classical Dictionary; Harper's Dictionary of Classical Literature and
Antiquities; Smith's History of Greece; Goodwin's Greek Grammar;
Goodwin's Greek Modes and Tenses.

HEBREW.

1, 2, 3. Grammar and Old Testament.

These are primarily courses in the Divinity School, but may be elected by students in the College of Liberal Arts whenever they are offered. Classes will be formed each year if a sufficient number of students apply.

It is the aim to give the student such a knowledge of the forms and structure of the Hebrew language as shall enable him to use it efficiently in the criticism and literary analysis of the Old Testament Scriptures. The text-books used are H. G. Mitchell's Hebrew Lessons and the Hebrew Old Testament. Three terms—Fall, Winter and Spring—each term counting as a course. Professor WHITE.

Open (under conditions as described above) to students who, in the judgment of the Instructor, are qualified by previous training to take the course.

MATHEMATICS.

The primary aim of this department is to cultivate habits of precision in thought, and power of abstract reasoning. It is believed that these qualities of mind can nowhere better be acquired than in mathematical study. In addition, mathematical facts and formulæ are learned, and practice is given in the solution of practical problems.

[For courses 1 to 4 inclusive, see Preparatory Department.]

5. Elementary Algebra.

This course embraces the Theory of Exponents, the solution of Quadratic, Simultaneous and Indeterminate Equations, Ratio and Proportion, and Arithmetical and Geometrical Progressions. Wells's College Algebra is used. Fall term. Professor WRIGHT.

Open to all students who have completed Mathematics 4.

6. Plane Geometry.

This course is designed to give students thorough drill in the first principles of Geometry. Each proposition is carefully analyzed and particular attention is given to correct reasoning and precise expression. Phillips and Fisher's Elements of Geometry is used. Winter term.

Professor WRIGHT.

Open to students who have completed Mathematics 5.

7. Plane and Solid Geometry.

A continuation of Mathematics 6. It is the design in these two courses to take up all the matter contained in the text-book. This includes the fundamental propositions of Plane Geometry, the circle, the polyhedron, the cylinder, the cone, and the sphere. Spring term.

Professor WRIGHT.

Open to students who have completed Mathematics 6.

8. Higher Algebra.

This course assumes a thorough knowledge on the part of the student of Mathematics 5, and also some knowledge of Plane Geometry. It embraces the study of Series, Undetermined Co-efficients, the Binomial Theorem, Logarithms, Permutations and Combinations, Probability, and the Theory of Equations. Fall term. Professor WRIGHT.

Open to students who have completed Mathematics 6.

9. Plane and Spherical Trigonometry.

This course includes the solution of trigonometrical equations, the solution of plane and spherical triangles, and problems involving an application of Trigonometry to Mensuration, Surveying, and Astronomy. Crockett's Plane and Spherical Trigonometry is used as a text-book. Winter term. Professor WRIGHT.

Open to students who have completed Mathematics 8.

10. Analytic Geometry.

This course treats of the straight line, the conic sections and higher plane curves. Hardy's Analytic Geometry is used. Mondays, Wednesdays, and Fridays. Spring term. Professor WRIGHT.

Open to students who have completed Mathematics 9.

11. Surveying and Leveling.

Field work and problems. Field work on Saturdays at the option of the instructor. Spring term. Professor WRIGHT.

Open to students who have completed Mathematics 9.

12. Differential Calculus.

Osborne's Differential and Integral Calculus is used. Mondays, Wednesdays, and Fridays. Fall term. Professor WRIGHT.

Open to students who have completed Mathematics 10.

13. Integral Calculus.

Mondays, Wednesdays, and Fridays. Winter term.

Professor WRIGHT.

Open to students who have completed Mathematics 12.

14. Descriptive Geometry.

This course embraces orthographic projection, shades and shadows, and perspective. Church's Descriptive Geometry is used. Mondays, Wednesdays, and Fridays. Fall term. Professor WRIGHT.

Open to students who have completed Mathematics 9.

15. Strength of Structures.

This course takes up the computation of the strains in bridge and roof trusses, by graphical and analytical methods. Shreve's Strength of Bridges and Roofs is used as a text-book. Mondays, Wednesdays and Fridays. Winter term. Professor WRIGHT.

Open to students who have completed Mathematics 13.

Mathematics 14 and 15 will be given in 1901-02, but will not be given in 1902-03, alternating with Mathematics 12 and 13.

16. Quaternions.

A class will be formed for the study of Quaternions when a sufficient number of advanced students apply. The class will meet once a week for a year at such hour as the instructor may appoint.

Professor WRIGHT.

ASTRONOMY.

1. General Astronomy.

This course is largely descriptive in character, though some of the simpler mathematical problems connected with Astronomy are solved. It embraces a study of the imaginary lines into which the heavens are divided: latitude, longitude, time; the sun, moon, and planets; comets, meteors, and the stars. Some attention is given to the constellations and the myths connected with them. The Nebular Hypothesis is presented and discussed. Young's Lessons in Astronomy is used. Fall term.

Professor WRIGHT.

Open to students who have completed Mathematics 9.

Given in the Fall term 1901, and in the Fall term of every alternate year thereafter.

2. Mathematical Astronomy.

This course will have to do with the solution of various Astronomical problems. Computations in latitude, longitude and time, eclipses, orbits, etc., will be among the subjects considered. Three hours a week. Winter term. Professor WRIGHT.

Open to students who have completed Mathematics 13 and Astronomy 1.

PHYSICS.

The work in Physics consists of a careful consideration of the various phenomena treated under mechanics, acoustics, heat, light, electricity, and magnetism. The student is led to note the general principles of mechanics that apply throughout, and the application of modern theories. The courses in Physics consist of recitations, lectures, with demonstrations, and laboratory work.

1. Mechanics, Hydrostatics, Pneumatics.

Fall Term.   Professor RICH.
Open to students who have completed Mathematics 9.

2. Acoustics, Optics, Heat.

Winter term. Musical students, taking the work in Acoustics, will be counted a half credit.   Professor RICH.
Open to students who have completed Mathematics 9.

3. Electricity, Magnetism.

Spring term.   Professor RICH.
Open to students who have completed Physics 2.

CHEMISTRY.

The aim of the course is: first, a general knowledge of chemical phenomena; second, a thorough knowledge of Theoretical Chemistry and Stoichiometry; third, a careful study of the elements and their more important compounds; fourth, methods and work in Analysis, Qualitative and Quantitative.

1. Inorganic Chemistry.

This work consists of four hours per week of recitations or lectures, and two hours per week of experimental work. Remsen's Inorganic Chemistry, or an equivalent, is used as the basis of courses 1 and 2. Fall term.   Professor RICH.
Open to all students.

2. Inorganic Chemistry.

This is a continuation of Chemistry 1, and consists of four hours per week of recitations or lectures, and of two hours per week of experimental work. The course consists chiefly of Theoretical Chemistry, Stoichiometry, and a study of metals. Winter term.
Professor RICH.
Open to students who have completed Chemistry 1 or its equivalent.

3. Organic Chemistry.

This course consists of recitations, lectures, with experimental demonstrations, and laboratory work. The lectures treat chiefly of new methods and of food-stuffs, their composition and adulteration. Remsen's Organic Chemistry is used. Spring term. Professor RICH.

Open to students who have completed Chemistry 2.

In each of the courses 1, 2, and 3, the work is profusely illustrated by experiments, and the laboratory gives opportunity for individual work on the principles discussed.

4. Analytical Chemistry.

Laboratory work. Fall term. Professor RICH.

Open to students who have completed Chemistry 2.

5. Analytical Chemistry.

Laboratory work. Winter term. Professor RICH.

Open to students who have completed Chemistry 4.

6. Analytical Chemistry.

Laboratory work. Spring term. Professor RICH.

Open to students who have completed Chemistry 5.

Chemistry 4, 5, and 6, form progressive courses in Qualitative and Quantitative Analysis. General Qualitative and Quantitative methods are studied, and analysis is made of such compounds as ores, soils, fertilizers, milk, butter, water, soaps, gas, drugs, etc.

For the present, no student is allowed to register for more than fifteen hours per week in laboratory courses.

BIOLOGY.

1. General Biology.

The course will consist of recitations, lectures and laboratory work. This course will be required of all students in Sociology, and Psychology. Fall term. Dr. KIMBLE.

Open to all College students.

2. Physiology.

Lectures, recitations, and demonstrations. Winter Term.

Dr. KIMBLE.

Open to students who have completed Biology 1.

3. Systematic Zoölogy.

A continuation of work begun in Biology 1, together with lectures in Natural History and Vertebrate Zoology. Winter term.

Dr. KIMBLE.

Open to students who have completed Biology 1.

4. Structural Botany.

A study of the structure of phanerogams, with a brief introduction to Ecology and Vegetable Physiology. Spring term. Dr. KIMBLE.
Open to all College students.

5. Cryptogamic Botany.

The life history of cryptogams, with special reference to the development and function of plant tissues. Fall term. Dr. KIMBLE.
Open to students who have completed Biology 4.

GEOLOGY AND MINERALOGY.

1. Geology.

The work in Geology is given by text-book recitations, supplemented by lectures and excursions for field work. The College has a valuable collection of minerals, which serves for purposes of illustration and study. Dana's work is used. Spring term. Professor RICH.
Open to students who have completed Chemistry 1, Biology 3 and Biology 4.

2. Mineralogy.

This course consists of a qualitative determination of minerals by means of the blow pipe. Winter term. Professor RICH.
Open to students who have completed Chemistry 2.

HISTORY.

[For History 1 to 4 inclusive, see courses in Preparatory School.]

5. History of the Christian Church.

A. The Ancient and Mediæval Eras (1-1517).

This course in Church History is primarily intended for the members of the Divinity School, but is also open to College students. It will require the investigation of the early organization and extension of Christianity, and the successive periods of the Church down to the time of Charlemagne; followed by a careful inquiry into the causes of the rise of the Papacy, of the political relations of the Church, and of the Crusades. Fisher's History of the Church will be used as a hand book and topics will be assigned to each member of the class for special investigation and reports. Fall term. Professor WHITE.
Open to students who have completed History 1 and 2.

6. History of the Christian Church.

B. The Modern Era (1517-1901).

This course will begin with the study of the Reformation, and trace the history of the Church down to the present time. It will include the history of Christian missions, revivals, social reforms and philanthropy. The same text-book will be used as in History 5. Winter term.

Professor WHITE.

Open to students who, in the judgment of the instructor, are qualified by previous training to take the course.

7. History of the United States.

Advanced course. Spring term.

Open to students who, in the judgment of the instructor, are qualified by previous training to take the course.

ECONOMICS.

1. Science of Government.

This course is designed to give students some insight into the nature and theory of government, especially of the National, State, and Municipal governments of the United States. It also deals briefly with the rights of citizens and the elements of common law. Texts, Fiske's Civil Government and Andrew's Constitution of the United States. Spring term.

Open to Preparatory and College students.

2. Political Economy.

The standard economic theories of production, exchange and distribution are developed before the class; and the bearing of these theories on vital economic questions of the day is frankly and freely discussed. Students are encouraged to write essays on economic topics and to read them for discussion. In preparing these essays, students will receive the personal aid of the instructor in directing their reading. A good reference library for this purpose is at the disposal of the class. Walker's Political Economy is used. Spring term. Professor WRIGHT.

Open to all College students.

3. Financial History of the United States.

This course embraces the finances of the Revolution; the financial administrations of Morris, Hamilton, and Gallatin; the bank struggle, tariff legislation, and the financial measures of the civil war and reconstruction period. This course will be conducted by lectures and frequent reviews. Fall term. Professor WRIGHT.

Open to students who have completed Economics 2.

[Economics 3 will not be given in 1901.]

JURISPRUDENCE.

1. International Law.

The general principles which govern the relations of States, as historically developed in express agreements and by usage, are elucidated, and these principles are discussed from the standpoints of reason and justice. Special study is made of current international problems and theses on these subjects are required. Particular attention is paid to terminology. Lawrence's International Law is used as a text-book. Frequent reference is made to the works on International Law by Woolsey, Wheaton, Glenn, etc. Spring term.

Open to students who, in the judgment of the instructor, are qualified by previous training to take the course.

[Jurisprudence 1 will not be given in 1902.]

SOCIOLOGY.

Series A.   The Development of Sociological Theory.

1. An Introduction to the Study of Sociology.

An outline study of the characteristic concepts of recent sociological thought.   Professor KIMBLE.

Open, by consultation, to all students.

2. Pre-Comtean Sociology.

A careful study of the earlier theories concerning social relations.
Professor KIMBLE.

3. Pre-Comtean Sociology.   (Continuation of Course 2.)
Professor KIMBLE.

*4. Modern Sociological Theory.

The chief works of the more prominent modern sociologists are studied with a view to the characteristic positions of each author and the relation borne by each to sociological theory as a whole.
Professor KIMBLE.

*5. Modern Sociological Theory.   (Continuation of Course 4.)
Professor KIMBLE.

*6. Types of Sociological Theory.

The Utopians, the organicists, the psychologists.
Professor KIMBLE.

Series B.   The Development of Association and of Society.

7. An Introduction to the Comparative Study of Association.

The method, scope, and aim of Comparative Sociology.
Professor KIMBLE

Open, by consultation, to all students.

---

*Will not be given in 1901-02.

8. Biogeography.

A general sketch of the influence of "natural conditions" upon the associative activities of living organisms.   Professor KIMBLE.

9. The Development of Association.

A study of the lower stages of the associative process with especial reference to the earlier forms of food, sex, and conflict association.

Professor KIMBLE.

10. The Development of Association. (Continuation of Course 9.)

The investigation begun in Course 9 is continued among organisms of a higher type than those there studied.   Professor KIMBLE.

*11. The Development of Association. (Continuation of Courses 9 and 10.)

The associational process as manifested among the natural races.

Professor KIMBLE.

*12. The Development of Association. (Continuation of Courses 9, 10 and 11.)

The associational life of a modern community. Study of the local environment.   Professor KIMBLE.

*13. Abnormal and Pathologic Variations of the Associative Process.

An introductory and outline study of the sociology of crime, pauperism, etc.   Professor KIMBLE.

*14. Abnormal and Pathologic Variations of the Associative Process. (Continuation of Course 13.)

A study of the preventive, curative, and ameliorative factors of associate life.   Professor KIMBLE.

15. Reproductive Association.

The family is taken as the most highly developed and best known example of this type of associational life; attention is given to its origin, development, and significance.   Professor KIMBLE.

*16. The Chief Types of Association.

Food, sex, and conflict. The characteristic associational activities centering about each. Origin, development, and significance.

Professor KIMBLE.

For the most advanced students only.

---

*Will not be given in 1901-02.

*17. The Sociology of Religion.

A consideration, from the stand-point of Sociology, of the phenomena of religion.   Professor KIMBLE.

PHILOSOPHY.

1 (a). Psychology.

After a somewhat detailed inquiry into the general relations of mind and body, followed by a close examination of the phenomena of perception, the more complex mental processes, as memory, association, apperception, hallucination, imagination, impulse, habit, volition, are taken up for careful study. Special emphasis is laid upon self-observation, and the indications for self-culture are attentively marked. Stress is also laid upon the definition and use of technical terms.

Professor KIMBLE.

Open to students who have completed Biology 2.

1 (b). Psychology.

A continuation of Philosophy 1 (a).

Professor KIMBLE.

Open to students who have completed Biology 2 and Philosophy 1.

2. Metaphysic.

This is primarily a course in the Divinity School, but it may be elected by students in the College of Liberal Arts whenever it is offered. Classes will be formed whenever a sufficient number of students apply. Lotze's Outlines of Metaphysic is used as a text-book. Fall term.

Professor WHITE.

Open to students who, in the judgment of the instructor, are qualified by previous training to take the course.

3. Logic.

Having first obtained a thorough grounding in the principles and methods of correct reasoning both deductive and inductive, at least one-half of the term is given to the detection and discrimination of fallacies in actual examples. Such examples the class is required to search out in current literature and bring in for discussion. Davis's Elements of Deductive Logic, and Davis's Elements of Inductive Logic are used. Winter term.   Professor FOWLER.

Open to students who, in the judgment of the instructor, are qualified by previous training to take the course.

---

*Will not be given in 1901-02.

4. Ethics.

Ethics is treated from the standpoint of Philosophy, and the different systems are discussed. The nature and grounds of obligation are investigated and applied to the practical affairs of life. Winter term.

Professor WHITE.

Open to students who, in the judgment of the instructor, are qualified by previous training to take the course.

5. Philosophy of Religion.

Caird's Introduction to the Philosophy of Religion is the text-book. Lotze, Sabatier, and Martineau are used as works of reference. The aim of the instructor is to acquaint the student with the proper office of reason in the effort to find argumentative grounds for religious ideas. Most of the modern theories respecting the nature and scope of the religious feeling pass under review; and in such discussions free questioning on the part of the student is encouraged. Winter term.

Professor WHITE.

Open to students who, in the judgment of the instructor, are qualified by previous training to take the course.

Philosophy 5 will alternate with Dogmatic Theology. See under Divinity School.

6. Ethical Theories.

Martineau's Types of Ethical Theory is used as a text-book with frequent references to the works of Sidgwick, Green, Smyth, and others. Much attention is paid to the elucidation and criticism of the modern ethical theories. Spring term.   Professor WHITE.

Open to students who, in the judgment of the instructor, are qualified by previous training to take the course.

Philosophy 6 will alternate with Comparative Religion. See under Divinity School.

FINE ARTS.

1. History of Art.

This course gives a brief survey of the progress of Art from the earliest to the present time. The course will consist of lectures, recitations, and frequent reviews. Students will study under direction of the instructor from numerous works of reference in the college and public libraries. The course is copiously illustrated with photographs and engravings of the masterpieces of painting and sculpture. Two hours a week. Spring term.   Miss BLOOD.

Open only to advanced students.

2, 3, 4. Drawing.

This course includes perspective, drawing from casts in charcoal and crayon, still life studies in crayon, etc. - It will count as one credit for the entire year.   Miss BLOOD.

Open to all students in the College.

MUSIC.

1, 2, 3. Harmony.

Class-room work, lectures, recitations, and written exercises, covering theory of the elements of music, triads, chords of the seventh, augmented chords, chords of the ninth and eleventh, modulation, suspension and harmonizing of melodies.   Text-books, Emery, Richter, and Jadassohn.   Three hours a week for one year.   Professor LUNDBERG.

Open to all students in the College.

4, 5, 6. Simple and Double Counterpoint.

Lectures, recitations and daily written exercises, based on the textbooks of Richter, Haupt, and others.   Three hours a week for one year.   Professor LUNDBERG.

Open to students who have completed Music 3.

7, 8, 9. Fugue, Canon, Musical Form, and the elements of Orchestration.

Lectures, recitations, and written exercises.   Text-books, Prout, Cherubini, Rieman, Berlioz.   Three hours a week for one year.
Professor LUNDBERG.

Open to students who have completed Music 6.

10. History of Music. (Half Course.)

Introductory course on the lives of the great composers.   Two hours a week.   Fall term.   Professor LUNDBERG.

Open to students who, in the judgment of the instructor, are qualified by previous training to take the course.

11. History of Music. (Half Course.)

Advanced course on the development of music from the earliest times until today, with special reference to critical analysis of the works of the greatest masters.   Text-books, Naumann, Langhans, Rieman. Two hours a week.   Winter term,   Professor LUNDBERG.

Open to students who have completed Music 10.

ELOCUTION.

[Not more than four credits can be counted in this department towards the degree of A. B.]

1. Elocution. [Half Course.]

The aim of this course is to rid the voice of all impurities, secure correct placing of the voice, proper breathing, and beauty of tone for conversational purposes. Notes will be given upon the anatomy of the vocal organs and the care of the voice. Physical exercises will be introduced as a means of securing grace and becoming deportment. Recitations Mondays, Wednesdays, and Fridays. Fall term.

Miss KIDDER.

Open to all students of the College.

2. Elocution. [Half Course.]

In this course attention will be given to the adaptation of the conversational voice to the requirements of platform speaking. Each pupil will be required to deliver three selections before the class for criticism. Work in pantomime and life study will be introduced. Recitations Mondays, Wednesdays, and Fridays. . Winter term.

Miss KIDDER.

Open to students who have completed Elocution 1.

3. Elocution. [Half Course.]

This course will consist of a continuation of the work outlined in Elocution 2. The analysis of some English Classic will be required. Recitations Mondays, Wednesdays, and Fridays. Spring term.

Miss KIDDER.

Open to students who have completed Elocution 2.

4. Elocution. [Half Course.]

The study of Masterpieces will be made the basis of this course. Recitations Mondays and Thursdays. Fall term. Miss KIDDER.

Open to students who have completed Elocution 3.

5. Elocution. [Half Course.]

The work in this course will be a continuation of that begun in Elocution 4, together with extemporaneous talks, critical and detailed life study for personation. Recitations Mondays and Thursdays. Winter term. Miss KIDDER.

Open to students who have completed Elocution 4.

6. Elocution. [Half Course.]

This course will consist of a continuation of Elocution 5. Recitations Mondays and Thursdays. Spring term. Miss KIDDER.

Open to students who have completed Elocution 5.

7. Oratory. [Half Course.]

In this course the aim will be to assist the students in gaining some knowledge of the great orators, both American and English. Each student is required to deliver before class for criticism a certain number of selections, chosen from the orators studied; also to give talks on subjects previously assigned. Recitations Mondays and Thursdays. Fall term.

Open to students who have completed Elocution 6. Miss KIDDER.

8. Oratory. [Half Course.]

Important features of this course are extemporaneous speaking, class debates and criticism. Two orations and one debate will be required from each member of the class. Recitations Mondays and Thursdays. Winter term. Miss KIDDER.

Open to students who have completed Elocution 7.

9. Dramatic Expression. [Half Course.]

This course consists of a study of two dramas for the purpose of character interpretation. Scenes will be committed and interpreted for public presentation. Recitations Tuesdays and Thursdays. Fall term,

Open to students who have completed Elocution 6. Miss KIDDER.

10, 11. Dramatic Expression. [Half Courses.]

These courses consist of a study of two Shakespearian plays. As in Elocution 9, scenes will be committed and interpreted for public presentation. Recitations Tuesdays and Thursdays. Winter and Spring terms. Miss KIDDER.

Open to students who have completed Elocution 9.

RECITALS.

Recitals will be given during the year to show the proficiency of pupils, and to give them assistance in acquiring confidence, ease and self control.

GYMNASIUM WORK.

Regular class work in the Gymnasium is required of all students in the institution during two years of their college course. This work will embrace Swedish Gymnastics; marching; Wand, Dumb-bell, and Indian Club drills. Instruction is also given in the use of the Apparatus and in Heavy Gymnastics. Especial attention is given to correct posture of the body and good form in walking and standing. Each student is given a thorough physical examination by the medical examiner, and private work is prescribed to him in accordance with his individual needs. All students will provide themselves with regular gymnasium uniforms. The price of the uniform is about $2.75 for the men and $6.50 for the women

TABULAR VIEW FOR THE YEAR 1901-1902.

Courses are given in 5 hours a week recitations unless otherwise stated.

HOUR.	FALL TERM.	WINTER TERM.	SPRING TERM.
8:00	Biblical History. *Economics 3. *English 9. English 10. *History 5. Homiletics 1. (3 h) Latin 4. Latin 7. Music 1. (3 h) Music 4. (3 h) Physics 1. Sociology 9. *Sociology 13.	Biblical History. Astronomy 2. *English 11. English 12. *History 1. *History 6. Homiletics 2. (1 h) Latin 5. Latin 8. Music 2. (3 h) Music 5. (3 h) Physics 2. Sociology 10. *Sociology 14.	Biblical Geography 　　and Archæology. *English 13. English 14. Greek 12. *Greek 13. *Hermeneutics. Homiletics 6. (1 h) Latin 6. Latin 9. *Latin 10. Music 3. (3 h) Music 6. (3 h) Physical Geography. Physics 3.
9:30	Chemistry 1. Elocution 7. (2 h) German 4. *German 5. Greek 7. Greek 14. *Greek 15. Homiletics 4. Mathematics 1. Mathematics 8. Music 10. (2 h) Philosophy 1. Sociology 8.	Chemistry 2. Elocution 8. (2 h) German 6. *German 7. *Greek 8. Greek 9. Homiletics 5. (3 h) Mathematics 2. Mathematics 9. Music 11. (2 h) Pastoral Theology. Philosophy 3. Philosophy 4. Sociology 15. *Sociology 12.	Chemistry 3. Economics 1. German 8. *German 9. Greek 10. *Greek 11. Homiletics 3. *Jurisprudence 1. Mathematics 10. (3 h) *Theo. of Universalism.
10:30	Astronomy 1. Biology 1. English 5. French 1. Greek 4. History 2. *Philosophy 2. Sociology 2. *Sociology 6.	Biology 2. Dogmatic Theology. English 6. English 7. French 2. Greek 5. History 3. Sociology 3. Sociology 16.	Biology 3. Economics 2. French 3. Greek 6. History 4. Pastoral Care.
11:30	Christian Evidences. Elocution 4. (2 h) English 2. (4 h) Fine Arts 1. (3 h) German 1. Greek 1. Mathematics 5. Sociology 1. *Sociology 4.	Elocution 5. (2 h) English 3. (4 h) German 2. Greek 2. Mathematics 3. Mathematics 6. Philosophy 5. Sociology 7. *Sociology 5.	Elocution 6. (2 h) English 4. (4 h) Philosophy 6. Geology 1. German 3. Greek 3. Mathematics 4. Mathematics 7.
2:00	Chemistry 4. Elocution 1. (3 h) Elocution 9. (2 h) English Bible. (1 h) French 4. (3 h) *French 5. (3 h) Latin 1. *Latin 11. Latin 12. *Mathematics 12. (3 h) Mathematics 14. (3 h) *Sociology 17.	Biblical Introduction. Chemistry 5. Elocution 2. (3 h) Elocution 10. (2 h) English Bible. (1 h) French 6. *French 7. Geology 2. Latin 2. Latin 13. *Latin 14. *Mathematics 13. (3 h) Mathematics 15. (3 h)	Chemistry 6. Comparative Religion Elocution 3. (3 h) Elocution 11. (2 h) English Bible. (1 h) English 8. (1 h) French 8. *French 9. Latin 3. Latin 15. *Latin 16. Mathematics 11.
3:00	Chemistry 4. Fine Arts 2.	Chemistry 5. Fine Arts 3. Geology 2.	Chemistry 6. Fine Arts 4.

*Not given in 1901-02.

PREPARATORY SCHOOL.

DEPARTMENT OF ELEMENTARY INSTRUCTION, INTRO-DUCTORY TO THE COLLEGE COURSES.

The primary object of this Department is to prepare students thoroughly for admission to College, but it also affords special advantages to those students who wish to become teachers or to fit themselves for active business, and who are unable to pursue a complete course.

Thorough preparation is the price of sure success both in and out of College.

Students may enter this department with the full assurance that they will receive thorough instruction in those subjects and principles which contribute to sound scholarship and success.

SUPERVISION.

The Preparatory School is under the general superintendence of the President and Faculty, and its students are under the same regulations as those of the College. Instruction is given by the regular College Professors, as well as by the Department Instructors.

ADVANTAGES.

All the advantages of the College, such as libraries, museums, lectures, and instruction in elocution, are open to all.

One hour is devoted to every recitation, and as the number in each class is not large, each student recites and receives individual drill every day. Contrast such opportunities with the disadvantages of membership in crowded classes and note the gain to the student here.

ATTENDANCE.

To secure the full benefit of all the opportunities here afforded, it is necessary for the student to enter at the beginning of the College year and remain until its close.

ABSENCE.

The vacations are so long and so arranged that it is unnecessary for students to visit their friends during term time, except for the most urgent reasons. The student's absence, even for a few days, entails upon him much greater injury than is commonly supposed. Parents are earnestly requested to co-operate with the Faculty in securing continuous attendance.

Faculty.

CHARLES ELLWOOD NASH, A. M., S. T. D., PRESIDENT.
JON WATSON GRUBB, M. S.
ISAAC AUGUSTUS PARKER, A. M., PH. D.
FREDERICK WILLIAM RICH, B. S.
PHILIP GREEN WRIGHT, A. M.
FRANK HAMILTON FOWLER, PH. D.
M. AGNES HATHAWAY.

Students in the Preparatory School.

Marie Adams..*Monmouth.*
William Andrew...*New Salem.*
William McCall Baird.....................................*Biggsville.*
Fred Daniel Boehm.............. ....*Muncie, Ind.*
Ida Brothers ....*Fincastle, Ind.*
Glenn Carlton Bruner.......................................*Gerlaw.*
Ross Elvin Bruner...*Gerlaw.*
Grace LaClare Clark.......................................*Galesburg.*
John Lawson Clay...*Galesburg.*
Walter Timothy Clay.....................................*Galesburg.*
Fielden W. Converse............................ ....*Dysart, Ia.*
Rauseldon Cooper, Jr..... ....*Oquawka.*
Laura Gladdis Cox.....................................*Augusta, Wis.*
Clifford Elmo Davis.....................................*Galesburg.*
Ida Amy Davis................... ... .*Otranto, Ia.*
Charles Walter Downs ....*Winslow, Ariz.*
Bert Miller Eustice ....*Stockton.*
James Wilson Frick............... ....*Kiethsburg.*
Emma Welton Grubb........ ....*Hamilton.*
Lois Pearl Hamilton............................ ....*Knoxville.*
Herschel Victor Harlan.............................*Walnut, Kan.*

Mary Lucy Harlan..................................*Corwin, O.*
Mary Arrah Hart................................*Eureka, Kan.*
Thomas Asher Hicks...............................*Stockton.*
Stephen Earle Hilliard.............................*Lafayette.*
Laura May Hobbs.....................*Benton Harbor, Mich.*
Guy Hungerford............................*Brookfield, Mo.*
Franklin Wilbur Kidder...............................*Monica.*
Ross Larnard Kidder..........................*Youngstown.*
Ira Porter Kimble...........................*Ridgeway, Kan.*
Calista Martin...........................*Poultney, Vt.*
John Calhoun McCrea..............................*Victoria.*
Anna Louisa Mitchell........................*Round Grove.*
Elsie Cora Newlin..............................*Hutsonville.*
Louis G. Palmer........................*Mt. Pleasant, Ia.*
Guy Clarence Pease................................*Galesburg.*
Clarence LeRoy Perrine.....................*Burlington, Ia.*
Myrtle Celestine Powell...............................*Avon.*
James Alexander Shaffer........................*Williamsfield.*
Joseph Earle Shearer.............................*Maquon.*
Celia May Smith.................................*Dahinda.*
Claud Bernard Tanney.................................*Avon.*
Nelle Louise Townsend.............................*Galesburg.*
Clyde Edson Tyrrell...............................*Stockton.*
Bertha Louisa Whitney.....................*Buffalo Prairie.*

Courses of Study.

The following courses of study are open to students in the Preparatory School. A student will be admitted to the College of Liberal Arts upon the successful completion of twenty-one of these courses. In arranging these courses he will consult with the Advisory Committee. (See pp. 19 and 28.)

ENGLISH.

2. Studies in English Literature and Composition.

Macaulay's Essays on Milton and Addison will be studied with care, and the class will be required to read specimens of the writings of Addison and of Lowell. It is expected that more than half the student's time will be given to work in Composition. Four hours a week. Fall term. Professor FOWLER.

Open to all Preparatory Students.

3. Studies in English Literature and Composition. (Continued.)

Work for careful study will be Burke's Speech on Conciliation with America. The class will read carefully Pope's Translation of the Iliad (books I, VI, XXII, and XXIV), Goldsmith's Vicar of Wakefield, Coleridge's Ancient Mariner, and Cooper's Last of the Mohicans. Four hours a week. Winter term. Professor FOWLER.

Open to students who have completed English 2.

4. Studies in English Literature and Composition. (Continued.)

Shakespeare's Macbeth and Milton's L'Allegro, Il Penseroso, Comus, and Lycidas will be carefully studied; and the class will read Shakespeare's Merchant of Venice, George Eliot's Silas Marner, Tennyson's Princess, and Scott's Ivanhoe. Four hours a week. Spring term. Professor FOWLER.

Open to students who have completed English 3.

ELOCUTION.

1, 2, 3. Elementary Courses. (Half Courses.)

These three courses are continuous through the year, each term counting as one-half a course. (See page 49.) Miss KIDDER.

Open to all students.

LATIN.

1. Latin Lessons.

Tuell and Fowler's First Book in Latin. Fall term.

Professor GRUBB.

Open to Preparatory and College Students.

2. Latin Lessons. (Continued.)

Winter term.   Professor GRUBB.

Open to students who have completed Latin 1.

3. Caesar.

Texts, Rolfe and Dennison's Junior Latin Book and Daniell's Latin Prose Composition. Spring term.   Professor GRUBB.

Open to students who have completed Latin 2.

4. Caesar. (Continued.)

Fall term.   Professor GRUBB.

Open to students who have completed Latin 3.

5. Cicero.

Kelsey's Cicero's Orations and Daniell's Latin Prose Composition. Winter term.   Professor GRUBB.

Open to students who have completed Latin 4.

6. Cicero. (Continued.)

Spring term.   Professor GRUBB.

Open to students who have completed Latin 5.

7. Virgil.

Greenough's Virgil's Aeneid. Fall term.   Professor PARKER.

Open to students who have completed Latin 6.

8. Virgil. (Continued.)

Winter term.   Professor PARKER.

Open to students who have completed Latin 7.

GREEK.

1. Grammar and Lessons.

Boise and Pattengill's Greek Lessons. Goodwin's Greek Grammar. Fall term.   Professor PARKER.

Open to all students in the College.

2. Grammar and Lessons. (Continued.)

Winter term. Professor PARKER.

Open to students who have completed Greek 1.

3. Anabasis.

Goodwin's Xenophon's Anabasis. Collar and Daniell's Greek Composition. Spring term. Professor PARKER.

Open to students who have completed Greek 2.

4. Anabasis. (Continued.)

Collar and Daniell's Greek Composition. Fall term.

Professor PARKER.

Open to students who have completed Greek 3.

5. Orations of Lysias.

Stevens' edition. Winter term. Professor PARKER.

Open to students who have completed Greek 4.

6. Iliad.

Keep's Homer's Iliad. Spring term. Professor PARKER.

Open to students who have completed Greek 5.

MATHEMATICS.

1. Arithmetic.

Robinson's Higher Arithmetic. Study of the subject matter of the text to Interest. This course includes thorough work in analysis and mental arithmetic. Fall term. Miss HATHAWAY.

Open to Preparatory students.

2. Arithmetic. (Continued.)

Interest and its applications, Alligation, Extraction of Roots, Mensuration, including the Metric System. This course is supplemented by seven hundred practical problems in mensuration from Mechanic's Arithmetic. Winter term. Miss HATHAWAY.

Open to Preparatory Students who have completed Mathematics 1.

Mathematics 1 and 2 do not count as credits for admission to the College of Liberal Arts.

3. Elementary Algebra.

Well's Academic Algebra is used. Winter term.

Miss HATHAWAY.

Open to Preparatory Students.

4. Elementary Algebra. (Continued.)

Spring term.   Miss HATHAWAY.
Open to Preparatory Students who have completed Mathematics 3.

Mathematics 3 and 4 are continuous through the winter and spring terms and include everything in the text-book preceding Quadratic Equations.

5. Elementary Algebra.

This course embraces the Theory of Exponents, the solution of Quadratic, Simultaneous, and Indeterminate Equations, Ratio and Proportion, and Arithmetical and Geometrical Progressions. Wells' College Algebra is used.   Fall term.   Professor WRIGHT.
Open to all students who have completed Mathematics 4.

6. Plane Geometry.

This course is designed to give students thorough drill in the first principles of Geometry.   Each proposition is carefully analyzed, and particular attention is given to correct reasoning and precise expression. Phillips and Fisher's Elements of Geometry is used.   Winter term.

Professor WRIGHT.
Open to students who have completed Mathematics 5.

7. Plane and Solid Geometry.

A continuation of Mathematics 6.   It is the design in these two courses to take up all the matter contained in the text-book.   This includes the fundamental propositions of Plane Geometry, the circle, the polyhedron, the cylinder, the cone, and the sphere.   Spring term.

Professor WRIGHT.
Open to students who have completed Mathematics 6.

PHYSICAL GEOGRAPHY.

1. Physical Geography.

Text-book, Tarr's Elementary Physical Geography.   Spring term.
Open to all students of the Preparatory School.

Physical Geography 1 will·alternate with Economics 1.

CHEMISTRY.

1. Inorganic Chemistry.

The work consists of four hours per week of recitations or lectures and two hours of experimental work.   Remsen's Inorganic Chemistry. Fall term.   Professor RICH,
Open to all students.

HISTORY.

1. United States.

History of the United States. Text-book, Channing's Student's History of the United States, with Scudder and Fiske for reference. Winter term.

Open to all students of the Preparatory School.

History 1 will not be given unless a considerable number of students apply.

2. Greece.

History of Greece. Text-book, Smith's History of Greece. Fall term. Miss HATHAWAY.

Open to all students of the Preparatory School.

3. Rome.

History of Rome. Text-book, Liddell's History of Rome. Winter term. Miss HATHAWAY.

Open to all students of the Preparatory School.

4. England.

History of England. Text-book. Montgomery's Leading Facts of English History. Spring term. Miss HATHAWAY.

Open to all students of the Preparatory School.

ECONOMICS.

1. Science of Government.

Text-books, Fiske's Civil Government in the United States, and Andrew's Manual of the Constitution. Spring term.

Open to all students.

[Economics 1 will alternate with Physical Geography 1.]

RYDER DIVINITY SCHOOL.

The Divinity School of Lombard College was opened for the admission of students on the 5th of September, 1881. The first class was graduated in 1885.

At the annual meeting of the Board of Trustees in 1890, it was voted to name the theological department of the College the RYDER DIVINITY SCHOOL, in honor of the late William Henry Ryder, D. D., whose munificent bequests to the College exceed fifty thousand dollars.

The largest benefaction to the Divinity School from any other source was received from the late Hon. A. G. Throop, founder of the Throop Polytechnic Institute at Pasedena, California. In 1890, Mr. Throop gave twenty thousand dollars towards the endowment of the Divinity School.

ADMISSION.

Applicants unknown to the faculty must bring satisfactory evidences of good moral and religious character. They should also bring certificates of their church membership.

Candidates for admission to the Divinity School must be prepared to sustain examination in the following subjects.

I. ENGLISH.

(a) **Grammar and Analysis.**

Reed and Kellogg's Higher Lessons in English, or an equivalent.

(b) **Composition.**

An extemporaneous composition on an assigned subject, correct as to paragraphing, grammar, and rhetorical form.

(c) **Literature.**

An equivalent of English 2, 3, and 4 as described on page 55 of this catalogue.

II. HISTORY.

(a) **Bible History.**

A general knowledge of the leading characters, events, and localities in the Bible record.

(b) **General History.**

Swinton's General History or an equivalent.

III. MATHEMATICS.

(a) **Arithmetic.**

Higher Arithmetic, including percentage, alligation, extraction of roots, mensuration and the metric system.

(b) **Elementary Algebra.**

Wells's Academic Algebra, or an equivalent.

IV. GEOGRAPHY.

Tarr's Elementary Geography, or an equivalent.

V. SCIENCE.

(a) **Physical Geography.**

Tarr's Elementary Physical Geography, or an equivalent.

(b) **Elementary Physics.**

Carhart and Chute's Elements of Physics, or an equivalent.

ADMISSION BY CERTIFICATE.

Satisfactory grades from approved schools will be accepted in lieu of examination. Students thus admitted by certificate will be regarded as on probation during the first term of their course.

ADMISSION TO ADVANCED STANDING.

Students who bring satisfactory evidence of work done beyond the requirements of admission will be given credit for the same on the regular course, so far as the faculty may deem consistent with the special aims of that course.

The members of the Divinity School are admitted to the advantages presented by the other departments of the College.

EXPENSES.

Tuition is free to all regular members of the Divinity School who are candidates for the ministry.

The charge for incidentals is the same as in the College of Liberal Arts, $5 per term.

For board in commons, see page 12.

Board in good families can be secured for from $2.50 to $3.25 per week. Students may greatly reduce their expenses by forming clubs, or boarding themselves.

PECUNIARY AID.

Students who are candidates for the ministry of the Universalist church, may, upon complying with the prescribed conditions and receiving the recommendation of the faculty, obtain assistance from the Universalist General Convention in the form of a gratuity, to an amount not exceeding $125 per year. Applications will be granted only when entirely satisfactory. The first installment of this gift will not be issued until January, the second will be issued in May. Students should therefore come with resources of their own sufficient to pay their expenses for at least one term.

Those who have not a definite purpose of entering the Universalist ministry are not eligible to the Convention gift.

During the two last years of their regular course, students who show due proficiency are permitted to secure appointments to preach, and thus to add to their pecuniary resources.

All who intend to enter the Divinity School the coming year, are advised to correspond immediately with the President.

Courses of Instruction.

1. Regular Course.

The full course of study occupies four years of three terms each, as exhibited in the schedule on page 65. Those who complete this course will be entitled to the degree of Bachelor of Divinity.

2. Special Work.

(a) Candidates for the ministry who cannot take the Regular Course, will be permitted to elect special studies, so far as their preparation warrants. Pastors already engaged in ministerial work, who can spare a period for further study, are particularly invited to avail themselves of this opportunity.

(b) The School is also open to persons who do not intend to enter the ministry. The pursuit of studies of a theological or religious character is an interesting and helpful means of personal culture. Such a course is especially recommended to those who desire to become better fitted for service in the Sunday school, the church, the Young People's Christian Union and similar societies, or for charitable and philanthropic work.

Upon those who come with these purposes, no denominational test will be imposed. Students of all denominations and beliefs will be welcome to the advantages of study and training in the Divinity School, as in other departments of the College.

Faculty of the Divinity School.

CHARLES ELLWOOD NASH, A. M., S. T. D., PRESIDENT,

NEHEMIAH WHITE, A. M., PH. D., S. T. D.,
*Hall Professor of Intellectual and Moral Philosophy.
In charge of the Ryder Divinity School, Professor of Biblical
Languages and Exegesis.

---

†Hull Professor of Biblical Geography and Archæology.

ISAAC AUGUSTUS PARKER, A. M., PH. D.,
Professor of Greek.

EVERETT L. CONGER, A. M., D. D.,
Instructor in Homiletics and Pastoral Care.

FRANK HAMILTON FOWLER, PH. D.,
Professor of English Literature.

RALPH GRIERSON KIMBLE,
Professor of Sociology.

CHARLES E. VARNEY,
Instructor in Biblical History and Archæology.

AMANDA KIDDER,
Instructor in Elocution.

NON-RESIDENT LECTURERS,

MARION D. SHUTTER, D. D.,
REV. ALAN RAY TILLINGHAST,
REV. GEORGE A. SAHLIN.

*In honor of the late E. G. HALL, of Chicago.
†In honor of the REV. STEPHEN HULL, of Kansas City, Mo.

Degree Conferred in 1900.

William David Buchanan.........................*Coon Rapids, Ia.*

Students in the Divinity School.

FOURTH YEAR.

Francis Britton Bishop.........................*New London, Ia.*

THIRD YEAR.

George Runyan Longbrake............................*Galesburg.*
Kiyoshi Satoh..................................*Miyagiken, Japan.*
George Francis Thompson......................*Stony Point, Mich.*
Mrs. Mecca Varney....................................*Galesburg.*

SECOND YEAR.

Deborah Davis.....................................*Otranto, Ia.*

FIRST YEAR.

Jacob John De Boer..........................*Benton Harbor, Mich.*
Clark West Greene............................*Brockwayville, Pa.*
Charles Kramer.................................*Reading, Pa.*
George Patterson...................................*Stockton.*

Course of Study

LEADING TO THE DEGREE OF BACHELOR OF DIVINITY.

FIRST YEAR.

FALL TERM.	WINTER TERM.	SPRING TERM.
Chemistry 1.	Chemistry 2.	Chemistry 3.
English 5.	English 6.	English 8.
Greek 1.	Greek 2.	Greek 3.
Biblical History.	Biblical History.	Biblical Geography and Archeology.

SECOND YEAR.

Philosophy 1.	Philosophy 3.	Comparative Religion.
Greek 4.	Greek 5.	Greek 12, 13.
Elocution.	Elocution.	Elocution.
*History 5.	*History 6.	*Hermeneutics.

THIRD YEAR.

Homiletics 1.	Homiletics 2.	Homiletics 3.
Sociology 1.	Sociology 15.	*Theology of Universalism.
*Philosophy 2.	*Dogmatic Theology.	Greek 12, 13.
Greek 14, 15.	Biblical Introduction.	

FOURTH YEAR.

Homiletics 4.	Homiletics 5.	Homiletics 6.
Sociology 9.	Sociology 10.	Ethical Theories.
Christian Evidences.	Philosophy of Religion.	Pastoral Care.
Greek 14, 15.	Philosophy 4.	

*Not given in 1901-02.

Description of Studies.

HEBREW.

1, 2, 3. Grammar and Old Testament

These are primarily courses in the Divinity School, but may be elected by students in the College of Liberal Arts whenever they are offered. Classes will be formed each year if a sufficient number of students apply.

It is the aim to give the student such a knowledge of the forms and structure of the Hebrew language as shall enable him to use it efficiently in the criticism and literary analysis of the Old Testament Scriptures. The text-books used are H. G. Mitchell's Hebrew Lessons and the Hebrew Old Testament. Three terms—Fall, Winter and Spring—each term counting as a course. Professor WHITE.

BIBLE STUDY.

1. Biblical History, A.

Kent's Studies in Biblical History and Literature is used. The aim is to present the contents of the Bible as they stand in our English version. Due account is made of contemporary history and the monumental data. In general the first term will be occupied with the material of the Old Testament; the second term with that of the New. Fall term. Mr. VARNEY.

2. Biblical History, B.

A continuation of the preceding. Winter term. Mr. VARNEY.

3. Biblical Geography and Archaeology.

A detailed study of the political and physical geography of the Bible countries, and a general study of the antiquities of the Bible peoples. Spring term. Mr. VARNEY.

4. Biblical Criticism.

Driver's Introduction to the Old Testament is used as a text-book, with references to Fripp, Ryle, Bacon, Robertson, and other works. A course of lectures is given on the Science of Documentary Analysis, the Principles and Methods of Historical Criticism, and the Religious aspects of the Higher Criticism. Winter term. Professor WHITE.

HERMENEUTICS.

The aim of Hermeneutics, rightly called "the science and art of interpretation," is to set forth those principles and processes whereby the true intent and meaning of an author may be ascertained from the language which he employs. Hermeneutics is therefore the basis of all sound exegesis and is an invaluable aid to the interpretation of the Scriptures. Instruction will be given both by text-book and by lectures. Spring term. Professor WHITE.

Hermeneutics will not be given in 1902.

PREPARATORY GREEK.

(For Greek 1, 2, 3, 4, 5, see page 35.)

THE GREEK NEW TESTAMENT.

(The courses are numbered continuously with the Greek courses of the College of Liberal Arts.)

12. Exegesis of the Synoptic Gospels.

Critical rendering of selections from the Synoptic Gospels. Exegesis of Mark's Gospel; Origin and peculiar characteristics of the Gospel, and its relation to the other Synoptists—their harmonies, divergencies, and interdependence. Date of Synoptic Gospels; their genuineness and authenticity. Theology and Christology of the Synoptic Gospels. Spring term. Professor WHITE.

13. The Acts of the Apostles.

Critical rendering of the Greek text of the Acts of the Apostles, their genuineness and authenticity, date of the work, sources of the narrative. Exegesis of the Acts. Spring term. Professor WHITE.

14. Thessalonians and Galatians.

Critical rendering of the Greek text of the Epistles to the Thessalonians. Exegesis of the Epistles. Eschatology of the Epistles. Primitive Paulinism. Critical rendering of the Greek text of the Epistle to the Galatians. Fall term. Professor WHITE.

15. Corinthians, Romans, and Apocalypse.

Selections from the first and the second Epistle to the Corinthians. Critical rendering of the Greek text of the Epistle to the Romans. Examination of the nature of Pauline Theology and Christology. Development of the doctrine of Paul. Character of later Paulinism. Critical rendering of the Greek text of the Apocalypse. Examination of the resemblances and differences in the style and language of the Apocalypse and of the fourth gospel. Fall term. Professor WHITE.

THEOLOGY.

1. Christian Evidences.

The study of Christian Evidences will include an examination of the bases of Christian belief, Evolutionary theories and their relation to Philosophy, Ethics and Religion, and the function and method of Apologetics. Comparison will be instituted between the modern methods in Apologetics and the methods of primitive Christianity. Instruction will be given mostly by lectures with frequent reference to Fisher, Schurman, Flint, Bruce, and others. Fall term. Professor WHITE.

2. Dogmatic Theology.

Martensen's Christian Dogmatics is used as a text-book. A thorough investigation is made of the several Christian doctrines, with an extended examination of associated questions and controversies. The widest liberty is given for questions and discussions on the various topics presented. Winter term. Professor WHITE.

Dogmatic Theology will not be given in 1901-02.

3. Theology of Universalism.

The Scriptural and rational bases of Universalism will be examined. Instruction will be given for the most part by lectures. Frequent reference will be made to such well known Universalist works as Manuals of Faith and Duty, Allin's Universalism Asserted, Thayer's Theology of Universalism, and Dr. Dodge's Purpose of God. Spring term.

Professor WHITE.

Theology of Universalism will not be given in 1902.

4. Comparative Religion.

The work of the students consists in the examination and comparison of the authorities upon the great Non-Christian religions. Special topics are investigated and reports made by each member of the class. Spring term. Professor WHITE.

APPLIED CHRISTIANITY.

The demand for a more thorough investigation of the bearings of Christian Doctrine upon the social, political, and industrial organisms, coupled with the demand for a more diversified and scientific administration of religion through the churches, is met at Lombard College by the establishment of a chair of Applied Christianity and Pastoral Theology. The course of study provided for will occupy five terms, four terms being devoted to Sociology, and one term to Pastoral Care.

A. SOCIOLOGY.

1. An Introduction to the Study of Sociology.

An outline study of the characteristic concepts of recent sociological thought.   Professor KIMBLE.
Open, by consultation, to all students.

9. The Development of Association.

A study of the lower stages of the associative process with especial reference to the earlier forms of food, sex, and conflict association.
                                                      Professor KIMBLE.

10. The Development of Association. (Continuation of Course 9.)

The investigation begun in Course 9 is continued among organisms of a higher type than those there studied.   Professor KIMBLE.

15. Reproductive Association.

The family is taken as the most highly developed and best known example of this type of associational life; attention is given to its origin, development, and significance.   Professor KIMBLE.

B. PASTORAL CARE.

The spiritual, mental, and social qualifications of the minister for his work will be noted, and his administration of the special services of the church—baptism, confirmation, the Lord's Supper, marriage, and the burial of the dead. A liberal portion of the term will be devoted to an examination of various methods of church organization, for the purpose of giving the minister facility in adapting himself to parish needs, especially to those peculiar to the locality in which he may be settled. Spring term.   Dr. CONGER.

PHILOSOPHY.

1 (a). Psychology.

After a somewhat detailed inquiry into the general relations of mind and body, followed by a close examination of the phenomena of perception, the more complex mental processes, as memory, association, apperception, hallucination, imagination, impulse, habit, volition, are taken up for careful study. Special emphasis is laid upon self-observation, and the indications for self-culture are attentively marked. Stress is also laid upon the definition and use of technical terms. Fall term.

Professor KIMBLE.

2. Metaphysic.

This is primarily a course in the Divinity School, but it may be elected by students in the College of Liberal Arts whenever it is offered. Classes will be formed whenever a sufficient number of students apply. Lotze's Outlines of Metaphysic is used as a text-book. Fall term.

Professor WHITE.

Philosophy 2 will not be given in 1901.

3. Logic.

Having first obtained a thorough grounding in the principles and methods of correct reasoning, both deductive and inductive, at least one-half of the term is given to the detection and discrimination of fallacies in actual examples. Such examples the class is required to search out in current literature and bring in for discussion. Davis's Elements of Deductive Logic, and Davis's Elements of Inductive Logic are used. Winter term.

Professor FOWLER.

4. Ethics.

Ethics is treated from the standpoint of Philosophy, and the different systems are discussed. The nature and grounds of obligation are investigated and applied to the practical affairs of life. Winter term.

Professor WHITE.

5. Philosophy of Religion.

Caird's Introduction to the Philosophy of Religion is the text-book. Lotze, Sabatier, and Martineau are used as works of reference. The aim of the instructor is to acquaint the student with the proper office of reason in the effort to find argumentative grounds for religious ideas. Most of the modern theories respecting the nature and scope of the religious feeling pass under review; and in such discussions free questioning on the part of the student is encouraged. Winter term.

Professor WHITE.

6. Ethical Theories.

Martineau's Types of Ethical Theory is used as a text-book with frequent reference to the works of Sidgwick, Green, Smythe, and others. Much attention is paid to the elucidation and criticism of the modern ethical theories. Spring term.

Professor WHITE.

CHURCH HISTORY.

(The courses in Church History are numbered continuously with the courses in History in the Preparatory School. See page 59.)

5. History of the Christian Church.

A. *The Ancient and Mediæval Eras. (1-1517.)*

This course in Church History is primarily intended for the members of the Divinity School, but is also open to College students. It will require the investigation of the early organization and extension of Christianity, and the successive periods of the Church down to the time of Charlemagne; followed by a careful inquiry into the causes of the rise of the Papacy, of the political relations of the Church, and of the Crusades. Fisher's History of the Church will be used as a hand book and topics will be assigned to each member of the class for special investigation and reports. Fall term. Professor WHITE.

History 5 will not be given in 1901.

6. History of the Christian Church.

B. *The Modern Era (1517-1901.)*

This course will begin with the study of the Reformation, and trace the history of the Church down to the present time. It will include the history of Christian missions, revivals, social reforms, and philanthropy. The same text-book will be used as in History 5. Winter term.

Professor WHITE.

History 6 will not be given in 1901-02.

HOMILETICS.

The course in Homiletics covers the third and fourth years. The primary aim is practical. Upon a general but adequate groundwork of theory and history of preaching the effort is made to construct an art of effective pulpit oratory. Elaborate and exacting drill in the logical conception and construction of the sermon plan, with constant application of rhetorical principles, occupies the major part of the first year. Inspiration and direction are sought in the frequent analysis of the discourses of great preachers of all styles, and in the study of their sources of power. Individuality and originality are emphasized as desiderata. In the second year the stress is laid upon flexibility and adaptability, upon invention, upon the rationale of interesting preaching, and upon the

acquisition of freedom in extempore address. Throughout the course the preparation and criticism of sermons by the class continues uninterruptedly.   President NASH,
                                              Dr. CONGER.

ELOCUTION.

In view of the fact that a good delivery is of inestimable advantage to the preacher, the students in the Divinity School are offered an extended course in Elocution and Physical Culture.

The students are not only admitted to all Elocution classes in the College, but also receive a large amount of individual training.

Courses 1, 2, 3, as outlined on p. 49 of this catalogue, are required.
                                              Miss KIDDER.

ENGLISH.

For English 5, 6, 8, which courses are required in the Divinity School, see p. 29 of this catalogue.

8. Daily Themes.

This course will be made a full course for students in the Divinity School. Besides the daily themes, fortnightly themes will be required. Spring term.   Professor FOWLER.

COLLEGE STUDIES.

Divinity students are permitted, with the consent of the Faculty, to pursue studies in the College of Liberal Arts. Graduates of the Divinity School may receive the additional degree of Bachelor of Arts, upon the satisfactory completion of an aggregate of twenty full courses taken in the classes of the College of Liberal Arts, beyond the full requirements of the Divinity School for the degree of Bachelor of Divinity.

In addition to the above twenty credits, the candidate must furnish the full quota of twenty-one credits required for admission to the College of Liberal Arts. Of these twenty-one credits, the courses required for admission to the Divinity School (see pp. 60 and 61) will count ten.

DEPARTMENT OF MUSIC.

Instruction is provided in the various branches of Theoretical, Vocal, and Instrumental Music. These courses are distinct from the work in the other departments of the College, and unless otherwise specified do not count toward a college degree. Students are classed and registered as private pupils of the several instructors, with whom arrangements may be made in regard to lessons. Instruction is given either at the college, or at the instruction-rooms of the teachers, as preferred.

Faculty.

KARL JACOB RUDOLPH LUNDBERG,
Director and Instructor in Voice, Piano, Organ, and Theory.

W. H. CHEESMAN,
Instructor in Violin.

Candidates for Diplomas in Instrumental Music.

Virginia Henney...........................Mitchellville, Iowa.
Cyrena Weir.................................Galesburg.

Students in the Department of Music.

THEORY (Harmony and Musical History).

Sarah Lucy Cook...........................Le Roy.
Mary Hart.................................Eureka, Kan.
Virginia Henney...........................Mitchellville, Iowa.
Jennie Eliza Marriott.....................La Moille.
Anna Louisa Mitchell......................Round Grove.
Maud Alvira Oldfield......................Mitchellville, Iowa.
Anne Marian Wrigley.......................Chicago.

PIANOFORTE.

Lillian Backman..*Galesburg.*
Ruth Chamberlain...*Galesburg.*
Sarah Lucy Cook..*Le Roy.*
Laura Gladdis Cox...................... ....*Augusta, Wis.*
Mrs. Alice Dunaway........ ....*Galesburg.*
Manda Hansen...*Galesburg.*
Mary Arrah Hart.....................,.................*Eureka, Kan.*
Virginia Henney...............................*Mitchellville, Iowa.*
Laura May Hobbs..........................*Benton Harbor, Mich.*
Mattie Johnson...*Galesburg.*
Ruth Ellen McAchran............................*Bloomfield, Iowa.*
Mary Markmann.................................*Muscatine, Iowa.*
Pauline Marsh...*Galesburg.*
Pearl Maxwell.................................*Burlington, Iowa.*
Anna Louisa Mitchell ....*Round Grove.*
Alvira Nelson...*Galesburg.*
Nettie Nelson.... ....*Galesburg.*
Elsie Cora Newlin.......................................*Hutsonville.*
Maud Alvira Oldfield......... ....*Mitchellville, Iowa.*
Amelia Olson...*Galesburg.*
Mila Parke..*Sycamore.*
Ruth Parke............. ....*Sycamore.*
Grace Olive Pingrey............................*Coon Rapids, Ia.*
Gertrude Rich...*Galesburg.*
Willis Rich...*Galesburg.*
Carrie Schroeder...*Galesburg.*
Elsie Sommers..................... ....*Burlington, Iowa.*
Hannah Swanson..................... ....*Galesburg.*
Vina May Ward..............................*Superior, Neb.*
Cyrena Weir..*Galesburg.*
Marian Wilcox..*Galesburg.*
Anne Marian Wrigley............... ....*Chicago.*

VOCAL MUSIC.

Kelley Alexander...*Galesburg.*
Lilah Anderson...*Galesburg.*
Julia Byloff...*Galesburg.*
Fanny Churchill...................... ....*Avon.*
Kate Clark...................... ....- ....*Maquon.*
Grace Elting..............................*Dodgeville, Iowa.*

Claude Fosher...*Galesburg.*
Manda Hansen..*Galesburg.*
Mary Arrah Hart.....................................*Eureka, Kan.*
Selma Hulstrum..................... ....*Galesburg.*
Frank H. Johnson......................................*Galesburg.*
Alice Lindstrum... .. ..*Galesburg.*
Ruth Ellen McAchran...........................*Bloomfield, Iowa.*
Mary Markmann.................................*Muscatine, Iowa.*
Jennie Eliza Marriott.....................................*La Moille.*
Anna Louisa Mitchell.................................*Round Grove.*
Faith Nash..*Galesburg.*
Ruth Nash..*Galesburg.*
Elsie Cora Newlin.....................................*Hutsonville.*
Vera Peck..*Galesburg.*
Rosa Raines...*Hutsonville.*
C. W. Sandusky..*Galesburg.*
Edward Smith.... ....*Galesburg.*
Nelle Townsend.......................................*Galesburg.*
Clyde Edson Tyrrell......................................*Stockton.*
Jesse Williams..*Galesburg.*
Anne Marian Wrigley....................................*Chicago.*

VIOLIN.

Mr. Anderson..*Galesburg.*
Zetta Boyer...*Galesburg.*
Chester Cedarholm....................................*Galesburg.*
Alta Elder...*Galesburg.*
Eva. Frailey..................... ....*Galesburg.*
Theo Golliday...*Galesburg.*
Ira Neifert..*Galesburg.*
Lorentz Offrell..*Galesburg.*
Willie Purington......................................*Galesburg.*
Willie Rhudman.......................................*Galesburg.*
Harry Swanson..*Galesburg.*
Louie Ware....................... ....*Altona.*

MANDOLIN.

Glenn Carlton Bruner....................................*Gerlaw.*
Cora Margaret Hanna................... .. ..*Roachdale, Ind.*

GUITAR.

Ida Brothers...*Fincastle, Ind.*
John Welcome...... ....*Galesburg.*

CORNET.

Mr. Nelson..*Galesburg.*

A. THEORETICAL COURSES.
Professor Lundberg.

1. Harmony. (Music 1, 2, 3.)

Class-room work, lectures, recitations, and written exercises covering theory of the elements of music, triads, chords of the seventh, augmented chords, chords of the ninth and eleventh, modulation, suspension, and harmonizing of melodies. ·Text-books, Emery, Richter, and Jadassohn. Three hours a week for one year.   Professor LUNDBERG.

Open to all students in the College.

2. Simple and Double Counterpart. (Music 4, 5, 6.)

Lectures, recitations and daily written exercises, based on the text-books of Richter, Haupt, and others. Three hours a week for one year.   Professor LUNDBERG.

Open to students who have completed Music 3.

3. Fugue, Canon, Musical Form, and the Elements of Orchestration. (Music 7, 8, 9.)

Lectures, recitations, and written exercises. Text-books, Prout, Cherubini, Rieman, Berlioz. Three hours a week for one year.
          Professor LUNDBERG.

Open to students who have completed Music 6.

4. History of Music. (Music 10.) [Half Course.]

Introductory course on the lives of the great composers. Two hours a week. · Fall term.   Professor LUNDBERG. ·

Open to students who, in the judgment of the instructor, are qualified by previous training to take the course.

5. History of Music. (Music 11.) [Half Course.]

Advanced course on the development of music from the earliest times until today, with special reference to critical analysis of the works of the greatest masters. Text-books, Naumann, Langhans, Rieman. Two hours a week. Winter term,   Professor LUNDBERG.

Open to students who have completed Music 10.

6. Acoustics.

Theory of sound in its connection with Music and musical instruments. Open to students who have finished Course 1. Text-books, Helmholtz, Tyndall.

Music 1 to 9 count each as a credit towards a degree in the College of Liberal Arts; Music 10, 11, and the course in Acoustics, each as a half credit.

B. PIANOFORTE COURSES.

Professor Lundberg.

1. Preparatory Year.

Five-finger exercises; scales in major and minor; triads; selected studies by Czerney, Vol. 1 (Germer Edition).

2. First Grade.

Finger exercises; scales; Czerney's studies, Vols. 1 and 2 (Germer edition); Sonatinen by Dussek, Clementi,. Diabelli, Kuhlau, Reinecke. Memorizing.

3. Second Grade.

Finger exercises; scales; arpeggios; Czerney's studies, Vol.. 3 (Germer edition); Sonatinas by Clementi, Kuhlau, Dussek, Haydn, Mozart, Beethoven. Pieces by American and foreign composers.

4. Third Grade.

Finger exercises with modulation to different keys. Scales in fourths, sixths, and thirds. Czerney's studies, Vol. 4; Bach's Inventions for two and three voices. Pieces by different composers.

5. Fourth Grade.

Finger exercises in different keys. Scales; études by Cramer; preludes and fugues by Bach. Easier sonatas by Haydn, Clementi, Mozart and Beethoven. . Memorizing; pieces by different composers.

6. Fifth Grade.

Finger exercises in different keys; scales. Clementi's Gradus ad Parnassum. Etudes by Moscheles, Chopin, etc. Sonatas by Bach, Mozart, Beethoven and Hummel. Memorizing. Pieces by different composers.

·VOICE CULTURE.

Professor Lundberg.

1. First Grade.

Exercises in breathing, tone placing, sustained tones, etc. Voice training exercises by Emil Behnke and C. W. Pearce. 50 vocalises by Concone. Easy songs.

2. Second Grade.

Masset's exercises; 30 exercises by Concone; 25 and 15 vocalises by Concone.   Songs by American and foreign composers.

3. Third Grade.

Vocalises by Reber, Panofka, and Masset.   Songs, and oratorios. Recitatives.   Practicing of duets, trios and quartets.

C. PIPE ORGAN COURSES.

Professor Lundberg.

Students who wish to begin the study of the Organ should have completed the Second Grade of the Piano Course.

The chief aim of this department is the thorough preparation of church organists.   Organ students should also make a conscientious study of Solo and Chorus Singing, with a view of becoming efficient chorus-masters and directors of church music.

The study of Harmony, Counterpoint, and History of Music is absolutely necessary to an intelligent study of the instrument.

1. First Grade.

Exercises in pedal playing, Ritter's Organ School, hymns, construction of interludes, Modulation, Transposing, and Elementary Registration.

2. Second Grade.

Studies in Pedal Phrasing by Buck, Volkmar, and Schneider.   Polyphonic compositions by Rink, Bach, Fisher.   Easy pieces by Merkel, Dubois, Guilmant, Mendelssohn, and others.   Registration, Structure of the Organ, Choir Accompaniment.

3. Third Grade.

Study of Sonatas and Fugues by Bach, Mendelssohn, Reinberger, and others.   Modern compositions of German, English and French masters.   Choir accompaniment.

D. VIOLIN COURSES.

Professor Cheesman.

1. Preparatory Grade.

Elementary exercises in position, bowing, etc.   Easy exercises in major and minor keys in the first book from Wichtl's Violin School. Pleyel's Duets, and twelve studies by H. E. Kayser, op. 20.   Memorizing.

2. Intermediate Grade.

Studies by Kayer and Wohlfahrt. Systematic progress through the various positions, beginning with the second book of F. Hermann. Studies from Schradieck for the development of technic and pure tone qualities. Selections from compositions by Dancla, Mazas, Weiss, De Beriot: also solos and fantasias based upon operatic themes.

3. Advanced Grade.

Technical studies from the works of Kreutzer, Fiorillo, Rode, together with duets, trios and quartets, arranged for strings; overtures; sight-reading. Sonatas and concertos by Bach, Haydn, Spohr, Beethoven, Mendelssohn, DeBeriot, Wieniawsky, Grieg, and others.

E. MANDOLIN AND GUITAR COURSES.
Professor Cheesman.

The study of these popular instruments has become a favorite recreation with those students of our colleges who may not have the time or inclination to pursue the study of music in its more serious forms.

At the conclusion of the first term of lessons (twelve weeks), a "Lombard Mandolin Club" will be organized, with rehearsals one evening a week. The Italian method is used entirely in the study of these instruments, thereby establishing the very best method of picking the strings and fingering, with special attention to the tone quality of the "tremolo," which relieves the mandolin of much of its so-called monotony. Solos, duets, and quartets, will also be prepared in addition to the regular club work, with special numbers to be given by the lady members of the club.

G. SIGHT SINGING AND CHORUS CLASSES.
Professor Lundberg.

1. Elementary Sight Singing Class.

The rudiments of Music, the intervals of the Major Scale, exercises in one and two parts, and easy songs. Ear-training. One college term.

2. Advanced Class.

Solfeggios in major and minor keys, three and four part songs. One college term.

3. Chorus Class.

Four part compositions, glees, sacred and secular choruses from our best classic and modern composers. Oratorios.

Only those students who have finished the work done in the Advanced Sight-Singing Class will be admitted into the Chorus Class.

Requirements for Graduation.

A diploma will be conferred upon any student who shall satisfactorily complete any of the following courses in instrumental or vocal music. In addition to the requirements enumerated below, the candidate will prepare a thesis, present an original musical composition, or perform other original work satisfactory to the instructor, and also appear in public at a graduating recital.

A. THE PIANOFORTE.

Musical Requirements.

Five grades of the Piano Courses, Nos. 1, 2, 3, 4, 5, 6, 10, and 11 of the Theoretical Courses; Acoustics; and one year's membership in the Chorus Class.

Literary Requirements.

English Grammar, English Composition, Rhetoric, English and American Literature, one year of French or German.

If the candidate upon entering brings satisfactory proof of proficiency in any of these courses, he is advised to take one study each term from such electives in the College of Liberal Arts as the Director may recommend.

B. THE PIPE ORGAN.

Musical Requirements.

The full Organ Course, Nos. 1, 2, 3, 4, 5, 6, 10, and 11 of the Theoretical Courses; and Acoustics.

Literary Requirements.

The same as for Piano students.

C. THE VOICE.

Musical Requirements.

All the prescribed studies for Voice Culture; grade 2 of the Piano Courses, with special view to accompaniments; and Nos. 1, 2, 3, 10, 11, of the Theoretical Courses.

Literary Requirements.

The same as for Piano students, except that Italian may be substituted for French or German.

TUITION.

The following prices are for a term of twelve weeks:

THEORETICAL COURSES—
  Music 1 to 9, each, $5.00.
  Music 10 and 11, each $3.00.

PIANOFORTE—
  Private Lessons—one hour per week, $18.00.
  Private Lessons—two half hours per week, $18.00.
  Private Lessons—one half hour per week, $10.00.
  Private Lessons—one 45-minute lesson per week, $14.00.

  Class Lessons, one hour per week, each—
      In classes of two, $10.00.
      In classes of three, $7.00.

VOICE CULTURE—
  Charges same as for piano forte.

RENT OF PIANO—1 hour per day, per term, $2.75.
  2 hours per day, per term, $5.00.
  3 hours per day, per term, $6.75.
  4 hours per day, per term, $8.00.

PIPE ORGAN—
  Private Lessons—one hour per week, $24.00.
  In classes of two, one hour per week, each person, $13.00.

VIOLIN—
  Private Lessons—one hour per week, $15.00.
  Private Lessons—two half hours per week, $15.00.
  Private Lessons—one 45-minute lesson per week, $12.00.

CLASS LESSONS, one hour per week, each—
  In classes of two, $8.00.
  In classes of three, $6.00.

MANDOLIN AND GUITAR—
  Private Lessons—one hour per week, $12.00.
  Private Lessons—two half hours per week, $12.00.

  Class Lessons—charges will be given on application to teacher.
(A weekly rehearsal for club practice without extra charge.)

SIGHT SINGING CLASSES—
  Each, $1.00.

CHORUS CLASS—
  A charge of $1.00 per term each will be made for the use of music to be supplied by the department.

  The privilege of joining the Lombard Mandolin and Guitar Club, or the Lombard String Orchestra is extended to any student outside of the private pupils of the instructor, by the payment of $1.25 per term of twelve weeks. Rehearsals one evening each week.

GENERAL REMARKS.

Tuition and other charges must be paid before lessons are assigned.

In case of protracted sickness only, will a proportionate deduction be made from term charges.

No visitors are allowed in practice rooms during practice hours.

All concerts and recitals given by the school of music or its faculty are free to music students.

A course of free lectures on musical culture will be given each year by the Director.

LADIES' HALL.

DEPARTMENT OF ART.

Instructor.

M. ISABELLE BLOOD.

Students in the Department of Art.

Jessie Baldwin..*Ipava.*
Mrs. Fred Barndt................................. ....*Galesburg.*
Maud Boydston......................................*Galesburg.*
Roland Buckley.....................................*Knoxville.*
Charles Caldwell ....*Knoxville.*
Lottie Cone...*Surrey.*
Willie Consor .... *Knoxville.*
Mrs. John Egan....................... ....*Galesburg.*
Carl Frasier...*Knoxville.*
Mrs. David Fuller....................................*Galesburg.*
Mima Gardiner......................................*Coldbrook.*
Gertrude Hartgrove...................... ....*Galesburg.*
Ida Hopkins............... ....*Galesburg.*
Pearl Luster...*Galesburg.*
Lodema McWilliams..................................*Knoxville.*
Helen Manny.......... ....*Galesburg.*
Mrs. W. H. Mason....................................*Knoxville.*
Jennie Miles...*Knoxville.*
Mrs. Charles Munson ....*Galesburg.*
Izal Phillips............................ ....*Knoxville.*
Grace Olive Pingrey..............................*Coon Rapids, Ia.*
Lulu Ramp...*Knoxville.*
Jennie Sims...*Galesburg.*
Maud Smith.......................................*Knoxville.*
Mrs. P. F. Swanson..................................*Galesburg.*
Frances White.......................................*Galesburg.*

Course in Art.

The Art Department affords a practical course in Drawing and Painting to those who wish to become teachers, designers, illustrators, or portrait artists. Regular students in this department who wish to take the entire course in Art will be given careful training in the following branches: Perspective drawing; drawing from casts in charcoal and crayon; still life studies in crayon, oil, water color, and pastel; landscape from nature; and copying from good studies.

The entire course will occupy from two to three years, according to the ability of the student and the amount of time given to the work. A thorough knowledge of the elements of drawing being necessary to independent work, at least one year's work will be required in drawing in black and white from models of simple form, casts, still life, and those studies which will best prepare the student for the special line of work preferred.

Students may enter the Art Department at any time; and though they are advised to take a full course in order to obtain the best results, arrangements can be made for lessons in any line desired.

While portrait work, pen and ink drawing, and china painting are not required in the regular course, credit will be given for good work in any of these branches if it is desired to substitute them in part for oil, water color, or pastel.

A course of study in the History of Art and a thesis upon some subject approved by the instructor will also be required of students wishing to graduate from this department.

Those who complete the work as outlined above will be entitled to a Diploma.

For a description of courses in the History of Art, and in Free Hand Drawing, and for credit allowed for these courses in the College of Liberal Arts, see pp. 47 and 48.

TUITION.

The tuition fees will be as follows:

Drawing or Sketching—3-hour lesson, 35 cents.
Painting in Water Colors—3-hour lesson, 50 cents.
Oil Painting—3-hour lesson, 50 cents.
Portrait and China Painting—3-hour lesson, 50 cents.

For those who work six hours per week for the entire year, a rebate will be made at the end of the Spring term, so that the lessons in drawing will be less than 35 cents.

If pupils in Art desire four or more lessons per week, special rates are made.

DEPARTMENT OF ELOCUTION AND DRAMATIC EXPRESSION.

The object of the work in this department is to acquire a knowledge of the Art of Expression by means of the cultivated voice and educated body. A complete and thorough course is offered in its various branches, affording a theoretical and practical training in all the principles upon which the art is based. The aim is to study the individual needs of the student mentally, vocally and pictorially, and to found upon this study a discipline which shall develop the powers of expression through intelligent grasp of thought and trained aesthetic conception. Three years are necessary for the fulfillment of all requirements in this department. Instruction is given in the class room or the auditorium of the gymnasium building, which is provided with a stage well equipped with curtain, scenery, appliances, etc., affording ample opportunity of obtaining facility in voice and action.

Recitals will be made a prominent feature during the year, to show the proficiency of pupils and to afford them assistance in acquiring confidence, ease and self-control. These recitals are to be considered, not as an end in themselves, but as an auxiliary to the course of the work.

Instructor.

AMANDA KIDDER.

SPECIAL PUPILS IN PHYSICAL CULTURE.

Ethel May Chamberlain.......... .... *Galesburg*.
Harry Knowles Chapman...... .... *Galesburg*.
Willis Rich .... *Galesburg*.
Helen Terry... *Galesburg*.
Nelly Williamson................... .... *Galesburg*.

The names of other pupils doing class work in Elocution and Dramatic Expression and in Physical Culture are included in the lists of students in the College of Liberal Arts and in the Preparatory and Divinity Schools.

DESCRIPTION OF STUDIES.

1. Elocution.

The aim of this course is to rid the voice of all impurities, secure correct placing of the voice, proper breathing and beauty of tone for conversational purposes. Notes will be given upon the anatomy of the vocal organs and the care of the voice. Physical exercises will be introduced as a means of securing grace and becoming deportment. Recitations Mondays, Wednesdays, and Fridays. Fall term.

2. Elocution.

In this course attention will be given to the adaptation of the conversational voice to the requirements of platform speaking. Each pupil will be required to deliver three selections before the class for criticism. Work in pantomime and life study will be introduced. Recitations Mondays, Wednesdays, and Fridays. Winter term.

3. Elocution.

This course will consist of a continuation of the work outlined in Elocution 2. The analysis of some English Classic will be required. Recitations Mondays, Wednesdays, and Fridays. Spring term.

4. Elocution.

The study of Masterpieces will be made the basis of this course. Recitations Mondays and Thursdays. Fall term.

5. Elocution.

The work in this course will be a continuation of that begun in Elocution 4, together with extemporaneous talks, critical and detailed life study for personation. Recitations Mondays and Thursdays. Winter term.

6. Elocution.

This course will consist of a continuation of Elocution 5. Recitations Mondays and Thursdays. Spring term.

7. Oratory.

In this course the aim will be to assist the students in gaining some knowledge of the great orators, both American and English. Each student is required to deliver before class for criticism a certain number of selections chosen from the orators studied; also to give talks on subjects previously assigned. Recitations Mondays and Thursdays. Fall term.

8. Oratory.

Important features of this course are extemporaneous speaking, class debates and criticism. Two orations and one debate will be required from each member of the class. Recitations Mondays and Thursdays. Winter term.

9. Dramatic Expression.

This course consists of a study of two dramas for the purpose of character interpretation. Scenes will be committed and interpreted for public presentation. Recitations Tuesdays and Thursdays. Fall term.

10, 11. Dramatic Expression.

These courses consist of a study of two Shakespearian plays. As in Elocution 9, scenes will be committed and interpreted for public presentation. Recitations Tuesdays and Thursdays. Winter and Spring terms.

REQUIREMENTS FOR GRADUATION IN ELOCUTION.

Elocution courses 1, 2, 3, 4, 5, 6; Oratory 7, 8; Dramatic Art 9, 10, 11. One private lesson a week for two years.

Literary Requirements.

English Grammar; English and American Literature; one year of French; one year of German; one year of Music; Roman and Grecian History.

A thesis upon some subject approved by the instructor.

TERMS.

CLASS LESSONS—
Regular charge in class per term, besides incidentals.....................$1.75
PRIVATE LESSONS—
One half hour a week, per term...$ 6.00
Two half hours a week, per term.. 10.00

THE GYMNASIUM.

General Summary.

COLLEGE OF LIBERAL ARTS.

Candidates for degree in 1901.
    Master of Arts.. 2
    Bachelor of Arts..10
                                                        — 12

Students in the College of Liberal Arts....................... 91

PREPARATORY SCHOOL.

Students in the Preparatory School............................ 45

RYDER DIVINITY SCHOOL.

Candidate for degree in 1901.
    Bachelor of Divinity.. 1
Students in the Divinity School.
    Fourth Year.. 1
    Third Year... 4
    Second Year.. 1
    First Year... 4
                                                        — 10

MUSIC.

Candidates for Diplomas in 1901............................... 2
Students in Harmony and Musical History....................... 7
Students in Pianoforte..32
Students in Vocal Culture.....................................27
Students in Violin..12
Students in Mandolin.. 2
Students in Guitar.. 2
Students in Cornet.. 1
                                                        — 85

ART.

Students in Art... 26

ELOCUTION AND DRAMATIC EXPRESSION.

Special Pupils in Physical Culture............................ 5
                                                            ———
                                                            275
Names entered twice... 60
                                                            ———
    Total...215

Association of Graduates.
1900-1901.

OFFICERS.

PRESIDENT,

RALPH GRIERSON KIMBLE, GALESBURG.

VICE PRESIDENT,

JAMES W. CARNEY, GALESBURG.

SECRETARY,

NINA ALTA HARRIS, GALESBURG.

TREASURER,

JON W. GRUBB, GALESBURG.

HISTORIAN,

LORA A. TOWNSEND, GALESBURG.

BOARD OF DIRECTORS.

RALPH G. KIMBLE. LORA A. TOWNSEND.

C. A. WEBSTER. C. ELLWOOD NASH.

J. J. WELSH. FRANCES WHITE.

R. D. BOWER. GUY A. LONGBRAKE.

NINA ALTA HARRIS.

Graduates.

The degree of A. M. or M. S. placed immediately after a name, implies that the corresponding Bachelor's degree (A. B. or B. S.) was received on graduation.

The person to whose name a star is attached is deceased. The date following designates the year of his death.

1856.

William Worth Burson, A. M.................Manufacturer, 322 Racine Ave, Chicago.
William Ramey Cole, A. M............................Clergyman. Mt. Pleasant, Iowa.
Hon. Thompson W. McNeeley, A. M..................Ex-M. C., Attorney, Petersburg.
Hon. Lewis Alden Simmons, A. M., *1889...........................Wellington, Kan.
Addie Hurd, A. M. (Mrs. Wm. Van Horn).........917 Sherbrooke St., Montreal, Can.
Jennie Miles, A. M., *1859..... ....Decatur.

1857.

Fielding B. Bond, A. B., *1862..Greenbush.
Floyd G. Brown, A. B., *1868....................., ...Mankato, Minn.
James Henry Chapin, A. M., Ph. D., *1892............................Meriden, Conn.
Hon. Edward D. Laning, A. B....................................Attorney, Petersburg.
Hon. Scott Wike, B. S., *1901...Barry.

1858.

Anson L. Claik, A. M., M. D., President Bennett Eclectic Medical College,
   Chicago.. ....Elgin.
Thomas Gorman, A. B., *1891...Columbus, O.

1859.

Hon. George W. Elwell, B. S., *1869.................................Chillicothe, Mo.
Eugene Beauharnais Hill, B. S............ ....Manufacturer, Ottumwa, Iowa.
Almon Kidder, A. M............. ....Attorney. Monmouth.
Mary Jane Fuller, B. S...Tarpon Springs, Fla.
Ruth Waldron Miller, M. S. (Mrs. Brower), *1892 ....Chicago.

1860.

Jonathan Eden Brown, A. B......................................Farmer, Peabody, Kan.
Arick Burr, B. S., *1860....................................... ....Charleston.
Hon. William Judah Frisbee, A. M..............................Druggist, Bushnell.
James Scott Lindsay, A. B., *1860..................................Onarga.
Albert Sidney Slater, M. S., M. D.................................Wataga.

1861.

Hon. Franklin Fayette Brower, A. M., *1869...............................Ottawa.
Everett Lorentus Conger, A. M., D. D.. ....Professor Lombard College, Galesburg.
Henry George Pollock, A. M...................:.........Clergyman, Madison, Ind.
Mary Stewart Miller, A. B. (Mrs. Catlin), *1867.......................Vinton, Iowa.

1862.

Hon. Edwin Hurd Conger, A. M..............U. S. Minister to China, Peking, China.
Samuel Alvus Dow, A. M., M. D..............Wyalong, New South Wales, Australia.
William Sampson Dow, B. S., *1863...Galesburg.
Hon. Charles Allen Holmes, A. M..................................Attorney, Cañon City, Colo.
Hamilton Lafayette Karr, A. M....................................Attorney, Osceola, Ia.
Frederick Warren Livingston, M. S.........................Teacher, San Diego, Cal.
Harvey Rowell, A. B...........................Solicitor of Patents, Columbus, Wis.
Hon. John Crocker Sherwin. M. S., Ex-M. C. Attorney,
                                1234 Columbus St., Denver, Colo.
Alfred Henry Trego, A. M. ....Manufacturer, Hoopeston.
George John Turner, A. M., M. D., *1899...........................Oskaloosa, Ia.
Eugenia Adaline Fuller, B. S. (Mrs. J. W. Ranstead) ....Elgin.

1863.

Samuel Addison Calhoun, A. B..........Adv. Solicitor "German Demokrat," Peoria.
Hon. John W. Ranstead, B. S..Attorney, Elgin.
Hannah Jane Biddlecombe, M. S...Bookkeeper Glendale Furnace Co., Columbus, O.
Oricy Villa Crocker, L. A., (Mrs. Nead) *1880.............................Galesburg.
Sarah Jane Miles, A. M. (Mrs. Bullman)....................................Galesburg.
Mary Addie Moore, M.S., (Mrs. Sumner Ellis)..............2734 Prairie Ave., Chicago.
Sarah Jane Pike, L. A.. (Mrs. E. H. Conger) ....-....Peking, China.

1864.

Elmore Chase, B. S... Teacher, Fair Oaks, Cal.
Leslie Greenwood, A. M..........With Farmers' Loan and Trust Co., Sioux City, Ia.
Laura Lavinia Pike, A. M., (Mrs. J. S. McConnell)...........4359 Lake Ave., Chicago.
Josephine Raymond, A. M., (Antioch College), (Mrs. Maxwell)............Champaign.
Sallie Raymond, L. A., (Mrs. J. B. Green)..................................Ramsey.

1865.

Elmore Chase, B. S., A. M............. ....Teacher, Fair Oaks, Cal.
John Henry McCormick, B. S..Caledonia, Mo.
Alice Caroline Chapin, B. S....Teacher, 222 West 3d South St., Salt Lake City, Utah.

1866.

Hon. Elwin Wallace Claycomb, A. M............... ....Farmer, Eureka, Kan.
Hon. Geo. R. Shook, B. S......................Teacher and Surveyor, Fruita, Colo.
James Smith McConnell, B. S..................Attorney, 84 Washington St., Chicago.
Emma N. H. Conger, A. M., (Mrs. S. W. Conger).....................Villa Park, Cal.

1867.

William Bryan Carlock, B. S................................ ...Attorney, Bloomington.
William Harvey Woods, B. S.......................................Farmer, Mendota.
Helen Maria Bingham, L. A., M. D..................................... Monroe, Wis.

1868.

Henry Moses Chase, A. B., *1870.................................Concord, Vt.
Hon. James O'Donnell, B. S...........................:Attorney, Cherokee, Ia.
Wellington Smith, B. S, *1870......................... ....,............Annawan.
Edward Keys Walbridge, B. S............Loan and Real Estate Agent, Girard, Kan.
Mary J. Claycomb, A. M.,(Mrs. J. W. Grubb)..............................Galesburg.

Josephine Marian Kirk, A. M., (Mrs. Kerr) *1879............................Chicago.
Almeda Beals, L. A., (Mrs. Chas. Wickwire)...........................Farmington.
Sarah Elvira Edwards, L. A., (Mrs. Otis Jones) *1899...............Los Angeles, Cal.
Grace Greenwood, L. A., (Mrs. E. E. Holroyd) *1898.......................Chicago.
Emeline Elizabeth Kirk, L. A., *1881...........,........................Rockford.
Frances Elizabeth Pike, L. A., (Mrs. J. Kirke Keller)............Artist, St. Louis, Mo.
Mary Ann Sparks, L. A., (Mrs. Milnor).................................Litchfield.
Florence Adeline Tenny, L. A., (Mrs. Edwards) *1871...................Omaha, Neb.
Mary Emeline Weston, L. A.. (Mrs. Woodman) *1888...................Portland, Me.

1869.

Rauseldon Cooper, B. S.......................................Attorney, Oquawka.
Hon. Samuel Kerr, A. M.........................Attorney, 189 La Salle St., Chicago.
Hon. Michael F. Knappenberger, B. S.....................Attorney, Jewel City, Kan.
Howard Knowles, B. S..Galesburg.
Patrick Talent, B. S...Attorney, Butte City, Mont.
John Ewalt Wiley, B. S.............. ....Farmer, Elmwood.
Mary Emily Dunton. A. M., (Mrs. Samuel Kerr).....1323 Washington Blvd., Chicago.
Ella May Greenwood, L. A., (Mrs. S. O. Snyder)....687 3rd St., Salt Lake City, Utah.
Mary Hartman, L. A., A. M., 1888............Teacher in State Normal Univ., Normal.

1870.

Jared Perkins Blood, A. B.........................Attorney, Sioux City, Iowa.
Hon. Abraham Miller Brown, A. M.............................Attorney, Galesburg.
Nathaniel Ray Chase, A. M., M. D....................................Newport, R. I.
Matthias Crum, M. S...Banker, Farmer City.
Hon. Chas. Electus Hasbrook, A. M., LL. B. (Chicago University),
          Business Manager Denver Republican, Denver, Colo.
Elmer Clifford Johnson, B. S..............Manufacturer, 36 Main St., Evansville, Ind.
Otis Jones, B. S. ....Real Estate dealer, San Antonio, Cal.
Israel Cyrus Stockton, M. S...........Clerk, Interior Department, Washington, D. C.
Hon. John Hill Walbridge, B. S.....................Farmer, West Concord, Vt.
Mary Ann Chapin, L. A., (Mrs. T. T. Perry) *1883.....................Girard, Kan.
Flora Amanda Edwards, L. A., (Mrs. J. F. Fargo).................San Antonio, Cal.

1871.

Hon. Martin Ireneus Brower, A. M......... ....Attorney, Fullerton, Neb.
Hon. Willis Hardin Fuson, A. M., *1884.............................Wa Keeney, Kan.
Frank Tenney Greenwood, A. B............................Druggist, Seneca, Kan.
Hon. Madison Reynolds Harris, A. B.....Att'y, 148 W. Madison St., Rm. 30, Chicago.
Hon. Samuel Parsons McConnell, A. B.,
        Ex-Circuit Judge, Attorney, Home Insurance Building, Chicago.
John DeBolt Stephenson, B. S., *1872...... ....Dexter, Ind.
Ida Bullock, L. A., (Mrs. Thatcher) *1894.............................Attleboro, Mass.
Hanna Laura Haight, B. S.....................................Teacher, Mendota.
Ada May Hasbrook, A. M., (Mrs. Hale),
        Matron Ladies' Hall, Lombard College, Galesburg.
Mary Knowles, L. A., (Mrs. J. S. Alspaugh).......................Washington, Kan.
Flora Adaline Prindle, L. A., (Mrs. A. G. Dow)........................Galesburg.

1872.

Albert Elmore Chase, B. S............Deputy U. S. Mining Surveyor, Boulder, Colo.
Joseph Albert Gates, A. B...........Nat. Military Home, Box 97, Leavenworth, Kan.
Alice M. Bingham, L. A., (Mrs. Copeland)..............School Trustee, Monroe, Wis.
Mattie Wilburn Burford, L. A., (Mrs. Bates)...............Merchant, Wichita, Kan.

1873.

Theodore C. Stevens, A. M., *1892....................................... Lincoln, Neb.
Ada D. Bingham, L. A., M. D............. ....1623 Gaylord St., Denver, Colo.
Ella M. Brown, L. A., (Mrs. Salley). *1883...............................Monroe, Wis.
Anna L. Nelson, L. A., (Mrs. Fuson).......................................Emporia, Kan.
Clara Richardson, L. A., (Mrs. G. F. Claycomb)........................Farragut, Ia.
Sarah A. Richardson, A. M............. ....Lawrence, Kan.
Mary M. Stevens, A. M.....................................871 East St., Lincoln, Neb.

1874.

William Albrecht, B. S., *1878...Tiskilwa.
Eugene E. Brunson, B. S., M. D.......................................Ganges, Mich.
Daniel Clingingsmith, B. S..Newton, Kan.
William E. Day, B. S....................Teacher, 198 Oakwood Boulevard, Chicago.
Morris W. Fletcher, B. S., M. D....................................Collierville, Tenn.
Irene A. Conger, L. A., (Mrs. Courtney). *1891................................Chicago.
Belle Sherman, B. S..Teacher, Ithaca, N. Y.

1875.

Charles A. Buck. L. A.. Merchant, LeRoy.
Lucien J. Dinsmore, B. S., A. M., 1886...........Clergyman, 1389 Perry St., Chicago.
Charles Ellwood Nash, A. M., S. T. D. (Tufts),
                              President Lombard College, Galesburg.
Carrie W. Brainard, A. M., B. D., (St. Lawrence)..... .....Clergyman, Caledonia, O.
Emma S. Collins, L. A., (Mrs. J. E. Buchanan).................Teacher, Lake Forest.
Lillie E. Conger, L. A., *1877.......................................Oneida.
Genie R. Edwards, L. A., (Mrs. Noteware), *1888.................Minneapolis, Minn.
Jennie C. Nelson, L. A., (Mrs. Nichols)..............................St. Charles.
Josie M. Pryne, L. A............................113 Hanover St., Mankato, Minn.
Luella R. Warner, L. A., (Mrs. Frank Hitchcock), Teacher of Painting, Mosca, Colo.

1876.

Hon. J. L. Hastings, B. S., *1894.. ..Galesburg.
Charlotte Fuller, M. S., (Mrs. S. M. Risley)..............................Harvard, Neb.
Stella Hale, L. A ....Galesburg.
Lottie E. Leighton, B. S., (Mrs. L. J. Dinsmore)............1389 Perry St., Chicago.
Izah T. Parker, A. M., *1891.. ...Banning, Cal.

1877.

George F. S. Baker, A. M., *1891.......................................Goodenow.
Charles C. Maynard, A. M.....................Dentist, 97 S. 1st St., San Jose, Cal.
Clara Z. Edwards, L. A., (Mrs. J. F. Calhoun),
                              2121 Bryant Ave., South, Minneapolis, Minn.
Emily L. Fuller, A. M...Teacher, Galesburg.

Eugenia Fuller, A. M..........................Principal High School, Riverside, Cal.
Lottie J. Humphrey, B. S., *1879...Tipton, Ia.
Ella McCullough, L. A., (Mrs. J. D. Welsh)................................Galesburg.

1878.

Ozro P. Bostwick, A. B...............................Supt. City Schools, Clinton, Ia.
Eben H. Chapin, A. M., B. D., (Tufts).......Clergyman, 18 Maple St., Rockland, Me.
Shirley C. Ransom, B. S., A. M. 1892......Agent Prudential Insurance Co., Kewanee.
Adah M. Mariner, M. S...Walnut Grove.

1879.

Jon W. Grubb, M. S.:........................Professor Lombard College, Galesburg.
Charles P. Hale, A. M................................Bank Cashier, Pittsburg, Kan.
Douglas A. Myers, B. S......................................Real Estate Agent, Peoria.
Charles A. Webster, B. S...................Treasurer Lombard College, Galesburg.
J. Edwin Webster, B. S..Merchant, Galesburg.

1880.

Henry S. Livingston, A. M., *1895...Galesburg.
William H. Livingston, A. B., Auditor Mercantile Mutual Building and Loan
 Association, 716 Delaware St., Kansas City, Mo.
William A. Parker, A. M...............Civil Engineer, U. P. R. R., Kansas City, Mo.
Otto H. Swigart, B. S............................Farmer and Stockman, Champaign.
Mollie B. Devendorf, B. S................Stenographer, 689 W. Adams St., Chicago.
Jennie B. Townsend, B. S., (Mrs. C. A. Webster)...........................Galesburg.

1881.

George F. Hughes, A. B.......................................Attorney, Yates City.
Milo C. Summers, M. S., War Department Clerk, Surgeon General's office,
 314 Seventh Street, Northeast, Washington, D. C.
Lura D. Bailey, A. B.. (Mrs. G. F. Hughes)..............................Yates City.

1882.

Reuben D. Bower, B. S..Clerk, Galesburg.
Henry M. Chase, A. M......................Loan and Real Estate Agent, Galesburg.
Lafayette Swart, B. S........................Farmer, Murfreesborough, Tenn.
Elmer H. West, M. S., *1894......................................Yates City.

1883.

Chas. E. Brewster, A. B., Loan and Real Estate Agent,
 1770 Emerson Avenue, South, Minneapolis, Minn.
James Weston Carney, B. S., B. D., (Tufts)....................Attorney, Galesburg.
Lloyd Z. Jones, B. S............................County Surveyor and Farmer, Galva.
John H. Miles, B. S...Farmer, Bushnell.
Fannie M. Edwards, A. B., (Mrs. C. E. Brewster),
 1770 Emerson Ave., South, Minneapolis, Minn.
Lizzie E. Furniss, B. S., (Mrs. W. J. Moring) Teacher 2200 Logan Ave., Denver, Colo.
Emma J. Livingston, L. A., (Mrs. A. T. Wing)......................Ottumwa, Iowa.
Elma E. Williams, A. M.......................................Teacher, Geneseo.

1884.

Anna M. Brewster, M. S., (Mrs. E. H. West)...........................Yates City.
Gay M. Brunson, B. S., M. D., D. D. S...............................Dentist, Joliet.
Lulu M. Burt, B. S., (Mrs. W. B. Cravens)..........2401 E. 11th St., Kansas City, Mo.

Charles L. Edwards, B. S., Ph. D. (Leipsic),
Professor of Biology, Trinity College, Hartford, Conn.
Jay C. Edwards, M. S...Teacher, Union Hill.
Frank R. Jones, B. S.......................Cashier American Well Works, Aurora.

1885.

Jennie B. Conger, A. M., (Mrs. Conger).....217 N. Los Angeles St., Los Angeles, Cal.
Eugene F. Carney, B. S., *1887...Galesburg.
Alma J. Devore, B. S., (Mrs. J. H. Miles)....................................Bushnell.
Lizzie B. Hughes, B. L., (Mrs. D. Perry)....................................Table Grove.
Ella Suiter, B. S., (Mrs. Geo. Pittard), *1894....................................Alexis.
Hon. Lyman McCarl, M. S.......................Attorney, 304 N. Sixth St., Quincy.
J. Douglas Welsh, B. S...Attorney, Galesburg.
George Crum, B. D..Clergyman, Cedar Rapids, Ia.
Wallace F. Small, B. D......... ....Everett, Wash.

1886.

Rainie Adamson, M. S., (Mrs. W. F. Small)..................Teacher, Everett, Wash.
L. Ward Brigham, M. S., M. D., B. D., (Canton)........Clergyman, Rochester, Minn.
John M. Davies, M. S.............................Teacher, 285 Ontario St., Chicago.
Anna H. Ebberd, B. S., (Mrs. Cyrus Hannum).........................Campbell, Neb.
Alice L. Roberts, B. S., (Mrs. J. L. Andrew)......................National City, Cal.
Rachel A. Watkins. M. S., (Mrs. Billings), B. D. 1894.....................Hico, Texas.
August Dellgren, B. D................................Clergyman, Minneapolis, Minn.
Hiram J. Orelup, B. D........................... ......Clergyman, Whitesville, N. Y.

1887.

Ella M. Grubb, A. M.....................................Teacher, Stevens Point, Wis.
Hon. Henry C. Morris, A. M...........Attorney, 188 Madison St., Suite 703, Chicago.
J. W. Crane, B. S...........Attorney, 908 Guarantee Loan Bldg., Minneapolis, Minn.
Perry B. Fuller, B. S.... ....Clerk, Elgin.
Jay Welsh, M. S..Teacher, Williamsfield.
Alva T. Wing, B. S... ....Clerk. Ottumwa, Ia.
John R. Carpenter, B. D...............................Clergyman, New Olmstead, O.
Osgood G. Colegrove, B. D..........·......................Clergyman, Woodstock, O.
Mary Garrard, B. D., (Mrs. I. Rollin Andrews).........3819 Charles St., Omaha, Neb.

1888.

Peter T. Hawley, B. S...Merchant, Ralston, Ia.
Harry H. Jones, M. S..............:·Manager American Well Works, Dallas, Texas.
Allen W. Lapham, M. S. M.. D., *1894...Victoria.
Elmer E. Taylor, B. S...............................Clergyman, Wellsville, Mo.
Elfreda L. Shaffer, B. D., (Mrs. Newport)..................Clergyman, Wauponsee.

1889.

Elmer E. Taylor, B. S., A. B.........:.....................Clergyman. Wellsville, Mo.
George E. Dutton, M. S...................President First National Bank, Sycamore.
Frank H. Fowler, B. S., Ph. D. (The Univ. of Chicago),
Professor Lombard College, Galesburg.
Edward P. McConnell, M. S..Chicago.
Allen F. Moore, B. S..Merchant, Monticello.

William T. Smith, M. S...Attorney, Galesburg.
Vanna R. Williams, B. L., (Mrs. W. W. Slaughter)................Francis, Oklahoma.
Charles A. C. Garst, B. D., *1896...Riverside, Cal.
Carrie A. Rice, B. D......................Clergyman, 6019 Prairie Ave., Chicago.

1890.

Frank H. Fowler, B. S., A. B., Ph. D. (The Univ. of Chicago),
　　　　　　　　　　　　Professor Lombard College, Galesburg.
Claude N. Anderson, B. S...........,........................Teacher, Tecumseh, Neb
Bert H. Brigham, M. S..............................Attorney, 803 Perry St., Chicago.
Elizabeth Gaile Durston, M. S., (Mrs. H. F. Simmons),
　　　　　　　　B. O. (Columbia School of Oratory), Woodhull.
Fred Farlow, B. S................. ....Stock Dealer, Camp Point.
Samuel D. Harsh, B. S., *1893..............................,.................Creston, Iowa.
Anna E. Ross, M. S., (Mrs. A. Lapham), M. D.,
　　　　　　　Physician, Langely Ave. and 431d St., Chicago.
Richard L. Slater, B. S., *1894..Wataga.
Loring Trott, M. S..Junction City, Kan.
James J. Welsh, B. S..Attorney, Galesburg.
Lizzie Wigle, B. S., (Mrs. C. N. Anderson)..........................Tecumseh, Neb.
Burtrust T. Wilson, M. S..............Professor Guadalupe College, Seguin, Texas.
Lilian J. Wiswell, B. L., (Mrs. E. P. McConnell)............4359 Lake Ave., Chicago.
Thomas E. Dotter, B. D.....................................Clergyman, Sullivan, Mo.

1891.

Willard J. White, A. M., M. D..................Professor Medicine, Longmont, Colo.
M. McClelland Case, M. S....................................Teacher, Williamsfield.
Villa A. Cole, B. S., (Mrs. M. M. Case)......................Teacher, Williamsfield.
S. Taylor Donohoe, M. S.......................United States Gauger, Pekin.
Jennie A. Grubb, B. S., (Mrs. F. H. Fowler)..............................Galesburg.
Robert D. Hill, M. S..Attorney, Lewistown.
Della M. Rogers, B. L., (Mrs. Chas. Garber)......................Reardan, Wash.
William Franklin Smith, B. D., *1897..............................Whitewater, Wis.

1892.

Frank N. Allen, B. S........................ ......Bookkeeper, 442 E. 45th St., Chicago.
Curtis P. Beale, M. S...............Agent New York Life Insurance Co., Yates City.
Harry A. Blount, B. S...Merchant, Macomb.
Ben F. Brady, B. S..Attorney, Ottawa.
Alice C. Durston, A. M...New Windsor.
Chas. W. Elliott, B. S......................................Jeweler, Williamsfield.
Grace S. Harsh, B. S...Creston, Ia.
Lissie Seeley, B. S., (Mrs. Leonard Crew) ....Salem, Ia.
Daniel P. Wild, M. S..Banker, Sycamore.
Luther E. Wyman, B. S...........................Broker, Board of Trade, Chicago.
Benjamin W. Jones, Jr., B. D.. *1898.....................................Barre, Vt.
Effie K. (McCollum) Jones, B. D., (Mrs. B. W. Jones)..........Clergyman, Barre, Vt.
George W. Skilling, B. D................................Clergyman, Iowa Falls, Ia.

1893.

Robert F. Anderson, A. B............................Principal Columbia School, Peoria.
Carl C. Countryman, A. M......................Impersonator and Author, Chicago.
Ethel M. Tompkins, A. M.. (Mrs. W. S. Clayberg)................................Avon.

F. Louise Bradford, B. S................ ....Teacher, Quincy.
Richard Brown, M. S...Attorney, Creston, Ia.
Kate A. Carlton, B. S., (Mrs. F. W. Smith)..............................DeLand, Fla.
J. Newton Conger, Jr., M. S.......................................Attorney, Galesburg.
States Dickson, B. S................ ....Attorney, Kewanee.
S. Hepsey Fuller, M. S., (Mrs. J. M. Earhart) ....Wyoming.
Daisy D. Wiswell, M. S., (Mrs. G. A. Franklin).....................Carpentaria, Cal.
Guy A. Longbrake, B. L., M. D..Galesburg.
Charles E. Varney, B. D....................Instructor Lombard College, Galesburg.

1894.

William Richard Tapper, A. B....................Attorney, 157 E. 47th St., Chicago.
Guy Henry Bernard, B. S......................................Teacher, Delphos, Kan.
Lucy Minerva Conger, B. S.......... ....Galesburg.
Joseph Amos Crum, B. S., M. D.......................................Oshkosh, Wis.
Maud Alice Crum, B. S...Boone, Ia.
Adelphia Gould Durston, B. S., (Mrs. George Ohse).........................Chicago.
Albert Prentice Smith, B. S...............................Merchant, Denver, Colo.
Lucy Titus, B. S., (Mrs. R. F. Anderson)...................................Peoria.
Eliza M. Drake Curtis, B. D., (Mrs. J. L. Everton)............Clergyman, Hoopeston.
Rachel C. Watkins Dellgren, B. D., (Mrs. Billings)......................Hico, Texas.
Jasper Leroy Everton, B. D.....................................Clergyman, Hoopeston.
Martha Dandridge Garner, B. D.,(Mrs. L. P. Jones)Clergyman, Blenheim, Ontario,Can.
Henry LaFayette Gillespie, B. D......................................Clergyman,Ohio.
Elijah Emmet Hamand, B. D..........Clergyman, 1222 Lyden Ave., Kansas City, Mo.
Rett E. Olmstead, B. D......................................Clergyman, Storm Lake, Ia.
Margaret Titus, B. D.,,(Mrs. R. E. Olmstead)...........Clergyman, Albert Lea, Minn.
Albert Ernest Menke, Ph. D..............................Chemist, Fayetteville, Ark.
Hans Schuler, Ph. D ....Teacher, Flushing, N. Y.

1895.

John McDuffie, Ph. D......................................Teacher, Springfield, Mass.
Lucile Bragg, A. B..Clerk, Humboldt, Kan.
William Robert Chapin, B. S....................................Bank Cashier, Kirkwood.
Frank Loren Conger, A. B...................................Bank Clerk, Galesburg.
Grace Winifred Conley, A. B...............................Postal Clerk, Galesburg.
Mabel Dow, A. B., (Mrs. F. L. Conger).............................. ....Galesburg.
Robert Pinckney Higgins, B. S..............................Attorney, Bloomington.
John Richard Stanley, A. B.............Agricultural Implement Dealer, Stronghurst.
Nellie Christine Tompkins, A. B........................... ....Avon.
Albert Orin Wakefield, A. B...............................Attorney, Sioux City, Ia.
Frances Elizabeth Cheney, B. D...............................Clergyman, Greenup.
Orrin Carlton Evans, B. D....................................Clergyman, Morrison.
Charles Robert Jones, B. D..........................Clergyman, Gould Farm, Mo.
Thomas Francis Rayon, B. D..............................Clergyman, Bellaire, Mich.

1896.

Jessie Beatrice Brown, A. B., (Mrs. A. C. Clock)......................Winona, Minn.
Fred Leo Camp, A. B...Druggist, Galesburg.
Bertha Alice Cook, A. B., (Mrs. O. C. Evans)............................Marseilles.
Almira Lowry Cheney, A. B...Saybrook.
Elice Crissey, A. B...Teacher, Avon.

Homer Franklin Harsh, A. B.................................Stockman, Lowell, Neb.
Hamilton Lafayette Karr, Jr., A. B.............................Attorney, Osceola, Ia.
Marion Alice Kendall, A. B..Brockton, Mass.
Harry McGee Lessig, A. B...Knoxville.
Ralph Grierson Kimble, A. B ....Professor Lombard College, Galesburg.
Iva Della Myers, A. B...Bookkeeper, Galesburg.
Edward Leroy Shinn, A. B., Sec. and Treas. Atlantic Fuel Co.,
       918 Stephen Girard Building, Philadelphia, Pa.
Emma Genevra Van Liew, A. M., (Mrs. Guy Tuttle).......................Galesburg.
Jean Gillette White, A. B., (Mrs. A. B. McGill)...........................Peoria.
James Alvin Clark, B. D................................Clergyman, Webster City, Ia.
Charles William Edward Gossow, B. D...........................Clergyman, Clinton.
Maurice Gilbert Linton, B. D..................................Clergyman, Roseville.
Eugene Southwick, B. D.............. ....Clergyman, Corfu, N. Y.

Georgia Stanley, Diploma in Art, (Mrs. C. H. Wickham).......Teacher, Stronghurst.

1897.

Frank Pierce Anderson. A. B.......................................Teacher, Yates City.
Loetta Frances Boyd, A. B..Teacher, Plano.
Flora May Cutter, A. B....................................... ....Camp Point.
Benjamin Downs, A. B ....Clerk, Winslow, Ariz.
Nina Alta Harris, A. B...Teacher, Galesburg.
Fred Louis Holcomb, A. B., M. D..Zenda, Kan.
Theodore Lindquist, A. B., Instructor Kansas State Agricultural
         College, Manhattan, Kan.
Carrie Alice Stickney. A. B.......Student New England Conservatory, Boston, Mass.
Elmer Joseph Tapper, A. B............................Insurance Solicitor, Riverside.
Claude Bryant Warnei, A. B., A. M.. ....Dentist, Avon.
Guy Henry Weeks, A. B...Teacher, Galesburg.
Frances Cora White, A. B........ ....Galesburg.
Fred Minosuke Yamaguchi, A. B.........Student Yale University, New Haven, Conn.
George Hilary Ashworth, B. D............................Clergyman, Mt. Gilead, O.
Edward Milton Minor, B. D................................Clergyman, Mt. Vernon.
George Burr Rogers, B. D....................................Clergyman, Decatur, Mich.
William Willis Slaughter, B. D...... ....Clergyman, Francis, Oklahoma.
Simeon Lafayette Taylor, B. D................................Clergyman, Osage, Ia.

1898.

Mervin Wallace Allen, A. B..............Agent Metropolitan Life Ins. Co., Maquon.
Alice Helen Bartlett, A. B..Galesburg.
Charles Reid Brown, A. B....With Knickerbocker Ice Co., 171 La Salle St., Chicago.
Joshua J. Bullman, A. B..Farmer, Galesburg.
Ida Galbreath, A. B..Teacher, Galveston, Ind.
Charles Edward Piper, A. B........Student Yale Divinity School, New Haven, Conn.
Simeon Lafayette Taylor, B. D., A. B...........................Clergyman, Osage, Ia.
Edna Madison McDonald, B. D................................Clergyman, Urbana.
John Willis Slaughter, B. D., Student University of Michigan,
       311 S. Division St., Ann Arbor, Mich.
Benjamin Franklin Stacey....................Fellow University of Chicago, Chicago.
Oluf Tandberg, B. D..Clergyman, Earlville.

Isal Caldwell, Diploma in Vocal Music, (Mrs. Lewis).......... ....Knoxville.

1899.

Christen Martin Alsager, A. B........................Principal City Schools, Fairdale.
Ella Berry Boston, A. B................Student Dvorak School of Oratory, Chicago.
Henry William Dubee, A. B..........Student Harvard University, Cambridge, Mass.
Howard Everett Foster, A. B., *1900..Galesburg.
Homer Edwin Garvin, A. B............................Traveling Salesman, Quincy.
Fannie Pauline Gingrich, A. B.....................................Clerk, Galesburg.
George Runyan Longbrake, A. B., Student Ryder Divinity School,
                                            Lombard College, Galesburg.
Nellie Stuart Russell, A. B.......................................Teacher, Woodhull.
Lora Adelle Townsend, A. B.......................................Teacher, Galesburg.
Lloyd Champlain, B. D...Clergyman, Galesburg.

Edith C. Crissey, Diploma in Instrumental Music....................Teacher, Avon.
Jennie Holmes, Diploma in Art...............................North Henderson.

1900.

Martha Belle Arnold, A. B...........Graduate Student Lombard College, Galesburg.
Fay Alexander Bulluck, A. B...................................Reporter, Galesburg.
Gertrude Grace Kidder, A. B..Galesburg.
Edwin Julius McCullough, A. B..........................Teacher, La Prairie Centre.
Carrie Ruth Nash, A. B............. Graduate Student Lombard College, Galesburg.
Charles Wait Orton, A. B..Tacoma, Wash.
Burt G. Shields, A. B....Supt. Storehouse Philadelphia-Colorado Mining Co.,
                                            Colorado Springs, Colo.
Iva May Steckel, A. B..........Law Student University of Colorado, Boulder, Colo.
Earle Wolcott Watson, A. B...........Clerk Simmons Hardware Co., St. Louis, Mo.
Harry William Weeks...Peoria.
William David Buchanan, B. D ....Clergyman, Mt. Pleasant, Ia.

*Deceased.

Honorary Degrees.

The degree placed immediately after the name is the honorary degree conferred by Lombard University.

An additional degree, followed by a date only, is one conferred by Lombard University.

An additional degree, without date, is one conferred by another institution, the name of which is given, if known.

1858. *Rev. Qtis A. Skinner, D. D .... Ex-President Lombard University.
1859. Rev. George S. Weaver, A. M .... Canton, N. Y.
1860. *Ansel Streeter, A. M .... Weston, Mo.
1862. *Rev. Ebenezer Fisher, D. D ..... Principal Theological School, Canton, N. Y.
1862. Rev. Joseph Selmon Dennis, A. M .....: .... Chicago.
1863. *Rev. William Henry Ryder, D. D.; A. M. (Harvard) .... Chicago.
1864. *Rev. Holden R. Nye, A. M .... Philadelphia, Pa.
1864. *Rev. Charles Woodhouse, A. M.; M. D .... Rutland, Vt.
1865. Rev. A. G. Hibbard, A. M .... Wheaton.
1865. *Rev. J. G. H. Hartzell, A. M.; D. D. (St. Lawrence). .... Detroit, Mich.
1867. *Rev. William Ethan Manley, A. M .... Denver, Colo.
1867. Rev. Thomas B. St. John, A. M ....
1868. *Rev. Clement G. Lefevre, D. D .... Milwaukee, Wis.
1868. William B. Powell, A. M .... Washington, D. C.
1868. Rev. James Harvey Tuttle, A. M.; D. D ....Minneapolis, Minn.
1869. Rev. John Wesley Hanson, A. M.; D. D. (Buchtel) .... Pasadena, Cal.
1869. Rev. William Wallace Curry, A. M .... Washington, D. C.
1869. *Rev. Daniel Parker Livermore, A. M .... Melrose, Mass.
1869. Rev. Augusta J. Chapin, A. M .... Mt. Vernon, N. Y.
1870. Rev. John S. Cantwell, A. M .... Chicago.
1870. Daniel Lovejoy Hurd, A. M.; M. D ....
1870. *Rev. George Truesdale Flanders, D. D .... Rockport, Mass.
1870. *Rev. Alfred Constantine Barry, D. D .... Lodi, Mass.
1872. *Rev. William Ethan Manley, D. D.; A. M. 1867..... .... Denver, Colo.
1872. Rev. R. H. Pullman, A. M .... Baltimore, Md.
1872. *Rev. Gamaliel Collins, A. M .... U. S. A., Chatham, Mass.
1872. *Rev. B. F. Rogers, A. M .... Fort Atkinson, Wis.
1875. *Rev. J. H. Chapin, Ph. D.; A. B. 1857; A. M. 1860 .... Meriden, Conn.
1876. Rev. George S. Weaver, D. D.; A. M. 1859 .... Canton, N. Y.
1876. Rev. John S. Cantwell, D. D.; A. M. 1870 .... Chicago.
1877. Rev. Q. Cone, D. D .... Canton, N. Y.
1879. Elias Fraunfelter, Ph. D .... Akron, O.
1879. Milton L. Comstock, Ph. D .... Professor Knox College, Galesburg.
1882. Rev. Charles W. Tomlinson, D D .... Taunton, Mass.
1883. *Rev. Amos Crum, A. M .... Webster City, Ia.

*Deceased.

1884. Matthew Andrews, A. M.....................,....................................Monmouth.
1886. Rev. L. A. Dinsmore, A. M.; B. S. 1875.......................................Chicago.
1887.. *Rev. Holden R. Nye, D. D.; A. M. 1864........................Towanda, Pa.
1887. Rev. Charles Fluhrer, D, D..Albion, N. Y.
1887. Hon. Lewis E. Payson, LL. D..Pontiac.
1887. Hon. George W. Wakefield, A. M...............................Sioux City, Ia.
1888. Rev. George H. Deere, D. D......................................Riverside, Cal.
1888. Homer M. Thomas, A. M.; M. D...Chicago.
1888. Rev. Charles A. Conklin, A. M..............................Springfield, Mass.
1888. Mary Hartman, A. M.; L. A. 1859.......................................Normal.
1890. Rev. Jacob Straub, D. D...Chicago.
1890. George B. Harrington, A. M......... ....Princeton.
1890. Carl F. Kolbe, Ph. D......... ....Akron, O.
1891. Rev. A. G. Gaines, LL. D.; D. D,
                    Ex-President St. Lawrence University, Canton, N. Y.
1892. Rev. George Thompson Knight, D. D.,
                    Professor Divinity School, Tufts College, Mass.
1892. Charles Kelsey Gaines, Ph. D.Professor St. Lawrence University, Canton, N. Y.
1892. Shirley C. Ransom, A. M.; B. S. 1878..............................Kewanee.
1893. Rev. Augusta J. Chapin. D. D.; A. M. 1869..................Mt. Vernon, N. Y.
1893. *Rev. Amos Crum, D. D.; A. M. 1885........................Webster City, Ia.
1895. John Huston Finley, Ph. D....................... ....New York City.
1893. Charles Loring Hutchinson, A. M.......................................Chicago.
1894. Rev. Royal Henry Pullman, D. D.; A. M. 1872.................Baltimore, Md.
1894. Rev. George B. Stocking, D. D......................................Galesburg.
1895. Rev. Aaron Aldrich Thayer, D. D....................................California.
1895. Rev. Andrew Jackson Canfield, Ph. D.; D. D.................Brooklyn, N. Y.
1897. Rev. Daniel Bragg Clayton, D. D..............................Columbia, S. C.
1897. Rev. Thomas Sander Guthrie, D. D..........................Logansport, Ind.
1898. Rev. Rodney F. Johonnot, D. D....................................Oak Park.
1898. Henry Priest, Ph. D., Professor St. Lawrence University........Canton, N. Y.
1899. John Wesley Hanson, Jr., A. M...Chicago.
1900. Rev. Alfred Howitzer Laing, D. D.............:. ....Joliet.

*Deceased.

HARVARD UNIVERSITY SCHOLARSHIP.

By request of the Harvard Club of Chicago we publish the following notice:

At its annual meeting December 14, 1897, The Harvard Club of Chicago established a scholarship at Harvard University of the annual value of three hundred dollars. This scholarship is open to the graduates of the universities and colleges of Illinois who wish to follow a graduate course of study at Harvard University. Applications must be made before May 1st in each year, and senior students about to finish their undergraduate course are eligible as candidates. Communications should be addressed to Murry Nelson, Jr., Chairman, 99 Randolph Street, Chicago.

INDEX.

MAIN BUILDING.

CATALOGUE

OF

LOMBARD COLLEGE

GALESBURG, ILLINOIS

FOR THE YEAR ENDING JUNE 5, 1902.

GALESBURG, ILL.
THE MAIL PRINTING COMPANY.
1902.

College Calendar.

1902.
MARCH 11—Tuesday ....Third Term Begins.
MARCH 11—Tuesday, 8 a. m............... ....Registration.
MAY 17—Saturday...Senior Vacation Begins.
MAY 28, 29—Wednesday, Thursday................. ....Examinations.
JUNE 1—Sunday..Baccalaureate Sermon.
JUNE 2—Monday...Field Day.
JUNE 2—Monday, Evening.. ....Townsend Prize Contest in Declamation.
JUNE 3—Tuesday.................Annual Meeting of Association of Graduates.
JUNE 3—Tuesday, Evening.....................................Senior Class Play.
JUNE 4—Wednesday............................Meeting of the Board of Trustees.
JUNE 4—Wednesday, Evening................................Class Day Program.
JUNE 5—Thursday...Commencement Day.

Summer Vacation.

SEPT. 2, 3, 4—Tuesday, Wednesday. Thursday..........Entrance Examinations.
SEPT. 2, 3, 4—Tuesday, Wednesday, Thursday.....................Registration.
SEPT. 4—Thursday ....Beginning of the College Year.
SEPT. 4—Thursday ....First Term Begins.
·NOV. 24, 25—Monday, Tuesday.......................................Examinations.
NOV. 25—Tuesday ....First Term Ends.

Thanksgiving Vacation.

DEC. 2—Tuesday...Second Term Begins.
DEC. 2—Tuesday, 8 a. m...Registration.
DEC. 23—Tuesday..........Last Day of Recitations preceding Christmas Recess.

Christmas Recess.

1903.
JAN. 6—Tuesday.........................Recitations of Second Term Resumed.
JAN. 23—Friday, Evening..... ....Swan Prize Contest in Oratory.
FEB. 12—Thursday.............. . ...Holiday, Lincoln's Birthday.
MARCH 4, 5—Wednesday, Thursday..... ....Examinations.
MARCH 5—Thursday................... ....Second Term Ends.

Spring Vacation.

MARCH 10—Tuesday..... ....Third Term Begins·
MARCH 10—Tuesday, 8 a. m...Registration.
MAY 16—Saturday.................................Senior Vacation Begins.
MAY 29, 31—Wednesday, Friday ....Examinations.
MAY 31—Sunday.................... ....Baccalaureate Sermon.
JUNE 1—Monday.................... ....Field Day.
JUNE 1—Monday................... ....Gymnasium Exhibition.
JUNE 1—Monday, Evening ....Townsend Prize Contest in Declamation.
JUNE 2—Tuesday ....Class Day.
JUNE 2—Tuesday...... . ....Annual Meeting of the Association of Graduates.
JUNE 2—Tuesday, Afternoon....................Annual Recital of Music Pupils.
JUNE 2—Tuesday, Evening... ..   ....Exhibition of Department of Elocution.
JUNE 3—Wednesday............................Meeting of the Board of Trustees.
JUNE 3—Wednesday, Evening.............................Commencement Rally.
JUNE 4—Thursday...Commencement Day.

Board of Trustees.

Officers of the Board.

Hon. SAMUEL KERR, Chicago,

PRESIDENT.

CHARLES A. WEBSTER, Galesburg,

TREASURER.

PHILIP G. WRIGHT, Galesburg,

SECRETARY.

W. F. CADWELL, Galesburg,

AUDITOR.

Executive Committee.

HOWARD KNOWLES, Chairman.

CHARLES A. WEBSTER, Secretary.

CHARLES ELLWOOD NASH, D. D.

ROBERT CHAPPELL.   J. DOUGLAS WELSH.

Board of Visitors.

Each Universalist State Convention, which adopts Lombard College as its Institution of Learning, is entitled to send two visitors, whose duty it is to examine into the condition of the College and to assist in the choice of Trustees.

GENERAL STATEMENT.

LOCATION.

Lombard College is located in Galesburg, Knox County, Illinois, a healthful and beautiful city of 20.000 inhabitants, noted for its public buildings, its elegant churches, and the good order, intelligence, thrift, and refinement of its people.

Galesburg is easily accessible by railroad from all parts of the West; being the center of the great Burlington System, leading to Chicago, Burlington, Quincy, Peoria, Rock Island, St. Louis, Kansas City, Omaha, Denver, and Minneapolis; and also on the main line of the Santa Fe system. It is the terminus of the Fulton County Narrow Gauge R. R., connecting with the great Wabash System.

THE COLLEGE CAMPUS.

The College Campus is situated in the southeastern part of the city and may readily be reached by the electric cars. It is thirteen acres in extent and affords ample space for base-ball, foot-ball, tennis, and other athletic sports. A large part is planted with trees, which have been growing many years and have attained noble size and graceful forms. Among them are pines, larches, hemlocks, cedars, maples, elms, ash-trees, tulip-trees, and others, embracing about forty species. The trees and lawns are well kept and cared for, and the beauty of the surroundings thus created is a pleasing and attractive feature of the College.

HISTORY.

The Illinois Liberal Institute was chartered in 1851, opened for students in the autumn of 1852, invested with College powers in 1853, and took the name of Lombard University (in honor of Mr. Benjamin Lombard, at that time the largest donor to its properties) in 1855. It was one of the first Colleges in the country to admit women as students on the same terms with men, allowing them to graduate in the same class and with the same honors. The first class was graduated in 1856. The Ryder Divinity School was opened September 5, 1881.

THE ELECTIVE SYSTEM.

Experience has demonstrated the soundness of the educational principle that the selection of studies, in some degree, at least, should be adapted to the needs, tastes, and talents of the student. At Lombard this principle is fully recognized and great liberty is given to students in the choice of their studies. At the same time the fact is recognized that there is a distinct educational gain to a student in pursuing a well matured and logically developed course of study. The method by which it is sought to reconcile these important principles of education at Lombard is fully explained later in the catalogue.

THE COLLEGE YEAR.

The College year begins early in September and closes early in June. It is divided into three terms of approximately equal length. (See Calendar, page 2.)

Students should, if possible, enter at the beginning of the College year, since much of the work is arranged progressively from that date. They will, however, be allowed to enter at any time when there seems a prospect of their being able to do so profitably.

Commencement day occurs the first Thursday in June.

NEW ADMISSION REQUIREMENTS.

Beginning with the Fall term 1902, the requirements for admission to the College of Liberal Arts for students who are candidates for a degree, will be raised to the highest standard recommended by the joint committee of the High School and College Sections of the Illinois State Teachers' Association. This is essentially the standard recommended by the Committee of Thirteen of the National Educational Association, being the standard in force at Harvard, The University of Chicago, and other leading colleges in the United States. [See p. 20.]

Students not candidates for a degree may enter on probation any class for which they are prepared, and at the end of their connection with the College they will be furnished a certificate, stating the amount and quality of the work accomplished while in the College.

APPORTIONMENT OF TIME.

The regular sessions of the College are held on Monday, Tuesday, Wednesday, Thursday, and Friday.

GRADES OF SCHOLARSHIP.

From the courses of study offered, each student is expected to elect work to an amount sufficient to keep him profitably employed. In all full courses each recitation occupies one hour. Absence from a recitation will forfeit the mark in that study for the day.

At the end of every term the standing of a student in each of his courses will be expressed, according to his proficiency, by one of four grades, designated respectively by the letters A, B, C, D.

The grade is determined by term work estimated on the basis of attendance, quality of recitations or laboratory work, occasional tests, written exercises, etc., and by final examinations at the end of the term, the term grade and the final examination being valued in the ratio of two to one.

Grade C is the lowest which will be accepted in any study as counting towards the fulfillment of the requirements of graduation.

Students who receive grade A in all their studies may pursue not more than four courses in the succeeding term.

Students whose lowest grade is B may pursue not more than three and one-half courses in the succeeding term.

Other students are not permitted to pursue more than three courses in any term.

CHAPEL EXERCISES.

Religious exercises, at which attendance is required, are conducted daily in the college chapel.

With the view of imparting additional interest and value to these exercises, relieving them of mere formality, brief addresses by members of the faculty or by invited speakers upon practical life questions or upon topics of the day, will be given from time to time. At intervals, also, special musical numbers will be introduced by the Director of the Musical Department.

LABORATORIES.

The department of Physics is well equipped with apparatus for experimentation. Students have an opportunity to obtain a practical acquaintance with the principles of Physics through a series of Laboratory experiments, which they perform for themselves under the direction of the instructor.

The extended courses in Chemistry, described elsewhere in this Catalogue, require a large amount of practical work on the part of the student. Each student in Chemistry has a desk provided with gas, water, re-agents and all necessary conveniences. The Laboratory is thoroughly equipped for work in General Chemistry, and in Qualitative and Quantitative Analysis.

A supply of superior microscopes has been imported during the past year, which, with other instruments and apparatus, affords a very satisfactory equipment for experimental work in Biology.

MUSEUM.

The Museum contains valuable collections duly classified and arranged, and available for purposes of instruction. The collection of corals is especially fine. A fine collection of minerals, birds, and ethnological specimens, the loan of A. B. Cowan, Esq., a former citizen of Galesburg, is known and designated as the Cowan collection.

LIBRARY.

The Library of the College contains about seven thousand volumes. It is located in the College building and is open daily. The books are systematically arranged and easy of access. They may be taken out by the students upon application to the Librarian. A considerable fund has been raised during the past year, which will be expended as occasion arises in the purchase of new books, thus assuring a substantial increment each year.

READING ROOM.

A Reading Room under the auspices of a Reading Room Association is supported by the voluntary efforts and contributions of the students, faculty, and friends. The leading newspapers and periodicals are kept on file. The Reading Room is open daily, except Sundays, for the use of the students, from 8:00 a. m. until 6:00 p. m.

GYMNASIUM.

The Gymnasium is a building 50 x 80 feet on the ground. On the ground floor, besides the Gymnasium proper, there is a large room, at present used as a recitation room, which can be thrown into the main room by withdrawing the movable partitions. There is also a stage, equipped with an adequate outfit of scenery, for the special use of the Department of Elocution. A gallery runs around the building, affording a suitable running track for indoor practice. The basement contains bathrooms and lockers and other conveniences.

Regular exercises are held in the Gymnasium daily, except Saturdays and Sundays. The exercises will consist of class drill, under the charge of a director, or of special work on the apparatus in accordance with the prescription of the medical examiner. It is intended that the instruction shall be thoroughly scientific, aiming not so much at special muscular or athletic development, as at a sound physical culture, which is the true basis of health and so of energy and endurance.

ATHLETICS.

The Athletic interests of the College are in charge of the Director of Physical Culture, assisted by a board of Management, consisting of two members chosen from the student body, one from the faculty, and two from the alumni. The Campus affords opportunity for foot-ball, base-ball, and track and field events. During

the winter basket ball is played in the Gymnasium. The Director
of Physical Culture will take personal charge of the coaching of the
foot-ball, basket-ball, base-ball, and track teams.

THE LADIES' HALL.

The new Ladies' Hall, finished and first opened for use in the
Fall of 1896, is a thoroughly modern building and complete in all
its appointments. It is heated by steam, lighted by gas, fitted with
sanitary plumbing, including porcelain baths, closets, lavatories,
etc., and supplied with every convenience of a well equipped home.
The Hall will accommodate forty young ladies; and all out-
of-town lady students, unless permission is obtained from the
President to live elsewhere, are expected to make their home in
this building.

Each room is finished with hard wood floor and furnished
with bedstead, springs, mattress, chairs, desk, dresser and rugs.
The occupants are expected to provide bedding, pillows, towels,
napkins, to pay for washing said articles, and to keep their own
rooms in order.

The charge for board is $42 per term for each person, payable
in advance. This does not include the Christmas recess. The
charge for room rent is from $6 to $15 per term, according to the
location of the room, payable to the Registrar in advance. Where
one person occupies a double room from choice an extra charge of
50 cents a week will be made; but the privilege of assigning two
persons to such room is reserved.

Board will be furnished to women students of the College who
do not have rooms in the Hall for $3.25 a week, payable in advance.

Applications for rooms in the Hall should be made during the
summer vacation to President C. Ellwood Nash, at other times to
Mrs. Ada M. H. Hale, Matron, Lombard Ladies' Hall.

THE LOMBARD REVIEW.

A College paper, called *The Lombard Review*, is published
monthly by the students. It makes a record of College events, and
serves as a medium of communication with the friends and alumni
of the College. Subscription price $1.00.

SOCIETIES.
The Erosophian.

The Erosophian Society was organized January 29, 1860. Any
gentleman connected with the College or Divinity School is eligible to membership, and is entitled to all the benefits of the society.
Its regular meetings are held on Thursday evening of each week.
The literary exercises consist of orations, debates, and essays.

The Zetecalian.

This Society was organized in 1863 for the ladies of the College. Its exercises consist of debates, essays, historical narrations, and general discussions. Regular meetings are held on Wednesday afternoon of each week. The officers are elected quarterly.

PRIZES.

1. The Swan Prizes.

Two prizes for excellence in Oratory are offered annually by Mrs. J. H. Swan, of Chicago. They are of the value of fifteen dollars and ten dollars, respectively. The contest for these prizes is held in January.

2. The Townsend Prizes.

Two prizes for excellence in Declamation are offered annually by Mrs. E. P. Townsend, of Sycamore. They are of the value of fifteen dollars and ten dollars, respectively. The contest for these prizes is held during Commencement week.

EXPENSES.

Boarding.

Board is furnished at the College Commons at cost. During the past year rates have been as follows:

Board, 37 weeks; Tuition, one year (without restriction of number of studies); incidentals, one year; payable annually or semi-annually in advance $117.25
Board, one term; Tuition, one term (without restriction of number of studies); Incidentals, one term; payable in advance................... 40.00
Board per week, payable in advance..................................... 2.00
Meal tickets, 7 tickets.. 1.00

The quality of the board furnished is not indicated by the price. Owing to the facts that provisions can be obtained at wholesale rates, that service at the table is co-operative, several students paying in part for their board in this manner, and that it is the purpose of the management to make no profit out of this department above actual operating expenses, the board is certainly equal in quality to that furnished in private families for $2.75 per week.

The yearly expenses may be estimated as follows:

Board at Commons, Tuition, Incidentals $117.25
Room rent 22.50
Washing 15.00
Books 15.00
_____
$169.75

Students, however, are not required to board at the Commons; some board themselves, and some board in private families. Students who board themselves may possibly cut their expenses a trifle below the above rates. In private families rates of from $2.75 and upwards per week for board, may be obtained.

A faculty committee will assist students in securing comfortable, home-like accommodations.

The charge for board in the Ladies' Hall is $42 per term, for each person, payable in advance. This does not include the Christmas recess. The charge for room rent is from $6 to $15 per term, according to location of room, payable to the Registrar in advance. Where one person occupies a double room from choice, an extra charge of 50 cents per week will be made, but the privilege of assigning two persons to such room is reserved. Board will be furnished to women students of the College who do not have rooms in the Hall at the rate of $3.25 per week, payable in advance.

Tuition and Incidentals.

Students in the College of Liberal Arts and Unclassified students will pay a tuition fee for each study pursued. The charge, except in theoretical music, is $3.50 per term for each full course, a course being a study taken for one term and counting as one credit toward graduation. The rate for each fractional course is in proportion to the credit allowed for such fractional course toward graduation. Thus, a half course is half rate; a third course, third rate, etc.

Students in Chemistry, Mineralogy, and Biology are required to deposit with the Registrar a sum sufficient to cover laboratory bills. Students in General Chemistry will deposit two dollars; students in Analytical Chemistry, five dollars; students in Mineralogy, three dollars; and students in Biology, three dollars each. At the close of the term there will be returned the balance remaining after deducting cost of chemicals and broken apparatus.

Students in Physics each pay one dollar per term as a laboratory fee.

The charge for incidentals, to be paid by all students of the College is $5.00 per term.

No student will be enrolled in any class until he presents the Registrar's receipt for the payment of tuition and incidentals. The registration fee is twenty-five cents. The payment of this fee will be remitted to all who register on the first day of the term.

Tuition and incidentals will not be refunded. In case a student is absent a half term or more from sickness or other adequate cause a certificate for a half term's tuition and incidentals will be given the student (at his request), said certificate good "to order" for its face value at any succeeding term.

Art and Music.

For information as to charges in Art and Music, see under these departments later in this Catalogue.

AID TO WORTHY STUDENTS.

Free tuition will be given to the student who graduates with highest rank from an approved high school. Students receiving this concession may be called upon for some College service.

Through the generosity of its friends the College is enabled to offer assistance to worthy students desiring to secure an education. The income of endowed scholarships is applied toward paying the tuition of a limited number.

Perpetual Scholarships.

Sixteen Perpetual Scholarships of $1,000 each have been founded by the following named persons.

The F. R. E. Cornell, Scholarship, by Mrs. E. O. Cornell.
The George B. Wright Scholarship, by Mrs. C. A. Wright.
The George Power Scholarship, by George and James E. Power.
The Mrs. Emma Mulliken Scholarship, by Mrs. Emma Mulliken.
The Clement F. LeFevre Scholarship, by William LeFevre and Mrs. Ellen R. Coleman.
The Samuel Bowles Scholarship, by Samuel Bowles.
The Dollie B. Lewis Scholarship, by Mrs. Dollie B. Lewis.
The O. B. Ayres Scholarship, by O. B. Ayres.
The Mary Chapin Perry Scholarship, by T. T. Perry.
The C. A. Newcomb Scholarship, by C. A. Newcomb.
The Mary W. Conger Scholarship, by the children of Mrs. Mary W. Conger.
The Hattie A. Drowne Scholarship, by Rev. E. L. Conger, D. D.
The A. R. Wolcott Scholarship, by A. R. Wolcott.
The Woman's Association Scholarship, by the U. W. A. of Illinois.
The Calista Waldron Slade Scholarship, by E. D. Waldron and sisters.
The Mary L. Pingrey Scholarship, by Mrs. Mary L. Pingrey.

BEQUESTS.

For the convenience of those who may wish to secure, by bequest, to the College, any given sum for a specific purpose, the accompanying form is here given:

I hereby give and bequeath to The Lombard College, located at Galesburg, Ill.,..... ....Dollars ($......)
for....... ..(state the object) ....and direct that my executor pay said bequest to the Treasurer of said College within ....after my death.

(Signed)................................

Dated .... Witness........................

CATALOGUES.

Former students of the College, whether graduates or not, are requested to inform the President of any change of residence, in order that the publications of the College may be sent to them. Catalogues and circulars of information will promptly be sent to those who apply for them.

MORALE AND SOCIAL POLICY.

Aside from a few obvious regulations designed to secure punctuality and regularity in attendance on college exercises, and to protect students and teachers from disturbance while at work, no formal rules are imposed upon the students.

It is expected that, as young men and women of somewhat mature years, they will observe the usual forms of good breeding, and enjoy the ordinary privileges of good society in so far as the latter do not conflict with the best interests of the institution or with their own health and intellectual advancement.

Should any student show a disposition to engage in conduct detrimental to his own best interests, or to those of his fellow students or of the college, the faculty will deal with the case in such manner as will protect the common welfare of all.

OFFICERS OF THE COLLEGE.

CHARLES ELLWOOD NASH, A. M., S. T. D., PRESIDENT,

A. B., Lombard University. 1875; B. D., Tufts College, 1878; A. M. Lombard University, 1878; S. T. D., Tufts College, 1891; President Lombard College, 1895—.

ISAAC AUGUSTUS PARKER, A. M., PH. D.,

*Williamson Professor of the Greek Language and Literature.

A. B., Dartmouth College. 1853; A. M., ibid, 1856; Ph. D., Buchtel College, 1892; Principal Orleans Liberal Institute, Glover, Vt., 1853-58; Professor of Ancient Languages, Lombard University, 1858-68; Professor of Greek Language and Literature, Lombard College, 1868—

NEHEMIAH WHITE, A. M., PH. D., S. T. D.,

†Hall Professor of Intellectual and Moral Philosophy.

In charge of the Ryder Divinity School, Professor of Biblical Languages and Exegesis.

A. B. Middlebury College 1857; A. M. ibid, 1860; Ph. D. St. Lawrence University, 1876; S. T. D., Tufts College, 1889; Associate Principal Green Mt. Perkins Institute, 1857-58; Principal Clinton Liberal Institute, 1859-60; Principal Pulaski Academy, 1865; Professor of Mathematics and Natural Science, St. Lawrence University, 1865-71; Professor Ancient Languages, Buchtel College, 1872-75; President Lombard University, 1875-92; In charge of the Ryder Divinity School, and Professor of Biblical Languages and Exegesis, 1892—.

JON WATSON GRUBB, M. S.

Instructor In Latin.

B. S., Lombard University, 1879; M. S., Lombard University, 1882; Adjunct Professor of Mathematics, Lombard University, 1882-94; Registrar, Lombard College, 1893—; Professor of Latin, Lombard College, 1894—.

FREDERICK WILLIAM RICH, D. Sc.,

‡ Conger Professor of Chemistry and Physics.

B. S., Cornell University, 1881; Graduate Student, Cornell University 1881; D. Sc., St. Lawrence University, 1900; Instructor in Analytical Chemistry, Cornell University, 1882-84; Professor of Natural Science, Lombard College, 1884—.

PHILIP GREEN WRIGHT. A. M.,

Professor of Mathematics, Astronomy, and Economics.

A. M. B., Tufts College, 1884; A. M., Harvard University, 1887; Teacher of Mathematics and Science, Goddard Seminary, Vt., 1883; Adjunct Professor of Mathematics, Buchtel College, 1884-86; Professor of Mathematics, Lombard College, 1892—.

---

*In honor of the late I. D. Williamson, D. D., of Cincinnati.
· †In honor of the late E. G. Hall, of Chicago.
‡In honor of the late L. E. Conger, of Dexter, Iowa.

FRANK HAMILTON FOWLER, PH. D.,

Professor of English Literature and Rhetoric.

A. B., Lombard University, 1890; Ph. D., The University of Chicago, 1896; Graduate Student, Johns Hopkins University, 1890-91; Principal Peaster Academy, 1891-92; Fellow in the University of Chicago, 1892-96; Professor of English, Lombard College, 1897—.

RALPH GRIERSON KIMBLE,

Professor of Sociology.

A. B., Lombard University, 1896; University Scholar University of Chicago, 1896-97, Fellow, ibid, 1897-1900; Professor of Sociology, Lombard College, 1900—.

THADDEUS CAREY KIMBLE, M. D.,

Instructor in Biology.

M. D. St. Louis College of Physicians and Surgeons, 1898 ; Supt. A., T. & S. F. R. R. Hospital, Ottawa, Ks., 1898-99; Instructor in Biology, Lombard College, 1900—.

CHARLES E. VARNEY,

Instructor in Biblical History and Archæology.

B. D., Lombard University, 1893; Instructor in Biblical History and Archæology, Lombard College, 1901—.

KARL JAKOB RUDOLPH LUNDBERG,

Director of Music Department and Instructor in Voice, Piano, Organ, and Theory.

Graduate Royal Musical Academy, of Stockholm, Sweden, in voice, piano, organ and theory, 1892; Studied voice with Prof. Ivar Hallstrom, 1893; organist and choir-master in Lindesberg, Sweden, 1894-97; Musical Director Burlington Institute College, Burlington, Iowa, 1897-99; Director Music Department, Lombard College, 1899—.

EMMA B. WAIT,

Professor of French and German.

Principal of School, Los Angeles, Cal., 1881-83: Student, École Sévigné, Sévres, 1891, Université de Généve, 1896-98, The University of Chicago, 1899: Professor of French and German, Lombard College, 1899—.

M. AGNES HATHAWAY.

Dean of Women and Instructor in Preparatory Courses.

Graduate from Genesee Wesleyan Seminary, Lima. New York, 1888; student at National Normal University, Lebanon, Ohio, 1895-96; Teacher in Public Schools of New York and Illinois; Dean of Women and Instructor in Preparatory School, Lombard College, 1900—.

AMANDA KIDDER,

Instructor in Elocution and Physical Culture.

Graduate from the Detroit Training School of Elocution and English Literature, 1890; Post-Graduate course, ibid, 1897; Darling College, Minn., 1891; Academy of Our Lady of Lourdes, 1892-94; Private Studio, LaCrosse, Wis., 1895-1900; Instructor in Elocution and Physical Culture, Lombard College, 1900—.

M. ISABELLE BLOOD,

Instructor in Drawing and Painting.

Studied with Dean Fletcher, N. Y.; William Bertram, Chicago; at the Art Institute and with Nellie Davis, St. Louis; Instructor in Drawing and Painting, Lombard College, 1889—

W. H. CHEESMAN,
Instructor in Violin.

EDNA UHLER,
Instructor in Piano.

ALICE HELEN BARTLETT, A. B.,
Instructor in Pipe Organ and Harmony.

ADA M. H. HALE,
Matron Ladies' Hall.

DR. GUY A. LONGBRAKE AND DR. DELIA M. RICE,
Medical Examiners.

NON-RESIDENT LECTURERS.

MARION D. SHUTTER, D. D.
REV. FRANK H. YORK.
REV. C. A. VINCENT, D. D.

FRANK HAMILTON FOWLER, PH.-D.,
Librarian.

CHARLES A. SANDBURG,
Librarian's Assistant.

JON WATSON GRUBB, M. S.,
Registrar,

FREDERICK WILLIAM RICH, D. Sc.,
Curator of the Museum.

PHILIP G. WRIGHT, A. M.,
Director of the Gymnasium.

ALLEN HARSHBARGER,
Janitor.

Standing Faculty Committees.

ADVISORY—
PROFESSORS WRIGHT AND FOWLER.

CREDITS—
PROFESSORS PARKER AND RICH.

HOMES FOR NEW STUDENTS—
PROFESSORS FOWLER AND KIMBLE.

CATALOGUE—
PROFESSORS WRIGHT AND FOWLER.

HIGHER DEGREES—
PRESIDENT NASH AND PROFESSOR PARKER.

LIBRARY—
PROFESSORS WHITE AND KIMBLE.

CHAPEL EXCUSES—
PROFESSORS KIMBLE AND FOWLER.

CHAPEL EXERCISES—
PRES. NASH, PROFS. WAIT AND LUNDBERG.

ATHLETICS—
PROFESSORS WRIGHT AND KIDDER.

ORDER AND DISCIPLINE—
PRES. NASH, PROF. RICH AND MISS HATHAWAY.

DEPARTMENTS OF THE COLLEGE.

Students at Lombard are divided primarily into Classified and Unclassified Students.

The Classified department includes all students who are candidates for a degree or diploma. It embraces the College of Liberal Arts, the Divinity School, and the schools of Music and Art.

The Unclassified department includes students who are pursuing studies at Lombard for a greater or less period without any express intention of obtaining a degree or diploma.

COLLEGE OF LIBERAL ARTS.

Faculty of Liberal Arts.

CHARLES ELLWOOD NASH, A. M., S. T. D., PRESIDENT.

ISAAC AUGUSTUS PARKER, A. M., PH. D.,
*Williamson Professor of the Greek Language and Literature.

NEHEMIAH WHITE, A. M., PH. D., S. T. D.,
†Hall Professor of Intellectual and Moral Philosophy.

JON WATSON GRUBB, M. S.,
Instructor in Latin.

FREDERICK WILLIAM RICH, D. Sc.,
‡Conger Professor of Chemistry and Physics.

PHILIP GREEN WRIGHT, A. M.,
Professor of Mathematics, Astronomy and Economics.

*In honor of the late I. D. Williamson, D. D., of Cincinnati.
†In honor of the late E. G. Hall, of Chicago,
‡In honor of the late L. E. Conger, of Dexter, Iowa.

FRANK HAMILTON FOWLER, Ph. D.,
Professor of English Literature and Rhetoric.

RALPH GRIERSON KIMBLE,
Professor of Sociology.

EMMA B. WAIT,
Professor of French and German.

THADDEUS CAREY KIMBLE. M. D.,
Instructor in Biology.

KARL JAKOB RUDOLPH LUNDBERG,
Professor of Musical Theory.

AMANDA KIDDER,
Instructor in Elocution and Physical Culture.

Degrees Conferred in 1901.

DOCTOR OF DIVINITY.

John Sharp Cook........... .... *Galesburg.*

DOCTOR OF LAWS.

Edwin Hurd Conger.........:... ... .*Pekin, China..*

MASTER OF ARTS.

Martha Belle Arnold.... · .. .. · ....*Galesburg.*
Carrie Ruth Nash..... .... *Galesburg.*

BACHELOR OF ARTS.

John Donington Bartlett. .... · ... .*Galesburg.*
Nannie Mer Buck...... .... *Le Roy.*
Gertrude West Hartgrove . ...*Galesburg.*
Julia Evelyn Lombard.... ....*East Orange, N. J.*
Jennie Eliza Marriott. ... .*La Moille.*
Donald P. McAlpine........ . ...*Charlotte, Mich.*
William J. Orton... ....*Mt. Pleasant, Ia.*
Grace Olive Pingrey ....*Coon Rapids, Ia.*
Frederick Preston ....*Boston, Mass.*
Grace Schnur................. .... · .. ..*Adams.*

Requirements for Admission.

Beginning with the fall term, 1902, all applicants for admission to the College of Liberal Arts, except those from certain approved High Schools and Academies, will be required to pass satisfactory examinations in studies selected from the following list, to an aggregate of sixteen units. The English examination will be required of all applicants without exception:

STUDY.	UNITS.	STUDY.	UNITS.
English	3	Physics	1
Greek	3	Chemistry	1
Latin	3	Physiography	½ to 1
German	1	Physiology	½ to 1
French	1	Botany	½ to 1
Ancient History	1	Astronomy	1
English and American History	1	Meteorology	1
Algebra	1½	Political Economy	½ to 1
Plane Geometry	½ to 1	Zoölogy	½ to 1
Solid Geometry	½ to 1		

CONSTANTS.

The studies presented must include the following constants:

STUDIES.	UNITS.
English	3
One Foreign Language	3
History	1
Algebra	1½
Geometry	½
Science	2
	11

The two units in Science, one of which must include laboratory work, may be chosen from the following, viz: Physics, Chemistry, Physiography, Anatomy and Physiology, Botany, Zoölogy.

EXAMINATIONS.

Examinations in the above studies will be held during the first week in September, as follows:

HOUR.	TUESDAY SEPT. 2.	WEDNESDAY, SEPT. 3.	THURSDAY, SEPT. 4.
7:30- 9:30	English.	French.	Plane Geometry.
9:30-11:30	Greek—Astronomy.	Ancient History.	Physics.
11:30-12:30	Physiology.	Physiography.	Botany.
2:00- 4:00	Latin.	Algebra.	Chemistry.
4:00- 6:00	German—Solid Geom.	Eng. and Am. Hist.	Zoölogy—Pol. Econ.

ADMISSION BY CERTIFICATE.

In harmony with the recommendation of the joint committee of the High School and College sections of the Illinois State Teachers' Association, certificates from the principals or other authorized officers of certain approved High Schools and Academies will be accepted in lieu of Examinations; except that in English an examination will be required of all students. *But these certificates must be presented during the examination week in order to be accepted,* and no certificate will be valid for more than two years after the completion of the course of study to which the certificate refers. The credit allowed on them will be based upon the work accomplished; in general, one unit being equal to a year's work in a study reciting five hours a week in recitation periods of not less than forty minutes.

The detailed descriptions given below indicate more fully the amount of work required in each study to obtain the number of units given in the table. Students admitted by certificate enter classes on probation, and if, after a week's trial, it is found that their previous training is insufficient to render it advisable for them to continue in these classes, they will be assigned other work.

SCOPE OF PREPARATORY STUDIES.

The amount of work required in the several Preparatory studies to obtain the units assigned in the foregoing table, either by examination or certificate, is indicated by the following outline of examination requirements:

ENGLISH.

The examination will occupy two hours and will consist of two parts, which, however, cannot be taken separately:—

I. The candidate will be required to write a paragraph or two on each of several topics chosen by him from a considerable number—perhaps ten or fifteen—set before him on the examination paper. In 1902 the topics will be drawn from the following works:—

Shakespeare's Merchant of Venice; Pope's Iliad, Books I, VI, XXII, and XXIV; The Sir Roger de Coverley Papers in the Spectator; Goldsmith's Vicar of Wakefield; Coleridge's Ancient Mariner; Scott's Ivanhoe; Cooper's Last of the Mohicans; Tennyson's Princess; Lowell's Vision of Sir Launfal; George Eliot's Silas Marner.

In 1903, 1904, and 1905, the topics will be drawn from the following works —:

Shakespeare's Merchant of Venice, and Julius Caesar; The Sir Roger de Coverley Papers in the Spectator; Goldsmith's Vicar of Wakefield; Coleridge's Ancient Mariner; Scott's Ivanhoe; Carlyle's

Essay on Burns; Tennyson's Princess; Lowell's Vision of Sir Launfal; George Eliot's Silas Marner.

The candidate is expected to read intelligently *all* the books prescribed. He should read them as he reads other books; he is expected, not to know them minutely, but to have freshly in mind their most important parts. In every case the examiner will regard knowledge of the book as less important than ability to write English.

II.   A certain number of books are prescribed for careful study. This part of the examination will be upon subject-matter, literary form, and logical structure, and will also test the candidate's ability to express his knowledge with clearness and accuracy.

The books prescribed for this part of the examination are:—

In 1902:   Shakespeare's Macbeth; Milton's Lycidas, Comus, L'Allegro, and Il Penseroso; Burke's Speech on Conciliation with America; Macaulay's Essays on Milton and Addison.

No candidate will be accepted in English whose work is seriously defective in point of spelling, punctuation, grammar, or division into paragraphs.

In connection with the reading and study of the prescribed books, parallel or subsidiary reading should be encouraged, and a considerable amount of English poetry should be committed to memory.   The essentials of English grammar should not be neglected in preparatory study.

The English written by a candidate in any of his examination-books may be regarded as part of his examination in English, in case the evidence afforded by the examination-book in English is insufficient.

As additional evidence of preparation the candidate may present an exercise book, properly certified by his instructor, containing compositions or other written work.

FRENCH.

(*a*) The translation at sight of ordinary Nineteenth Century prose. (The passages set for translation must be rendered into simple and idiomatic English.)

(*b*) The translation into French of simple English sentences or of easy connected prose, to test the candidate's familiarity with elementary grammar.   Proficiency in grammar may also be tested by direct questions, based on the passages set for translation under (*a*).

The passages set for translation into English will be suited to the proficiency of candidates who have read not less than four hundred pages (including reading at sight in class) from the works of at least three different authors.   It is desirable that a portion of the reading should be from works other than works of fiction.

Grammar should be studied concurrently with the reading as an indispensable means of ensuring thoroughness and accuracy in the understanding of the language. The requirement in elementary grammar includes the conjugations of regular verbs, of the more frequent irregular verbs, such as *aller, envoyer, tenir, pouvoir, voir, vouloir, dire, savoir, faire,* and those belonging to the classes represented by *ouvrir, dormir, connaître, conduire,* and *craindre;* the forms and positions of personal pronouns and of possessive, demonstrative, and interrogative adjectives; the inflection of nouns and adjectives for gender and number, except rare cases; the uses of articles, and the partitive constructions.

Pronunciation should be carefully taught, and pupils should have frequent opportunities to hear French spoken or read aloud. The writing of French from dictation is recommended as a useful exercise.

GERMAN.

(*a*) The translation at sight of simple German prose. (The passages set for translation must be rendered into simple and idiomatic English.)

(*b*) The translation into German of simple English sentences, or of easy connected prose, to test the candidate's familiarity with elementary grammar.

The passages set for translation into English will be suited to the proficiency of candidates who have read not less than two hundred pages of easy German (including reading at sight in class.)

Grammar should be studied concurrently with the reading as an indispensable means of ensuring thoroughness and accuracy in the understanding of the language. The requirement in elementary grammar includes the conjugation of the weak and the more usual strong verbs; the declension of articles, adjectives, pronouns, and such nouns as are readily classified; the commoner prepositions; the simpler uses of the modal auxiliaries; the elements of syntax, especially the rules governing the order of words.

Pronunciation should be carefully taught, and the pupils should have frequent opportunities to hear German spoken or read aloud. The writing of German from dictation is recommended as a useful exercise.

LATIN.

The examination in Latin for admission to the Collegiate Department will be calculated to test the proficiency of students who have pursued a Latin course of five lessons a week for three years.

The translation at sight of simple Latin prose will be required.

Passages from Cæsar and Cicero will be assigned for translation and such questions will be asked as will test the candidate's knowledge of forms and constructions. The writing of simple Latin prose will be required.

For those who have pursued a Latin course of five lessons a week for four years, the examination will be extended so as to include a test in Vergil and additional tests in Cicero.

MATHEMATICS.

Algebra. The examination in Algebra will demand accuracy in the several processes of literal Arithmetic. Special emphasis will be laid on factoring, and the correct manipulation of negative and fractional exponents.   It will include the solution of simple and quadratic equations (together with a knowledge of the theory of quadratic equations) and elimination in the case of simultaneous equations of the first and second degrees.

Plane Geometry.   The examination in Plane Geometry will emphasize precision in the definition of Geometric terms, and accuracy in the demonstration of Geometric theorems.   In scope it will demand a knowledge of all the propositions in Plane Geometry preceding solid Geometry, included in such a standard text book in this subject as Phillips and Fisher's Elements.

Solid Geometry.   As in Plane Geometry emphasis will be laid upon accuracy in definition and demonstration.   In scope the examination will cover the propositions in Solid Geometry included in such a standard text book as Phillips and Fisher's Elements.

ASTRONOMY.

The examination in this subject will demand knowledge of descriptive rather than mathematical Astronomy.   The student will be expected to understand the theory of the celestial sphere, simple methods of computing latitude, time, and longitude, the astronomical features of the earth, the sun, and the moon, the principles of spectrum analysis, the motions and characteristics of the planets, the names and myths of the principal stars and constellations, the facts in regard to aberration, parallax, and proper motion of the stars, and the principles of a rational cosmogony as developed in La Place's nebular hypothesis.   Young's Lessons in Astronomy is suggested as a text book embracing the matter with which students are expected to be acquainted who wish to prepare for this examination.

PHYSICS.

Students offering physics for entrance credit must show an acquaintance with the more important phenomena and with the principles involved in the explanation of them.   They must, in addition to the text book work, have completed a course of laboratory experiments and be able to work simple numerical problems, involving the laws of falling bodies; pendulum; properties of liquids and gases; thermometry and calorimetry; current strength, resistance, and electromotive force; properties of sound; refraction and reflection with the size and position of images.

CHEMISTRY.

The Elementary Course in Chemistry offered for entrance credit must include a knowledge of the elements and compounds equivalent to that given in Remsen's Introduction to the study of Chemistry. In addition, students must have had a series of laboratory experiments illustrating the text book work and be able to write equations and solve problems in the calculation of gas volumes and in Stoichiometry.

BOTANY.

Students presenting work in Botany for entrance credit should have a knowledge of the general laws and fundamental principles of plant nutrition, assimilation, growth, etc., as exemplified by plants chosen from the different groups, as well as the general comparative morphology and the broader relationships of plants. He should present an herbarium of at least twenty-five specimens, collected and mounted by himself, and certified to by his instructor.

ZOOLOGY.

Students desiring entrance credit for Zoology should have devoted the equivalent of five periods a week for at least one-half year to the study of general Zoology. A portion of this work must have been laboratory practice in the observation of living forms and dissection. His laboratory notes and drawings, endorsed by the instructor, should be presented at the time of registration as evidence of the nature of this part of the work. This laboratory practice should include a study of at least twelve of the forms named in the following list: Amœba, paramœcium, sea-anemone, star-fish, sea-urchin, earth-worm, cray-fish, lobster, spider, centipede, locust (grasshopper), dragon-fly, squash-bug, bumblebee, clam, snail, a simple tunicate, shark, any soft rayed-fish, snake, turtle, frog, pigeon, rabbit, and cat.

PHYSIOLOGY.

Students presenting work in human Physiology for entrance credit should have a general knowledge of the human skeleton, muscular, circulatory, and nervous systems, the vital organs, viscera, and organs of special sense, and the processes of respiration and digestion.

The text-book used should cover the ground treated in such books as Martin's Human Body (briefer course), or Huxley's Elementary Physiology (Lee's Revision).

PHYSIOGRAPHY.

A course of study equivalent to Tarr's Elementary Physical Geography.

The examination will include a thorough test on all the leading subjects treated in Physical Geography, with maps to illustrate relief forms, currents, ocean beds, and the distribution of animal and plant life.

HISTORY (including Historical Geography).

Either of the two following groups, each including two fields of historical study:—

1. *Greek and Roman History.*—(*a*) Greek History to the death of Alexander, with due reference to Greek life, literature, and art. (*b*) Roman History to the downfall of the Western Roman Empire, with due reference to literature and government.

2. *English and American History.*—(*a*) English History, with due reference to social and political development. (*b*) American History, with the elements of Civil Government.

For preparation in each of the two historical fields presented, a course of study equivalent to at least three lessons a week for one year will be necessary.

The candidate will be expected to show on examination such general knowledge of each field as may be acquired from the study of an accurate text-book of not less than 300 pages, supplemented by suitable parallel readings amounting to not less than 500 pages. The examination will call for comparison of historical characters, periods, and events, and in general for the exercise of judgment as well as of memory. Geographical knowledge will be tested by means of an outline map.

It is desirable that Greek and Roman History be offered as a part of the preparation of every candidate.

POLITICAL ECONOMY.

The examination in Political Economy will demand a thorough knowledge of the fundamental economic laws relating to Production, Exchange, Distribution, and Consumption. The applicant will also be expected to discuss intelligently from an economic standpoint such questions as Free Trade, Socialism, Strikes, and Taxation. Bullock's Introduction to the Study of Economics is suggested as a text covering the ground required for the examination.

ADMISSION TO ADVANCED STANDING.

Students from other institutions, who present letters of honorable dismissal, may be admitted to such standing and upon such terms as the Faculty may deem equitable. Every such student is required to present, along with the catalogue of the institution in which he has studied, a full statement, duly certified, of the studies he has completed, including preparatory studies. Candidates for advanced standing who wish to receive credit for work accomplished in private study, are permitted to take examinations in such subjects upon payment of the regular term fee for the course in which the examination is taken. A minimum residence of the two terms next preceeding the completion of the requirements for graduation, and a minimum of eight courses taken in this College, are required of all applicants for a baccalaureate degree.

Requirements for Graduation.

GROUP SYSTEM.

Having been admitted to the College of Liberal Arts, the student will elect one of the following groups as a course of study leading to his degree. These groups consist of certain required studies arranged logically with reference to some central subject, in addition to which considerable option is allowed in the way of free electives. All the required studies, together with a sufficient number of electives to bring the total up to an aggregate of thirty-eight credits, must be completed before the degree will be conferred. A credit is obtained by the satisfactory completion of one full course pursued for one term. Of the thirty-eight credits at least twenty-four must be above grade C. Two credits may be obtained by two full year's work in the Gymnasium classes.

THESIS.

In addition to the above requirements, every student who is a candidate for a degree, or a diploma, will present a graduation thesis upon some subject in which he, or she, has prosecuted original research or special study.

The subject selected for treatment must be approved by the President within four weeks after the opening of the Fall term.

A syllabus of the thesis must be handed to the President at least six weeks before the close of the Winter term.

The completed thesis is limited to fifteen hundred words, and must be handed in for criticism at least ten weeks before Commencement.

In lieu of a thesis, original work, performed under the direction of some member of the Faculty, may be accepted.

Degrees will be conferred only on the annual Commencement Day.

CORRESPONDENCE COURSES.

Certain courses may be taken *in absentia* by correspondence. Of the total number of courses required for the bachelor's degree, not more than one-fourth may be so taken. Full particulars will be given upon application to the President.

ADVANCED DEGREE.

The Master's degree will be conferred upon graduates of this College, or of other institutions of equal rank, on the satisfactory completion of ten courses, pursued in actual study at this College, beyond the requirements for the baccalaureate degree. The candidate must present a thesis showing original research in the special line of study pursued.

GROUPS.

On being admitted to the College of Liberal Arts, each student, who is a candidate for a degree, will elect one of these groups:

ENGLISH.

STUDY.	CREDITS.	STUDY.	CREDITS.
English	9	History	2
Foreign Language	9[1]	Science	2[2]
Mathematics	3	Psychology	1
English (5 and 6)	2	Sociology	1
Elocution	1		

MODERN LANGUAGES.

German	9[3]	History	2
French	9[3]	Science	2[2]
Mathematics	3	Psychology	1
English (5 and 6)	2	Sociology	1
Elocution	1		

CLASSICS.[3]

Latin	7	History	2
Greek	12[4]	Science	2[2]
German or French	6[4]	Psychology	1
English	2	Sociology	1
Elocution	1		

LATIN SCIENTIFIC.

Latin	7	English	
Chemistry	6	Elocution	1
Physics	3	History	
Biology	3	Psychology	1
German or French	6[4]	Sociology	1

MATHEMATICS.

Mathematics and Astronomy	12	History	2
Physics	3	Psychology	1
Chemistry	3	Sociology	1
English	2	Elocution	1
Modern Language	6		

SOCIAL SCIENCE.

Sociology	10	Mathematics	5
Biology	3	Modern Language	4
Economics	1	Chemistry	2
Psychology	2	Physics	2
English	2		

BIOLOGY AND CHEMISTRY.

STUDY.	CREDITS.	STUDY.	CREDITS
Chemistry	6	Psychology	1
Biology	12	Geology	1
Mathematics	3	German	6[4]
English	3		

PREPARATORY MEDICAL.

Chemistry	3	German	6[4]
Biology	9	Latin	3[5]
Mathematics	5	Psychology	2
English	3		

CHEMISTRY AND PHYSICS.

Physics	3	Mathematics	3
Chemistry	8	English	3
Geology	1	Psychology	1
Biology	3	Astronomy	1
German or French	6[4]		

1. Of these, at least six must be in a modern language.

2. If a Biological Science is offered for entrance, Physics or Chemistry must be chosen. If Physics or Chemistry is offered a Biological science must be chosen.

3. Students choosing this group must offer at least four units in Ancient Languages for admission.

4. By offering German or French for admission the prescribed courses in several groups may be reduced and the number of free electives correspondingly increased. The same is true of Greek in the Classics group.

5. Unless entrance Latin is presented.

Courses of Instruction.

RECITATIONS AND CREDITS.

The following studies are classed as full courses or fractional courses, according to the estimated amount of work in each, and its value in fulfilling the requirements for graduation. Unless otherwise stated, a course in any study consists of five hours of recitations or lectures, per week, for one term. Certain courses, however, are given in three hours per week recitations. Laboratory courses require ten hours of work per week in the Laboratory, in addition to a considerable amount of study outside. Certain other studies, as indicated in each case, count only as half courses, or less.

ENGLISH.

For courses 2 to 4 inclusive, see page 54.

5. Rhetoric and Composition.

A general introduction to the principles of Rhetoric and their application. Frequent exercises and fortnightly themes will be required. Fall term.   Professor FOWLER.

Open to all college students.

6. The Forms of Discourse.

Baldwin's Specimens of Prose Description and Baker's Specimens of Argumentation will be used as texts. Fortnightly themes will be required. Tuesday, Wednesday, Thursday and Friday. Winter term.   Professor FOWLER.

Prerequisite, English 5.

7. The Forms of Discourse. (Continued.)

Brewster's Specimens of Narration and Lamont's Specimens of Exposition will be used as texts. Fortnightly themes will be required. Tuesday, Wednesday, Thursday and Friday. Spring Term.   Professor FOWLER.

Prerequisite, English 5.

8. Daily Themes. (Half Course.)

The object of this course is the attainment of rapidity and skill in composition. Each student will be required to hand in a short theme daily for one term. Class meets for conference and criticism every Friday. Winter term.   Professor WRIGHT.

Prerequisite, English 5.

9. English Lyric Poetry.

Wordsworth, Tennyson, Browning. Fall term.
                              Professor FOWLER.
Prerequisite, English 5.

English 9 will not be given in 1902.

10. English Prose.

A study of English prose writers. Fall term.
                              Professor FOWLER.
Prerequisite, English 5.

English 10 will not be given in 1902.

11. Old English.

An introduction to the older language. The relations between Old and Modern English will be studied. Winter term.

Professor FOWLER.

Prerequisite, English 5.

English 11 will not be given in 1902–03.

12. History of the English Language.

Lectures and text-book recitations. Winter term.

Professor FOWLER.

Prerequisite, English 5.

English 12 will not be given in 1902–03.

13. The English Drama.

Shakespeare will form the center of the work. Two or three plays will be studied critically and the class will read a number of plays by different authors. Spring term.

Professor FOWLER.

Prerequisite, English 5.

English 13 will not be given in 1903.

14. Epic Poetry.

Milton. Spring term. Professor FOWLER.

Prerequisite, English 5.

English 14 will not be given in 1903.

15. American Literature.

A general survey of the history of literature in the United States with a more careful study of a few representative authors. Fall term. Professor FOWLER.

Prerequisite, English 5.

16. Epochs in the History of English Literature.

Winter term. Professor FOWLER.

Prerequisite, English 5.

17. English Novelists.

Spring term. Professor FOWLER.

Prerequisite, English 5.

18. Oratory.

The preparation and delivery of five original orations. Fall term. Professor FOWLER.

Miss KIDDER.

Prerequisite, English 5.

FRENCH.

1. How to Think in French.

Petites Causeries. Conversation. Elementary Grammar. Fall
term.   Miss WAIT.

Open to all students.

2. Foundations of French.

Petites Causeries.   Memorizing. Conversation. Winter term.
                                         Miss WAIT.

Prerequisite, French 1.

3. Foundations of French.

Kuhn's French Readings.   Sight reading.   Conversation.
Spring term.   Miss WAIT.

Prerequisite, French 2.

4. Grammar, Conversation, and Reading.

Edgren's Grammar. François' Composition.   George Sand's
La Mare au Diable. Fall term.   Miss WAIT.

Prerequisite, French 3.

French 4 will not be given in 1902.

5. Grammar, Conversation, and Reading.

Edgren's Grammar. François' Composition. Corneille's Le
Cid. Dumas' La Tulipe Noire. Fall term.   Miss WAIT.

Prerequisite, French 3.

6. Grammar, Conversation, and Reading.

L'Avare, Colomba. Sight Reading. Winter term.
                                         Miss WAIT.

Prerequisite, French 4.

French 6 will not be given in 1902-03.

7. Grammar, Conversation, and Reading.

Le Verre d' Eau. Sept Auteurs Français. Winter term.
                                         Miss WAIT.

Prerequisite, French 5.

8. Grammar, Conversation, and Reading.

Pêcheurs d' Islande.   Gazier's Histoire de La Littérature
Française. Spring term.   Miss WAIT.

Prerequisite, French 6.

French 8 will not be given in 1903.

9. Grammar, Conversation, and Reading.

Study of authors of the 17th and 19th centuries. Reading, Balzac, Hugo, Thiers. Spring term. Miss WAIT.

Prerequisite, French 7.

10, 11, 12. Scientific French. [Half Courses].

Reading of Scientific French, especially for the benefit of students in courses using French text and reference books. Class meets one hour per week. Fall, winter and spring terms, each term counting as a half credit. Miss WAIT.

Prerequisite, French 3.

Grammar, Composition, Sight Reading and Conversation constitute an important part of 4 to 9 inclusive.

GERMAN.

1. Elementary German.

Das Deutsche Buch. Elementary Grammar. Conversation. Fall term. Miss WAIT.

Open to all students.

2. Elementary German.

Das Deutsche Buch. Grammar. Conversation. Sight Reading. Committing to Memory. Winter term. Miss WAIT.

Prerequisite, German 1.

3. Grammar and Reading.

Collars's Eysenbach's Grammar. Immensee. Sight Reading. Conversation. Memorizing. Spring term. Miss WAIT.

Prerequisite, German 2.

4. Grammar, Conversation, and Reading.

Collar's Eysenbach's Grammar. Stein's Exercises for Translation. Schrakamp's German Conversation Grammar. L'Arrabbiata. Sight Reading. Fall term. Miss WAIT.

Prerequisite, German 3.

German 4 will not be given in 1902.

5. Grammar, Conversation, and Reading.

Maria Stuart, Götz von Berlichingen. Fall term.

Miss WAIT.

Prerequisite, German 3.

6. Grammar, Conversation, and Reading.

Hermann und Dorothea. Meereskunde. Winter term.

Miss WAIT.

Prerequisite, German 4.

German 6 will not be given in 1902-'03.

7. Grammar, Conversation, and Reading.

Nathan der Weise, Freytag's Bilder aus der deutschen Vergan-genheit. Winter term. Miss WAIT.

Prerequisite, German 5.

8. Grammar, Conversation, and Reading.

Meereskunde. Bötticher's German Literature. Spring term.

Miss WAIT.

Prerequisite, German 6.

German 8 will not be given in 1903.

9. Grammar, Conversation, and Reading.

German Classics. Spring term. Miss WAIT.

Prerequisite, German 7.

10, 11, 12. Scientific German. [Half Courses,].

Readings from Scientific German, especially for the benefit of students in courses using German text and reference books. Class meets one hour per week. Fall, winter, and spring terms, each term counting as a half credit. Miss WAIT.

Prerequisite, German, 3.

Grammar, Composition, Sight Reading, and Conversation constitute an important part of courses 4 to 9 inclusive.

LATIN.

1. Latin Lessons.

Tuell and Fowler's First Book in Latin. Fall term.

Professor GRUBB.

Open to all students.

2. Latin Lessons. (Continued). Winter term.

Professor GRUBB.

Prerequisite, Latin 1.

3. Viri Romae.

Texts, Rolfe and Dennison's Junior Latin-Book and Daniell's Latin Prose Composition. Spring term. Professor GRUBB.

Prerequisite, Latin 2.

4. Caesar.

Texts, Rolfe and Dennison's Junior Latin Book and Daniell's Latin Prose Composition. Fall term. Professor GRUBB.

Prerequisite, Latin 3.

5. Caesar. (Continued.)

Winter term Professor GRUBB.

Prerequisite, Latin 4.

6. Cicero.

Kelsey's Cicero's Orations and Daniell's Latin Prose Composition. Spring term. Professor GRUBB.

Prerequisite, Latin 5.

7. Cicero. (Continued.)

Fall term. Professor PARKER.

Prerequisite, Latin 6.

8. Vergil.

Greenough's Vergil's Aeneid. Winter term.

Professor PARKER.

Prerequisite, Latin 7.

9. Vergil. (Continued.)

Spring term. Professor PARKER.

Prerequisite, Latin 8.

10. Horace (Satires and Epistles), or Ovid.

Fall term. Professor PARKER.

Prerequisite, Latin 9.

*11. Horace, Odes and Epodes.

Chase and Stuart's edition. Fall term.

Professor PARKER.

Prerequisite, Latin 9.

*12. Livy, First Book.

Westcott's edition. Fall term. Professor PARKER.

Prerequisite, Latin 9.

---

*Latin 10, 13, 16, will be given in 1902-3; Latin 11, 14, 17, in 1903-4; Latin 12, 15, 18, in 1904-5.

13. Cicero's DeSenectute and De Amicitia.

Kelsey's Edition.   Winter term.   Professor PARKER.

Prerequisite, Latin 9.

*14. Curtius Rufus's Life of Alexander.

Crosby's Edition.   Winter term.   Professor PARKER.

Prerequisite, Latin 9.

*15. Livy, Twenty-first Book.

Winter term.   Professor PARKER.

Prerequisite, Latin 9.

16. Tacitus's Germania and Agricola.

Hopkins's Edition.   Spring term.   Professor PARKER.

Prerequisite, Latin 9.

*17. Juvenal.

Anthon's Edition.   Spring term.   Professor PARKER.

Prerequisite, Latin 9.

*18. Plautus.

Spring term.   Professor PARKER.

Prerequisite, Latin 9.

Latin Composition may be given in connection with Latin 10 to 18 inclusive.

BOOKS OF REFERENCE.

The following books are recommended for reference to students pursuing the study of Latin:

Harper's Latin Lexicon; White's Junior Student's Latin Lexicon; Doederlein's Latin Synonyms; Liddell's History of Rome; Long's, or Ginn & Co.'s Classical Atlas; Anthon's or Smith's Classical Dictionary; Harper's Dictionary of Classical Literature and Antiquities; Harkness's and Bennett's Latin Grammar.

GREEK.

1. Grammar and Lessons.

Boise and Pattengill's Greek Lessons. Goodwin's Greek Grammar.   Fall term.   Professor PARKER.

Open to all students in the college.

---

*Latin 10, 13, 16, will be given in 1902-3; Latin 11, 14, 17, in 1903-4; Latin 12, 15, 18, in 1904-5.

2. Grammar and Lessons. (Continued.)

Winter term. Professor PARKER.

Prerequisite, Greek 1.

3. Anabasis.

Goodwin's Xenophon's Anabasis. Collar and Daniell's Greek Composition. Spring term. Professor PARKER.

Prerequisite, Greek 2.

4. Anabasis. (Continued.)

Collar and Daniéll's Greek Composition. Fall term.

Professor PARKER.

Prerequisite, Greek 3.

5. Orations of Lysias.

Stevens' Edition. Winter term. Professor PARKER.

Prerequisite, Greek 4.

6. Iliad.

Keep's Homer's Iliad. Spring term.

Professor PARKER.

Prerequisite, Greek 5.

7. Odyssey.

Merry's Homer's Odyssey. Fall term.

Professor PARKER.

Prerequisite, Greek 6.

8. Plato's Apology of Socrates.

Dyer's Edition. Winter term of 1902–03 and the Winter term of every alternate year thereafter. Professor PARKER.

Prerequisite, Greek 5.

9. Plato's Gorgias.

Lodge's Edition. Winter term of 1903-04 and the Winter term of every alternate year thereafter. Professor PARKER.

Prerequisite, Greek 5.

10. Herodotus.

Fernald's Selections. Spring term of 1902 and the Spring term of every alternate year thereafter. Professor PARKER.

Prerequisite, Greek 8 or 9.

11. Prometheus of Aeschylus, or Medea of Euripides.

Wecklein's Prometheus, Allen's Medea. Spring term of 1903, and the Spring term of every alternate year thereafter.

Professor PARKER.

Prerequisite, Greek 8 or 9.

12, 13, 14, 15. Greek New Testament.

These classes, while primarily intended for theological students, are open also to College students who have the requisite preparation. A full description is given in the Divinity School courses.

BOOKS OF REFERENCE.

The following books are recommended for reference to those pursuing the study of Greek:

Liddell and Scott's Greek Lexicon; Autenrieth's Homeric Dictionary; Long's, or Ginn & Co.'s Classical Atlas; Anthon's, or Smith's Classical Dictionary; Harper's Dictionary of Classical Literature and Antiquities; Smith's History of Greece; Goodwin's Greek Grammar; Goodwin's Greek Modes and Tenses.

HEBREW.

1, 2, 3. Grammar and Old Testament.

These are primarily courses in the Divinity School, but may be elected by students in the College of Liberal 'Arts whenever they are offered. Classes will be formed each year if a sufficient number of students apply.

It is the aim to give the students such a knowledge of the forms and structure of the Hebrew language as shall enable him to use it efficiently in the criticism and literary analysis of the Old Testament Scriptures. The text-books used are H. G. Mitchell's Hebrew Lessons and the Hebrew Old Testament. Three terms—Fall, Winter and Spring—each term counting as a course.

Professor WHITE.

Open (under conditions as described above) to students who, in the judgment of the Instructor, are qualified by previous training to take the course.

MATHEMATICS.

The primary aim of this department is to cultivate habits of precision in thought, and power of abstract reasoning. It is believed that these qualities of mind can nowhere better be acquired than in mathematical study. In addition, mathematical facts and formulæ are learned, and practice is given in the solution of practical problems.

For courses 1 to 4 inclusive, see Preparatory Courses, p. 55.

5. Algebra.

This course presupposes a thorough grounding in Elementary Algebra on the part of the student: [See Entrance Requirements in Algebra, p. 23.] After a brief review of Quadratic Equations, with especial reference to theory, the subjects of simultaneous equations of the second degree, indeterminate equations, ratio and proportion, arithmetical and geometrical progression, series, undetermined coefficients, the binomial theorem, and logarithms, will be considered. Wells's College Algebra is used. Fall term.

Professor WRIGHT.

Prerequisite, entrance Algebra or Mathematics 4.

6.(a) Plane Geometry.

This course is designed to give students thorough drill in the first principles of Geometry. Each proposition is carefully analyzed and particular attention is given to correct reasoning and precise expression. Phillips and Fisher's Elements of Geometry is used.

Mathematics 6 (a) may be taken by students who are deficient in Entrance Geometry. It will not count as one of the thirty-eight credits required for a degree. Winter term.

Professor WRIGHT.

6.(b) Plane Geometry.

This course consists of a review of Mathematics 6 (a) together with the demonstration of a large number of original propositions. Winter term.   Professor WRIGHT.

Prerequisite, Mathematics 6 (a.)

7. Solid Geometry.

This course is continuous with Mathematics 6 (a). Spring term.   Professor WRIGHT.

Prerequisite, Mathematics 6 (a.)

8. Higher Algebra.

This course assumes a thorough knowledge on the part of the student of Mathematics 5 and also some knowledge of Plane Geometry. It embraces the study of Permutations and. Combinations, Probability, Determinants, and the Theory of Equations. Fall term.   Professor WRIGHT.

Prerequisite, Mathematics 5 and Mathematics 6 (a).

9. Plane and Spherical Trigonometry.

This course includes the solution of trigonometric equations, the solution of plane and spherical triangles, and problems involving an application of Trigonometry to Mensuration, Surveying, and Astronomy. Crockett's Plane and Spherical Trigonometry is used as a text-book. Winter term.   Professor WRIGHT.

Prerequisite, Mathematics 8.

10. Analytic Geometry.

This course treats of the straight line, the conic sections, and higher plane curves. Spring term. Professor WRIGHT.

Prerequisite, Mathematics 9.

11. Surveying and Leveling.

Field work and problems. Field work on Saturdays at the option of the instructor. Spring term. Professor WRIGHT.

Prerequisite, Mathematics 9.

*12. Differential Calculus.

Osborne's Differential and Integral Calculus is used. Fall term. Professor WRIGHT.

Prerequisite, Mathematics 10.

*13. Integral Calculus.

Winter term. Professor WRIGHT.

Prerequisite, Mathematics 12.

*14. Descriptive Geometry.

This course embraces orthographic projection, shades and shadows, and perspective. Church's Descriptive Geometry is used. Fall term. Professor WRIGHT.

Prerequisite, Mathematics 9.

*15. Strength of Structures.

This course takes up the computation of the strains in bridge and roof trusses, by graphical and analytical methods. Shreve's Strength of Bridges and Roofs is used as a text book. Winter term. Professor WRIGHT.

Prerequisite, Mathematics 13.

16. Quaternions.

A class will be formed for the study of Quaternions when a sufficient number of advanced students apply. The class will meet once a week for a year at such hour as the instructor may appoint. Professor WRIGHT.

In addition to the foregoing courses, classes will be formed, when there is a sufficient demand on the part of advanced students, to pursue work in the solution of original problems in the Calculus, and in the study of infinitesimals, probability, elliptic functions, and other topics.

---

*Mathematics 14 and 15 will be given in 1902-3, but will not be given in 1903-4, alternating with Mathematics 12 and 13.

ASTRONOMY.

1. General Astronomy.

This course is largely descriptive in character, though some of the simpler mathematical problems connected with Astronomy are solved. It embraces a study of the imaginary lines into which the heavens are divided; latitude, longitude, time; the sun, moon and planets; comets, meteors, and the stars. Some attention is given to the constellations and the myths connected with them. The Nebular Hypothesis is presented and discussed. Young's Lessons in Astronomy is used. Fall term.   Professor Wright.

Prerequisite, Mathematics 8.

Astronomy 1 will not be given in 1902.

2. Mathematical Astronomy.

This course will have to do with the solution of various Astronomical problems. Computations in latitude, longitude and time; eclipses, orbits, etc., will be among the subjects considered. Three hours a week. Winter term.   Professor Wright.

Prerequisites, Mathematics 13 and Astronomy 1.

PHYSICS.

The work in Physics consist of a careful consideration of the various phenomena treated under mechanics, acoustics, heat, light, electricity, and magnetism. The student is led to note the general principles of mechanics that apply throughout, and the application of modern theories. The courses in Physics consist of recitations, lectures, with demonstrations, and laboratory work.

1. Mechanics, Hydrostatics, Pneumatics.

Text-book, Carhart's University Physics. Fall term.
                                        Professor Rich.

Prerequisite, Mathematies 9.

2. Acoustics, Optics, Heat.

Winter term. Musical students, taking the work in Acoustics, will be counted a half credit.   Professor Rich.

Prerequisite, Mathematics 9.

3. Electricity, Magnetism.

Spring term.   Professor Rich.

Prerequisite, Physics 2.

CHEMISTRY.

The aim of the course is: first, a general knowledge of chemical phenomena; second, a thorough knowledge of Theoretical Chemistry and Stoichiometry; third, a careful study of the elements and their more important compounds; fourth, methods and work in Analysis, Qualitative and Quantitative.

1. Inorganic Chemistry.

This work consists of four hours per week of recitations or lectures and two hours per week of experimental work. Remsen's College Chemistry is used as the basis of courses 1 and 2. Fall term.   Professor RICH.

Open to all students.

2. Inorganic Chemistry.

This is a continuation of Chemistry 1, and consists of four hours per week of recitations or lectures, and of two hours per week of experimental work. The course consists chiefly of Theoretical Chemistry, Stoichiometry, and a study of metals. Winter term.   Professor RICH.

Prerequisite, Chemistry 1.

3. Organic Chemistry.

This course consists of recitations, lectures, with experimental demonstrations, and laboratory work. The lectures treat chiefly of food-stuffs, their composition, adulteration, and new methods of preparation. Remsen's Organic Chemistry is used. Spring term.
                    Professor RICH.

Prerequisite, Chemistry 2.

In each of the courses 1, 2, and 3, the work is profusely illustrated by experiments, and the laboratory gives opportunity for individual work on the principles discussed.

4. Analytical Chemistry.

Laboratory work. Fall term.   Professor RICH.

Prerequisite, Chemistry 2.

5. Analytical Chemistry.

Laboratory work. Winter term.   Professor RICH.

Prerequisite, Chemistry 4.

6. Analytical Chemistry.

Laboratory work. Spring term.   Professor RICH.

Prerequisite, Chemistry 5.

Chemistry 4, 5, and 6, form progressive courses in Qualitative and Quantitative Analysis. General Qualitative and Quantitative methods are studied, and analysis is made of such compounds as ores, soils, fertilizers, milk, butter, water, soaps, gas, drugs, etc.

For the present, no student is allowed to register for more than fifteen hours per week in laboratory courses.

GEOLOGY AND MINERALOGY.

1. Geology.

The work in Geology is given by text-book recitations, supplemented by lectures and excursions for field work. The College has a valuable collection of minerals, which serves for purposes of illustration and study. Dana's work is used. Spring term.

Professor RICH.

Prerequisite, Chemistry 1, Biology 3 and Biology 4.

2. Mineralogy.

This course consists of a qualitative determination of minerals by means of the blow pipe. Winter term. Professor RICH.

Prerequisite, Chemistry 2.

BIOLOGY.

1. General Biology.

This course will furnish a sketch of the history of the science of Biology and discuss the aims and methods of biological research, composition of living substance, and the elementary vital phenomena. Recitations and laboratory work. Fall term.

Dr. KIMBLE.

Prerequisite, entrance Physics or Chemistry, and Botany.

2. General Biology. (Continuation of Course 1.)

A study of the general conditions of life, of stimuli, and their actions, and of the mechanism of life. Winter term.

Dr. KIMBLE.

Prerequisite, Biology 1.

*3. Elementary Physiology.

This course is intended for students desiring a general knowledge of human physiology. Fall term. Dr. KIMBLE.

Prerequisites, Chemistry 2 and Entrance Physics, also Biology 12.

*4. Physiology and Anatomy of the Sense Organs.

This course deals with the physiology and anatomy of the organs of special sense. It is especially adapted to the needs of stu-

---

*Biology 3, 4, 6, 7, 10, not given in 1902-03.

dents preparing for work in Psychology more advanced than that of Psychology 1 and 2, and Pre-Medical students.　Winter term.

Dr. KIMBLE.

Prerequisites, Biology 2, 3, 12; Chemistry 2, and Entrance Physics.

5.　Human Anatomy.

Lectures and recitations, three hours per week ; Laboratory work, ten hours per week.　Winter term.　　　　Dr. KIMBLE.

Prerequisites, Biology 2, 3, Chemistry 2.

*6.　Advanced Physiology.

This course is designed to meet the needs of Pre-Medical students.　Lectures, recitations and Laboratory work.　Fall term.

Dr. KIMBLE.

Prerequisites, Biology 2 and 3.

*7.　General Botany.

This course is intended to acquaint the student with the general field of Botany, including plant Ecology and Cartography.　Fall term.　　　　　　　　　　　　　　　Dr. KIMBLE.

Prerequisites, Entrance Chemistry, Biology 2.

8.　Cryptogamic Botany.

This will be a study of the life history of Cryptogams, with special reference to their systematic relations.　Winter term.

Dr. KIMBLE.

Prerequisite, Biology 7.

9.　Invertebrate Zoology.

This course will treat of the Invertebrata, with special reference to their systematic relations. · Recitations, laboratory and reference work.　Fall term.　　　　　　　　　Dr. KIMBLE.

Prerequisites, Entrance Credits in Zoology and Chemistry.

*10.　Vertebrate Zoology.

In this course typical forms will be studied in the laboratory. Drawings and explanatory notes of dissected specimens will be required.　Winter term.　　　　　　　　　Dr. KIMBLE.

Prerequisite, Biology 9.

11.　Animal Ecology.

This will be a study of the life relations of animals.　Extensive collateral reading will be required.　Winter term.

Dr. KIMBLE.

Prerequisite, Biology 9.

---

*Biology 3, 4, 6, 7, 10, not given in 1902-03.

12. Introductory Course in Practical Hygiene and Sanitation. [Half Course.]

Lectures, two hours per week. Fall term.   Dr. KIMBLE.

HISTORY.

[For History 1 to 4 inclusive, see page 56.]

5. History of the Christian Church.

A. The Ancient and Mediæval Eras [1-1517.]

This course in Church History is primarily intended for the members of the Divinity School, but is also open to College students. It will require the investigation of the early organization and extension of Christianity, and the successive periods of the Church down to the time of Charlemagne; followed by a careful inquiry into the causes of the rise of the Papacy, of the political relations of the Church, and of the Crusades. Fisher's History of the Church will be used as a hand book and topics will be assigned to each member of the class for special investigation and reports. Fall term.   Professor WHITE.

Prerequisites, History 1 and 2.

6. History of the Christian Church.

B. The Modern Era 1517-1902.)

This course will begin with the study of the Reformation, and trace the history of the Church down to the present time. It will include the history of Christian missions, revivals, social reforms, and philanthropy. The same text-book will be used as in History 5. Winter term.   Professor WHITE.

Open to students who, in the judgment of the instructor, are qualified by previous training to take the course.

ECONOMICS.

[For Economics 1 see page 56.]

2. Political Economy.

The standard economic theories of production, exchange and distribution are developed before the class; and the bearing of these theories on vital economic questions of the day is frankly and freely discussed. Students are encouraged to write essays on economic topics and to read them for discussion. In preparing essays, students will receive the personal aid of the instructor in directing their reading. A good reference library for this purpose is at the disposal of the class. Bullock's Introduction to the study of Economics is used. Spring term. Professor WRIGHT.

Prerequisite, Sociology 1.

3. Financial History of the United States.

This course embraces the finances of the Revolution; the financial administrations of Morris, Hamilton, and Gallatin; the bank struggle, tariff legislation, and the financial measures of the civil war and reconstruction periods. This course will be conducted by lectures and frequent reviews. Fall term. Professor WRIGHT.

Prerequisite, Economics 2.

JURISPRUDENCE.

1. International Law.

The general principles which govern the relations of States, as historically developed in express agreements and by usage, are elucidated, and these principles are discussed from the standpoints of reason and justice. Special study is made of current international problems and theses on these subjects are required. Particular attention is paid to terminology. Lawrence's International Law is used as a text-book. Frequent reference is made to the works on International Law by Woolsey, Wheaton, Glenn, etc. Spring term.

Open to students who, in the judgment of the instructor, are qualified by previous training to take the course.

SOCIOLOGY.

The Development of Sociological Theory.

1. An Introduction to Sociological Theory.

A study of the characteristics of general sociological theory.
Professor KIMBLE.

Open to all college students.

2. Pre-Comtean Sociological Theory.

A study of the earlier theories of social relations.
Professor KIMBLE.

Prerequisite, Sociology 1.

3. Modern Sociological Theory.

The chief works of the more prominent modern sociologists, are studied with a view to the characteristic positions of each, and the relations sustained by each to sociological theory as a whole.
Professor KIMBLE.

Prerequisite, Sociology 1.

4. Modern Sociological Theory. (Continuation of Course 3.)

Professor KIMBLE.

Prerequisite, Sociology 3.

5. Types of Sociological Theory.

Outline study of the principle types of sociological theory.

Professor KIMBLE.

Prerequisites, Sociology 1 to 4 inclusive.

The Development of Association.

6. An Introduction to the Comparative Study of Association.

The method, scope, and aim of Comparative Sociology.

Professor KIMBLE.

Prerequisites, Sociology 1, Biology 1 and 2. After 1902-03 Biology 12 will also be required of all students registering for this course.

7. Biogeography.

An outline study of the influence of the inanimate environment upon the development of association.   Professor KIMBLE.

Prerequisites, Sociology 1, reading knowledge of German.

8. Nutritive Association.

A study of association as developed about the process of nutrition.   Professor KIMBLE.

Prerequisite, as in Sociology 6.

9. Reproductive Association.

A study of association as developed about the reproductive process.   Professor KIMBLE.

Prerequisites, as in Sociology 6.

10. Conflictive Association.

A study of association as developed about the various stages of struggle and conflict.   Professor KIMBLE.

Prerequisites, as in Sociology 6.

11. Types of Association.

A critical study of the process of association as set forth in Courses 7 to 10 inclusive   Professor KIMBLE.

Prerequisites, Sociology 8 to 10.

12. Abnormal and Pathologic Variations in Association.

A course introductory to the study of crime, pauperism, etc.

Professor KIMBLE.

Course to be taken only after consultation with instructor.

The Development of Certain Social Institutions.

13. The Family.

A study of the origin, development and significance of the family.   Professor KIMBLE.

Prerequisites, as in Sociology 11.

14. The Sociology of Religion.

An outline study of certain of the phenomena of religion from the standpoint of the sociologist.   Professor KIMBLE.

Course to be taken only after consultation with instructor.

Students who contemplate doing more than the required constant in Sociology should note that Sociology 1 and Biology 1, 2, and 12 are prerequisites for the major portion of the work in Sociology. These prerequisites should, if possible, be taken by such student during the first year in college work.

A reading knowledge of German and French is highly desirable for all students expecting to register for more than introductory work in Sociology. Those proposing to complete the Social Science group will be required to possess a reading knowledge of German and French by the time they have completed the second year in the College.

PSYCHOLOGY.

1. Introductory Psychology.

The purpose of the course is to guide the beginner in gaining the fundamentals of a thorough knowledge of psychology and of psychic life. The course is organized about a careful study of the commoner characteristics of the more accessible mental processes. Emphasis is laid upon the ready and accurate use of the more important psychological terms. Some knowledge of the chief standpoints and methods of the science is gained. Collateral reading in connection with the text will be regularly assigned and a correct appreciation of the relation of this reading to the treatment presented in the text will be a requirement of the course. Experiments described in text and reading will be fully discussed, and where circumstances will permit, the student will see performed by others, or will himself perform in the laboratory certain type experiments.   Professor KIMBLE.

Prerequisites, Physiology 3, Nichols' Outlines of Physics or equivalent.

2. Introductory Psychology.

Continuation of Psychology 1. These two courses are practically one course, and in electing the first the student should also arrange to elect the second.   Professor KIMBLE.

Prerequisite, Psychology 1.

METAPHYSIC.

This is primarily a course in the Divinity School, but it may be elected by students in the College of Liberal Arts whenever it is offered. Classes will be formed whenever a sufficient number of students apply. Lotze's Outline of Metaphysic is used as a textbook. Fall term. Professor WHITE.

Open to students who, in the judgment of the instructor, are qualified by previous training to take the course.

LOGIC.

Having first obtained a thorough grounding in the principles and methods of correct reasoning both deductive and inductive, at least one-half of the term is given to the detection and discrimination of fallacies in actual examples. Such examples the class is required to search out in current literature and bring in for discussion. Davis's Elements of Deductive Logic, and Davis's Elements of Inductive Logic are used. Winter term.

Professor FOWLER.

Open to students who, in the judgment of the instructor, are qualified by previous training to take the course.

Logic will not be given in 1902–03.

ETHICS.

Ethics is treated from the standpoint of Philosophy, and the different systems are discussed. The nature and grounds of obligation are investigated and applied to the practical affairs of life. Winter term. Professor WHITE.

Open to students who, in the judgment of the instructor, are qualified by previous training to take the course.

PHILOSOPHY OF RELIGION.

Caird's Introduction to the Philosophy of Religion is the textbook. Lotze, Sabatier, and Martineau are used as works of reference. The aim of the instructor is to acquaint the student with the proper offices of reason in the effort to find argumentative grounds for religious ideas. Most of the modern theories respecting the nature and scope of the religious feeling pass under review; and in such discussions free questioning on the part of the student is encouraged. Winter term. Professor WHITE.

Open to students who, in the judgment of the Instructor, are qualified by previous training to take the course.

Philosophy of Religion will alternate with Dogmatic Theology. See under Divinity School.

ETHICAL THEORIES.

Martineau's Types of Ethical Theory is used as a text-book with frequent references to the works of Sidgwick, Green, Smyth, and others. Much attention is paid to the elucidation and criticism of the modern ethical theories. Spring term.

Professor WHITE.

Open to students who, in the judgment of the instructor, are qualified by previous training to take the course.

Ethical theories will alternate with Comparative Religion, See under Divinity School.

FINE ARTS.

2, 3, 4. Drawing.

This course includes perspective, drawing from casts in charcoal and crayon, still life studies in crayon, etc. It will count as one credit for the entire year. Miss BLOOD.

Open to all students in the college.

MUSIC.

1. Harmony.

Keys, scales and signatures, intervals, formation of the triad, chord connection, simple part writing begun. Stephen A. Emery's text book is used. Two hours a week. Fall term.

Miss BARTLETT.

Open to all students in the College.

2. Harmony.

Harmonizing basses, including all chords of the seventh and their inversions. Key board work. Modulation begun. Two hours a week. Winter term. Miss BARTLETT.

Prerequisite, Music 1.

3. Harmony.

Altered and Augmented Chords explained and worked out from basses given for harmonization. Modulation continued. Two hours a week. Spring term. Miss BARTLETT.

Prerequisite, Music 2.

4. Harmony.

Harmonizing melodies continued. Double chants and chorals. Two hours a week. Fall term. Miss BARTLETT.

Prerequisite, Music 3.

5. Harmony.

Harmonizing melodies continued. Suspensions. Passing chords. Passing and changing notes. Modulation completed. Two hours a week. Winter term. Miss BARTLETT.

Prerequisite, Music 4.

6. Single Counterpoint.

Single counterpoint in all forms in two and three voices. Spring term. Miss BARTLETT.

Prerequisite, Music 5.

7. Single Counterpoint.

Single counterpoint in four voices. Double counterpoint begun. Fall term. Miss BARTLETT.

Prerequisite, Music 6.

8. Double Counterpoint.

Double counterpoint in tenth and twelfth. Triple and quadruple counterpoint. Winter term. Miss BARTLETT.

Prerequisite, Music 7.

9. Canon and Fugue.

Canon in two voices in all intervals. Free imitation. Fugues in two, three, and four voices. Double fugue. Spring term.
Miss BARTLETT.

Prerequisite, Music 8.

ELOCUTION.

Not more than four credits can be counted in this department towards the degree of A. B.

1. Elocution. [Half Course.]

The aim of this course is to rid the voice of all impurities, secure correct placing of the voice, proper breathing, and beauty of tone for conversational purposes. Notes will be given upon the anatomy of the vocal organs and the care of the voice. Physical exercises will be introduced as a means of securing grace and becoming deportment. Recitations Mondays, Wednesdays, and Fridays. Fall term. Miss KIDDER.

Open to all students of the College.

2. Elocution. [Half Course.]

In this course attention will be given to the adaptation of the conversational voice to the requirements of platform speaking.

Each pupil will be required to deliver three selections before the class for criticism. Work in pantomime and life study will be introduced. Recitations Mondays, Wednesdays, and Fridays. Winter term.   Miss KIDDER.

Prerequisite, Elocution 1.

3. Elocution. [Half Course.]

This course will consist of a continuation of the work outlined in Elocution 2. The analysis of some English Classic will be required. Recitations Mondays, Wednesdays, and Fridays. Spring term.   Miss KIDDER.

Prerequisite, Elocution 2.

4. Elocution. [Half Course.]

The study of Masterpieces will be made the basis of this course. Recitations Mondays and Thursdays. Fall term.
Miss KIDDER.

Prerequisite, Elocution 3.

5. Elocution. [Half Course.]

The work in this course will be a continuation of that begun in Elocution 4, together with extemporaneous talks, critical and detailed life study for personation. Recitations Mondays and Thursdays. Winter term.   Miss KIDDER.

Prerequisite, Elocution 4.

6. Elocution. [Half Course.]

This course will consist of a continuation of Elocution 5. Recitations Mondays and Thursdays. Spring term.
Miss KIDDER.

Prerequisite, Elocution 5.

7. Oratory. [Half Course.]

In this course the aim will be to assist the student in gaining some knowledge of the great orators, both American and English. Each student is required to deliver before class for criticism a certain number of selections, chosen from the orators studied; also to give talks on subjects previously assigned. Recitations Mondays and Thursdays. Fall term.   Miss KIDDER.

Prerequisite, Elocution 6.

8. Oratory. [Half Course.]

Important features of this course are extemporaneous speaking, class debates and criticism. Two orations and one debate will

be required from each member of the class. Recitations Mondays
and Thursdays. Winter term.   Miss KIDDER.

Prerequisite Elocution 7.

9. Elocution. [Half Course.]

This course consists of a study of the works of Dickens, Eliot,
Shakespeare, and other authors, for the purpose of character interpretation. Scenes will be committed and interpreted for public
presentation.   Miss KIDDER.

Prerequisite, Elocution 6.

10, 11. Elocution. [Half Courses.]

These courses will consist of a continuation of elocution 9.
                                                    Miss KIDDER.

Prerequisite, Elocution 9.

RECITALS.

Recitals will be given during the year to show the proficiency
of pupils, and to give them assistance in acquiring confidence, ease,
and self control.

GYMNASIUM WORK.

Regular class work in the Gymnasium may be elected by any
student in the institution.   When taken by students in the College
of Liberal Arts it will count towards the requirements for graduation to an amount not to exceed two credits; a term's work counting as one-third of a credit.   This work will embrace Swedish
Gymnastics; marching; Wand. Dumb-bell. and Indian Club drills.
Instruction is also given in the use of the Apparatus and in Heavy
Gymnastics. Especial attention is given to correct posture of the
body and good form in walking and standing.   Each student is
given a thorough physical examination by the medical examiner,
and private work is prescribed to him in accordance with his individual needs.   All students will provide themselves with regular
gymnasium uniforms.   The cost of the uniform is about $2.75
for the men and $6.50 for the women.

PREPARATORY COURSES.

The following courses are designed chiefly for the benefit of those Unclassified Students who wish to complete the entrance requirements for admission to the College of Liberal Arts. They are, however, open to all students, *but if taken by students in the College of Liberal Arts they will not be counted on the thirty-eight credits required for graduation.*

ENGLISH.

The following courses are offered for the benefit of those wishing to pass the English examination for admission as outlined on pages 21-22. The work for the members of the class will be varied according to individual needs. In many cases it will be necessary for the student to repeat one or more of the courses in order to acquire sufficient proficiency to pass the examination.

2. Studies in English Literature and Composition.

Macaulay's Essays on Milton and Addison will be studied with care, and the class will be required to read specimens of the writings of Addison and of Lowell. It is expected that more than half the student's time will be given to work in Composition. Four hours a week. Fall term. Professor FOWLER.

Open to all students.

3. Studies in English Literature and Composition. (Continued.)

Work for careful study will be Burke's Speech on Conciliation with America. The class will read carefully Pope's Translation of the Iliad (books I, VI, XXII, XXIV), Goldsmith's Vicar of Wakefield, Coleridge's Ancient Mariner, and Cooper's Last of the Mohicans. Four hours a week. Winter term. Professor FOWLER.

Prerequisite, English 2.

4. Studies in English Literature and Composition. (Continued.)

Shakespeare's Macbeth and Milton's L'Allegro, Il Penseroso, Comus, and Lycidas will be carefully studied; and the class will read Shakespeare's Merchant of Venice, George Eliot's Silas Marner, Tennyson's Princess, and Scott's Ivanhoe. Four hours a week. Spring term. Professor FOWLER.

Prerequisite, English 3.

MATHEMATICS.

1. Arithmetic.

Robinson's Higher Arithmetic. Study of the subject matter of the text to Interest. This coure includes thorough work in analysis and mental arithmetic. Fall term. Miss HATHAWAY.

Open to all students.

Mathematics 1 will not be given unless at least six students apply for the course.

2. Elementary Algebra.

Wells's Academic Algebra is used. Fall term.
Miss HATHAWAY.

Open to all students.

3. Elementary Algebra. (Continued.) Winter term.
Miss HATHAWAY.

Prerequisite, Mathematics 2.

4. Elementary Algebra. (Continued.)

Spring term. Miss HATHAWAY.

Prerequisite, Mathematics 3.

6 (a) Plane Geometry.

This course is designed to give students thorough drill in the first principles of Geometry. Each proposition is carefully analyzed and particular attention is given to correct reasoning and. precise expression. Phillips and Fisher's Elements of Geometry is used. Winter term. Professor WRIGHT.

Open to all students.

Mathematics 2, 3, 4, and 6(a) are designed to meet the entrance requirements in Algebra and Plane Geometry. [See pp. 23–24.]

PHYSICAL GEOGRAPHY.

1. Physical Geography.

Text-book, Tarr's Elementary Physical Geography. Spring term.

Open to all students.

Physical Geography 1 will alternate with Economics 1.

HISTORY.

1. United States.

History of the United States. Text-book, Channing's Students' History of the United States, with Scudder and Fiske for reference. Winter term.

Open to all students.

[History 1 will not be given unless a considerable number of students apply.]

2. Greece.

History of Greece. Text-book, Smith's History of Greece. Fall term.   Miss HATHAWAY.

Open to all students.

3. Rome.

History of Rome. Text-book, Liddell's History of Rome. Winter term.   Miss HATHAWAY.

Open to all students.

4. England.

History of England. Text-book. Montgomery's Leading Facts of English History. Spring term.   Miss HATHAWAY.

Open to all students.

ECONOMICS.

1. Science of Government.

Text-books, Fiske's Civil Government in the United States, and Andrew's Manual of the Constitution. Spring term.

Open to all students.

Economics 1 will alternate with Physical Geography 1.

UNCLASSIFIED STUDENTS.

Persons who wish to pursue studies at Lombard without becoming candidates for a degree will be admitted on probation to any class for which they are fitted by previous training. In case the class in question demands a prerequisite, the applicant must bring a certificate in this prerequisite from an approved school, or pass an examination.

On severing their connection with the College, these students will receive, upon request, a certificate, signed by the President and their several instructors, stating the amount and quality of the work done.

If at any time such students wish to become candidates for a degree, they must fulfill all the requirements for admission to the department in which the degree is to be taken.

Among these also will be placed all students who have an ultimate purpose of taking a degree, but who need to pursue one or more of the preparatory courses to fulfill the requirements for admission to the College of Liberal Arts.

RYDER DIVINITY SCHOOL.

The Divinity School of Lombard College was opened for the admission of students on the 5th of September, 1881. The first class was graduated in 1885.

At the annual meeting of the Board of Trustees in 1890, it was voted to name the theological department of the College the RYDER DIVINITY SCHOOL, in honor of the late William Henry Ryder, D. D., whose munificent bequests to the College exceed fifty thousand dollars.

The largest benefaction to the Divinity School from any other source was received from the late Hon. A. G. Throop, founder of the Throop Polytechnic Institute at Pasadena, California. In 1890, Mr. Throop gave twenty thousand dollars towards the endowment of the Divinity School.

ADMISSION.

Applicants unknown to the faculty must bring satisfactory evidences of good moral and religious character. They should also bring certificates of their church membership.

Candidates for admission to the Divinity School must be prepared to sustain examination in the following subjects.

I. ENGLISH.

(*a*) Grammar and Analysis.

Reed and Kellogg's Higher Lessons in English, or an equivalent.

(*b*) Composition.

An extemporaneous composition on an assigned subject, correct as to paragraphing, grammar, and rhetorical form.

(*c*) **Literature.**

An equivalent of English 2, 3, and 4 as described on page 54 of this catalogue.

II HISTORY.

(*a*) **Bible History.**

A competent knowledge of the Bible as history, including the so-called Old Testament Apocrypha. The ground covered is given in the ten volume Historical Series for Bible Students, edited by Kent and Sanders, and published by Scribner's Sons.

(*b*) **Bible Geography and Archeology.**

A general knowledge of localities, customs, manners, etc., of Bible times.

Rand and McNally's Manual of Biblical Geography, and Jahn's Archeology, or equivalents.

(*c*) **General History.**

Swinton's General History or an equivalent.

III. MATHEMATICS.

(*a*) **Arithmetic.**

Higher Arithmetic, including percentage, alligation, extraction of roots, mensuration, and the metric system.

(*b*) **Elementary Algebra.**

Wells's Academic Algebra, or an equivalent.

IV. GEOGRAPHY.

Tarr's Elementary Geography, or an equivalent.

V. SCIENCE.

(*a*) **Chemistry.**

The equivalent of Chemistry 1 and 2 as described on page 42. (Equivalent work in Physics and Botany may be accepted in lieu of Chemistry.)

(*b*) **Physiology.**

This calls for a general knowledge of the human skeleton, muscular, circulatory, and nervous systems, the vital organs, viscera, and organs of special sense, and the processes of respiration and digestion. The preparation required is covered in such text-books as Martin's Human Body (briefer course), or Huxley's Elementary Physiology (Lee's Revision).

Preliminary Year.

To accommodate those candidates for admission who are not fully prepared to satisfy the admission requirements an opportunity is given to complete their preparation in the School, and a preliminary year's work is mapped out (page 62), which, however, is susceptible of some modification to meet the special needs of the candate.

As a further encouragement to candidates to avail themselves of this opportunity the Universalist General Convention will permit its grant of financial aid to be spread over five years, instead of four as hitherto. Thus the candidate who requires five years for the full course, including the Preliminary year, may receive, under the usual conditions, a maximum grant of $100 each year for the five years, or a maximum grant of $125 a year for four years as he may prefer.

ADMISSION BY CERTIFICATE.

Satisfactory grades from approved schools will be accepted in lieu of examination. Students thus admitted by certificate will be regarded as on probation during the first term of their course.

ADMISSION TO ADVANCED STANDING.

Students who bring satisfactory evidence of work done beyond the requirements of admission will be given credit for the same on the regular course, so far as the faculty may deem consistent with the special aims of that course.

The members of the Divinity School are admitted to the advantages presented by the other departments of the College.

EXPENSES.

Tuition is free to all regular members of the Divinity School who are candidates for the ministry.

The charge for incidentals is the same as in the College of Liberal Arts, $5 per term.

For board in commons, see page 10.

Board in good families can be secured for from $2.50 to $3.25 per week. Students may greatly reduce their expenses by forming clubs, or boarding themselves.

PECUNIARY AID.

Students who are candidates for the ministry of the Universalist Church may, upon complying with the prescribed conditions

and receiving the recommendations of the faculty, obtain assistance from the Universalist General Convention in the form of a
gratituity, to an amount not exceeding $125 a year for four years.
Applications will be granted by the Convention only when entirely
satisfactory.   The first installment of this gift will not be issued to
entering students until January, the second will be issued in May.
Students should therefore come with resources of their own sufficient to pay their expenses for at least one term.

Those who have not a definite purpose of entering the Universalist ministry are not eligible to the Convention gift.

Membership in some.Universalist Church is also required as a
condition of the gift.

The use of tobacco or other narcotic or stimulants is an absolute bar to to the grant of the Convention aid.

The Convention aid may be withheld at any time, should the
work or behavior of the candidate prove unsatisfactory.

After having had two terms in homiletics, students who show
due proficiency are permitted to secure appointments to preach,
and thus to add to their pecuniary resources.

Courses of Instruction.

1. Regular Course.

Candidates for the degree of B. D. will be expected to complete
the course scheduled on page 62.   This course, it will be observed,
prescribes a certain amount of work in Greek, which is regarded
as indispensable to the degree.   In addition to the studies indicated in the schedule, a year's work in Hebrew will be offered
to those who desire it, at some time during their residence.   It is
earnestly recommended that all students whose circumstances do
not positively forbid their spending the requisite time, take the
Regular Course.

2. Alternative Course.

It is, however, permitted to those who, after due deliberation,
prefer to do so, to omit the Greek and Hebrew, and to substitute
therefor an equivalent amount of elective work in English, Modern
Languages, Science, Mathematics, or Sociology, with the approval
of the faculty.   Those who complete such a course will be graduated at the Annual Commencement, and will be furnished a certificate showing what work they have done; but they will not be
given the degree of B. D. nor any other degree.

3. Special Work.

(*a*) Candidates for the ministry who cannot take either of the above described courses, will be permitted to elect particular studies, so far as their preparation warrants. Pastors already engaged in ministerial work, who can spare a period for further study, are particularly invited to avail themselves of this opportunity.

(*b*) The School is also open to persons who do not intend to enter the ministry. The pursuit of studies of a theological or religious character is an interesting and helpful means of personal culture. Such a course is especially recommended to those who desire to become better fitted for service in the Sunday School, the Church, the Young People's Christian Union and similar societies, or for charitable and philanthropic work. Upon those who come with these purposes, no denominational test will be imposed. Students of all denominations and beliefs will be welcome to the advantages of study and training in the Divinity School, as in other departments of the College.

Faculty of the Divinity School.

CHARLES ELLWOOD NASH, A. M., S. T. D., PRESIDENT,
Instructor in Homiletics and Pastoral Care.

NEHEMIAH WHITE, A. M., PH. D., S. T. D.,
*Hall Professor of Intellectual and Moral Philosophy.
In charge of the Ryder Divinity School, Professor of Biblical Languages and Exegesis.

†Hull Professor of Biblical Geography and Archæology.

ISAAC AUGUSTUS PARKER, A. M., PH. D.,
Professor of Greek.

FRANK HAMILTON FOWLER, PH. D.,
Professor of English Literature.

RALPH GRIERSON KIMBLE,
Professor of Sociology.

*In honor of the late E. G. HALL, of Chicago.
†In honor of the REV. STEPHEN HULL, of Kansas City, Mo.

CHARLES E. VARNEY,
Instructor in Biblical History and Archæology.

AMANDA KIDDER,
Instructor in Elocution.

NON-RESIDENT LECTURERS.

MARION D. SHUTTER, D. D.
REV. FRANK H. YORK.

Degree Conferred in 1901.

BACHELOR OF DIVINITY.

Francis Britton Bishop..............................*Marseilles.*

Schedule.

1. Preliminary Year.

FALL TERM.	WINTER TERM.	SPRING TERM.
English 2.	English 3.	English 4.
Biblical History.	Biblical History.	Biblical Geography and
Chemistry.	Chemistry.	Archæology.
		Physiology.

---

2. Regular Course.

Leading to the Degree of Bachelor of Divinity.

FIRST YEAR.

FALL TERM.	WINTER TERM.	SPRING TERM.
English 5.	English 6.	English 18.
Greek 1.	Greek 2.	Greek 3.
History 5.	History 6.	History 7.

SECOND YEAR.

Psychology 1.	Psychology 2.	Hermeneutics.
Greek 4.	Greek Testament.	Greek Testament.
Homiletics 1.	Homiletics 2.	Homiletics 3.
Elocution.	Elocution.	Elocution.

THIRD YEAR.

Homiletics 4.	Homiletics 5.	Homiletics 6.
Metaphysic.	Greek Testament.	Greek Testament.
Sociology 1.	Logic.	Dogmatic Theology.
	Dogmatic Theology.	

FOURTH YEAR.

Sociology D. 1.	Sociology D. 2.	Pastoral Care.
Philosophy of Relig'n.	Ethics.	Ethical Theories.
*Hebrew.	*Hebrew.	*Hebrew.
Preaching.	Preaching.	Preaching.

---

*Elective.

Description of Studies.

HEBREW.

1, 2, 3. Grammar and Old Testament.

These are primarily courses in the Divinity School, but may be elected by students in the College of Liberal Arts whenever they are offered. Classes will be formed each year if a sufficient number of students apply.

It is the aim to give the student such a knowledge of the forms and structure of the Hebrew language as shall enable him to use it efficiently in the criticism and literary analysis of the Old Testament Scriptures. The text-books used are H. G. Mitchell's Hebrew Lessons and the Hebrew Old Testament. Three terms—Fall, Winter and Spring—each term counting as a course.

Professor WHITE.

BIBLE STUDY.

1. Biblical History, A.

Kent's Studies in Biblical History and Literature is used. The aim is to present the contents of the Bible as they stand in our English version. Due account is made of contemporary history and the monumental data. In general the first term will be occupied with the material of the Old Testament; the second term with that of the New. Fall term. Mr. VARNEY.

2. Biblical History, B.

A continuation of the preceding. Winter term.

Mr. VARNEY.

3. Biblical Geography and Archaeology.

A detailed study of the political and physical geography of the Bible countries, and a general study of the antiquities of the Bible peoples. Spring term. Mr. VARNEY.

4. Biblical Criticism.

Driver's Introduction to the Old Testament is used as a textbook, with references to Fripp, Ryle, Bacon, Robertson, and other works. A course of lectures is given on the Science of Documentary Analysis, the Principles and Methods of Historical Criticism, and the Religious aspects of the Higher Criticism. Winter term.

Professor WHITE.

HERMENEUTICS.

The aim of Hermeneutics, rightly called "the science and art of interpretation," is to set forth those principles and processes whereby the true intent and meaning of an author may be ascertained from the language which he employs. Hermeneutics is therefore the basis of all sound exegesis and is an invaluable aid to the interpretation of the Scriptures. Instruction will be given both by text-book and by lectures. Spring term.

Professor WHITE.

Hermeneutics will not be given in 1902.

PREPARATORY GREEK.

(For Greek 1, 2, 3, 4, 5, see pp. 36, 37.

THE GREEK NEW TESTAMENT.

(The courses are numbered continuously with the Greek Courses of the College of Liberal Arts.)

12. Exegesis of the Synoptic Gospels.

Critical rendering of selections from the Synoptic Gospels. Exegesis of Mark's Gospel; Origin and peculiar characteristics of the Gospel, and its relation to the other Synoptists—their harmonies, divergencies, and interdependence. Date of Synoptic Gospels; their genuineness and authenticity. Theology and Christology of the Synoptic Gospels. Spring term.   Professor WHITE.

13. Acts of the Apostles.

Critical rendering of the Greek text of the Acts of the Apostles, their genuineness and authenticity, date of the work, sources of the narrative. Exegesis of the Acts. Spring term.

Professor WHITE.

14. Thessalonians and Galatians.

Critical rendering of the Greek text of the Epistles to the Thessalonians. Exegesis of the Epistles. Eschatology of the Epistles. Primitive Paulinism. Critical rendering of the Greek text of the Epistle to the Galatians. Fall term.   Professor WHITE.

15. Corinthians, Romans, and Apocalypse.

Selections from the first and the second Epistle to the Corinthians. Critical rendering of the Greek text of the Epistle to the Romans. Examination of the nature of Pauline Theology and Christology. Development of the doctrine of Paul. Character of later Paulinism. Critical rendering of the Greek text of the Apocalypse. Examination of the resemblances and differences in the style and language of the Apocalypse and of the fourth gospel. Fall term.   Professor WHITE.

THEOLOGY.

1. Christian Evidences.

The study of Christian Evidences will include an examination of the bases of Christian belief, Evolutionary theories and their relation to Philosophy, Ethics and Religion, and the function and method of Apologetics. Comparison will be instituted between the modern methods in Apologetics and the methods of primitive Christianity. Instruction will be given mostly by lectures with frequent reference to Fisher, Schurman, Flint, Bruce, and others. Fall term. Professor WHITE.

2. Dogmatic Theology.

Martensen's Christian Dogmatics is used as a text-book. A thorough investigation is made of the several Christian doctrines, with an extended examination of associated questions and controversies. The widest liberty is given for questions and discussions on the various topics presented. Winter and spring terms.

Professor WHITE.

3. Comparative Religion.

The work of the students consists in the examination and comparison of the authorities upon the great Non-Christian religions. Special topics are investigated and reports made by each member of the class. Spring term. Professor WHITE.

APPLIED CHRISTIANITY.

The demand for a more thorough investigation of the bearings of Christian Doctrine upon the social, political, and industrial organisms, coupled with the demand for a more diversified and scientific administration of religion through the churches, is met at Lombard College by the establishment of a chair of Applied Christianity and Pastoral Theology. The course of study provided for will occupy four terms, three terms being devoted to Sociology, and one term to Pastoral Care.

SOCIOLOGY.

1. An Introduction to Sociological Theory.

A study of the characteristics of general sociological theory.

D. 1. Pathologic Factors of the Modern Community.

The discrimination and definition of the dependant, defective, and delinquent classes, together with a brief study of current attempts to deal with the same.

D. 2. Pathologic Factors of the Modern Community.

A continuation of Sociology D. 1.

Sociology D. 1, and D. 2 are designed expressly to meet the needs of Divinity Students. If taken by students in the College of Liberal Arts they will not count on the thirty-eight credits required for the A. B. degree.

PASTORAL CARE.

The spiritual, mental and social qualifications of the minister for his work will be noted, and his administration of the special services of the church—baptism, confirmation, the Lord's Supper, marriage, and the burial of the dead. A liberal portion of the term will be devoted to an examination of various methods of church organization, for the purpose of giving the minister facility in adapting himself to parish needs, especially to those peculiar to the locality in which he may be settled. Also a study is made of the Manual of the Universalist General Convention. Spring term.

Pres. NASH.

PSYCHOLOGY.

1. Introductory Psychology.

The purpose of the course is to guide the beginner in gaining the fundamentals of a thorough knowledge of psychology and of psychic life. The course is organized about a careful study of the commoner characteristics of the more accessible mental processes. Emphasis is laid upon the ready and accurate use of the more important psychological terms. Some knowledge of the chief standpoints and methods of the science is gained. Collateral reading in connection with the text will be regularly assigned and a correct appreciation of the relation of this reading to the treatment presented in the text will be a requirement of the course. Experiments described in text and reading will be fully discussed, and where circumstances will permit, the student will see performed by others, or will himself perform in the laboratory certain type experiments.

Professor KIMBLE.

2. Introductory Psychology.

Continuation of Psychology 1.

Professor KIMBLE.

METAPHYSIC.

This is primarily a course in the Divinity School, but it may be elected by students in the College of Liberal Arts whenever it is offered. Classes will be formed whenever a sufficient number of students apply. Lotze's Outlines of Metaphysic is used as a textbook. Fall term.

Professor WHITE.

LOGIC.

Having first obtained a thorough grounding in the principles and methods of correct reasoning, both deductive and inductive, at least one-half of the term is given to the detection and discrimination of fallacies in actual examples. Such examples the class is required to search out in current literature and bring in for discussion. Davis's Elements of Deductive Logic, and Davis's Elements of Inductive Logic are used. Winter term.

Professor FOWLER.

ETHICS.

Ethics is treated from the standpoint of Philosophy, and the different systems are discussed. The nature and grounds of obligation are investigated and applied to the practical affairs of life. Winter term. Professor WHITE.

PHILOSOPHY OF RELIGION.

Caird's Introduction to the Philosophy of Religion is the text-book. Lotze, Sabatier, and Martineau are used as works of reference. The aim of the instructor is to acquaint the student with the proper office of reason in the effort to find argumentative grounds for religious ideas. Most of the modern theories respecting the nature and scope of the religious feeling pass under review; and in such discussions free questioning on the part of the student is encouraged. Winter term. Professor WHITE.

ETHICAL THEORIES.

Martineau's Types of Ethical Theory is used as a text-book with frequent reference to the works of Sidgwick, Green, Smythe, and others. Much attention is paid to the elucidation and criticism of the modern ethical theories. Spring term.

Professor WHITE.

CHURCH HISTORY.

(The courses in Church History are numbered continuously with the Preparatory courses in History. See page 56.)

5. **History of the Christian Church.**

A. The Ancient and Mediæval Eras. (1-1517.)

This course in Church History is primarily intended for the members of the Divinity School, but is also open to College students. It will require the investigation of the early organization and extension of Christianity, and the successive periods of the Church down to the time of Charlemagne; followed by a careful inquiry into the causes of the rise of Papacy, of the political relations of the Church, and of the Crusades. Fisher's History of the Church will be used as a hand-book and topics will be assigned to each member of the class for special investigation and reports. Fall term. Professor WHITE.

6. History of the Christian Church.

B.　The Modern Era (1517-1902.)

This course will begin with the study of the Reformation, and trace the history of the Church down to the present time. It will include the history of Christian missions, revivals, social reforms, and philanthropy. The same text-book will be used as in History 5. Winter term. Professor WHITE.

7. History of Christian Doctrine.

Special pains will be taken to make clear the aim of the History of Christian Doctrine, and to indicate the process of its development. Professor WHITE.

HOMILETICS.

The course in Homiletics covers the second, third, and fourth years. The primary aim is practical. Upon a general but adequate groundwork of theory and history of preaching the effort is made to construct an art of effective pulpit oratory. Elaborate and exacting drill in the logical conception and construction of the sermon plan, with constant application of rhetorical principles, occupies the major part of the first year. Inspiration and direction are sought in the frequent analysis of the discourses of great preachers of all styles, and in the study of their sources of power. Individuality and originality are emphasized as desiderata. In the second year the stress is laid upon flexibility and adaptability, upon invention, upon the rationale of interesting preaching, and upon the acquisition of freedom in extempore address. Throughout the course the preparation and criticism of sermons by the class continues uninterruptedly. President NASH.

ELOCUTION.

In view of the fact that a good delivery is of inestimable advantage to the preacher, the students in the Divinity School are offered an extended course in Elocution and Physical Culture.

The students are not only admitted to all Elocution classes in the College, but also receive a large amount of individual training.

Courses 1, 2, 3, as outlined on pp. 51 and 52 of this catalogue, are required. Miss KIDDER.

ENGLISH.

For English 5, 6, 8, which courses are required in the Divinity School, see p. 30 of this catalogue.

8. Daily Themes.

This course will be made a full course for students in the Divinity School. Besides the daily themes, fortnightly themes will be required. Spring term.   Professor FOWLER.

COLLEGE STUDIES.

Divinity students are permitted, with the consent of the Faculty, to pursue studies in the College of Liberal Arts. Graduates of the Divinity School may receive the additional degree of Bachelor of Arts, upon the satisfactory completion of an aggregate of twenty full courses taken in the classes of the College of Liberal Arts, beyond the full requirements of the Divinity School for the degree of Bachelor of Divinity.

In addition to the above twenty credits, the candidate must furnish the full quota of twenty-one credits required for admission to the College of Liberal Arts. Of these twenty-one credits, the courses required for admission to the Divinity School (see pp. 57 and 58) will count ten.

THE GYMNASIUM.

DEPARTMENT OF MUSIC.

Instruction is provided in the various branches of Theoretical, Vocal, and Instrumental Music. These courses are distinct from the work in the other departments of the College, and unless otherwise specified do not count toward a college degree. Students are classed and registered as private pupils of the several instructors, with whom arrangements may be made in regard to lessons. Instruction is given either at the College, or at the instruction-rooms of the teachers, as preferred.

Faculty.

KARL JACOB RUDOLPH LUNDBERG,
Director, and Instructor in Voice and Piano.

W. H. CHEESMAN,
Instructor in Violin.

EDNA UHLER,
Instructor in Piano.

ALICE HELEN BARTLETT,
Instructor in Pipe Organ and Harmony.

THEORETICAL COURSES.

Miss Bartlett.

1. Harmony.

Keys, scales and signatures, intervals, formation of the triad, chord connection, simple part writing begun. Stephen A. Emery's text book is used. Two hours a week. Fall term.

2. Harmony.

Harmonizing basses, including all chords of the seventh and their inversions. Key board work. Modulation begun. Two hours a week. Winter term.

3. Harmony.

Altered and Augmented Chords explained and worked out from basses given for harmonization. Modulation continued. Two hours a week. Spring term.

4. Harmony.

Harmonizing melodies continued. Double chants and chorals. Two hours a week. Fall term.

5. Harmony.

Harmonizing melodies continued. Suspensions. Passing chords. Passing and changing notes. Modulation completed. Two hours a week. Winter term.

6. Single Counterpoint.

Single counterpoint in all forms in two and three voices. Spring term.

7. Single Counterpoint.

Single counterpoint in four voices. Double counterpoint begun. Fall term.

8. Double Counterpoint.

Double counterpoint in tenth and twelfth. Triple and quadruple counterpoint. Winter term.

9. Canon and Fugue.

Canon in two voices in all intervals. Free imitation. Fugues in two, three, and four voices. Double fugue. Spring term.

10, 11, 12. History of Music. [Half Courses.]

These courses embrace a history of the development of music from the earliest times until to-day, with special reference to critical analysis of the works of the great masters. They also furnish an introduction to the lives of the great composers. One hour a week for the year.   PROFESSOR LUNDBERG.

PIANOFORTE COURSES.

Professor Lundberg and Miss Uhler.

1. Preparatory Year.

Five-finger exercises; scales in major and minor; triads; selected studies by Czerney, Vol. 1 (Germer Edition).

2. First Grade.

Finger exercises; scales; Czerney's studies, Vols. 1 and 2 (Germer edition); Sonatinen by Dussek, Clementi, Diabelli, Kuhlau, Reinecke. Memorizing.

3. Second Grade.

Finger exercises; scales; arpeggios; Czerney's studies, Vol. 3 (Germer edition); Sonatinas by Clementi, Kuhlau, Dussek, Haydn, Mozart, Beethoven. Pieces by American and foreign composers.

4. Third Grade.

Finger exercises with modulation to different keys. Scales in fourths, sixths, and thirds. Czerney's studies, Vol. 4; Bach's Inventions for two and three voices. Pieces by different composers.

5. Fourth Grade.

Finger exercises in different keys. Scales; études by Cramer; preludes and fugues by Bach. Easier sonatas by Haydn, Clementi, Mozart and Beethoven. Memorizing; pieces by different composers.

6. Fifth Grade.

Finger exercises in different keys; scales. Clementi's Gradus ad Parnassum. Etudes by Moscheles, Chopin, etc. Sonatas by Bach, Mozart, Beethoven and Hummel. Memorizing. Pieces by different composers.

VOICE CULTURE.

Professor Lundberg.

1. First Grade.

Exercises in breathing, tone placing, sustained tones, etc. Voice training exercises by Emil Behnke and C. W. Pearce. 50 vocalises by Concone. Easy songs.

2. Second Grade.

Masset's exercises; 30 exercises by Concone; 25 and 15 vocalises by Concone. Songs by American and foreign composers.

3. Third Grade.

Vocalises by Reber, Panofka, and Masset. Songs, and oratorios. Recitatives. Practicing of duets, trios and quartets.

PIPE ORGAN COURSES.

Miss Bartlett.

Students who wish to begin the study of the Organ should have completed the Second Grade of the Piano Course.

The chief aim of this department is the thorough preparation of church organists. Organ students should also make a conscientious study of Solo and Chorus Singing, with a view of becoming efficient chorus-masters and directors of church music.

The study of Harmony, Counterpoint, and History of Music is absolutely necessary to an intelligent study of the instrument.

1. First Grade.

Exercises in pedal playing. Ritter's Organ School. Hymns. Thayer's Pedal Studies. Elementary Registration.

2. Second Grade.

Studies in Pedal Phrasing by Buck, Volkmar, and Schneider. Polyphonic composition by Rink, Bach, Fisher. Easy pieces by Merkel, Dubois, Guilmant, Mendelssohn, and others. Registration, Structure of the Organ, Choir Accompaniment.

3. Third Grade.

Study of Sonatas and Fugues by Bach, Mendelssohn, Reinberger, and others. Modern compositions of German, English and French masters. Choir accompaniment.

VIOLIN COURSES.

Professor Cheesman.

1. Preparatory Grade.

Elementary exercises in position, bowing, etc. Easy exercises in major and minor keys in the first book from Wichtl's Violin School. Pleyel's Duets, and twelve studies by H. E. Kayser, op. 20. Memorizing.

2. Intermediate Grade.

Studies by Kayer and Wohlfahrt. Systematic progress through the various positions, beginning with the second book of F. Hermann. Studies from Shradieck for the development of technic and pure tone qualities. Selections from compositions by Dancla, Mazas, Weiss, De Beriot: also solos and fantasias based upon operatic themes.

3. Advanced Grade.

Technical studies from the works of Kreutzer, Fiorillo, Rode, together with duets, trios and quartets, arranged for strings; overtures; sight-reading. Sonatas and concertos by Bach, Haydn, Spohr, Beethoven, Mendelssohn, DeBeriot, Wieniawsky, Grieg, and others.

MANDOLIN AND GUITAR COURSES.

Professor Cheesman.

The study of these popular instruments has become a favorite recreation with those students of our colleges who may not have the time or inclination to pursue the study of music in its more serious forms.

At the conclusion of the first term of lessons (twelve weeks) a "Lombard Mandolin Club" will be organized, with rehersals one evening a week. The Italian method is used entirely in the study of these instruments, thereby establishing the very best method of picking the strings and fingering, with special attention to the tone quality of the "tremolo," which relieves the mandolin of much of its so-called monotony. Solos, duets, and quartets, will also be prepared in addition to the regular club work, with special numbers to be given by the lady members of the club.

SIGHT SINGING AND CHORUS CLASSES.

Professor Lundberg.

1. Elementary Sight Singing Class.

The rudiments of Music, the intervals of the Major Scale, exerercises in one and two parts, and easy songs. Ear-training. One college term.

2. Advanced Class.

Solfeggios in major and minor keys, three and four part songs. One college term.

3. Chorus Class.

Four part compositions, glees, sacred and secular choruses from our best classic and modern composers. Oratorios.

Only those students who have finished the work done in the Advanced Sight-Singing Class will be admitted into the Chorus Class.

Requirements for Graduation.

A diploma will be conferred upon any student who shall satisfactorily complete any of the following courses in instrumental or vocal music. In addition to the requirements enumerated below, the candidate will prepare a thesis, present an original musical composition, or perform other original work satisfactory to the instructor, and also appear in public at a graduating recital.

A. THE PIANOFORTE.

Musical Requirements.

Five grades of the Piano Courses, Nos. 1, 2, 3, 4, 5, 6, 10, and 11 of the Theoretical Courses; Acoustics; and one year's membership in the Chorus Class.

Literary Requirements.

English Grammar, English Composition, Rhetoric, English and American Literature, one year of French or German.

If the candidate upon entering brings satisfactory proof of proficiency in any of these courses he is advised to take one study each term from such electives in the College of Liberal Arts as the Director may recommend.

B. THE PIPE ORGAN.

Musical Requirements.

The full Organ Course, Nos. 1, 2, 3, 4, 5, 6, 10, and 11 of the Theoretical Courses; and Acoustics.

Literary Requirements.

The same as for Piano students.

C. THE VOICE.

Musical Requirements.

All the prescribed studies for Voice Culture; grade 2 of the Piano Courses, with special view to accompaniments; and Nos. 1, 2, 3, 10, 11, of the Theoretical Courses.

Literary Requirements.

The same as for Piano students, except that Italian may be substituted for French or German.

TUITION.

The following prices are for a term of twelve weeks:

THEORETICAL COURSES—

 Music 1 to 9, each, $5.00.
 Music 10, 11 and 12, each $3.00.

PIANOFORTE—

 Private Lessons—one hour per week, $18.00.
 Private Lessons—two half hours per week, $18.00.
 Private Lessons—one-half hour per week, $10.00.
 Private Lessons—one 45-minute lesson per week, $14.00.

 Class Lessons, one hour per week, each—
   In classes of two, $10.00.
   In classes of three, $7.00.

VOICE CULTURE—

 Charges same as for pianoforte.

RENT OF PIANO—1 hour per day, per term, $2.75.

 2 hours per day, per term, $5.00.
 3 hours per day, per term, $6.75.
 4 hours per day, per term, $8.00.

PIPE ORGAN—

Private Lessons—one hour per week, $24.00.
In classes of two, one hour per week, each person, $13.00.

VIOLIN—

Private Lessons—one hour per week, $15.00.
Private Lessons—two half hours per week, $15.00.
Private Lessons—one 45-minute lesson per week, $12.00.

CLASS LESSONS, one hour per week, each—

In classes of two, $8.00.
In classes of three, $6.00.

MANDOLIN AND GUITAR—

Private Lessons—one hour per week, $12.00.
Private Lessons—two half hours per week, $12.00.

Class Lessons—charges will be given on application to teacher.
(A weekly rehearsal for club practice without extra charge.)

SIGHT SINGING CLASSES—

Each, $1.00.

CHORUS CLASS—

A charge of $1.00 per term each will be made for the use of music to be supplied by the department.

The privilege of joining the Lombard Mandolin and Guitar Club, or the Lombard String Orchestra is extended to any student outside of the private pupils of the instructor, by the payment of $1 25 per term of twelve weeks. Rehearsals one evening each week.

GENERAL REMARKS.

Tuition and other charges must be paid before lessons are assigned.

In cases of protracted sickness only, will a proportionate deduction be made from term charges.

No visitors are allowed in practice rooms during practice hours.

All concerts and recitals given by the school of music or its faculty are free to music students.

A course of free lectures on musical culture will be given each year by the Director.

THE LADIES' HALL.

DEPARTMENT OF ART.

Instructor.

M. ISABELLE BLOOD.

Course in Art.

The Art Department affords a practical course in Drawing and Painting to those who wish to become teachers, designers, illustrators, or portrait artists. Regular students in this department who wish to take the entire course in Art will be given careful training in the following branches: Perspective drawing; drawing from casts in charcoal and crayon; still life studies in crayon, oil, water color, and pastel; landscape from nature; and copying from good studies.

The entire course will occupy from two to three years, according to the ability of the student and the amount of time given to the work. A thorough knowledge of the elements of drawing being necessary to independent work, at least one year's work will be required in drawing in black and white from models of simple form, casts, still life, and those studies which will best prepare the student for the special line of work preferred.

Students may enter the Art Department at any time; and though they are advised to take a full course in order to obtain the best results, arrangements can be made for lessons in any line desired.

While portrait work, pen and ink drawing, and china painting are not required in the regular course, credit will be given for good work in any of these branches if it is desired to substitute them in part for oil, water color, or pastel.

A course of study in the History of Art and a thesis upon some subject approved by the instructor will also be required of students wishing to graduate from this department.

Those who complete the work as outlined above will be entitled to a Diploma.

For a description of courses in Free Hand Drawing, and for credit allowed for these courses in the College of Liberal Arts, p. 50.

TUITION.

The tuition fees will be as follows:

Drawing of Sketching—3-hour lessons, 35 cents.
Painting in Water Colors—3-hour lesson, 50 cents.
Oil Painting—3-hour lesson, 50 cents.
Portrait and China Painting—3-hour lesson, 50 cents.

For those who work six hours per week for the entire year, a rebate will be made at the end of the Spring term, so that the lessons in drawing will be less than 35 cents.

If pupils in Art desire four or more lessons per week, special rates are made.

STUDENTS IN ALL DEPARTMENTS.

Candidates for Degrees in 1902.

BACHELOR OF ARTS.

Alspaugh, Charlotte...Washington, Kan
Andrew, John, Jr..New Salem
Cranston, Edna Mae..Hermon.
Efner, Charles Julius..Galesburg.
Epperson, Edna Ethel..Rio.
Ericson, Henry..Galesburg.
Hitchcock, Augusta Eaton..Osage, Ia.
Kimble, Thaddeus Carey..Carbondale, Kan.
Lauer, Howard Walter..Hutchinson, Kan.
Muffler, Emma Annette...Serena.
Smith, Edward Milton..Edinburg.
Stokes, Alice...Galesburg.
Stoughton, Herbert Leonard..Osage, Ia.
Varney, Charles E...Clinton.

BACHELOR OF DIVINITY.

Satoh, Kiyoshi..Miyagiken, Japan.
Thompson, George Francis..Stony Point, Mich.

Students in the College of Liberal Arts.

*Having credits sufficient in number to enter College, but one or more required studies lacking.

Allen, Blanche.	Ayars, Frank Cope.
Alspaugh, Charlotte.	Baker, Walter Graves.
Andreen, Frank G.	Belcher, Roy Swan.
Andrew, John, Jr.	Bird, Charles.
Andrew, Mary Maud.	Bowles, James Earle.

Brown, Athol Ray.
Campbell, Raymond R.
Chamberlain, Ethel Mary.
Clark, Fred Andrew.
Clay, Walter Timothy.*
Cook, Sarah Lucy.
Cooper, Harry, Mac.
Cranston, Edna Mae.
Dickinson, Frederick.
Efner, Charles Julius.
Epperson, Edna Ethel.
Ericson, Henry.
Fosher, Cora M.*
Fosher, Dudley Claude.
Gibson, John Kendall.
Gillis, Anna Moore.
Gillis, Hudson McBain.
Grier, Ethelwyn Sophia.
Grimes, Lloyd Owen.
Grubb, Emma Welton.*
Hall, Jesse A.
Hall, Olive.
Hartgrove, Claude Webster.
Hicks, Thomas Asher.*
Hilliard, Stephen Earle.*
Hitchcock, Augusta Eaton.
Hopkins, Roy Victor.
Howard, Ola Agnes.
Howell, Spencer P.*
Hurd, Jay Clinton.*
Jansen, Harry Albin.
Kidder, Ross Larned.*
Kimble, Olin Arvin.
Kimble, Thaddeus Carey.
Kober, Frances Leclerc.
Lauer, Howard Walter.

Lewis Bert Anson.*
Linderholm, Ernest Arthur.*
Long, Katherine Temple.*
McAchran, Ruth Ellen.
McCoy, Albert Graham.
Metcalf, Harold.
Miller, Edith Louise.*
Miller, Ralph Todd.
Mitchell, Anna Louise.*
Muffler, Emma Annetta.
Nash, Faith Tenney.
Needham, Nelle Jeannette.
Oldfield, Maud Alivia.
Parke, Mila.
Philbrook, Elizabeth Freeman.
Porter, Gail Quincy.*
Rees, Jenkins Bennett.
Rich, Willis Horton.
Ross, Frances Lunette.
Sammons, Mabel Alta.*
Sandburg, Charles August.*
Scott Preston Brown.
Schaffer, James Alexander.
Smith, Edward Milton.
Smith, Gilbert Wesley.
Stockton, Mary Elizabeth.*
Stokes, Alice.
Stoughton, Herbert Leonard.
Thomson, Anna Laura.*
Tyrrell, Clyde Edson.*
Van Camp, Raymond E.*
Van Cise, Ethel.
Varney, Charles E.
Ward, Vina Maye.*
Webster, Albert Sanger.
Wrigley, Anne Marion.

Students in the Divinity School.

FOURTH YEAR.

Longbrake, George Runyan.
Satoh, Kiyoshi.

Thompson, George Francis.
Varney, Mrs. Mecca.

SECOND YEAR.

DeBoer, Jacob John.
Kramer, Charles.

Patterson, George.

FIRST YEAR.

Bartholomew, Jennie Lind.
Brock, Horace Mann.
Ells, Harry Hugh.
Manning, Stanley.

Ohlmacher, Gertrude Annie.
Phillips, William.
Varney, Frank G.

SPECIAL STUDENTS.

Mary Stella Fiske.

Blanche L. Young.

Students in the Department of Music.

THEORY, HARMONY, AND HISTORY OF MUSIC.

Byloff, Julia.
Cook, Sarah Lucy.
Elting, Grace Helen.
Grant, Ethel.
Gunder, Edith Eileen.
Hobbs, Laura May.
Kimble, Thaddeus Carey.
Long, Katherine Temple.
McAchran, Ruth Ellen.
Mitchell, Anna Louise.
Multer, Lucille.
Nash, Faith Tenney.
Oldfield, Maud Alivia.
Patterson, Anna.
Peck, Vera.
Wrigley, Anne Marion.

VOCAL MUSIC.

Anderson, Lilah.
Ayars, Frank Cope.
Breece, Amber Lorena.
Byloff, Julia.
Dahlburg, Esther.
Elting, Grace Helen.
Fosher, Dudley Claude.
Grant, Ethel.
Geyer, Rosa.
Hansen, Marie.
Harmon, Winifred Grace.
Linderholm, Ernest Arthur.
Mitchell, Anna Louise.
Multer, Lucille.
Nash, Faith Tenney.
Nations, Maude Bernice.
Peck, Clyde.
Peck, Vera.
Perrine, Clarence Le Roy.
Sandusky, C. W.
Smith, Edward Milton.
Stephens, Anna.
Stockton, Mary Elizabeth.
Wrigley, Anne Marion.

PIANOFORTE.

Allen, Blanche.
Ayars, Frank Cope.
Blackman, Lillian.
Brock, Horace Mann.
Byloff, Julia.
Chamberlain, Ruth.
Chambers, Pearl.
Cook, Sarah Lucy.
Elting, Grace Helen.
Gingrich, Fannie Pauline.
Gordon, Luella.
Grant, Ethel.
Gunder, Edith Eileen.
Harmon, Winifred Grace.
Hobbs, Laura May.
Huffman, Edith.
Imai, Tame.
Johnson, Mattie.
Kenison, Lulu.
Kidder, Clytia.
Long, Katherine Temple.
Mason, Marguerite.
McAchran, Ruth Ellen.
Miller, Edith Louise.
Multer, Lucille.
Nations, Maud Bernice.
Nelson, Elvira.
Oldfield, Maud Alivia.
Oleen, Evelyn.
Olson, Amelia.
Olson, Hattie.
Parke, Eleanor.
Patterson, Anna.
Peterson, Mabelle.
Rich, Gertrude May.
Rich, Willis Horton.
Sandusky, C. W.
Schroeder, Carrie.
Sommers, Elsie.
Stockton, Mary Elizabeth.
Swanson, Hannah.
Tyner, Mrs. W. J.
Van Cise, Ethel.
Ward, Vina Maye.
Wrigley, Anne Marion.

VIOLIN.

Blair, Marie.
Boyer, Zetta.
Burnside, Orpha.
Cedarholm, Chester.
Golliday, Theo.
Hedstrom, Mary.
Hughes, Dora.

Johnson, Lyman B.
Morris, Guy.
Neifert, Ira.
O'Conner, Joseph.
Schaffer, Charles.
Swanson, Harry.
Williamson, Hugh.

MANDOLIN.

Hedstrom, Ida.
Kitchen, Everett.

Jarl, Edward.
Lueder, John.

GUITAR.

Mitchell, Anna

Williamson, Howard.

Students in the Department of Art.

Cline, Mrs. A. J.
Fiske, Mary Stella.
Fuller, Mrs. David.
Hartgrove, Gertrude West.
Kenison, Lulu.
Luster, Pearl.

Miles, Jennie.
Munson, Mrs. Charles.
Myers, Emma.
Swanson, Mrs. P. F.
White, Frances Cora.

Directory of Teachers and Students.

Col. denotes College; Unc., Unclassified; Mus., Music; Div., Divinity School.

Alexander, John.....................................Unc..........Winchester, Kan.
Allen, Blanche...Col...................Galesburg.
Alspaugh, Charlotte................................Col..........Washington, Kan.
Anderson, Lilah.....................................Mus................Galesburg.
Andreen, Frank G....................................Col. ....Woodhull.
Andrew, John, Jr.....................................Col.................New Salem.
Andrew, Mary Maud................................Col.................New Salem.
Andrew, William.....................................Unc................New Salem.
Atterberry, Archie C...............................Unc.............Atlanta, Mo.
Atterberry, Fred A...................................Unc.............Atlanta, Mo.
Atterberry, Ralph M.................................Unc.............Atlanta, Mo.
Ayars, Frank Cope....................................Col...............Seneca, Kan.
Backman, Lillian......................................Mus................Galesburg.
Baker, Walter Graves................................Col....................Morrison.
Barlow, Lawrence W..................................Unc.................Galesburg.
Bartholomew, Jennie Lynn.........................Div..............Table Grove.
Bartlett, William Almon............................Unc..................Galesburg.
Belcher, Roy Swan....................................Col...................Galesburg.
Bird, Charles...Col..................Yates City.

Blair, Marie........................ ....Unc..........New Madison, O.
Blood, M. Isabelle, Teacher in Art Department....................64 N. West St.
Boehm, Fred Daniel...............................Unc..............Muncie, Ind.
Bowles, James Earle..............................Col.............. ......Astoria.
Boyer, Zetta ....Mus................Galesburg.
Breece, Amber Lorena...........................Unc..................Dahinda.
Brock, Horace Mann..............................Div................Sheldon, Ia.
Brockman, William May...........................Unc........... ....Atlanta, Mo.
Brown, Athol Ray................................Col.............N. Henderson.
Bruner, Glenn Carlton...........................Unc................Monmouth.
Burnside, Orpha................................Mus.................Knoxville.
Byloff, Julia..................... ....Mus. ....Galesburg.
Campbell, Raymond R............................Col....................De Land.
Cedarholm,/Chester.. ....Mus. ....Galesburg.
Chamberlain, Ethel Mary.. ....Col ....Galesburg.
Chamberlain, Ruth..............................Mus.................Galesburg.
Chambers, Pearl...............................Mus.................Galesburg.
Clarke, Fred Andrew............. ....Col....................Maquon.
Clay, Walter Timothy*.....................Col..................Galesburg.
Cline, Mrs. A. J...............................Art.................Galesburg.
Cook, Grace Jane................................Unc................Galesburg.
Cook, Richard Clarence...........................Unc... ....Galesburg.
Cook, Sarah Lucy..................................Col.................Galesburg.
Cooper, Harry Mac..............................Col. ....Oquakwa.
Cranston, Edna Mae.............. ....Col..................Hermon.
Custer, Harry W................................Unc.............Galesburg.
Dahlberg, Esther...............................Mus.................Galesburg.
Davis, Ida Amy...............................Unc................Otranto, Ia.
De Boer, Jacob John ....Div......Benton Harbor, Mich.
Dickinson, Frederick ....Col......... ....Chicago.
Downes, Charles Walter..........................Unc.......... ......Winslow, Ariz.
Edwards, Russell............................,....Unc....................Cadiz, O.
Efner, Charles Julius........ ....Col ....Galesburg.
Ells, Harry Hugh.................................Div............Charlotte, Mich.
Elting, Grace Helen.............................Mus............ Burlington, Ia.
Epperson, Edna Ethel............................Col......................Rio.
Ericson, Henry..... ....Col................Galesburg.
Eustice, Bert Miller..............................Unc.............. ....Stockton.
Ferris, Mamie....................................Unc. ....Galesburg.
Fisher, Fred Bradbury............................Unc...............New Salem.
Fiske, Mary Stella..............................Div.........Pleasant Lake, Ind.
Fosher, Cora Margaret*........ ....Col..................Galesburg.
Fosher, Dudley Claude............................Col..................Galesburg.
Fowler, Prof. Frank Hamilton...................................1155 E. Knox St.
Fuller, Mrs. David..............................Art..................Galesburg.
Geyer, Rosa.......... ....Mus.................Galesburg.
Gibson, John Kendall............................Col..... ....Kirkwood.
Gillis, Anna M...................................Col..........Mt. Pleasant, Ia.
Gillis, Hudson McBain............................Col.............Mt. Pleasant, Ia.
Gingrich, Fannie Pauline...........................Mus...............Galesburg.
Golliday, Theo..................................Mus...... ....Galesburg.
Gordon, Lueille.................................Unc.......St. Joseph Mo.
Grant, Ethel....................................Mus.................Galesburg.
Grier, Ethelwyn Sophia...........................Col............. Racine, Wis.
Grimes, Lloyd Owen,.............................Col.. ....Blue Hill, Neb.
Grubb, Emma Welton*..:..........................Col..................Hamilton.

Grubb, Prof. Jon Watson ....1427 E. Knox St.
Gunder, Edyth Eileen....................... ....Unc.................Arcanum, O.
Hale, Mrs. Ada M. H., Matron of Ladies' Hall..........................Galesburg.
Hall, Jesse........................ ....Col............. Lansing, Kan.
Hall, Olive...Col...................Sycamore.
Hansen, Marie.................................... ....Mus.................Galesburg.
Harmon, Winifred Grace......................... Mus.................Galesburg.
Harris, Dell Ransom....................................Unc.............Blandinsville.
Harshbarger, Allen, Janitor...859 Day St.
Hartgrove, Claude Webster......................Col.... ....Galesburg.
Hartgrove. Gertrude West.....................Art.................Galesburg.
Hathaway, M. Agnes, Dean of Women...............................Ladies' Hall.
Hedstrom, Ida.... ....Mus....................Victoria.
Hedstrom, Mary.................................Mus... ....Victoria.
Hicks, Thomas Asher*............... ....Col.. ....Stockton.
Hillard Stephen Earle*...................................Col...................Lafayette.
Hitchcock, Augusta Eaton......................Col...................Osage, Ia.
Hobbs, Laura May..............................Unc......Benton Harbor, Mich.
Hopkins, Roy Victor. ....Col...................Princeville.
Howard, Ola Agnes........... ....Col.................Walton, Ind.
Howell, Spencer Pritchard*.. ....Col................ Woodhull.
Huffman, Edith...Mus......................Woodhull.
Hughes, Dora.....................................Mus................ Monmouth.
Hughes, George Edward..........................Unc.......New Athens, O.
Hurd, Jay Clinton*..............................Col.................... Maquon.
Imai, Tame........ ....Unc.................Tokio, Jap.
Jansen, Harry Albin..............................Col..................Woodhull.
Jarl, Edward.......................................Mus.................Galesburg.
Johnson, Lyman B......................... ....Mus...............Galesburg.
Johnson, Mattie...............................Mus...............Galesburg.
Johnson, Winfield G............................Unc...................Brimfield.
Kenison, Lulu........................ . ...Mus. and Art.....Waterloo, Ia.
Kidder, Amanda, Teacher in Elocution...........................1044 E. Knox St.
Kidder, Clythia..Mus....................Galesburg.
Kidder, Ross Larned*..................................Col.............Youngstown.
Kimble, Olin Arvin............................Col........... Carbondale Kan.
Kimble, Prof. Ralph Grierson.......................................427 Locust St.
Kimble, Thaddeus Carey............... ....Col ....Carbondale.
Kitchen, Everett...............................Mus.................Galesburg.
Kober, Florence Leclerc...... ....Col.............Ft. Bidwell, Cal.
Kramer, Charles...................................Div................Galesburg.
Lauer, Howard Walter.....:...................Col ... .Hutchinson, Kan.
Lessig, Raymond Stuart........................Div................Knoxville.
Lewis, Bert Anson*...............................Col...... West Mitchell, Ia.
Linderholm, Ernest Arthur*.......................Col........................Altona.
Long, Katherine Temple*.................... ......Col.................Galesburg.
Longbrake, George Runyan......................Div..........Albert Lea, Minn.
Longbrake, Dr. Guy A., Medical Examiner.....................347 E. Main St.
Lueder, John.................... .. ..Mus...... ....Galesburg.
Lundberg, Prof. Karl Jakob Rudolph........... ....572 Lombard St.
Luster, Pearl.....................................Art.................Galesburg.
Manning, Stanley...................................Div...................Chicago.
Martin, Calista.................................Unc..............Poultney, Vt.
Mason, Marguerite...............................Mus.................Galesburg.
McAchran, Ruth Ellen............................Col.............Bloomfield, Ia.
McCoy, Albert Graham..........................Col...................Monmouth.

McCreight, Harry C................................Unc......................Aledo.
Metcalf, Harold...................................Col.............Blandinsville.
Miles, Jennie...................................Art..............Knoxville.
Miller, Edith Louise*...............................Col .. ..Monmouth.
Miller, Lee Warren ....Unc ....Fairdale.
Miller, Ralph Todd................................Col................Monmouth.
Mitchell, Anna Louise*.. .. ..Col..............Round Grove.
Morris, Guy...Mus................:Galesburg.
Muffler, Emma Annetta................................Col............. ....Serena.
Multer, Lucille D................................Unc....... ....Altona.
Munson, Mrs. Charles...............................Art.................Galesburg.
Myers, Emma...Art.................Galesburg.
Nash, Pres. Charles Ellwood..... .... 1115 E. Knox St.
Nash, Faith Tenney,.................................Col.................Galesburg.
Nations, Maud Bernice......... ....Unc.................. Barry.
Neifert, Ira..Mus...... ......Galesburg.
Needham, Nelle Jeannette......................Col............Racine, Wis.
Nelson, Elvira.................... ....Mus..........Galesburg.
Ober, Floyd Hitchcock....... ....Unc......Sheldon, Ia.
O'Conner, Joseph.....................................Mus.................Galesburg.
Ohlmacher, Gertrude Anna......................Div............... Sycamore.
Oldfield, Maud Alivia............................Col..........Mitchellville, Ia.
Oleen, Evelyn ....Mus............ Galesburg.
Olson, Amelia ....Mus............ Galesburg.
Olson, Hattie......................................Mus.................Woodhull.
Parke, Eleanor J ....,..........Unc.................Sycamore.
Parke, Mila...Col.................Sycamore.
Parker, Prof. Isaac Augustus.....................................488 Lombard St.
Patterson, Anna...................................Mus...... ....Galveston, Ind.
Patterson, George...............................Div...................Stockton.
Peck, Clyde...Mus..................Galesburg.
Peck, Vera.....,...................................Mus............. Galesburg.
Perrine, Clarence...................................Mus...... Burlington, Ia.
Peterson, Mabelle...............................Mus...................Galesburg.
Philbrook, Elizabeth Freeman ....Col..............Racine, Wis.
Phillips, William...............................Div...................Chicago.
Porter, Gail Quincy*.................................Col................De Land.
Ray, William Franklin............................Unc..........New Madison, O.
Rees, Jenkins Bennett............................Col.................Galesburg,
Rice, Dr. Delia M., Medical Examiner.........................84 N. Prairie St.
Rich, Prof. Frederick William....................................1379 E. Knox St.
Rich, Gertrude May...............................Mus.............Galesburg.
Rich, Willis Horton...............................Col.............Galesburg·
Rogers, Charles Clinton............................Unc.................Galesburg.
Ross, Frances Lunette...........................Col.....................Avon.
Sammons, Mabel Alta*.................,...........Col..................Joliet.
Sandburg, Charles August*......................Col.... . ...Galesburg.
Sandusky, C. W.....................................Mus.................Galesburg.
Satoh Kiyoshi......................................Div..........Miyagiken, Jap.
Schaeffer, Charles.................................Mus.................Galesburg.
Schroeder, Carrie........... .. ..Mus.:................Galesburg.
Scott, Preston Brown...............................Col................. Galesburg.
Shaffer, James Alexander*........................Col.....:.........Williamsfield.
Smith, Celia May.....,...........................Unc...................Dahinda.
Smith, Edward Milton..............................Col...................Edinburg.
Smith, Gilbert Wesley................... ....Col.................Galesburg.

Smith, Thomas Huse................................Unc.................Colchester.
Sommers. Elsie....................................Mus.............Burlington, Ia.
Stephens, Agnes...................................Mus................Woodhull.
Stickney, Eva Jane. ....Unc.............Chester, Vt.
Stockton, Mary Elizabeth*.........................Col.................Monmouth.
Stokes, Alice Grace...............................Col.................Galesburg.
Stoughton, Herbert Leonard........................Col.................Osage, Ia.
Swanson, Hannah...................................Mus.............Galesburg.
Swanson, Harry....................................Mus.............Galesburg.
Swanson, Mrs. P. F................................Art.............Galesburg.
Tanney, Claude Bernard... ....Unc....................Avon.
Thompson, George Francis..........................Div........Stony Point, Mich.
Thomson, Anna Laura*..............................Col.............Table Grove.
Thorp, Joel Rex...................................Unc...........Merriam, Kan.
Tipton, Fred Lincoln..............................Unc..................Girard.
Tyner, Mrs. W. J..................................Mus.............Galesburg.
Tyrrell, Clyde Edson*.............................Col.................Stockton.
Uhler, Edna, Teacher in Music...Ladies' Hall.
Van Camp, Raymond E.*.............................Col.............Otranto, Ia.
Van Cise, Ethel......... ....Col.............Denver, Col.
Varney, Charles Edward............................Col.................Clinton.
Varney, Frank G...................................Div.................Galesburg.
Varney, Mrs. Mecca................................Div.................Clinton.
Wait, Prof. Emma B...................................1347 E. Knox St.
Ward, Vina Maye*..................................Col.............Superior, Neb.
Webster, Albert Sanger............................Col.................Galesburg.
Webster, Charles A., Treasurer...........................328 Holmes Building.
Welsh, Frank Edward............................ Unc............Williamsfield.
White, Frances Cora...............................Art.................Galesburg.
White, Prof. Nehemiah................................1473 E Knox St.
Whitney, Bertha Louise............................Unc............Buffalo Prairie.
Williamson, Howard................................Mus.............Galesburg.
Williamson, Hugh ....Mus.............Galesburg.
Wright, Prof. Philip Green...........................1443 E. Knox St.
Wrigley, Anne Marion..............................Col.................Chicago.
Young, Blanche L..................................Div.................Galesburg.

*Having credits sufficient in number to enter College, but one or more required studies lacking.

GENERAL SUMMARY.

COLLEGE OF LIBERAL ARTS.

Candidates for degrees in 1902.

    Bachelor of Arts............................. 14
                   — 14

Students in the College of Liberal Arts.................... 82

UNCLASSIFIED STUDENTS.

Unclassified Students............................ 45

RYDER DIVINITY SCHOOL.

Candidate for a degree in 1902.

    Bachelor of Divinity.......................... 1

Students in Divinity School.
    Fourth Year.......... 4
    Second Year 3
    First Year........ 7
    Special Students 2
                   — 17

MUSIC.

Students in Harmony and Musical History..... 16
Students in Pianoforte. 45
Students in Vocal Culture............ 24
Students in Violin.................... 14
Students in Mandolin...................................... 4
Students in Guitar............ 2
                 —105

ART.

Students in Art.............. 11
Names entered twice................ 71

    Total 204

ASSOCIATION OF GRADUATES.
1902-1903.

OFFICERS.

PRESIDENT,

W. R. TAPPER, CHICAGO.

VICE PRESIDENT,

C. E. VARNEY, CLINTON.

SECRETARY,

FANNIE P. GINGRICH, GALESBURG.

TREASURER,

JON W. GRUBB, GALESBURG.

HISTORIAN,

LORA A. TOWNSEND, GALESBURG.

BOARD OF DIRECTORS.

W. R. TAPPER.	R. D. BOWER.
C. A. WEBSTER.	FANNIE P. GINGRICH.
G. A. LONGBRAKE.	C. ELLWOOD NASH.
R. G. KIMBLE.	NELLIE TOMPKINS.

ADA HASBROOK HALE.

Graduates.

The degree of A. M. or M. S. placed immediately after a name, implies that the corresponding Bachelor's degree (A. B. or B. S.) was received on graduation.

The person to whose name a star is attached is deceased. The date following designates the year of his death.

1856.

William Worth Burson, A. M.......Manufacturer, 3424 Sheridan Drive, Chicago.
William Ramey Cole, A. M.....................Clergyman, Mt. Pleasant, Iowa.
Hon. Thompson W. McNeeley, A. M............Ex-M. C., Attorney, Petersburg.
Hon. Lewis Alden Simmons, A. M., *1889.......................Wellington, Kan.
Addie Hurd, A. M. (Mrs. Wm. Van Horn)......917 Sherbrook St., Montreal, Can.
Jennie Miles, A. M., *1859..Decatur.

1857.

Fielding B. Bond, A. B., *1862... Greenbush.
Floyd G. Brown, A. B., *1868...Mankato, Minn.
James Henry Chapin, A. M., Ph. D., *1892..........................Meriden, Conn.
Hon. Edward D. Laning, A. B..... ....Attorney, Petersburg.
Hon. Scott Wike, B. S., *1901..Barry.

1858.

Anson L. Clark, A. M., M. D. President Bennett Eclectic Medical College, Chicago...Elgin.
Thomas Gorman, A. B., *1891...Columbus, O.

1859.

Hon. George W. Elwell, B. S., *1869.............................Chillicothe, Mo.
Eugene Beauharnais Hill, B. S..................Manufacturer, Ottumwa, Iowa.
Almon Kidder, A. M...Attorney, Monmouth.
Mary Jane Fuller, B. S......................................Tarpon Springs, Fla.
Ruth Waldron Miller, M. S. (Mrs. Brower). *1892...................... Chicago.

1860.

Jonathan Eden Brown, A. B.................................Farmer, Peabody, Kan.
Arick Burr, B. S., *1860..Charleston.
Hon. William Judah Frisbee, A. M..........................Druggist, Bushnell.
James Scott Lindsay, A. B., *1860...Onarga.
Albert Sidney Slater, M. S., M. D...Wataga.

1861.

Hon. Franklin Fayette Brower, A. M., *1869............................. ..Ottawa.
Everett Lorentus Conger, A. M., D. D.................Clergyman, Pasadena, Cal.
Henry George Pollock, A. M.......................... Clergyman, Madison, Ind.
Mary Stewart Miller, A. B. (Mrs. Catlin), *1867.....................Vinton, Iowa.

1862.

Hon. Edwin Hurd Conger, A. M..........U. S. Minister to China, Peking, China.
Samuel Alvus Dow, A. M., M. D........Wyalong, New South Wales, Australia.
William Sampson Dow, B. S., *1863.......................................Galesburg.
Hon. Charles Allen Holmes, A. M..................Attorney, New London, Wis.
Hamilton Lafayette Karr, A. M............................Attorney, Osceola, Ia.
Frederick Warren Livingston, M. S....................Teacher, San Diego, Cal.
Harvey Rowell, A. B.......................Solicitor of Patents, Columbus, Wis.
Hon. John Crocker Sherwin, M. S., Ex-M. C., Attorney,
                                            1234 Columbus St., Denver, Colo.
Alfred Henry Trego, A. M.............................Manufacturer, Hoopeston.
George John Turner, A. M., M. D., *1899...........................Oskaloosa, Ia.
Eugenia Adaline Fuller, B. S. (Mrs. J. W. Ranstead).......................Elgin.

1863.

Samuel Addison Calhoun, A. B......Adv. Solicitor "German Demokrat," Peoria.
Hon. John W. Ranstead, B. S.......................................Attorney, Elgin.
Hannah Jane Biddlecombe, M. S.Bookkeeper Glendale Furnace Co.,Columbus,O.
Oricy Villa Crocker, L. A., (Mrs. Nead) *1880...........................Galesburg.
Sara Jane Miles, A. M., (Mrs. Bullman) ....Galesburg.
Mary Addie Moore. M. S., (Mrs. Sumner Ellis).........2734 Prairie Ave., Chicago.
Sarah Jane Pike, L. A., Mrs. E. H. Conger).....................Peking, China.

1864.

Elmore Chase, B. S.......................................Teacher, Fair Oaks, Cal.
Leslie Greenwood, A. M .....With Farmers' Loan and Trust Co., Sioux City, Ia.
Laura Lavinia Pike, A. M., (Mrs. J. S. McConnell)......4359 Lake Ave., Chicago.
Josephine Raymond, A. M., (Antioch College), (Mrs. Maxwell)......Champaign.
Sallie Raymond, L. A., (Mrs. J. B. Green)................................Ramsey.

1865.

Elmore Chase, B. S., A. M..............................Teacher, Fair Oaks, Cal.
John Henry McCormick, B. S............. ....Caledonia, Mo.
Alice Caroline Chapin, B. S.Teacher, 222 West 3d South St., Salt Lake City,Utah.

1866.

Hon. Elwin Wallace Claycomb, A. M..................... Farmer, Eureka, Kan.
Hon. Geo. R. Shook, B. S..................Teacher and Surveyor, Fruita, Colo.
James Smith McConnell, B. S.............Attorney, 84 Washington St., Chicago.
Emma N. H. Conger, A. M., (Mrs. S. W. Conger)................. Villa Park, Cal.

1867.

William Bryan Carlock, B. S............................ Attorney, Bloomington.
William Harvey Woods, B. S.....................................Farmer, Mendota.
Helen Maria Bingham, L. A., M. D..................................Monroe, Wis.

1868.

Henry Moses Chase, A. B., *1870......................................Concord, Vt.
Hon. James O'Donnell, B. S., *1901...................................Cherokee, Ia.
Wellington Smith, B. S., *1870......................................Annawan.
Edward Keys Walbridge, B. S.......Loan and Real Estate Agent, Girard, Kan.
Mary J. Claycomb, A. M., (Mrs. J. W. Grubb).........................Galesburg.
Josephine Marian Kirk, A. M., (Mrs. Kerr) *1879.......................Chicago.

Almeda Beals, L. A., (Mrs. Charles Wickwire)......................Farmington.
Sarah Elvira Edwards, L. A.. (Mrs. Otis Jones) *1899...........Los Angeles, Cal.
Grace Greenwood, L. A., (Mrs. E. E. Holroyd) *1898.....................Chicago.
Emeline Elizabeth Kirk, L. A., *1881....................................Rockford.
Frances Elizabeth Pike, L. A., (Mrs. J. Kirk Keller).......Artist, St. Louis, Mo.
Mary Ann Sparks, L. A., (Mrs. Milnor)..............................Litchfield.
Florence Adeline Tenney, L. A., (Mrs. Edwards) *1871..............Omaha, Neb.
Mary Emeline Weston, L. A., (Mrs. Woodman), *1888..............Portland, Me.

1869.

Ráuseldon Cooper, B. S....................................Attorney, Oquawka.
Hon. Samuel Kerr, A. M....................Attorney, 189 La Salle St., Chicago.
Hon. Michael F. Knappenberger, B. S.............Attorney, Jewel City, Kan.
Howard Knowles, B. S...Galesburg.
Patrick Talent, B. S...........................Attorney, Butte City, Mont.
John Ewalt Wiley, B. S................................Farmer, Elmwood.
Mary Emily Dunton,A.M.,(Mrs. Samuel Kerr)..1323 Washington Blvd., Chicago.
Ella May Greenwood L.A.,(Mrs.S.O.Snyder)....687 3rd St., Salt Lake City, Utah.
Mary Hartman, L. A., A. M. 1888.......Teacher in State Normal Univ., Normal.

1870.

Jared Perkins Blood, A. B...................Attorney, Sioux City, Iowa.
Hon. Abraham Miller Brown, A. M.....................Attorney, Galesburg.
Nathaniel Ray Chase, A. M., M. D................................Newport, R. I.
Matthias Crum, M. S........................Banker, Farmer City.
Hon. Chas. Electus Hasbrook, A. M., LL. B. (Chicago University),
                Publisher Minneapolis Times, Minneapolis, Minn.
Elmer Clifford Johnson, B. S........Manufacturer, 36 Main St., Evansville, Ind.
Otis Jones, B. S..................................115 Monroe St., Chicago.
Israel Cyrus Stockton, M. S......Clerk, Interior Department, Washington, D. C.
Hon. John Hill Walbridge, B. S.....................Farmer, West Concord, Vt.
Mary Ann Chapin, L. A.. (Mrs. T. T. Perry) *1883...................Girard, Kan.
Flora Amanda Edwards, L. A., (Mrs. J. F. Fargo).............San Antonio, Cal.

1871.

Hon. Martin Ireneus·Brower, A. M.....................Attorney, Fullerton, Neb.
Hon. Willis Hardin Fuson, A. M., *1884......................Wa Keeney, Kan.
Frank Tenney Greenwood, A. B.....................Druggist, Seneca, Kan.
Hon. Madison Reynolds Harris, A.B.,Att'y, 148 W.Madison St., Rm. 30,Chicago.
Hon. Samuel Parsons McConnell, A. B.,
                Ex-Circuit Judge, Attorney, Home Insurance Building, Chicago.
John DeBolt Stephenson, B. S., *1872....................................Dexter, Ind.
Ida Bullock, L. A., (Mrs. Thatcher) *1894........................Attleboro, Mass.
Hanna Laura Haight, B. S..................................Teacher, Mendota.
Ada May Hasbrook, A. M., (Mrs. Hale),
                Matron Ladies' Hall, Lombard College, Galesburg.
Mary Knowles, L. A., (Mrs. J. S. Alspaugh)................Washington, Kan.
Flora Adaline Prindle, L. A., (Mrs. A. G. Dow).................... Galesburg.

1872.

Albert Elmore Chase, B. S....... Deputy U. S. Mining Surveyor, Boulder, Colo.
Joseph Albert Gates, A. B.......Nat. Military Home, Box 97, Leavenworth, Kan.
Alice M. Bingham, L. A., (Mrs. Copeland)........School Trustee, Monroe, Wis.
Mattie Wilburn Burford, L. A., (Mrs. Bates)...........Merchant, Wichita, Kan.

1873.

Theodore C. Stevens, A. M., *1892....................................Lincoln, Neb.
Ada D. Bingham, L. A., M. D....................1623 Gaylord St., Denver, Colo.
Ella M. Brown, L. A., (Mrs. Salley) *1883.......................... ..Monroe, Wis.
Anna L. Nelson, L. A., (Mrs. Fuson)...............................Emporia, Kan.
Clara Richardson, L. A., (Mrs. G. F. Claycomb)....................Farragut, Ia.
Sarah A. Richardson, A. M.................................... Lawrence, Kan.
Mary M. Stevens, A. M...............................871 East St., Lincoln, Neb.

1874.

William Albrecht, B. S., *1878...Tiskilwa.
Eugene E. Brunson, B. S., M. D ....Ganges, Mich.
Daniel Clingingsmith, B. S................................... ....Newton, Kan.
William E. Day, B. S............... .Teacher, 198 Oakwood Boulevard, Chicago.
Morris W. Fletcher, B. S., M. D. ....Collierville, Tenn.
Irene A. Conger, L. A., (Mrs. Courtney), *1891.............................Chicago.
Belle Sherman, B. S........................:..................Teacher, Ithica, N. Y.

1875.

Charles A. Buck, L. A...Merchant, LeRoy.
Lucien J. Dinsmore, B. S., A. M., 1886.......Clergyman, 1389 Perry St., Chicago.
Charles Ellwood Nash, A. M., S. T. D. (Tufts),
                        President Lombard College, Galesburg.
Carrie W. Brainard, A. M., B. D., (St. Lawrence)...Clergyman, Rome City, Ind.
Emma S. Collins, L. A., (Mrs. J. E. Buchanan)............Teacher, Lake Forest.
Lillie E. Conger, L. A., *1877...Oneida.
Genie R. Edwards, L. A. (Mrs. Noteware), *1888..............Minneapolis, Minn.
Jennie C. Nelson, L. A., (Mrs. Nichols)...............................St. Charles.
Josie M. Pryne, L. A...... ....113 Hanover St., Mankato, Minn.
Luella R. Warner, L. A., (Mrs. Frank Hitchcock)
                        Teacher of Painting, Mosca, Colo.

1876.

Hon. J. L. Hastings, B. S., *1894...Galesburg.
Charlette Fuller, M. S., (Mrs. S. M. Risley).......................Harvard, Neb.
Stella Hale, L. A...Galesburg.
Lottie E. Leighton, B. S., (Mrs. L. J. Dinsmore)..... ....1389 Perry St., Chicago.
Izah T. Parker, A. M., *1891...Banning Cal.

1877.

George F. S. Baker, A. M., *1891..Goodenow.
Charles C. Maynard, A. M....................Dentist, 97 S. 1st St., San Jose, Cal.
Clara Z. Edwards, L. A., (Mrs. J. F. Calhoun),
                        2121 Bryant Ave., South, Minneapolis, Minn.
Emily L. Fuller, A. M.....................................Teacher, Galesburg.
Eugenia Fuller, A. M....................Principal High School, Riverside, Cal.
Lottie J. Humphrey, B. S., *1879...Tipton, Ia.
Ella McCullough, L. A., (Mrs. J. D. Welsh)...........................Galesburg.

1878.

Ozro P. Bostwick, A. B.............................Supt. City Schools, Clinton, Ia.
Eben H. Chapin, A. M., B. D., (Tufts)...Clergyman, 18 Maple St. Rockland, Me.
Shirley C. Ransom, B. S., A. M.,1892,
                Agent Home Building Co., Holmes Building, Galesburg.
Adah M. Mariner, M. S., (Mrs. Stewart) ....Monmouth.

1879.

Jon W. Grubb, M. S..................Professor Lombard College, Galesburg.
Charles P. Hale, A. M...........................Bank Cashier, Pittsburg, Kan.
Douglas A. Myers, B. S..............................Real Estate Agent, Peoria.
Charles A. Webster, B. S...............Treasurer Lombard College, Galesburg.
J. Edwin Webster, B. S..Merchant, Galesburg.

1880.

Henry S. Livingston, A. M., *1895..................................Galesburg.
\William H. Livingston, A. B., Auditor Mercantile Mutual Building and
           Loan Association, 716 Delaware St., Kansas City, Mo.
William A. Parker, A. M........ .....Civil Engineer, U. P. R. R., Kansas City, Mo.
Otto H. Swigart, B. S........................Farmer and Stockman, Champaign.
Mollie B. Devendorf, B. S.............Stenographer, 689 W. Adams St., Chicago.
Jennie B. Townsend, B. S., (Mrs. C. A. Webster).....................Galesburg.

1881.

George F. Hughes, A. B...................................Attorney, Yates City.
Milo C. Summers, M. S., War Department Clerk, Surgeon General's office,
           314 Seventh Street, Northeast, Washington, D. C.
Lura D. Bailey, A. B., Mrs. G. F. Hughes).....................Yates City.

1882.

Reuben D. Bower, B. S...Clerk, Galesburg.
Henry M. Chase, A. M.................Loan and Real Estate Agent, Galesburg.
Lafayette Swart, B. S.......................Farmer, Murfreesborough, Tenn.
Elmer H. West, M. S., '1894.................................Yates City.

1883.

Chas. E. Brewster, A. B., Loan and Real Estate Agent,
           1770 Emerson Avenue, South, Minneapolis, Minn.
James Weston Carney, B. S., B. D., (Tufts).................Attorney, Galesburg.
Lloyd Z. Jones, B. S......................County Surveyor and Farmer, Galva.
John H. Miles, B. S......................................Farmer, Bushnell.
Fannie M. Edwards, A. B., (Mrs. C. E. Brewster),
           1770 Emerson Ave., South, Minneapolis, Minn.
Lizzie E. Furniss, B. S., (Mrs. W. J. Moring)
           Teacher, 2200 Logan Ave., Denver, Col.
Emma J. Livingston, L. A., (Mrs. A. T. Wing)..................Maryville, Mo.
Elma E. Williams, A. M ....Teacher, Geneseo.

1884.

Anna M. Brewster, M. S., (Mrs. E. H. West)..................Yates City.
Gay M. Brunson, B. S., M. D., D. D. S..........................Dentist, Joliet.
Lulu M. Burt, B. S , (Mrs. W. B. Cravens)......2401 E. 11th St., Kansas City, Mo.
Charles L. Edwards, B S., Ph. D. (Leipsic)
           Professor of Biology, Trinity College, Hartford, Conn.
Jay C. Edwards, M. S........................... .4000 Vincennes Ave., Chicago.
Frank R. Jones, B. S....................Cashier American Well Works, Aurora.

1885.

Jennie B. Conger, A. M., (Mrs. Conger)........1059 E. 34th St., Los Angeles, Cal.
Eugene F. Carney, B. S., *1887..Galesburg.
Alma J. Devore, B. S., (Mrs. J. H. Miles)...............................Bushnell.

Lizzie B. Hughes, B L., (Mrs. D. Perry)......................... ....Table Grove.
Ella Suiter, B. S., (Mrs. Geo. Pittard), *1894 ....Alexis.
Hon. Lyman McCarl, M. S ....Attorney, 304 N. Sixth St., Quincy.
J. Douglas Welsh, B. S........ ....Attorney, Galesburg.
George Crum, B. D...............................Clergyman, Cedar Rapids, Ia.
Wallace F. Small, B. D..Everett, Wash.

1886.

Rainie Adamson, M. S. (Mrs. W. F. Small)....Co. Supt. Schools, Everett, Wash.
L. Ward Brigham, M. S., M. D., B. D., (Canton)....Clergyman, Rochester, Minn.
John M. Davies, M. S...Teacher, Maywood.
Anna H. Ebberd, B. S., (Mrs. Cyrus Hannum)......................Campbell, Neb.
Alice L. Roberts, B. S., (Mrs. J. L. Andrew)...................National City, Cal.
Rachel A. Watkins, M. S., (Mrs. Billings , B. D., 1894......................Texas.
August Dellgren, B. D...........................Clergyman, Minneapolis, Minn.
Hiram J. Orelup, B. D...............................Clergyman, Whitesville, N. Y.

1887.

Ella M. Grubb, A. M.................................Teacher, Stevens Point, Wis.
Hon. Henry C. Morris, A. M.......Attorney, 188 Madison St., Suite 703, Chicago·
J. W. Crane, B. S.......Attorney, 908 Guarantee Loan Bldg., Minneapolis. Minn.
Perry B. Fuller, B. S.................................. ....Clerk, Elgin.
Jay Welsh, M. S...:..Teacher, Williamsfield.
Alva T. Wing, B. S........ ....Merchant, Maryville, Mo.
John R. Carpenter, B. D..................... ......Clergyman, New Olmstead, O.
Osgood G. Colegrove, B. D...............................Clergyman, Woodstock, O.
Mary Garrard, B. D., (Mrs. I. Rollin Andrews)....3819 Charles St., Omaha, Neb.

1888.

Peter T. Hawley, B. S...... ....Merchant, Ralston, Ia.
Harry H. Jones, M. S...........Manager American Well Works, Dallas, Texas.
Allen W. Lapham, M. S., M. D., *1894............. ....:.............Victoria.
Elmer E. Taylor, B. S............................. ....Clergyman.
Elfreda L. Shaffer, B. D., (Mrs. Newport)...............Clergyman, Wauponsee.

1889.

Elmer E. Taylor, B. S., A. B. ....Clergyman, Wellsville, Mo.
George E. Dutton, M. S......................... ....Banker, Sycamore.
Frank H. Fowler, B. S., Ph. D. (The Univ. of Chicago),
                    Professor Lombard College, Galesburg.
Edward P. McConnell, M. S..............................4359 Lake Ave., Chicago.
Allen F. Moore, B. S.................................. ....Merchant, Monticello.
William T. Smith, M. S.... ....Attorney, Galesburg.
Vanna R. Williams, B. L., (Mrs. W. W. Slaughter).........Francis, Oklahoma.
Charles A. C. Garst, B. D., *1896....................................Riverside, Cal.
Carrie A. Rice, B. D.....................Clergyman, 6019 Prairie Ave., Chicago.

1890.

Frank H. Fowler, B. S., A. B., Ph. D. (The Univ. of Chicago)
                    Professor Lombard College, Galesburg.
Claude N Anderson, B. S................................Teacher, Tecumseh, Neb.
Bret H. Brigham, M. S....................Attorney, 778 Bosworth Ave., Chicago.
Elizabeth Gaile Durston, M. S., (Mrs. H. F, Simmons),
                    B. O. (Columbia School of Oratory), Woodhull.

Fred Farlow, B. S..Stock Dealer, Camp Point.
Samuel D. Harsh, B. S., *1893...Creston, Iowa.
Anna E. Ross, M. S., (Mrs. A. Lapham), M. D.,
                            Physician, 4256 Langley Ave., Chicago.
Richard L. Slater, B. S., *1894..... ....Wataga.
Loring Trott, M. S...Junction City, Kan.
James J. Welsh, B. S................................. ..... Attorney, Galesburg.
Lizzie Wigle, B. S., (Mrs. C. N. Anderson).........................Tecumseh, Neb.
Burtrust T. Wilson, M. S...........Professor Guadalupe College, Seguin, Texas.
Lilian J. Wiswell, B. L., (Mrs. E. P. McConnell)...... 4359 Lake Ave., Chicago.
Thomas E. Dotter, B. D.... ....Clergyman, Sullivan, Mo.

1891.

Willard J. White, A. M., M. D..............Professor Medicine, Longmont, Colo.
M. McClelland Case, M. S.................................Teacher, Williamsfield.
Villa A. Cole, B. S., (Mrs. M. M. Case) ....Teacher, Williamsfield.
S. Taylor Donohoe, M. S.....................United States Gauger, Pekin.
Jennie A. Grubb, B. S., (Mrs. F H. Fowler)...........................Galesburg.
Robert D. Hill, M. S ....Attorney, Lewistown.
Della M. Rogers, B. L., (Mrs. Chas. Garber).............. ....Reardan, Wash.
William Franklin Smith, B. D., *1897...........................Whitewater, Wis.

1892.

Frank N. Allen, B. S..................... ....Bookkeeper. 442 E. 45th St., Chicago.
Curtis P. Beale, M. S...........................Insurance Agent, Fairfield, Iowa.
Harry A. Blount, B. S.. Merchant, Macomb.
Ben F. Brady, B. S..Attorney, Ottawa.
Alice C. Durston, A. M...New Windsor.
Chas. W. Elliott, M. S............... ....Jeweler, Williamsfield.
Grace S. Harsh, B. S ....Creston, Ia.
Lissie Seeley, B. S., (Mrs. Leonard Crew............. ....Salem, Ia.
Daniel P. Wild, M. S...Banker, Sycamore.
Luther E. Wyman, B. S.....................Broker, Board of Trade, Chicago.
Benjamin W. Jones, Jr., B. D., *1898.... ....Barre, Vt.
Effie K. (McCollum) Jones, B. D., (Mrs. B. W. Jones)······Clergyman, Barre, Vt.
George W. Skilling, B. D..............................Clergyman, Iowa Falls, Ia.

1893.

Robert F. Anderson, A. B.. Principal Columbia School, 1402 Peoria Ave.,Peoria.
Carl C. Countryman, A. M....................Impersonator and Author, Chicago.
Ethel M. Tompkins, A. M., (Mrs. W. S. Clayberg)...........................Avon.
F. Louise Bradford, B. S ....Teacher, Quincy.
Richard Brown, M. S................................. .... Attorney, Creston, Ia.
Kate A. Carlton, B. S., (Mrs. F. W. Smith)............................DeLand, Fla.
J. Newton Conger, Jr., M. S............ ....Attorney, Galesburg.
States Dickson, B. S......................................Attorney, Kewanee.
S. Hepsey Fuller, M. S., (Mrs. J. M. Earhart)............................Wyoming.
Daisy D. Wiswell, M. S., (Mrs. G. A. Franklin)............... Carpintaria, Cal.
Guy A. Longbrake, B. L., M. D............................Physician, Galesburg.
Charles E. Varney, B. D................... ....Clergyman, Clinton.

1894.

William Richard Tapper, A. B. ....Attorney, 157 E. 47th St., Chicago.
Guy Henry Bernard, B. S..........................Bank Cashier, Glasco, Kan.

Lucy Minerva Conger, B. S.,.....Teacher Boston Conservatory of Music, Boston.
Joseph Amos Crum, B. S., M. D.......................................Oshkosh, Wis.
Maud Alice Crum, B. S..Boone, Ia.
Adelphia Gould Durston, B. S., (Mrs. George Ohse). ....Yorkville, Ill.
Albert Prentice Smith, B. S.............................Merchant, Denver, Colo.
Lucy Titus, B. S., (Mrs. R. F. Anderson)..............1402 Peoria Ave., Peoria.
Eliza M. Drake Curtis, B. D., (Mrs. J. L. Everton).......Clergyman, Hoopeston.
Rachel C. Watkins Dellgreen, B. D., (Mrs. Billings)................................
Jasper Leroy Everton, B. D....................................Clergyman, Hoopeston.
Martha Dandridge Garner, B. D., (Mrs. L. P. Jones),
..Clergyman, Blenheim, Ontario, Can.
Henry LaFayette Gillespie, B. D ... .Clergyman, Newtown, Ohio.
Elijah Emmett Hamand, B. D...Clergyman, 1222 Lyden Ave., Kansas City, Mo.
Rett E. Olmstead, B. D................ ....Clergyman, Storm Lake, Ia.
Margaret Titus, B. D., (Mrs. R. E. Olm0tead).....Clergyman, Albert Lea, Minn.
Albert Ernest Menke, Ph. D........... ....Chemist, Fayetteville, Ark.
Hans Schuler, Ph. D................................ ...Teacher, Flushing. N. Y.

1895.

John McDuffie, Ph. D....................................Teacher, Springfield, Mass.
Lucile Bragg, A. B......................................Clerk, Humboldt, Kan.
William Robert Chapin, B. S............................Bank Cashier, Kirkwood.
Frank Loren Conger, A. B..'........................... Bank Clerk, Galesburg.
Grace Winifred Conley, A. B...........................Postal Clerk, Galesburg.
Mabel Dow, A. B., (Mrs. F. L. Conger)................................Galesburg.
Robert Pinckney Higgins, B. S......................Attorney, Bloomington.
John Richard Stanley, A. B.......Agricultural Implement Dealer, Stronghurst.
Nellie Christine Tompkins, A. B...Avon.
Albert Orin Wakefield, A. B.................. ....Attorney, Sioux City, Ia.
Frances Elizabeth Cheney, B. D. *1902....................................Greenup.
Orrin Carlton Evans, B. D........ ....Clergyman, Morrison.
Charles Robert Jones, B. D.......................Clergyman, Gould Farm, Mo.
Thomas Francis Rayon, B. D..................Clergyman, Rapid River, Mich.

1896.

Jessie Beatrice Brown, A. B., (Mrs. A. C. Clock).... ....Winona, Minn.
Fred Leo Camp, A. B..................................... .....Druggist, Galesburg.
Bertha Alice Cook, A. B., (Mrs. O. C. Evans)................ ....Marseilles.
Almira Lowrey Cheney, A. B...Saybrook.
Elice Crissey, A. B...Teacher, Avon.
Homer Franklin Harsh, A. B...... ....Stockman, Lowell, Neb.
Hamilton Lafayette Karr, Jr., A. B.......................Attorney, Osceola, Ia.
Marion Alice Kendall, A. B...........................,........Brockton, Mass.
Harry McGee Lessig, A. B..Knoxville.
Ralph Grierson Kimble, A. B...........Professor Lombard College, Galesburg.
Iva Della Myers, A. B................. ....Bookkeeper, Galesburg.
Edward Leroy Shinn, A. B...N. E. Sales Agt. W. F. Jacobs & Co.,
147 Milk St , Boston, Mass.
Emma Genevra Van Liew, A. M., (Mrs. Guy Tuttle).. ....Bushnell.
Jean Gillette White, A. B., (Mrs. A. B. McGill)...........................Peoria.
James Alvin Clark, B. D...................... ....Clergyman, Webster City, Ia.
Charles William Edward Gossow, B. D................Clergyman, Seneca, Kan.
Maurice Gilbert Linton, B. D............................. Clergyman, Roseville.
Eugene Southwick, B. D................................ .... Clergyman, Corfu, N. Y.

Georgia Stanley, Diploma in Art, (Mrs. C. H. Wickham)..Teacher, Stronghurst.

1897.

Frank Pierce Anderson, A. B......,.........................Teacher, Yates City.
Loetta Frances Boyd, A. B...Teacher, Plano.
Flora May Cutter, A. B..Camp Point.
Benjamin Downs, A. B...Clerk, Winslow, Ariz.
Nina Alta Harris, A. B...Teacher, Galesburg.
Fred Louis Holcomb, A. B., M. D......................................Zenda, Kan.
Theodore Lindquist, A. B., Instructor Kansas State Agricultural
College, Manhattan, Kan.
Carrie Alice Stickney, A. B..Student New England Conservatory, Boston, Mass.
Elmer Joseph Tapper, A. B.......................Insurance Solicitor, Riverside.
Claud Bryant Warner, A. B., A. M..........................Dentist, Avon.
Guy Henry Weeks, A. B..Teacher, Galesburg.
Frances Cora White, A. B..Galesburg.
Fred Minosuke Yamaguchi, A. B..Student Yale University, New Haven, Conn.
George Hilary Ashworth, B. D.............................Clergyman, Bryan, O.
Edward Milton Minor, B. D ....Clergyman, Decatur, Mich.
George Burr Rogers, B. D ....Clergyman, Decatur, Mich.
William Willis Slaughter, B. D., *1901......................Francis, Oklahoma.
Simeon Lafayette Taylor, B. D............................Clergyman, Osage, Ia.

1898.

Mervin Wallace Allen, A. B...............................,.........Farmer, Maquon.
Alice Helen Bartlett, A. B....Instructor in Music, Lombard College, Galesburg.
Charles Reid Brown, A. B., With Knickerbocker Ice Co., 171 La Salle St., Chicago.
Joshua J. Bullman, A. B......... .. ..Farmer, Galesburg.
Ida Galbreath, A. B.... .... Teacher, Galveston, Ind.
Charles Edward Piper, A. B..Student Yale Divinity School, New Haven, Conn.
Simeon Lafayette Taylor, B. D., A. B......... ....Clergyman, Osage, Ia.
Edna Madison McDonald, B. D...............................Clergyman, Urbana.
Helen Jessie Mackay..Galesburg.
John Willis Slaughter; B. D., Student University of Michigan,
311 S Division St., Ann Arbor, Mich.
Benjamin Franklin Stacey, B. D................ ...Journalist, Las Vegas, N. M.
Oluf Tandberg, B. D......... ....Clergyman, Earlville.

Isal Caldwell, Diploma in Vocal Music, (Mrs. Lewis)..................Knoxville.

1899.

Christen Martin Alsager, A. B ....Principal City Schools, Winnebago.
Ella Berry Boston, A. B.............................. ....Galesburg.
Henry William Dubee, A. B., Professor of German, University of
Cincinnati, Cincinnati, O.
Howard Everett Foster, A. B., *1900... . ...Galesburg.
Homer Edwin Garvin, A. B.....................Traveling Salesman, Quincy.
Fannie Pauline Gingrich, A. B.................................Clerk, Galesburg.
George Runyan Longbrake, A. B.................Clergyman, Albert Lea, Minn.
Nellie Stuart Russell, A. B.....................................Teacher, Woodhull.
Lora Adelle Townsend, A. B............. ....Teacher, Galesburg.
Lloyd Chaplain, B. D., Manager Co-Operative League of Photo Art,
330 Main St., Galesburg.

Edith C. Crissey, Diploma in Instrumental Music ....Teacher, Avon.
Jennie Holmes, Diploma in Art...............................North Henderson.

1900.

Martha Belle Arnold, A. B..................................Teacher, Galesburg.
Fay Alexander Bulluck, A. B..................City Editor Rep.-Reg., Galesburg.
Gertrude Grace Kidder, A. B ....Galesburg.
Edwin Julius McCullough, A. B......................Teacher, La Prairie Centre.
Carrie Ruth Nash, A. B....................................Teacher, Galesburg.
Charles Wait Orton, A. B..Tacoma, Wash.
Burt G. Shields, B. S.......................................Stock Broker, Golden, Colo.
Iva May Steckel, A. B......Law Student, University of Colorado, Boulder, Colo.
Earl Wolcott Watson, A. B...........................Hardware Merchant, Barry.
Harry William Weeks, A. B..............Student Univ. of Illinois, Champaign.
William David Buchanan, B. D.....................Clergyman, Mt. Pleasant, Ia.

1901.

Martha Belle Arnold, A. M...................................Teacher, Galesburg.
Carrie Ruth Nash, A. M.....................................Teacher, Galesburg.
John Donington Bartlett, A. B......Medical Student Univ. of Chicago, Chicago.
Nannie Mer Buck, B. S..Teacher, Galesburg.
Gertrude West Hartgrove, A. B..Galesburg.
Julia Evelyn Lombard, A. B...............................East Orange, N. J.
Jennie Eliza Marriott, A. B., (Mrs. Buchanan)............Mount Pleasant, Iowa.
Donald P. McAlpine, A. B............................Teacher, Charlotte, Mich.
William J. Orton, A. B......................................Mount Pleasant, Iowa.
Grace Olive Pingrey, A. B....................................Coon Rapids, Iowa.
Frederick Preston, A. B..Boston, Mass
Grace Schnur, A. B...Teacher, Rio.
Francis Britton Bishop, B. D..Marseilles.

Virginia Henney, Diploma in Music..........................Mitchellville, Iowa.
Cyrena Weir, Diploma in Music...................................Galesburg.

HONORARY DEGREES.

The degreee placed immediately after the name is the honorary degree conferred by Lombard College.

An additional degree, followed by a date only, is one conferred by Lombard College.

An Additional degree, without date, is one conferred by another institution, the name of which is given, if known.

1858. *Rev. Otis A. Skinner, D. D ....Ex-President Lombard University.
1859. Rev. George S. Weaver, A. M........................ ....Canton, N. Y.
1860. *Ansel Streeter, A. M.... ....Weston, Mo.
1862. *Rev. Ebenezer Fisher, D. D.,.Principal Theological School, Canton, N.Y.
1862. Rev. Joseph Selmon Dennis, A. M...................................Chicago.
1863. *Rev. William Henry Ryder, D. D.; A. M. (Harvard).............Chicago.
1864. *Rev. Holden R. Nye, A. M................................Philadelphia, Pa.
1864. Rev. Charles Woodhouse, A. M.; M. D.............. ....Rutland, Vt.
1865. Rev. A. G. Hibbard, A. M...Wheaton.
1865. *Rev. J. G. H. Hartzell, A. M.; D. D. (St. Lawrence)..........Detroit, Mich.
1867. *Rev. William Ethan Manley, A. M............................Denver, Colo.
1867. Rev. Thomas B. St. John, A. M...
1868. *Rev. Clement G. Lefevre, D. D............................Milwaukee, Wis.
1868. William B. Powell, A. M ....Washington, D. C.
1868. Rev. James Harvey Tuttle, A. M.; D. D. ....Minneapolis, Minn.
1869. Rev. John Wesley Hanson, A. M., D. D., (Buchtel)..........Pasadena, Cal.
1869. Rev. William Wallace Curry, A. M....................Washington, D. C.
1869. ·Dev. Daniel Parker Livermore, A. M......................Melrose, Mass.
1869. Rev. Augusta J. Chapin, A. M............................Mt. Vernon, N. Y.
1870. Rev. John S. Cantwell, A. M.................................Chicago.
1870. Daniel Lovejoy Hurd, A. M.; M. D..
1870. *Rev. George Truesdale Flanders, D. D....................Rockport, Mass.
1870. *Rev. Alfred Constantine Barry, D. D.......... ....Lodi, Mass.
1872. *Rev. William Ethan Manley, D. D.; A. M., 1867.............Denver, Colo.
1872. Rev. R. H. Pullman, A. M...................................Baltimore, Md.
1872. *Rev. Gamaliel Collins, A. M.....................U. S. A., Chatham, Mass.
1872. *Rev. B. F. Rogers, A. M..................... ....Fort Atkinson, Wis.
1875. *Rev. J. H. Chapin, Ph. D.; A. B., 1857; A. M., 1860.........Meriden, Conn.
1876. Rev. George S. Weaver, D. D.; A. M., 1859. ....Canton, N. Y.
1876. Rev. John S. Cantwell, D. D.; A. M , 1870.........................Chicago.
1877. Rev. O. Cone, D. D.. Canton, N. Y.
1879. Elias Fraunfelter, Ph. D...Akron, O.
1879. Milton L. Comstock, Ph. D...........Professor, Knox College, Galesburg.
1882. Rev. Charles W Tomlinson, D. D.........·..............Taunton, Mass.
1883. *Rev. Amos Crum, A. M.................................Webster City, Ia.
1884. Matthew Andrews, A. M ....Monmouth.
1886. Rev. L. A. Dinsmore, A. M.; B. S., 1875.... ....Chicago.
1887. *Rev. Holden R. Nye, D. D.; A. M., 1864.................:.......Towanda, Pa.
1887. Rev. Charles Fluhrer, D. D.......... ....Albion, N. Y.

*Deceased.

1887. Hon Lewis E. Payson, LL. D..Pontiac.
1887. Hon. George W. Wakefield, A. M.............................Sioux City, Ia.
1888. Rev. George H. Deere, D. D...................................Riverside, Cal.
1888. Homer M. Thomas, A. M.; M. D............................ ... .Chicago.
1888. Rev. Charles A. Conklin, A. M...................... ....Springfield, Mass.
1888. Mary Hartman, A. M.; L. A , 1859...............................Normal.
1890. Rev. Jacob Straub, D. D..Chicago.
1890. George B. Harrington, A. M.......................................Princeton.
1890. Carl F. Kolbe, Ph. D ....Akron, O.
1891. Rev. A. G. Gaines, LL. D.; D. D..............................Canton, N. Y.
1892. Rev. George Thompson Knight, D. D.................Tufts College, Mass.
1892. Charles Kelsey Gaines, Ph. D., Professor St. Lawrence Univ., Canton, N.Y.
1892. Shirley C. Ransom, A. M.; B. S., 1878..........................Galesburg.
1893. Rev. Augusta J. Chapin, D. D.; A. M., 1869 ....Mt. Vernon,, N. Y.
1893. *Rev. Amos Crum, D. D.; A. M., 1885.....................Webster City, Ia.
1895. John Huston Finley, Ph. D...................................Princeton, N. J.
1893. Charles Loring Hutchinson, A. M...................... ....Chicago.
1894. Rev. Royal Henry Pullman, D. D.; A. M., 1872.............Baltimore, Md.
1894. Rev. George B. Stocking, D. D................................Lansing, Mich.
1895. Rev. Aaron Aldrich Thayer, D. D.. ....California.
1895. Rev. Andrew Jackson Canfield, Ph. D.; D. D..............Brooklyn, N. Y.
1897. Rev. Daniel Bragg Clayton, D. D......................Columbia, S. C.
1897. Rev. Thomas Sander Guthrie, D. D......................Logansport, Ind.
1898. Rev. Rodney F. Johonnot, D. D...................................Oak Park.
1898. Henry Priest, Ph. D.,.........Professor St. Lawrence Univ., Canton, N. Y.
1899. John Wesley Hanson, Jr., A. M..............................Chicago.
1900. Rev. Alfred Howitzer Laing, D. D ....Joliet.
1901. Edwin Hurd Conger, LL. D...............................Peking, China.
1901. John Sharp Cook, D. D...Galesburg.

*Deceased.

HARVARD UNIVERSITY SCHOLARSHIP.

By request of the Harvard Club of Chicago we publish the following notice:
At its annual meeting December 14, 1897, The Harvard Club of Chicago established a scholarship at Harvard University of the annual value of three hundred dollars. This scholarship is open to the graduates of the universities and colleges of Illinois who wish to follow a graduate course of study at Harvard University. Applications must be made before May 1st in each year, and senior students about to finish their undergraduate course are eligible as candidates. Communications should be addressed to Murry Nelson, Jr., Chairman, 99 Randolph Street, Chicago.

INDEX.

LOMBARD COLLEGE PUBLICATIONS—Series I., Vol. II.

[Issued Quarterly by Lombard College.]

CATALOGUE

OF

LOMBARD COLLEGE,

GALESBURG, ILLINOIS,

FOR THE YEAR ENDING JUNE 4, 1903.

GALESBURG, ILL.:
REPUBLICAN-REGISTER PRINT.
1903.

College Calendar.

1903.

MARCH 10 Tuesday............................Registration. Third Term Begins.
MARCH 26—Thursday...Senior Theses Due.
MAY 9—Saturday.................................Townsend Preliminary Contest.
MAY 16—Saturday.................................Senior Vacation Begins.
MAY 28, 29—Thursday, Friday..Examinations.
MAY 31—Sunday...Baccalaureate Sermon.
JUNE 1—Monday.............................Field Day. Gymnasium Exhibition.
JUNE 1—Monday, Evening.................Townsend Prize Contest in Declamation.
JUNE 2—Tuesday.......................Annual Meeting of Association of Graduates.
JUNE 3—Wednesday.......................Annual Meeting of the Board of Trustees.
JUNE 4—Thursday...Commencement Day

Summer Vacation.

SEPT. 1—Tuesday...Entrance Examinations.
SEPT. 2—Wednesday...........................Registration. College Year Begins.
SEPT. 7—Monday..Holiday, Labor Day.
SEPT. 30—Wednesday.......................Senior Topics for Theses Due.
NOV. 14—Saturday...........................Orations for Swan Contest Due.
NOV. 24, 25—Tuesday, Wednesday.......................................Examinations.
NOV. 25—Wednesday...First Term Ends.
NOV. 26—Thursday...................................Holiday, Thanksgiving Day.
NOV. 27—Friday.............................Registration. Second Term Begins.
DEC. 12—Saturday..................................Swan Preliminary Contest.
DEC. 23—Wednesday..........Last Day of Recitations preceding Christmas Recess.

1904.

Christmas Recess.

JAN. 5—Tuesday............................Recitations of Second Term Resumed.
JAN. 21—Thursday...Senior Syllabi Due.
JAN. 29—Friday.......................................Swan Prize Contest in Oratory.
FEB. 12—Friday..................................Holiday, Lincoln's Birthday.
FEB. 22—Monday...............................Holiday, Washington's Birthday.
MARCH 2, 3—Wednesday, Thursday.......................................Examinations.
MARCH 3—Thursday...Second Term Ends.

Spring Vacation.

MARCH 8—Tuesday.*............................Registration. Third Term Begins.
MARCH 24—Thursday...Senior Theses Due.
MAY 7—Saturday...........................Townsend Preliminary Contest.
MAY 14—Saturday...........................Senior Vacation Begins.
MAY 26, 27—Thursday, Friday...Examinations.
MAY 28—Saturday...........................Field Day. Gymnasium Exhibition.
MAY 29—Sunday...........................Baccalaureate Sermon.
MAY 30—Monday...Memorial Day.
MAY 30—Monday, Evening.................Townsend Prize Contest in Declamation.
MAY 31—Tuesday.......................Annual Meeting of Association of Graduates.
JUNE 1—Wednesday.......................Annual Meeting of the Board of Trustees.
JUNE 2—Thursday...Commencement Day.

BOARD OF TRUSTEES.

OFFICERS OF THE BOARD.

HON. J. B. HARSH, Creston, Iowa.
PRESIDENT.

CHARLES A. WEBSTER, Galesburg,
TREASURER.   Holmes Building.

PHILIP G. WRIGHT, Galesburg,
SECRETARY.   1443 East Knox St.

W. F. CADWELL, Galesburg,
AUDITOR.

Executive Committee.

HOWARD KNOWLES, Chairman.

CHARLES A. WEBSTER, Secretary.

CHARLES ELLWOOD NASH, D. D.

ROBERT CHAPPELL.   J. DOUGLAS WELSH.

Board of Visitors.

Each Universalist State Convention, which adopts Lombard College as its Institution of Learning, is entitled to send two visitors, whose duty it is to examine into the condition of the College and to assist in the choice of Trustees.

SCOPE AND IDEALS.

Between the high school or academy and the graduate, professional or technical school, American educators are coming to recognize a distinct and imperative educational function which is discharged only by the college, properly so called. This function is not so much "practical," in the commercial sense, as cultural in purpose; yet the broad results aimed at in character and in grasp of general principles, constitute the only adequate foundation in which to base the special training of the crafts and professions. Within the limits thus indicated, Lombard College is content to do its work.

Owing to differing standards and degrees of efficiency the interval between the high school and the graduate school varies greatly. At Lombard College it has seemed wise to prescribe admission requirements which presume a four years' high school course; and thus the Lombard graduation requirements are expected to meet the entrance requirements of the most advanced graduate institutions.

Inasmuch as many applicants have not had access to a four years' high school period, a considerable number of preparatory subjects are still offered at Lombard, sufficient in fact to comprise an academic course of at least three years. Further, as there are some who desire to pursue certain subjects without claiming full college standing, provision is made for such special students upon equitable terms. The pure college ideal, however, enjoins us to regard these concessions as temporary, to be granted only so long as conditions necessitate them.

On the other hand, it is believed to be not inconsistent with the college idea to allow those students who intend to enter a graduate, professional or technical school after graduation, to expedite the later course and shorten the whole period of study by directly matching the graduation requirements with the prospective entrance requirements. Thus by using his elective privilege in mapping out his college course, the Lombard A. B. may complete the subsequent Divinity course leading to the degree of B. D. in two additional years, the Medical course leading to the degree of M. D. in three years, and an Engineering course in three years.

While the number of subjects offered at Lombard is largely in excess of graduation requirements and equalled by few of the "small" American colleges, thus allowing exceptional opportunity for adapting the course to the individual student, the emphasis is laid upon quality rather than amount of work, upon principles, more than upon mere facts, and the cultivation of orderly, self-active mental life is the constant endeavor.

GENERAL STATEMENT.

LOCATION.

LOMBARD COLLEGE is located in Galesburg, Knox County, Illinois, a healthful and beautiful city of 20,000 inhabitants, noted for its public buildings, its strong churches, and the good order, intelligence, thrift and refinement of its people.

Galesburg is easily accessible by railroad from all parts of the West; being the center of the great Burlington system, leading to Chicago, Burlington, Quincy, Peoria, Rock Island, St Louis, Kansas City, Omaha, Denver, and Minneapolis; and also on the main line of the Santa Fe system. It is the northern terminus of the Fulton County Narrow Gauge R. R., connecting with the great Wabash system.

THE COLLEGE CAMPUS.

The College Campus is situated in the southeastern part of the city, and may readily be reached by the electric cars. It is thirteen acres in extent and affords ample space for base-ball, foot-ball, tennis, and other athletic sports. A large part is planted with trees which have been growing many years and have attained noble size and graceful forms. Among them are pines, larches, hemlocks, cedars, maples, elms, ash-trees, tulip-trees, and others, embracing about forty species. The trees and lawns are well kept and cared for, and the beauty of the surroundings thus created is a pleasing and attractive feature of the College.

HISTORY.

The Illinois Liberal Institute was chartered in 1851, opened for students in the autumn of 1852, invested with College powers in 1853, and took the name of Lombard University (in honor of Mr. Benjamin Lombard, at that time the largest donor to its properties) in 1855. It was one of the first Colleges in the country to admit women as students on the same terms with men, allowing them to graduate in the same class and with the same honors. The first class was graduated in 1856. The Ryder Divinity School was opened September 5, 1881. The official title of the institution was changed in 1899 to Lombard College.

THE ELECTIVE SYSTEM.

Experience has demonstrated the soundness of the educational principle that the selection of studies, in some degree, at least, should be adapted to the needs, tastes, and talents of the student. At Lombard this principle is fully recognized, and great liberty is given to students in the choice of their studies. At the same time the fact is recognized that there is a distinct educational gain to a student in pursuing a well matured and logically developed course of study. The method by which it is sought to reconcile these important principles of education at Lombard is fully explained later in the catalogue.

THE COLLEGE YEAR.

The College year begins early in September and closes early in June. It is divided into three terms of approximately equal length. (See Calendar, page 4.)

Students should, if possible, enter at the beginning of the College year, since much of the work is arranged progressively from that date. They will, however, be allowed to enter at any time when there seems a prospect of their being able to do so profitably.

Commencement day occurs the first Thursday in June.

ADMISSION REQUIREMENTS.

The requirements for admission to the College of Liberal Arts for students who are candidates for a degree, is the highest standard recommended by the joint committee of the High School and College Sections of the Illinois State Teachers' Association. This is essentially the standard recommended by the Committee of Thirteen of the National Educational Association, being the standard in force at Harvard, The University of Chicago, and other leading colleges in the United States. (See pages 23-30.)

Students not candidates for a degree may enter on probation any class for which they are prepared, and at the end of their connection with the College they will be furnished a certificate, stating the amount and quality of the work accomplished while in the College.

APPORTIONMENT OF TIME.

The regular sessions of the College are held on Monday, Tuesday, Wednesday, Thursday, and Friday.

GRADES OF SCHOLARSHIP.

From the courses of study offered, each student is expected to elect work to an amount sufficient to keep him profitably employed. In all full courses each recitation occupies one hour. Absence from a recitation will forfeit the mark in that study for the day.

At the end of every term the standing of a student in each of his courses will be expressed, according to his proficiency, by one of four grades, designated respectively by the letters, A, B, C, D.

The grade is determined by term work, estimated on the basis of attendance, quality of recitations or laboratory work, occasional tests, written exercises, etc., and by final examinations at the end of the term, the term grade and the final examination being valued in the ratio of two to one.

Grade C is the lowest which will be accepted in any study as counting towards the fulfillment of the requirements of graduation.

Students who receive grade A in all their studies may pursue not more than four courses in the succeeding term.

Students whose lowest grade is B may pursue not more than three and one-half courses in the succeeding term.

Other students are not permitted to pursue more than three courses in any term.

CHAPEL EXERCISES.

Religious exercises, at which attendance is required, are conducted daily in the College chapel.

With the view of imparting additional interest and value to these exercises, relieving them of mere formality, brief addresses by members of the faculty, or by invited speakers, upon practical life questions, or upon topics of the day, will be given from time to time. At intervals, also, special musical numbers will be introduced by the Director of the Musical Department.

LABORATORIES.

The department of Physics is well equipped with apparatus for experimentation. Students have an opportunity to obtain a practical acquaintance with the principles of Physics, through a series of Laboratory experiments, which they perform for themselves under the direction of the instructor.

The extended courses in Chemistry, described elsewhere in this Catalogue, require a large amount of practical work on the part of the student. Each student in Chemistry has a desk provided with gas, water, re-agents and all necessary conveniences. The Laboratory is well equipped for work in General Chemistry, and in Qualitative and Quantitative Analysis.

A supply of superior microscopes, with other instruments and apparatus, affords a very satisfactory equipment for experimental work in Biology.

MUSEUM.

The Museum contains valuable collections duly classified and arranged, and available for purposes of instruction. The collection of corals is especially fine. A fine collection of minerals, birds, and ethnological specimens, the loan of A. B. Cowan, Esq., a former citizen of Galesburg, is known and designated as the Cowan Collection.

LIBRARY.

The Library of the College contains about seven thousand volumes. It is located in the College building and is open daily. The books are systematically arranged and easy of access. They may be taken out by the students upon application to the librarian. A considerable fund has been raised during the past year, which will be expended as occasion arises, in the purchase of new books, thus assuring a substantial increment each year.

READING ROOM.

A Reading Room, under the auspices of a Reading Room Association, is supported by the voluntary efforts and contributions of the students, faculty, and friends. The leading newspapers and periodicals are kept on file. The Reading Room is open daily, except Sundays, for the use of the students, from 8:00 a. m. until 6:00 p. m.

GYMNASIUM.

The Gymnasium is a building 50x80 feet on the ground. On the ground floor, besides the Gymnasium proper, there is a large room, at present used as a recitation room, which can be thrown into the main room by withdrawing the movable partitions. There is also a stage, equipped with an adequate outfit of scenery, for the special use of the Department of Elocution. The apparatus, consisting of chest weights, dumb bells, Indian clubs, parallel bars, horizontal bar, flying rings, travelling rings, rowing machine, etc., is of approved patterns. The basement contains bathrooms and lockers and other conveniences.

Regular exercises are held in the Gymnasium daily, except Saturdays and Sundays. The exercises will consist of class drill, under the

charge of a director, or of special work on the apparatus in accordance
with the prescription of the medical examiner. It is intended that the
instruction shall be thoroughly scientific, aiming not so much at special
muscular or athletic development as at a sound physical culture, which
is the true basis of health and so of energy and endurance.

ATHLETICS.

The Athletic interests of the College are in charge of the Director
of Physical Culture, assisted by a Board of Management, consisting of
two members chosen from the student body, one from the faculty, and
two from the alumni. The Campus affords opportunity for foot-ball,
base-ball, and track and field events. During the winter basket-ball is
played in the Gymnasium. The Director of Physical Culture will take
personal charge of the coaching of the foot-ball, basket-ball, base-ball
and track teams.

THE LADIES' HALL.

The new Ladies' Hall, finished and first opened for use in the fall
of 1896, is a thoroughly modern building and complete in all its appointments. It is heated by steam, lighted by gas, fitted with sanitary
plumbing, including porcelain baths, closets, lavatories, etc., and supplied with every convenience of a well equipped home. The Hall will
accommodate forty young women; and all out-of-town women students,
unless permission is obtained from the President to live elsewhere, are
expected to make their home in this building.

Each room is finished with hard wood floor and furnished with
bedstead, springs, mattress, chairs, desk, dresser, and rugs. The occupants are expected to provide bedding, pillows, towels, napkins, to pay
for washing said articles, and to keep their own rooms in order.

Rates are stated on page 14.

Applications for rooms in the Hall should be made during the summer vacation to President C. Ellwood Nash, at other times to Mrs, Ada
M. H. Hale, Matron, Lombard Ladies' Hall.

LOMBARD COLLEGE PUBLICATIONS.

A series of papers is issued quarterly by the College, including the annual catalogue, containing announcements, articles discussing educational
questions, and other matter calculated to keep the College in touch with
its friends, and to extend a knowledge of educational data, processes and
theories. Copies will be sent free upon application.

The Lombard Review.

A College paper called *The Lombard Review*, is published monthly
by the students. It makes a record of College events; and serves as a

medium of communication with the friends and alumni of the College. Subscription price $1.00.

SOCIETIES.

The Erosophian.

The Erosophian Society was organized January 29, 1860. Any male student connected with the College or Divinity School is eligible to membership, and is entitled to all the benefits of the society. Its regular meetings are held on Thursday evening of each week. The literary exercises consist of orations, debates and essays.

The Zetecalian.

This Society was organized in 1863 for the women of the College. Its exercises consist of debates, essays, historical narrations, and general discussions. Regular meetings are held fortnightly on Friday afternoons. The officers are elected quarterly.

Lombard Oratorical and Debating Association.

The Lombard Oratorical and Debating Association is the local branch of the Northern Illinois Intercollegiate Oratorical League. The League holds an annual prize contest in oratory on the last Friday in April. There are two prizes of twenty and ten dollars respectively. The local organization holds a preliminary contest to decide who shall represent the College in the contest of the League. All male students of the College are eligible for membership.

PRIZES.

1. The Swan Prizes.

Two prizes for excellence in Oratory are offered annually by Mrs. J. H. Swan, of Chicago. They consist of fifteen dollars and ten dollars respectively. The contest for these prizes is held in January.

2. The Townsend Prizes.

Two prizes for excellence in Declamation are offered annually by Mrs. E. P. Townsend, of Sycamore. They consist of fifteen dollars and ten dollars, respectively. The contest for these prizes is held during Commencement week.

EXPENSES.

Boarding.

Board is furnished at the College Commons at cost.   During the past year the maximum rates have been as follows:

Board, 37 weeks: Tuition, one year (without restriction of number of
    studies); incidentals, one year; payable annually or semi-annually in
    advance.. $126.50
Board, one term; Tuition, one term (without restriction of number of stu-
    dies); Incidentals, one term, payable in advance........................   43.00
Board per week, payable in advance........... ....,   2.25
Meal tickets, 7 tickets... ....   1.05

The quality of the board furnished is not indicated by the price. Owing to the facts that provisions can be obtained at wholesale rates; that service at the table is co-operative, several students paying in part for their board in this manner; and that it is the purpose of the management to make no profit out of this department above actual operating expenses, the board is certainly equal in quality to that furnished in private families for $2.75 per week.

The yearly expenses may be estimated as follows:

Board at Commons, Tuition, Incidentals.............................. .... $126.50
Room rent...   22.50
Washing...   15.00
Books...   15.00
                                                                $179.00

Students, however, are not required to board at the Commons; some board themselves, and some board in private families. Students who board themselves may possibly cut their expenses a trifle below the above rates.   In private families rates of from $2.75 and upwards per week for board, may be obtained.

A faculty committee will assist students in securing comfortable, home-like accommodations.

The charge for board in the Ladies' Hall is $42 per term, for each person, payable in advance. This does not include the Christmas recess. The charge for room rent is from $6 to $15 per term, according to location of room, payable to the Registrar in advance. Where one person occupies a double room from choice, an extra charge of 50 cents per week will be made, but the privilege of assigning two persons to such room is reserved. Board will be furnished to women students of the College who do not have rooms in the Hall at the rate of $3.25 per week, payable in advance.

Tuition and Incidentals.

Students in the College of Liberal Arts and Unclassified students will pay a tuition fee for each study pursued. The charge, except in theoretical music and certain medical courses, is $3.50 per term for each full course, a course being a study taken for one term and counting as one credit toward graduation. The rate for each fractional course is in proportion to the credit allowed for such fractional course toward graduation. Thus, a half course is half rate; a third course, third rate, etc.

Students in Chemistry, Mineralogy, and Biology are required to deposit with the Registrar a sum sufficient to cover laboratory bills. Students in General Chemistry will deposit two dollars; students in Analytical Chemistry, five dollars; students in Mineralogy, three dollars; and students in Biology, two dollars each. At the close of the term there will be returned the balance remaining, after deducting cost of chemicals and broken apparatus.

Students in Physics each pay one dollar per term as a laboratory fee.

The charge for incidentals, to be paid by all students of the College is $5.00 per term.

No student will be enrolled in any class until he presents the Registrar's receipt for the payment of tuition and incidentals. The registration fee is one dollar. The payment of this fee will be remitted to all who register on the first day of the term.

Tuition and incidentals will not be refunded. In case a student is absent a half term or more from sickness or other adequate cause a certificate for a half term's tuition and incidentals will be given the student (at his request), said certificate good "to order" for its face value at any succeeding term.

Art and Music.

For information as to charges in Art and Music, see under these departments later in this Catalogue.

AID TO WORTHY STUDENTS.

Free tuition will be given to the student who graduates with highest rank from an approved high school. Students receiving this concession may be called upon for some College service.

Perpetual Scholarship.

Through the generosity of its friends the College is enabled to offer assistance to worthy students desiring to secure an education. The income of endowed scholarships is applied toward paying the tuition of a limited number.

Sixteen Perpetual Scholarships of $1,000 each have been founded by the following named persons:

\ The F. R. E. Cornell Scholarship, by Mrs. E. O. Cornell.
The George B. Wright Scholarship, by Mrs. C. A. Wright.
The George Power Scholarship, by George and James E. Power.
The Mrs. Emma Mulliken Scholarship, by Mrs. Emma Mulliken.
The Clement F. LeFevre Scholarship, by William LeFevre and Mrs. Ellen R. Coleman.
The Samuel Bowles Scholarship, by Samuel Bowles. *
The Dollie B. Lewis Scholarship, by Mrs. Dollie B. Lewis.
The O. B. Ayres Scholarship, by O. B. Ayres.
The Mary Chapin Perry Scholarship, by T. T. Perry.
The C. A. Newcomb Scholarship, by C. A. Newcomb.
The Mary W. Conger Scholarship, by the children of Mrs. Mary W. Conger.
The Hattie A. Drowne Scholarship, by Rev. E. L. Conger, D. D.
The A. R. Wolcott Scholarship, by A. R. Wolcott.
The Woman's Association Scholarship, by the Universalist Women's Association, of Illinois.
The Calista Waldron Slade Scholarship, by E. D. Waldron and sisters.
The Mary L. Pingrey Scholarship, by Mrs. Mary L. Pingrey.

BEQUESTS.

For the convenience of those who may wish to secure by bequest, to the College, any given sum for a specific purpose, the accompanying form is here given:

I hereby give and bequeath to The Lombard College, located at Galesburg, Ill ....Dollars ($......) for.............,.(state the object) ....and direct that my executor pay said bequest to the Treasurer of said College within ....after my death.

(Signed) ....

Dated....................... Witness ......:...............

CATALOGUES.

Former students of the College, whether graduates or not, are requested to inform the President of any change of residence in order that the publications of the College may be sent to them. Catalogues and circulars of information will promptly be sent to those who apply for them.

DISCIPLINE AND SOCIAL POLICY.

Aside from a few obvious regulations designed to secure punctuality and regularity in attendance on College exercises, and to protect students and teachers from disturbance while at work, no formal rules are imposed upon the students.

It is expected that, as young men and women of somewhat mature years, they will observe the usual forms of good breeding, and enjoy the ordinary privileges of good society in so far as the latter do not conflict with the best interests of the institution or with their own health and intellectual advancement.

Should any student show a disposition to engage in conduct detrimental to his own best interests, or to those of his fellow students or of the College, the faculty will deal with the case in such manner as will protect the common welfare of all.

OFFICERS OF THE COLLEGE.

CHARLES ELLWOOD NASH, A. M., S. T. D., PRESIDENT,

A. B., Lombard University, 1875; B. D., Tufts College, 1878; A. M., Lombard University, 1878; S. T. D., Tufts College, 1891; President Lombard College, 1895—.

FREDERICK WILLIAM RICH, D. Sc.,

ACTING DEAN OF THE COLLEGE OF LIBERAL ARTS.

‡Conger Professor of Chemistry and Physics.

B. S., Cornell University, 1881; Graduate Student, Cornell University, 1881; D. Sc., St. Lawrence University, 1900; Instructor in Analytical Chemistry, Cornell University, 1882-84; Professor of Natural Science, Lombard College, 1884—.

ISAAC AUGUSTUS PARKER, A. M., PH. D.

*Williamson Professor of the Greek Language and Literature.

A. B., Dartmouth College, 1853; A. M., ibid. 1856; Ph. D., Buchtel College. 1892; Principal Orleans Liberal Institute, Glover, Vt., 1853-58; Professor of Ancient Languages, Lombard University, 1858-68; Professor of Greek Language and Literature, Lombard College, 1868—.

NEHEMIAH WHITE, A. M., PH. D., S. T. D.

†Hall Professor of Intellectual and Moral Philosophy.

In charge of the Ryder Divinity School, Professor of Biblical Languages and Exegesis.

A. B., Middlebury College, 1857; A. M., ibid, 1860; Ph. D., St. Lawrence University, 1876; S. T. D., Tufts College, 1889; Associate Principal Green Mt. Perkins Institute, 1857-58; Principal Clinton Liberal Institute, 1859-60; Principal Pulaski Academy, 1865; Professor of Mathematics and Natural Science, St. Lawrence University, 1865-71; Professor Ancient Languages, Buchtel College, 1872-75; President Lombard University, 1875-92: in charge of Ryder Divinity School, and Professor of Biblical Languages and Exegesis, 1892—.

JON WATSON GRUBB, M. S.,

Instructor in Latin.

B. S., Lombard University, 1879; M. S., Lombard University, 1882; Adjunct Professor of Mathematics, Lombard University, 1882-94; Registrar Lombard College, 1893—; Professor of Latin, Lombard College, 1894—.

PHILIP GREEN WRIGHT, A. M.,

Professor of Mathematics, Astronomy and Economics.

A. M. B., Tufts College, 1884; A. M. Harvard University, 1887; Teacher of Mathematics and Science, Goddard Seminary, Vt., 1883; Adjunct Professor of Mathematics, Buchtel College, 1884-86; Professor of Mathematics, Lombard College, 1892—.

FRANK HAMILTON FOWLER, PH. D.,

Professor of English Literature and Rhetoric.

A. B., Lombard University, 1890; Ph. D., The University of Chicago, 1896; Graduate Student, Johns Hopkins University, 1890-91; Principal Peaster Academy, 1891-92; Fellow in the University of Chicago, 1892-96; Professor of English, Lombard College, 1897—.

---

* In honor of the late I. D. Williamson, D. D., of Cincinnati.
† In honor of the late E. G. Hall, of Chicago.
‡ In honor of the late L. E. Conger, of Dexter, Iowa.

RALPH GRIERSON KIMBLE,
Professor of Sociology.

A. B., Lombard College, 1896; University Scholar in Sociology, University of Chicago, 1896-97; Senior Fellow in Sociology, ibid, 1897-1901; Special Lecturer in Sociology, Lombard College, Spring term, 1899; ibid, 1900; Special Lecturer in Sociological Theory, University of Wisconsin, Spring of 1902; Professor of Sociology, Lombard College, 1901—.

THADDEUS CAREY KIMBLE, A. B., M. D.,
Instructor in Medical Courses and in Biology.

A. B., Lombard College, 1902; M. D., St. Louis College of Physicians and Surgeons, 1898; Instructor in Biology, Lombard College, 1900-02; Instructor in Medical Courses, Lombard College, 1902—.

JOHN S. COOK, M. D., D. D.,
Lecturer on Regional Anatomy.

KARL JAKOB RUDOLPH LUNDBERG,
Director of Music Department and Instructor in Voice, Piano, Organ and Theory.

Graduate Royal Musical Academy, of Stockholm, Sweden, in voice, piano, organ and theory, 1892; Studied voice with Prof Ivar Hallstrom, 1893; organist and choir-master in Lindesberg, Sweden, 1894-97; Musical Director Burlington Institute College, Burlington, Iowa, 1897-99; Director Music Department, Lombard College, 1899—.

EMMA B. WAIT,
Professor of French and German.

Principal of School, Los Angeles, California, 1881-83; Student Ecole Sévigné, Sévres, 1891; Université de Généve, 1896-98; The University of Chicago. 1899; Professor of French and German, Lombard College, 1899—.

M. AGNES HATHAWAY,
Dean of Women and Instructor in Preparatory Courses.

Graduate from Genesee Wesleyan Seminary, Lima, New York, 1888; Student at National Normal University, Lebanon, Ohio, 1895-96; Teacher in Public Schools of New York and Illinois; Dean of Women and Instructor in Preparatory School, Lombard College, 1900—.

WILLIS S. KIENHOLZ,
Physical Director and Instructor in Zoology.

Special student in Biological Science, University of Minnesota, 1897-1901; Member of Minnesota Zoological Survey, 1898-1901; Assistant in University of Minnesota Botanical Herbarium. 1899-1900; Member of foot-ball, basket-ball, and track teams University of Minnesota, 1897-1901; Instructor in Biology and Athletics, Crookston High School 1901-02; Physical Director, Coach, and Instructor in Zoology, Lombard College, 1902—.

AMANDA KIDDER.
Instructor in Oratory.

Graduate from the Detroit Training School of Elocution and English Literature, 1890; Post-Graduate course, ibid, 1897; Instructor in Elocution, Darling College, Minnesota, 1891; Instructor in Elocution, Academy of Our Lady of Lourdes, 1892-94; Private Studio, LaCrosse, Wisconsin, 1895-1900; Instructor in Elocution and Physical Culture, Lombard College, 1900—.

M. ISABELLE BLOOD,
Instructor in Drawing and Painting.

Studied with Dean Fletcher, N. Y.; William Bertram, Chicago; at the Art Institute and with Nellie Davis, St. Louis; Instructor in Drawing and Painting, Lombard College, 1889—.

RAYMOND R. CAMPBELL,
Instructor in Mathematics.

JENKINS BENNETT REES,
Instructor in Physics.

ANNA M. GILLIS,
Instructor in English.

W. H. CHEESMAN,
Instructor in Violin.

EDNA UHLER,
Instructor in Piano.

ALICE HELEN BARTLETT, A. B.,
Instructor in Pipe Organ and Harmony.

ADA M. H. HALE,
Matron Ladies' Hall.

DR. GUY A. LONGBRAKE AND DR. DELIA M. RICE,
Medical Examiners.

_____

NON-RESIDENT LECTURERS.

REV. MARION D. SHUTTER, D. D.

REV. I. M. ATWOOD, D. D.

REV. F. C. PRIEST, D. D.

EDNA CHAFFEE NOBLE.

_____

FRANK HAMILTON FOWLER, PH. D.,
Librarian.

JON WATSON GRUBB, M. S.,
Registrar.

FREDERICK WILLIAM RICH, D. Sc.,
Curator of the Museum.

WILLIS S. KIENHOLZ,
Director of the Gymnasium.

_____

ALLEN HARSHBARGER,
Janitor.

Standing Faculty Committees.

ADVISORY—
PROFESSORS WRIGHT AND FOWLER.

CREDITS—
PROFESSORS PARKER AND RICH.

HOMES FOR NEW STUDENTS—
PROFESSORS FOWLER AND KIMBLE.

CATALOGUE—
PROFESSORS WRIGHT AND FOWLER.

HIGHER DEGREES—
PRESIDENT NASH AND PROFESSOR PARKER.

LIBRARY—
PROFESSORS WHITE AND KIMBLE.

CHAPEL EXCUSES—
PROFESSORS KIMBLE AND FOWLER.

CHAPEL EXERCISES—
PRESIDENT NASH, PROFS. WAIT AND LUNDBERG.

ATHLETICS—
PROFESSORS KIENHOLZ AND WRIGHT.

ORDER AND DISCIPLINE—
PRESIDENT NASH, PROF. RICH AND MISS HATHAWAY.

Departments of the College.

Students at Lombard are divided primarily into Classified and Unclassified Students.

The Classified department includes all students who are candidates for a degree or diploma. It embraces the College of Liberal Arts, the Divinity School, and the Schools of Music and Art.

The Unclassified department includes students who are pursuing studies at Lombard for a greater or less period, without any express intention of obtaining a degree or diploma.

COLLEGE OF LIBERAL ARTS.

Faculty of Liberal Arts.

CHARLES ELLWOOD NASH, A. M., S. T. D., PRESIDENT.

ISAAC AUGUSTUS PARKER, A. M., PH. D.,
* Williamson Professor of the Greek Language and Literature.

NEHEMIAH WHITE, A. M., PH. D., S. T. D.,
† Hall Professor of Intellectual and Moral Philosophy.

JON WATSON GRUBB, M. S.,
Instructor in Latin.

FREDERICK WILLIAM RICH, D. Sc.,
‡ Conger Professor of Chemistry and Physics.

PHILIP GREEN WRIGHT, A. M.,
Professor of Mathematics, Astronomy and Economics.

FRANK HAMILTON FOWLER, PH. D.,
Professor of English Literature and Rhetoric.

RALPH GRIERSON KIMBLE,
Professor of Sociology.

EMMA B WAIT,
Professor of French and German.

THADDEUS CAREY KIMBLE, M. D.,
Instructor in Biology.

KARL JAKOB RUDOLPH LUNDBERG,
Professor of Musical Theory.

AMANDA KIDDER,
Instructor in Oratory.

WILLIS S. KIENHOLZ,
Physical Director and Instructor in Zoology.

* In honor of the late I. D. Williamson, D. D., of Cincinnati.
† In honor of the late E. G. Hall, of Chicago.
‡ In honor of the late L. E. Conger, of Dexter, Iowa.

Degrees Conferred in 1902.

DOCTOR OF DIVINITY.

Frederick Clarence Priest..Chicago.

BACHELORS OF ARTS.

Alspaugh, Charlotte.. Washington, Kan.
Andrew, John, Jr..... ....New Salem.
Cranston, Edna Mae..Hermon.

By action of the Faculty, May 4, 1903, the requirement of an examination in English from accredited high schools has been dropped. English will, therefore, be on the same basis as other subjects.

Requirements for Admission.

All applicants for admission to the College of Liberal Arts, except those from certain approved High Schools and Academies, are required to pass satisfactory examinations in studies selected from the following list, to an aggregate of sixteen units. The English examination will be required of all applicants, without exception:

STUDY.	UNITS.	STUDY.	UNITS.
English	3	Physics	1
Greek	3	Chemistry	1
Latin	3	Physiography	½ to 1
German	1	Physiology	½ to 1
French	1	Botany	½ to 1
Ancient History	1	Astronomy	1
English and American History	1	Meteorology	1
Algebra	1½	Political Economy	½ to 1
Plane Geometry	½ to 1	Zoology	½ to 1
Solid Geometry	½ to 1		

COLLEGE OF LIBERAL ARTS.

Faculty of Liberal Arts.

CHARLES ELLWOOD NASH, A. M., S. T. D., PRESIDENT.

ISAAC AUGUSTUS PARKER, A. M., PH. D.,
* Williamson Professor of the Greek Language and Literature.

RALPH GRIERSON KIMBLE,
Professor of Sociology.

EMMA B WAIT,
Professor of French and German.

THADDEUS CAREY KIMBLE, M. D.,
Instructor in Biology.

KARL JAKOB RUDOLPH LUNDBERG,
Professor of Musical Theory.

AMANDA KIDDER,
Instructor in Oratory.

WILLIS S. KIENHOLZ,
Physical Director and Instructor in Zoology.

* In honor of the late I. D. Williamson, D. D., of Cincinnati.
† In honor of the late E. G. Hall, of Chicago.
‡ In honor of the late L. E. Conger, of Dexter, Iowa.

Degrees Conferred in 1902.

DOCTOR OF DIVINITY.

Frederick Clarence Priest..Chicago.

BACHELORS OF ARTS.

Alspaugh, Charlotte.. Washington, Kan.
Andrew, John, Jr..................... ....New Salem.
Cranston, Edna Mae...Hermon.
Efner, Charles Julius...Galesburg.
Epperson, Edna Ethel...... ....Rio.
Ericson, Henry ....Galesburg.
Hitchcock, Augusta Eaton...Osage, Ia.
Kimble. Thaddeus Carey..Carbondale, Kan.
Lauer, Howard Walter...Hutchinson, Kan.
Muffler, Emma Annette...Serena.
Smith, Edward Milton..Edinburg.
Stokes, Alice...Galesburg.
Stoughton, Herbert Leonard...Osage, Ia.
Varney, Charles E...Clinton.

Requirements for Admission.

All applicants for admission to the College of Liberal Arts, except those from certain approved High Schools and Academies, are required to pass satisfactory examinations in studies selected from the following list, to an aggregate of sixteen units. The English examination will be required of all applicants, without exception:

STUDY.	UNITS.	STUDY.	UNITS.
English....................	3	Physics.	1
Greek	3	Chemistry......................	1
Latin.............	3	Physiography....................	½ to 1
German.........................	1	Physiology.....................	½ to 1
French.........................	1	Botany....	½ to 1
Ancient History.................	1	Astronomy......................	1
English and American History...	1	Meteorology	1
Algebra........................	1½	Political Economy.............	½ to 1
Plane Geometry...............½ to 1		Zoology........................	½ to 1
Solid Geometry..... ....½ to 1			

CONSTANTS.

The studies presented must include the following constants:

STUDIES.	UNITS.
English........	3
One Foreign Language........	3
History........	I
Algebra........	1½
Geometry........	½
Science........	2
	II

The two units in Science, one of which must include laboratory work, may be chosen from the following, viz: Physics, Chemistry, Physiography, Anatomy and Physiology, Botany, Zoology.

EXAMINATIONS.

Examinations in the above studies will be held during the first week in September, as follows:

HOUR.	TUESDAY, SEPT. I.	WEDNESDAY, SEPT. 2.	THURSDAY, SEPT. 3.
7:30– 9:30	English.	French.	Plane Geometry.
9:30–11:30	Greek—Astronomy.	Ancient History.	Physics.
11:30–12:30	Physiology.	Physiography.	Botany.
2:00– 4:00	Latin.	Algebra.	Chemistry.
4:00– 6:00	German—Solid Geom.	Eng. and Am. History.	Zoology—Pol. Econ.

ADMISSION BY CERTIFICATE.

In harmony with the recommendation of the joint committee of the High School and College sections of the Illinois State Teachers' Association, certificates from the principals or other authorized officers of certain approved High Schools and Academies will be accepted in lieu of examinations; except that in English an examination will be required of all students. *But these certificates must be presented during the term in which the student applies for admission in order to be accepted,* and no certificate will be valid for more than two years after the completion of the course of study to which the certificate refers. The credit allowed on them will be based upon the work accomplished; in general, one unit being equal to a year's work in a study reciting five hours a week in recitation periods of not less than forty minutes.

The detailed descriptions given below indicate more fully the amount of work required in each study to obtain the number of units given in the table. Students admitted by certificate enter classes on probation, and if after a week's trial, it is found that their previous training is insufficient to render it advisable for them to continue in these classes, they will be assigned other work.

SCOPE OF PREPARATORY STUDIES.

The amount of work required in the several Preparatory studies to obtain the units assigned in the foregoing table, either by examination or certificate, is indicated by the following outline of examination requirements:

ENGLISH.

The examination will occupy two hours and will consist of two parts, which, however, cannot be taken separately:—

I. The candidate will be required to write a paragraph or two on each of several topics chosen by him from a considerable number—perhaps ten or fifteen—set before him on the examination paper.

In 1903, 1904, and 1905, the topics will be drawn from the following works:

Shakespeare's Merchant of Venice, and Julius Caesar; The Sir Roger de Coverley Papers in the Spectator; Goldsmith's Vicar of Wakefield; Coleridge's Ancient Mariner; Scott's Ivanhoe; Carlyle's Essay on Burns; Tennyson's Princess; Lowell's Vision of Sir Launfal; George Eliot's Silas Marner.

The candidate is expected to read intelligently *all* the books prescribed. He should read them as he reads other books; he is expected, not to know them minutely, but to have freshly in mind their most important parts. In every case the examiner will regard knowledge of the book as less important than ability to write English.

II. A certain number of books are prescribed for careful study. This part of the examination will be upon subject-matter, literary form and logical structure, and will also test the candidate's ability to express his knowledge with clearness and accuracy.

The books prescribed for this part of the examination in 1903, 1904, and 1905 are: Shakespeare's Macbeth; Milton's Lycidas, Comus, L'Allegro, and Il Penseroso; Burke's Speech on Conciliation with America; Macaulay's Essays on Milton and Addison.

No candidate will be accepted in English whose work is seriously defective in point of spelling, punctuation, grammar, or division into paragraphs.

In connection with the reading and study of the prescribed books, parallel or subsidiary reading should be encouraged, and a considerable amount of English poetry should be committed to memory. The essentials of English grammar should not be neglected in preparatory study.

The English written by a candidate in any of his examination-books may be regarded as part of his examination in English, in case the evidence afforded by the examination-book in English is insufficient.

As additional evidence of preparation the candidate may present an exercise book, properly certified by his instructor, containing compositions or other written work.

FRENCH.

(a) The translation at sight of ordinary Nineteenth Century prose. (The passages set for translation must be rendered into simple and idiomatic English.)

(b) The translation into French of simple English sentences or of easy connected prose, to test the candidate's familiarity with elementary grammar. Proficiency in grammar may also be tested by direct questions, based on the passages set for translation under (a).

The passages set for translation into English will be suited to the proficiency of candidates who have read not less than four hundred pages (including reading at sight in class) from the works of at least three different authors. It is desirable that a portion of the reading should be from works other than works of fiction.

Grammar should be studied concurrently with the reading as an indispensable means of insuring thoroughness and accuracy in the understanding of the language. The requirement in elementary grammar includes the conjugations of regular verbs, of the more frequent irregular verbs, such as *aller, envoyer, tenir, pouvoir, voir, vouloir, dire, savoir, faire*, and those belonging to the classes represented by *ouvrir, dormir, connaitre, conduire*, and *craindre;* the forms and positions of personal pronouns and of possessive, demonstrative, and interrogative adjectives; the inflection of nouns and adjectives for gender and number, except rare cases; the uses of articles, and the partitive constructions.

Pronunciation should be carefully taught, and pupils should have frequent opportunities to hear French spoken or read aloud. The writing of French from dictation is recommended as a useful exercise.

GERMAN.

(a) The translation at sight of simple German prose. (The passages set for translation must be rendered into simple and idiomatic English.)

(b) The translation into German of simple English sentences, or of easy connected prose, to test the candidate's familiarity with elementary grammar.

The passages set for translation into English will be suited to the proficiency of candidates who have read not less than two hundred pages of easy German (including reading at sight in class).

Grammar should be studied concurrently with the reading as an indispensable means of insuring thoroughness and accuracy in the understanding of the language. The requirement in elementary grammar includes the conjugation of the weak and the more usual strong verbs; the declension of articles, adjectives, pronouns and such nouns as are readily classified; the commoner prepositions; the simpler uses of the modal auxiliaries; the elements of syntax, especially the rules governing the order of words.

Pronunciation should be carefully taught, and the pupils should have frequent opportunities to hear German spoken or read aloud. The writing of German from dictation is recommended as a useful exercise.

LATIN.

The examination in Latin for admission to the Collegiate Department will be calculated to test the proficiency of students who have pursued a Latin course of five lessons a week for three years.

The translation at sight of simple Latin prose will be required.

Passages from Cæsar and Cicero will be assigned for translation and such questions will be asked as will test the candidate's knowledge of forms and constructions. The writing of simple Latin prose will be required.

For those who have pursued a Latin course of five lessons a week for four years, the examination will be extended so as to include a test in Vergil and additional tests in Cicero.

MATHEMATICS.

Algebra. The examination in Algebra will demand accuracy in the several processes of literal Arithmetic. Special emphasis will be laid on factoring, and the correct manipulation of negative and fractional exponents. It will include the solution of simple and quadratic equations (together with a knowledge of the theory of quadratic equations) and elimination in the case of simultaneous equations of the first and second degrees.

Plane Geometry. The examination in Plane Geometry will emphasize precision in the definition of Geometric terms, and accuracy in the demonstration of Geometric theorems. In scope it will demand a knowledge of all the propositions in Plane Geometry preceding Solid Geometry, included in such a standard text book in this subject as Phillips and Fisher's Elements.

Solid Geometry. As in Plane Geometry emphasis will be laid upon accuracy in definition and demonstration. In scope the examination will cover the propositions in Solid Geometry included in such a standard text book as Phillips and Fisher's Elements.

ASTRONOMY.

The examination in this subject will demand knowledge of descriptive rather than mathematical Astronomy. The student will be expected to understand the theory of the celestial sphere, simple methods of computing latitude, time and longitude, the astronomical features of the earth, the sun and the moon, the principles of spectrum analysis, the motions and characteristics of the planets, the names and myths of the principal stars and constellations, the facts in regard to aberration, parallax, and proper motion of the stars, and the principles of a rational cosmogony as developed in La Place's nebular hypothesis. ' Young's Lessons in Astronomy is suggested as a text book embracing the matter with which students are expected to be acquainted who wish to prepare for this examination.

PHYSICS.

Students offering Physics for entrance credit must show an acquaintance with the more important phenomena and with the principles involved in the explanation of them. They must, in addition to the text book work, have completed a course of laboratory experiments and be able to work simple numerical problems, involving the laws of falling bodies; pendulum; properties of liquids and gases; thermometry and calorimetry; current strength, resistance, and electromotive force; properties of sound, refraction and reflection with the size and position of images.

CHEMISTRY.

The Elementary Course in Chemistry offered for entrance credit must include a knowledge of the elements and compounds equivalent to that given in Remsen's Introduction to the study of Chemistry. In addition, students must have had a series of laboratory experiments illustrating the text book work and be able to write equations and solve simple chemical problems.

BOTANY.

Students presenting work in botany for entrance credit should have a knowledge of the general laws and fundamental principles of plant nutrition, assimilation, growth, etc., as exemplified by plants chosen from the different groups, as well as the general comparative morphology and the broader relationships of plants. He should present an herbarium of at least twenty-five specimens, collected and mounted by himself, and certified to by his instructor.

ZOOLOGY.

Students desiring entrance credit for Zoology should have devoted the equivalent of five periods a week for at least one-half year to the study of general Zoology. A portion of this work must have been laboratory practice in the observation of living forms and dissection. His laboratory notes and drawings, endorsed by the instructor, should be presented at the time of registration as evidence of the nature of this part of the work. This laboratory practice should include a study of at least twelve of the forms named in the following list: Amœba, paramœcium, sea-anemone, star-fish, sea-urchin, earth-worm, cray-fish, lobster, spider, centipede, locust (grasshopper), dragon-fly, squash-bug, bumblebee, clam, snail, a simple tunicate, shark, any soft rayed-fish, snake, turtle, frog, pigeon, rabbit, and cat.

PHYSIOLOGY.

Students presenting work in human Physiology for entrance credit should have a general knowledge of the human skeleton, muscular, circulatory, and nervous systems, the vital organs, viscera, and organs of special sense, and the processes of respiration and digestion.

The text-book used should cover the ground treated in such books as Martin's Human Body, or Huxley's Elementary Physiology (Lee's Revision).

PHYSIOGRAPHY.

A course of study equivalent to Tarr's Elementary Physical Geography.

The examination will include a thorough test on all the leading subjects treated in Physical Geography, with maps to illustrate relief forms, currents, ocean beds, and the distribution of animal and plant life.

HISTORY (including Historical Geography).

Either of the two following groups, each including two fields of historical study:—

1. *Greek and Roman History.*—(a) Greek History to the death of Alexander, with due reference to Greek life, literature, and art. (b) Roman History to the downfall of the Western Roman Empire, with due reference to literature and government.

2. *English and American History.*—(a) English History, with due reference to social and political development. (b) American History, with the elements of Civil Government.

For preparation in each of the two historical fields presented, a course of study equivalent to at least three lessons a week for one year will be necessary.

· The candidate will be expected to show on examination such general knowledge of each field as may be acquired from the study of an accurate text book of not less than 300 pages, supplemented by suitable parallel readings amounting to not less than 500 pages. The examination will call for comparison of historical characters, periods, and events, and in general for the exercise of judgment as well as of memory. Geographical knowledge will be tested by means of an outline map.

It is desirable that Greek and Roman History be offered as a part of the preparation of every candidate.

POLITICAL ECONOMY.

The examination in Political Economy will demand a thorough knowledge of the fundamental economic laws relating to Production, Exchange, Distribution, and Consumption. The applicant will also be expected to discuss intelligently from an economic standpoint such questions as Free Trade, Socialism, Strikes, and Taxation. Bullock's Introduction to the Study of Economics is suggested as a text covering the ground required for the examination.

ADMISSION TO ADVANCED STANDING.

Students from other institutions, who present letters of honorable dismissal, may be admitted to such standing and upon such terms as the Faculty may deem equitable. Every such student is required to present, along with the catalogue of the institution in which he has studied, a full statement, duly certified, of the studies he has completed, including preparatory studies. Candidates for advanced standing who wish to receive credit for work accomplished in private study, are permitted to take examinations in such subjects upon payment of the regular term fee for the course in which the examination is taken. A minimum residence of the two terms next preceeding the completion of the requirements for graduation, and a minimum of eight courses taken in this College, are required of all applicants for a baccalaureate degree.

Requirements for Graduation.

GROUP SYSTEM.

Having been admitted to the College of Liberal Arts, the student will elect one of the following groups as a course of study leading to his degree. These groups consist of certain required studies arranged logically with reference to some central subject, in addition to which, considerable option is allowed in the way of free electives. All the required studies, together with a sufficient number of electives to bring the total up to an aggregate of thirty-eight credits, must be completed before the degree will be conferred. A credit is obtained by the satisfactory completion of one full course pursued for one term. Of the thirty-eight credits at least twenty-four must be above grade C. Two credits may be obtained by two full years' work in the Gymnasium classes.

THESIS.

In addition to the above requirements, every student who is a candidate for a degree, or a diploma, will present a graduation thesis upon some subject in which he, or she, has prosecuted original research or special study.

The subject selected for treatment must be approved by the President within four weeks after the opening of the Fall term.

A syllabus of the thesis must be handed to the President at least six weeks before the close of the Winter term.

The completed thesis is limited to fifteen hundred words, and must be handed in for criticism at least ten weeks before Commencement.

In lieu of a thesis, original work, performed under the direction of some member of the Faculty, may be accepted.

Degrees will be conferred only on the annual Commencement Day.

ADVANCED DEGREE.

The degree of Master of Arts will be conferred upon graduates of this college or other institutions of equal rank, on the satisfactory completion of one year's residence work upon a course of study or research which shall have been submitted to and approved by the Faculty beyond the requirements for the baccalaureate degree. The candidate must present a thesis showing original research in the special line of study pursued.

GROUPS.

On being admitted to the College of Liberal Arts, each student, who is a candidate for a degree, will elect one of these groups :

ENGLISH.

STUDY.	CREDITS.	STUDY.	CREDITS.
English	9	History	2
Foreign Language	9^1	Science	2^2
Mathematics	3	Psychology	1
English (5 and 6)	2	Sociology	1
Elocution	1		

MODERN LANGUAGES.

STUDY.	CREDITS.	STUDY.	CREDITS.
German	9^3	History	2
French	9^3	Science	2^2
Mathematics	3	Psychology	1
English (5 and 6)	2	Sociology	1
Elocution	1		

CLASSICS.

STUDY.	CREDITS.	STUDY.	CREDITS.
Latin	7	History	2
Greek	12[4]	Science	2[2]
German or French	6[4]	Psychology	1
English	2	Sociology	1
Elocution	1		

LATIN SCIENTIFIC.

Latin	7	English	2
Chemistry	6	Elocution	1
Physics	3	History	2
Biology	3	Psychology	1
German or French	6[4]	Sociology	1

MATHEMATICS.

Mathematics and Astronomy	12	History	2
Physics	3	Psychology	1
Chemistry	3	Sociology	1
English	2	Elocution	1
Modern Language	6		

SOCIAL SCIENCE.

Sociology	10	Mathematics	5
Biology	3	Modern Language	4
Economics	1	Chemistry	2
Psychology	2	Physics	2
English	2		

BIOLOGY AND CHEMISTRY.

Chemistry	6	Psychology	1
Biology	9	Geology	1
Mathematics	3	German	6[4]
English	3		

PREPARATORY MEDICAL.

Chemistry	5	German or French	6[4]
Biology	12	Latin	3[5]
Mathematics (including Trig.)	5	Psychology	2
English	3	Physics	1

CHEMISTRY AND PHYSICS.

Physics	3	Mathematics	3
Chemistry	8	English	3
Geology	1	Psychology	1
Biology	3	Astronomy	1
German or French	6[4]		

1. Of these, at least six must be in a modern language.

2. If a Biological science is offered for entrance, Physics or Chemistry must be chosen. If Physics or Chemistry is offered a Biological science must be chosen.

3. Students choosing this group must offer at least four units in Ancient Languages for admission.

4. By offering German or French for admission the prescribed courses in several groups may be reduced and the number of free electives correspondingly increased. The same is true of Greek in the Classics group.

5. Unless entrance Latin is presented.

Courses of Instruction.

RECITATIONS AND CREDITS.

The following studies are classed as full courses or fractional courses, according to the estimated amount of work in each, and its value in fulfilling the requirements for graduation. Unless otherwise stated, a course in any study consists of five hours of recitations or lectures, per week, for one term. Certain full courses, however, are given in three hours per week recitations. Laboratory courses require ten hours of work per week in the Laboratory, in addition to a considerable amount of study outside. Certain other studies, as indicated in each case, count only as half courses, or less. It is intended to give each course during the year and term indicated. But the faculty reserves the right to make any change when it seems desirable to do so.

The general descriptions at the head of each department and the brief outline accompanying each course are designed to give in simple language the scope and purpose of the course to assist the student in making his elections.

The student is urged especially to notice the dependence of one course on another, so that in arranging his group, before electing any course, the prerequisite shall have been completed.

ENGLISH.

The study of English is considered of fundamental importance. For this reason thorough preparation in English is insisted on for admission to the College proper. . As will be seen by reference to p. 23, certificates in this subject are not accepted, but all candidates are required to pass the examination in English before being admitted to full college standing. The practical value of this study need hardly be mentioned. No matter what the occupation, there will be. the necessity for expression, and this is to be obtained by the study of English. Closely related to this is the value attaching to the study as a preparation for other work of the college course. The ability to gather thought from the printed page rapidly and accurately, and the power of expression just mentioned, are prime requisites for the student. A peculiar value attaching to the study of English is that of correlating the studies of the curriculum, of making the college course more of a unit. History, Philosophy, Linguistics, Æsthetics, and Sociology may here find a common ground of meeting. As a corollary to this it may be said that English to an especial degree possesses the power of enlarging the student's mental horizon, of making a broader man of him. It is the aim of the department to utilize all these values of the study, and in order to do that to the full the endeavor is made so to foster a love of literature that the study will be pursued after the student has left college.

Primarily the object of the courses in English Composition (5, 6, 7, and 18) is the acquiring on the part of the student the ability to write good English prose. It is believed, however, that the study properly pursued has a considerable disciplinary value. In these courses there is a minimum of theory and a maximum of practice. The important principles are given in lectures; these principles are illustrated in the specimens of the writings of others; and the student is required to exemplify them in the preparation of daily and fortnightly themes. Courses 5 and 6 are required courses and, together with course 7, should be taken during the first year of college work.

In the courses in English Literature emphasis is laid on criticism rather than on the history. An introduction is made to the several forms of literature, special attention being given to the chief representative authors of each department. One course is given in Old English and one in the History of the English Language. The nine courses dealing with the Literature and Language are arranged in a cycle covering three years. The student is enabled to specialize in this study to such a degree that he may, without further preparation, undertake graduate work in the Universities.

5. Rhetoric and Composition.

Fall Term.   Professor FOWLER.

Open to all college students.

6. The Forms of Discourse.

Winter term.   Professor FOWLER.

Prerequisite, English 5.

7. The Forms of Discourse. (Continued.)

Spring term.   Professor FOWLER.

Prerequisite, English 5.

8. Daily Themes. (Half Course.)

Winter term. Professor FOWLER.
Prerequisite, English 5.

9. English Lyric Poetry.

Wordsworth, Tennyson, Browning. Fall term.
Professor FOWLER.
Prerequisite, English 5.

10. English Prose.

A study of English prose writers. Fall term.
Professor FOWLER.
Prerequisite, English 5.

[English 10 will not be given in 1903.]

11. Old English.

An introduction to the older language. The relations between Old and Modern English will be studied. Winter term.
Professor FOWLER.
Prerequisite, English 5.

12. History of the English Language.

Lectures and text-book recitations. Winter term.
Professor FOWLER.
Prerequisite, English 5.

[English 12 will not be given in 1903–04.]

13. The English Drama.

Shakespeare will form the center of the work. Two or three plays will be studied critically, and the class will read a number of other plays by different authors. Spring term. Professor FOWLER.
Prerequisite, English 5.

14. Epic Poetry.

Milton. Spring term. Professor FOWLER.
Prerequisite, English 5.

[English 14 will not be given in 1904.]

15. American Literature.

A general survey of the history of literature in the United States with a more careful study of a few representative authors. Fall term.
Professor FOWLER.
Prerequisite, English 5.

[English 15 will not be given in 1903.]

16. Epochs in the History of English Literature.

Winter term. Professor FOWLER.

Prerequisite, English 5.

[English 16 will not be given in 1903-4.]

17. English Novelists.

Spring term. Professor FOWLER.

Prerequisite, English 5.

[English 17 will not be given in 1904.]

18. Oratory.

The preparation and delivery of five original orations. Students may register in any one of the terms and have two terms in which to complete the work. Professor FOWLER.

Miss KIDDER.

Prerequisite, English 5.

MODERN LANGUAGES.

It is needless at the present day to insist upon the advisability of knowing one or more of the modern languages; we, as Americans, are awakening to the fact that to know English alone is to be seriously handicapped in the circles of polite society or commerce, or in the pursuits of science or literature.

The effort in this department of our College work is to impart a sound knowledge of grammar and syntax and a correct pronunciation, preparing the way to a complete mastery of the spoken and written language.

FRENCH.

1. How to Think in French.

Petites Causeries. Conversation. Elementary Grammar. Fall term.

Miss WAIT.

Open to all students.

2. Foundations of French.

Petites Causeries. Memorizing. Conversation. Winter Term.

Miss WAIT.

Prerequisite, French 1.

3. Foundations of French.

Kuhn's French Readings. Sight reading. Conversation. Spring term. Miss WAIT.

Prerequisite, French 2.

4. Grammar, Conversation, and Reading.

Fraser & Squair's Grammar. François' Composition. George Sand's La Mare au Diable. Fall term. Miss WAIT.

Prerequisite, French 3.

5. Grammar, Conversation, and Reading.

Fraser & Squair's Grammar. François' Composition. Corneille's Le Cid. Dumas' La Tulipe Noire. Fall term. Miss WAIT.

Prerequisite, French 3.

[French 5 will not be given in 1903.]

6. Grammar, Conversation, and Reading.

L'Avare, Colomba. Sight reading. Winter term.

Miss WAIT.

Prerequisite, French 4.

7. Grammar, Conversation, and Reading.

Le Verre d'Eau. Sept Auteurs Français. Winter term.

Miss WAIT.

Prerequisite, French 5.

[French 7 will not be given in 1903–04.]

8. Grammar, Conversation, and Reading.

Pêcheurs d'Islande. Gazier's Histoire de La Littérature Française. Spring term. Miss WAIT.

Prerequisite, French 6.

9. Grammar, Conversation, and Reading.,

Study of the authors of the 17th and 19th centuries. Reading, Balzac, Hugo, Thiers. Spring term. Miss. WAIT.

Prerequisite, French 7.

[French 9 will not be given in 1904.]

10, 11, 12. Scientific French. (Half Courses.)

Reading of Scientific French, especially for the benefit of students in courses using French text and reference books. Class meets one hour per week. Fall, winter, and spring terms, each term counting as a half credit. Miss WAIT.

Prerequisite, French 3.

Grammar, Composition, Sight Reading, and Conversation constitute an important part of 4 to 9 inclusive.

GERMAN.

1. Elementary German.

Das Deutsche Buch.   Elementary Grammar.   Conversation.   Fall term.   Miss WAIT,
Open to all students.

2. Elementary German.

Das Deutsche Buch.   Grammar.   Conversation.   Sight reading. Committing to memory.   Winter term.   Miss WAIT.
Prerequisite, German 1.

3. Grammar and Reading.

Collar's Eysenbach's Grammar.   Immensee.   Sight reading.   Conversation.   Memorizing.   Spring term.   Miss WAIT.
Prerequisite, German 2.

4. Grammar, Conversation, and Reading.

Collar's Eysenbach's Grammar.   Stein's Exercises for Translation. Schrakamp's German Conversation Grammar.   L'Arrabbiata.   Sight reading.   Fall term.   Miss WAIT.
Prerequisite, German 3.

5. Grammar, Conversation, and Reading.

Maria Stuart, Götz von Berlichingen.   Fall term.

Miss WAIT.
Prerequisite, German 3.
[German 5 will not be given in 1903.]

6. Grammar, Conversation, and Reading.

Hermann und Dorothea.   Meereskunde.   Winter term.

Miss WAIT.
Prerequisite, German 4.

7. Grammar, Conversation, and Reading.

Nathan der Weise, Freytag's Bilder aus der deutschen Vergangenheit. Winter term.   Miss WAIT.
Prerequisite, German 5.
[German 7 will not be given in 1903-04.]

8. Grammar, Conversation, and Reading.

Meereskunde.   Bötticher's German Literature.   Spring term.

Miss WAIT,
Prerequisite, German 6.

9. Grammar, Conversation, and Reading.

German Classics.   Spring term.   Miss WAIT.

Prerequisite, German 7.

[German 9 will not be given in 1904.]

10, 11, 12. Scientific German. (Half Courses.)

Readings from Scientific German, especially for the benefit of students in courses using German text and reference books.   Class meets one hour per week.   Fall, winter, and spring terms, each term counting as a half credit.   Miss WAIT.

Prerequisite, German 3.

Grammar, Composition, Sight Reading, and Conversation constitute an important part of courses 4 to 9 inclusive.

LATIN AND GREEK.

It is the purpose in this department to give the student the ability to read understandingly the writings of the Latin and the Greek authors and to enter into their spirit, and, also, to give him a general acquaintance with Greek and Latin literature.   Thoroughness in instruction is aimed at.   The student is required to learn the forms of words, so that he can decline each noun and adjective occurring in his lessons, tell the conjugation, voice, mood, tense, number, and person of each verb, and to know the construction of sentences, so that he can tell how to dispose of each word.   A correct translation gains no credit for a student, if upon questioning it is found that he has not a knowledge of words and constructions and has evidently obtained his translation from notes or some other source.

Approved English sentences are required in translation, and where the literal is not allowable in English, the student is expected to know the construction in the Latin, or the Greek, and to render into idiomatic English.

The closest attention is required in the hour of recitation.   The student cannot succeed, relying on what he has learned by rote, but he must perceive and understand each word at the time of recitation.

In reading poetry attention is given to prosody.   Instruction is given in the meters used in the Odes of Horace and their scanning is required.

The student is required to present an essay on each work read, stating its scope and the peculiarities of its style, and giving a brief biography of its author.

Latin composition is taken in connection with translations from Latin into English.

Frequent reference is made to a Dictionary of Classical Antiquities to elucidate allusions to the mythology and the manners and customs of the ancient Greeks and Romans.

Much attention is paid to the derivation and composition of words, and English words derived from the Latin and the Greek are noted.

In the study of the Greek language instruction is carefully given in the principles of Greek accent, and from the beginning, in writing Greek exercises, students are required to be careful to accent correctly.

For the more advanced students in Latin and Greek different courses are given in different years. This enables the student desiring to do so, to elect more of these courses than are usually taken.

The student who meets the requirements in this department, not only learns to read with pleasure and profit the language which he is studying, but, what is more, he acquires a mental discipline and a habit of carefulness and accuracy which will aid him in the business of life. The discipline of mind and the knowledge which he gains will greatly assist him in other studies, especially those of the sciences and medicine and law, since the terms with which he will meet in these studies are mostly derived from the Latin and the Greek.

LATIN.

1. Latin Lessons.
Bennett's Latin Lessons.   Bennett's Latin Grammar.   Fall term.
Professor GRUBB.
Open to all students.

2. Latin Lessons. (Continued.)
Winter term.   Professor GRUBB.
Prerequisite, Latin 1.

3. Latin Lessons. (Continued.)
Spring term.   Professor GRUBB.
Prerequisite, Latin 2.

4. Caesar.
Texts, Harkness and Forbes's Caesar's Gallic War and Daniell's Latin Prose Composition.   Fall term.   Professor GRUBB.
Prerequisite, Latin 3.

5. Caesar. (Continued.)
Winter term.   Professor GRUBB.
Prerequisite, Latin 4.

6. Cicero.

Kelsey's Cicero's Orations and Daniell's Latin Prose Composition.
Spring term. Professor GRUBB.
Prerequisite, Latin 5.

7. Cicero. (Continued.)

Fall term. Professor PARKER.
Prerequisite, Latin 6.

8. Vergil.

Dennison's Frieze's Vergil's Æneid. Winter term.
Professor PARKER.
Prerequisite, Latin 7.

9. Vergil. (Continued.)

Spring term. Professor PARKER.
Prerequisite Latin 8.

*10. Horace (Satires and Epistles) or Ovid.

Fall term. Professor PARKER.
Prerequisite, Latin 9.

*11. Horace, Odes and Epodes.

Chase and Stuart's edition. Fall term. Professor PARKER.
Prerequisite, Latin 9.

*12. Sallust.

Chase and Stuart's edition. Fall term. Professor PARKER.
Prerequisite, Latin 9.

13. Cicero's De Senectute and De Amicitia.

Kelsey's edition. Winter term. Professor PARKER.
Prerequisite, Latin 9.

*14. Curtius Rufus's Life of Alexander.

Crosby's edition. Winter term. Professor PARKER.
Prerequisite, Latin 9.

*15. Livy, Twenty-first Book.

Westcott's edition. Winter term. Professor PARKER.
Prerequisite, Latin 9.

---

*Latin 10, 13, 16, will be given in 1902-03; Latin 11, 14, 17, in 1903-04; Latin 12, 15, 18, in 1904-05.

*16. Tacitus's Germania and Agricola.

Hopkins's edition. Spring term. Professor PARKER.
Prerequisite, Latin 9.

*17. Juvenal.

Anthon's edition. Spring term. Professor PARKER.
Prerequisite, Latin 9.

*18. Plautus.
Spring term. Professor PARKER.
Prerequisite, Latin 9.

Latin Composition may be given in connection with Latin 10 to 18 inclusive.

BOOKS OF REFERENCE.

The following books are recommended for reference to students pursuing the study of Latin:

Harper's Latin Lexicon; White's Junior Student's Latin Lexicon; Doederlein's Latin Synonyms; Liddell's History of Rome; Long's, or Ginn & Co.'s Classical Atlas; Anthon's or Smith's Classical Dictionary; Harper's Dictionary of Classical Literature and Antiquities; Harkness's and Bennett's Latin Grammars.

GREEK.

1. Grammar and Lessons.

Boise and Pattengill's Greek Lessons. Goodwin's Greek Grammar.
Fall term. Professor PARKER.
Open to all students in the College.

2. Grammar and Lessons. (Continued.)

Winter term. Professor PARKER.
Prerequisite, Greek 1.

3. Anabasis.

Goodwin's Xenophon's Anabasis. Collar and Daniell's Greek Composition. Spring term. Professor PARKER.
Prerequisite, Greek 2.

4. Anabasis. (Continued.)

Collar and Daniell's Greek Composition. Fall term.
Professor PARKER.
Prerequisite, Greek 3.

---

*Latin 10, 13, 16, will be given in 1902-03; Latin 11, 14, 17, in 1903-04; Latin 12, 15, 18, in 1904-05.

5. Orations of Lysias.

Stevens' edition.   Winter term.   Professor PARKER.
Prerequisite, Greek 4.

6. Iliad.

Keep's Homer's Iliad.   Spring term.   Professor PARKER.
Prerequisite, Greek 5.

7. Odyssey..

Merry's Homer's Odyssey.   Fall term.   Professor PARKER.
Prerequisite, Greek 6.

8. Plato's Apology of Socrates.

Kitchel's edition.   Winter term of 1904–05 and the winter term of every alternate year thereafter.   Professor PARKER.
Prerequisite, Greek 5.

9. Plato's Gorgias.

Lodge's edition.   Winter term of 1903–04 and the Winter term of every alternate year thereafter.   Professor PARKER.
Prerequisite, Greek 5.

10. Herodotus.

Fernald's Selections.   Spring term of 1904 and the Spring term of every alternate year thereafter.   Professor PARKER.
Prerequisite, Greek 8 or 9.

11. Prometheus of Aeschylus, or Medea of Euripides.

Wecklein's Prometheus, Allen's Medea.   Spring term of 1903, and the Spring term of every alternate year thereafter.
                                            Professor PARKER.
Prerequisite, Greek 8 or 9.

12, 13, 14, 15.   Greek New Testament.

These classes, while primarily intended for theological students, are open also to College students who have the requisite preparation.   A full description is given in the Divinity School Courses.
                                            Professor WHITE.
Prerequisite, Greek 5.

BOOKS OF REFERENCE.

The following books are recommended for reference to those pursuing the study of Greek:

Liddell and Scott's Greek Lexicon; Autenrieth's Homeric Dictionary; Long's, or Ginn & Co's Classical Atlas; Anthon's, or Smith's Classical Dictionary; Harper's Dictionary of Classical Literaturé and Antiquities; Smith's History of Greece; Goodwin's Greek Grammar; Goodwin's Greek Modes and Tenses.

HEBREW.

1, 2, 3. Grammar and Old Testament.

These are primarily courses in the Divinity School, but may be elected by students in the College of Liberal Arts whenever they are offered. Classes will be formed each year if a sufficient number of students apply.

It is the aim to give the students such a knowledge of the forms and structure of the Hebrew language as shall enable them to use it efficiently in the criticism and literary analysis of the Old Testament Scriptures. The text-books used are H. G. Mitchell's Hebrew Lessons and the Hebrew Old Testament. Three terms—Fall, Winter and Spring—each term counting as a course.   Professor WHITE.

Open (under conditions as described above) to students who, in the judgment of the Instructor, are qualified by previous training to take the course.

MATHEMATICS.

The study of Mathematics is useful to the student in two ways. In the first place, it affords an admirable mental discipline, developing habits of precise thought and accurate statement. In the second place, as the necessary tool of the civil and electrical engineer, the architect, and all persons engaged in higher scientific work, it has a practical value to those intending to enter these professions.

It is the purpose of the department to keep these two objects steadily in view. Students are required to show their understanding of mathematical principles and reasoning by rigid demonstrations, subject to the criticism of other members of the class. Problems are selected for solution which arise in the actual practice of surveying, engineering, physical research, and the like.

Students who intend to enter any of the above mentioned professions may profitably take a large part of their work at Lombard, completing their course in some technical school.

For courses 1 to 4 inclusive, see Preparatory Courses, p. 68.

5. Algebra.

This course presupposes a thorough grounding in Elementary Algebra on the part of the student: [See Entrance Requirements in Algebra, p. 27.] After a brief review of Quadratic Equations, with especial reference to theory, the subjects of Simultaneous Equations of the second degree, Indeterminate Equations, Ratio and Proportion, Arithmetical and

Geometrical Progression, Series, Undetermined Coefficients, the Binomial theorem, and Logarithms, will be considered. Wells's College Algebra is used. Fall term. Mr. Campbell.

Prerequisite, entrance Algebra or Mathematics 4.

6. (a) Plane Geometry.

This course is designed to give students thorough drill in the first principles of Geometry. Phillips and Fisher's Elements of Geometry is used.

Mathematics 6 (a) may be taken by students who are deficient in Entrance Geometry. It will not count as one of the thirty-eight credits required for a degree. Winter term. Mr. Campbell.

6. (b) Plane Geometry.

This course consists of a review of Mathematics 6 (a) together with the demonstration of a large number of original propositions. Winter term. Professor Wright.

Prerequisite, Mathematics 6 (a).

7. Solid Geometry.

This course is continuous with Mathematics 6 (a). Spring term.
Mr. Campbell.

Prerequisite, Mathematics 6 (a).

8. Higher Algebra.

This course assumes a thorough knowledge on the part of the student of Mathematics 5 and also some knowledge of Plane Geometry. It embraces the study of Permutations and Combinations, Probability, Determinants, and the Theory of Equations. Fall term.

Professor Wright.

Prerequisite, Mathematics 5 and Mathematics 6 (a).

9. Plane and Spherical Trigonometry.

This course includes the solution of trigonometric equations, the solution of plane and spherical triangles and problems involving an application of Trigonometry to Mensuration, Surveying, and Astronomy. Crockett's Plane and Spherical Trigonometry is used as a text-book. Winter term. Professor Wright.

Prerequisite, Mathematics 8.

10. Analytic Geometry.

This course treats of the straight line, the conic sections, and higher plane curves. Spring term. Professor Wright.

Prerequisite, Mathematics 9.

11. Surveying and Leveling.

Field work and problems.　Field work on Saturdays at the option of the instructor.　Spring term.　　　　　Professor Wright.

Prerequisite, Mathematics 9.

*12. Differential Calculus.

Byerly's Differential Calculus is used.　Fall term.

Professor Wright.

Prerequisite, Mathematics 10.

*13. Integral Calculus.

Winter term.　　　　　　　　　　Professor Wright.

Prerequisite, Mathematics 12.

*14. Descriptive Geometry.

This course embraces mechanical drawing, orthographic projection, shades and shadows, and perspective.　Church's Descriptive Geometry is used.　Fall term.　　　　　　　Professor Wright.

Prerequisite, Mathematics 9.

*15. Strength of Structures.

This course takes up the computation of the strains in bridge and roof trusses, by graphical and analytical methods.　Shreve's Strength of Bridges and Roofs is used as a text-book.　Winter term.

Professor Wright.

Prerequisite, Mathematics 13.

16. Quaternions.

A class will be formed for the study of Quaternions when a sufficient number of advanced students apply.　The class will meet once a week for a year at such hour as the instructor may appoint.

Professor Wright.

17. Life Insurance.

This course will embrace a discussion of the fundamental principles of Life Insurance, a brief historical review, and a thorough though necessarily elementary treatment of actuarial science.　Methods of computing premium, reserve, insurance value, etc., will be studied, and the class will have practice in making such computations.　The policies issued by leading American companies will be examined, and such questions as loading, forfeiture, surplus distribution, and the like will be discussed.

---

*Mathematics 12 and 13 will be given in 1903-04, but will not be given in 1904-05, alternating with mathematics 14 and 15.

Reference will be made to the methods of fraternal insurance, and their practice compared with that of the "old line companies."

It is the purpose of the course to fit the student for efficient service in the actuarial department of a life company or to make independent actuarial computations. Winter term. Professor WRIGHT.

In addition to the foregoing courses, classes will be formed, when there is a sufficient demand on the part of advanced students, to pursue work in the solution of original problems in the Calculus, and in the study of infinitesimals, probability, elliptic functions, and other topics.

ASTRONOMY.

1. General Astronomy.

This course is largely descriptive in character, though some of the simpler mathematical problems connected with Astronomy are solved. It embraces a study of the imaginary lines, of the celestial phere latitude, longitude, time; the sun, moon, and planets; comets, meteors, and the stars. Some attention is given to the constellations and the myths connected with them. The Nebular Hypothesis is presented and discussed. Young's Lessons in Astronomy is used. Fall term.
Professor WRIGHT.
Prerequisite, Mathematics 9.

2. Mathematical Astronomy.

This course will have to do with the solution of various Astronomical problems. Computations in latitude, longitude, and time, eclipses, orbits, etc., will be among the tasks assigned. Three hours a week. Winter term. Professor WRIGHT.
Prerequisites, Mathematics 13 and Astronomy 1.

PHYSICS.

The course in Physics extends through the year, four periods per week being devoted to lectures and recitations and one to laboratory work. The aim is to present the science of Physics as a whole, that students may be led to note the general principles of mechanics that apply throughout, and which furnish the basis of explanation of all the various phenomena.

The work of this course consists of a careful consideration of the various laws treated under the six main divisions of the subject.

It is intended for the general student and no Mathematics higher than Plane Trigonometry is required. A special effort is made to make the work as practical as possible. Numerous problems given, test the student's ability to think clearly and make a correct application of the principles involved.

The laboratory experiments are chiefly quantitative and give opportunity for the verification of fundamental laws and general formulae. Each student is required to present carefully prepared notes which shall include the data obtained from observation and computed results.

1. Mechanics, Hydrostatics, Pneumatics.

Text-book, Carhart's University Physics.   Fall term.

Professor RICH.

Prerequisite, Mathematics 9.

2. Heat, Electricity, and Magnetism.

Winter term.   Professor RICH.

Prerequisite, Mathematics 9.

3. Acoustics and Optics.

Spring term.   Professor RICH.

Prerequisite, Physics 2.

CHEMISTRY.

The courses in Chemistry have been arranged with several distinct objects in view: First—A clear understanding of the underlying principles of chemical changes. This involves a thorough knowledge of the theory of the structure of matter. Students who understand well this theory will avoid many of the difficulties ordinarily met with in the study of Chemistry and Physics.

Second—The principles of Stoichiometry, or Chemical Arithmetic, are to be thoroughly mastered and applied in a large series of practical chemical problems.

Third—A study of the elements and their compounds with careful attention given to the writing of equations.

Fourth—A systematic course in the laboratory, designed to give the student practice in careful manipulation and also opportunity for verification of the laws of chemical combination. The experiments of this course include the preparation of common elements and compounds.

Fifth—A general course in Qualitative analysis in which the student becomes familiar with the methods of determining the composition of native and manufactured substances.

Sixth—A well graded course in Quantitative analysis which gives the student practice in the various gravimetric and volumetric methods.

This gives the student the basis for technical work and enables him, in the minimum time, to become familiar with special, practical methods in the arts, and in fact to take the position of chemist in many lines of trade or manufacture without further preparation.

The course includes the analysis of such substances as ores, soils, fertilizers, soaps, milk, butter, gas, air, water, etc.

1. Inorganic Chemistry

Remsen's College Chemistry is used as the basis of courses 1 and 2. Fall term. Professor Rich.
Open to all students.

2. Inorganic Chemistry.

Winter term. Professor Rich.

Prerequisite, Chemistry 1.

3. Organic Chemistry.

This course consists of recitations, lectures with experimental demonstrations, and laboratory work. The consideration of food-stuffs is an important part of the work. Their composition, adulteration, and the new methods of preparation are carefully studied. Remsen's Organic Chemistry is used. Spring term. Professor Rich.

Prerequisite, Chemistry 2.

In each of the courses 1, 2, and 3, the work is profusely illustrated by experiments, and individual work by the student in the laboratory demonstrates the principles discussed.

4. Analytical Chemistry.

Qualitative analysis, laboratory work, and recitations. Fall term.
-- Professor Rich.

Prerequisite, Chemistry 2.

5. Analytical Chemistry.

Qualitative, and quantitative analysis, laboratory work. Winter term. Professor Rich.

Prerequisite, Chemistry 4.

6. Analytical Chemistry.

Quantitative analysis. Laboratory work. Spring term.
Professor Rich.

Prerequisite, Chemistry 5.

7. Physiological Chemistry.

A study of the organic compounds, and the chemical processes of physiological change. Specially useful in subsequent study of practical medicine. Spring term. Professor Rich.

Prerequisites, Chemistry 3 and 4.

GEOLOGY AND MINERALOGY.

1. Geology.

The work in Geology is given by text-book recitations, supplemented by lectures and excursions for field work. The College has a valuable collection of minerals, which serves for purposes of illustration and study. Dana's work is used.   Spring term.   Professor RICH.

Prerequisite, Chemistry 1, Biology 3, and Biology 4.

2. Mineralogy.

The course consists of a qualitative determination of minerals by means of the blow-pipe and a careful study of the principles of classification.   Winter term.   Professor RICH.

Prerequisite, Chemistry 2.

Biological Sciences.

The courses offered in biology have been prepared to meet the requirements of students who desire instruction in the Biological Sciences either for general culture, as a preparation for teaching, for original research in Physiology and Zoology, or as foundation for the professional course in medicine.

To meet these needs the College offers the "Biologico-Chemical Group," the "Chemico-Physical and Pre-Medical Group," and the "Pre-Medical Group."

These courses are offered in the belief that the education of the professional man or woman should in no sense be a narrow one, and that the subsequent success of the individual depends upon the thoroughness and upon the breadth of his education.

The courses offered in this department give the student a general knowledge of life from its simplest to its most complex form.   They build a broad foundation for graduate work in Physiology, Zoology, Sociology, Botany, Psychology, and Medicine.   The student who faithfully does the work as outlined in these courses will be well prepared to teach them in secondary schools.   In this department the student learns of life, of the structure and functions of the various organs of which the organism is composed, and of their relations to each other.   He learns how to observe and appreciate the wonderful phenomena of nature.   The numerous unsolved problems in this field offer many opportunities for investigation and advancement.

BIOLOGY.

1. General Biology.

This course will furnish a sketch of the history of the science of Biology and discuss the aims and methods of biological research, composi-

tion of living substance, and the elementary vital phenomena. Recitations and laboratory work. Dr. KIMBLE.
Open to all College students.

2. General Biology. (Continuation of Course 1.)

A study of the general conditions of life, of stimuli, and their actions, and of the mechanisms of life. Dr. KIMBLE.
Prerequisite, Biology 1.

PHYSIOLOGY.

1. Elementary Physiology.

This course is intended for students desiring a general knowledge of Physiology, but will not count as a credit for the "Pre-Medical Group." Fall term. Dr. KIMBLE.
Open to all College students.

2. Advanced Physiology.

This will be a study of the blood, the tissues of movement, and the vascular mechanism. Primarily for medical students, but may be taken by any student in the College of Liberal Arts. Fall term.
Dr. KIMBLE.
Prerequisite, Chemistry 2.

3. Advanced Physiology. (Continuation of Course 2.)

In this course the student is given an opportunity for a thorough knowledge of the tissues and mechanisms of digestion, and respiration, the elimination of waste products, and nutrition. Winter term.
Dr. KIMBLE.
Prerequisites, Chemistry 3 and Physiology 2.

4. Physiology of the Nervous System.

A study of the central nervous system, including a brief sketch of the anatomy of the same. Laboratory, recitations, and lectures. Fall term.
Dr. KIMBLE.
Prerequisites, same as in Physiology 2.

5. Physiology and Anatomy of the Sense Organs.

This course deals with the Physiology and Anatomy of the organs of sense. It is especially adapted to the needs of students in medicine, but those wanting to do advanced work in Psychology will find it of decided advantage to have the knowledge which this course offers. Winter term.
Dr. KIMBLE.
Prerequisites, Biology 2 or Physiology 1 and Entrance Physics.

6. Practical Hygiene.

In this course it is intended to give the student such knowledge as will best fit him properly to care for himself in his surroundings while pursuing his college work. A series of about ten lectures given at the beginning of the Fall term. Dr. KIMBLE.

Required of all students.

ANATOMY.

1. Osteology.

This course consists of laboratory work, lectures, and demonstrations. Each student is required to make a drawing of each bone of the human skeleton, and model it in clay. Fall term. Dr. KIMBLE.

This course is primarily for medical students.

2. General Anatomy.

This course consists of practical work in the laboratory; each student is required to make at least one complete dissection of the human body. Most students find it necessary to devote to this course five hours a day, or to continue it in the Spring term. Winter term. Dr. KIMBLE.

Prerequisite, Anatomy 1.

3. Histology.

The construction and use of the microscope, the methods of preparing microscopical sections of tissues, and of the normal histology of the various tissues and organs of the body. Two hours daily.

Dr. KIMBLE.

BOTANY.

1. General Botany.

This course is intended to acquaint the student with the general field of Botany, including plant ecology and cartography. Fall term.

DR. KIMBLE.

Prerequisites, Entrance Chemistry and Botany, Biology 2.

*2. Morphological Botany.

A view of mossworts, ferns, and flowering plants, with special problems in structure, life history, and phylogeny. Text, lectures, laboratory work, and reference reading. Spring term.

Mr. KIENHOLZ.

Prerequisite, Botany 1.

*3. Physiological Botany.

This course consists of a series of qualitative experiments dealing with the functions of plants and plant tissues, behavior of plant growth in different environments. Lectures on absorption, metabolism, excretion, respiration, foods, actions of enzymes, plant constituents, and relation of growth to environments. Text, MacDougal. Plant Physiology. Spring term. Mr. KIENHOLZ.

Prerequisite, Botany 1.

*Botany 2 alternates with Botany 3. Botany 3 will be given in 1904.

ZOOLOGY.

1. Invertebrate Zoology.

This course will treat of the Invertebrata, with special reference to their systematic relations. Recitations, laboratory, and reference work. Fall term. Mr. KIENHOLZ.

Prerequisites, entrance credits in Zoology and Chemistry.

2. Vertebrate Zoology.

In this course typical forms will be studied in the laboratory. Drawings and explanatory notes of dissected specimens will be required. Winter term. Mr. KIENHOLZ.

Prerequisite, Zoology 1.

3. Animal Ecology.

This will be a study of life relations of animals and the effects of the environment on the individual and the phylum. Extensive collateral reading will be required. This course will be given whenever a sufficient number of adequately prepared students apply for it. Dr. KIMBLE.

HISTORY.

[For History 1 to 4 inclusive, see page 69.]

5. History of the Christian Church.

A. The Ancient and Mediaeval Eras [1-1517.]

This course in Church History is primarily intended for the members of the Divinity School but is also open to College students. It will require the investigation of the early organization and extension of Christianity and the successive periods of the Church down to the time of Charlemagne; followed by a careful inquiry into the causes of the rise of the Papacy, of the political relations of the Church, and of the Crusades. Fisher's History of the Church will be used as a hand book and topics will be assigned to each member of the class for special investigation and reports. Fall term. Professor WHITE.

6. History of the Christian Church.

B. The Modern Era [1517-1903.]

This course will begin with the study of the Reformation, and trace the history of the Church down to the present time. It will include the history of Christian missions, revivals, social reforms, and philanthropy. The same text-book will be used as in History 5. Winter term.
Professor WHITE.

Prerequisite, History 5.

7. History of Christian Doctrines.

Fisher is used for text. Spring term. Professor WHITE.

8. Development of English Nationality.

Text, Terry. Fall Term. Miss HATHAWAY,

Prerequisite, History 4.

9. United States from 1760 to 1889.

Lectures and reference work.   Winter term.

Miss HATHAWAY.

Prerequisite, entrance History of the United States.

10. Europe from 1789 to 1815.

The Revolutionary and Napoleonic Era.   Text, Rose.   Spring term.

Open to all College students.   Miss HATHAWAY.

11. History of Civilization.

Text, Guizot.   Spring term.   Professor WHITE.

ECONOMICS.

In the first place the student becomes acquainted with the idea that in human relations there are laws of cause and effect, as there are in nature.   There are certain attributes of human nature and certain phenomena of physical nature which may be regarded as fundamental; and on account of these fundamental attributes human beings in their relations to one another may be expected to react in a perfectly definite and predicable way.   In other words the student learns that a Social Law may be formulated, and that a Social Science is possible.   This feature of the work, however, is more exhaustively brought out in the more general science of Sociology, one course in which the student is expected to have pursued before taking up Economics.

In the second place such social laws as have reference to men's actions in the ordinary business of life, are developed.   These are the familiar economic laws which form the subject matter of text-books in Political Economy: the law of diminishing returns; the doctrine of Malthus; the laws of market, normal, and monopoly value; the principles of international trade; and the principles governing the distribution of the products of labor among landowners, capitalists, employers, and wage earners.

A third feature of the work is the study of certain historical periods with reference to the actual operation of economic laws; a verification of the truths developed from economic premises.

Finally, as human society is progressive rather than static, economic ideals are discussed and practical problems relating to the improvement of the present economic order are investigated.   Under this head are discussed such subjects as free trade, bimetallism, the labor question, monopoly, land tenure reform, socialism, and the like.

A prominent feature of the work is its investigatory character.   In many cases the student is thrown upon his own resources to determine an economic point by studying and comparing the views of different authorities, rather than by simply learning the statement of the text. Throughout, a great deal of collateral reading is required. The way is thus paved for subsequent independent research.

It is believed that the study of Economics is of great value in fitting a student for the duties of citizenship, and in the growing complexity of our economic life the importance of this consideration can hardly be over-estimated. The problems of international trade, of money, of monopoly, of socialism, and the like are demanding attention, and in a popular form of government it is important that the individual citizen with whom ultimately the decision in regard to these questions will rest should have an opinion independent of party affiliation.

(For Economics 1 see page 70.)

2. Political Economy.
General Political Economy. Bullock's Introduction to the Study of Economics is used. Fall term. Professor WRIGHT.
Prerequisite, Sociology 1.

3. Financial History of the United States.
This course embraces the finances of the Revolution; the financial administrations of Morris, Hamilton, and Gallatin; the bank struggle; tariff legislation, and the financial measures up to the time of the civil war. This course will be conducted by lectures and frequent reviews. Fall term. Professor WRIGHT.
Prerequisite. Economics 2.

4. Current Economic Problems.
It is the purpose in this course to investigate from a standpoint somewhat broader than that of purely economic considerations certain vital economic problems and reforms. Different topics will be discussed different years. The subject for 1903 is the Labor Question. Spring term.
Prerequisite, Economics 2. Professor WRIGHT.

JURISPRUDENCE.
1. International Law.
The general principles which govern the relations of States, as historically developed in express agreements and by usage, are elucidated; and these principles are discussed from the standpoints of reason and justice. Special study is made of current international problems, and theses on these subjects are required. Particular attention is paid to terminology. Lawrence's International Law is used as a text-book. Frequent reference is made to the works on International Law by Woolsey, Wheaton, Glenn, etc. Spring term. Professor WHITE.

Open to students who, in the judgment of the instructor, are qualified by previous training to take the course.
International Law will not be given in 1903-04.

SOCIOLOGY.*

Nature and Scope of the Science.

The comparative recency with which this department has taken its place in the college course and the consequent unfamiliarity of the public with the nature of its work, coupled with the fundamental importance of that work, seem to warrant a slightly extended statement concerning it.

Sociology may be defined as the primary and fundamental science of society. What are the conditions and laws under which societies originate, develop, and decay? What are the elementary social laws upon which the more special laws of economics, jurisprudence, civics, and religion depend? What are the fundamental and necessary relationships which must obtain in any given community of men if that community is to be a safe, stable, and progressive community? Under what conditions do the great social institutions of law, religion, the state, commercial relationships, the family, etc., have their origin, development, and decline? What are their history and their present status in the social structure? How do they react upon each other and upon the individual? What are the methods by which a student should make a study of a given community or social class or institution, and how and when can these methods be applied? These and others are the questions which it is the business of the science to answer. To the discovery, organization, and dissemination of knowledge calculated to answer these questions, it devotes itself. It is this knowledge which the student gets from a study of the science. The great importance of such knowledge to every member of society, no matter what his station in life may be, cannot possibly need emphasis to the mind of any thoughtful person.

Methods.

The method of instruction is a combination of the lecture, laboratory, and recitation methods, dependent upon the nature of the subject and the

---

*SOCIOLOGY AND SOCIAL REFORM.—Because of certain widely current misconceptions it cannot be too clearly stated that Sociology is in no possible sense to be identified with any scheme or program of social reform, ancient or modern. The sociologist as such is a scientist pure and simple. He has no thought of shaping or molding the phenomena which constitute the subject matter of his science. As a sociologist he no more proposes to reform society than the anatomist proposes to remodel the vertebrate skeleton. He studies social reform, its methods, its varieties, its history, results, etc., but in a perfectly critical and dispassionate manner, and with no other motive than to discover and set forth the facts pertaining to it. Moreover it is to be remembered that social reform comprises only a very small, and relatively very unimportant portion of the subject matter of Sociology. One of the greatest of living sociologists has well said that the study of social reform comes about as near to being the sole business of Sociology as does the mending of broken rails to being the chief business of a railroad company. The sociologist's studies must undoubtedly form the chief source of reliable knowledge concerning social reform. This fact cannot be overlooked; but anyone who looks to Sociology as a champion of any particular reform, or of reform in general, is wholly in error. Sociology is no more a part of social reform than is the microscope a part of the amoeba which is seen through its lenses.

characteristics of the student. The constant aim is to furnish to the student such knowledge of the primary facts of the associational life as will be most useful to him both in his college course and in his ensuing career. Any and all methods fruitfully contributing to this result are used as occasion suggests.

Library.

A good working library is being accumulated for the use of students of the department. Additions are made from time to time as the needs of the department and the resources of the institution seem to warrant.

General Courses.

1. An Introduction to Sociology.

This course together with course 1 (*a*) will furnish the student an introductory knowledge of the more elementary principles of the science and of the fundamental facts of the associational life. They are particularly designed to meet the needs of the general college student, and besides affording him a broad basis for further study in Sociology, Logic, Ethics, Economics, Political Science, and Law, also to provide him with information and training which will be of high practical value in the various walks of life. Wherever possible, students should arrange to take the two courses consecutively. Certain of the subjects dealt with are as follows: the province and aim of the science, its relation to other sciences and to practical life; the primary social institutions, their history, characteristics, functions; the chief associative processes, their nature, their causes, and their place in the structure and life of society; the origin, development, and decline of societies; critical study of certain leading ideas of prominent modern sociologists; illustrative study of an actual community. Lectures, personal investigation, recitations, and assigned readings. Fall term.

Professor KIMBLE.

Open regularly to all students who have acquired the sixteen units requisite for college standing; open to others only on consultation with instructor.

1 (*a*). An Introduction to Sociology.

See announcement of Course 1 of which course this is a continuation. Winter term. Professor KIMBLE.

Prerequisite, Sociology 1.

The Development of Sociological Theory.

The courses in sociological theory are practically continuous, though any one of them can be taken without taking those later than itself. Collectively they are designed to offer the student opportunity to make a somewhat extended study of the chief works in the literature of sociology.

In so doing he is taught to see each work in its relation to each of the others and to the common whole. Each work is first subjected to a careful analysis; the results of this analysis are then compared with the results of similar analysis of other works, and through critical evaluation and constructive synthesis of the factors thus discriminated the development of sociological theory as a whole is made clear to the mind.

*2. Pre-Comtean Sociological Theory.

A study of the earlier theories of social relations.

Professor KIMBLE.

Prerequisite, reading knowledge of French or German.

*3. Modern Sociological Theory.

The chief works of the more prominent modern sociologists are studied with a view to the characteristic positions of each and the relations sustained by each to sociological theory as a whole.

Professor KIMBLE.

Prerequisite, reading knowledge of French or German.

*4. Modern Sociological Theory.

(Continuation of Course 3.) Professor KIMBLE.

Prerequisite, Sociology 3.

The Development of Association.

The courses under this head are intended to afford the student opportunity to study certain of the chief factors of the associate life in a more detailed manner than is allowed in courses 1 and 1 (*a*).

*6. An Introduction to Comparative Study of Association.

The method, scope, and problems of Comparative Sociology. The development of association from the earlier to the later forms. Chief stages and factors. Fundamental laws and processes.

Professor KIMBLE.

*7. Biogeography.

An outline study of the influence of the inanimate environment upon the development of association. Professor KIMBLE.

Prerequisite, reading knowledge of German.

9. Reproductive Association.

A study of association as developed about the reproductive process. This course is designed to furnish a solid basis for Course 13. The various forms of reproductive association, commencing with the crudest and most simple, are considered as steps in the development of one great process having its beginning among the lowest animals and its ending in the highest form of the human family.   Fall term.

Professor KIMBLE.

Open by consultation to all college students who have completed the entrance requirements.   The elementary courses in Zoology, Biology, Sociology, and Psychology, will be of great assistance to students taking this course.

12.   Abnormal and Pathological Variations in Association.

A course in the study of dependents, defectives, and delinquents. Crime and the criminal classes.   Methods of organized charity work. Winter term.   Professor KIMBLE.

Open regularly to all students who have had Course 1.   Open to others by consultation only.   Ordinarily Course 12 will not be given the same year with Courses 9 and 13.

13.   The Family.

A study of the development and present significance of the human family.   The various forms of marriage and the family.   The function of the family in modern society.   The relations by which the family is constituted.   The influence of certain other institutions upon the family: the family and the church, the family and the state, the family and economic institutions, the family and educational and moral institutions. Winter term.   Professor KIMBLE.

Open to all college students.   Students will find Courses 1, 1a, and 9 of great value in connection with Course 13.

PSYCHOLOGY.

1.   Physiology and Psychology of the Senses.

Experience has shown the need of a course in which special attention shall be given to the correlation of the study of the physiology and anatomy of the sense organs with that of the psychology of the elementary psychic processes.   This course has been designed to meet this need. Fall term.   Professor KIMBLE and Dr. KIMBLE.

2.   Introductory Psychology.

The purpose of the course is to guide the beginner in gaining the fundamentals of a thorough knowledge of psychology and of psychic life. The course is organized about a careful study of the commoner characteristics of the more accessible mental processes.   Emphasis is laid upon the ready and accurate use of the more important psychological terms.

*Courses so marked are special courses and are at present given only when a sufficient number of adequately prepared students present themselves for registration therein.   Students desiring to arrange for work in such courses are requested to consult the instructor personally.

Some knowledge of the chief standpoints and methods of the science is gained. Collateral reading in connection with the text will be regularly assigned and a correct appreciation of the relation of this reading to the treatment presented in the text will be a requirement of the course. Experiments described in text and reading will be fully discussed; and, where circumstances will permit, the student will see performed by others or will himself perform in the laboratory certain type experiments. Winter term. Professor KIMBLE.

Prerequisite, Psychology 1, or equivalent.

METAPHYSIC.

This is primarily a course in the Divinity School, but it may be elected by students in the College of Liberal Arts whenever it is offered. Classes will be formed whenever a sufficient number of students apply. Lotze's Outline of Metaphysic is used as a text-book. Fall term.

Professor WHITE.

Open to students, who in the judgment of the instructor, are qualified by previous training to take the course.

LOGIC.

Having first obtained a thorough grounding in the principles and methods of correct reasoning both deductive and inductive, at least one-half of the term is given to the detection and discrimination of fallacies in actual examples. Such examples the class is required to search out in current literature and bring in for discussion. Davis's Elements of Deductive Logic and Davis's Elements of Inductive Logic are used. Winter term. Professor FOWLER.

Open to students who, in the judgment of the instructor, are qualified by previous training to take the course.

ETHICS.

Ethics is treated from the standpoint of Philosophy, and the different systems are discussed. The nature and grounds of obligation are investigated and applied to the practical affairs of life. Winter term.

Professor WHITE.

Open to students who, in the judgment of the instructor, are qualified by previous training to take the course.

PHILOSOPHY OF RELIGION.

Fairbairn's Philosophy of the Christian Religion is the text-book. Lotze, Sabatier, and Martineau are used as works of reference. The aim of the instructor is to acquaint the student with the proper offices of reason in the effort to find argumentative grounds for religious ideas. Most of the modern theories respecting the nature and scope of the religious feeling pass under review; and in such discussions free questioning on the part of the student is encouraged. Winter term.

Professor WHITE.

Open to students who, in the judgment of the instructor, are qualified by previous training to take the course.

ETHICAL THEORIES.

Martineau's Types of Ethical Theory is used as a text-book with frequent references to the works of Sidgwick, Green, Smyth, and others. Much attention is paid to the elucidation and criticism of the modern ethical theories. Spring term. Professor WHITE.

Open to students who, in the judgment of the instructor, are qualified by previous training to take the course.

COMPARATIVE RELIGION.

The work consists in the examination and comparison of the authorities upon the great Non-Christian religions. Special topics are investigated and reports made by each member of the class. Spring term.

Professor WHITE.

FINE ARTS.

2, 3, 4. Drawing.

This course includes perspective, drawing from casts in charcoal and crayon, still life studies in crayon, etc. It will count as one credit for the entire year. Miss BLOOD.

Open to all students in the College.

MUSIC.

1. Harmony.

Keys, scales and signatures, intervals, formation of the triad, chord connection, simple part writing begun. Stephen A. Emery's text-book is used. Two hours a week. Fall term. Miss BARTLETT.

Open to all students in the College.

2. Harmony.

Harmonizing basses, including all chords of the seventh and their inversions. Key board work. Modulation begun. Two hours a week. Winter term. Miss BARTLETT.

Prerequisite, Music 1.

3. Harmony.

Altered and augmented chords explained and worked out from basses given for harmonization. Modulation continued, Two hours a week. Spring term. . Miss BARTLETT.

Prerequisite, Music 2.

4. Harmony. ·

Harmonizing melodies continued. Double chants and chorals. Two hours a week. Fall term. MISS BARTLETT.

Prerequisite, Music 3.

5. Harmony.

Harmonizing melodies continued. Suspensions. Passing chords and changing notes. Modulation completed. Two hours a week. Winter term. Miss BARTLETT.

Prequisite, Music 4.

6. Single Counterpoint.

Single counterpoint in all forms in two and three voices. Spring term. Miss BARTLETT.

Prerequisite, Music 5.

7. Single Counterpoint.

Single counterpoint in four voices. Double counterpoint begun. Fall term. Miss BARTLETT.

Prerequisite, Music 6.

8. Double Counterpoint.

Double counterpoint in tenth and twelfth. Triple and quadruple counterpoint. Winter term. Miss BARTLETT.

Prerequisite, Music 7.

9. Canon and Fugue.

Canon in two voices in all intervals. Free imitation. Fugues in two, three, and four voices. Double fugue. Spring term.

Miss BARTLETT.

Prerequisite, Music 8.

10, 11, 12. History of Music. [Half Courses.]

These courses embrace a history of the development of music from the earliest times until to-day, with special reference to critical analysis of the works of the great masters. They also furnish an introduction to the lives of the great composers. One hour a week for the year.

Professor LUNDBERG.

ELOCUTION.

Not more than four credits can be counted in this department towards the degree of A. B.

1. Elocution. [Half Course.]

The aim of this course is to rid the voice of all impurities, secure correct placing of the voice, proper breathing, and beauty of tone for conversational purposes. Notes will be given upon the anatomy of the vocal organs and the care of the voice. Physical exercises will be introduced as a means of securing grace and becoming deportment. Recitations Mondays, Wednesdays, and Fridays. Fall term. Miss KIDDER.

Open to all students of the College.

2. Elocution. [Half Course.]

In this course attention will be given to the adaptation of the conversational voice to the requirements of platform speaking. Each pupil will be required to deliver three selections before the class for criticism. Work in pantomime and life study will be introduced. Recitations Mondays, Wednesdays, and Fridays. Winter term. Miss KIDDER.

Prerequisite, Elocution 1.

3. Elocution. [Half Course.]

This course will consist of a continuation of the work outlined in Elocution 2. The analysis of some English Classic will be required. Recitations Mondays, Wednesdays, and Fridays. Spring term.

Miss KIDDER.

Prerequisite, Elocution 2.

4. Elocution. [Half Course.]

The study of masterpieces will be made the basis of this course. Recitations Mondays and Thursdays. Fall term. Miss KIDDER.

Prerequisite, Elocution 3.

5. Elocution. [Half Course,]

The work in this course will be a continuation of that begun in Elocution 4, together with extemporaneous talks, critical and detailed life study for personation. Recitations Mondays and Thursdays, Winter term. Miss KIDDER.

Prerequisite, Elocution 4.

6. Elocution. [Half Course.]

This course will consist of a continuation of Elocution 5. Recitations Mondays and Thursdays. Spring term. Miss KIDDER.

Prerequisite, Elocution 5.

7. Oratory. [Half Course.]

In this course the aim will be to assist the student in gaining some knowledge of the great orators, both American and English. Each student is required to deliver before class for criticism a certain number of selections, chosen from the orators studied; also to give talks on subjects previously assigned. Recitations Mondays and Thursdays. Fall term.

Miss KIDDER.

Prerequisite, Elocution 6.

8. Oratory. [Half Course.]

Important features of this course are extemporaneous speaking, class debates, and criticism. Two orations and one debate will be required from each member of the class. Recitations Mondays and Thursdays. Winter term.   Miss KIDDER.
Prerequisite, Elocution 7.

9. Elocution. [Half Course.]

This course consists of a study of the works of Dickens, Eliot, Shakespeare, and other authors, for the purpose of character interpretation. Scenes will be committed and interpreted for public presentation. Spring term.   Miss KIDDER.
Prerequisite, Elocution 6.

10, 11. Elocution. [Half Courses.]

These courses will consist of a continuation of Elocution 9. Fall and Winter terms.   Miss KIDDER.
Prerequisite. Elocution 9.

Recitals.

Recitals will be given during the year to show the proficiency of pupils, and to give them assistance in acquiring confidence, ease, and self control.

GYMNASIUM WORK.

The new system of physical education as pursued at Lombard College does not aim to make athletes and gymnasts, ball players, prize fighters, or wrestlers. The old idea that the gymnasium was solely for those already strong, or for the development of candidates for field honors, is not primarily considered. Incidentally the gymnasium affords ample facilities for indoor training of athletes, but this work is necessarily given a secondary place. Our system of physical education maintains that the development of mind and body go together and that one must not be sacrificed for the other. Its aim is not only to give a better and more useful physique, but to develop a will, a resolution of purpose, and to create a college spirit, which bring with them loyalty and help to dignify American citizenship. When the student enters the gymnasium he is subjected to a rigid medical examination which is made the basis of all gymnasium work. It determines the condition of the heart and circulation, the lungs and respiration, the stomach and its appendages, vision, hearing, size and consistency of muscles, and the temperament of the nervous system. Deformities, or bodily defects, are carefully sought for. From this examination a scientific application of physical exercises as a means of development is made. Occasionally in such examinations organic heart trouble is revealed. Such persons are not permitted to take the usual gymnasium work, but are given special exercises of a milder nature which are helpful. Functional derangements of nutrition, circulation, respiration, etc., are often discovered. Here again special exercises are prescribed.

The greater part of gymnasium work is conducted in classes which meet daily. Dumb-bell and club work are taken with a snap that puts life and vigor into every move. Class work is also done on the heavy apparatus, such as the buck and the parallel bars. Individual work is done with the chest weights and horizontal bars, traveling rings, climbing poles, etc. Wrestling and boxing are given special attention. Special work is also done on the rowing machine.

Besides the dumb-bell and light apparatus work, the ladies are offered a course in the Preece System of Physical Culture. During their respective seasons much attention is paid to foot-ball, basket-ball, base-ball, lawn tennis, and track athletics. Attention is now also given to boating in the spring of the year at Lombard. The gymnasium is made the cradle of college spirit.

All students will provide themselves with regular gymnasium uniforms. The cost of the uniform is about $2.50 for the men, and $4.50 for the women.

MEDICAL COURSES.

GENERAL ANNOUNCEMENTS.

The work offered in medical studies covers the first year of the four-year course now required in the medical colleges of the United States. None of the strictly professional branches are given, and no attempt will be made to offer these until proper facilities for thorough hospital work have been procured.   Of the scientific courses, however, all are given that are usually taught during the freshman year in the best medical colleges of this country.   The work in these branches is exceptionally thorough and complete, the time devoted to them being thirty-six weeks, as compared with about twenty-eight weeks of the usual medical course.

The courses are so arranged as to secure in a large measure concentration of attention upon single or closely allied subjects.

The work accomplished during the past three years has demonstrated both the need of medical instruction at Lombard College and the possibilities of its advancement and improvement.   At the opening of the fall term of 1904 we expect to be prepared to offer the first two years of the four-year course in medicine.

GROUPS.

Two groups are offered to students intending to become physicians: one of four years, leading to the degree of Bachelor of Arts; the other of one year, at the completion of which a certificate will be given.   All students are earnestly advised to elect the four-year group, because it will give them that training in natural sciences and modern languages now so important to the medical practitioner.   It is the intention of the College to require all students registering in the medical courses after June 1st, 1905, to have obtained nine credits in the college, and after June 1st, 1906, to have obtained eighteen credits in the college, before entering upon their medical curriculum.

CERTIFICATES.

Any student who has completed the work as outlined in the "Premedical Group" will be given the degree of Bachelor of Arts.

To all students who satisfactorily complete the studies of the one-year group a "Certificate of Proficiency" will be given, showing the amount and character of the work done.   This certificate will now be accepted by the leading colleges of the "American Medical Association" as satisfactory evidence of having completed the freshman year of the four-year course in medicine, admitting the student to the sophomore year.

ADMISSION REQUIREMENTS.

First—The student must be regularily registered in the College of Liberal Arts,   (See page 23.)

Second—The student must present creditable certificates of good moral character signed by two physicians of good standing in the state in which the applicant last resided.   .

Third—The student must have had at least three years of preliminary training in Latin.

CURRICULUM.

FOUR-YEAR GROUP.*

FIRST YEAR.

Chemistry, 1, 2, 3.
Zoology, 1.
Botany, 1.
German or French, 1, 2, 3.

SECOND YEAR.

Chemistry, 4, 7.
General Biology, 1, 2.
German or French, 10, 11, 12.
Mathematics, 5, 6 (a), 7.

THIRD YEAR.

Physiology, 2, 3.
Botany, 2.
Anatomy, 1, 2, 3.
Psychology.
Mathematics, 8, 9.

FOURTH YEAR.

Physiology, 4, 5.
Botany, 3.
Physics.
English, 5, 6, 7.
†Materia Medica.

In addition to the above studies 3½ electives must be taken, 2 of which may be taken in tbe Gymnasium.

ONE-YEAR GROUP.

FALL TERM.

Anatomy, 1.
Physiology, 2.
Chemistry, 1.
†Materia Medica.

WINTER TERM.

Anatomy, 2.
Physiology, 3.
Chemistry, 2.
†English, 8.

SPRING TERM.

Anatomy, 3.
Chemistry, 3.
Botany, 2 or 3.
Physiology, 4.

---

*While it will be advantageous for every student to follow the group as outlined, it may be varied to meet the prerequisites for the different studies.

†One-half course. Class meets three days per week.

PREPARATORY COURSES.

The following courses are designed chiefly for the benefit of those Unclassified Students who wish to complete the entrance requirements for admission to the College of Liberal Arts. They are, however, open to all students, *but if taken by students in the College of Liberal Arts they will not be counted on the thirty-eight credits required for graduation.*

ENGLISH.

The following courses are offered for the benefit of those wishing to pass the English Examination for admission as outlined on pages 25, 26. Courses 2, 3, and 4 are full courses and will deal with composition and with the study of the books prescribed for careful study. Courses 2*b*, 3*b*, and 4*b* are half courses and will deal with the books prescribed for reading. The work of the classes may be varied somewhat and the completing of the courses is not a guarantee that the student is able to pass the examination mentioned above.

2. Studies in English Literature and Composition.
Fall term.   Professor FOWLER.

2 (*b*). Studies in Literature.
Fall term.   Miss GILLIS.

3. Studies in Literature and Composition.
Winter term.   Professor FOWLER.

3 (*b*). Studies in Literature.
Winter term.   Miss GILLIS.

4. Studies in Literature and Composition.
Spring term.   Professor FOWLER.

4 (*b*). Studies in Literature.
Spring term.

MATHEMATICS.

1. Arithmetic.
Robinson's Higher Arithmetic. Study of the subject matter of the text to Interest. This course includes thorough work in analysis and mental arithmetic. Fall term.   Miss HATHAWAY.
Open to all students.

Mathematics 1 will not be given unless at least six students apply for the course.

2. Elementary Algebra.

Wells's Essentials of Algebra is used.   Fall term.

Open to all students.   Professor GRUBB.

3. Elementary Algebra.   (Continued.)
Winter term.   Professor GRUBB.

Prerequisite, Mathematics 2.

4. Elementary Algebra.   (Continued.)
Spring term.   Professor GRUBB.

Prerequisite, Mathematics 3.

6 (a) Plane Geometry.

This course is designed to give students thorough drill in the first principles of Geometry.   Each proposition is carefully analyzed and particular attention is given to correct reasoning and precise expression. Phillips and Fisher's Elements of Geometry is used.   Winter term.

Open to all students.   Mr. CAMPBELL.

Mathematics 2, 3, 4, and 6 (a) are designed to meet the entrance requirements in Algebra and Plane Geometry.   (See page 27.)

PHYSICAL GEOGRAPHY.

1. Physical Geography.

Text-book, Tarr's Elementary Physical Geography.   Spring term.

Open to all students.

Physical Geography 1 will alternate with Economics 1.   Given in 1903.   Miss HATHAWAY.

HISTORY.

2. Greece.

History of Greece.   Fall term.   Miss HATHAWAY.

Open to all students.

3. Rome.

History of Rome.   Text-book, Morey.   Winter term.

Miss HATHAWAY.

Open to all students.

4. England.

History of England.   Text-book, Higginson and Channing.   Spring term.   Miss HATHAWAY.

Open to all students.

ECONOMICS.

1. Science of Government.

Text-books, Fiske's Civil Government in the United States, and Andrew's Manual of the Constitution.   Spring term.

Miss HATHAWAY.

Open to all students.

Economics 1 will alternate with Physical Geography 1.   Given in 1904.

UNCLASSIFIED STUDENTS.

Persons who wish to pursue studies at Lombard without becoming candidates for a degree will be admitted on probation to any class for which they are fitted by previous training.   In case the class in question demands a prerequisite, the applicant must bring a certificate in this prerequisite from an approved school, or pass an examination.

On severing their connection with the College, these students will receive, upon request, a certificate, signed by the President and their several instructors, stating the amount and quality of the work done.

If at any time such students wish to become candidates for a degree, they must fulfill all the requirements for admission to the department in which the degree is to be taken.

Among these also will be listed all students who have an ultimate purpose of taking a degree, but who need to pursue one or more of the preparatory courses to fulfill the requirements for admission to the College of Liberal Arts.

RYDER DIVINITY SCHOOL.

The Divinity School of Lombard College was opened for the admission of students on the 5th of September, 1881.   The first class was graduated in 1885.

At the annual meeting of the Board of Trustees in 1890, it was voted to name the theological department of the College the RYDER DIVINITY SCHOOL, in honor of the late William Henry Ryder, D. D., whose munificent bequests to the College exceed fifty thousand dollars.

The largest benefaction to the Divinity School from any other source was received from the late Hon. A. G. Throop, founder of the Throop Polytechnic Institute at Pasadena, California.   In 1890, Mr. Throop gave twenty thousand dollars toward the endowment of the Divinity School.

ADMISSION.

Applicants unknown to the faculty must bring satisfactory evidences of good moral and religious character.   They should also bring certificates of their church membership.

Candidates for admission to the Divinity School must be prepared to sustain examination in the following subjects.

I. ENGLISH.

(a) **Grammar and Analysis.**

Reed and Kellogg's Higher Lessons in English, or an equivalent.

(b) **Composition.**

An extemporaneous composition on an assigned subject, correct as to spelling, paragraphing, grammar, and rhetorical form.

(c) **Literature.**

An equivalent of English 2, 2b, 3, 3b, 4, and 4b as described on page 58 of this catalogue.

II. HISTORY.

(a) **Bible History.**

A competent knowledge of the Bible as History, including the so-called Old Testament Apocrypha.   The ground covered is given in the ten volume Historical Series for Bible Students, edited by Kent and Sanders, and published by Scribner's Sons.

(*b*) **Bible Geography and Archaeology.**

A general knowledge of localities, customs, manners, etc., of Bible times.

Rand and McNally's Manual of Biblical Geography and Jahn's Archeology or equivalents.

(*c*) **General History.**

Swinton's General History or an equivalent.

III. MATHEMATICS.

(*a*) **Arithmetic.**

Higher Arithmetic, including percentage, alligation, extraction of roots, mensuration, and the metric system.

(*b*) **Elementary Algebra.**

Wells's Academic Algebra, or an equivalent.

IV. GEOGRAPHY.

Tarr's Elementary Geography, or an equivalent.

V. SCIENCE.

(*a*) **Chemistry.**

The equivalent of Chemistry 1 and 2 as described on page 49. (Equivalent work in Physics and Botany may be accepted in lieu of Chemistry.)

(*b*) **Physiology.**

This calls for a general knowledge of the human skeleton, muscular, circulatory, and nervous systems, the vital organs, viscera, and organs of special sense, and the processes of respiration and digestion. The preparation required is covered in such text-books as Martin's Human Body (advanced course), or Huxley's Elementary Physiology (Lee's Revision).

Preliminary Year.

To accommodate those candidates for admission who are not fully prepared to satisfy the admission requirements an opportunity is given to complete their preparation in the School, and a preliminary year's work is mapped out (page 76), which, however, is susceptible of some modification to meet the special needs of the candidate.

As a further encouragement to candidates to avail themselves of this opportunity the Universalist General Convention will permit its grant of financial aid to be spread over five years, instead of four as hitherto. Thus the candidate who requires five years for the full course, including the Preliminary year, may receive, under the usual conditions, a maximum grant of $100 each year for the five years, or a maximum grant of $125 a year for four years as he may prefer.

ADMISSION BY CERTIFICATE.

Satisfactory grades from approved schools will be accepted in lieu of examination. Students thus admitted by certificate will be regarded as on probation during the first term of their course.

ADMISSION TO ADVANCED STANDING.

Students who bring satisfactory evidence of work done beyond the requirements of admission will be given credit for the same on the regular course, so far as the faculty may deem consistent with the special aims of that course:

The members of the Divinity School are admitted to the advantages presented by the other departments of the College.

EXPENSES.

Tuition is free to all regular members of the Divinity School who are candidates for the ministry, on condition that the student maintains an average grade of at least 70 per cent.

The charge for incidentals is the same as in the College of Liberal Arts, $5 per term.

For board in Commons, see page 14.

Board in good families can be secured for from $2.50 to $3.25 per week. Students may somewhat reduce their expenses by forming clubs or boarding themselves.

PECUNIARY AID.

Students who are candidates for the ministry of the Universalist Church may, upon complying with the prescribed conditions and receiving the recommendation of the faculty, obtain assistance from the Universalist General Convention in the form of a gratuity, to an amount not exceeding $125 a year for four years. Applications will be granted by the Convention only when entirely satisfactory. The first installment of this gift will not be issued to entering students until January, the second will be issued in May. Students should therefore come with resources of their own sufficient to pay their expenses for at least one term.

Those who have not a definite purpose of entering the Universalist ministry are not eligible to the Convention gift.

Membership in some Universalist Church is also required as a condition of the gift.

The use of tobacco or other narcotic or stimulants is an absolute bar to the grant of the Convention aid.

The Convention aid may be withheld at any time, should the work or behavior of the candidate prove unsatisfactory.

After having had two terms in homiletics, students who show due proficiency are permitted to secure appointments to preach, and thus to add to their pecuniary resources.

Courses of Instruction.

1. Regular Course.

Candidates for the degree of B. D. will be expected to complete the course scheduled on pages 76, 77. This course, it will be observed, prescribes a certain amount of work in Greek, which is regarded as indispensable to the degree. In addition to the studies indicated in the schedule, a year's work in Hebrew will be offered to those who desire it, at some time during their residence. It is earnestly recommended that all students whose circumstances do not positively forbid their spending the requisite time, take the Regular Course.

2. Alternative Course.

It is, however, permitted to those who, after due deliberation, prefer to do so, to omit the Greek and Hebrew, and to substitute therefor an equivalent amount of elective work in English, Modern Languages, Science, Mathematics, or Sociology, with the approval of the faculty. Those who complete such a course will be graduated at the Annual Commencement, and will be furnished a certificate showing what work they have done; but they will not be given the degree of B. D. nor any other degree.

3. Special Work.

(a) Candidates for the ministry who cannot take either of the above described courses, will be permitted to elect particular studies, so far as their preparation warrants. Pastors already engaged in ministerial work who can spare a period for further study, are particularly invited to avail themselves of this opportunity.

(b) The School is also open to persons who do not intend to enter the ministry. The pursuit of studies of a theological or religious character is an interesting and helpful means of personal culture. Such a course is especially recommended to those who desire to become better fitted for service in the Sunday School, the Church, the Young People's Christian Union and similar societies, or for charitable and philanthropic work. Upon those who come with these purposes, no denominational test will be imposed. Students of all denominations and beliefs will be welcome to the advantages of study and training in the Divinity School, as in other departments of the College.

Faculty of the Divinity School.

CHARLES ELLWOOD NASH, A. M., S. T. D., PRESIDENT,
Instructor in Homiletics and Pastoral Care.

NEHEMIAH WHITE, A. M., PH. D., S. T. D.
*Hall Professor of Intellectual and Moral Philosophy.
In charge of the Ryder Divinity School, Professor of Biblical Languages and Exegesis.

†Hull Professor of Biblical Geography and Archæology.

ISAAC AUGUSTUS PARKER, A. M., PH. D.,
Professor of Greek.

FRANK HAMILTON FOWLER, A. M., PH. D.,
Professor of English Literature.

RALPH GRIERSON KIMBLE,
Professor of Sociology.

EDSON REIFSNIDER, B. D.
Instructor in Homiletics and Pastoral Care. Spring term.

*In honor of the late E. G. HALL, of Chicago.
†In honor of the REV. STEPHEN HULL, of Kansas City, Mo.

AMANDA KIDDER,
Instructor in Elocution.

NON-RESIDENT LECTURERS.

MARION D. SHUTTER, D. D.

I. M. ATWOOD, D. D.,

FRED'K C. PRIEST, D. D.

Degrees Conferred in 1902.

BACHELOR OF DIVINITY.

Kiyoshi Satoh ....*Myagiken, Japan.*
George Francis Thompson.. ....*Stony Point, Mich.*
Mecca Varney................. .. ..*Clinton.*

Schedule.

---

1. Preliminary Year.

FALL TERM.	WINTER TERM.	SPRING TERM.
English 2, 2*b*.	English 3, 3*b*.	English 4, 4*b*.
Biblical History.	Biblical History.	Biblical Geography and Archæology.
Chemistry.	Elementary Physiology.	Elementary Botany.

---

2. Regular Course.

Leading to the Degree of Bachelor of Divinity.

FIRST YEAR.

FALL TERM.	WINTER TERM.	SPRING TERM.
English 5.	English 6.	English 7.
Greek 1.	Greek 2.	Greek 3.
History 5.	History 6.	History 7.

SECOND YEAR.

Psychology 1.	Psychology 2.	Hermeneutics.
Greek 4.	Greek Testament.	Greek Testament.
Homiletics 1.	Homiletics 2.	Homiletics 3.
Elocution.	Elocution.	Elocution.

THIRD YEAR.

Homiletics 4.	Homiletics 5.	Homiletics 6.
Sociology 1.	Greek Testament.	Greek Testament.
Apologetics.	Dogmatic Theology.	Dogmatic Theology.
	Logic.	

FOURTH YEAR.

Sociology D. 1.	Sociology D. 2.	Pastoral Care.
Philosophy of Religion.	Ethics.	Ethical Theories.
or	*Hebrew.	or
Metaphysic,	Preaching.	History of Civilization.
or		*Hebrew.
Comparative Religions.		Preaching.
*Hebrew.		
Preaching.		

*Elective.

Description of Studies.

HEBREW.

1, 2, 3. Grammar and Old Testament.

These are primarily courses in the Divinity School, but may be elected by students in the College of Liberal Arts whenever they are offered. Classes will be formed each year if a sufficient number of students apply.

It is the aim to give the student such a knowledge of the forms and structure of the Hebrew language as will enable him to use it efficiently in the criticism and literary analysis of the Old Testament Scriptures. The text-books used are H. G. Mitchell's Hebrew Lessons, and the Hebrew Old Testament. Three terms—Fall, Winter, and Spring—each term counting as a course. Professor WHITE.

BIBLE STUDY.

1. Biblical History, A.

Kent's Studies in Biblical History and Literature is used. The aim is to present the contents of the Bible as they stand in our English version.   Due account is made of contemporary history and the monumental data.   In general the first term will be occupied with the material of the Old Testament; the second term with that of the New.   Fall term.

Miss KIDDER.

2. Biblical History, B.

A continuation of the preceding.   Winter term.   Miss KIDDER.

3. Biblical Geography and Archaeology.

A detailed study of the political and physical geography of the Bible countries, and a general study of the antiquities of the Bible peoples. Spring term.

4. Biblical Criticism.

Driver's Introduction to the Old Testament is used as a text-book, with reference to Fripp, Ryle, Bacon, Robertson, and other works.   A course of lectures is given on the Science of Documentary Analysis, the Principles and Methods of Historical Criticism, and the Religious aspects of the Higher Criticism.   Winter term.   Professor WHITE.

HERMENEUTICS.

The aim of Hermeneutics, rightly called "the science and art of interpretation," is to set forth those principles and processes whereby the true intent and meaning of an author may be ascertained from the language which he employs.   Hermeneutics is therefore the basis of all sound exegesis and is an invaluable aid to the interpretation of the Scriptures.   Instruction will be given both by text-book and by lectures. Spring term.   Professor WHITE.

PREPARATORY GREEK.

(For Greek 1, 2, 3, 4, 5, see pages 42, 43).

THE GREEK NEW TESTAMENT.

12. Exegesis of the Synoptic Gospels.

Critical rendering of selections from the Synoptic Gospels.   Exegesis of Mark's Gospel; origin and peculiar characteristics of the Gospel, and its relation to the other Synoptists—their harmonies, divergencies, and interdependence.   Date of Synoptic Gospels; their genuineness and authenticity.   Theology and Christology of the Synoptic Gospels.   Winter term.   Professor WHITE.

13. Acts of the Apostles.

Critical rendering of the Greek text of the Acts of the Apostles, their genuineness and authenticity, date of the work, sources of the narrative. Exegesis of the Acts.   Spring term.   Professor WHITE.

14. Thessalonians and Galatians.

Critical rendering of the Greek text of the Epistles to the Thessalonians and Galatians. Exegesis and eschatology of the Epistles. Primitive Paulinism. Winter term. Professor WHITE.

15. Corinthians, Romans, and Apocalypse.

Selections from the first and the second Epistles to the Corinthians, the Epistle to the Romans, and the Apocalypse. Critical rendering of the Greek text of the Epistle to the Romans. Examination of the nature of Pauline Theology and Christology. Development of the doctrine of Paul. Character of later Paulinism. Examination of the resemblances and differences in the style and language of the Apocalypse and of the fourth gospel. Spring term. Professor WHITE.

THEOLOGY.

1. Christian Evidences.

The study of Christian Evidences will include an examination of the bases of Christian belief, Evolutionary theories and their relation to Philosophy, Ethics, and Religion, and the function and method of Apologetics. Comparison will be instituted between the modern methods in Apologetics and the methods of primitive Christianity. Instruction will be given mostly by lectures with frequent reference to Fisher, Schurman, Flint, Bruce, and others. Fall term. Professor WHITE.

2. Dogmatic Theology.

Martensen's Christian Dogmatics is used as a text-book. A thorough investigation is made of the several Christian doctrines, with an extended examination of associated questions and controversies. The widest liberty is given for questions and discussions on the various topics presented. Winter and spring terms. Professor WHITE.

3. Comparative Religions.

The work of the students consists in the examination and comparison of the authorities upon the great Non-Christian religions. Special topics are investigated and reports made by each member of the class. Fall term. Professor WHITE.

APPLIED CHRISTIANITY.

The demand for a more thorough investigation of the bearings of Christian Doctrine upon the social, political, and industrial organisms, coupled with the demand for a more diversified and scientific administration of religion through the churches, is met at Lombard College by the establishment of a chair of Sociology. The course of study provided for will occupy four terms, three terms being devoted to Sociology, and one term to Pastoral Care.

SOCIOLOGY.

1. An Introduction to Sociological Theory.

A study of the characteristics of general sociological theory.

D. 1. Pathologic Factors of the Modern Community.

The discrimination and definition of the dependent, defective, and delinquent classes, together with a brief study of current attempts to deal with the same.

D. 2. Pathologic Factors of the Modern Community.

A continuation of Sociology D. 1.

Sociology D. 1, and D. 2 are designed expressly to meet the needs of Divinity Students. If taken by students in the College of Liberal Arts they will not count on the thirty-eight credits required for the A. B. degree.

PASTORAL CARE.

A study of the spiritual, mental, and social qualifications of the minister for his work, and his administration of the special services of the church—baptism, confirmation, the Lord's Supper, marriage, and the burial of the dead. A liberal portion of the term will be devoted to an examination of various methods of church organization, for the purpose of giving the minister facility in adapting himself to parish needs, especially to those peculiar to the locality in which he may be settled. Also a study is made of the Manual of the Universalist General Convention. Spring term.   Mr. REIFSNIDER.

PSYCHOLOGY.

1. Introductory Psychology.

The purpose of the course is to guide the beginner in gaining the fundamentals of a thorough knowledge of psychology and of psychic life. The course is organized about a careful study of the commoner characteristics of the more accessible mental processes. Emphasis is laid upon the ready and accurate use of the more important psychological terms. Some knowledge of the chief standpoints and methods of the science is gained. Collateral reading in connection with the text will be regularly assigned and a correct appreciation of the relation of this reading to the treatment presented in the text will be a requirement of the course. Experiments described in text and reading will be fully discussed, and where circumstances permit, the student will see performed by others or will himself perform in the laboratory certain type experiments. Fall term.

Professor KIMBLE.

2. Introductory Psychology.

Continuation of Psychology 1. Winter term.

METAPHYSIC.

This is primarily a course in the Divinity School, but it may be elected by students in the College of Liberal Arts whenever it is offered. Classes will be formed whenever a sufficient number of students apply. Lotze's Outlines of Metaphysic is used as a text-book. Fall term.

Professor WHITE.

LOGIC.

Having first obtained a thorough grounding in the principles and methods of correct reasoning, both deductive and inductive, at least one-half of the term is given to the detection and discrimination of fallacies in actual examples. Such examples the class is required to search out in current literature and bring in for discussion. Davis's Elements of Deductive Logic, and Davis's Elements of Inductive Logic are used. Winter term.

Professor FOWLER.

ETHICS.

Ethics is treated from the standpoint of Philosophy, and the different systems are discussed. The nature and grounds of obligation are investigated and applied to the practical affairs of life. Winter term.

Professor WHITE.

PHILOSOPHY OF RELIGION.

Fairbairn's Philosophy of the Christian Religion is the text-book. Lotze, Sabatier, and Martineau are used as works of reference. The aim of the instructor is to acquaint the student with the proper office of reason in the effort to find argumentative grounds for religious ideas. Most of the modern theories respecting the nature and scope of the religious feeling pass under review; and in such discussions free questioning on the part of the student is encouraged. Winter term.

Professor WHITE.

ETHICAL THEORIES.

Martineau's Types of Ethical Theory is used as a text-book with frequent reference to the works of Sidgwick, Green, Smythe, and others.

Much attention is paid to the elucidation and criticism of the modern ethical theories.   Spring term.   Professor WHITE.

CHURCH HISTORY.

(The courses in Church History are numbered continuously with the Preparatory courses in History.   See page 69).

5. History of the Christian Church.

A.   The Ancient and Mediæval Eras [1-1517.]

This course in Church History is primarily intended for the members of the Divinity School, but is also open to College students.   It will require the investigation of the early organization and extension of Christianity, and the successive periods of the Church down to the time of Charlemagne; followed by a careful inquiry into the causes of the rise of Papacy, of the political relations of the Church, and of the Crusades. Fisher's History of the Church will be used as a hand-book and topics will be assigned to each member of the class for special investigation and reports.   Fall term.   Professor WHITE.

6. History of the Christian Church.

B.   The Modern Era [1517-1903.]

This course will begin with the study of the Reformation, and trace the history of the Church down to the present time.   It will include the history of the Christian missions, revivals, social reforms, and philanthropy.   The same text-book will be used as in History 5.   Winter term.

Professor WHITE.

7. History of Christian Doctrine.

Special pains will be taken to make clear the aim of the History of Christian Doctrine, and to indicate the process of its development.

Professor WHITE.

HOMILETICS.

The course in Homiletics covers the second, third, and fourth years. The primary aim is practical.   Upon a general but adequate groundwork of theory and history of preaching the effort is made to construct an art of effective pulpit oratory.   Elaborate and exacting drill in the logical conception and construction of the sermon plan, with constant application of rhetorical principles, occupies the major part of the first year. Inspiration and direction are sought in the frequent analysis of the discourses of great preachers of all styles, and in the study of their sources of power.   Individuality and originality are emphasized as desiderata.   In the second year the stress is laid upon flexibility and adaptability, upon invention, upon the rationale of interesting preaching, and upon the acquisition of freedom in extempore address. Throughout the course the preparation and criticism of sermons by the class continues uninterruptedly.   President NASH.

                                    Mr. REIFSNIDER.

ELOCUTION.

In view of the fact that a good delivery is of inestimable advantage to the preacher, the students in the Divinity School are offered an extended course in Elocution and Physical Culture.

The students are not only admitted to all Elocution classes in the College, but also receive a large amount of individual training.

Courses 1, 2, 3, as outlined on pages 62 and 63 of this catalogue, are required, as well as regular drill and rehearsals for the preaching exercises.   Miss KIDDER.

ENGLISH.

For English 2, 3, 4, required for entrance to full standing in the Divinity School, and taught in the Preliminary year, see p. 68. For English 5, 6, 7, which courses are required in the Divinity School, see p. 34 of this catalogue.

8. Daily Themes.

This course will be made a full course for students in the Divinity School. Besides the daily themes, fortnightly themes will be required. Spring term.   Professor FOWLER.

COLLEGE STUDIES AND THE A. B. DEGREE.

Divinity students are permitted, with the consent of the Faculty, to pursue studies in the College of Liberal Arts. Graduates of the Divinity School may receive the additional degree of Bachelor of Arts, upon the satisfactory completion of an aggregate of twenty full courses taken in the classes of the College of Liberal Arts, beyond the full requirements of the Divinity School for the degree of Bachelor of Divinity.

In addition to the above twenty credits, the candidate must furnish the full quota of sixteen units required for admission to the College of Liberal Arts. Of these sixteen units, the courses required for admission to the Divinity School (see pp. 71 and 72) will count six.

LADIES' HALL.

DEPARTMENT OF MUSIC.

Instruction is provided in the various branches of Theoretical, Vocal, and Instrumental Music. These courses are distinct from the work in the other departments of the College, and unless otherwise specified do not count toward a college degree. Students are classed and registered as private pupils of the several instructors, with whom arrangements may be made in regard to lessons. Instruction is given either at the College, or at the instruction-rooms of the teachers, as preferred.

Faculty.

KARL JACOB RUDOLPH LUNDBERG,
Director, and Instructor in Voice and Piano.

W. H. CHEESMAN,
Instructor in Violin.

EDNA UHLER,
Instructor in Piano.

ALICE HELEN BARTLETT,
Instructor in Pipe Organ and Harmony.

THEORETICAL COURSES.

Miss Bartlett.

1. Harmony.

Keys, scales and signatures, intervals, formation of the triad, chord connection, simple part writing begun. Stephen A. Emery's text-book is used. Two hours a week. Fall term.

2. Harmony.

Harmonizing basses, including all chords of the seventh and their inversions.   Key board work.   Modulation begun.   Two hours a week. Winter term.

3. Harmony.

Altered and Augmented Chords explained and worked out from basses given for harmonization.   Modulation continued.   Two hours a week.   Spring term.

4. Harmony.

Harmonizing melodies continued.   Double chants and chorals.   Two hours a week.   Fall term.

5. Harmony.

Harmonizing melodies continued. Suspensions. Passing chords. Passing and changing notes.   Modulation completed.   Two hours a week.   Winter term.

6. Single Counterpoint.

Single counterpoint in all forms in two and three voices.   Spring term.

7. Single Counterpoint.

Single counterpoint in four voices.   Double counterpoint begun. Fall term.

8. Double Counterpoint.

Double counterpoint in tenth and twelfth.   Triple and quadruple counterpoint.   Winter term.

9. Canon and Fugue.

Canon in two voices in all intervals.   Free imitation.   Fugues in two, three, and four voices.   Double fugue.   Spring term.

10, 11, 12. History of Music.   [Half Courses.]

These courses embrace a history of the development of music from the earliest time until to-day, with special reference to critical analysis of the works of the great masters.   They also furnish an introduction to the lives of the great composers.   One hour a week for the year.

Professor LUNDBERG.

PIANOFORTE COURSES.

Professor Lundberg and Miss Uhler.

1. Preparatory.

Five-finger exercises; scales in major and minor; triads; selected studies by Czerny, Vol. 1 (Germer Edition.)

2. First Grade.

Finger exercises; scales; Czerny's studies, Vols. 1 and 2 (Germer edition); Sonatinas by Dussek, Clementi, Diabelli, Kuhlau, Reinecke. Memorizing.

3. Second Grade.

Finger exercises; scales; arpeggios; Czerny's studies, Vol. 3 (Germer edition); Sonatinas by Clementi, Kuhlau, Dussek, Haydn, Mozart, Beethoven. Pieces by American and foreign composers.

4. Third Grade.

Finger exercises with modulation to different keys. Scales in fourths, sixths, and thirds. Czerny's studies, Vol. 4; Bach's Inventions for two and three voices. Pieces by different composers.

5. Fourth Grade.

Finger exercises in different keys. Scales; études by Cramer; preludes and fugues by Bach. Easier sonatas by Haydn, Clementi, Mozart, and Beethoven. Memorizing; pieces by different composers.

6. Fifth Grade.

Finger exercises in different keys; scales. Clementi's Gradus ad Parnassum. Etudes by Moscheles; Chopin, etc. Sonatas by Bach, Mozart, Beethoven, and Hummel. Memorizing. Pieces by different composers.

VOICE CULTURE.

Professor Lundberg.

1. First Grade.

Exercises in breathing, tone placing, sustained tones, etc. Voice training exercises by Emil Behnke and C. W. Pearce. Fifty vocalises by Concone. Easy songs.

2. Second Grade.

Massett's exercises; 30 exercises by Concone; 25 and 15 vocalises by Concone. Songs by American and foreign composers.

3. Third Grade.

Vocalises by Reber, Panofka, and Masset. Songs and oratorios. Recitatives. Practicing of duets, trios, and quartets.

PIPE ORGAN COURSES.

Miss Bartlett.

Students who wish to begin the study of the Organ should have completed the Second Grade of the Piano Course.

The chief aim of this department is the thorough preparation of church organists. Organ students should also make a conscientious study of Solo and Chorus Singing, with a view of becoming efficient chorusmasters and directors of church music.

The study of Harmony, Counterpoint, and History of Music is absolutely necessary to an intelligent study of the instrument.

1. First Grade.

Exercises in pedal playing. Ritter's Organ School. Hymns. Thayer's Pedal Studies. Elementary Registration.

2. Second Grade.

Studies in Pedal Phrasing by Buck, Volkmar, and Schneider. Polyphonic composition by Rink, Bach, Fisher. Easy pieces by Merkel, Dubois, Guilmant, Mendelssohn, and others. Registration, Structure of the Organ, Choir Accompaniment.

3. Third Grade.

Study of Sonatas and Fugues by Bach, Mendelssohn, Reinberger, and others. Modern compositions of German, English, and French masters. Choir Accompaniment.

VIOLIN COURSES.

Professor Cheesman.

1. Preparatory Grade.

Elementary exercises in position, bowing, etc. Easy exercises in major and minor keys in the first book from Wichtl's Violin School. Pleyel's Duets, and twelve studies by H. E. Kayser, op. 20. Memorizing.

2. Intermediate Grade.

Studies by Kayer and Wohlfahrt. Systematic progress through the various positions, beginning with the second book of F. Hermann. Studies from Shradieck for the development of technic and pure tone qualities. Sections from compositions by Dancla, Mazas, Weiss, De Beriot: also solos and fantasias based upon operatic themes.

3. Advance Grade.

Technical studies from the works of Kreutzer, Fiorillo, Rode, together with duets, trios, and quartets, arranged for strings; overtures; sight-reading. Sonatas and concertos by Bach, Haydn, Spohr, Beethoven, Mendelssohn, De Beriot, Wieniawsky, Grieg, and others.

MANDOLIN AND GUITAR COURSES.

Professor Cheesman.

The study of these popular instruments has become a favorite recreation with those students of our colleges who may not have the time or inclination to pursue the study of music in its more serious forms.

At the conclusion of the first term of lessons (twelve weeks) a "Lombard Mandolin Club" will be organized, with rehearsals one evening a week. The Italian method is used entirely in the study of these instruments, thereby establishing the very best method of picking the strings and fingering, with special attention to the tone quality of the "tremolo," which relieves the mandolin of much of its so-called monotony. Solos, duets, and quartets, will also be prepared in addition to the regular club work, with special numbers to be given by the lady members of the club.

SIGHT SINGING AND CHORUS CLASSES.

Professor Lundberg.

1. Elementary Sight Singing Class.

The rudiments of Music, the intervals of the Major Scale, exercises in one and two parts, and easy songs. Ear-training. One college term.

2. Advanced Class.

Solfeggios in major and minor keys, three and four part songs. One college term.

3. Chorus Class.

Four part compositions, glees, sacred and secular choruses from our best classic and modern composers. Oratorios.

Only those students who have finished the work done in the Advanced Sight-Singing Class will be admitted into the Chorus Class.

Requirements for Graduation.

A diploma will be conferred upon any student who shall satisfactorily complete one of the following courses in instrumental or vocal music. In addition to the requirements enumerated below, the candidate will prepare a thesis, present an original musical composition, or perform other original work satisfactory to the instructor, and also appear in public at a graduating recital.

A. THE PIANOFORTE.

Musical Requirements.

Five grades of the Piano Courses, Nos. 1, 2, 3, 4, 5, 6, 10, and 11 of the Theoretical Courses; Acoustics; and one year's membership in the Chorus Class.

Literary Requirements.

English 2, 3, 4, 5, and two English electives; one year of French or German.

If the candidate upon entering brings satisfactory proof of proficiency in any of these courses he is advised to take one study each term from such electives in the College of Liberal Arts as the Advisory Committee may recommend.

B. THE PIPE ORGAN.

Musical Requirements.

The full Organ Course, Nos. 1, 2, 3, 4, 5, 6, 10, and 11 of the Theoretical Courses; and Acoustics.

Literary Requirements.

The same as for Piano students.

C. THE VOICE.

Musical Requirements.

All the prescribed studies for Voice Culture; grade 2 of the Piano Courses, with special view to accompaniments; and Nos. 1, 2, 3, 10, 11, of the Theoretical Courses.

Literary Requirements.

The same as for Piano students, except that Italian may be substituted for French or German.

TUITION.

The following prices are for a term of twelve weeks:

THEORETICAL COURSES—

    Music 1 to 9, each, $5.00.
    Music 10, 11 and 12, each, $3.00.

PIANOFORTE—

    Private Lessons—one hour per week, $18.00.
    Private Lessons—two half hours per week, $18.00.
    Private Lessons—one half hour per week, $10.00.
    Private Lessons—one forty-five-minute lesson per week, $14.00.

    Class Lessons, one hour per week—

        In classes of two, each, $10.00.
        In classes of three, each, $7.00.

VOICE CULTURE—

Charges same as for pianoforte.

RENT OF PIANO—

1 hour per day, per term, $2.75.
2 hours per day, per term, $5.00.
3 hours per day, per term, $6.75.
4 hours per day, per term, $8.00.

PIPE ORGAN—

Private Lessons—one hour per week, $24.00.
In classes of two, one hour per week, each person, $13.00.

VIOLIN—

Private Lessons—one hour per week, $15.00.
Private Lessons—two half hours per week, $15.00.
Private Lessons—one 45-minute lesson per week, $12.00.

CLASS LESSONS, one hour per week—

In classes of two, each, $8.00.
In classes of three, each, $6.00.

MANDOLIN AND GUITAR—

Private Lessons—one hour per week, $12.00.
Private Lessons—two half hours per week, $12.00.
Class Lessons—charges will be given on application to teacher.
(A weekly rehearsal for club practice without extra charge.)

SIGHT SINGING CLASSES—

Each, $1.00.

CHORUS CLASS—

A charge of $1.00 per term each will be made for the use of music to be supplied by the department.

The privilege of joining the Lombard Mandolin and Guitar Club, or the Lombard String Orchestra, is extended to any student outside of the private pupils of the instructor, by the payment of $1.25 per term of twelve weeks. Rehearsals one evening each week.

GENERAL REMARKS.

Tuition and other charges must be paid before lessons are assigned.

In cases of protracted sickness only will a proportionate deduction be made from term charges.

No visitors are allowed in practice rooms during practice hours.

All concerts and recitals given by the school of music or its faculty are free to music students.

A course of free lectures on musical culture will be given each year by the Director.

LADIES' HALL.

DEPARTMENT OF ART.

Instructor,

M. ISABELLE BLOOD.

Course in Art.

The Art Department affords a practical course in Drawing and Painting to those who wish to become teachers, designers, illustrators, or portrait artists. Regular students in this department who wish to take the entire course in Art will be given careful training in the following branches: Perspective drawing; drawing from casts, in charcoal and crayon; still life studies in crayon, oil, water color, and pastel; landscape from nature; and copying from good studies.

The entire course will occupy from two to three years, according to the ability of the student and the amount of time given to the work. A thorough knowledge of the elements of drawing being necessary to independent work, at least one year's work will be required in drawing in black and white from models of simple form, casts, still life, and those studies which will best prepare the student for the special line of work preferred.

Students may enter the Art Department at any time; and, though they are advised to take a full course in order to obtain the best results, arrangements can be made for lessons in any line desired.

While portrait work, pen and ink drawing, and china painting, are not required in the regular course, credit will be given for good work in any of these branches if it is desired to substitute them in part for oil, water color, or pastel.

A course of study in the History of Art and a thesis upon some subject approved by the instructor will also be required of students wishing to graduate from this department.

Those who complete the work as outlined above will be entitled to a Diploma.

For a description of courses in Free Hand Drawing, and for credit allowed for these courses in the College of Liberal Arts, p. 61.

TUITION.

·The tuition fees will be as follows:

Drawing or Sketching—3-hour lessons, 35 cents.
Painting in Water Colors—3-hour lesson, 50 cents.
Oil Painting—3-hour lesson, 50 cents.
Portrait and China Painting—3-hour lesson, 50 cents.

For those who work six hours per week for the entire year, a rebate will be made at the end of the Spring term, so that the lessons in drawing will be less than 35 cents.

If pupils in Art desire four or more lessons per week, special rates are made.

SCHEDULE FOR THE YEAR 1903-1904.

Classes Recite 5 Hours per Week, Except as Indicated.

HOUR	FALL TERM	WINTER TERM	SPRING TERM
8:00	Astronomy 1 Biblical History English 9, 10*, 15* French 1 Greek 7 History 2, 5 Homiletics 1 (3h) Latin 4 Physics 1 Physiology 2, 4* Sociology D. 1	Astronomy 2 Biblical History English 11, 12*, 16* French 2 Greek 8*, 9 History 3, 6 Homiletics 2 (3h) Latin 5 Mathematics 17 Physics 2 Physiology 3, 5* Sociology D. 2	Biblical Geography English 13, 14*, 17* French 3 Greek 10, 11* History 4, 7 Homiletics 3 (3h) Latin 6 Physics 3
9:30	Chemistry 1 †Comparative Religions Economics 2 Elocution 4 (T. Th.) German 1 Homiletics 4 (2h) Latin 7 Mathematics 1 †Metaphysic Music 7 †Philosophy of Religion Physiology 1 Psychology 1	Chemistry 2 Economics 3 Elementary Physiology Elocution 5 (T. Th.) Ethics German 2 Latin 8 Logic Music 8 Psychology 2	Chemistry 3 Economics 1, 4 Elementary Botany Elocution 6 (T. Th.) †Ethical Theories German 3 †History 11 Homiletics 6 (2h) Latin 9 Music 9 *Physical Geography
10:30	Biology 1 Elocution 7 (T. Th.) English 2b (T. Th.) English 5 (M.W.F) German 4, 5*, 10 (M.) Greek 4 †Hebrew 1 Mathematics 8 Music 1, (M. Th) Music 10, (W.) Sociology 1	Biology 2 Elocution 8 (T. Th.) English 3b (T.Th.) English 6 (M.W.F.) German 6, 7*, 11 (M.) Greek 5, 12, 14* Mathematics 9 Music 2, (M. Th.) Music 11, (W.) Sociology 1a	Botany 2*, 3 Elocution 9 (T. Th.) English 4b (T.Th.) English 7 (M.W.F.) German 8, 9*, 12 (M.) Geology 1 Greek 6, 13, 15* Hermeneutics Mathematics 10 Music 3, (M. Th.) Music 12, (W.) Pastoral Care (2h)

11:30	Apologetics English 2 (T.W.Th.F.) French 4, 5*, 10 (Th.) Greek 1 Mathematics 2. 5 Music 4, (M. Th.) Zoology 1	English 3 (T.W.Th.F.) French 6, 7*, 11 (Th.) Greek 2 †Hebrew 2 Homiletics 5 (2h) Mathematics 3. 6a, 6b Music 5, (M. Th.) Sociology 12 Zoology 2	English 4 (T.W.Th.F.) French 8, 9*, 12 (Th.) Botany 1 English 8 (Tu.) Greek 3 †Hebrew 3 Jurisprudence 1 Mathematics 4. 7, 11 Music 6, (M. Th.) Zoology 3*
1:45	Anatomy 1 Art 2 Chemistry 4, 7 Elocution 1, (M.W.F.) Elocution 10 (T.Th.) English 18 History 8 Latin 1, 10*, 11, 12* Mathematics 12, 14*	Anatomy 2 Art 3 Chemistry 5 Dogmatic Theology Elocution 2, (M.W.F.) Elocution 11 .T.Th.) English 18 Geology 2 History 9 Latin 2, 13*, 14. 15* Mathematics 13. 15*	Anatomy 3 Art 4 Chemistry 6 Dogmatic Theology Elocution 3 (M.W.F.) English 18 History 10 Latin 3, 16*, 17, 18*
2:45	Physiology 6 Preaching	Preaching	Preaching

*Not given in 1903-1904.   †Given only when there is a considerable demand

STUDENTS IN ALL DEPARTMENTS.

Candidates for Degrees in 1903.

MASTER OF ARTS

Edwin Julius McCullough,..... ....*Sparland*

BACHELOR OF ARTS

Andrew, Mary Maud, ...*New Salem*
Brown, Athol Ray,............................. .....*N. Henderson*
Campbell, Raymond R.,........................ ....*De Land*
Fosher, Claude Dudley, ...*Galesburg*
Gillis, Anna Moore,.............................*Mt. Pleasant, Ia.*
Hartgrove, Claude Webster,.........................*Galesburg*
Kienholz, Willis Simon,...........................*Galesburg*
Miller, Ralph Todd,... ....*Monmouth*
Needham, Nellie Jeanette, ...*Racine, Wis.*
Rees, Jenkins B.,.... ....*Oneida*

BACHELOR OF DIVINITY

Nieveen, S. Martin,............................. ....*Platte, S. Dak*

CANDIDATES FOR DIPLOMAS IN MUSIC

Cook, Sarah Lucy,............................... .....*Galesburg*
Elting, Grace Helen,........................ ....*Sperry, Ia.*
Nash, Faith Tenney,...............................*Galesburg*
Sommers, Elsie Dorothy,..........................*Burlington, Ia.*
Willis, Leura, ...*Table Grove*
Wrigley, Anne Marion,...............................*Chicago*

Students in the Divinity School.

FOURTH YEAR.

S. Martin Nieveen.

THIRD YEAR.

Charles Kramer.   George Patterson.

SECOND YEAR.

Jennie L. Bartholomew. Stanley Manning.
John Jacob DeBoer. Frank C. Varley.

FIRST YEAR.

Horace M. Brock. William Phillips.
Edith Morden. David E. Young.

PREPARATORY YEAR.

W. O. Bodell.

SPECIAL STUDENT.

Blanche L. Young.

Students in the College of Liberal Arts.

Andreen, Frank G.
Andrew, Mary Maud
Andrew, William B.
Ayars, Frank Cope
Baker, Walter Graves
Boehm, Fred Daniel*
Bowles, James E.
Brown, Athol Ray
Bruner, Glenn Carlton*
Campbell, Raymond R.
Chamberlain, Ethel Mary
Clarke, Fred Andrew
Clay, Walter Timothy
Conger, Delia Chase
Cook, Sarah Lucy
Cooper, Harry Mac
Dickson, Arthur A.
†Ericson, Henry, A. B.
Fosher, Cora Margaret*
Fosher, Dudley Claude
Gillis, Anna Moore
Gillis, Hudson McBain
Grimes, Lloyd Owen
Grubb, Emma Welton
Hart, Mary Arrah
Hartgrove, Claude Webster
Hopkins, Roy Victor
Howell, Spencer Pritchard
Hurd, Jay Clinton
Jansen, Harry Albin
Kidder, Ross Larned*
Kienholz, Willis S.
Kimble, Olin Arvin
Kober, Florence Leclerc
Lauer, Herbert Louis
Lewis, Bert Anson*
Linderholm, Ernest Arthur*
McAlpine, Roy Kenneth*
†McCullough, Edwin Julius, A. B.
Metcalf, Harold
Miller, Ralph Todd
Musgrave, Estella*
Nash, Faith Tenney
Needham, Nellie Jeanette
Ober, Floyd H.*
Porter, Gail Quincy*
Rees, Jenkins B.
Rich, Willis Horton
Sammons, Mabel Alta
Scott, Preston B.
Shaffer, James Alexander*
Van Cise, Ethel
Ward, Vina Maye*
Webster, Albert Sanger
Whitney, Bertha Louise*
Willis, Leura*
Wise, Lorena
Wrigley, Anne Marion

*Having credits sufficient in number to enter college, but one or more required studies lacking.

†Graduate student.

Students in the Department of Music.

THEORY AND HISTORY OF MUSIC.

Andrew, Maud
Backman, Lillian
Byloff, Julia
Chambers, Pearl
Claycomb, Eleanor
Cook, Sallie
Dresing, Carrie
East, Ida
Elting, Grace
Farr, May
Fosher, Claude
Galbreath, Minnie
Jones, Minnie
Long, Katherine
Nash, Faith
Nelson, Alvira
Oleen, Evelyn
Olson, Hattie
Rains, Bertha
Rich, Willis
Sommers, Elsie
Tyner, Mrs. W. J.
Willis, Leura
Wrigley, Anne Marion

VOCAL MUSIC.

Brock, Horace
Byloff, Julia
Curtis, Naida
Dahlberg, Esther
Dove, Genevieve
East, Ida
Elting, Grace
Farr, May
Fosher, Claude

Gates, Carroll
Jones, Minnie
Linderholm, Ernest
Nash, Faith
Olson, Amelia
Sandusky, C. W.
Swanson, Florence Aletta
Ward, Maye
Wrigley, Anne Marion

PIANOFORTE.

Backman, Lillian
Biklen, Marie
Black, Ethel
Bruner, Glenn
Byloff, Julia
Chamberlain, Ruth
Chambers, Pearl
Claycomb, Eleanor
Cook, Sallie
Dresing, Carrie
Duty, Gertrude
East, Ida
Eisenhart, Marie
Elting, Grace
Farr, May
Galbreath, Minnie
Gillette, Ora
Harler, Myrtle
Hollister, Florence
Johnson, Mattie
Kidder, Clytia
Linderholm, Ernest
Long, Katherine
Mason, Marguerite
Murphy, Mrs. Clara

Nelson, Alvira
Nelson, Lilah
Oleen, Evelyn
Olson, Amelia
Olson, Hattie
Peterson, Mabelle
Pittman, Clio
Pittman, Eskridge
Rains, Bertha
Reed, Grace
Rich, Gertrude May
Rich, Willis
Schroeder, Carrie
Shontz, Mary
Sommers, Elsie
Tenchert, Alma
Tyner, Mrs. W. J.
Van Cise, Ethel
Ward, Florence
Ward, Maye
Willis, Leura
Wilson, Helen
Wrigley, Anne Marion
Young, Bessie

VIOLIN.

Allison, Ira
Boyer, Zetta
Brown, Carrie
Burnside, Orpha
Cedarholm, Chester
Hall, Daisy

Neifert, Ira
North, Felix B.
Ottrell, Blenda
Schaffer, Charles
Snider, Retta
Williams, Jesson

MANDOLIN.

Halliday, Eugene
Higgins, Lucy

Lueder, John
Sapp, Bessie

GUITAR.

Anderson, C. E.
Halliday, Herschel

Johnson, Minnie
Nelson, Carrie

VIOLONCELLO.

Stromberg, Edward

Students in the Department of Art.

Brockway, Marcia
Fuller, Mrs. David
Hart, Mary
Hartgrove, Gertrude
Johnson, Myrtle
Lacey, Retta
Mason, Mrs.
Miles, Emma

Miles, Jennie
Nelson, Emma
Roe, Amy
Sims, Jennie
Smith, Maud
Swanson, Mrs. P. F.
White, Frances Cora

Directory of Teachers and Students.

'Col. denotes College; Unc., Unclassified; Mus., Music; Div., Divinity School.

Allison, Ira.......................... ....Mus........................Galesburg
Anderson, C. E..... ....Mus................ ... .Galesburg
Andreen, Frank G...... ....Col.........................Woodhull
Andrew, Mary Maud........... ....Col ....New Salem
Andrew, William B.............................Col ....New Salem
Ayars, Frank Cope.... ....· Col....................Brookfield, Mo.
Backman, Lillian.......... ...., ...Mus .. ..Galesburg
Baker, Walter Graves.........................Col ....Morrison
Bartholomew, Jennie Lind........ ....Div.....................Table Grove
Bartlett, Alice Helen, Instructor in Music....................117 Division Street
Beatty, Dwight Curtis ....Unc ....Fairview
Biklen, Marie ....Mus....................Burlington, Ia.
Black, Ethel................... ... . Mus ....Galesburg
Blood, M. Isabelle, Instructor in Art ....64 North West Street
Bodell, Willard Orpha ....Div........................ ....Avon
Boehm, Fred Daniel*.........................Col.......................Muncie, Ind.
Bourgeois, Arthur J............................Unc ....Chicago
Bowles, James E. ....Col...........................Astoria
Boyer, Zetta.............................Mus..... ....Galesburg
Brock, Horace Mann...............:.........Div ....Sheldon, Ia.
Brockway, Marcia...........................Art...................,....Galesburg
Brown, Athol Ray.......................Col..................North Henderson
Brown, Carrie.............................Mus...................... Galesburg
Brown, Marguerite B..:....... ....Unc...................... Sycamore
Bruner, Glenn Carlton*......................Col........................... Gerlaw
Burnside, Orpha ....Mus....................Galesburg
Byloff, Julia.............................. Mus .... Galesburg
Campbell, Raymond R......................Col............ .... Deland
Cedarholm, Chester ....Mus......................Galesburg
Chamberlain, Ethel Mary ....Col.................... Galesburg
Chamberlain, Ruth............................Unc .... Galesburg
Chambers, Pearl ....Mus....................... Galesburg
Cheesman, Prof. W. H., Instructor in Violin.. ....1198 North Cherry Street

Clarke, Fred Andrew......................Col......................Maquon
Clay, Walter Timothy......................Col......................Galesburg
Claycomb, Eleanor Pierce ....Mus.............. ....Sycamore
Conger, Delia Chase ....:....Col................. .....Galesburg
Cook, Grace Jane ....Unc......................Galesburg
Cook, Richard Clarence. ....Unc......................Galesburg
Cook, Sarah Lucy ....Col..... .... Galesburg
Cooper, Harry Mac........................Col...................... Oquawka
Curfman, Harry M.........................Unc......................Galesburg
Curtis, Naida................................Mus...................... Galesburg
DeBoer, Jacob John ....Div............Benton Harbor, Mich.
Dickerson, Orval Melcher.................Unc................................Mt. Vernon
Dickson, Arthur A..........................Col......................Galesburg
Dove, Genevieve ....Mus....................Burlington, Ia.
Dresing, Carrie ....Unc.......... .... Girard
Duty, Gertrude.............................Mus......................Galesburg
East, Ida Ritter ....Mus...............:.....Reading, Pa.
Eisenhart, Marie ....Mus....................Burlington, Ia.
Elting, Grace Helen......... ....Mus.:....................... Sperry, Ia.
Ericson, Henry.............. ....Col......................... Galesburg
Eustice, Bert Miller........................Unc...................... Stockton
Farr, May ....Mus...................Galesburg
Fosher, Cora Margaret*...................Col...................'. Galesburg
Fosher, Dudley Claude.... ....Col......................Galesburg
Fowler, Prof. Frank Hamilton....... .... 1155 East Knox Street
Fuller, Mrs. David..........................Art......................Galesburg
Galbreath, Minnie May.....................Unc...................Galveston, Ind.
Garver, Ora Beatrice........................Unc......................Pecatonica
Garvin, Benton..............................Unc..............................Quincy
Gates, Carroll ....Mus............................Galesburg
Gillette, Ora...............................Mus...................... Galesburg
Gillis, Anna Moore...........................Col...............Mt. Pleasant, Ia.
Gillis, Hudson McBain......................Col............. .... Mt. Pleasant. Ia.
Gordon, Robert Davis......................Unc..... ....: St. Joseph, Mo.
Grimes, Lloyd Owen   ....Col...................Blue Hill, Neb.
Grubb, Emma Welton*.....................Col......................Hamilton
Grubb, Prof. Jon Watson.................. .... 1427 E. Knox Street
Hale, Mrs. Ada M. H......................................Matron at Ladies' Hall
Hall, Daisy.................................Mus......................Galesburg
Halliday, Eugene............. .. ..Mus...................... Galesburg
Halliday, Herschel........................Mus..................... Galesburg
Harler, Myrtle ....Unc.................. ..... Rapatee
Hart, Mary Arrah ....Col...................... Eureka, Kan.
Hartgrove, Claude Webster.................Col...................... Galesburg
Hartgrove, Gertrude ....Art......................Galesburg
Hathaway, M. Agnes, Dean of Women.................................Ladies' Hall
Herlocker, Webb A..........................Unc...................... Table Grove
Higgins, Lucy ....Mus...................... Galesburg
Hollister, Florence Gertrude.................Unc...................... Pecatonica
Hopkins, Roy Victor ....Col......................Princeville
Howell, Spencer Pritchard.................:Col......................Woodhull
Hull, Lee C..................................Unc......................Eureka, Kan.

Hurd, Jay Clinton.............................Col...........,..................Maquon
Jansen, Harry Albin...........................Col ....Woodhull
Johnson, Mattie ....,.............Mus.......................... Galesburg
Johnson, Minnie............................ Mus........................ Galesburg
Johnson, Myrtle.................................Art........................ Knoxville
Jones, Minnie...........................Mus........................ Galesburg
Justus, Ray W. ....Unc................... Stockton
Keefe, Statia ......:............................Art......................Galesburg
Kienholz, Willis Simon, Director of Athletics..Col............ ...665 Locust Street
Kidder, Amanda, Instructor in Elocution.........................1284 E. Brooks Street
Kidder, Clytia...............................Mus........................ Galesburg
Kidder, Ross Larned*....... ....Col.......................Youngstown
Kimble, Olin A. ....Col....................Carbondale, Kan.
Kimble, Prof. Ralph Grierson.............................427 Locust Street
Kimble, Prof. Thaddeus Carey...............................1214 E. Berrien Street
Kirker, George H.............................. Unc......,.............. Moweaqua
Kober, Florence Leclerc ....Col.......................... Macomb
Koethe, Ella E..... ....Unc.................La Crosse, Wis.
Kramer, Charles..............................Div..................... Reading, Pa.
Lacey, Retta.......................... ....Art......................... Knoxville
Lauer, Herbert Louis ....Col...............Hutchinson, Kan.
Lewis, Bert Anson*............................Col............ ..West Mitchell, Ia.
Linderholm, Ernest Arthur*................Col...... ....Altona
Long, Katherine Temple ....Mus.... ....Galesburg
Longbrake, Dr. Guy A., Medical Examiner....................74 N. Chambers Street
Lueder, John...............................Mus........................ Galesburg
Lundberg, Prof. Karl Jacob Rudolph............................548 Lombard Street
McAlpine, Roy Kenneth*......................Col..................... Jackson, Mich.
McCullough, Edwin Julius....................Col................................Sparland
McDavitt, Arthur Woodford...................Unc.................LaPlata, Mo.
McDonald, Garnette ....Unc......... ....:....Galesburg
Main, Albert...........................Unc.................... .... Galesburg
Manning, Stanley.............................Div........................... Chicago
Marsh, Dora Ione ....Unc..................... .. Stockton
Mason, Marguerite ....Mus........................ Galesburg
Mason, Mrs..............................Art......................... Knoxville
Mertz, Leven George...........................Unc...........................Stockton
Metcalf, Harold ....Col................ Blandinsville
Miles, Emma.............................Art...................... Knoxville
Miles, Jennie...............................Art...................... Knoxville
Miller, Ralph Todd ....Col..................... Monmouth
Morden, Edith ....Div................... Maquoketa, Ia.
Murphy, Mrs. Clara.................... ......Mus................... Burlington, Ia.
Musgrave, Estella*...........................Col........................ Hutsonville
Nash, Beth............................Unc .... Galesburg
Nash, Pres. Charles Ellwood. . ... 1115 East Knox Street
Nash, Faith Tenney..........................Col......: .... Galesburg
Needham, Nellie Jeannette...................Col.......................Racine, Wis.
Neifert, Ira..................................Mus...................... Galesburg
Nelson, Alvira..............................Mus........................ Galesburg
Nelson, Carrie..... ....Mus................. .... Galesburg
Nelson, Emma ....Art........................ Knoxville

Nelson, Lilah ....Mus........................ Galesburg
Nieveen, S. Martin... ....Div.....................Platte, S. Dak.
North, Felix B..............................Mus.......... .... Galesburg
Ober, Floyd H.*.............................Col........................ Sheldon, Ia.
Offrell, Blenda ....Mus........................ Galesburg
Oleen, Evelyn Marie ....Mus........................ Galesburg
Olson, Amelia ....Mus........................ Galesburg
Olson, Hattie................................Mus........................ Woodhull
Orton, Edward Charles.......................Unc.................. Mt. Pleasant, Ia.
Parke, Eleanor G. ....Unc........................ Sycamore
Parker, Prof. Isaac Augustus...............................488 Lombard Street
Patterson, George...........................Div......................... Morrison
Peterson, Mabelle...........................Mus........................ Galesburg
Phillips, William...........................Div...................... ....Chicago
Pittman, Clio...............................Unc................... Prescott, Ark.
Pittman, Eskridge...........................Unc.................... Prescott, Ark.
Porter, Gail Quincy *.......................Col........................DeLand
Rains, Bertha Ellen...... ....Unc.................... Hutsonville
Reed, Grace.................................Mus........................ Galesburg
Rees, Jenkins B. ....Col.......................Oneida
Reifsnider, Rev. Edson, Instructor in Homiletics and Pastoral Care..257 E. North St.
Rice, Dr. Delia M., Medical Examiner ....84 North Prairie Street
Rich, Prof. Frederick William.................................1379 East Knox Street
Rich, Gertrude May..........................Mus.......... .... Galesburg
Rich, Willis Horton.........................Col................... ...... Galesburg
Roe, Amy....................................Art.................. .... Knoxville
Sammons, Mabel Alta.........................Col................ .... Joliet
Sandusky, C. W. ....Mus........................ Galesburg
Sapp, Bessie ....Mus........................ Galesburg
Schaffer Chas.........................Mus........... .... Galesburg
Schroeder, Carrie ....Mus.... ....Galesburg
Scott, Preston B............................Col..... .... Galesburg.
Shaffer, James Alexander* ....Col..... ..... Galesburg
Shontz, Mary................................Mus.....................Burlington, Ia.
Sims, Jennie................................Art..................../...........Galesburg
Smith, Maude ....Art .... Knoxville
Snodderly, Ellsworth........................Unc......................Galesburg
Snyder, Retta...............................Mus........................ Galesburg
Snyder, Roy.................................Unc.......................Moweaqua
Sommers, Elsie Dorothy ....Mus.....................Burlington, Ia.
Starr, Fred Schumme ....Unc.....................Muncie, Ind.
Stickney, Eva Jane........ ....Unc....................Nashua, Minn.
Stromberg, Edward ....Mus........................ Galesburg
Swanson, Florence Aletta ....Mus........................ Galesburg
Swanson, Mrs. P. F..........................Art..... ....Galesburg
Tausche. Arthur.............................Unc....................La Crosse, Wis.
Teuchert, Alma ....Mus.....................Burlington, Ia.
Thorpe, Joel Rex............................Unc...... .... Merriam, Kan.
Tipton, Fred Lincoln........................Unc.................. ....Girard
Tolan, Lena.................................Unc........................ Girard
Tyner, Mrs. W. J. ....Mus........................ Galesburg
Uhler, Edna, Instructor in Music ....Ladies' Hall

Van Cise, Ethel..............................Col.......................Denver, Col.
Varney, Franklin G...........................Div...... ....Clinton
Wait, Prof. Emma B...447 Locust Street
Ward, Florence ....Mus........................Galesburg
Ward, Vina Maye* ....Col......................... Galesburg
Webster, Albert Sanger ....Col...... .. .. Galesburg
Webster, Charles A., Treasurer...................................328 Holmes Building
Webster, Inez ....Unc.......................Galesburg
Wertman, Albert J...........................Unc...... .... Villisca, Ia.
Wheeler, Lynn Virgil ....Unc........................Sangamon
Wheeler, Nathaniel Herbert ... .Unc.......................Sangamon
White, Frances Cora..........................Art........................Galesburg
White, Prof. Nehemiah.....................................1473 East Knox Street
Whitney, Bertha Louise*.....................Col....................Buffalo Prairie
Wilkins, Louis Guy ....Unc.............. Logansport, Ind.
Williams, Jesse Edward.......................Unc.......................Galesburg
Williams, Jesson ....Mus............. .... Galesburg
Willis, Leura*.............................Col......................Table Grove
Wilson, Harlan R........................Unc...................... Knoxville
Wilson, Helen..................... ....Mus....................Burlington, Ia.
Wise, Lorena Myrtle......................Col ....Winfield, Ia.
Wright, Prof. Philip Green.......... .... 1443 East Knox Street
Wrigley, Anne Marion........... ....Col........................... Chicago
Young, Bessie............... ....Mus.......................Galesburg
Young, Blanche L. ....Div...................... Galesburg
Young, David Ernest ....Div...................... Adel, Ia.

*Having credits sufficient in number to enter college, but one or more required studies lacking.

GENERAL SUMMARY.

COLLEGE OF LIBERAL ARTS.

Candidates for degrees in 1902.
  Master of Arts... 1
  Bachelor of Arts 10-11
Students in the College of Liberal Arts .... :...... 58

UNCLASSIFIED STUDENTS.

Unclassified Students 47

RYDER DIVINITY SCHOOL.

Candidate for a degree in 1902.
  Bachelor of. Divinity 1
Students in Divinity School.
  Fourth Year 1
  Third Year... 2
  Second Year 4
  First Year.. 4
  Prepaiatory Year.................................... 1
  Special Student 1-13

MUSIC.

Candidates for Diploma in Music............................. 6
Students in Harmony and Musical History 24
Students in Pianoforte 49
Students in Vocal Culture 18
Students in Violin..12
Students in Mandolin 4
Students in Guitar....................................... 4
Students in Violoncello...................................1-118

ART.

Students in Art............. 15
                     263
Names entered twice....................................... 70

  Total... 193

ASSOCIATION OF GRADUATES.
1902-1903.

OFFICERS.

PRESIDENT,

T. C. KIMBLE, GALESBURG.

VICE PRESIDENT,

J. J. WELSH.

SECRETARY,

MRS. CLARENCE L. PERRINE. MILWAUKEE, WIS.

TREASURER,

JON W. GRUBB, GALESBURG.

HISTORIAN,

LORA A. TOWNSEND, GALESBURG.

BOARD OF DIRECTORS.

J. D. WELSH.	R. D. BOWER.
C. A. WEBSTER.	MRS. C. L. PERRINE.
MRS. F. H. FOWLER.	MRS. JON W. GRUBB.
T. C. KIMBLE.	J. N. CARNEY.

MRS. ADA HASBROOK HALE.

Graduates.

The degree of A. M. or M. S. placed immediately after a name, implies that the corresponding Bachelor's degree (A. B. or B. S.) was received on graduation.

The person to whose name a star is attached is deceased. The date following designates the year of his death.

Addresses known to be incorrect are bracketed.

1856.

William Worth Burson, A. M..... .....Manufacturer, 3424 Sheridan Drive, Chicago.
William Ramey Cole, A. M.......................... Clergyman, Mt. Pleasant, Iowa.
Hon. Thompson W. McNeeley, A. M.................Ex-M. C., Attorney, Petersburg.
Hon. Lewis Alden Simmons, A. M., *1889.............................Wellington, Kan.
Addie Hurd, A. M. (Mrs. Wm. Van Horn).........917 Sherbrook St., Montreal, Can.
Jennie Miles, A. M., *1859......... ....Decatur.

1857.

Fielding B. Bond, A. B., *1862.............. ....Greenbush.
Floyd G. Brown, A. B., *1868.............. .... Mankato, Minn.
James Henry Chapin, A. M., Ph. D., *1892........................... Meriden, Conn.
Hon. Edward D. Laning, A. B...............................Attorney, Petersburg.
Hon. Scott Wike, B. S., *1901...Barry.

1858.

Anson L. Clark, A. M., M. D.   President Bennett Eclectic Medical Col-
        lege, Chicago....... ....: Elgin.
Thomas Gorman, A. B., *1891...Columbus, O.

1859.

Hon. George W. Elwell, B. S., *1869................................ Chillicothe, Mo.
Eugene Beauharnais Hill, B. S........... ....Manufacturer, Ottumwa, Iowa.
Almon Kidder, A. M..Attorney, Monmouth.
Mary Jane Fuller, B. S...Tarpon Springs, Fla.
Ruth Waldron Miller, M. S. (Mrs. Brower), *1892... ....:......Chicago.

1860.

Jonathan Eden Brown, A. B...................................Farmer, Peabody, Kan.
Arick Burr, B. S., *1860...Charleston.
Hon. William Judah Frisbee, A. M...............................Druggist, Bushnell.
James Scott Lindsay, A. B., *1860...................,.........................Onarga.
Albert Sidney Slater, M. S., M. D...Wataga.

1861.

Hon. Franklin Fayette Brower, A. M., *1869...................................Ottawa.
Everett Lorentus Conger, A. M., D. D.....................Clergyman, Pasadena, Cal.
Henry George Pollock, A. M..............................Clergyman, Madison, Ind.
Mary Stewart Miller, A. B. (Mrs. Catlin), *1867.........................Vinton, Iowa.

1862.

Hon. Edwin Hurd Conger, A. M...............U. S. Minister to China, Pekin, China.
Samuel Alvus Dow, A. M., M. D..............Wyalong, New South Wales, Australia.
William Sampson Dow, B. S., *1863 ....Galesburg.
Hon. Charles Allen Holmes, A. M.................Attorney, New London, Wis.
Hamilton Lafayette Karr, A. M......................... Attorney, Osceola, Ia.
Frederick Warren Livingston, M. S................Teacher, San Diego, Cal.
Harvey Rowell, A. B.......................... Solicitor of Patents, Columbus, Wis.
Hon. John Crocker Sherwin, M. S., Ex-M. C.,...............................
.............................Attorney, [1234 Columbus Street, Denver, Colo.]
Alfred Henry Trego, A. M...................... Manufacturer, Hoopeston.
George John Turner. A. M., M. D., *1899............................Oskaloosa, Ia.
Eugenia Adaline Fuller, B. S. (Mrs. J. W. Ranstead).........................Elgin.

1863.

Samuel Addison Calhoun, A. B..........Adv. Solicitor "German Demokrat," Peoria.
Hon. John W. Ranstead, B. S..Attorney, Elgin.
Hanna Jane Biddlecombe, M. S.,..Bookkeeper Glendale Furnace Co., Columbus, O.
Oricy Villa Crocker, L. A., (Mrs. Nead). *1880 ....Galesburg.
Sarah Jane Pike, L. A., (Mrs. E. H. Conger).........................Pekin, China.

1864.

Elmore Chase, B. S.......................................Teacher, Fair Oaks, Cal.
Leslie Greenwood, A. M..........With Farmers' Loan and Trust Co.. Sioux City, Ia.
Laura Lavinia Pike, A. M., (Mrs. J. S. McConnell).......4359 Lake Avenue, Chicago.
Josephine Raymond, A. M. (Antioch College), (Mrs Maxwell)............Champaign.
Sallie Raymond, L. A., (Mrs. J. B. Green).......................................Ramsey.

1865.

Elmore Chase, B. S., A. M.....................................Teacher, Fair Oaks, Cal.
John Henry McCormick, B. S..Caledonia, Mo.
Alice Caroline Chapin, B. S. Teacher. .[222 West 3d South St., Salt Lake City, Utah.]

1866.

Hon. Elwin Wallace Claycomb, A. M. ....Farmer, Eureka, Kan.
Hon. Geo. R. Shook. B. S.......:..............Teacher and Surveyor, Fruita, Colo.
James Smith McConnell, B. S..............Attorney, 84 Washington Street, Chicago.
Emma N. H. Conger, A. M., (Mrs. S. W. Conger)................... Villa Park, Cal.

1867.

William Bryan Carlock, B. S.......................... Attorney, Bloomington.
William Harvey Woods, B. S.............................. Farmer, [Mendota.]
Helen Maria Bingham, L. A., M. D..............................Monroe, Wis.

1868.

Henry Moses Chase, A. B., *1870...Concord, Vt.
Hon. James O'Donnell, B. S., *1901 ....,.... ....Cherokee, Ia.
Wellington Smith, B. S., *1870... Annawan.
Edward Keys Walbridge, B. S............. Loan and Real Estate Agent, Girard, Kan.
Mary J. Claycomb, A. M. (Mrs. J. W. Grubb).............................Galesburg
Josephine Marian Kirk, A. M. (Mrs. Kerr) *1879.............................Chicago.
Almeda Beals, L. A. (Mrs. Charles Wickwire).... ....Farmington.
Sarah Elvira Edwards, L. A., (Mrs. Otis Jones), *1899..............Los Angeles, Cal.
Grace Greenwood, L. A. (Mrs. E. E. Holroyd), *1898... ....Chicago.
Emeline Elizabeth Kirk, L. A., *1881.....................................'.Rockford.
Frances Elizabeth Pike, L. A., (Mrs. J. Kirk Keller)............Artist, Paris, France.
Mary Ann Sparks, L. A., (Mrs. Milnor) ....Litchfield.
Florence Adeline Tenney, L. A. (Mrs. Edwards) *1871.................. Omaha, Neb.
Mary Emeline Weston, L. A. (Mrs. Woodman), *1888..................Portland, Me.

1869.

Rauseldon Cooper, B. S..................................... ..... Attorney, Oquawka.
Hon. Samuel Kerr, A. M................. ....Attorney, 189 La Salle St., Chicago.
Hon. Michael F. Knappenberger, B. S..................... Attorney, Jewel City, Kan.
Howard Knowles, B. S.,.. Galesburg.
Patrick Talent, B. S............................. ....Attorney, Hanford, Cal.
John Ewalt Wiley, B. S.......... .... Farmer. Elmwood.
Mary Emily Dunton, A. M., (Mrs. Samuel Kerr).............................Oak Park.
Ella May Greenwood, L. A., (Mrs. S. O. Snyder),.687 Third St., Salt Lake City, Utah.
Mary Hartman, L. A., A. M. *1888......Teacher in State Normal University, Normal.

1870.

Jared Perkins Blood, A. B............................. ....Attorney, Sioux City, Iowa.
Hon. Abraham Miller Brown, A. M............................ Attorney, Galesburg.
Nathaniel Ray Chase, A. M., M. D..........................'....... Newport, R. I.
Matthias Crum, M. S................................. ....Stockman, Mendon, Mo.
Hon. Chas. Electus Hasbrook, A. M., LL. B., (Chicago University), ...
.. .. Publisher Minneapolis Times, Minneapolis, Minn.
Elmer Clifford Johnson, B. S............. Manufacturer, 36 Main St., Evansville, Ind.
Otis Jones, B. S..115 Monroe St., Chicago.
Israel Cyrus Stockton, M. S. ....
        Clerk, Interior Department, 1514 New Jersey Ave., N. W., Washington, D. C.
Hon. John Hill Walbridge, B. S..........................Farmer. West Concord, Vt.
Mary Ann Chapin, L. A. (Mrs. T. T. Perry) *1883....................... Girard, Kan.
Flora Amanda Edwards, L. A. (Mrs. J. F. Fargo)................. San Antonio, Cal.

1871.

Hon. Martin Ireneus Brower, A. M.......................Attorney, Fullerton, Neb.
Hon. Willis Hardin Fuson, A. M.. *1884............................. Wa Keeney, Kan.
Frank Tenney Greenwood, A. B.................. Druggist, Seneca, Kan.
Hon. Madison Reynolds Harris, A. B., Attorney, 148 W. Madison St., Rm. 30, Chicago.
Hon. Samuel Parsons McConnell, A. B., Ex-Circuit Judge, Attorney, New York, N. Y.
John DeBolt Stephenson, B. S., *1872.............................Dexter, Ind.
Ida Bullock, L. A. (Mrs. Thatcher), *1894............................ Attleboro, Mass.

Hanna Laura Haight, B. S..................... ....Teacher, Mendota.
Ada May Hasbrook, A. M., (Mrs. Hale).......................................
.......................Matron Ladies' Hall, Lombard College, Galesburg.
Mary Knowles, L. A., (Mrs. J. S. Alspaugh)........................Washington, Kan.
Flora Adaline Prindle, L. A., (Mrs.˙A. G. Dow) ....Galesburg.

1872.

Albert Elmore Chase, B. S............ Deputy U. S. Mining Surveyor, Boulder, Colo.
Joseph Albert Gates, A. B......National Military Home, Box 97, Leavenworth, Kan.
Alice M. Bingham, L. A., (Mrs. Copeland)............. School Trustee, Monroe, Wis.
Mattie Wilburn Burford, L. A., (Mrs. Bates)................Merchant, Wichita, Kan.

1873.

Theodore C. Stevens, A. M., *1892.....................................Lincoln, Neb.
Ada D. Bingham, L. A., M. D........................ 1623 Gaylord St., Denver, Colo.
Ella M. Brown, L. A., (Mrs. Salley) *1883 .... Monroe, Wis.
Anna L. Nelson, L. A. (Mrs. Fuson)....................................Emporia, Kan.
Clara Richardson, L. A., (Mrs. G. F. Claycomb).............................
.................................3927 Woodlawn Park Ave., Seattle, Wash.
Sarah A. Richardson, A. M........................ ....,..........Lawrence, Kan.
Mary M. Stevens, A. M...................................... 871 East St., Lincoln, Neb.

1874.

William Albrecht, B. S., *1878.. Tiskilwa.
Eugene E. Brunson, B. S., M. D.......................................Ganges, Mich.
Daniel Clingingsmith, B. S.....................................Newton, Kan.
William E. Day, B. S.................˙.....Teacher, 198 Oakwood Boulevard, Chicago.
Morris W. Fletcher, B. S., M. D....................................... Collierville, Tenn.
Irene A. Conger, L. A., (Mrs. Courtney), *1891..................................Chicago.
Belle Sherman, B. S... Teacher, Ithaca, N. Y.

1875.

Charles A. Buck, L. A.. Merchant, LeRoy.
Lucien J. Dinsmore, B. S., A. M., *1866..........Clergyman, 1389 Perry St., Chicago.
Charles Ellwood Nash, A. M., S. T. D. (Tufts), President Lombard College, Galesburg.
Carrie W. Brainard, A. M., B. D. (St. Lawrence)........ Clergyman, Rome City, Ind.
Emma S. Collins, L. A., (Mrs. J. E. Buchanan)................Teacher, Lake Forest.
Lillie E. Conger, L. A., *1877............................ .... Oneida
Genie R. Edwards, L. A. (Mrs. Noteware), *1888.................Minneapolis, Minn.
Jennie C. Nelson, L. A., (Mrs. Nichols)....................................St. Charles.
Josie M. Pryne, L. A..............................113 Hanover St., Mankato, Minn.
Luella R. Warner, B. S., (Mrs. Frank Hitchcock)..Teacher of Painting, Mosca, Colo.

1876.

Hon. J. L. Hastings, B. S., *1894.. Galesburg.
Charlette Fuller, M. S., (Mrs. S. M. Risley)......................... Harvard, Neb.
Stella Hale, L. A.. ....Galesburg.
Lottie E. Leighton, B. S., (Mrs. L. J. Dinsmore)..............1389 Perry St. Chicago.
Izah T. Parker, A. M., *1891..Banning, Cal.

1877.

George F. S. Baker, A. M., *1891.............. .... Goodenow.
Charles C. Maynard, A. M.................. Dentist, 97 South First St., San Jose, Cal.

Clara Z. Edwards, L. A., (Mrs. J. F. Calhoun)...............................
..........................,.......... 2121 Bryant Ave., South, Mlnneapolis, Minn.
Emily L. Fuller, A. M................. ....Teacher, Galesburg.
Eugenia Fuller, A. M...................... ...... Principal High School, Riverside, Cal.
Lottie J. Humphrey, B. S., *1879... Tipton, Ia.
Ella McCullough, L. A., (Mrs. J. D. Welsh)...............................Galesburg.

1878.

Ozro P. Bostwick, A. B.............................Supt. City Schools, Clinton, Ia.
Eben H. Chapin, A. M., B. D., (Tufts).......Clergyman, 18 Maple St., Rockland, Me.
Shirley C. Ransom, B. S., A. M., 1892 ....
.................Agent Home Building Co., [Holmes Building, Galesburg.]
Adah M. Mariner, M. S., (Mrs. Stewart)...................................Bushnell.

1879.

Jon W. Grubb, M. S.........................Professor Lombard College, Galesburg.
Charles P. Hale, A. M., Insurance and Real Estate Agt.1087 Broadway, Denver, Colo.
Douglas A. Myers, B. S.................................... Real Estate Agent, Peoria.
Charles A. Webster, B. S....................Treasurer Lombard College, Galesburg.
J. Edwin Webster, B. S........... ....Merchant, Galesburg.

1880.

Henry S. Livingston, A. M., *1895...Galesburg.
Wiliam H. Livtngston, A. B.,....................Auditor Mercantile Mutual
        Building and Loan Association, 301 New England B'i'd'g, Kansas City, Mo.
William A. Parker, A. M... ....Civil Engineer, U. P. R. R., Kansas City, Mo.
Otto H. Swigart, B. S...........................Farmer and Stockman, Champaign.
Mollie B. Davendorf, B. S...........Stenographer, 682 N. California Ave., Chicago.
Jennie B. Townsend, B. S., (Mrs. C. A. Webster) ....Galesburg.

1881.

George F. Hughes, A. B.............................. ....Attorney, Yates City.
Milo C. Summers, M. S...................... .....War Department Clerk,
        Surgeon General's Office, 314 Seventh Street, Northeast, Washington, D. C.
Lura D. Bailey, A. B., (Mrs. G. F. Hughes)...............................Yates City.

1882.

Reuben D. Bower, B. S.............................. .... Clerk, Galesburg.
Henry M. Chase, A. M.....................Loan and Real Estate Agent, Galesburg.
Lafayette Swart, B. S.... ....Farmer, Murfreesborough, Tenn.
Elmer H. West, M. S., *1894..... .... Yates City.

1883.

Chas. E. Brewster, A. B. ....:...............,..................Loan
        and Real Estate Agent, 1770 Emerson Avenue, South, Minneapolis, Minn.
James Weston Carney, B. S., B. D., (Tufts).......................Attorney, Galesburg.
Lloyd Z. Jones, B. S..................... ......County Surveyor and Farmer, Galva.
John H. Miles, B. S...... ....Farmer, Bushnell
Fannie M. Edwards, A. B. (Mrs. C. E. Erewster),........................
:.........../......... .... 1770 Emerson Ave., South, Minneapolis, Minn.
Lizzie E. Furniss, B. S., (Mrs. W. J. Moring), Teacher. 2200 Logan Ave., Denver, Col.

Emma J. Livingston, L. A., (Mrs. A. T. Wing)..........................Maryville, Mo.
Elma E. Williams, A. M..Teacher, Geneseo.

1884.

Anna M. Brewster, M. S., (Mrs. E. H. West)...... ....Brewster.
Gay M. Brunson, B. S., M. D., D. D. S...............................Dentist, Joliet.
Lulu M. Burt, B. S., (Mrs. W. B. Cravens)..........2401 E. 11th St., Kansas City, Mo.
Charles L. Edwards, B. S., Ph. D. (Leipsic)
              Professor of Biology, Trinity College, Hartford, Conn.
Jay C. Edwards, M. S ... .4000 Vincennes Ave., Chicago.
Frank R. Jones, B. S..........................Cashier American Well Works, Aurora.

1885.

Jennie B. Conger, A. M., (Mrs. Conger)............1059 E. 34th St. Los Angeles, Cal.
Eugene F. Carney, B. S., *1887..Galesburg.
Alma J. Devore, B. S., (Mrs. J. H. Miles)....................................Bushnell.
Lizzie B. Hughes, B. L., (Mrs. D. Perry).............................Table Grove.
Ella Suiter, B. S., (Mrs. Geo. Pittard), *1894....................................Alexis.
Hon. Lyman McCarl, M. S.................... .....Attorney, 304 N. Sixth St., Quincy.
J. Douglas Welsh, B. S...............;...................... County Judge, Galesburg.
George Crum, B. D. ....Clergyman, Cedar Rapids, Ia.
Wallace F. Small, B. D... Everett, Wash.

1886.

Rainie Adamson, M. S. (Mrs. W. F. Small)........Co. Supt. Schools, Everett, Wash.
L. Ward Brigham, M. S., M. D., B. D., (Canton) Clergyman........573 Bedford Ave.,
....Brooklyn, N. Y.
John M. Davies, M. S.......... ....Teacher, 612 Fifth St., Maywood.
Anna H. Ebberd, B. S., (Mrs. Cyrus Hannum)........................Campbell Neb.
Alice L. Roberts, B. S., (Mrs. J. L. Andrew)..............r............National City, Cal.
Rachel A. Watkins, M. S., (Mrs. Billings, B. D., 1894).....Siloam Springs, Arkansas.
August Dellgren, B. D............................. Clergyman, Minneapolis, Minn.
Hiram J. Orelup, B. D....... ....Clergyman, 221 Penn. Ave., Aurora.

1887.

Ella M. Grubb, A. M. (Mrs. James Simmons,) ....Owasso, Mich.
Hon. Henry C. Morris, A. M.......... Attorney, 188 Madison St., Suite 703, Chicago.
J. W. Crane, B. S............Attorney, 908 Guarantee Loan Bldg., Minneapolis, Minn.
Perry B. Fuller, B. S.. Clerk, Elgin.
Jay Welsh, M. S..Teacher, Williamsfield.
Alva T. Wing, B. S................................Merchant, Maryville, Mo.
John R. Carpenter, B. D.............................Clergyman, New Olmstead, O.
Osgood G. Colegrove, B. D............................ Clergyman, Woodstock, O.
Mary Garrard, B. D., (Mrs. l. Rollln Andrews).........3819 Charles St., Omaha, Neb.

1888.

Peter T. Hawley, B. S..Merchant, Ralston, Ia.
Harry H. Jones, M. S.................Manager American Well Works, Dallas, Texas.
Allen W. Lapham, M. S., M. D., *1894...Victoria.
Elmer E. Taylor, B. S.......President McGee Holiness College, College Mound, Mo.
Elfreda L. Shaffer, B. D., (Mrs. Newport).................. Clergyman, Wauponsee.

1889.

Elmer E. Taylor, B. S., A. B. President McGee. Holiness College, College Mound, Mo.
George E. Dulton, M. S...Banker, Sycamore.
Frank H. Fowler, B. S., Ph. D. (The University of Chicago)...............
.................................Professor Lombard College, Galesburg.
Edward P. McConnell, M. S., *1902... Chicago.
Allen F. Moore, B. S.. Merchant, Monticello.
William T. Smith, M. S...................................Attorney, Galesburg.
Vanna R. Williams, B. L., (Mrs. W. W. Slaughter).................. Brookston, Ind.
Charles A. C. Garst, B. D., *1896.................................... Riverside, Cal.
Carrie A. Rice, B. D..........................Clergyman, 6019 Prairie Ave., Chicago.

1890.

Frank H. Fowler, B. S., A. B., Ph. D., (The University of Chicago).........
.................................Professor Lombard College, Galesburg.
Claude N. Anderson, B. S.................................. Teacher, Tecumseh, Neb.
Bret H. Brigham, M. S.......................................Attorney, Milwaukee, Wis.
Elizabeth Gaile Durston, M. S., B. O., (Columbia School of Oratory), (Mrs.
        H. F. Simmons)..................... ....Woodhull.
Fred Farlow, B. S.......................................,.....Stock Dealer, Camp Point.
Samnel D. Harsh, B. S., *1893.................................Creston, Iowa.
Anna E. Ross, M. S., (Mrs. A. Lapham), M. D., Physician, 4256 Langley Ave., Chicago.
Richard L. Slater, B. S., *1894................................ .... Wataga.
Loring Trott, M. S...Junction City, Kan.
James J. Welsh, B. S...Attorney, Galesburg.
Lizzie Wigle, B. S., (Mrs. C. N. Anderson)........................ Tecumseh, Neb.
Burtrust T. Wilson, M. S.............. Professor Guadalúpe College, Seguin, Texas.
Lilian J. Wiswell, B. L., (Mrs. E. P. McConnell)...................... ....Cameron.
Thomas E. Dotter, B. D................................. Clergyman, Sullivan, Mo.

1891.

Willard J. White, A. M., M. D.............. Professor of Medicine, Longmont, Colo.
M. McClelland Case, M. S.......................................Draughtsman, Chicago.
Villa A. Cole, B. S., (Mrs. M. M. Case)...Chicago.
S. Taylor Donohoe, M. S..............................United States Gauger, Pekin.
Jennie A. Grubb, B. S., (Mrs. F. H. Fowler)................................Galesburg.
Robert D. Hill, M. S...Teacher, Hopedale.
Della M. Rogers, B. L., (Mrs. Chas. Garber).........................Reardan, Wash.
William Franklin Smith, B. D., *1897.............................. Whitewater, Wis.

1892.

Frank N. Allen, B. S......................Bookkeeper, 442 E. Forty-fifth St., Chicago.
Curtis P. Beale, M. S...............................Insurance Agent, Farragut, Iowa.
Harry A. Blount, B. S.. Merchant, Macomb.
Ben. F. Brady, B. S... ..... Attorney, Ottawa.
Alice C. Durston, A. M.. New Windsor.
Chas. W. Elliott, M. S...Jeweler, Williamsfield.
Grace S. Harsh, B. S..Creston, Ia.
Lissie Seeley, B. S., (Mrs. Leonard Crew)................................Salem, Ia.
Daniel P. Wild, M. S...... ....Banker, Sycamore.
Luther E. Wyman, B. S.............................Broker, Board of Trade, Chicago.

Benjamin W. Jones, Jr. B. D., *1898..Barre, Vt.
Effie K. McCollum Jones, B. D., (Mrs. B. W. Jones)...........Clergyman, Barre, Vt.
George W. Skilling, B. D..................................Clergyman, Iowa Falls, Ia.

1893.

Robert F. Anderson, A. B.......Principal Columbia School, 1402 Peoria Ave., Peoria.
Carl C. Countryman, A. M...................... Impersonator and Author, [Chicago.]
Ethel M. Tompkins, A. M. (Mrs. W. S. Clayberg) ....Avon.
F. Louise Bradford, B. S...................... ....Teacher, Quincy.
Richard Brown, M. S..Attorney, Creston, Ia.
Kate A. Carlton, B. S., (Mrs. F. W. Smith).......................... DeLand, Fla.
J. Newton Conger, Jr., M. S.......................................Attorney, Galesburg.
States Dickson, B. S.................................. ....Attorney, Kewanee.
S. Hepsey Fuller, M. S., (Mrs. J. M. Earhart)... ....Wyoming.
Daisy D. Wiswell. M. S., (Mrs. G. A. Franklin)....................Carpintaria, Cal.
Guy A. Longbrake, B. L., M. D........................... ....Physician, Galesburg.
Charles E. Varney, B. D..Clergyman. Clinton.

1894.

William Richard Tapper, A. B.......... Attorney, 157 E. Forty-seventh St., Chicago.
Guy Henry Bernard, B. S...................................Bank Cashier, Glasco, Kan.
Lucy Minerva Conger, B. S., (Mrs. E. P. May)...12 Gibbs St., Newton Center, Mass.
Joseph Amos Crum, B. S., M. D..Oshkosh, Wis.
Maud Alice Crum, B. L... ....Boone, Ia.
Adelphia Gould Durston, B. S., (Mrs. George Ohse)....................Yorkville, Ill.
Albert Prentice Smith, B. S............................... Merchant, Denver, Colo.
Lucy Titus, B. S., (Mrs. R. F. Anderson)................. 1402 Peoria Ave., Peoria.
Eliza M. Drake Cuttis, B. D., (Mrs. J. L. Everton)............Clergyman, Hoopeston.
Rachel C. Watkins Dellgren, B. D., (Mrs. Billings).......Siloam Springs, Arkansas.
Jasper Leroy Everton, B. D......................................Clergyman, Hoopeston.
Martha Dandridge Garner, B. D., (Mrs. L. P Jones).....................
....Clergyman. Blenheim, Ontario, Can.
Henry LaFayette Gillespie, B. D.......................Clergyman, Newtown, Ohio.
Elijah Emmett Hamand, B. D.........Clergyman, 1222 Lyden Ave., Kansas City, Mo.
Rett E. Olmstead, B. D.............................. Clergyman, Cherokee, Ia.
Margaret Titus, B. D., (Mrs. R. E. Olmstead)............. Clergyman, Cherokee, Ia.
Albert Ernest Menke, Ph. D...............................Chemist, Fayetteville, Ark.
Hans Schuler, Ph. D...................................Teacher, Flushing, N. Y.

1895.

John McDuffie, Ph. D......................................Teacher, Springfield, Mass.
Lucile Bragg, A. B...Clerk, Humboldt, Kan.
William Robert Chapin, B. S..Buyer, Internat'l Harvester Co., 7 Monroe St., Chicago.
Frank Loren Conger, A. B....................................Bank Clerk, Galesburg.
Grace Winifred Conley, A. B............................. Postal Clerk, Galesburg.
Mabel Dow, A. B., (Mrs. F. L. Conger)....................................Galesburg.
Robert Pinckney Higgins, B. S.............................. Attorney, Bloomington.
John Richard Stanley, A. B............. Agricultural Implement Dealer, Stronghurst.
Nellie Christine Tompkins, A. B... Avon.
Albert Orin Wakefield, A. B............................:........Attorney, Sioux City, Ia.
Frances Elizabeth Cheney, B. D., *1902.....................................Greenup.

Orrin Carlton Evans, B. D...............................Clergyman, Rochester, Minn.
Charles Robert Jones, B. D............................... Clergyman, Nettleton, Mo
Thomas Francis Rayon, B. D........................ .. Clergyman, Rapid River, Mich.

1896.

Jessie Beatrice Brown, A. B., (Mrs. A. C. Clock)......................Winona, Minn.
Fred Leo. Camp, A. B...Expressman, Galesburg.
Bertha Alice Cook, A. B., (Mrs. O. C. Evans)........................ Rochester, Minn.
Almira Lowrey Cheney, A. B.................... ....Saybrook.
Elice Crissey, A. B...Teacher, Avon.
Homer Franklin Harsh, A. B.......... ....Stockman, Lowell, Neb.
Hamilton Lafayette Karr, Jr., A. B..............................Attorney, Osceola, Ia.
Marion Alice Kendall, A. B...Ithica, N. Y.
Harry McGee Lessig, A. B..[Knoxville.]
Ralph Grierson Kimble, A. B.................Professor Lombard College, Galesburg.
Iva Della Myers, A. B.. Bookkeeper, Galesburg.
Edward Leroy Shinn, A. B., Penn Collieries Co.. ....147 Milk St., Boston, Mass.
Emma Genevra Van Liew, A. M., (Mrs. Guy Tuttle)........................Bushnell
Jean Gillette White, A. B., (Mrs. A. B. McGill)...................................Peoria.
James Alvin Clark, B. D. ....Clergyman, Webster City, Ia.
Charles William Edward Gossow, B. D................... Clergyman, Wichita, Kan.
Maurice Gilbert Linton, B. D...........................Clergyman, Janesville, Ohio.
Eugene Southwick, B. D................................ Clergyman, Corfu, N. Y.

Georgia Stanley, Diploma in Art, (Mrs. C. H. Wickham).......Teacher, Stronghurst.

1897.

Frank Pierce Anderson, A. B............. ....Teacher, Yates City.
Loetta Frances Boyd, A. B...Teacher, Oneida.
Flora May Cutter, A. B...Camp Point.
Benjamin Downs, A. B...Clerk, Winslow, Ariz.
Nina Alta Harris, A. B., (Mrs. C. E. Hunter).. ... 619 W. Fourth St., Des Moines, Ia.
Fred Louis Holcomb, A. B., M. D... Zenda, Kan.
Theodore Lindquist, A. B...................................... Teacher, Kankakee.
Carrie Alice Stickney, A. B.......Student New England Conservatory, Boston, Mass.
Elmer Joseph Tapper, A. B............................Insurance Solicitor, Riverside.
Claud Bryant Warner, A. B., A. M......................................Dentist, Avon.
Guy Henry Weeks, A. B...Teacher, Galesburg.
Frances Cora White, A. B..Galesburg.
Fred Minosuke Yamaguchi, A. B.......Student Yale University, New Haven, Conn.
George Hilary Ashworth, B. D........... ....Clergyman, Bryan, O.
Edward Mllton Minor, B. D.............................Clergyman, Decatur, Mich.
George Burr Rogers, B. D. .... Clergyman, Decatur, Mich.
William Willis Slaughter, B. D., *1901....................... .... Francis, Okla.
Simeon Lafayette Taylor, B. D............................ Student, Des Moimes, Ia.

1898.

Mervin Wallace Allen, A. B.....................................Farmer, Maquon.
Alice Helen Bartlett, A. B........Instructor in Music, Lombard College, Galesburg.
Charles Reid Brown, A. B... With Knickerbrocker Ice Co., 171 La Salle St., Chicago.
Joshua J. Bullman, A. B..Farmer, Galesburg.
Ida Galbreath, A. B................................Teacher, Columbia City, Ind.

Charles Edward Piper, A. B........Student Yale Divinity School, New Haven, Conn●
Simeon Lafayette Taylor, B. D., A. B...................... Student, Des Moines, Ia.
Edna Madison McDonald, B. D., (Mrs. Bonser)........:...Clergyman, Cheney, Wash.
Helen Jessie Mackay...Galesburg.
John Willis Slaughter, B. D..
.... Student Univ. of Mich. 311 S. Division St., Ann Arbor, Mich.
Benjamin Franklin Stacey, B. D., A. B.,...Professor Univ. Arizona, Tucson, Arizona.
Oluf Tandberg, B. D...................................:Clergyman, Gardiner, Maine.

Isal Caldwell, Diploma in Vocal Music, (Mrs. Lewis) ....Knoxville.

1899.

Christen Martin Alsager, A. B....................Principal City Schools, Winnebago.
Ella Berry Boston, A. B., (Mrs. J. L. Lieb).................................Springfield.
Henry William Dubee, A. B..:...............Instructor in German, Harvard College.
Howard Everett Foster, A. B., *1900............... .... Galesburg.
Homer Edwin Garvin, A. B...............................Traveling Salesman, Quincy.
Fannie Pauline Gingrich, A. B., (Mrs. Clarence Perrine)............ Milwaukee, Wis.
George Runyan Longbrake, A. B........................Clergyman, Seneca, Kansas.
Nellie Stuart Russell, A. B.. Teacher, Woodhull.
Lora Adelle Townsend, A. B.................................. Teacher, Galesburg.
Lloyd Champlain, B. D............................ ....
.......Manager Co-Operative League of Photo Art, 330 Main St., Galesburg.

Edith C. Crissey, Diploma in Instrumental Music....................Teacher, Avon.
Jennie Holmes, Diploma in Art..... ....North Henderson.

1900.

Martha Belle Arnold, A. B.........-............................. Teacher, Galesburg.
Fay Alexander Bulluck, A. B.........Business Department Evening Mail, Galesburg.
Gertrude Grace Kidder, A. B., (Mrs. Kerr)...........................Winona, Minn.
Edwin Julius McCullough, A. B.....Graduate, Student-Lombard College, Galesburg.
Carrie Ruth Nash, A. B., (Mrs. Donald P. McAlpine)................Charlotte, Mich.
Charles Wait Orton, A. B...................................... Grocer, Tacoma, Wash.
Burt G. Shields, B. S.................................... Stock Broker, Golden, Colo.
Iva May Steckel, A. B..........Law Student, University of Colorado, Boulder, Colo.
Earl Wolcott Watson, A. B............................. Hardware Merchant, Barry.
Harry William Weeks, A. B.................... Student Univ. of Illinois, Champaign.
William David Buchanan, B. D............... ....Clergyman, Mt. Pleasant, Ia.

1901.

Martha Belle Arnold, A. M.......................................Teacher, Galesburg.
Carrie Ruth Nash, A. M., (Mrs. Donald P. McAlpine).............. Charlotte, Mich.
John Donington Bartlett, A. B...........Medical Student, Univ. of Chicago, Chicago.
Nannie Mer Buck, B. S................................ ....Teacher, Galesburg.
Gertrude West Hartgrove, A. B... Galesburg.
Julia Evelyn Lombard, A. B...... ....East Orange, N. J.
Jennie Eliza Marriott, A. B., (Mrs. W. D. Buchanan)............... Mt. Pleasant, Ia.
Donald Palmer McAlpine, A. B..:...........Principal High School, Charlotte, Mich.
William J. Orton, A. B............................ ..... Bank Clerk, Tacoma, Wash.
Grace Oliver Pingrey, A. B....................................... .Coon Rapids, Ia.

Frederick Preston, A. B...Boston, Mass.
Grace Schnur, A. B.................................317 N. Thirteenth St., Quincy.
Francis Britton Bishop, B. D.. Marseilles.

Virginia Henney, Diploma in Music............................... Mitchellville, Ia.
Cyrena Weir, Diploma in Music.....................................Clerk, Galesburg.

1902.

Charlotte Alspaugh, A. B... Washington, Kan.
John Andrew, Jr., A. B..........Medical Student, Univ. of Colorado, Boulder, Colo.
Edna Mae Cranston, A B., (Mrs. Mugg)..........................Indianapolis, Ind.
Charles Junius Efner, A. B..... ....Galesburg.
Edna Ethel Epperson, A. B......................................Teacher, Hanover.
Henry Ericson, A. B...............Graduate Student, Lombard College, Galesburg.
Augusta Eaton Hitchcock, A. B........Graduate Student, Univ. of Chicago, Chicago.
Thaddeus Carey Kimble, A. B... Instructor of Biology, Lombard College, Galesburg.
Howard Walter Lauer, A. B.....With Latrobe Steel and Coupler Co., Melrose Park.
Emma Annette Muffler, A. B..Serena.
Edward Milton Smith, A. B.......................Principal High School, Maquon.
Alice Stokes, A. B.......... ....Galesbuig.
Herbert Leonard Stoughton, A. B....... ....Law Student, Los Angeles, Cal.
Charles E. Varney, B. D., A. B.... .... Clergyman, Clinton.
Kiyoshi Satoh, B. D....... .... Theological Student, Tufts College, Mass.
George Francis Thompson, B. D...........Ass't Supt. of Churches, Plain City, Ohio.
Mecca Varney, B. D., (Mrs. C. E. Varney) ....Clergyman, Clinton.

HONORARY DEGREES.

The degree placed immediately after the name is the honorary degree conferred by Lombard College.

An additional degree, followed by a date only, is one conferred by Lombard College.

An additional degree, without date, is one conferred by another institution, the name of which is given, if known.

1858. *Rev. Otis A. Skinner, D. D................Ex-President Lombard University.
1859. Rev. George S. Weaver, A. M....................................Canton, N. Y.
1860. *Ansel Streeter, A. M..........:.......................................Weston, Mo.
1862. *Rev. Ebenezer Fisher, D. D....:..Principal Theological School, Canton, N. Y.
1862. Rev. Joseph Selmon Dennis, A. M.................................. Chicago.
1863. *Rev. William Henry Ryder, D D.; A. M. (Harvard)......:...........Chicago.
1864. *Rev. Holden R. Nye, A. M...................................Philadelphia, Pa.
1864. Rev. Charles Woodhouse, A. M.; M. D............................Rutland, Vt.
1865. Rev. A. G. Hibbard, A. M..Wheaton.
1865. *Rev. J. G. H. Hartzell, A. M.; D. D. (St. Lawrence)............Detroit, Mich.
1867. *Rev. William Ethan Manley, A. M................................Denver, Col.
1867. Rev. Thomas B. St. John, A. M...
1868. *Rev. Clement G. Lefevre, D. D............................Milwaukee, Wis.
1868. William B. Powell, A. M......................... ....Washington, D. C.
1868. Rev. James Harvey Tuttle, A. M.; D. D............38 W. 53d St., N. Y. City.
1869. Rev. John Wesley Hanson, A. M.; D. D. (Buchtel)..............Pasadena, Cal.
1869. Rev. William Wallace Curry, A. M........................Washington, D. C.
1869. *Rev. Daniel Parker Livermore. A. M........................ Melrose, Mass.
1869. Rev. Augusta J. Chapin, A. M..............· ....459 W. 144th St., N. Y. City.
1870. Rev. John S. Cantwell, A. M.......... ....Chicago.
1870. Daniel Lovejoy Hurd, A. M.; M. D..
1870. *Rev. George Truesdale Flanders, D. D.......................Rockport, Mass.
1870. *Rev. Alfred Constantine Barry, D. D...... ....Lodi, Mass.
1872. *Rev. William Ethan Manley, D. D.; A. M., 1867.................Denver, Col.
1872. *Rev. R. H. Pullman, A. M....................................Baltimore, Md.
1872. *Rev. Gamaliel Collins, A. M.....................U. S. A., Chatham, Mass.
1872. *Rev. B. F. Rogers, A. M....... ....Fort Atkinson, Wis.
1875. *Rev. J. H. Chapin, Ph. D.; A. B., 1857; A. M., 1860....,......Meriden, Conn.
1876. Rev. George S. Weaver, D. D.; A. M., 1859.....................Canton, N. Y.
1876. Rev. John S. Cantwell, D. D.; A. M., 1870..........................Chicago.
1877. Rev. O. Cone, D. D...................:...........................Canton, N. Y.
1879. Elias Fraunfelter, Ph. D....................·.......................Akron, O.
1879. Milton L. Comstock, Ph. D...............Professor, Knox College, Galesburg.
1882. Rev. Charles W. Tomlinson, D. D.........................Huntington, L. I.
1883. *Rev. Amos Crum, A. M....................................:....Webster City, Ia.
1884. Matthew Andrews, A. M..Monmouth.
1886. Rev. L. J. Dinsmore, A. M.; B. S., 1875 ....Chicago.
1887. *Rev. Holden R. Nye, D. D.; A. M., 1864......................Towanda, Pa.
1887. *Rev. Charles Fluhrer, D. D....................................Albion, N. Y·

*Deceased.

1887. Hon. Lewis E. Payson, LL. D...Pontiac.
1887. Hon. George W. Wakefield, A. M...............................Sioux City, Ia.
1888. Rev. George H. Deere, D. D...............................Riverside, Cal.
1888. Homer M. Thomas, A. M.; M. D...................................Chicago.
1888. Rev. Charles A. Conklin, A. M.............. ....Boston, Mass.
1888. Mary Hartman, A., M.; L. A., 1859.....................................Normal.
1890. Rev. Jacob Straub, D. D.......................................Columbia, Cuba.
1890. George B. Harrington, A. M...Princeton.
1890. Carl F. Kolbe, Ph. D...Akron, O.
1891. *Rev. A. G. Gaines, LL. D.; D. D.............................Canton, N. Y.
1892. Rev. George Thompson Knight, D. D.....................Tufts College, Mass.
1892. Charles Kelsey Gaines, Ph. D. ....Professor St. Lawrence Univ., Canton. N. Y.
1892. Shirley C. Ransom, A. M.; B. S., 1878...............................Galesburg.
1893. Rev. Augusta J. Chapin, D. D.; A. M., 1869.........459 W. 144th St., N. Y. City.
1893. *Rev. Amos Crum, D. D.; A. M., 1885......................Webster City, Ia.
1895. John Huston Finley, Ph. D.................................Princeton, N. J.
1893. Charles Loring Hutchinson, A. M................................Chicago.
1894. *Rev. Royal Henry Pullman, D. D.; A. M., 1872.................Baltimore, Md.
1894. Rev. George B. Stocking, D. D...............................Lansing, Mich.
1895. Rev. Aaron Aldrich Thayer, D. D.................................California.
1895. Rev. Andrew Jackson Canfield, Ph. D.; D. D...............Worcester, Mass.
1897. Rev. Daniel Bragg Clayton, D. D..............................Columbia, S. C.
1897. Rev. Thomas Sander Guthrie, D. D.............................Muncie, Ind.
1898. Rev. Rodney F. Johonnot, D. D...................................Oak Park.
1898. Henry Priest, Ph. D..............Professor St. Lawrence Univ., Canton, N. Y.
1899. *John Wesley Hanson, Jr., A. M......................................Chicago.
1900. Rev. Alfred Howitzer Laing, D. D...................................Joliet.
1901. Edwin Hurd Conger, LL. D.....................................Pekin, China.
1901. John Sharp Cook, D. D...Galesburg.
1902. Frederick Clarence Priest, D. D.,............ 691½ Washington Bvd., Chicago.
_____
*Deceased.

HARVARD UNIVERSITY SCHOLARSHIP.

Established by the Harvard Club of Chicago.

By request of the Harvard Club of Chicago we publish the following notice.

At its annual meeting, December 14, 1897, the Harvard Club of Chicago established a scholarship at Harvard University of the annual value of three hundred dollars. This scholarship is open to the graduates of the universities and colleges of Illinois who wish to follow a course of study at the Graduate School of Harvard University. Applications must be made before May 1st in each year, and senior students about to finish their under graduate course are eligible as candidates. Communications from candidates for the year 1903-1904 should be addressed to Louis M. Greeley, 906 Tacoma Block, Chicago.

INDEX.

LU   ERIES 11, No. 1.

[Issued Bi-Monthly by Lombard College.]

CATALOGUE

OF

LOMBARD COLLEGE

GALESBURG, ILLINOIS,

FOR THE YEAR ENDING JUNE 2, 1904.

❖   ❖   ❖

GALESBURG, ILL.:
MAIL PRINTING COMPANY.
1904.

College Calendar.

1904.

MARCH 8—Tuesday......................Registration.　Third Term Begins.
MAY 7—Saturday...........................Townsend Preliminary Contest.
MAY 14—Saturday.................................Senior Vacation Begins.
MAY 19—Thursday.........................Senior Theses Due.
MAY 26, 27—Thursday, Friday..............................Examinations.
MAY 28—Saturday....................Field Day.　Gymnasium Exhibition.
MAY 29—Sunday....................................Baccalaureate Sermon.
MAY 30—Monday..Memorial Day.
MAY 30—Monday, Evening.........Townsend Prize Contest in Declamation.
MAY 31—Tuesday..............Annual Meeting of Association of Graduates.
JUNE 1—Wednesday..............Annual Meeting of the Board of Trustees.
JUNE 2—Thursday.....................................Commencement Day.

Summer Vacation.

SEPT. 5—Monday..................................Entrance Examinations.
SEPT. 6—Tuesday......................Registration.　College Year Begins.
Nov. 19—Saturday........................Orations for Swan Contest Due.
Nov. 22, 23—Tuesday, Wednesday............................Examinations.
Nov. 23—Wednesday.......................................First Term Ends.
Nov. 24—Thursday.........................Holiday, Thanksgiving Day.
Nov. 28—Monday.....................Registration.　Second Term Begins.
DEC. 23—Friday........Last Day of Recitations preceding Christmas Recess.

Christmas Recess.

1905.

JAN. 3—Tuesday.....................Recitations of Second Term Resumed.
JAN. 21—Saturday.............................Swan Preliminary Contest.
FEB. 22—Wednesday......................Holiday, Washington's Birthday.
FEB. 24—Friday..........................Swan Prize Contest in Oratory.
MARCH 1, 2—Wednesday, Thursday........................Examinations.
MARCH 2—Thursday..............Senior Syllabi Due.　Second Term Ends.

Spring Vacation.

MARCH 7—Tuesday......................Registration.　Third Term Begins.
MAY 6—Saturday...........................Townsend Preliminary Contest.
MAY 13—Saturday.................................Senior Vacation Begins.
MAY 18—Thursday..............................Senior Theses Due.
MAY 25, 26—Thursday, Friday..............................Examinations.
MAY 28—Sunday....................................Baccalaureate Sermon.
MAY 29—Monday......................Field Day.　Gymnasium Exhibition.
MAY 29—Monday, Evening.........Townsend Prize Contest in Declamation.
MAY 30—Tuesday.Memorial Day. Annual Meeting of Association of Graduates.
MAY 31—Wednesday..............Annual Meeting of the Board of Trustees.
JUNE 1—Thursday.....................................Commencement Day.

BOARD OF TRUSTEES.

OFFICERS OF THE BOARD.

HON. J. B. HARSH, CRESTON, IOWA.
PRESIDENT.

CHARLES A. WEBSTER, GALESBURG.
TREASURER.   Holmes Building.

PHILIP. G. WRIGHT, GALESBURG.
SECRETARY.   1443 East Knox St.

Executive Committee.

HOWARD KNOWLES, CHAIRMAN.

CHARLES A. WEBSTER, SECRETARY.

CHARLES ELLWOOD NASH, D. D.

ROBERT CHAPPELL.   J. DOUGLAS WELSH.

Board of Visitors.

Each Universalist State Convention, which adopts Lombard College as its Institution of Learning, is entitled to send two visitors, whose duty it is to examine into the condition of the College and to assist in the choice of Trustees.

SCOPE AND IDEALS.

Between the high school or academy and the graduate, professional or technical school, American educators are coming to recognize a distinct and imperative educational function which is discharged only by the college, properly so called. This function is not so much "practical," in the commercial sense, as cultural in purpose; yet the broad results aimed at in character and in grasp of general principles, constitute the only adequate foundation in which to base the special training of the crafts and professions. Within the limits thus indicated, Lombard College is content to do its work.

Owing to differing standards and degrees of efficiency the interval between the high school and the graduate school varies greatly. At Lombard College it has seemed wise to prescribe admission requirements which presume a four years' high school course; and thus the Lombard graduation requirements are expected to meet the entrance requirements of the most advanced graduate institutions.

Inasmuch as many applicants have not had access to a four years' high school period, a considerable number of preparatory subjects are still offered at Lombard, sufficient in fact to comprise an academic course of at least three years. Further, as there are some who desire to pursue certain subjects without claiming full college standing, provision is made for such special students upon equitable terms. The pure college ideal, however, enjoins us to regard these concessions as temporary, to be granted only so long as conditions necessitate them.

On the other hand, it is believed to be not inconsistent with the college idea to allow those students who intend to enter a graduate, professional, or technical school after graduation, to expedite the later course and shorten the whole period of study by directly matching the graduation requirements with the prospective entrance requirements. Thus by using his elective privilege in mapping out his college course, the Lombard A. B. may complete the subsequent Divinity course leading to the degree of B. D. in two additional years, the Medical course leading to the degree of M. D. in three years, and an Engineering course in three years.

While the number of subjects offered at Lombard is largely in excess of graduation requirements and equalled by few of the "small" American colleges, thus allowing exceptional opportunity for adapting the course to the individual student, the emphasis is laid upon quality rather than amount of work, upon principles, more than upon mere facts, and the cultivation of orderly, self-active mental life is the constant endeavor.

GENERAL STATEMENT.

LOCATION.

LOMBARD COLLEGE is located in Galesburg, Knox County, Illinois, a healthful and beautiful city of 20,000 inhabitants, noted for its public buildings, its strong churches, and the good order, intelligence, thrift and refinement of its people.

Galesburg is easily accessible by railroad from all parts of the West; being the center of the great Burlington system, leading to Chicago, Burlington, Quincy, Peoria, Rock Island, St. Louis, Kansas City, Omaha, Denver, and Minneapolis; and also on the main line of the Santa Fé system. It is the northern terminus of the Fulton County Narrow Gauge R. R., connecting with the great Wabash system.

THE COLLEGE CAMPUS.

The College Campus is situated in the southeastern part of the city, and may readily be reached by the electric cars. It is thirteen acres in extent and affords ample space for base-ball, foot-ball, tennis, and other athletic sports. A large part is planted with trees which have been growing many years and have attained noble size and graceful forms. Among them are pines, larches, hemlocks, cedars, maples, elms, ash-trees, tulip-trees, and others, embracing about forty species. The trees and lawns are well kept and cared for, and the beauty of the surroundings thus created is a pleasing and attractive feature of the College.

HISTORY.

The Illinois Liberal Institute was chartered in 1851, opened for students in the autumn of 1852, invested with College powers in 1853, and took the name of Lombard University (in honor of Mr. Benjamin Lombard, at that time the largest donor to its properties) in 1855. It was one of the first Colleges in the country to admit women as students on the same terms with men, allowing them to graduate in the same class and with the same honors. The first class was graduated in 1856. The Ryder Divinity School was opened September 5, 1881. The official title of the institution was changed in 1899 to Lombard College.

THE ELECTIVE SYSTEM.

Experience has demonstrated the soundness of the educational principle that the selection of studies, in some degree, at least, should be adapted to the needs, tastes, and talents of the student. At Lombard this principle is fully recognized, and great liberty is given to students in the choice of their studies. At the same time the fact is recognized that there is a distinct educational gain to a student in pursuing a well matured and logically developed course of study. The method by which it is sought to reconcile these important principles of education at Lombard is fully explained later in the catalogue.

THE COLLEGE YEAR.

The College year begins early in September and closes early in June. It is divided into three terms of approximately equal length. (See Calendar, page 2.)

Students should, if impossible, enter at the beginning of the College year, since much of the work is arranged progressively from that date. They will, however, be allowed to enter at any time when there seems a prospect of their being able to do so profitably.

Commencement day occurs the first Thursday in June.

ADMISSION REQUIREMENTS.

The requirements for admission to the College of Liberal Arts for students who are candidates for a degree, is the highest standard recommended by the joint committee of the High School and College Sections of the Illinois State Teachers' Association. This is essentially the standard recommended by the Committee of Thirteen of the National Educational Association. (See pages 22-30.)

Students not candidates for a degree may enter on probation any class for which they are prepared, and at the end of their connection with the College they will be furnished a certificate, stating the amount and quality of the work accomplished while in the College.

APPORTIONMENT OF TIME.

The regular sessions of the College are held on Monday, Tuesday, Wednesday, Thursday, and Friday.

GRADES OF SCHOLARSHIP.

From the courses of study offered, each student is expected to elect work to an amount sufficient to keep him profitably employed.

In all full courses each recitation occupies one hour. Absence from a recitation will forfeit the mark in that study for the day.

At the end of every term the standing of a student in each of his courses will be expressed, according to his proficiency, by one of four grades, designated respectively by the letters, A, B, C, D.

The grade is determined by term work, estimated on the basis of attendance, quality of recitations or laboratory work, occasional tests, written exercises, etc., and by final examinations at the end of the term, the term grade and the final examination being valued in the ratio of two to one.

Grade C is the lowest which will be accepted in any study as counting towards the fulfillment of the requirements of graduation.

Students who receive grade A in all their studies may pursue not more than four courses in the succeeding term.

Students whose lowest grade is B may pursue not more than three and one-half courses in the succeeding term.

Other students are not permitted to pursue more than three courses in any term.

CHAPEL EXERCISES.

Religious exercises, at which attendance is required, are conducted daily in the College chapel.

With the view of imparting additional interest and value to these exercises, relieving them of mere formality, brief addresses by members of the faculty, or by invited speakers, upon practical life questions, or upon topics of the day, will be given from time to time. At intervals, also, special musical numbers will be introduced by the Director of the Musical Department.

LABORATORIES.

The department of Physics is well equipped with apparatus for experimentation. Students have an opportunity to obtain a practical acquaintance with the principles of Physics, through a series of Laboratory experiments, which they perform for themselves under the direction of the instructor.

The extended courses in Chemistry, described elsewhere in this Catalogue, require a large amount of practical work on the part of the student. Each student in Chemistry has a desk provided with gas, water, re-agents and all necessary conveniences. The Laboratory is well equipped for work in General Chemistry, and in Qualitative and Quantitative Analysis.

A supply of superior microscopes, with other instruments and apparatus, affords a very satisfactory equipment for experimental work in Biology.

MUSEUM.

The Museum contains valuable collections duly classified and arranged, and available for purposes of instruction. The collection of corals is especially fine. A fine collection of minerals, birds, and ethnological specimens, the loan of A. B. Cowan, Esq., a former citizen of Galesburg, is known and designated as the Cowan Collection.

LIBRARY.

The Library of the College contains about seven thousand volumes. It is located in the College building and is open daily. The books are systematically arranged and easy of access. They may be taken out by the students upon application to the librarian. A considerable fund has been raised during the past year, which will be expended as occasion arises, in the purchase of new books, thus assuring a substantial increment each year.

READING ROOM.

A Reading Room, under the auspices of a Reading Room Association, is supported by the voluntary efforts and contributions of the students, faculty, and friends. The leading newspapers and periodicals are kept on file. The Reading Room is open daily, except Sundays, for the use of the students, from 8:00 a. m. until 6:00 p. m.

GYMNASIUM.—

The Gymnasium is a building 50x80 feet on the ground. On the ground floor, besides the Gymnasium proper, there is a large room, at present used as a recitation room, which can be thrown into the main room by withdrawing the movable partitions. There is also a stage, equipped with an adequate outfit of scenery, for the special use of the Department of Elocution. The apparatus, consisting of chest weights, dumb bells, Indian clubs, parallel bars, horizontal bar, flying rings, travelling rings, rowing machine, etc., is of approved patterns. The basement contains bathrooms and lockers and other conveniences.

Regular exercises are held in the Gymnasium daily, except Saturdays and Sundays. The exercises will consist of class drill, under the charge of a director, or of special work on the apparatus in accordance with the prescription of the medical examiner. It is intended that the instruction shall be thoroughly scientific, aiming not so much at special muscular or athletic development as at a sound physical culture, which is the true basis of health and so of energy and endurance.

ATHLETICS.

The Athletic interests of the College are in charge of the Director of Physical Culture, assisted by a Board of Management, consisting of two members chosen from the student body, one from the faculty, and two from the alumni. The Campus affords opportunity for foot-ball, base-ball, and track and field events. During the winter basket-ball is played in the Gymnasium. The Director of Physical Culture will take personal charge of the coaching of the foot-ball, basket-ball, base-ball, and track teams.

THE LADIES' HALL.

The new Ladies' Hall, finished and first opened for use in the fall of 1896, is a thoroughly modern building and complete in all its appointments. It is heated by steam, lighted by gas, fitted with sanitary plumbing, including porcelain baths, closets, lavatories, etc., and supplied with every convenience of a well equipped home. The Hall will accommodate forty young women; and all out-of-town women students, unless permission is obtained from the President to live elsewhere, are expected to make their home in this building.

Each room is finished with hard wood floor and furnished with bedstead, springs, mattress, chairs, desk, dresser, and rugs. The occupants are expected to provide bedding, pillows, towels, napkins, to pay for washing said articles, and to keep their own rooms in order.

Rates are stated on page 12.

Applications for rooms in the Hall should be made during the summer vacation to Prof. Frederick W. Rich, at other times to Mrs. Ada M. H. Hale, Matron, Lombard Ladies' Hall.

LOMBARD COLLEGE PUBLICATIONS.

Lombard College Bulletin.

A series of papers is issued bi-monthly by the College, including the annual Catalogue, containing announcements, articles discussing educational questions, and other matter calculated to keep the College in touch with its friends, and to extend a knowledge of educational data, processes, and theories. Copies will be sent free upon application.

The Lombard Review.

A College paper called *The Lombard Review,* is published monthly by the students. It makes a record of College events, and serves as a medium of communication with the friends and alumni of the College. Subscription price $1.00.

SOCIETIES.

The Erosophian.

The Erosophian Society was organized January 29, 1860. Any male student connected with the College or Divinity School is eligible to membership, and is entitled to all the benefits of the society. Its regular meetings are held on Monday evenings of each week. The literary exercises consist of orations, debates and essays.

The Zetecalian.

This society was organized in 1863 for the women of the College. Its exercises consist of debates, essays, historical narrations, and general discussions. Regular meetings are held fortnightly on Friday afternoons. The officers are elected quarterly.

Lombard Oratorical and Debating Association.

The Lombard Oratorical and Debating Association is the local branch of the Northern Illinois Intercollegiate Oratorical League. The League holds an annual prize contest in oratory on the last Friday in April. There are two prizes of twenty and ten dollars respectively. The local organization holds a preliminary contest to decide who shall represent the College in the contest of the League. All male students of the College are eligible for membership.

PRIZES.

1. The Swan Prizes.

Two prizes for excellence in Oratory are offered annually by Mrs. J. H. Swan, of Chicago. They consist of fifteen dollars and ten dollars respectively. The contest for these prizes is held in January.

2. The Townsend Prizes.

Two prizes for excellence in Declamation are offered annually by Mrs. E. P. Townsend, of Sycamore. They consist of fifteen dollars and ten dollars, respectively. The contest for these prizes is held during Commencement week.

EXPENSES.

Boarding.

Board is furnished at the College Commons at cost. During the past year the maximum rates have been as follows:

Board, 37 weeks: Tuition, one year (without restriction of number of studies); incidentals, one year; payable annually or semi-annually in advance $126.50
Board, one Term; Tuition, one term (without restriction of number of studies); Incidentals, one term, payable in advance.............. 43.00
Board per week, payable in advance................................. 2.25
Meal tickets, 7 tickets... 1.05

The quality of the board furnished is not indicated by the price. Owing to the facts that provisions can be obtained at wholesale rates; that service at the table is co-operative, several students paying in part for their board in this manner; and that it is the purpose of the management to make no profit out of this department above actual operating expenses, the board is certainly equal in quality to that furnished in private families for $2.75 per week.

The yearly expenses may be estimated as follows:

```
Board at Commons, Tuition, Incidentals..........................$126.50
Room rent ..........................................................  22.50
Washing ...........................................................  15.00
Books .............................................................  15.00
                                                              ----------
                                                                 $179.00
```

Students, however are not required to board at the Commons; some board themselves, and some board in private families. Students who board themselves may possibly cut their expenses a trifle below the above rates. In private families rates of from $2.75 and upwards per week for board, may be obtained.

A faculty committee will assist students in securing comfortable, home-like accommodations.

The charge for board in the Ladies' Hall is $42 per term, for each person, payable in advance. This does not include the Christmas recess. The charge for room rent is from $6 to $15 per term, according to location of room, payable to the Registrar in advance. Where one person occupies a double room from choice, an extra charge of 50 cents per week will be made, but the privilege of assigning two persons to such room is reserved. Board will be furnished to women students of the College who do not have rooms in the Hall at the rate of $3.25 per week, payable in advance.

Tuition and Incidentals.

Students in the College of Liberal Arts and Unclassified students will pay a tuition fee for each study pursued. The charge, except in theoretical music and certain medical courses, is $3.50 per term for each full course, a course being a study taken for one term and counting as one credit toward graduation. The rate for each fractional course is in proportion to the credit allowed for such fractional course toward graduation. Thus, a half course is half rate; a third course, third rate, etc.

Students in Chemistry, Mineralogy, Histology, and Osteology, are required to deposit with the Registrar a sum sufficient to cover laboratory bills. Students in General Chemistry will deposit two dollars; students in Analytical Chemistry, five dollars; students in Mineralogy, three dollars; students in Histology, five dollars; students in Osteology, ten dollars each. At the close of the term there will be returned the balance remaining, after deducting cost of chemicals and broken apparatus.

Regular term fees are charged in each of the following laboratory courses: in Physics, one dollar; in Anatomy, five dollars; in Biology, two dollars; in Physiology, two dollars; in Zoology, two dollars; and in Botany, two dollars.

The charge for incidentals, to be paid by all students of the College, is $5.00 per term.

No students will be enrolled in any class until he presents the Registrar's receipt for the payment of tuition and incidentals. The registration fee is one dollar. The payment of this fee will be remitted to all who register on the first day of the term. For any change in registration not advised by the faculty a fee of one dollar will be charged.

Tuition and incidentals will not be refunded. In case a student is absent a half term or more from sickness or other adequate cause a certificate for a half term's tuition and incidentals will be given the student (at his request), said certificate good "to order" for its face value at any succeeding term.

Art and Music.

For information as to charges in Art and Music, see under these departments later in this Catalogue.

AID TO WORTHY STUDENTS.

Free tuition, beginning with the fall term after graduation, will be given to the student who graduates with highest rank from an approved High School. Students receiving this concession may be called upon for some College service.

Perpetual Scholarship.

Through the generosity of its friends the College is enabled to offer assistance to worthy students desiring to secure an education. The income of endowed scholarships is applied toward paying the tuition of a limited number.

Sixteen Perpetual scholarships of $1,000 each have been founded by the following named persons:

The F. R. E. Cornell Scholarship, by Mrs. E. O. Cornell.
The George B. Wright Scholarship, by Mrs. C. A. Wright.
The George Power Scholarship, by George and James E. Power.
The Mrs. Emma Mulliken Scholarship, by Mrs. Emma Mulliken.
The Clement F. LeFevre Scholarship, by William LeFevre and Mrs. Ellen R. Coleman.
The Samuel Bowles Scholarship, by Samuel Bowles.
The Dollie B. Lewis Scholarship, by Mrs. Dollie B. Lewis.

The O. B. Ayres Scholarship, by O. B. Ayres.
The Mary Chapin Perry Scholarship, by T. T. Perry.
The. C. A. Newcomb Scholarship, by C. A. Newcomb.
The Mary W. Conger Scholarship, by the children of Mrs. Mary W. Conger.
The Hattie A. Drowne, Scholarship, by Rev. E. L. Conger, D. D.
The A. R. Wolcott Scholarship, by A. R. Wolcott.
The Woman's Association Scholarship, by the Universalist Women's Association, of Illinois.
The Calista Waldron Slade Scholarship, by E. D. Waldron and sisters.
The Mary L. Pingrey Scholarship, by Mrs. Mary L. Pingrey.

BEQUESTS.

For the convenience of those who may wish to secure by bequest to the College, any given sum for a specific purpose, the accompanying form is here given

˙I hereby give and bequeath to The Lombard College, located at Galesburg, Ill............................Dollars ($......) for...............(state the object)............and direct that my executor pay said bequest to the Treasurer of said College within ....after my death.

(Signed)...............................
Dated......................... Witness.......................

CATALOGUES.

Former students of the College, whether graduates or not, are requested to inform the President of any change of residence in order that the publications of the College may be sent to them. Catalogues and circulars of information will promptly be sent to those who apply for them.

DISCIPLINE AND SOCIAL POLICY.

Aside from a few obvious regulations designed to secure punctuality and regularity in attendance on College exercises, and to protect students and teachers from disturbance while at work, no formal rules are imposed upon the students.

It is expected that, as young men and women of somewhat mature years, they will observe the usual forms of good breeding, and enjoy the ordinary privileges of good society in so far as the latter do not conflict with the best interests of the institution or with their own health and intellectual advancement.

Should any student show a disposition to engage in conduct detrimental to his own best interests, or to those of his fellow students or of the College, the faculty will deal with the case in such manner as will protect the common welfare of all.

THE GYMNASIUM.

OFFICERS OF THE COLLEGE.

CHARLES ELLWOOD NASH, A. M., S. T. D., PRESIDENT.

A. B., Lombard University, 1875; B. D., Tufts College, 1878; A. M., Lombard University, 1878; S. T. D., Tufts College, 1891; President Lombard College, 1895—1904.

FREDERICK WILLIAM RICH, D. Sc.

DEAN OF THE COLLEGE OF LIBERAL ARTS.

‡Conger Professor of Chemistry and Physics.

B. S., Cornell University, 1881; Graduate Student, Cornell University, 1881; D. Sc., St. Lawrence University, 1900; Instructor in Analytical Chemistry, Cornell University, 1882-84; Professor of Natural Science, Lombard College, 1884-1900; Professor of Chemistry and Physics, 1900—.

ALICE BERTHA CURTIS, B. DI., PH B.,

DEAN OF WOMEN.

Professor of English and Public Speaking.

B. Di., Iowa State Normal School, 1896; Student University of Iowa, 1900; Student University of Wisconsin, 1902; Ph. B., University of Iowa, 1903; Graduate student and tutor in English, University of Iowa, 1903; Professor of English and Public Speaking, and Dean of Women, Lombard College, 1903—.

ISAAC AUGUSTUS PARKER, A. M., PH. D.

*Williamson Professor of the Greek Language and Literature.

A. B., Dartmouth College, 1853; A. M., ibid, 1856; Ph. D., Buchtel College, 1892; Principal Orleans Liberal Institute, Glover, Vt., 1853-58; Professor of Ancient Languages, Lombard University, 1858-68; Professor of Greek Language and Literature, Lombard College, 1868—.

NEHEMIAH WHITE, A. M., PH. D., S. T. D.

†Hall Professor of Intellectual and Moral Philosophy.

In charge of the Ryder Divinity School, Professor of Biblical Languages and Exegesis.

A. B., Middlebury College, 1857; A. M., ibid, 1860; Ph. D., St. Lawrence University, 1876; S. T. D.. Tufts College, 1889; Associate Principal Green Mt. Perkins Institute, 1857-58; Principal Clinton Liberal Institute, 1859-60; Principal Pulaski Academy, 1865; Professor of Mathematics and Natural Science, St. Lawrence University, 1865-71; Professor of Ancient Languages Buchtel College, 1872-75; President Lombard University, 1875-92; in charge of Ryder Divinity School, and Professor of Biblical Languages and Exegesis, 1892—.

---

*In honor of the late I. D. Williamson, D. D., of Cincinnati.
†In honor of the late E. G. Hall, of Chicago.
‡In honor of the late L. E. Conger, of Dexter, Iowa.

JON WATSON GRUBB, M. S., REGISTRAR,
Instructor in Mathematics.

B. S., Lombard University, 1879; M. S., Lombard University, 1882; Adjunct Professor of Mathematics, Lombard University, 1882-94; Registrar Lombard College, 1893—; Professor of Latin, Lombard College, 1894-1903; Instructor in Mathematics, Lombard College, 1903—.

PHILIP GREEN WRIGHT, A. M.,
Professor of Mathematics, Astronomy and Economics.

A. M. B., Tufts College, 1884; A. M., Harvard University, 1887; Teacher of Mathematics and Science, Goddard Seminary, Vt., 1883; Adjunct Professor of Mathematics, Buchtel College, 1884-86; Professor of Mathematics, Lombard College, 1892—.

FRANK HAMILTON FOWLER, PH. D.,
Professor of Latin Language and Literature.

A. B., Lombard University, 1890; Ph. D., The University of Chicago, 1896; Graduate Student, Johns Hopkins University, 1890-91; Principal Peaster Academy, 1891-92; Fellow in the University of Chicago, 1892-96; Professor of English, Lombard College, 1897-1903; Professor Latin Language and Literature, Lombard College, 1903—.

RALPH GRIERSON KIMBLE, A. B.,
Professor of Sociology.

A. B., Lombard College, 1896; University Scholar in Sociology, University of Chicago, 1896-97; Senior Fellow in Sociology, ibid, 1897-1901; Special Lecturer in Sociology, Lombard College, Spring term, 1899; ibid, 1900; Special Lecturer in Sociological Theory, University of Wisconsin, Spring of 1902; Professor of Sociology, Lombard College, 1901—.

THADDEUS CAREY KIMBLE, A. B., M. D.,
Professor of Physiology and Biology, in charge of Medical Courses.

A. B., Lombard College, 1902; M. D., St. Louis College of Physicians and Surgeons, 1898; Instructor in Biology, Lombard College, 1900-02; Instructor in Medical Courses, Lombard College, 1902—.

EMMA B. WAIT,
Professor of French and German.

Principal of School, Los Angeles, California, 1881-83; Student École Sévigné, Sèvres, 1891; Université de Genève, 1896-98; The University of Chicago, 1899; Professor of French and German, Lombard College, 1899—.

WILLIS S. KIENHOLZ, B. S.,
Physical Director and Professor of Zoology and Botany.

Special student in Biological Science, University of Minnesota, 1897-1901; Member of Minnesota Zoological Survey, 1898-1901; B. S., Lombard College, 1903; Assistant in University of Minnesota Botanical Herbarium, 1899-1900; Member of foot-ball, basket-ball, and track teams, University of Minnesota, 1897-1901; Instructor in Biology and Athletcis, Crookston High School, 1901-02; Physical Director, Coach, and Instructor in Zoology, Lombard College, 1902—.

EDSON REIFSNIDER, B. D.,
Instructor in Homiletics and Pastoral Care.

B. D., Tufts College, 1898; Instructor in Homiletics and Pastoral Care, Lombard College, 1903—.

M. AGNES HATHAWAY,
Instructor in History.

Graduate from Genesee Wesleyan Seminary, Lima, New York, 1888; Student at National Normal University, Lebanon, Ohio, 1895-96; Teacher in Public Schools of New York and Illinois; Dean of Women and Instructor in Preparatory School, Lombard College, 1900-03; Instructor in History, Lombard College, 1903—.

ANNA GILLIS KIMBLE,
Instructor in English.

ALEXANDER STEWART THOMPSON,
Director of Department of Music.

Springfield, Mass., Conservatory of Music, 1875-79; Private Studio, Albany, N. Y., 1879-84; Director of Music, Saratoga Springs, N. Y., Public Schools, 1884-87; Student of Voice, William Courtney, New York City, 1887; Private Studio, Utica, N. Y., 1887-90; Student of Piano, Kelso and Sherwood, 1890; Director of Music, Kansas State Normal, 1890-91; Norfolk, Va., Ladies College, 1891-92; Student Guildhall School of Music (Sims Reeves) London, Eng., and Dr. W. E. Gladstone, Royal College of Music, London, Eng., 1892-93; Oneida Conservatory of Music and Utica School of Music, Utica, N. Y., 1893-97; Director of Music, Lincoln, Ill., College, 1897-1903; Director of Music, Lombard College, 1903—.

CLARA DUTTON THOMPSON,
Associate Director of Department of Music.

Graduate in Music, Cazenovia, N. Y., Seminary, 1886; Church Singer, Syracuse and Utica, N. Y., 1886-90; Teacher of Voice, Kansas State Normal, 1890-91; Norfolk, Va., Ladies' College, 1891-92, Student Alberto Randegger, London, Eng., Guildhall School of Music (Sims Reeves) London, England, 1892-93; Teacher of Voice, Houghton Seminary, Clinton, N. Y., and Utica, N. Y., 1893-97; Teacher of Voice, Lincoln, Ill., College, 1897-1903; Teacher of Voice, Lombard College, 1903—.

W. H. CHEESMAN,
Instructor in Violin.

M. ISABELLE BLOOD,
Instructor in Drawing and Painting.

Studied with Dean Fletcher, N. Y., William Bertram, Chicago; at the Art Institute and with Nellie Davis, St. Louis; Instructor in Drawing and Painting, Lombard College, 1889—.

ADA M. H. HALE,
Matron Ladies' Hall.

DR. GUY A. LONGBRAKE AND DR. DELIA M. RICE,
Medical Examiners.

NON-RESIDENT LECTURER.
REV. I. M. ATWOOD, D. D.

FRANK HAMILTON FOWLER, PH. D.,
Librarian.

JON WATSON GRUBB, M. S.,
Registrar.

FREDERICK WILLIAM RICH, D. Sc.,
Curator of the Museum.

WILLIS S. KIENHOLZ, B. S.,
Director of the Gymnasium.

ALLEN HARSHBARGER,
Janitor.

Standing Faculty Committees.

ADVISORY—
PROFESSORS WRIGHT AND FOWLER.

CREDITS—
PROFESSORS PARKER AND RICH.

HOMES FOR NEW STUDENTS—
PROFESSORS FOWLER AND T. C. KIMBLE.

CATALOGUE—
PROFESSORS WRIGHT AND FOWLER.

HIGHER DEGREES—
PRESIDENT NASH AND PROFESSOR PARKER.

LIBRARY—
PROFESSORS WHITE AND R. G. KIMBLE.

CHAPEL EXCUSES—
PROFESSORS RICH AND FOWLER.

CHAPEL EXERCISES—
PRESIDENT NASH, PROFS. WAIT AND THOMPSON.

ATHLETICS—
PROFESSORS KIENHOLZ AND WRIGHT.

ORDER AND DISCIPLINE—
PRESIDENT NASH, PROF. RICH AND MISS CURTIS.

Departments of the College.

Students at Lombard are divided primarily into Classified and Unclassified Students.

The Classified department includes all students who are candidates for a degree or diploma. It embraces the College of Liberal Arts, the Divinity School, and the Schools of Music and Art.

The Unclassified department includes students who are pursuing studies at Lombard for a greater or less period, without any express intention of obtaining a degree or diploma.

COLLEGE OF LIBERAL ARTS.

Faculty of Liberal Arts.

CHARLES ELLWOOD NASH, A. M., S. T. D., PRESIDENT.

FREDERICK WILLIAM RICH, D. Sc.
‡ Dean and Conger Professor of Chemistry and Physics.

ALICE BERTHA CURTIS, B. DI., PH. B.,
Dean of Women and Professor of English and Public Speaking.

ISAAC AUGUSTUS PARKER, A. M., PH. D.,
*Williamson Professor of the Greek Language and Literature.

NEHEMIAH WHITE, A. M., PH. D., S. T. D.,
† Hall Professor of Intellectual and Moral Philosophy.

JON WATSON GRUBB, M. S.,
Instructor in Mathematics.

PHILIP GREEN WRIGHT, A. M.,
Professor of Mathematics, Astronomy and Economics.

* In honor of the late I. D. Williamson, D. D., of Cincinnati.
† In honor of the late E. G. Hall, of Chicago.
‡ In honor of the late L. E. Conger, of Dexter, Iowa.

FRANK HAMILTON FOWLER, Ph. D.,
Professor of Latin Language and Literature.

RALPH GRIERSON KIMBLE, A. B.,
Professor of Sociology.

THADDEUS CAREY KIMBLE, A. B., M. D.,
Professor of Physiology and Biology, in charge of Medical Courses.

WILLIS S. KIENHOLZ, B. S.,
Physical Director and Instructor in Zoology and Botany.

EMMA B. WAIT,
Professor of French and German.

Degrees Conferred in 1903.

MASTER OF ARTS.

Edwin Julius McCullough.........................*Sparland*

BACHELOR OF ARTS.

Andrew, Mary Maud.............................*New Salem*
Brown, Athol Ray................................*N. Henderson*
Campbell, Raymond R............................*De Land*
Fosher, Claude Dudley..........................*Galesburg*
Gillis, Anna Moore.............................*Mt. Pleasant, Ia.*
Hartgrove, Claude Webster......................*Galesburg*
Miller, Ralph Todd.............................*Monmouth*
Needham, Nellie Jeanette.......................*Racine, Wis.*
Rees, Jenkins B................................*Oneida*

BACHELOR OF SCIENCE.

Kienholz, Willis Simon.........................*Galesburg*

BACHELOR OF DIVINITY.

Nieveen, S. Martin.............................*Platte, S. Dak.*

DIPLOMAS IN MUSIC.

Cook, Sarah Lucy...............................*Galesburg*
Elting, Grace Helen............................*Sperry, Ia.*
Nash, Faith Tenney.............................*Galesburg*
Sommers, Elsie Dorothy.........................*Burlington, Ia.*
Willis, Leura..................................*Table Grove*
Wrigley, Anne Marion...........................*Chicago*

Requirements for Admission.

All applicants for admission to the College of Liberal Arts, except those from certain approved High Schools and Academies, are required to pass satisfactory examinations in studies selected from the following list, to an aggregate of sixteen units:

STUDY.	UNITS.	STUDY.	UNITS.
English	3	Physics	1
Greek	3	Chemistry	1
Latin	3	Physiography	½ to 1
German	1	Physiology	½ to 1
French	1	Botany	½ to 1
Ancient History	1	Astronomy	1
English and American His.	1	Meteorology	1
Algebra	1½	Political Economy	½ to 1
Plane Geometry	½ to 1	Zoology	½ to 1
Solid Geometry	½ to 1		

CONSTANTS.

The studies presented must include the following constants:

STUDIES.	UNITS.
English	3
One Foreign Language	3
History	1
Algebra	1½
Geometry	½
Science	2
	11

The two units in Science, one of which must include laboratory work, may be chosen from the following, viz: Physics, Chemistry, Physiography, Anatomy and Physiology, Botany, Zoology.

EXAMINATIONS.

Examinations in the above studies will be held during the first week in September, as follows:

HOUR.	TUESDAY, SEPT. 5.	WEDNESDAY, SEPT. 6.	THURS., SEPT. 7.
7:30- 9:30	English.	French.	Plane Geometry.
9:30-11:30	Greek—Astronomy.	Ancient History.	Physics.
11:30-12:30	Physiology.	Physiography.	Botany.
2:00- 4:00	Latin.	Algebra.	Chemistry.
4:00- 6:00	German—Solid Geom.	Eng. and Am. Hist.	Zoology—Pol. Ec.

ADMISSION BY CERTIFICATE.

In harmony with the recommendation of the joint committee of the High School and College sections of the Illinois State Teachers' Association, certificates from the principals or other authorized officers of certain approved High Schools and Academies will be accepted in lieu of examinations. *But these certificates must be presented during the term in which the student applies for admission in order to be accepted,* and no certificate will be valid for more than two years after the completion of the course of study to which the certificate refers. The credit allowed on them will be based upon the work accomplished; in general, one unit being equal to a year's work in a study reciting five hours a week in recitation periods of not less than forty minutes.

The detailed descriptions given below indicate more fully the amount of work required in each study to obtain the number of units given in the table. Students admitted by certificate enter classes on probation, and if after a week's trial it is found that their previous training is insufficient to render it advisable for them to continue in these classes, they will be assigned other work.

SCOPE OF PREPARATORY STUDIES.

The amount of work required in the several Preparatory studies to obtain the units assigned in the foregoing table, either by examination or certificate, is indicated by the following outline of examination requirements:

ENGLISH.

The examination will occupy two hours and will consist of two parts, which, however, cannot be taken separately:—

I. The candidate will be required to write a paragraph or two on each of several topics chosen by him from a considerable number—perhaps ten or fifteen—set before him on the examination paper.

In 1904, 1905, and 1906, the topics will be drawn from the following works:

Shakespeare's Merchant of Venice, and Julius Cæsar; The Sir Roger de Coverley Papers in the Spectator; Goldsmith's Vicar of Wakefield; Coleridge's Ancient Mariner; Scott's Ivanhoe; Carlyle's Essay on Burns; Tennyson's Princess; Lowell's Vision of Sir Launfal; George Eliot's Silas Marner.

The candidate is expected to read intelligently *all* the books prescribed. He should read them as he reads other books; he is expected, not to know them minutely, but to have freshly in mind their most important parts. In every case the examiner will regard knowledge of the book as less important than ability to write English.

II. A certain number of books are prescribed for careful study. This part of the examination will be upon subject-matter, literary form and logical structure, and will also test the candidate's ability to express his knowledge with clearness and accuracy.

The books prescribed for this part of the examination in 1904, 1905, and 1906, are: Shakespeare's Macbeth; Milton's Lycidas, Comus, L'Allegro, and Il Penseroso; Burke's Speech on Conciliation with America; Macaulay's Essays on Milton and Addison.

No candidate will be accepted in English whose work is seriously defective in point of spelling, punctuation, grammar, or division into paragraphs.

In connection with the reading and study of the prescribed books, parallel or subsidary reading should be encouraged, and a considerable amount of English poetry should be committed to memory. The essentials of English grammar should not be neglected in preparatory study.

The English written by a candidate in any of his examination-books may be regarded as part of his examination in English, in case the evidence afforded by the examination-book in English is insufficient.

As additional evidence of preparation the candidate may present an exercise book, properly certified by his instructor, containing compositions or other written work.

FRENCH.

(a) The translation at sight of ordinary Nineteenth Century prose. (The passages set for translation must be rendered into simple and idiomatic English.)

(b) The translation into French of simple English sentences or of easy connected prose, to test the candidate's familiarity with elementary grammar. Proficiency in grammar may also be tested by direct questions, based on the passages set for translation under *(a)*.

The passages set for translation into English will be suited to the proficiency of candidates who have read not less than four hundred pages (including reading at sight in class) from the works of at least three different auhors. It is desirable that a portion of the reading should be from works other than works of fiction.

Grammar should be studied concurrently with the reading as an indispensable means of insuring thoroughness and accuracy in the understanding of the language. The requirement in elementary grammar includes the conjugations of regular verbs, of the more frequent irregular verbs, such as *aller, envoyer, tenir, pouvoir, voir, vouloir, dire, savoir, faire,* and those belonging to the classes represented by *ouvrir, dormir, connaitre, conduire,* and *craindre;* the forms and positions of personal pronouns and of possessive, demonstrative, and interrogative adjectives; the inflection of nouns and adjectives for gender and number, except rare cases; the uses of articles, and the partitive constructions.

Pronunciation should be carefully taught, and pupils should have frequent opportunities to hear French spoken or read aloud. The writing of French from dictation is recommended as a useful exercise.

GERMAN.

(a) The translation at sight of simple German prose. (The passages set for translation must be rendered into simple and idiomatic English.)

(b) The translation into German of simple English sentences, or of easy connected prose, to test the candidate's familiarity with elementary grammar.

The passages set for translation into English will be suited to the proficiency of candidates who have read not less than two hundred pages of easy German (including reading at sight in class.)

Grammar should be studied concurrently with the reading as an indispensable means of insuring thoroughness and accuracy in the understanding of the language. The requirement in elementary grammar includes the conjugation of the weak and the more usual strong verbs; the declension of articles, adjectives, pronouns and such nouns as are readily classified; the commoner prepositions; the simpler uses of the modal auxiliaries; the elements of syntax, especially the rules governing the order of words.

Pronunciation should be carefully taught, and the pupils should have frequent opportunities to hear German spoken or read aloud. The writing of German from dictation is recommended as a useful exercise.

LATIN.

The examination in Latin will consist of two parts.

I. Elementary Latin.

This examination will be designed to test the proficiency of those who have studied Latin in the high school for two years, and will count as two admission units. The student should have read at least four books of the Gallic War or an equivalent. (The use of a Second Year Latin Book is recommended.) The examination will include:—

(a) Translation at sight of Latin prose, with questions on ordinary forms, constructions, and idioms of the language.

(b) The translation into Latin of English sentences involving a knowledge of the more common words and constructions used by Cæsar.

II. Advanced Latin.

This examination will be designed to test the proficiency of those who have studied Latin in the high school for four years and together with I will count as four admission units. In preparation for this examination the candidate should have read, besides the four books of Cæsar mentioned under I, at least six orations of Cicero and six books of Vergil's Aeneid, and should have had considerable practice in reading at sight and in Latin composition. The examination will include:—

(a) Translation at sight of passages of Latin prose and hexameter verse, with questions on ordinary forms, constructions, and idioms, and the principles of Latin verse.

(b) The translation into Latin prose of a passage of connected English narrative, limited in subject matter to the works usually read in preparation.

MATHEMATICS.

Algebra. The examination in Algebra will demand accuracy in the several processes of literal Arithmetic. Special emphasis will be laid on factoring, and the correct manipulation of negative and fractional exponents. It will include the solution of simple and quadratic equations (together with a knowledge of the theory of quadratic equations) and elimination in the case of simultaneous equations of the first and second degrees.

Plane Geometry. The examination in Plane Geometry will emphasize precision in the definition of Geometric terms, and accuracy in the demonstration of Geometric theorems. In scope it will demand a knowledge of all the propositions in Plane Geometry preceding Solid Geometry, included in such a standard text book in this subject as Phillips and Fisher's Elements.

Solid Geometry. As in Plane Geometry emphasis will be laid upon accuracy in definition and demonstration. In scope the examination will cover the propositions in Solid Geometry included in such a standard text book as Phillips and Fisher's Elements.

ASTRONOMY.

The examination in this subject will demand knowledge of descriptive rather than mathematical Astronomy. The student will be expected to understand the theory of the celestial sphere; simple methods of computing latitude, time, and longitude; the astronomical features of the earth, the sun, and the moon; the principles of spectrum analysis; the motions and characteristics of the planets; the names and myths of the principal stars and constellations; the facts in regard to aberration, parallax, and proper motion of the stars; and the principles of a rational cosmogony as developed in La Place's nebular hypothesis. Young's Lessons in Astronomy is suggested as a text book embracing the matter with which students are expected to be acquainted who wish to prepare for this examination.

PHYSICS.

Students offering Physics for entrance credit must show an acquaintance with the more important phenomena and with the principles involved in the explanation of them. They must, in addition to the text book work, have completed a course of laboratory experiments and be able to work simple numerical problems, involving the laws of falling bodies; pendulum; properties of liquids and gases; thermometry and calorimetry; current strength, resistance, and electromotive force; properties of sound, refraction and reflection with the size and position of images.

CHEMISTRY.

The Elementary Course in Chemistry offered for entrance credit must include a knowledge of the elements and compounds equivalent to that given in Remsen's Introduction to the study of Chemistry. In addition, students must have had a series of laboratory experiments illustrating the text book work and be able to write equations and solve simple chemical problems.

BOTANY.

Students presenting work in Botany for entrance credit should have a knowledge of the general laws and fundamental principles of plant nutrition, assimilation, growth, etc., as exemplified by plants chosen from the different groups, as well as the general comparative morphology and the broader relationships of plants. They should present an herbarium of at least twenty-five specimens, collected and mounted by themselves and certified to by their instructor.

ZOOLOGY.

Students desiring entrance credit for Zoology should have devoted the equivalent of five periods a week for at least one-half year to the study of general Zoology. A portion of this work must have been laboratory practice in the observation of living forms and dissection. Their laboratory notes and drawings, endorsed by the instructor, should be presented at the time of registration as evidence of the nature of this part of the work. This laboratory practice should include a study of at least twelve of the forms named in the following list: Amœba, paramœcium, sea-anemone, star-fish, sea-urchin, earth-worm, cray-fish, lobster, spider, centipede, locust, (grasshopper), dragon-fly, squash-bug, bumblebee, clam, snail, a simple tunicate, shark, any soft rayed-fish, snake, turtle, frog, pigeon, rabbit, and cat.

PHYSIOLOGY.

Students presenting work in human Physiology for entrance credit should have a general knowledge of the human skeleton, muscular, circulatory, and nervous systems, the vital organs, viscera, and organs of special sense, and the processes of respiration and digestion.

The text-book used should cover the ground treated in such books as Martin's Human Body, or Huxley's Elementary Physiology (Lee's Revision.)

PHYSIOGRAPHY.

A course of study equivalent to Tarr's Elementary Physical Geography.

The examination will include a thorough test on all the leading subjects treated in Physical Geography, with maps to illustrate relief forms, currents, ocean beds, and the distribution of animal and plant life.

HISTORY (including Historical Geography).

Either of the two following groups, each including two fields of historical study :—

1. *Greek and Roman History.—(a)* Greek History to the death of Alexander, with due reference to Greek life, literature, and art. *(b)* Roman History to the downfall of the Western Roman Empire, with due reference to literature and government.

2. *English and American History.—(a)* English History, with due reference to social and political development. *(b)* American History, with the elements of Civil Government.

For preparation in each of the two historical fields presented, a course of study equivalent to at least three lessons a week for one year will be necessary.

The candidate will be expected to show on examination such general knowledge of each field as may be acquired from the study of an accurate text book of not less than 300 pages, supplemented by suitable parallel readings amounting to less than 500 pages.. The examination will call for comparison of historical characters, periods, and events, and in general for the exercise of judgment as well as of memory. Geographical knowledge will be tested by means of an outline map.

It is desirable that Greek and Roman History be offered as a part of the preparation of every candidate.

POLITICAL ECONOMY.

The examination in Political Economy will demand a thorough knowledge of the fundamental economic laws relating to Production, Exchange, Distribution, and Consumption. The applicant will also be expected to discuss intelligently from an economic standpoint such questions as Free Trade, Socialism, Strikes, and Taxation. Bullock's Introduction to the Study of Economics is suggested as a text covering the ground required for the examination.

ADMISSION TO ADVANCED STANDING.

Students from other institutions, who present letters of honorable dismissal, may be admitted to such standing and upon such terms as the Faculty may deem equitable. Every such student is required to present, along with the catalogue of the institution in which he has studied, a full statement, duly certified, of the studies he has completed, including preparatory studies. Candidates for advanced standing who wish to receive credit for work accomplished in private study, are permitted to take examinations in such subjects upon payment of the regular term fee for the course in which the examination is taken. A minimum residence of the two terms next preceding the completion of the requirements for graduation, and a minimum of eight courses taken in this College, are required of all applicants for a baccalaureate degree.

Requirements for Graduation.

GROUP SYSTEM.

Having been admitted to the College of Liberal Arts, the student will elect one of the following groups as a course of study leading to his degree. These groups consist of certain required studies arranged logically with reference to some central subject, in addition to which, considerable option is allowed in the way of free electives. All the required studies, together with a sufficient number of electives to bring the total up to an aggregate of thirty-eight credits, must be completed before the degree will be conferred. A credit is obtained by the satisfactory completion of one full course pursued for one term. Of the thirty-eight credits at least twenty-four must be above grade C. Two credits may be obtained by two full years' work in the Gymnasium classes.

THESIS.

In addition to the above requirements, every student who is a candidate for a degree, or a diploma, will present a graduation thesis upon some subject in which he, or she, has prosecuted original research or special study.

The subject for the thesis is to be approved by the professor under whose direction the work is to be done and by the advisory committee and is to be recorded as a part of the regular registration at the beginning of the fall term. The student will prepare monthly reports on the work done and these reports, approved by the professor, will be filed in the office of the President. At the end of the winter term the student will prepare a syllabus of the dissertation on the chosen subject, to be approved and filed as in the case of reports. Two weeks before commencement the student will present a dissertation embodying the results of his work, this dissertation to meet the approval of the faculty before recommendation for a degree is made.

For work done in preparing his thesis the student will receive college credits to such an extent as the professor in whose department the work is done shall deem him entitled. The number of credits received in this way, however, is not to exceed three.

ADVANCED DEGREE.

The degree of Master of Arts will be conferred upon graduates of this college or other institutions of equal rank, on the satisfactory completion of one year's residence work upon a course of study or research which shall have been submitted to and approved by the Faculty beyond the requirements for the baccalaureate degree. The candidate must present a thesis showing original research in the special line of study pursued.

GROUPS.

On being admitted to the College of Liberal Arts, each student, who is a candidate for a degree, will elect one of these groups:

ENGLISH GROUP.

YEAR.	HOUR.	FALL TERM.	WINTER TERM.	SPRING TERM.
1st yr.	8:00 9:30 10:30	Germ. 1. Chem. 1. Eng. 5.	Germ. 2. Chem. 2. Eng. 6.	Germ. 3. Sociology. Eng. 7.
2nd yr.	8:00 10:30 1:45	Eng. 25 and 28. Germ. 4 or 5. Lat. 10.	Eng. 26 and 29. Germ. 6 or 7. Lat. 11.	Eng. 27 and 30. Germ. 8 or 9. Lat. 12.
3rd yr.	8:00 10:30 11:30 1:45	Eng. 31 and 34. Math. 7. Hist. 8.	Eng. 32 and 35. Math. 8. Hist. 9.	Eng. 33 and 36. Psychology. Math. 9.
4th yr.	8:00	Eng. 19 and 22. Elective. Elective.	Eng. 20 and 23. Elective. Elective.	Eng. 21 and 24. Elective. Elective.

LATIN SCIENTIFIC.

YEAR.	HOUR.	FALL TERM.	WINTER TERM.	SPRING TERM.
1st yr.	9:30 10:30 1:45	{ Chem. 1 or { French 1 Eng. 5. Lat. 10.	{ Chem. 2 or { French 2. Eng. 6. Lat. 11.	j Chem. 3 or ı French 3. Lat. 12.
2nd yr.	8:00 9:30 10:30 11:30	{ Germ. 1 or ı Chem. 1. Math. 7.	{ Germ. 2 or ı Chem. 2. Math. 8.	j Germ. 3 or ı Chem. 3. Psychology. Math. 9.
3rd yr.	8:00 9:30 10:30 11:30	Physics 1. Gen. Biol. 1. { Germ. 4 or 5, { or { French 4 or 5.	Physics 2. Biol. 2. { Germ. 6 or 7, { or { French 6 or 7.	Physics 3. Sociology. { Germ. 8 or 9, { or { French 8 or 9.
4th yr.	1:45	Elective. Elective. Hist. 8.	Elective. Elective. Hist. 9,	Elective. Elective.

MODERN LANGUAGE.

YEAR	HOUR.	FALL TERM.	WINTER TERM.	SPRING TERM.
1st yr.	8:00 9:30 10:30	Germ. 1. Chem. 1. Eng. 5	Germ. 2. Chem. 2. Eng. 6.	Germ. 3. Sociology.
2nd yr.	9:30 10:30 11:30	French 1. Germ. 4 or 5. Math. 7.	French 2. Germ. 6 or 7. Math. 8.	French 3. Germ. 8 or 9. Math. 9.
3rd yr.	9:30 10:30 11:30 1:45	Germ. 4 or 5. French 4 or 5. Hist. 8.	Germ. 6 or 7. French 6 or 7. Hist. 9.	Psychology. Germ. 8 or 9. French 8 or 9.
4th yr.	11:30	French 4 or 5.	French 6 or 7.	French 8 or 9.

CLASSICAL GROUP.

YEAR.	HOUR.	FALL TERM.	WINTER TERM.	SPRING TERM.
1st yr.	11:30 10:30 1:45	Greek 1. Eng. 5. Lat. 10.	Greek 2. Eng. 6. Lat. 11.	Greek 3. Psychology. Lat. 12.
2nd yr.	8:00 9:30 10:30	Germ. 1. Chem. 1. Greek 4.	Germ. 2. Chem. 2. Greek 5.	Germ. 3. Chem. 3. Greek 6.
3rd yr.	8:00 10:30 1:45 9:30	Greek 7 or 10. Germ. 4, 5. Hist. 8.	Greek 8 or 11. Germ. 6, 7. Hist. 9.	Greek 9 or 12. Germ. 8, 9. Sociology.
4th yr.	8:00	Elective.	Elective.	Elective.

MATHEMATICS.

YEAR.	HOUR.	FALL TERM.	WINTER TERM.	SPRING TERM.
1st yr.	9:00 10:30 11:30	Chem. 1. Eng. 5. Math. 7.	Chem. 2. Eng. 6. Math. 8.	Chem. 3. Math. 9.
2nd yr.	8:00 9:30 10:30 1:45	Ger. 1 or French 1. Math. 10. or Ast. 1.	Germ. 2 or French 2. Math. 12 or 14.	Germ. 3 or French 3. Psychology 1. Math. 13 or 16.
3rd yr.	8:00 10:30 11:30 1:45	Physics 1. German 4 or 5. or French 4 or 5. Ast. 1 or Math. 10.	Physics 2 Ger. 6 or 7. or French 6 or 7 Math. 14 or 12.	Physics 3. Germ. 8 or 9 or French 8 or 9. Math. 16 or 13.
4th yr.	9:30 1:45	Hist. 8.	Hist. 9.	Sociology.

BIOLOGY AND CHEMISTRY.

YEAR.	HOUR.	FALL TERM.	WINTER TERM.	SPRING TERM.
1st yr.	9:30 11:30 11:30	Chem. 1. Bot. 1 or Zool. 1.	Chem. 2. Bot. 2 or Zool. 2.	Chem. 3. Bot. 3 or Zool. 3.
2nd yr.	* 8:00 ‡ 9:30 10:30 1:45	Germ. 1 or French 1. Eng. 5. Chem. 4.	Germ. 2 or French 2. Eng. 6. Chem. 7.	Germ. 3 or French 3. Psychology. Chem. 5 or 6.
3rd yr.	9:30 8:00 *10:30 11:30	Biol. 1. Physiology 2. Germ. 10 ($\frac{1}{2}$). Math. 7.	Biol. 2. Physiology 2b. Germ. 11 ($\frac{1}{2}$) Math. 8.	Physiology 3. Germ. 12 ($\frac{1}{2}$). Math. 9.
4th yr.	8:00 9:30 10:30 ‡11:30	Physics 1. French 10 ($\frac{1}{2}$)	Physics 2. Geology. French 11 ($\frac{1}{2}$).	Physics 3. Sociology. French 12 ($\frac{1}{2}$)

*If German is chosen as the modern language, German 10, 11, and 12 must be taken in the 4th year.
‡If French is chosen as the modern language, French 10, 11, and 12 must be taken in the 4th year.

CHEMISTRY AND PHYSICS.

YEAR.	HOUR.	FALL TERM.	WINTER TERM.	SPRING TERM.
1st yr.	8:00 9:30 10:30 11:30	Germ. 1 or French 1. Eng. 5. Math. 7.	Germ. 2 or French 2. Eng. 6. Math. 8.	Germ. 3 or French 3. Math. 9.
2nd yr.	9:30 10:30 11:30	Chem. 1. Germ. 4 or 5. or French 4 or 5.	Chem. 2. Germ. 6 or 7. or French 6 or 7.	Chem. 3. Germ, 8 or 9 or French 8 or 9.
3rd yr.	8:00 9:30 10:30 1:45	Astronomy. Biol. 1. Chem. 4.	Biol. 2. Geology. Chem 5.	Sociology. Psychology. Chem. 6.
4th yr.	8:00 1:45	Physics 1. Chem. 8.	Physics 2. Chem. 7.	Physics 3.

SOCIAL SCIENCE.

YEAR.	HOUR.	FALL TERM.	WINTER TERM.	SPRING TERM.
1st yr.	9:30 10:30 11:30	Chem. 1. Eng. 5. Math. 7.	Chem. 3. Eng. Lit. Math. 8.	Sociology 1. Psychology 1. Math. 9.
2nd yr.	*8:00 *9:30 1:45	Germ. 1 or French 1. Hist. 8.	Germ. 2 or French 2. Hist. 9.	Germ 3 or French 3. Hist. 10.
3rd yr.	9:30 11:30	Economics 2.	Economics 3.	Economics 4. Sociology 2.
4th yr.	9:30 10:30		Gen. Biol. 1. —— Ethics.	Gen. Biol. 2.

PREPARATORY MEDICAL.

YEAR.	HOUR.	FALL TERM.	WINTER TERM.	SPRING TERM.
1st yr.	9:30 10:30 11:30	Chem. 1. Eng. 5. Math. 7.	Chem. 2. Eng. Lit. Math. 8.	Chem. 3. Sociology 1. Math. 9.
2nd yr.	8:00 9:30 1:45	Germ. 1. Biol. 1. Chem. 4.	Germ. 2. Biol. 2. Hist. (a) ½.	Germ. 3. Psychology 1. Hist. (b) ½.
3rd yr.	8:00 9:30 10:30 1:45	Physics 1. Germ. 4 or 5. Chem. 5.	Physics 2. Zool. 2 or 3. Chem. 7.	Physics 3. Botany 1 or 2. Osteol. ¼.
4th yr.	8:00 11:30 1:45	Physiology 2. Mat. Med. ½. Osteol. ½.	Physiology 2b. Mat. Med. ½. Anatomy 2.	Physiology 3. Embryology.

*A student must obtain a reading knowledge of one of these languages before entering upon his third year.

Courses of Instruction.

RECITATIONS AND CREDITS.

The following studies are classed as full courses or fractional courses, according to the estimated amount of work in each, and its value in fulfilling the requirements for graduation. Unless otherwise stated, a course in any study consists of five hours of recitations or lectures, per week, for one term. Certain full courses, however, are given in three hours per week recitations. Laboratory courses require ten hours of work per week in the Laboratory, in addition to a considerable amount of study outside. Certain other studies, as indicated in each case, count only as half courses, or less. It is intended to give each course during the year and term indicated. But the faculty reserves the right to make any change when it seems desirable to do so.

The general descriptions at the head of each department and the brief outline accompanying each course are designed to give in simple language the scope and purpose of the course to assist the student in making his elections.

The student is urged especially to notice the dependence of one course on another, so that in arranging his group, before electing any course, the prerequisite shall have been completed.

Courses in brackets will not be given in 1904-1905.

ENGLISH.

The study of English is considered of fundamental importance. For this reason thorough preparation in English is insisted on for admission to the College proper. The practical value of this study need hardly be mentioned. No matter what the occupation, there will be the necessity for expression, and this is to be obtained by the study of English. Closely related to this is the value attaching to the study as a preparation for other work of the College course. The ability to gather thought from the printed page rapidly and accurately, and the power of expression just mentioned, are prime requisites for the student. A peculiar value attaching to the study of English is that of correlating the studies of the curriculum, of making the college course more of a unit. History, Philosophy, Linguistics, Aesthetics, and Sociology may here find a common ground of meeting. As a corollary to this it may be said that English to an especial degree possesses the power of enlarging the student's mental horizon, of making a broader man of him. It is the aim of the department to utilize all these values of the study, and in order to do that to the full the endeavor is made so to foster a love of literature that the study will be pursued after the student has left college.

Primarily the object of the courses in English Composition (5, 6, and 7) is the acquiring on the part of the student the ability to write good English prose. It is believed, however, that the study properly pursued has a considerable disciplinary value. In these courses there is a minimum of theory and a maximum of practice. The important principles are given in lectures; these principles are illustrated in the specimens of the writings of others; and the student is required to exemplify them in the preparation of daily and fortnightly themes. Courses 5 and 6 are required courses and, together with course 7, should be taken during the first year of college work.

In the courses in English Literature emphasis is laid on criticism rather than on the history. An introduction is made to the several forms of literature, special attention being given to the chief representative authors of each department. One course is given in Old English and one in the History of the English Language. The courses dealing with the Literature and Language are arranged in a cycle covering three years. The student is enabled to specialize in this study to such a degree that he may, without further preparation, undertake graduate work in the Universities.

5. Rhetoric and Composition.
Fall term.   Professor Curtis.
Open to all college students.

6. The Forms of Discourse.
Winter term.   Professor Curtis.
Prerequisite, English 5.

7. The Forms of Discourse. (Continued.)
Spring term.   Professor Curtis.
Prerequisite, English 5.

[19. Middle English. (Two-fifths course.)]
Lectures on the life and times of Chaucer. Chaucer's shorter poems and "Canterbury Tales" will form the basis of the work. Tuesdays and Thursdays. Fall term.   Professor Curtis.
Prerequisite, English 5.

[20. **English Essayists.** (Two-fifths course.)]

A study of typical essays of Macaulay, DeQuincy, Carlyle, Burke, and Arnold, with special reference to style. Tuesdays and Thursdays. Winter term.   Professor CURTIS.

Prerequisite, English 5.

[21. **The Novel.** (Two-fifths course.)]

This art form will be considered. Some of the great novels of the Victorian Age will be read and criticised. Tuesdays and Thursdays. Spring term.   Professor CURTIS.

Prerequisite, English 5.

[22. **Art of Shakespeare.** (Three-fifths course.)]

The elements of literary art as exemplified in Shakespeare. A detailed study of "Hamlet." Mondays, Wednesdays, and Fridays. Fall term.   Professor CURTIS.

Prerequisite, English 5.

[23. **Art of Shakespeare.** (Three-fifths course.)]

Detailed study of "King Lear." Mondays, Wednesdays, and Fridays. Winter term.   Professor CURTIS.

Prerequisite, English 22.

[24. **Art of Shakespeare.** (Three-fifths course.)]

"The Tempest," "As You Like It," "Antony and Cleopatra," "Julius Cæsar." Mondays, Wednesdays, and Fridays. Spring term.
     Professor CURTIS.

Prerequisite, English 22 and 23.

25. **History of English Literature to the time of Chaucer.**
[Two-fifths course.]

Tuesdays and Thursdays. Fall. term.
     Professor CURTIS.

Prerequisite, English 5.

26. **History of English Literature from Chaucer to Shakespeare.**
[Two-fifths course.]

Tuesdays and Thursdays. Winter term.
     Professor CURTIS.

Prerequisite, English 5.

27. **History of English Literature from Shakespeare to Browning.**
[Two-fifths course.]

Tuesdays and Thursdays. Spring term.
     Professor CURTIS.

Prerequisite, English 26.

28. Browning. [Three-fifths course.]

Studies in the poems of Robert Browning. Mondays, Wednesdays, and Fridays. Fall term.   Professor CURTIS.

Prerequisite, English 5.

29. Tennyson. [Three-fifths course.]

Studies in the shorter poems and "Idylls of the King." Mondays, Wednesdays, and Fridays. Winter term.

Professor CURTIS.

Prerequisite, English 5.

30. English and Scottish Ballads. [Three-fifths course.]

The nature of ballad poetry together with reading and interpretation of selected ballads. Mondays, Wednesdays, and Fridays. Spring term.   Professor CURTIS.

Prerequisite, English 5.

[31. Old English. (Three-fifths course.)]

A study of the grammar of Old English and of the relatives between Old and Modern English. Mondays, Wednesdays, and Fridays. Fall term.   Professor CURTIS.

Prerequisite, English 5.

[32. Milton. (Three-fifths course.)]

The shorter poems and "Paradise Lost" will be studied. Mondays, Wednesdays, and Fridays. Winter term.

Professor CURTIS.

Prerequisite; English 5.

[33. Pre Shakespearean Drama. (Three-fifths course.)]

A history of the English drama before the time of Shakespeare. Some of the old Miracle and Morality plays will be studied. Mondays, Wednesdays, and Fridays. Spring term.   Professor CURTIS.

Prerequisite, English 5.

[34. American Literature. (Two-fifths course.)]

A consideration of the representative poets and prose writers of America. Tuesdays and Thursdays. Fall term.

Professor CURTIS.

Prerequisite, English 5.

[35. The Short Story. (Two-fifths course.)]

Criticism of the best representative short stories of French, English, and American writers. The short story as an art form will be studied. Tuesdays and Thursdays. Winter term.

Professor CURTIS.

Prerequisite, English 5.

[36. The Short Story. (Continued.) (Two-fifths course.)]

Practice in advanced composition. Short stories will be written by the members of the class. Tuesdays and Thursdays. Spring term.

Professor CURTIS.

Prerequisite, English 35.

MODERN LANGUAGES.

It is needless at the present day to insist upon the advisability of knowing one or more of the modern languages; we, as Americans, are awakening to the fact that to know English alone is to be seriously handicapped in the circles of polite society or commerce, or in the pursuits of science or literature.

The effort in this department of our College work is to impart a sound knowledge of grammar and syntax and a correct pronunciation, preparing the way to a complete mastery of the spoken and written language.

FRENCH.

1. How to Think in French.

Petites Causeries. Conversation. Elementary Grammar. Fall term.

Professor WAIT.

Open to all college students.

2. Foundations of French.

Petites Causeries. Memorizing. Conversation. Winter term.

Professor WAIT.

Prerequisite, French 1,

3. Foundations of French.

Kuhn's French Readings. Sight reading. Conversation. Spring term.

Professor WAIT.

Prerequisite, French 2.

[4. Grammar, Conversation, and Reading.]

Fraser & Squair's Grammar. François's Composition. George Sand's La Mare au Diable. Fall term.

Professor WAIT.

Prerequisite, French 3.

5. Grammar, Conversation, and Reading.

Fraser & Squair's Grammar. François's Composition. Corneille's Le Cid. Dumas's La Tulipe Noire. Fall term.

Professor WAIT.

Prerequisite, French 3.

[6. Grammar, Conversation, and Reading.]

L'Avare, Colomba. Sight reading. Winter term.

Professor WAIT.

Prerequisite, French 4.

7. Grammar, Conversation, and Reading.

Le Verre d'Eau.. Sept Auteurs Français. Winter term.

Professor WAIT.

Prerequisite, French 5.

[8. Grammar, Conversation, and Reading.]

Pécheurs d' Islande. Gazier's Histoire de La Littérature Française. Spring term.

Professor WAIT.

Prerequisite, French 6.

9. Grammar, Conversation, and Reading.

Study of the authors of the 17th and 19th centuries. Reading, Balzac, Hugo, Thiers. Spring term.

Professor WAIT.

Prerequisite, French 7.

10, 11, 12. Scientific French (Half Courses.)

Reading of Scientific French, especially for the benefit of students in courses using French text and reference books. Class meets one hour per week. Fall, winter, and spring terms, each term counting as a half credit.

Professor WAIT.

Prerequisite, French 3.

Grammar, Composition, Sight Reading, and Conversation constitute an important part of 4 to 9 inclusive.

GERMAN.

1. Elementary German.

Das Deutsche Buch. Elementary Grammar. Conversation. Fall term.

Professor WAIT.

Open to all students.

2. Elementary German.

Das Deutsche Buch. Grammar. Conversation. Sight reading. Committing to memory. Winter term.   Professor WAIT.

Prerequisite, German 1.

3. Grammar and Reading.

Collar's Eysenbach's Grammar. Immensee. Sight reading. Conversation. Memorizing. Spring term.   Professor WAIT.

Prerequisite, German 2.

[4. Grammar, Conversation, and Reading.]

Collar's Eysenbach's Grammar. Stein's Exercises for Translation. Schrakamp's German Conversation Grammar. L'Arrabbiata. Sight reading. Fall term.   Professor WAIT.

Prerequisite, German 3.

5. Grammar, Conversation, and Reading.

Maria Stuart, Götz von Berlichingen. Fall term.
         Professor WAIT.

Prerequisite, German 3.

[6. Grammar, Conversation, and Reading.]

Hermann und Dorothea. Meereskunde. Winter term.
         Professor WAIT.

Prerequisite, German 4.

7. Grammar, Conversation, and Reading.

Nathan der Weise, Freytag's Bilder aus der deutschen Vergangenheit. Winter term.   Professor WAIT.

Prerequisite, German 5.

[8. Grammar, Conversation, and Reading.]

Meereskunde. Bötticher's German Literature. Spring term.
         Professor WAIT.

Prerequisite, German 6.

9. Grammar, Conversation, and Reading.

German Classics. Spring term.   Professor WAIT.

Prerequisite, German 7.

10, 11, 12. Scientific German. (Half Courses.)

Readings from Scientific German, especially for the benefit of students in courses using German text and reference books. Class meets one hour per week. Fall, winter, and spring terms, each term counting as a half credit. Professor WAIT.

Prerequisite, German 3.

Grammar, Composition, Sight Reading, and Conversation constitute an important part of courses 4 to 9 inclusive.

LATIN.

Of the courses enumerated below, Latin 5 to 8 inclusive are intended for those entering college with two units of credit in Latin. They may be taken with college credit or to secure additional credit for admission, two courses being necessary to secure one unit. Latin 9, given in the spring, and Latin 10, given in the fall term, are intended as introductory college courses for those entering with four units of credit in Latin. Either or both may be taken. Courses 13 to 21, inclusive, are arranged in a cycle of three years and, if taken, will enable the student to specialize in Latin, that he may easily undertake graduate work in that subject in the Universities.

In courses 3 and following, the work for the most part will be literary; and even students taking Latin 5 should have previously obtained such proficiency in the art of reading Latin that they may be able to give the major portion of their attention to the study of the literature.

5. Cicero's Orations and Latin Prose Composition.
Winter term. Professor FOWLER.

6. Cicero's Orations and Latin Prose Composition.
Spring term. Professor FOWLER.

7. Vergil.
Fall term. Professor FOWLER.

8. Vergil.
Winter term. Professor FOWLER.

9. Livy.
One object of this course and of the two next following is to develop and increase the ability of the student to read Latin. Books XXI and XXII will be read in class and portions of Book I privately. Exercises in translating at sight and at hearing will be given. The relations existing between Rome and Carthage will be noticed. Spring term. Professor FOWLER.

Open to all students who have completed Latin 8 or who have four units of credit for admission.

10. Cicero, De Senectute and De Amicitia.

Besides the reading of the above mentioned essays portions of the De Officiis will be assigned for private reading, a part of Wilkin's Primer will be studied, and the life and times of Cicero will be discussed. Fall term.   Professor FOWLER.

Open to all students who have completed Latin 8 or who have four units of credit for admission.

11. Rapid Reading Course.

Selections from a number of authors will be read, including Phædrus, Livy, Aulus Gellius, and Nepos. This course is intended to afford a large amount of practice in the reading of Latin and so to be a preparation for more advanced courses. Winter term.
                              Professor FOWLER.

Prerequisite, Latin 9 or Latin 10.

12. Horace, Odes and Epodes.

It is expected that students taking this course will be able to give nearly or quite all of their attention to the study of the literature. The odes will be read with due attention to the quantitative pronunciation in order that the true rhythmical character of Latin poetry may be appreciated and enjoyed. The Carmen Sæculare will be assigned as private reading. Spring term.
                              Professor FOWLER.

Prerequisite, Latin 11.

13. Roman Comedy.

The Trinummus and the Captives of Plautus and the Phormio of Terence will be read; the sources and history of Latin Comedy will be studied and the peculiarities of early Latin will be noted. Fall term.   Professor FOWLER.

Prerequisite, Latin 12.

14. Prose Literature of the Silver Age.

The Dialogas and Agricola of Tacitus and selected letters of Pliny will be read. The history of the Literature of the Silver Age will be studied. Winter term.   Professor FOWLER.

Prerequisite, Latin 12.

15. Catullus.

The poems of Catullus will be read. The influences exerted upon him, the characteristics of his genius, and his relation to his times will be studied. Spring term.   Professor FOWLER.

Prerequisite, Latin 12.

[16. Roman Satire.]

The Satires of Horace will be read, together with the extant fragments of the Satires of Ennius, Pacuvius, Lucilius, and Varro, and the history of Roman Satire will be studied. Fall term.

Professor FOWLER.

Prerequisite, Latin 12.

[17. Roman Satire.]

The Satires of Juvenal with selections from Martial and Persius will be read. The private life of the Romans will be studied. Winter term. Professor FOWLER.

Prerequisite, Latin 12.

[18. Cicero, Brutus, and Quintilian, Book X.]

The books will be read as a study in literary criticism among the Romans. Spring term. Professor FOWLER.

Prerequisite, Latin 12.

[19. Lucretius.]

A study of the De Rerum Natura from literary and philosophical standpoints. Fall term. Professor FOWLER.

Prerequisite, Latin 12.

[20. Roman History.]

Selections from the Annals and the Histories of Tacitus will be read and the work of the more important Roman historians will be reviewed and compared. Winter term. Professor FOWLER.

Prerequisite, Latin 12.

[21. Cicero. Selected Letters.]

As many as possible of the letters will be read and studied with especial reference to the light which they shed on Roman History and Roman political institutions. Spring term.

Professor FOWLER.

Prerequisite, Latin 12.

GREEK.

It is the purpose in this department to give the student the ability to read understandingly the writings of the Greek authors and to enter into their spirit, and, also, to give him a general acquaintance with Greek literature. Thoroughness in instruction is aimed at. The student is required to learn the forms of words, so that he can decline each noun and adjective occurring in his lessons, tell the conjugation, voice, mood, tense, number, and person of each verb, and to know the construction of sentences, so that he can tell how to dispose of each word. A correct translation gains no credit for a student, if upon questioning it is found that he has not a knowledge of words and constructions and has evidently obtained his translation from notes or some other source.

Approved English sentences are required in translation, and where the literal is not allowable in English, the student is expected to know the construction in the Greek, and to render into idiomatic English.

The closest attention is required in the hour of recitation. The student cannot succeed, relying on what he has learned by rote, but he must perceive and understand each word at the time of recitation.

The student is required to present an essay on each work read, stating its scope and the peculiarities of its style, and giving a brief biography of its author.

Frequent reference is made to a dictionary of Classical Antiquities to elucidate allusions to the mythology and the manners and customs of the Ancient Greeks.

Much attention is paid to the derivation and composition of words, and English words derived from the Greek are noted.

Instruction is carefully given in the principles of accent, and from the beginning, in writing Greek exercises, students are required to be careful to accent correctly.

The student who meets the requirements in this department, not only learns to read with pleasure and profit the language which he is studying, but, what is more, he acquires a mental discipline and a habit of carefulness and accuracy which will aid him in the business of life. The discipline of mind and the knowledge which he gains will greatly assist him in other studies, especially those of the sciences and medicine, since the terms with which he will meet in these studies are to a great extent derived from the Greek.

1. Grammar and Lessons.

Boise and Pattengill's Greek Lessons. Goodwin's Greek Grammar. Fall term. Professor PARKER.

Open to all college students.

2. Grammar and Lessons. (Continued.)

Winter term. Professor PARKER.

Prerequisite, Greek 1.

3. Anabasis.

Goodwin's Xenophon's Anabasis. Collar and Daniell's Greek Composition. Spring term. Professor PARKER.

Prerequisite, Greek 2.

4. Anabasis. (Continued.)

Collar and Daniell's Greek Composition. Fall term.

Professor PARKER.

Prerequisite, Greek 3.

5. Orations of Lysias.

Stevens's Edition   Winter term.   Professor PARKER.

Prerequisite, Greek 4.

6. Greek Historians.

Fernald's Selections.   Spring term.   Professor PARKER.

Prerequisite, Greek. 5.

7. Iliad.

Keep's Homer's Iliad.   Fall term.   Professor PARKER.

Prerequisite, Greek 6.

8. Plato's Apology of Socrates.

Dyer's Edition.   Winter term.   Professor PARKER.

Prerequisite, Greek 6.

[9. Prometheus of Aeschylus.]

Wecklein's Edition.   Spring term.

Professor PARKER.

Prerequisite, Greek 6.

[10. Odyssey.]

Merry's Homer's Odyssey.   Fall term.

Professor PARKER.

Prerequisite, Greek 6.

[11. Plato's Gorgias.]

Lodge's Edition.   Winter term.   Professor PARKER.

Prerequisite, Greek 6.

12. Medea of Euripides.

Allen's Edition.   Spring term.   Professor PARKER.

Prerequisite, Greek. 6.

13, 14, 15, 16. Greek New Testament.

These classes, while primarily intended for theological students, are open also to College students who have the requisite preparation. A full description is given in the Divinity School Courses.

Professor PARKER.

Prerequisite, Greek 5.

The following books are recommended for reference to those pursuing the study of Greek:

Liddell and Scott's Greek Lexicon; Autenrieth's Homeric Dictionary; Long's, or Ginn & Co.'s Classical Atlas; Anthon's, or Smith's Classical Dictionary; Harper's Dictionary of Classical Literature and Antiquities; Smith's History of Greece; Goodwin's Greek Grammar; Goodwin's Greek Modes and Tenses.

HEBREW.

1, 2, 3. Grammar and Old Testament.

These are primarily courses in the Divinity School, but may be elected by students in the College of Liberal Arts whenever they are offered. Classes will be formed each year if a sufficient number of students apply.

It is the aim to give the students such a knowledge of the forms and structure of the Hebrew Language as shall enable them to use it efficiently in the criticism and literary analysis of the Old Testament Scriptures. The text-books used are H. G. Mitchell's Hebrew Lessons and the Hebrew Old Testament. Three terms—Fall, Winter and Spring—each term counting as a course.

Professor WHITE.

Open (under conditions as described above) to students who, in the judgment of the Instructor, are qualified by previous training to take the course.

MATHEMATICS.

The study of Mathematics is useful to the student in two ways. In the first place, it affords an admirable mental discipline, developing habits of precise thought and accurate statement. In the second place, as the necessary tool of the civil and electrical engineer, the architect, and all persons engaged in higher scientific work, it has a practical value to those intending to enter these professions.

It is the purpose of the department to keep these two objects steadily in view. Students are required to show their understanding of mathematical principles and reasoning by rigid demonstrations, subject to the criticism of other members of the class. Problems are selected for solution which arise in the actual practice of surveying, engineering, physical research, and the like.

Students who intend to enter any of the above mentioned professions may profitably take a large part of their work at Lombard, completing their course in some technical school.

7. Solid Geometry.

This course is continuous with Mathematics 6 (a). Fall term.

Professor GRUBB.

Prerequisite, Mathematics 6(a).

8. Higher Algebra.

This course assumes a thorough knowledge on the part of the student of Mathematics 5 and also some knowledge of Plane Geometry. It embraces the study of Permutations and Combinations, Probability, Determinants, and the Theory of Equations. Winter term.

Professor WRIGHT.

Prerequisite, Mathematics 5 and Mathematics 6(a).

9. Plane and Spherical Trigonometry.

This course includes the solution of trigonometric equations, the solution of plane and spherical triangles and problems involving an application of Trigonometry to Mensuration, Surveying, and Astronomy. Crockett's Plane and Spherical Trigonometry is used as a text-book. Spring term. Professor WRIGHT.

Prerequisite, Mathematics 8.

10. Analytic Geometry.

This course treats of the straight line, the conic sections, and higher plane curves. Fall term. Professor WRIGHT.

Prerequisite, Mathematics 9.

11. Surveying and Leveling.

Field work and problems. Field work on Saturdays at the option of the instructor. Spring term. Professor WRIGHT.

Prerequisite, Mathematics 9.

12. Differential Calculus.

Byerly's Differential Calculus is used. Winter term.

Professor WRIGHT.

Prerequisite, 10.

13. Integral Calculus.

Spring term. Professor WRIGHT.

Prerequisite, Mathematics 12.

[14. Descriptive Geometry.]

This course embraces mechanical drawing, orthographic projection, shades and shadows, and perspective. Church's Descriptive Geometry is used. Winter term. Professor WRIGHT.

Prerequisite, Mathematics 9.

[16. Quaternions.]

Kelland and Tait's text is used. Spring term.

Prerequisite, Mathematics 13. Professor Wright.

In addition to the foregoing courses, classes will be formed, when there is a sufficient demand on the part of advanced students, to pursue work in the solution of original problems in the Calculus, and in the study of infinitesimals, probability, elliptic functions, life insurance and other topics.

ASTRONOMY.

1. General Astronomy.

This course is largely descriptive in character, though some of the simpler mathematical problems connected with Astronomy are solved. It embraces a study of the imaginary lines of the celestial sphere; latitude, longitude, time; the sun, moon, and planets; comets, meteors, and the stars. Some attention is given to the constellations and the myths connected with them. The Nebular Hypothesis is presented and discussed. Young's General Astronomy is used. Fall term. Professor Wright.

Prerequisite, Mathematics 9.

PHYSICS.

The course in Physics extends through the year, four periods per week being devoted to lectures and recitations and four to laboratory work. The aim is to present the science of Physics as a whole, that students may be led to note the general principles of mechanics that apply throughout, and which furnish the basis of explanation of all the various phenomena.

The work of this course consists of a careful consideration of the various laws treated under the six main divisions of the subject.

It is intended for the general student and no Mathematics higher than Plane Trigonometry is required. Numerous problems given test the student's ability to think clearly and make a correct application of the principles involved.

The laboratory experiments are chiefly quantitative and give opportunity for the verification of fundamental laws and general formulæ. Each student is required to present carefully prepared notes which shall include the data obtained from observation and computed results.

1. Mechanics, Hydrostatics, Pneumatics.

Text-book, Hastings and Beach's Physics. Fall term.

Prerequisite, Mathematics 9. Professor Rich.

2. Heat, Electricity, and Magnetism.

Winter term. Professor RICH.

Prerequisite, Mathematics 9.

3. Acoustics and Optics.

Spring term. Professor RICH.

Prerequisite, Physics 2.

CHEMISTRY.

The courses in Chemistry have been arranged with several distinct objects in view: First—A clear understanding of the underlying principles of chemical changes. This involves a thorough knowledge of the theory of the structure of matter. Students who understand well this theory will avoid many of the difficulties ordinarily met with in the study of Chemistry and Physics.

Second—The principles of Stoichiometry, or Chemical Arithmetic, are to be thoroughly mastered and applied in a large series of practical chemical problems.

Third—A study of the elements and their compounds with careful attention given to the writing of equations.

Fourth—A systematic course in the laboratory, designed to give the student practice in careful manipulation and also opportunity for verification of the laws of chemical combination. The experiments of this course include the preparation of common elements and compounds.

Fifth—A general course in Qualitative analysis in which the student becomes familiar with the methods of determining the composition of native and manufactured substances.

Sixth—A well graded course in Quantitative analysis which gives the student practice in the various gravimetric and volumetric methods.

This gives the student the basis for technical work and enables him, in the minimum time, to become familiar with special, practical methods in the arts, and in fact to take the position of chemist in many lines of trade or manufacture without further preparation.

The course includes the analysis of such substances as ores, soils, fertilizers, soaps, milk, butter, gas, air, water, etc.

1. Inorganic Chemistry.

Remsen's College Chemistry is used as the basis of courses 1 and 2. Fall term. Professor RICH.

Open to all students.

2. Inorganic Chemistry.

Winter term.   Professor RICH.

Prerequisite, Chemistry 1.

3. Organic Chemistry.

This course consists of recitations, lectures with experimental demonstrations, and laboratory work. The consideration of food-stuffs is an important part of the work. Their composition, adulteration, and the new methods of preparation are carefully studied. Remsen's Organic Chemistry is used. Spring term.

Prerequisite, Chemistry 2.   Professor RICH.

In each of the courses 1, 2, and 3, the work is profusely illustrated by experiments, and individual work. by the student in the laboratory demonstrates the principles discussed. Four hours per week are devoted to recitations and lectures and four hours to laboratory work.

4. Analytical Chemistry.

Qualitative analysis, laboratory work, and recitations. Fall term.

Prerequisite, Chemistry 2.   Professor RICH.

5. Analytical Chemistry.

Qualitative, and quantitative analysis, laboratory work. Winter term.   Professor RICH.

Prerequisite, Chemistry 4.

6. Analytical Chemistry.

Quantitative analysis. Laboratory work. Spring term.

Prerequisite, Chemistry 5.   Professor RICH.

7. Physiological Chemistry.

A study of the organic compounds, and the chemical processes of physiological change. Specially useful in subsequent study of practical medicine. Spring term.   Professor RICH.

Prerequisites, Chemistry 3 and 4.

GEOLOGY AND MINERALOGY.

1. Geology.

The work in Geology is given by text-book recitations, supplemented by lectures and excursions for field work. The College has a valuable collection of minerals, which serves for purposes of illustration and study. Dana's work is used. Spring term.

Professor RICH.

Prerequisites, Chemistry 1, Biology 3, and Biology 4.

2. Mineralogy.

The course consists of a qualitative determination of minerals by means of the blow-pipe and a careful study of the principles of classification. Winter term. Professor RICH.

Prerequisite, Chemistry 2.

Biological Sciences.

The courses offered in Biology have been prepared to meet the requirements of students who desire instruction in the Biological Sciences either for general culture, as a preparation for teaching, for original research in Physiology and Zoology, or as foundation for the professional course in medicine.

To meet these needs the College offers the "Biologico-Chemical Group," the "Chemico-Physical and Pre-Medical Group," and the "Pre-Medical Group."

These courses are offered in the belief that the education of the professional man or woman should in no sense be a narrow one, and that the subsequent success of the individual depends upon the thoroughness and upon the breadth of his education.

The courses offered in this department give the student a general knowledge of life from its simplest to its most complex form. They build a broad foundation for graduate work in Physiology, Zoology, Sociology, Botany, Psychology, and Medicine. The student who faithfully does the work as outlined in these courses will be well prepared to teach them in secondary schools. In this department the student learns of life, of the structure and functions of the various organs of which the organism is composed, and of their relations to each other. He learns how to observe and appreciate the wonderful phenomena of nature. The numerous unsolved problems in this field offer many opportunities for investigation and advancement.

The Physiological and Anatomical laboratories have recently been equipped with the latest apparatus. An ample number of instruments have been supplied. These include the apparatus necessary for experiments and demonstrations in blood pressure, heart-beat, muscle, nerve phenomena, respiration, digestion, phenomena of stimulation, etc., etc.

BIOLOGY.

1. General Biology.

This course will furnish a sketch of the history of the science of Biology and discuss the aims and methods of biological research, composition of living substance, and the elementary vital phenomena. Recitations and laboratory work. Dr. KIMBLE.

Open to all students.

2. General Biology. (Continuation of Course 1.)

A study of the general conditions of life, of stimuli, and their actions, and of the mechanisms of life. Dr. KIMBLE.

Prerequisite, Biology 1.

PHYSIOLOGY.

1. Elementary Physiology.

This course is intended for students desiring a general knowledge of Physiology, but will not count as a credit for the "Pre-Medical Group." Fall term. Dr. KIMBLE.

Open to all students.

2. Advanced Physiology.

This will be a study of the blood, the tissues of movement, and the vascular mechanism. Primarily for medical students, but may be taken by any student in the College of Liberal Arts. Fall term.
Dr. KIMBLE.

Prerequisite, Chemistry 2.

3. Advanced Physiology. (Continuation of Course 2.)

In this course the student is given an opportunity for a thorough knowledge of the tissues and mechanisms of digestion, and respiration, the elimination of waste products, and nutrition. Winter term.
Dr. KIMBLE.

Prerequisites, Chemistry 3 and Physiology 2.

4. Physiology of the Nervous System.

A study of the central nervous system, including a brief sketch of the anatomy of the same. Laboratory, recitations, and lectures. Fall term. Dr. KIMBLE.

Prerequisites, same as in Physiology 2.

5. Physiology and Anatomy of the Sense Organs.

This course deals with the Physiology and Anatomy of the organs of sense. It is especially adapted to the needs of students in medicine, but those wanting to do advanced work in Psychology will find it of decided advantage to have the knowledge which this course offers. Winter term. Dr. KIMBLE.

Prerequisites, Biology 2 or Physiology 1 and Entrance Physics.

6. Practical Hygiene.

In this course it is intended to give the student such knowledge as will best fit him properly to care for himself in his surroundings while pursuing his college work. A series of about ten lectures given at the beginning of the Fall term.   Dr. KIMBLE.

Required of all students.

[Materia Medica.]

Under this course students will be taught the appearance and physical properties of the crude drugs and the preparations derived therefrom, illustrated by actual specimens. The elements of pharmacology, incompatabilities, and the art of prescription writing will be given thorough consideration during the term. The student is required to familiarize himself with the drugs and their characteristics. Fall term.   Dr. KIMBLE.

ANATOMY.

1. Osteology.

This course in Osteology is primarily intended for medical students. Each student is required to make a drawing of, and to model in clay each bone of the human skeleton. Each student is supplied with a disarticulated skeleton to be retained by the student during the entire course, at the end of which it is returned to the professor in charge. The museum contains many skeletons to which the student is frequently referred for comparative study. This course requires three laboratory periods and two recitation periods each week. Laboratory, recitations, and demonstrations. Mondays, Tuesdays, and Wednesdays. Fall and Winter terms.

Dr. KIMBLE and Professor KIMBLE.

[2. General Anatomy.]

This course consists of practical work in the laboratory, lectures and demonstrations. Each student will be required to make one dissection and to keep a note book in which he shall make drawings of the various dissections of the principal organs, vessels, and nerves showing their chief relations. No more than two students will be permitted to dissect at one table and Dr. Kimble or a demonstrator will be in charge of each class. Frequent quizzes will be given and the student will be required to demonstrate a thorough knowledge of each dissection before he will be permitted to begin another. Fifteen hours per week for fifteen weeks. Fall and winter terms, after November 1.   Dr. KIMBLE.

Prerequisites, Anatomy 1 and Zoology 3.

[3. Histology.]

The course in Histology will be divided into two parts. (a) The construction and use of the microscope, the methods of preparing microscopical sections of tissues, and work upon the fundamental mammalian tissues. (b) A study of the finer anatomy of mammalian organs. The material used is human tissue in large part, supplemented by tissue from other mammals. Eight hours per week. Winter and Spring terms. Dr. KIMBLE and Prof. KIENHOLZ.

Prerequisites, Zoology 1 and Biology 2.

4. Embryology.

Lectures, demonstrations, and laboratory work. Designed especially for medical students. The laboratory work deals with cleavage and gastrulation followed by a study of the development of the chick. Certain later periods of development are studied in mammalian embryos. The recitations deal with the development of the human embryo and the relations of the various stages as studied in the laboratory. Laboratory, five hours, and recitations two hours. Winter and spring terms. Dr. KIMBLE and ASSISTANT.

Prerequisite, Anatomy 3.

BOTANY.

1. General Botany.

This course is intended to acquaint the student with the general field of Botany, including plant ecology and cartography. Fall term.
Dr. KIMBLE.

Prerequisites, Entrance Chemistry and Botany,. Biology 2.

2. Morphological Botany.

A view of mossworts, ferns, and flowering plants, with special problems in structure, life history, and phylogeny. Text, lectures, laboratory work, and reference reading. Spring term.
Professor KIENHOLZ.

Prerequisite, Botany 1.

[3. Physiological Botany.]

This course consists of a series of qualitative experiments dealing with the functions of plants and plant tissues, behavior of plant growth in different environments. Lectures on absorption, metabolism, excretion, respiration, foods, actions of enzymes, plant constituents, and relation of growth to environments. Text, MacDougal. Plant Physiology. Spring term. Professor KIENHOLZ.

Prerequisite, Botany 1.

ZOOLOGY.

1. Invertebrate Zoology.

This course will treat of the Invertebrata, with special reference to their life history, anatomy, and sytematic relations. Recitations, laboratory, and reference work. Fall term.

Professor KIENHOLZ.

Prerequisites, Entrance credits in Zoology and Chemistry.

2. Vertebrate Zoology.

In this course typical forms will be studied in the laboratory. Drawings and explanatory notes of dissected specimens will be required. Winter term. Professor KIENHOLZ.

Prerequisite, Zoology 1.

3. Vertebrate Anatomy.

This course is designed to prepare the student for a general course in human anatomy. Careful dissections of vertebrate forms, with special reference to the cat, will be carried out. The order of the work will follow that of human anatomy as nearly as possible.

Prerequisite, Zoology 2. Professor KIENHOLZ.

HISTORY.

5. History of the Christian Church.

A. *The Ancient and Mediaeval Eras* [*1-1517.*]

This course in Church History is primarily intended for the members of the Divinity School but is also open to College students. It will require the investigation of the early organization and extension of Christianity and the successive periods of the Church down to the time of Charlemagne; followed by a careful inquiry into the causes of the rise of the Papacy, of the political relations of the Church, and of the Crusades. Fisher's History of the Church will be used as a hand book and topics will be assigned to each member of the class for special investigation and reports. Fall term.

Professor WHITE.

6. History of the Christian Church.

B. *The Modern Era* [*1517-1904.*]

This course will begin with the study of the Reformation, and trace the history of the Church down to the present time. It will include the history of Christian missions, revivals, social reforms, and philanthropy. The same text-book will be used as in History 5. Winter term. Professor WHITE.

Prerequisite, History 5.

7. History of Christian Doctrines.

Fisher is used for text.   Spring term.   Professor WHITE.

8. Development of English Nationality.

Text, Terry.   Fall term.   Miss HATHAWAY.

Prerequisite, History 4.

9. United States from 1760 to 1889.

Lectures and reference work.   Winter term.
                                        Miss HATHAWAY.

Prerequisite, Entrance History of the United States.

10. Europe from 1789 to 1815.

The Revolutionary and Napoleonic Era.   Text, Rose.   Spring
term.   Miss HATHAWAY.

Open to all college students.

11. History of Civilization.

Text, Guizot.   Spring term.   Professor WHITE.

ECONOMICS.

In the first place the student becomes acquainted with the idea
that in human relations there are laws of cause and effect, as there
are in nature.   There are certain attributes of human nature and
certain phenomena of physical nature which may be regarded as
fundamental; and on account of these fundamental attributes human
beings in their relations to one another may be expected to react in a
perfectly definite and predicable way.   In other words the student
learns that a Social Law may be formulated, and that a Social Science is possible.   This feature of the work, however, is more exhaustively brought out in the more general science of Sociology, one
course in which the student is expected to have pursued before taking up Economics.

In the second place such social laws as have reference to men's
actions in the ordinary business of life, are developed. These are the
familiar economic laws which form the subject matter of text-books
in Political Economy; the law of diminishing returns; the doctrine
of Malthus; the laws of market, normal, and monopoly value; the
principles of international trade; and the principles governing the
distribution of the products of labor among landowners, capitalists,
employers, and wage earners.

A third feature of the work is the study of certain historical
periods with reference to the actual operation of economic laws; a
verification of the truths developed from economic premises.

Finally, as human society is progressive rather than static, economic ideals are discussed and practical problems relating to the improvement of the present economic order are investigated. Under this head are discussed such subjects as free trade, bimetallism, the labor question, monopoly, land tenure reform, socialism, and the like.

A prominent feature of the work is its investigatory character. In many cases the student is thrown upon his own resources to determine an economic point by studying and comparing the views of different authorities, rather than by simply learning the statement of the text. Throughout, a great deal of collateral reading is required. The way is thus paved for subsequent independent research.

It is believed that the study of Economics is of great value in fitting a student for the duties of citizenship, and in the growing complexity of our economic life the importance of this consideration can hardly be over-estimated. The problems of international trade, of money, of monopoly, of socialism, and the like are demanding attention, and in a popular form of government it is important that the individual citizen with whom ultimately the decision in regard to these questions will rest should have an opinion independent of party affiliation.

2. Political Economy.

General Political Economy. Bullock's Introduction to the Study of Economics is used. Fall term. Professor WRIGHT.

Prerequisite, Sociology 1.

3. Financial History of the United States.

This course embraces the finances of the Revolution; the financial administrations of Morris, Hamilton, and Gallatin; the bank struggle; tariff legislation, the financial measures of the Civil War, and reconstruction periods to the present time. Dewey's Financial History of the United States is used as a text, collateral reading is required, and frequent lectures are given. Winter term.

Prerequisite, Economics 2. Professor WRIGHT.

4. Current Economic Problems.

It is the purpose in this course to investigate from a standpoint somewhat broader than that of purely economic considerations certain vital economic problems and reforms. Different topics will be discussed different years. The subject for 1904 is Schemes for Economic improvement. Spring term. Professor WRIGHT.

Prerequisite, Economics 2.

JURISPRUDENCE.

[1. International Law.]

The general principles which govern the relations of States, as historically developed in express agreements and by usuage, are elucidated; and these principles are discussed from the standpoints of reason and justice. Special study is made of current international problems, and theses on these subjects are required. Particular attention is paid to terminology. Lawrence's International Law is used as a text book. Frequent reference is made to the works on International Law by Woolsey, Wheaton, Glenn, etc. Spring term.

Professor WHITE.

Open to all students who, in the judgment of the instructor, are qualified by previous training to take the course.

SOCIOLOGY.*

Nature and Scope of the Science.

The comparative recency with which this department has taken its place in the college course and the consequent unfamiliarity of the public with the nature of its work, coupled with the fundamental importance of that work, seem to warrant a slightly extended statement concerning it.

Sociology may be defined as the primary and fundamental science of society. What are the conditions and laws under which societies originate, develop, and decay? What are the elementary social laws upon which the more special laws of economics, jurisprudence, civics, and religion depend? What are the fundamental and necessary relationships which must obtain in any given community of men if that community is to be a safe, stable, and progressive community? Under what conditions do the great social institutions of law, religion, the state, commercial relationships,

---

*SOCIOLOGY AND SOCIAL REFORM.—Because of certain widely current misconceptions it cannot be too clearly stated that Sociology is in no possible sense to be identified with any scheme or program of social reform, ancient or modern. The sociologist as such is a scientist pure and simple. He has no thought of shaping or molding the phenomena which constitute the subject matter of his science. As a sociologist he no more proposes to reform society than the anatomist proposes to remodel the vertebrate skeleton. He studies social reform, its methods, its varieties, its history, results, etc., but in a perfectly critical and dispassionate manner, and with no other motive than to discover and set forth the facts pertaining to it. Moreover it is to be remembered that social reform comprises only a very small, and relatively very unimportant portion of the subject matter of Sociology. One of the greatest of living sociologists has well said that the study of social reform comes about as near to being the sole business of Sociology as does the mending of broken rails to being the chief business of a railroad company. The sociologist's studies must undobtedly form the chief source of reliable knowledge concerning a social reform. This fact cannot be overlooked; but anyone who looks to Sociology as a champion of any particular reform, or of reform in general, is wholly in error. Sociology is no more a part of social reform than is the microscope a part of the amœba which is seen through its lenses.

the family, etc., have their origin, development, and decline? What are their history and their present status in the social structure? How do they react upon each other and upon the individual? What are the methods by which a student should make a study of a given community or social class or institution, and how and when can these methods be applied? These and others are the questions which it is the business of the science to answer. To the discovery, organization, and dissemination of knowledge calculated to answer these questions, it devotes itself. It is this knowledge which the student gets from a study of the science. The great importance of such knowledge to every member of society, no matter what his station in life may be, cannot possibly need emphasis to the mind of any thoughtful person.

Methods.

The method of instruction is a combination of the lecture, laboratory, and recitation methods, dependent upon the nature of the subject and the characteristics of the student. The constant aim is to furnish to the student such knowledge of the primary facts of the associational life as will be most useful to him both in his college course and in his ensuing career. Any and all methods fruitfully contributing to this result are used as occasion suggests.

Library.

A good working library is being accumulated for the use of students of the department. Additions are made from time to time as the needs of the department and the resources of the institution seem to warrant.

General Courses.

1. An Introduction to Sociology.

This course together with course 1 *(a)* will furnish the student an introductory knowledge of the more elementary principles of the science and of the fundamental facts of the associational life. They are particularly designed to meet the needs of the general college student, and besides affording him a broad basis for further study in Sociology, Logic, Ethics, Economics, Political Science, and Law, also to provide him with information and training which will be of high practical value in the various walks of life. Wherever possible, students should arrange to take the two courses consecutively. Certain of the subjects dealt with are as follows: the province and aim of the science, its relation to other sciences and to practical life; the primary social institutions, their history, characteristics, functions; the chief associative processes, their nature, their causes, and their place in the structure and life of society; the origin, development, and decline of societies; critical study of certain leading ideas of prominent modern sociologists.; illustrative study of an actual community. Lectures, personal investigation, recitations, and assigned readings. Fall term. Professor KIMBLE.

Open regularly to all students who have acquired the sixteen units requisite for college standing; open to others only on consultation with instructor.

1 (a). An Introduction to Sociology.

See announcement of Course 1 of which course this is a continuation. Winter term. Professor KIMBLE.

Prerequisite, Sociology 1.

The Development of Sociological Theory.

The courses in sociological theory are practically continuous, though any one of them can be taken without taking those later than itself. Collectively they are designed to offer the student opportunity to make a somewhat extended study of the chief works in the literature of sociology. In so doing he is taught to see each work in its relation to each of the others and to the common whole. Each work is first subjected to a careful analysis; the results of this analysis are then compared with the results of similar analysis of other works, and through critical evaluation and constructive synthesis of the factors thus discriminated the development of sociological theory as a whole is made clear to the mind.

*2. Pre-Comtean Sociological Theory.

A study of the earlier theories of social relations.
Professor KIMBLE.

Prerequisite, reading knowledge of French or German.

*3. Modern Sociological Theory.

The chief works of the more prominent modern sociologists are studied with a view to the characteristic positions of each and the relations sustained by each to sociological theory as a whole.
Professor KIMBLE.

Prerequisite, reading knowledge of French or German.

*4. Modern Sociological Theory.

(Continuation of Course 3.) Professor KIMBLE.

Prerequisite, Sociology 3.

---

*Courses so marked are special courses and are at present given only when a sufficient number of adequately prepared students present themselves for registration therein. Students desiring to arrange for work in such courses are requested to consult the instructor personally.

The Development of Association.

The courses under this head are intended to afford the student opportunity to study certain of the chief factors of the associate life in a more detailed manner than is allowed in courses 1 and 1 *(a)*.

*6. An Introduction to Comparative Study of Association.

The method, scope, and problems of Comparative Sociology. The development of association from the earlier to the later forms. Chief stages and factors. Fundamental laws and processes.

Professor KIMBLE.

*7. Biogeography.

An outline study of the influence of the inanimate environment upon the development of association. Professor KIMBLE.

Prerequisite, reading knowledge of German.

9. Reproductive Association.

A study of association as developed about the reproductive process. This course is designed to furnish a solid basis for Course 13. The various forms of reproductive association, commencing with the crudest and most simple, are considered as steps in the development of one great process having its beginning among the lowest animals and its ending in the highest form of the human family. Fall term: Professor KIMBLE.

Open by consultation to all college students who have completed the entrance requirements. The elementary courses in Zoology, Biology, Sociology, and Psychology, will be of great assistance to students taking this course.

12. Abnormal and Pathological Variations in Association.

A course in the study of dependents, defectives, and delinquents. Crime and the criminal classes. Methods of organized charity work. Winter term. Professor KIMBLE.

Open regularly to all students who have had Course 1. Open to others by consultation only. Ordinarily Course 12 will not be given the same year with Courses 9 and 13.

13. The Family.

A study of the development and present significance of the human family. The various forms of marriage and the family. The function of the family in modern society. The relations by which the family is constituted. The influence of certain other institutions upon the family; the family and the church, the family and the state, the family and economic institutions, the family and educational and moral institutions. Winter term.

Professor KIMBLE.

Open to all college students. Students will find Courses 1, 1a, and 9 of great value in connection with Course 13.

PSYCHOLOGY.

1. Physiology and Psychology of the Senses.

Experience has shown the need of a course in which special attention shall be given to the correlation of the study of the physiology and anatomy of the sense organs with that of the psychology of the elementary psychic processes. This course has been designed to meet this need. Fall term

Professor KIMBLE and Dr. KIMBLE.

2. Introductory Psychology.

The purpose of the course is to guide the beginner in gaining the fundamentals of a thorough knowledge of psychology and of psychic life. The course is organized about a careful study of the commoner characteristics of the more accessible mental processes. Emphasis is laid upon the ready and accurate use of the more important psychological terms. Some knowledge of the chief standpoints and methods of the science is gained. Collateral reading in connection with the text will be regularly assigned and a correct appreciation of the relation of this reading to the treatment presented in the text will be a requirement of the course. Experiments described in text and reading will be fully discussed; and, where circumstances will permit, the student will see performed by others or will himself perform in the laboratory certain type experiments. Winter term.   Professor KIMBLE.

Prerequisite, Psychology 1, or equivalent.

METAPHYSIC.

This is primarily a course in the Divinity School, but it may be elected by students in the College of Liberal Arts whenever it is offered. Classes will be formed whenever a sufficient number of students apply. Lotze's Outline of Metaphysic is used as a textbook. Fall term.   Professor WHITE.

Open to students who, in the judgment of the instructor, are qualified by previous training to take the course.

LOGIC.

Having first obtained a thorough grounding in the principles and methods of correct reasoning both deductive and inductive, at least one-half of the term is given to the detection and discrimination of fallacies in actual examples. Such examples the class is required to search out in current literature and bring in for discussion. Davis's Elements of Deductive Logic and Davis's Elements of Inductive Logic are used. Winter term.

Open to students who, in the judgment of the instructor, are qualified by previous training to take the course.

ETHICS.

Ethics is treated from the standpoint of Philosophy, and the different systems are discussed. The nature and grounds of obligation are investigated and applied to the practical affairs of life. Winter term. Professor WHITE.

Open to students who, in the judgment of the instructor, are qualified by previous training to take the course.

PHILOSOPHY OF RELIGION.

Fairbairn's Philosophy of the Christian Religion is the textbook. Lotze, Sabatier, and Martineau are used as works of reference. The aim of the instructor is to acquaint the student with the proper offices of reason in the effort to find argumentative grounds for religious ideas. Most of the modern theories respecting the nature and scope of the religious feeling pass under review; and in such discussions free questioning on the part of the student is encouraged. Winter term. Professor WHITE.

Open to students who, in the judgment of the instructor, are qualified by previous training to take the course.

ETHICAL THEORIES.

Martineau's Types of Ethical Theory is used as a text-book with frequent references to the works of Sidgwick, Green, Smyth, and others. Much attention is paid to the elucidation and criticism of the modern ethical theories. Spring term.

Professor WHITE.

Open to students who, in the judgment of the instructor, are qualified by previous training to take the course.

COMPARATIVE RELIGION.

The work consists in the examination and comparison of the authorities upon the great Non-Christian religions. Special topics are investigated and reports made by each member of the class. Spring term. Professor WHITE.

FINE ARTS.

2, 3, 4. Drawing.

This course includes perspective, drawing from casts in charcoal and crayon, still life studies in crayon, etc. It will count as one credit for the entire year. Miss BLOOD.

Open to all students.

MUSIC.

1. Harmony.

Keys, scales and signatures, intervals, formation of the triad, chord connection, simple part writing begun. Normal and Foreign progressions. All common chords and the rules governing their treatment in part writing. Goetchin's "The Materials of Composition" is the text-book used. Two hours a week.

Open to all college students.　　　　Professor THOMPSON.

2. Harmony.

Part writing continued. The inversion of chords. Chords of the sixth and six-four, chords of the seventh and their inversions. Key-board work. Modulation begun. Two hours a week. Winter term.　　　　Professor THOMPSON.

Prerequisite, Music 1.

3. Harmony.

Chords of the seventh continued. Altered and augmented chords explained and employed in harmonization. Modulation continued. Two hours a week. Spring term.

Prerequisite, Music 2.　　　　Professor THOMPSON.

4. Single Counterpoint.

Writing from *canti fermi.* First species, note against note. Second species, two notes against one. Third species four notes against one. John Frederick Bridge's Counterpoint is the text-book used. Fall term.　　　　Professor THOMPSON.

Prerequisite, Music 3.

5. Single Counterpoint.

Writing from *canti fermi* continued in fourth species. Syncopation-suspensions, retardations. Fifth species florid counterpoint. Winter term.　　　　·　Professor THOMPSON.

Prerequisite, Music 4.

6. Single and Double Counterpoint.

Florid counterpoint continued. Double counterpoint in all forms. Spring term.　　　　Professor THOMPSON.

Prerequisite, Music 5.

7. Musical Form.

The section and phrase. The period. The small primary forms. The large primary forms. The motive and its development. The study (Etude), dance forms, Rondo form. Vocal song. Sonata form. Musical form. Bussler-Cornell. Fall term.

　　　　Professor THOMPSON.

This course open to any student of the college, especially music students of medium advancement.

8. Canon and Fugue.

Canon in two voices in all intervals. Fugue in two, three, and four voices. Text-books. Richter, Double Counterpoint and Fugue; Higg's Fugue. Winter term. Professor THOMPSON.

Prerequisite, Music 6.

9. Instrumentation.

Study of Berlioz on instrumentation, also Prout's work on same subject. Study of orchestral scores. Orchestral scoring of various musical passages, and of original work. Orchestral writing without recourse to piano scoring. Spring term.

Prerequisites, Music 7 and 8. Professor THOMPSON.

10, 11, 12. History of Music. (Half Courses.)

These courses embrace a history of the development of music from the earliest times until to-day, with special reference to critical analysis of the works of the great masters. They also furnish an introduction to the lives of the great composers. One hour a week for the year. Mrs. THOMPSON.

PUBLIC SPEAKING.

1. Expression. (Half Course.)

A consideration of the elements of Expression. Physical exercises are given for purposes of control and vocal development. The conversational tone and its acquirement are made a matter of special study. Fall term. Professor CURTIS.

Open to all students.

2. Expression. (Half Course.)

Literary interpretation of masterpieces. Programs from various authors will be given throughout the term. Extemporaneous speaking will form a part of the work. Winter term.

Prerequisite, Public Speaking 1. Professor CURTIS.

3. Expression. (Half Course.)

Each student will be required to give a recital. The work will be criticised and special drill given by the instructor. Spring term.

Prerequisite, Public Speaking 2. Professor CURTIS.

4. Oratory. (Half Course.)

Study of the theory of oratory. Each student will be required to commit to memory and deliver various oratorical selections. Each student will prepare and deliver an oration under the supervision of the instructor. Fall term. Professor CURTIS.

Open to all students.

5. Oratory. (Half Course.)

The preparation and delivery of several orations. Winter term.

Prerequisite, Public Speaking 4.   Professor CURTIS.

6. Argumentation.

A study of the principals of argumentation. The handling of refutation, preparation of brief, writing of the forensic, and actual debate will form part of the work. Spring term.

Open to all students.   Professor CURTIS.

GYMNASIUM WORK.

The new system of physical education as pursued at Lombard College does not aim to make athletes and gymnasts, ball players, prize fighters, or wrestlers. The old idea that the gymnasium was solely for those already strong, or for the development of candidates for field honors, is not primarily considered. Incidentally the gymnasium affords ample facilities for indoor training of athletes, but this work is necessarily given a secondary place. Our system of physical education maintains that the development of mind and body go together and that one must not be sacrificed for the other. Its aim is not only to give a better and more useful physique, but to develop a will, a resolution of purpose, and to create a college spirit, which will bring with them loyalty and help to dignify American citizenship. When the student enters the gymnasium he is subjected to a rigid medical examination which is made the basis of all gymnasium work. It determines the condition of the heart and circulation, the lungs and respiration, the stomach and its appendages, vision, hearing, size and consistency of muscles, and the temperament of the nervous system. Deformities, or bodily defects, are carefully sought for. From this examination a scientific application of physical exercises as a means of development is made. Occasionally in such examination organic heart trouble is revealed. Such persons are not permitted to take the usual gymnasium work, but are given special exercises of a milder nature which are helpful. Functional derangements of nutrition, circulation, respiration, etc., are often discovered. Here again special exercises are prescribed.

The greater part of gymnasium work is conducted in classes which meet daily. Dumb-bell and club work are taken with a snap that puts life and vigor into every move. Class work is also done on the heavy apparatus, such as the buck and the parallel bars. Individual work is done with the chest weights and horizontal bars, traveling rings, climbing poles, etc. Wrestling and boxing are given special attention. Special work is also done on the rowing machine.

Besides the dumb-bell and light appartus work, the ladies are offered a course in the Preece System of Physical Culture. During their respective seasons much attention is paid to foot-ball, basket-ball, base-ball, lawn tennis, and track athletics. The gymnasium is made the cradle of college spirit.

All students will provide themselves with regular gymnasium uniforms. The cost of the uniform is about $2.50 for the men, and $4.50 for the women.

MEDICAL COURSES.

GENERAL ANNOUNCEMENT.

The work offered in medical studies covers the first year of the four-year course now required in the medical colleges of the United States. The work in these branches is exceptionally thorough and complete, the time devoted to them being thirty-six weeks, as compared with about twenty-eight weeks of the usual medical course.

The courses are so arranged as to secure in a large measure concentration of attention upon single or closely allied subjects.

The work accomplished during the past three years has demonstrated both the need of medical instruction at Lombard College and the possibilities of its advancement and improvement. At the opening of the fall term of 1904 we expect to be prepared to offer the first two years of the four-year course in medicine.

GROUPS.

Two groups are offered to students intending to become physicians; one of four years leading to the degree of B. A.; the other of one year, at the completion of which a certificate of proficiency will be given showing the amount and nature of the work done.

All medical students are required to take two years of preliminary college training, the strictly professional courses being taken as electives during the junior and senior years of the four-year college course. During the first years of his college course the student builds that broader foundation which will better enable him to meet those problems that inevitably await him in his professional career. We aim at the well-rounded development of the man rather than at the production of the specialist. The professional man in general and the physician in particular, should have his reasoning and seeing powers sharpened, should be the fully matured and equipped man. In accord with this ideal we offer the "Pre-Medical Group" in the last years of which are placed those studies that are required in the first year of the four-year course leading to the degree of M. D.

For list of schools accrediting our work and any questions not answered in our catalogue, write to Dr. T. C. Kimble, Galesburg, Ill.

CERTIFICATES.

Any student who has completed the work as outlined in the "Pre-medical Group" will be given the degree of Bachelor of Arts.

To all students who satisfactorily complete the studies of the one-year group a "Certificate of Proficiency" will be given, showing the amount and character of the work done. This certificate will now be accepted by the leading colleges of the "American Medical Association" as satisfactory evidence of having completed the freshman year of the four-year course in medicine, admitting the student to the sophomore year.

ADMISSION REQUIREMENTS.

First—The student must be regularly registered in the College.

Second—He must have completed at least eighteen (18) credits in the College. It is required that a student have a reading knowledge of French or German; Mathematics through Trigonometry; History, two courses; Psychology, one course; General Biology, two courses; Physics, two or three courses; Chemistry, three courses, and Zoology and Botany, three courses.

Third—He must present certificates of good moral character signed by at least two physicians of good standing in the state in which the student last resided.

Fourth—At the beginning of his senior year he must register as a medical student and as a college student. No fee will be charged for the extra registration.

CURRICULUM.

FIRST YEAR.

8:00 ....*German 1	German 2	German 3
9:30 .... Chemistry 1	Chemistry 2	Chemistry 3
10:30 .... English 5	English 6	Sociology 1

SECOND YEAR.

9:30 .... Biology 1	Biology 2	Psychology 1
11:30 .... Math. 7	Math. 8	Math. 9
1:45 .... History 8	History 9	Histology or Embryology

THIRD YEAR.

8:00 ..:......... Physics 1	Physics 2	Physics 3
10:30 .... Zoology 2	Zoology 3	Botany 1
1:45 .... Chem. 4	Chem. 5	Chem. 7

FOURTH YEAR

8:00 .... Physiology 2	Physiology 2b	Physiology 3
1:45 .... Materia Medica (½)	Materia Med. (½)	
Osteology (½)	Osteology (½)	Anatomy

*NOTE—A student must obtain a reading knowledge of either French or German from these courses and those offered for entrance.

The studies following, constituting the first year's medical course, require the number of hours as indicated.

STUDY.	LABORATORY.	RECITATIONS AND LECTURES.
*Chemistry	360 hrs.	72 hrs.
Physiology	72 hrs.	180 hrs.
Osteology	144 hrs.	72 hrs.
Anatomy	200 hrs.	100 hrs.
Histology	152 hrs.	48 hrs.
Embryology	120 hrs.	36 hrs.
Materia Medica	144 hrs.	108 hrs.
	1192 hrs.	616 hrs.

*NOTE.—General and organic chemistry are taken by the student during the first year in the college. In many medical colleges these courses supplemented by courses 4, 5, and 7 will exempt the student from farther work in chemistry and thus permit him to devote the time to the more strictly technical studies.

For further particulars see medical announcement for the year ending June 2nd, 1904, or write Dr. T. C. Kimble, Galesburg, Ill.

PREPARATORY COURSES.

The following courses are designed chiefly for the benefit of those Unclassified Students who wish to complete the entrance requirements for admission to the College of Liberal Arts. They are, however, open to all students, *but if taken by students in the College of Liberal Arts they will not be counted on the thirty-eight credits required for graduation.*

ENGLISH.

The following courses are offered for the benefit of those wishing to pass the English Examination for admission as outlined on pages 23, 24. Courses 2, 3, and 4 are full courses and will deal with composition and with the study of the books prescribed for careful study. Courses *2b, 3b,* and *4b* are half courses and will deal with the books prescribed for reading.

2. Macaulay's Essays on Milton and Addison, and Milton's L'Allegro and Il Penseroso.

Three days per week. Composition (Scott and Denney), one day per week. Fall term. Mrs. KIMBLE.

3. Milton's Comus and Lycidas, and Burke's Speech on Conciliation with America.

Three days per week. Composition (Scott and Denney), one day per week. Winter term. Mrs. KIMBLE.

4. Shakespeare's Macbeth.

Three days per week. Composition (Scott and Denney), one day per week. Spring term. Mrs. KIMBLE.

2 (b). Addison's Sir Roger de Coverly Papers in the Spectator, Goldsmith's Vicar of Wakefield, Lowell's Vision of Sir Launfal.

Three days per week. Fall term. Mrs. KIMBLE.

3 (b). Scott's Ivanhoe, Coleridge's Ancient Mariner, Carlyle's Essay on Burns, Shakespeare's Merchant of Venice.

Three days per week. Winter term. Mrs. KIMBLE.

4 (*b*). George Eliot's Silas Marner, Tennyson's Princess, Shakespeare's Julius Caesar.

Three days per week. Spring term. Mrs. KIMBLE.

English 2, 3, and 4 are given as full courses.
English 2b, 3b, and 4b are given as half courses.

LATIN.

1. Latin Lessons.

Collar and Daniell's First Year Latin. Fall term.

2. Latin Lessons. (Continuation of 1.)

Winter term.

3. Readings from Eutropius and Viri Romae.

Miller and Beeson's Second Year Latin. Spring term.

4. Caesar and Latin Prose Composition.

Miller and Beeson's Second Year Latin. Fall term.

Professor FOWLER.

MATHEMATICS.

2. Elementary Algebra.

Well's Essentials of Algebra is used. Fall term.

Open to all students. Professor GRUBB.

3. Elementary Algebra. (Continued.)

Winter term. Professor GRUBB.

Prerequisite, Mathematics 2.

4. Elementary Algebra. (Continued.)

Spring term. Professor GRUBB.

Prerequisite, Mathematics 3.

5. Algebra.

After a brief review of Quadratic Equations, with especial reference to theory, the subjects of Simultaneous Equations of the second degree, Indeterminate Equations, Ratio and Proportion, Arithmetical and Geometrical progression will be considered. Wells's College Algebra is used. Fall term. Professor GRUBB.

Prerequisite, Mathematics 4.

6. (*a*) Plane Geometry.

This course is designed to give students thorough drill in the first principles of Geometry. Phillips and Fisher's Elements of Geometry is used. Winter term. Professor GRUBB.

Open to all students.

6. (b) Plane Geometry.

This course consists of a review of Mathematics 6 (a) together with the demonstration of a large number of original propositions. Spring term. Professor WRIGHT.

Prerequisite, Mathematics 6 (a).

Mathematics 2, 3, 4, 5, and 6 (a) are designed to meet the entrance requirements in Algebra and Plane Geometry. (See page 26.)

PHYSICAL GEOGRAPHY.

1. Physical Geography.

Text-book, Tarr's Elementary Physical Geography. Spring term.

Open to all students.

Physical Geography 1 will alternate with Economics 1. Given in 1905. Miss HATHAWAY.

HISTORY.

1. Greece.

History of Greece. Fall term. Miss HATHAWAY.

Open to all students.

3. Rome.

History of Rome. Text-book, Morey. Winter term.

Open to all students. Miss HATHAWAY.

4. England.

History of England. Text-book, Higginson and Channing. Spring term. Miss HATHAWAY.

Open to all students.

ECONOMICS.

1. Science of Government.

Text-book, Fiske's Civil Government in the United States, and Andrew's Manual of the Constitution. Spring term.

Open to all students. Miss HATHAWAY.

Economics 1 will alternate with Physical Geography 1. Given in 1904.

UNCLASSIFIED STUDENTS.

Persons who wish to pursue studies at Lombard without becoming candidates for a degree will be admitted on probation to any class for which they are fitted by previous training. In case the class in question demands a prerequisite, the applicant must bring a certificate in this prerequisite from an approved school, or pass an examination.

On severing their connection with the College, these students will receive, upon request, a certificate, signed by the President and their several instructors, stating the amount and quality of the work done.

If at any time such students wish to become candidates for a degree, they must fulfill all the requirements for admission to the department in which the degree is to be taken.

Among these also will be listed all students who have an ultimate purpose of taking a degree, but who need to pusue one or more of the preparatory courses to fulfill the requirements for admission to the College of Liberal Arts.

RYDER DIVINITY SCHOOL.

The Divinity School of Lombard College was opened for the admission of students on the 5th of September, 1881. The first class was graduated in 1885.

At the annual meeting of the Board of Trustees in 1890, it was voted to name the theological department of the College the RYDER DIVINITY SCHOOL, in honor or the late William Henry Ryder, D. D., whose munificent bequests to the College exceed fifty thousand dollars.

The largest benefaction to the Divinity School from any other source was received from the late Hon. A. G. Throop, founder of the Throop Polytechnic Institute at Pasadena, California. In 1890, Mr. Throop gave twenty thousand dollars towards the endowment of the Divinity School.

ADMISSION.

Applicants unknown to the faculty must bring satisfactory evidences of good moral and religious character. They should also bring certificates of their church membership.

Candidates for admission to the Divinity School must be prepared to sustain examination in the following subjects:

I. ENGLISH.

(a) Grammar and Analysis.

Reed and Kellogg's Higher Lessons in English, or an equivalent.

(b) Composition.

An extemporaneous composition on an assigned subject, correct as to spelling, paragraphing, grammar, and rhetorical form.

(c) Literature.

An equivalent of English 2, 2b, 3, 3b, 4, and 4b as described on page 71 of this catalogue.

II. HISTORY.

(a) Bible History,

A competent knowledge of the Bible as History, including the so-called Old Testament Apocrypha. The ground covered is given in the ten volume Historical Series for Bible Students, edited by Kent and Sanders, and published by Scribner's Sons.

(*b*) **Bible Geography and Archaeology.**

A general knowledge of localities, customs, manners, etc., of Bible times.

Rand and McNally's Manual of Biblical Geography and Jahn's Archeology or equivalents.

(*c*) **General History.**

Swinton's General History or an equivalent.

III. MATHEMATICS.

(*a*) **Arithmetic.**

Higher Arithmetic, including percentage, alligation, extraction of roots, mensuration, and the metric system.

(*b*) **Elementary Algebra.**

Wells's Academic Algebra, or an equivalent.

IV. GEOGRAPHY.

Tarr's Elementary Geography, or an equivalent.

V. SCIENCE.

(*a*) **Chemistry.**

The equivalent of Chemistry 1 and 2 as described on page 49. (Equivalent work in Physics and Botany may be accepted in lieu of Chemistry.)

(*b*) **Physiology.**

This calls for a general knowledge of the human skeleton, muscular, circulatory, and nervous systems, the vital organs, viscera, and organs of special sense, and the processes of respiration and digestion. The preparation required is covered in such text-books as Martin's Human Body (advanced course), or Huxley's Elementary Physiology (Lee's Revision).

Preliminary Year.

To accommodate those candidates for admission who are not fully prepared to satisfy the admission requirements an opportunity is given to complete their preparation in the School, and a preliminary year's work is mapped out (page 80), which, however, is susceptible of some modification to meet the special needs of the candidate.

As a further encouragement to candidates to avail themselves of this opportunity the Universalist General Convention will permit its grant of financial aid to be spread over five years, instead of four as hitherto. Thus the candidate who requires five years for the full course, including the Preliminary year, may receive, under the usual conditions, a maximum grant of $100 each year for the five years, or a maximum grant of $125 a year for four years as he may prefer.

ADMISSION BY CERTIFICATE.

Satisfactory grades from approved schools will be accepted in lieu of examination. Students thus admitted by certificate will be regarded as on probation during the first term of their course.

ADMISSION TO ADVANCED STANDING

Students who bring satisfactory evidence of work done beyond the requirements of admission will be given credit for the same on the regular course, so far as the faculty may deem consistent with the special aims of that course.

The members of the Divinity School are admitted to the advantages presented by the other departments of the College.

EXPENSES.

Tuition is free to all regular members of the Divinity School who are candidates for the ministry, on condition that the student maintains an average grade of at least 70 per cent.

The charge for incidentals is the same as in the College of Liberal Arts, $5 per term.

For board in Commons, see page 11.

Board in good families can be secured for from $2.50 to $3.25 per week. Students may somewhat reduce their expenses by forming clubs or boarding themselves.

PECUNIARY AID.

Students who are candidates for the ministry of the Universalist Church may, upon complying with the prescribed conditions and receiving the recommendation of the faculty, obtain assistance from the Universalist General Convention in the form of a gratuity, to an amount not exceeding $125 a year for four years. Applications will be granted by the Convention only when entirely satisfactory. The first installment of this gift will not be issued to entering students until January, the second will be issued in May. Students should therefore come with resources of their own sufficient to pay their expenses for at least one term.

Those who have not a definite purpose of entering the Universalist ministry are not eligible to the Convention gift.

Membership in some Universalist Church is also required as a condition of the gift.

The use of tobacco or other narcotic or stimulants is an absolute bar to the grant of the Convention aid.

The Convention aid may be withheld at any time, should the work or behavior of the candidate prove unsatisfactory.

After having had two terms in Homiletics, students who show due proficiency are permitted to secure appointments to preach, and thus to add to their pecuniary resources.

Courses of Instruction.

1. Regular Course.

Candidates for the degree of B. D. will be expected to complete the course scheduled on page 80. This course, it will be observed, prescribes a certain amount of work in Greek, which is regarded as indispensable to the degree. In addition to the studies indicated in the schedule, a year's work in Hebrew will be offered to those who desire it, at some time during their residence. It is earnestly recommended that all students whose circumstances do not positively forbid their spending the requisite time, take the Regular Course.

2. Alternative Course.

It is, however, permitted to those who, after due deliberation, prefer to do so, omit the Greek and Hebrew, and to substitute therefor an equivalent amount of elective work in English, Modern Languages, Science, Mathematics, or Sociology, with the approval of the faculty. Those who complete such a course will be graduated at the Annual Commencement, and will be furnished a certificate showing what work they have done; but they will not be given the degree of B. D. or any other degree.

3. Special Work.

(a) Candidates for the ministry who cannot take either of the above described courses, will be permitted to elect particular studies, so far as their preparation warrants. Pastors already engaged in ministerial work who can spare a period for further study, are particularly invited to avail themselves of this opportunity.

(b) The School is also open to persons who do not intend to enter the ministry. The pursuit of studies of a theological or religious character is an interesting and helpful means of personal culture. Such a course is especially recommended to those who desire to become better fitted for service in the Sunday School, the Church, the Young People's Christian Union and similar societies, or for charitable and philanthropic work. Upon those who come with these purposes, no denominational test will be imposed. Students of all denominations and beliefs will be welcome to the advantages of study and training in the Divinity School, as in other departments of the College.

Faculty of the Divinity School.

CHARLES ELLWOOD NASH, A. M., S. T. D., PRESIDENT.
Instructor in Homiletics and Pastoral Care.

NEHEMIAH WHITE, A. M., PH. D., S. T. D.
*Hall Professor of Intellectual and Moral Philosophy.
In charge of the Ryder Divinity School, Professor of Biblical Languages and Exegesis.

†Hull Professor of Biblical Geography and Archæology.

ISAAC AUGUSTUS PARKER, A. M., PH. D.
Professor of Greek.

RALPH GRIERSON KIMBLE,
Professor of Sociology.

EDSON REIFSNIDER, B. D.,
Instructor in Homiletics and Pastoral Care.

ALICE BERTHA CURTIS, B. DI., PH B.,
Professor of English and Public Speaking.

NON-RESIDENT LECTURERS.
MARION D. SHUTTER, D. D.,
I. M. ATWOOD, D. D.

*In honor of the late E. G. Hall, of Chicago.
†In honor of the Rev. Stephen Hull, of Kansas City, Mo.

Degrees Conferred in 1903.

BACHELOR OF DIVINITY.

S. Martin Nieveen..............................*Platte, S. Dak.*

Schedule.

1. Preliminary Year.

FALL TERM.	WINTER TERM.	SPRING TERM.
English 2, 2b.	English 3, 3b.	English 4, 4b.
Biblical History.	Biblical History.	Biblical Geography and Archæology.
Chemistry.	Elementary Physiology.	Elementary Botany.

2. Regular Course.

Leading to the degree of Bachelor of Divinity.

FIRST YEAR.

FALL TERM.	WINTER TERM.	SPRING TERM.
English 5.	English 6.	English 7.
Greek 1.	Greek 2.	Greek 3.
History 5.	History 6.	History 7.

SECOND YEAR.

Psychology 1.	Psychology 2.	Hermeneutics.
Greek 4.	Greek Testament.	Greek Testament.
Homiletics 1.	Homiletics 2.	Homiletics 3.
Elocution.	Elocution.	Elocution.

THIRD YEAR.

Homiletics 4.	Homiletics 5.	Homiletics 6.
Sociology 1.	Greek Testament.	Greek Testament.
Apologetics.	Dogmatic Theology.	Dogmatic Theology.
	Logic.	

FOURTH YEAR.

Sociology D 1.	Sociology D 2.	Pastoral Care.
Economics 2.	Ethics.	O. T. Introduction (2hrs.)
*Hebrew.	*Hebrew.	Ethical Theories, or
Preaching.	Preaching.	Philosophy of Religion, or
		Metaphysic, or
		Comparative Religions.

*Elective.

Description of Studies.

HEBREW

1, 2, 3. Grammar and Old Testament.

These are primarily courses in the Divinity School, but may be elected by students in the College of Liberal Arts whenever they are offered. Classes will be formed each year if a sufficient number of students apply.

It is the aim to give the students such a knowledge of the forms and structure of the Hebrew Language as shall enable them to use it efficiently in the criticism and literary analysis of the Old Testament Scriptures. The text-books used are H. G. Mitchell's Hebrew Lessons and the Hebrew Old Testament. Three terms—Fall, Winter and Spring—each term counting as a course.

Professor WHITE.

BIBLE STUDY.

1. Biblical History, A.

Kent's Studies in Biblical History and Literature is used. The aim is to present the contents of the Bible as they stand in our English version. Due account is made of contemporary history and the monumental data. In general the first term will be occupied with the material of the Old Testament; the second term with that of the New. Fall term.

2. Biblical History, B.

A continuation of the preceding. Winter term.

3. Biblical Geography and Archæology.

A detailed study of the political and physical geography of the Bible countries, and a general study of the antiquities of the Bible peoples. Spring term.

4. Biblical Criticism.

Driver's Introduction to the Old Testament is used as a text-book, with reference to Fripp, Ryle, Bacon, Robertson, and other works. A course of lectures is given on the Science of Documentary Analysis, the Principles and Methods of Historical Criticism, and the Religious aspects of the Higher Criticism. Winter term.

Professor WHITE.

HERMENEUTICS.

It is the aim to set forth the principles of interpretation in connection with the translation and exposition of the portions of the Greek Testament to which attention is given.

Lectures intended to aid the student in interpreting the Greek Testament, and also on the History of Interpretation are given in the winter and the spring term. Professor PARKER.

PREPARATORY GREEK.

(Greek 1, 2, 3, 4, see pages 44, 45.)

THE GREEK TESTAMENT.

13. Translation and Exegesis of the Gospel of John.

Its date and genuineness. Portions of the Acts of the Apostles. Winter term. Professor PARKER.

14. Translation and Exegesis of Selections from the Gospel of Matthew and the Epistles of Paul.

Spring term. Professor PARKER.

THEOLOGY.

1. Christian Evidences.

The study of Christian Evidences will include an examination of the bases of Christian belief, Evolutionary theories and their relation to Philosophy, Ethics, and Religion, and the function and method of Apologetics. Comparison will be instituted between the modern methods in Apologetics and the methods of primitive Christianity. Instruction will be given mostly by lectures with frequent reference to Fisher, Schurman, Flint, Bruce, and others. Fall term.
Professor WHITE.

2. Dogmatic Theology.

Martensen's Christian Dogmatics is used as a text-book. A thorough investigation is made of the several Christian doctrines, with an extended examination of associated questions and controversies. The widest liberty is given for questions and discussions on the various topics presented. Winter and spring terms.
Professor WHITE.

3 Comparative Religions.

The work of the students consists in the examination and comparison of the authorities upon the great Non-Christian religions. Special topics are investigated and reports made by each member of the class. Spring term. Professor WHITE.

APPLIED CHRISTIANITY.

The demand for a more thorough investigation of the bearings of Christian Doctrine upon the social, political, and industrial organisms, coupled with the demand for a more diversified and scientific administration of religion through the churches, is met at Lombard College by the establishment of a chair of Sociology. The course of study provided for will occupy four terms, three terms being devoted to Sociology, and one term to Pastoral Care.

SOCIOLOGY.

1. An Introduction to Sociological Theory.

A study of the characteristics of general sociological theory.

D. 1. Pathologic Factors of the Modern Community.

The discrimination and definition of the dependent, defective and delinquent classes, together with a brief study of current attempts to deal with the same.

D. 2. Pathologic Factors of the Modern Community.

A continuation of Sociology D. 1.

Sociology D. 1, and D. 2 are designed expressly to meet the needs of Divinity students. If taken by students in the College of Liberal Arts they will not count on the thirty-eight credits required for the A. B. degree.

PASTORAL CARE.

A study of the spiritual, mental, and social qualifications of the minister for his work, and his administration of the special services of the church—baptism, confirmation, the Lord's Supper, marriage, and the burial of the dead. A liberal portion of the term will be devoted to an examination of various methods of church organization, for the purpose of giving the minister facility in adapting himself to parish needs, especially to those peculiar to the locality in which he may be settled. Also a study is made of the Manual of the Universalist General Convention. Spring term. Mr. REIFSNIDER.

PSYCHOLOGY.

1. Introductory Psychology.

The purpose of the course is to guide the beginner in gaining the fundamentals of a thorough knowledge of psychology and of psychic life. The course is organized about a careful study of the commoner characteristics of the more accessible mental processes. Emphasis is laid upon the ready and accurate use of the more important psychological terms. Some knowledge of the chief standpoints and methods of the science is gained. Collateral reading in connection with the text will be regularly assigned and a correct appreciation of the relation of this reading to the treatment presented in the text will be a requirement of the course. Experiments described in text and reading will be fully discussed; and, where circumstances will permit, the student will see performed by others or will himself perform in the laboratory certain type experiments. Fall term. Professor KIMBLE.

2. Introductory Psychology.

Continuation of Psychology 1. Winter term.

METAPHYSIC.

This is primarily a course in the Divinity School, but it may be elected by students in the College of Liberal Arts whenever it is offered. Lotze's Outlines of Metaphysic is used as a text-book. Spring term. Professor WHITE.

LOGIC.

Having first obtained a thorough grounding in the principles and methods of correct reasoning both deductive and inductive, at least one-half of the term is given to the detection and discrimination of fallacies in actual examples. Such examples the class is required to search out in current literature and bring in for discussion. Davis's Elements of Deductive Logic and Davis's Elements of Inductive Logic are used. Winter term.

ETHICS.

Ethics is treated from the standpoint of Philosophy, and the different systems are discussed. The nature and grounds of obligation are investigated and applied to the practical affairs of life. Winter term. Professor WHITE.

PHILOSOPHY OF RELIGION.

Fairbairn's Philosophy of the Christian Religion is the text-book. Lotze, Sabatier, and Martineau are used as works of reference. The aim of the instructor is to acquaint the student with the proper office of reason in the effort to find argumentative grounds for religious ideas. Most of the modern theories respecting the nature and scope of the religious feeling pass under review; and in such discussions free questioning on the part of the student is encouraged. Spring term. Professor WHITE.

ETHICAL THEORIES.

Martineau's Types of Ethical Theory is used as a text-book with frequent references to the works of Sidgwick, Green, Smyth, and others. Much attention is paid to the elucidation and criticism of the modern ethical theories. Spring term.

Professor WHITE.

CHURCH HISTORY.

5. History of the Christian Church.

A. *The Ancient and Mediaeval Eras* [*1-1517.*]

This course in Church History is primarily intended for the members of the Divinity School but is also open to College students. It will require the investigation of the early organization and extension of Christianity and the successive periods of the Church down to the time of Charlemagne; followed by a careful inquiry into the causes of the rise of the Papacy, of the political relations of the Church, and of the Crusades. Fisher's History of the Church will be used as a hand book and topics will be assigned to each member of the class for special investigation and reports. Fall term.

Professor WHITE.

6. History of the Christian Church.

B. *The Modern Era* [*1517-1904.*]

This course will begin with the study of the Reformation, and trace the history of the Church down to the present time. It will include the history of Christian missions, revivals, social reforms, and philanthropy. The same text-book will be used as in History 5. Winter term.

Professor WHITE.

7. History of Christian Doctrine.

Special pains will be taken to make clear the aim of the History of Christian Doctrine, and to indicate the process of its development.

Professor WHITE.

HOMILETICS.

The course in Homiletics covers the second, third, and fourth years. The primary aim is practical. Upon a general but adequate groundwork of theory and history of preaching the effort is made to construct an art of effective pulpit oratory. Elaborate and exacting drill in the logical conception and construction of the sermon plan, with constant application of rhetorical principles, occupies the major part of the first year. Inspiration and direction are sought in the frequent analysis of the discourses of great preachers of all styles, and in the study of their sources of power. Individuality and originality are emphasized as desiderata. In the second year the stress is laid upon flexibility and adaptability, upon invention, upon the rationale of interesting preaching, and upon the acquisition of freedom in extempore address. Throughout the course the preparation and criticism of sermons by the class continues uninterruptedly.

President NASH and Mr. REIFSNIDER.

ELOCUTION.

In view of the fact that a good delivery is of inestimable advantage to the preacher, the students in the Divinity School are offered an extended course in Elocution and Physical Culture.

The students are not only admitted to all Elocution classes in the College, but also receive a large amount of individual training.

Courses 1, 2, 3, as outlined on page 65 of this catalogue, are required, as well as regular drill and rehearsals for the preaching exercises.   Professor CURTIS.

ENGLISH.

For English 2, 3, 4, required for entrance to full standing in the Divinity School, and taught in the Preliminary year, see page 71 For English 5, 6, 7, which courses are required in the Divinity School, see page 35 of this catalogue.

COLLEGE STUDIES AND THE A. B. DEGREE.

Divinity students are permitted, with the consent of the Faculty, to pursue studies in the College of Liberal Arts. Graduates of the Divinity School may receive the additional degree of Bachelor of Arts, upon the satisfactory completion of an aggregate of twenty full courses taken in the classes of the college of Liberal Arts, beyond the full requirements of the Divinity School for the degree of Bachelor of Divinity.

In addition to the above twenty credits, the candidate must furnish the full quota of sixteen units required for admission to the College of Liberal Arts. Of these sixteen units, the courses required for admission to the Divinity School (see pages 75 and 76) will count six.

DEPARTMENT OF MUSIC.

Instruction is provided in the various branches of Theoretical, Vocal, and Instrumental Music. These courses, except the courses in Theoretical Music and Musical History, are distinct from the work in the other departments of the College, and do not count toward a college degree. Students are classed and registered as private pupils of the several instructors, with whom arrangements may be made in regard to lessons.

Faculty.

ALEXANDER S. THOMPSON,.
DIRECTOR.
Instructor in Piano and Voice, all Theoretical Courses, and Organ.

CLARA DUTTON THOMPSON,
ASSOCIATE DIRECTOR.
Instructor in Voice, Piano, and Organ.

W. H. CHEESMAN,
Instructor in Violin.

THEORETICAL COURSES.

Professor Thompson.

1. Harmony.

Keys, scales and signatures, intervals, formation of the triad, chord connection, simple part writing begun. Normal and Foreign progressions. All common chords and the rules governing their treatment in part writing. Goetchius, "The Materials of Composition" is the text-book used. Two hours a week. Fall term.

2. Harmony.

Part writing continued. The inversion of chords. Chords of the sixth and six-four, chords of the seventh and their inversions. Key-board work. Modulation begun. Two hours a week. Winter term.

3. Harmony.

Chords of the seventh continued. Altered and augmented chords explained and employed in harmonization. Modulation continued. Two hours a week. Spring term.

4. Single Counterpoint.

Writing from *canti fermi*. First species, note against note. Second species, two notes against one. Third species four notes against one. John Frederick Bridge's Counterpoint is the text-book used. Fall term.

5. Single Counterpoint.

Writing from *canti fermi* continued in fourth species. Syncopation-suspensions, retardations. Fifth species florid counterpoint. Winter term.

6. Single and Double Counterpoint.

Florid counterpoint continued. Double counterpoint in all forms. Spring term.

(Students who expect to finish only the six courses may substitute 7 for 6, with the advice and consent of the Director.)

7. Musical Form.

The section and phrase. The period. The small primary forms. The large primary forms. The motive and its development. The study (Etude), dance forms, Rondo form. Vocal song. Sonata form. Musical form. Bussler-Cornell. Fall term.

8. Canon and Fugue.

Canon in two voices in all intervals. Fugue in two, three, and four voices. Text-books. Richter, Double Counterpoint and Fugue; Higgs, Fugue. Winter term.

9. Instrumentation.

Study of Berlioz on instrumentation, also Prout's work on same subject. Study of orchestral scores. Orchestral scoring of various musical passages, and of original work. Orchestral writing without recourse to piano scoring. Spring term.

10, 11, 12. History of Music. (Half Courses.)

These courses embrace a history of the development of music from the earliest time until to-day, with special reference to critical analysis of the works of the great masters. They also furnish an introduction to the lives of the great composers. One hour a week for the year. Professor THOMPSON.

PIANOFORTE COURSES.

Professor Thompson or Mrs. Thompson.

1. Preparatory.

Stephen Emory's Foundation Studies; Herz Scales or Handrock's Mechanical Studies; Enckhausen Progressive Melodious Studies or Ehmant Petite Ecole Melodique; Mathew's Graded Course first four books. The major and minor scales and major and minor chords must be played from memory.

The above fundamentals must be fully mastered before a pupil can be classified as a student in the Collegiate Musical Course. The mastery of these principles is of the greatest importance, as it is the only way to secure intelligent and sure progress in the advanced stages. No effort will be spared to induce the student to work with that personal relish so necessary to good work.

COLLEGE PIANOFORTE COURSE.

Professor Thompson.

Some flexibility will and must be allowed in the course, to meet the peculiarities of the pupil; at the same time care will be taken not to graduate one-sided musicians.

1. First Year.

Mathew's Graded Course, Books 5 and 6; Daily Technical Exercises, Scales, Thirds and Sixths, Handstroke and Staccato, Arm Touch; Beren's New School of Velocity, Books 1 and 2; Selections from Clementi and Kuhlau Sonatinas; pieces by Bohm, Thome, Godard, Lebierre, Sapelnikoff and other suitable practice pieces.

2. Second Year.

Mathew's Graded Course, Book 7; Beren's New School of Velocity, Books 3 and 4; Low's Octave Studies; Selections from Haydn and Mozart Sonatas; Bach's Inventions, Selections from Mendelssohn's Songs without Words; pieces by modern authors including Grieg, Chaminade, Rachmaninoff, Rubinstein.

3. Third Year.

Mathew's Graded Course 8 and 9; Hasert's Modern Finger Exercises, Books 1 and 2; Kullak's Octave Studies; Bach's Preludes and Fugues; Selections from Chopin and Schumann; Beethoven's Sonatas; Cramer's Etudes.

4. Fourth Year.

Chopin's Etudes; Bach's Advanced Works, Chromatic Fantasie and Fugue in D minor, Bach-Tausig Toccata and Fugue D minor; Joseffy's Advanced School of Piano Playing; Beethoven Sonatas continued; Selections from Chopin and Schumann; Selections from Liszt's Compositions. Liberal recognition is accorded the works of American composers in the entire course.

VOICE CULTURE.

Mrs. Thompson and Professor Thompson.

1. Preparatory.

Elementary sight singing, Solfeggio practice and application of sol-fa syllables to staff in simple music; breathing and voice placing exercises—sustained tones and scale work according to the Italian method as taught by Sims Reeves of London, Eng., (pupil of Mazzucato, an acknowledged descendant of the famous Porpora) also by Vannucini of Florence, Italy. Concone's Fifty Lessons; Concone's Forty Lessons for Bass; Marchesi's Exercises, op. 1, First Part; Vaccai's Studies.

COLLEGE COURSE.

No student can be classified in the Collegiate Course in voice without passing examination in Solfeggio, or demonstrating to the satisfaction of the director the ability to read music of moderate difficulty at sight.

1. First Year.

Voice placing exercises, scales, sustained tones, and articulation exercises, Marchesi's Studies; Concone's Twenty-five Lessons; songs by American authors, Mendelssohn, Jensen, Grieg, Gastaldon, Denza, Cowen, and other good foreign authors.

2. Second Year.

Voice placing exercises, scales, etc. Marchesi's Studies; Concone's Fifteen Lessons; songs or solos by Schubert, Schumann. Mendelssohn, Grieg, Handel, Jensen, and American authors.

3. Third Year.

Voice placing exercises; Marchesi and Bordogni exercises; solos from standard oratorios and operas, Sullivan, Mendelssohn, Handel, Mozart, and other authors.

4. Fourth Year.

Handelian Oratorio Solos, German Lieder, Wagnerian, and other opera solos.

PIPE ORGAN COURSES.

Mrs. Thompson and Professor Thompson.

Students who wish to begin the study of the Organ should have completed the Second Grade of the Piano Course.

The chief aim of this department is the thorough preparation of church organists. Organ students should also make a conscientious study of Solo and Chorus Singing, with a view of becoming efficient chorus-masters and directors of church music.

The study of Harmony, Counterpoint, and History of Music is absolutely necessary to an intelligent study of the instrument.

1. First Grade.

Exercises in pedal playing. Ritter's Organ School. Hymns Thayer's Pedal Studies. Elementary Registration.

2. Second Grade.

Studies in Pedal Phrasing by Buck, Volckmar, and Schneider. Polyphonic composition by Rink, Bach, Fisher. Easy pieces by Merkel, Dubois, Guilmant, Mendelssohn, and others. Registration, Structure of the Organ, Choir Accompaniment.

3. Third Grade.

Study of Sonatas and Fugues by Bach, Mendelssohn, Reinberger, and others. Modern compositions of German, English, and French masters. Choir Accompaniment.

VIOLIN COURSES.

Professor Cheesman.

1. Preparatory Grade.

Elementary exercises in position, bowing, etc. Easy exercises in major and minor keys in the first book from Wichtl's Violin School. Pleyel's Duets, and twelve studies by H. E. Kayser, op. 20. Memorizing.

2. Intermediate Grade.

Studies by Kayer and Wohlfahrt. Systematic progress through the various positions, beginning with the second book of F. Hermann. Studies from Shradieck for the development of technic and pure tone qualities. Sections from compositions by Dancla, Mazas, Weiss, DeBeriot; also solos and fantasias based upon operatic themes.

3. Advance Grade.

Technical studies from the works of Kreutzer, Fiorillo, Rode, together with duets, trios, and quartets, arranged for strings; overtures; sight reading. Sonatas and concertos by Bach, Haydn, Spohr, Beethoven; Mendelssohn, DeBeriot, Wieniawski, Grieg, and others.

MANDOLIN AND GUITAR COURSES.

Professor Cheesman.

The study of these popular instruments has become a favorite recreation with those students of our colleges who may not have the time or inclination to pursue the study of music in its more serious forms.

At the conclusion of the first term of lessons (twelve weeks) a "Lombard Mandolin Club" will be organized, with rehearsals one evening a week. The Italian method is used entirely in the study of these instruments, thereby establishing the very best method of picking the strings and fingering, with special attention to the tone quality of the "tremolo," which relieves the mandolin of much of its so-called monotony. Solos, duets, and quartets, will also be prepared in addition to the regular club work, with special numbers to be given by the lady members of the club.

SIGHT SINGING AND CHORUS CLASSES.

1. Elementary Sight Singing Class.

The rudiments of Music, the intervals of the Major Scale, exercises in one and two parts, and easy songs. Ear-training. One college term.

2. Advanced Class.

Solfeggios in major and minor keys, three and four part songs. One college term.

3. Chorus Class.

Four part compositions, glees, sacred and secular choruses from our best classic and modern composers. Oratorios.

Only those students who have finished the work done in the advanced Sight-Singing Class will be admitted into the Chorus Class.

Requirements for Graduation.

A diploma will be conferred upon any student who shall satisfactorily complete one of the following courses in instrumental or vocal music. In addition to the requirements enumerated below, the candidate will prepare a thesis, present an original musical composition, or perform other original work satisfactory to the instructor, and also appear in public at a graduating recital.

A. THE PIANOFORTE.

Musical Requirements.

The complete College Course, Nos. 1, 2, 3, 4, 5, 6, 10, and 11 of the Theoretical Courses; Acoustics; and one year's membership in the Chorus Class.

Literary Requirements.

English 2, 3, 4, 5, and two English electives; one year of French or German.

If the candidate upon entering brings satisfactory proof of proficiency in any of these courses he is advised to take one study each term from such electives in the College of Liberal Arts as the Advisory Committee may recommend.

B. THE PIPE ORGAN.

Musical Requirements.

The full Organ Course, Nos. 1, 2, 3, 4, 5, 6, 10, and 11 of the Theoretical Courses; and Acoustics.

Literary Requirements.

The same as for Piano students.

C. THE VOICE.

Musical Requirements.

All the prescribed studies for Voice Culture; 1 and 2 of the CollegePiano Courses, with special view to accompaniments; and Nos. 1, 2, 3, 10, and 11, of the Theoretical Courses.

Literary Requirements.

The same as for Piano students, except that Italian may be substituted for French or German.

D. THE VIOLIN.

Musical Requirements.

All the prescribed studies laid down in the Violin Courses, Nos. 1, 2, 3, 4, 5, 6, 10, and 11 of the Theoretical Courses; Acoustics; and proficiency in all kinds of ensemble playing.

Literary Requirements.

The same as for Piano students.

TUITION.

The following prices are for a term of twelve weeks:

THEORETICAL COURSES—

    Music 1 to 9, each, $5.00.
    Music 10, 11, and 12, each, $3.00.

PIANOFORTE—

    Private Lessons—one hour per week, $20.00.
    Private Lessons—two half hours per week, $20.00.
    Private Lessons—one half hour per week, $11.00.
    Private Lessons—one forty-minute lesson per week, $15.00.
    Class Lessons may be specially arranged for.

VOICE CULTURE—

    Charges same as for pianoforte.

RENT OF PIANO—

    1 hour per day, per term, $2.75.
    2 hours per day, per term, $5.00.
    3 hours per day, per term, $6.75.
    4 hours per day, per term, $8.00.

PIPE ORGAN—

    Private Lessons—one hour per week, $24.00.
    In classes of two one hour per week, each person, $13.00.

VIOLIN—

    Private Lessons—one hour per week, $15.00.
    Private Lessons—two half hours per week, $15.00.
    Private Lessons, one 45-minute lesson per week, $12.00.

CLASS LESSONS, one hour per week—

    In classes of two, each, $8.00.
    In classes of three, each, $6,00.

MANDOLIN AND GUITAR—

    Private Lessons—one hour per week, $12.00.
    Private Lessons—two half hours per week, $12.00.
    Class Lessons—charges will be given on application to teacher.
    (A weekly rehearsal for club practice without extra charge.)

SIGHT SINGING CLASSES—

    Each, $1.00.

CHORUS CLASS—

A charge of $1.00 per term each will be made for the use of music to be supplied by the department.

The privilege of joining the Lombard Mandolin and Guitar Clubs, or the Lombard String Orchestra, is extended to any student outside of the private pupils of the instructor by the payment of $1.25 per term of twelve weeks. Rehearsals one evening each week.

GENERAL REMARKS.

Tuition and other charges must be paid before lessons are assigned.

In cases of protracted sickness only, will a proportionate deduction be made from term charges.

No visitors are allowed in practice rooms during practice hours.

All concerts and recitals given by the school of music or its faculty are free to music students, and attendance upon them is obligatory for music students.

A course of free lectures on musical culture will be given each year by the Director.

Holidays will be observed according to the calendar.

Pupils will be received at all times but should begin, if possible, with the term.

DEPARTMENT OF ART.

Instructor,

M. ISABELLE BLOOD.

Course in Art.

The Art Department affords a practical course in Drawing and Painting to those who wish to become teachers, designers, illustrators, or portrait artists. Regular students in this department who wish to take the entire course in Art will be given careful training in the following branches: Perspective drawing; drawing from casts, in charcoal and crayon; still life studies in crayon, oil, water color, and pastel; landscape from nature; and copying from good studies.

The entire course will occupy from two to three years, according to the ability of the student and the amount of time given to the work. A thorough knowledge of the elements of drawing being necessary to independent work, at least one year's work will be required in drawing in black and white from models of simple form, casts, still life, and those studies which will best prepare the student for the special line of work preferred.

Students may enter the Art Department at any time; and, though they are advised to take a full course in order to obtain the best results, arrangements can be made for lessons in any line desired.

While portrait work, pen and ink drawing, and china painting, are not required in the regular course, credit will be given for good work in any of these branches if it is desired to substitute them in part for oil, water color, or pastel.

A course of study in the History of Art and a thesis upon some subject approved by the instructor will also be required of students wishing to graduate from this department.

Those who complete the work as outlined above will be entitled to a Diploma.

For a description of courses in Free Hand Drawing, and for credit allowed for these courses in the College of Liberal Arts, see page 63.

TUITION.

The tuition fees will be as follows:

Drawing or Sketching—3-hour lesson, 35 cents.
Painting in Water Colors—3-hour lesson, 50 cents.
Oil Painting—3-hour lesson, 50 cents.
Portrait and China Painting—3-hour lesson, 50 cents.

For those who work six hours per week for the entire year, a rebate will be made at the end of the Spring term, so that the lessons in drawing will be less than 35 cents.

If pupils in Art desire four or more lessons per week, special rates are made.

SCHEDULE FOR THE YEAR 1904-1905.

Classes Recite 5 Hours Per Week, Except as Indicated.

HOUR	FALL TERM	WINTER TERM	SPRING TERM
8:00	Astronomy 1 Biblical History Economics 1* English 19*, 22*, 25, 28, 31*, 34ᵇ German 1 Greek 7*, 10 History 2 Homiletics 1 (3 h) Latin 4 Mathematics 2 Physics 1 Physiology 2, 4 Sociology D 1	Biblical History English 20*, 23*, 26, 29, 32*, 35* German 2 Greek 8*, 11 History 3 Homiletics 2 (3 h) Latin 5 Mathematics 3 Physics 2 Physiology 2b, 4b Sociology D2	Biblical Geography English 21*, 24*, 27, 30, 33*, 36* German 3 Greek 9*, 12 History 4 Homiletics 3 (3 h) Latin 6 Mathematics 4 Physical Geography Physics 3 Physiology 3, 5*
9:30	Biology 1 Chemistry 1 Economics 2 French 1 Homiletics 4 (2 h) Latin 7 Sociology 6*, 9	Biology 2 Chemistry 2 Economics 3 French 2 Latin 8 Logic Psychology 2 Sociology 7*, 12	Botany 1*, 2*, 3 Chemistry 3 †Compar. Religions Economics 4 French 3 Homiletics 6 (2 h) Latin 9 †Metaphysic †Philos. of Religion Physiology 1*
10:30	English 2b, 5 German 4*, 5, 10 (M) Greek 4 †Hebrew 1 History 5 Latin 1, 13, 16*, 19* Sociology 3* Zoology 1	English 3b, 6 Ethics German 6*, 7, 11 (M) Greek 5 †Hebrew 2 History 6 Latin 2, 14, 17*, 20* Sociology 1A*, 4* Zoology 2	English 4b, 7 Geology 1* German 8*, 9, 12 (M) Greek 6 †Hebrew 3 Hermeneutics History 7, 11* Latin 3, 15, 18*, 21* Mathematics 11 Pastoral Care Psychology 1 Zoology 3

HOUR	FALL TERM	WINTER TERM	SPRING TERM
11:30	Apologetics English 2 (T, W, Th, F) French 4*, 5, 10 (Th) Greek 1 Materia Medica (3h) Mathematics 5, 7	English 3 (T, W, Th, F) French 6*, 7, 11 (Th) Greek 2 Materia Medica (3h) Mathematics 6a, 8	English 4 (T, W, Th, F) French 8*, 9, 12 (Th) Greek 3 Jurisprudence 1 Math 6b, 9 Sociology 2*
1:45	Anatomy 1 (3h) Art 2 Chemistry 4 History 8 Hygiene Latin 10 Mathematics 10 Public Speaking 1	Anatomy 1 (3h), 2* Art 3 Chemistry 5 Dogmatic Theology Greek 13, 15* History 9 Latin 11 Mathematics 12, 14* Mineralogy Public Speaking 2, 5	Anatomy 1 (3h), 3a*, 3b* 4 Art 4 Chemistry 6, 7 Dogmatic Theology Greek 14, 16* Histology 3a*, 3b History 10 Latin 12 Mathematics 13, 16* Public Speaking 3, 6

*Not given in 1904-1905.

†Given at the option of the professor.

STUDENTS IN ALL DEPARTMENTS.

Candidates for Degrees in 1904.

MASTER OF ARTS.

Kimble, Olin Arvin..............................*Carbondale, Kan.*

BACHELOR OF ARTS.

Andreen, Frank G.....................................*Woodhull*
Ayars, Frank Cope................................*La Plata, Mo.*
Cooper, Harry Mac.....................................*Oquawka*
Grier, Ethelwyn Sophia............................*Racine, Wis.*
Hopkins, Roy Victor.................................*Princeville*
Howell, Spencer Pritchard..........................*Woodhull*
Hurd, Jay Clinton.......................................*Maquon*
Jansen, Harry Albin...................................*Woodhull*
Kimble, Olin Arvin..............................*Carbondale, Kan.*
Kober, Florence Leclerc...............................*Macomb*
Philbrook, Elizabeth Freeman.......................*Racine, Wis.*
Sammons, Mabel Alta....................................*Joliet.*
Scott, Preston Brown................................*Galesburg*
Varney, Franklin G.......................................*Clinton*

BACHELOR OF DIVINITY.

Varney, Franklin G.......................................*Clinton* .

CANDIDATE FOR DIPLOMA IN MUSIC.

Cease, Charles H.....................................*Belleville*

Candidates for Degrees in 1905.

CANDIDATES FOR THE DEGREE OF BACHELOR OF ARTS IN 1905.

Andrew, William B.

Clark, Fred Andrew

Clay, Walter Timothy

Grubb, Emma Welton

Hathaway, M. Agnes

Hills, Robert Asa

Linderholm, Ernest Arthur

Metcalf, Harold

Porter, Gail Quincy

Ross, Frances

CANDIDATES FOR THE DEGREE OF BACHELOR OF SCIENCE.

Rich, Willis Horton

Gillis, Hudson McBain

CANDIDATES FOR THE DEGREE OF BACHELOR OF DIVINITY IN 1905.

Bartholomew, Jennie L.
Fosher, Dudley C.

Manning, Stanley
Phillips, William

CANDIDATES FOR A DIPLOMA IN MUSIC IN 1905.

Nelson, Alvira
Rautenberg, Clare Marie

Rich, Willis Horton

Students in the Divinity School.

FOURTH YEAR.

Varney, Frank G.

THIRD YEAR.

Bartholomew, Jennie L.
Fosher, Claude Dudley

Manning, Stanley
Phillips, William

SECOND YEAR.

Ells, Harry Hugh

Hillstren, Charles W.

FIRST YEAR.

Bodell, Willard O.

Martin, Nellie Ruth

SPECIAL STUDENT.

Blood, Orrin Judson

Students in the College of Liberal Arts.

---

*Alvord, Francis M.
Andreen, Frank G.
Andrew, William B.
*Andrews, Euseba
Atterberry, Ralph Marshall
Austin, Ralph
Ayars, Frank Cope
Bignall, Roy E.
Blout, Charles J.
*Boehm, Fred Daniel
Chamberlain, Ethel Mary
Clark, Fred Andrew
Clay, Walter Timothy
*Conger, Delia Chase
*Conser, William H.
Cook, Grace Jane
Cooper, Harry Mac
Dickerson, Orval Melcher
Fennessy, Clinton L.

*Fennessy, Ethel C.
Fosher, Cora M.
Garlick, Elsie M.
Gibbs, Minnie Carroll
Gillis, Hudson McBain
*Golliday, Theo
Grier, Ethelwyn Sophia
Grubb, Emma Welton
Hathaway, M. Agnes
Herlocker, Webb A.
Hills, Robert Asa
*Hoffman, Arthur
*Hollister, Florence Gertrude
Hopkins, Roy Victor
Howell, Spencer Pritchard
Hurd, Jay Clinton
Jones, Mabel
Kimble, Anna Gillis
Kimble, Olin Arvin

Kober, Florence Leclerc
*Linderholm, Ernest Arthur
McAlpine, Roy Kenneth
*McDaniel, Levi Burt
Metcalf, Harold
*Parke, Eleanor
Philbrook, Elizabeth Freeman
Pittman, Eskridge
Porter, Gail Quincy
Potter, Albert M.
Potter, Warren J.
*Predmore, Pearl
Rich, Willis Horton
*Richey, Frances
*Robinson, Le Roy
Ross, Frances
*Ross, Louise
Sammons, Mabel Alta
Scott, Preston Brown
*Shaffer, James Alexander
Skinner, Albert Newton
Stryker, Elizabeth B.
*Tipton, Fred Lincoln
*Tolan, Lena
Varney, Frank G.
*Webster, Inez
Westfall, Curtis C.
*White, Bertha E.
*Wilson, Arthur J.
Wise, Lorena Myrtle

*Having credits sufficient in number to enter college, but one or more required studies lacking.

Students in the Department of Music.

HARMONY.

Cease, Charles
Hamerton, Lizzie
Hanson, Hildred
Nelson, Alvira
Randolph, Mollie
Rautenberg, Clare

HISTORY OF MUSIC.

Andrew, William B.
Cease, Charles
Clarke, Fred A.
Clay, Walter T.
Golliday, Theo
Hanson, Hildred
Porter, Gail Q.
Randolph, Mollie
Rautenberg, Clare

COUNTERPOINT.

Cease, Charles
Hanson, Hildred

VOCAL MUSIC.

Alexander, Kelley L.
Ayars, Frank C.
Bartholomew, Hattie
Buck, Hiram H.
Byloff, Julia
Cease, Charles
Crissey, Elice
Fosher, Dudley C.
Foster, June
Foster, May
Hanson, Hildred
Kienholz, Mrs. W. S.
Linderholm, Ernest A.
Long, Katherine
Randolph, Mollie
Riggs, Harlan
Rhodes, Simon
Rowan, Thomas
Smith, Celia M.
Snyder, Nina
VanBuren, Laura
White, Bertha
Williams, Jesse E.

PIANO.

Cease, Charles
Chamberlain, Ruth
Chambers, Pearl
Chapman, Jeannette
Clark, Katherine
Conger, Ethelin
Hamerton, Lizzie
Haffner, Mable A.
McLaughlin, Jessie Myrtle
Nash, Hope
Nash, Joy
Nelson, Alvira

Pittman, Clio
Pittman, Eskridge
Randolph, Mollie
Rautenberg, Clare
Rich, Gertrude
Rich, Willis H.
Smith, Celia M.
Smith, Cora B.
Snyder, Nina
Weber, Edna Mae
Webster, Marion

VIOLIN.

Brown, Carrie A.
Boyer, Zetta
Cederholm, Chester
Golliday, Theo.
Hanson, Hildred
Hall, Daisy
Marsh, Maggie
Meeks, William
Mizelle, Florence

Neifert, Ira
Peterson, Willis
Rosenfeld, Albert
Schaeffer, Charles
Shadley, Harold
Telford, Forrest
Telford, George
Williams, Jesse E.

MANDOLIN.

Leuder, John

Telford, Dora

GUITAR.

Dolbin, Stephen

Students in the Department of Art.

Clark, Kate
Coffman, Mrs. W. E.
Conser, William H.
Denny, Mrs. A. R.
Fletcher, Mildred A.
Foster, May
Fuller, Mrs. David
Green, Edith
Johnson, Myrtle

Munson, Mrs. Charles
Nash, Joy
Nelson, Alvira
Stoner, Leslie
Swanson, Mrs. R. F.
VanBuren, Laura
Weber, Edna Mae
White, Calvin
White, Frances

Directory of Teachers and Students.

Col. denotes College; Unc., Unclassified; Mus., Music; Div., Divinity School.

Alexander, Kelley S.................Mus .... Galesburg
*Alvord, Francis M...................Col............Friendship, N. Y.
Andreen, Frank G.................Col .... Woodhull

Andrew, William B.....................Col ....New Salem
*Andrews, J. Euseba....................Col .... Abingdon
Atterberry, Ralph Marshall.............Col................. Atlanta, Mo.
Austin, Ralph ....Col................. Morrison
Ayars, Frank Cope.....................Col.................La Plata, Mo.
Bartholomew, Hattie ....Mus................. Table Grove
Bartholomew, Jennie L.................Div................. Table Grove
Beattie, Dwight C.....................Unc .... Fairview
Bignall, Roy E........................Col .... Marseilles
Blood, Orrin Judson...................Div .... Petersburg
Blood, M. Isabelle, Instructor in Art.................64 North West street
Blout, Charles J......................Col .... Ellisville
*Boehm, Fred Daniel...................Col.................. Muncie, Ind.
Bodell, Willard Orpha.................Div .... Avon
Bower, Verner ....Unc .... Galesburg
Bowling, Lex ....Unc .... Galesburg
Boyer, Zetta ....Mus .... Galesburg
Briggs, Judson Clinton................Unc .... DeLong
Brown, Carrie A.......................Mus .... Galesburg
Brown, Talent ....Unc .... Galesburg
Buck, Hiram Harrison..................Unc .... LeRoy
Burns, Frank ....Unc ....Dalton City
Byloff, Julia Arvilla.................Mus .... Galesburg
Cease, Charles H......................Mus .... Belleville
Cederholm, Chester ....Mus .... Galesburg
Chamberlain, Ethel Mary...............Col .... Galesburg
Chamberlain, Ruth ....Mus .... Galesburg
Chambers, Pearl ....Mus .... Galesburg
Chapman, Jeannette ....Mus .... Galesburg
Cheesman, Prof. W. H..................1198 North Cherry Street
Clarke, Fred Andrew...................Col .... Maquon
Clarke, Katherine ....Art and Mus.............Maquon
Clay, Walter Timothy..................Col .... Galesburg
Claycomb, Eleanor Pierce..............Unc .... Sycamore
Coffman, Mrs. W. E....................Art .... Galesburg
*Conger, Delia Chase..................Col .... Galesburg
Conger, Ethelin ....Mus .... Galesburg
*Conser, William H....................Col .... Galesburg
Cook, Grace Jane......................Col .... Beecher City
Cooper, Harry Mac.....................Col .... Oquawka
Cooper, Leona ....Unc .... Oquawka
Crissey, Elice ....Mus .... Avon
Curtis, Prof. Alice B.................Ladies' Boarding Hall
Denny, Mrs. A. R......................Art .... Galesburg
Dickerson, Orval Melcher..............Col .... Mt. Vernon
Dixon, Ralph C........................Unc .... Yates City
Dolbin, Stephen ....Mus .... Galesburg
Eden, Joe ....Unc .... Sullivan
Ells, Harry Hugh......................Div ....Charlotte, Mich.
Fennessy, Clinton L...................Col .... Litchfield
*Fennessy, Ethel C....................Col .... Avon
Fletcher, Mildred Allen...............Art .... Smithshire
Fosher, Cora M........................Col .... Galesburg
Fosher, Dudley C......................Div .... Galesburg

Foster, June Leah.....................Unc .... Bradford
Foster, May ....Art .... Bradford
Fowler, Prof. Frank Hamilton.........................1155 East Knox Street
Fuller, Mrs. David......................Art .... Galesburg
Garlick, Elsie M.......................Col .... Joliet
Gibbs, Minnie Carroll..................Col................ Anoka, Minn.
Gillis, Hudson McBain...................Col............Mt. Pleasant, Ia.
Goad, Charles Howard...................Unc .... Blandinsville
*Golliday, Theo ....Col .... Galesburg
Greene, Edith ....Art .... Galesburg
Greene, Nina ....Unc .... Galesburg
Grier, Ethelwyn Sophia...................Col .... Racine, Wis.
Grubb, Emma Welton.....................Col .... Hamilton
Grubb, Prof. Jon Watson.....................1427 East Knox Street
Hale, Mrs. Ada M. H.............................Matron at Ladies' Hall
Hall, Daisy ....Mus .... Galesburg
Haffner, Grover Cleveland................Unc .... Anderson, Ind.
Haffner, Mabel Alice...................Unc .... Anderson, Ind.
Hamerton, Lizzie ....Mus .... Beason
Hanson, Hildred ....Mus .... Creston, Ia.
Harris, Dell Ransom.....................Unc .... Blandinsville
Hathaway, M. Agnes.....................Col .... Galesburg
Herlocker, Webb A.....................Col .... Table Grove
Hills, Robert Asa......................Col .... Mt. Pleasant, Ia..
Hillstren, Charles W....................Div .... Falun, Sweden
*Hoffman, Arthur ....Col .... Knoxville
*Hollister, Florence Gertrude...........Col .... Pecatonica
Hopkins, Roy Victor....................Col .... Princeville
Howell, Spencer Pritchard...............Col .... Woodhull
Hurd, Jay Clinton......................Col .... Maquon
Johnson, Myrtle ....Art .... Galesburg
Jones, Mabel ....Col .... Farragut, Ia.
Justus, Ray W.........................Unc .... Stockton
Kienholz, Prof. Willis S.....................809 East Berrien Street
Kienholz, Mrs. W. S...................Mus .... Galesburg
Kimble, Mrs. Anna Gillis................Col .... Galesburg
Kimble, Olin Arvin.....................Col .... Carbondale, Kan.
Kimble, Prof. Ralph G.............................427 Locust Street
Kimble, Prof. Thaddeus C............................1026 Maiden Lane
Kober, Florence Leclerc.................Col .... Macomb
Koons, Anna Pearle.....................Unc .... Galesburg
Leuder, John ....Mus .... Galesburg
*Linderholm, Ernest Arthur..............Col .... Altona
Linrothe, Luthera ....Mus .... Galesburg
Long, Katherine ....Mus .... Galesburg
Longbrake, Dr. Guy A., Medical Examiner........74 North Chambers Street
Manning, Stanley ....Div .... Chicago
Marsh Maggie ....Mus .... Galesburg
Martin, John Homer....................Unc .... LeRoy
Martin, Nellie Ruth...................Div .... Alexis
McAlpine, Roy Kenneth.................Col .... Jackson, Mich.
*McDaniel, Levi Bert...................Col .... Barry
Meeks, William ....Mus .... Galesburg
McLaughlin, Jessie Myrtle...............Mus .... Knoxville

Metcalf, Harold ....Col .... Blandinsville
Metcalf, Roscoe Flemming..............Unc .... Blandinsville
Mizelle, Florence ....Mus .... Galesburg
Munson, Mrs. Charles..................Art .... Galesburg
Myzner, C. Fred......................Unc............Mt. Moriah, Mo.
Nash, President Charles Ellwood.....................1115 East Knox Street
Nash, Hope ....Mus .... Galesburg
Nash, Joy ....Mus .... Galesburg
Neifert, Ira ....Mus .... Galesburg
Nelson, Alvira ....Mus .... Galesburg
Orton, Charles Edward.................Unc..............Mt. Pleasant, Ia.
Palmer, Louis G.......................Col...............Mt. Pleasant, Ia.
*Parke, Eleanor ....Col .... Sycamore
Parker, Prof. Isaac Augustus...........................488 Lombard street
Peterson, Willis ....Mus .... Galesburg
Philbrook, Elizabeth Freeman............Col .... Racine, Wis.
Phillips, William ....Div .... Chicago
Pittman, Clio ....Unc .... Prescott, Ark.
Pittman, Eskridge ....Col ....Prescott, Ark.
Porter, Gail Quincy....................Col .... DeLand
Potter, Albert M......................Col .... Morrison
Potter, Warren J......................Col .... Morrison
*Predmore, Pearl ....Col .... Avon
Randolph, Mary ....Mus .... School
Rautenberg, Clare Marie...............Mus .... Lincoln
Reifsnider, Rev. Edson, Instructor in Homiletics, and Pastoral Care,
...................................257 North Street
Rhodes, Simon ....Mus .... Bloomington
Rice, Dr. Delia M., Medical Examiner...............84 North Prairie Street
Rich, Prof, Frederick William.......................1379 East Knox Street
Rich, Gertrude ....Mus .... Galesburg
Rich, Willis Horton...................Col .... Galesburg
*Richey, Frances ....Col .... Galesburg
Riggs, Harlan ....Mus.............. Newbern, Ia.
*Robinson, LeRoy ....Col..............Mt. Pleasant, Ia.
Rosenfeld, Albert ....Mus .... Galesburg
Ross, Frances ....Col .... Avon
*Ross, Louise ....Col .... Avon
Rowan, Thomas ....Mus .... Galesburg
Sammons, Mabel Alta..................Col .... Joliet
Schaeffer, Charles ....Mus .... Galesburg
Scott, Preston Brown..................Col .... Galesburg
Shadley, Harold ....Mus .... Galesburg
*Shaffer, James Alexander.............Col .... Galesburg
Skinner, Albert Newton................Col .... Yates City
Smith, Celia May......................Mus .... Dahinda
Smith, Cora B.........................Mus .... Ellisville
Snyder, Nina Florence.................Mus .... Littleton
Stoner, Leslie ....Art .... Galesburg
Stryker, Elizabeth Bell.................Col .... Joliet
Swanson, Mrs. R. F...................Art .... Galesburg
Sykes, Kathryne Anna.................Unc .... Knoxville
Telford, Dora ....Mus .... Galesburg
Telford, Forrest ....Mus .... Galesburg

Telford, George ....Mus .... Galesburg
Thompson, Prof. Alexander S., Musical Director.....1248 East Brooks Street
Thompson, Mrs. Clara D., Teacher of Music, Piano, and Vocal
..............................1284 East Brooks Street
*Tipton, Fred Lincoln...................Col .... Girard
*Tolan, Lena ....Col .... Girard
Upham, Walter L.......................Unc .... Crossville, Tenn.
VanBuren, Laura ....Unc .... Marseilles
Varney, Frank G.......................Col. and Div.............Clinton
Wait, Prof. Emma B.............................1279 East Knox Street
Weber, Edna Mae......................Art .... Rochester, Minn.
Weber, George C.......................Unc ....Rochester, Minn.
*Webster, Inez ....Col .... Galesburg
Webster, Marion ....Unc .... Galesburg
Welcome, Eva Elsie ....Unc .... Galesburg
Wertman, Albert J.....................Unc .... Villisca, Ia.
Westfall, Curtis C.....................Col .... Bushnell
*White, Bertha E.......................Col .... Barry
White, Calvin ....Art .... Galesburg
White, Frances C.......................Art .... Galesburg
White, Prof. Nehemiah............................1473 East Knox Street
Williams, Jesse E......................Mus .... Galesburg
Williamson, Bessie B...................Unc .... Galesburg
*Wilson, Arthur J.....................Col .... Knoxville
Wilson, Harlan ....Unc .... Knoxville
Wise, Lorena Myrtle...................Col .... Winfield, Ia.
Wright, Prof. Philip G..............................1443 East Knox Street
Young, Trella Juanita..................Unc .... Gilson

*Having credits sufficient in number to enter college, but one or more required studies lacking.

GENERAL SUMMARY.

COLLEGE OF LIBERAL ARTS.

Candidates for degrees in 1904.
    Master of Arts...................................... 1
    Bachelor of Arts......................................14-15
Students in the College of Liberal Arts.................... 67

UNCLASSIFIED STUDENTS.

Unclassified Students 27

RYDER DIVINITY SCHOOL.

Candidate for a degree in 1904.
    Bachelor of Divinity.............................. 1
Students in Divinity School.
    Fourth Year 1
    Third Year 4
    Second Year 2
    First Year 2
    Special Student 1-10

MUSIC.

Candidate for Diploma in Music........................... 1
Students in Theory and Musical History...................11
Students in Pianoforte...................................23
Students in Vocal Culture...............................23
Students in Violin......................................17
Students in Mandolin...................................... 2
Student in Guitar.. 1-78

ART.

Students in Art.. 18
                                     216
Names entered twice....................................... 35

      Total.. 181

ASSOCIATION OF GRADUATES.
1903-1904.

OFFICERS.

PRESIDENT,

T. C. KIMBLE, GALESBURG.

VICE PRESIDENT,

HARRY A. BLOUNT.

SECRETARY,

NANNIE MER BUCK, GALESBURG.

TREASURER,

JON W. GRUBB, GALESBURG.

HISTORIAN,

LORA A. TOWNSEND, GALESBURG.

BOARD OF DIRECTORS.

J. D. WELSH.	ALICE BARTLETT.
J. J. WELSH.	NANNIE MER BUCK.
MRS. F. H. FOWLER	ALICE C. DURSTON.
T. C. KIMBLE.	WILLIS S. KIENHOLZ.

MRS. ADA HASBROOK HALE.

Graduates.

The degree of A. M. or M. S. placed immediately after a name, implies that the corresponding Bachelor's degree (A. B. or B. S.) was received on graduation.

The person to whose name a star is attached is deceased. The date following designates the year of his death.

Addresses known to be incorrect are bracketed.

1856.

William Worth Burson, A. M....Manufacturer, 3424 Sheridan Drive, Chicago.
William Ramey Cole, A. M.................Clergyman, Mt. Pleasant, Iowa.
Hon. Thompson W. McNeeley, A. M..........Ex-M. C., Attorney, Petersburg.
Hon. Lewis Alden Simmons, A. M., *1889.................Wellington, Kan.
Addie Hurd, A. M. (Mrs. Wm. Van Horn)..917 Sherbrook St., Montreal, Can.
Jennie Miles, A. M., *1859.......................................Decatur.

1857.

Fielding B. Bond, A. B., *1862...................................Greenbush.
Floyd G. Brown, A. B., *1868............................Mankato, Minn.
James Henry Chapin, A. M., Ph. D., *1892.................Meriden, Conn.
Hon. Edward D. Laning, A. B......................Attorney, Petersburg.
Hon. Scott Wike, B. S., *1901.......................................Barry

1858.

Anson L. Clark, A. M., M. D. President Bennett Eclectic Medical College, Chicago..Elgin.
Thomas Gorman, A. B., *1891...............................Columbus, O.

1859.

Hon. George W. Elwell,. B. S., *1869.....................Chillicothe, Mo.
Eugene Beauharnais Hill, B. S.,..............Manufacturer, Ottumwa, Iowa.
Almon Kidder, A. M.,................................Attorney, Monmouth.
Mary Jane Fuller, B. S...........................[Tarpon Springs, Fla.]
. Ruth Waldron Miller, M. S., (Mrs. Brower), *1892................Chicago.

1860.

Jonathan Eden Brown, A. B......................Farmer, Peabody, Kan.
Arick Burr, B. S., *1860.......................................Charleston.
Hon. William Judah Frisbee, A. M., *1903....................Bushnell.
James Scott Lindsay, A. B. *1860................................Onarga.
Albert Sidney Slater, M. S., M. D..............................Wataga.

1861.

Hon. Franklin Lafayette Brower, A. M., *1869....................Ottawa.
Everett Lorentus Conger, A. M., D. D...........Clergyman, Pasadena, Cal.
Henry George Pollock, A. M.,....................Clergyman, Madison, Ind.
Mary Stewart Miller, A. B., (Mrs. Catlin), 1867................Vinton, Ia.

1862.

Hon. Edwin Hurd Conger, A. M.....U. S. Minister to China, Pekin, China.
Samuel Alvus Dow, A. M., M. D.......Wyalong, New South Wales, Australia.
William Sampson Dow, B. S., *1863.............................Galesburg.
Hon. Charles Allen Holmes, A. M.,..............Attorney, New London, Wis.
Hamilton Lafayette Karr, A. M.....................Attorney, Osceola, Ia.
Frederick Warren Livingston, M. S................Teacher, San Diego, Cal.
Harvey Rowell, A. B...................Solicitor of Patents, Columbus, Wis.
Hon. John Crocker Sherwin, M. S., Ex-M. C....................
.............Attorney, [1234 Columbus Street, Denver, Colo.]
Alfred Henry Trego, A. M......................Manufacturer, Hoopeston.
George John Turner, A. M., M. D., *1899..................Oskaloosa, Ia.
Eugenia Adaline Fuller, B. S, (Mrs. J. W. Ranstead)................Elgin.

1863.

Samuel Addison Calhoun, A. B....Adv. Solicitor "German Demokrat," Peoria.
Hon. John W. Ranstead, B. S............................Attorney, Elgin.
Hanna Jane Biddlecombe, M. S. Bookkeeper Glendale Furnace Co., Columbus, O.
Oricy Villa Crocker, L. A., (Mrs. Nead), *1880................Galesburg.
Sarah Jane Pike, L. A., (Mrs. E. H. Conger)..................Pekin, China.

1864.

Elmore Chase, B. S................................Teacher, Fair Oaks, Cal.
Leslie Greenwood, A. M....With Farmers' Loan and Trust Co., Sioux City, Ia.
Laura Lavinia Pike, A. M., (Mrs. J. S. McConnell)..4359 Lake Ave., Chicago.
Josephine Raymond, A. M., (Antioch College), (Mrs. Maxwell)....Champaign.
Sallie Raymond, L. A., (Mrs. J. B. Green)........................Ramsey.

1865.

Elmore Chase, B. S., A. M........................Teacher, Fair Oaks, Cal.
John Henry McCormick, B. S...............................Caledonia, Mo.
Alice Caroline Chapin, B. S.......Teacher, 140 A St., Salt Lake City, Utah.

1866.

Hon. Elwin Wallace Claycomb, A. M.................Farmer, Eureka, Kan.
Hon. Geo. R. Shook, B. S..............Teacher and Surveyor, Fruita, Colo.
James Smith McConnell, B. S........Attorney, 84 Washington Street, Chicago.
Emma N. H. Conger, A. M., (Mrs. S. W. Conger)...........Villa Park, Cal.

1867.

William Bryan Carlock, B. S......................Attorney, Bloomington.
William Harvey Woods, B. S...........................Farmer, [Mendota.]
Helen Maria Bingham, L. A., M. D.........................Monroe, Wis.

1868.

Henry Moses Chase, A. B., *1870............................Concord, Vt.
Hon. James O'Donnell, B. S., *1901.........................Cherokee, Ia.
Wellington Smith, B. S., *1870................................Annawan.
Edward Keys Walbridge, B. S....Loan and Real Estate Agent, Girard, Kan.

Mary J. Claycomb, A. M., (Mrs. J. W. Grubb)...................Galesburg.
Josephine Marian Kirk, A. M., (Mrs. Kerr) *1879.................Chicago.
Almeda Beals, L. A., (Mrs. Charles Wickwire).................Farmington.
Sarah Elvira Edwards, L. A., (Mrs. Otis Jones), *1899....Los Angeles, Cal.
Grace Greenwood, L. A., (Mrs. E. E. Holroyd), *1898..............Chicago.
Emeline Elizabeth Kirk, L. A., *1881............................Rockford.
Frances Elizabeth Pike, L. A., (Mrs. J. Kirk Keller)............
.................Artist, 4509 Shenandoah Ave., St. Louis, Mo.
Mary Ann Sparks, L. A., (Mrs. Milnor).........................Litchfield.
Florence Adeline Tenney, L. A., (Mrs. Edwards) *1871.........Omaha, Neb.
Mary Emeline Weston, L. A., (Mrs. Woodman), *1888..........Portland, Me.

1869.

Rauseldon Cooper, B. S., *1903.....................................Oquawka.
Hon. Samuel Kerr, A. M.................Attorney, 189 LaSalle St., Chicago.
Hon. Michael F. Knappenberger, B. S., *1902..............Jewel City, Kan.
Howard Knowles, B. S...Galesburg.
Patrick Talent, B. S...............................Attorney, Hanford, Cal.
John Ewalt Wiley, B. S.............................Farmer, Elmwood.
Mary Emily Dunton, A. M., (Mrs. Samuel Kerr)...................Oak Park.
Ella May Greenwood, L. A., (Mrs. S. O. Snyder),................
......................687 Third St., Salt Lake City, Utah.
Mary Hartman, L. A., A. M....Teacher in State Normal University, Normal.

1870.

Jared Perkins Blood, A. B......................Attorney, Sioux City, Iowa.
Hon. Abraham Miller Brown, A. M.....................Attorney, Galesburg.
Nathaniel Ray Chase, A. M., M. D........................Newport, R. I.
Matthias Crum, M. S...........................Stockman, Mendon, Mo.
Hon. Chas. Electus Hasbrook, A. M., LL. B., (Chicago University)......
.................Publisher, Times Building, New York City.
Elmer Clifford Johnson, B. S.....Manufacturer, 36 Main St., Evansville, Ind.
Otis Jones, B. S...El Toro, Cal.
Israel Cyrus Stockton, M. S.....:...............................
Clerk, Interior Dept., 1514 New Jersey Ave., N. W., Washington, D. C.
Hon. John Hill Walbridge, B. S.................Farmer, West Concord, Vt.
Mary Ann Chapin, L. A., (Mrs. T. T. Perry) *1883.............Girard, Kan.
Flora Amanda Edwards, L. A., (Mrs. J. F. Fargo).........San Antonio, Cal.

1871.

Hon. Martin Ireneus Brower, A. M................Attorney, Fullerton, Neb.
Hon. Willis Hardin Fuson, A. M., *1884..................Wa Keeney, Kan.
Frank Tenney Greenwood, A. B...................Druggist, Seneca, Kan.
Hon. Madison Reynolds Harris, A. B.......Attorney, Reaper Block, Chicago.
Hon. Samuel Parsons McConnell, A. B......................
..............Attorney, 135 Bond St., New York, N. Y.
John DeBolt Stephenson, B. S., *1872........................Dexter, Ind.
Ida Bullock, L. A., (Mrs. Thatcher), *1894................Attleboro, Mass.
Hanna Laura Haight, B. S.............................Teacher, Mendota.
Ada May Hasbrook, A. M., (Mrs. Hale)............
..............Matron Ladies' Hall, Lombard College, Galesburg.
Mary Knowles, L. A., (Mrs. J. S. Alspaugh).............Washington, Kan.
Flora Adaline Prindle, L. A., (Mrs. A. G. Dow).................Galesburg.

1872.

Albert Elmore Chase, B. S....Deputy U. S. Mining Surveyor, Boulder, Colo.
Joseph Albert Gates, A. B., National Military Home, Box 97, Leavenworth, Kan.
Alice M. Bingham, L. A., (Mrs. Copeland)......School Trustee, Monroe, Wis.
Mattie Wilburn Burford, L. A., (Mrs. Bates)......Merchant, [Wichita, Kan.]

1873.

Theodore C. Stevens, A. M., *1892...........................Lincoln, Neb.
Ada D. Bingham, L. A., M. D.................................Monroe, Wis.
Elless M. Brown, L. A., (Mrs. Salley), *1883................Monroe, Wis.
Anna L. Nelson, L. A., (Mrs. Fuson).........................Emporia, Kan.
Clara Richardson, L. A., (Mrs. G. F. Claycomb)..............
..................3927 Woodlawn Park Ave., Seattle, Wash.
Sarah A. Richardson, A. M..................................Lawrence, Kan.
Mary M. Stevens, A. M.·.................871 East St., Lincoln, Neb.

1874.

William Albrecht, B. S., *1878......................................Tiskilwa.
Eugene E. Brunson, B. S., M. D.............................Ganges, Mich.
Daniel Clingingsmith, B. S..................................Newton, Kan.
William E. Day, B. S.....Christian Science Healer, 4335 Lake Ave., Chicago.
Morris W. Fletcher, B. S., M. D...................,...Collierville, Tenn.
Irene A. Conger, L. A., (Mrs. Courtney), *1891...................Chicago.
Belle Sherman, B. S................................Teacher, Ithaca, N. Y.

1875.

Charles A. Buck, L. A......................................Merchant, LeRoy.
Lucien J. Dinsmore, B. S., A. M...Clergyman, 2155 N. Ashland Ave., Chicago.
Charles Ellwood Nash, A. M., S. T. D., (Tufts)...............
....................President Lombard College, Galesburg.
Carrie W. Brainard, A. M., B. D. (St. Lawrence)..Clergyman, Rome City, Ind.
Emma S. Collins, L. A., (Mrs. J. E. Buchanan)........Teacher, Lake Forest.
Lillie E. Conger, L. A., *1877.......................................Oneida.
Genie R. Edwards, L. A., (Mrs. Noteware), *1888........Minneapolis, Minn.
Jennie C. Nelson, L. A., (Mrs. Nichols)....................St. Charles.
Josie M. Pryne, L. A.....................118 Hanover St., Mankato, Minn.
Luella R. Warner, B. S., (Mrs. Frank Hitchcock).............
.................Teacher of Painting, Mosca, Colo.

1876.

Hon. J. L. Hastings, B. S., *1894.............................Galesburg.
Charlotte Fuller, M. S., (Mrs. S. M. Risley)...................Harvard, Neb.
Stella Hale, L. A..Galesburg.
Lottie E. Leighton, B. S., (Mrs. L. J. Dinsmore)............
.......................2155 N. Ashland Ave., Chicago.
Izah T. Parker, A. M., *1891...............................Banning, Cal.

1877.

George F. S. Baker, A. M., *1891...............................Goodenow.
Charles C. Maynard, A. M........Dentist, 97 South First St., San Jose, Cal.
Clara Z. Edwards, L. A., (Mrs. J. F. Calhoun).................
.............2121 Bryant Ave., South, Minneapolis, Minn.

Emily L. Fuller, A. M...............................Teacher, Galesburg.
Eugenia Fuller, A. M..................Principal High School, Riverside, Cal.
Lottie J. Humphrey, B. S., *1879......................Tipton, Ia.
Ella McCullough, L. A., (Mrs. J. D. Welsh).....................Galesburg.

1878.

Ozro P. Bostwick, A. B.....................Supt. City Schools, Clinton, Ia.
Eben H. Chapin, A. M., B. D., (Tufts) Clergyman, 18 Maple St., Rockland, Me.
Shirley C. Ransom, B. S., A. M., 1892...........Insurance Agent, Abingdon.
Adah M. Mariner, M. S., (Mrs. Stewart)........................Bushnell.

1879.

Jon W. Grubb, M. S..................Professor Lombard College, Galesburg.
Charles P. Hale, A. M.....................................
........Insurance and Real Estate Agt., 1087 Broadway, Denver, Colo.
Douglas A. Myers, B. S ....Real Estate Agent, Peoria.
Charles A. Webster, B. S..............Treasurer Lombard College, Galesburg.
J. Edwin Webster, B. S...................`...............Merchant, Galesburg.

1880.

Henry S. Livingston, A. M., *1895..............................Galesburg.
William H. Livingston, A. B..............Auditor Mercantile Mutual
.. Building and Loan Association, 301 New England Bldg., Kansas City, Mo.
William A. Parker, A. M......Civil Engineer, U. P. R. R., Kansas City, Mo.
Otto H. Swigart, B. S...................Farmer and Stockman, Champaign.
Mollie B. Devendorf, B. S.....Stenographer, 682 N. California Ave., Chicago.
Jennie B. Townsend, B. S., (Mrs. C. A. Webster)................Galesburg.

1881.

George F. Hughes, A. B.............................Attorney, Yates City.
Milo C. Summers, M. S.....................War Department Clerk
    Surgeon's General's Office, 314 Seventh St., Northeast, Washington, D. C.
Lura D. Bailey, A. B., (Mrs. G. F. Hughes)...................Yates City.

1882.

Reuben D. Bower, B. S.....,..............'.................Clerk, Galesburg.
Henry M. Chase, A. M..............Loan and Real Estate Agent, Galesburg.
Lafayette Swart, B. S..........................Farmer, Christiana, Tenn.
Elmer H. West, M. S., *1894.......................'.............Yates City.

1883.

Chas. E. Brewster, A. B........................Loan and
        Real Estate Agent, 1770 Emerson Ave., South, Minneapolis, Minn.
James Weston Carney, B. S., B. D., (Tufts)............Attorney, Galesburg.
Lloyd Z. Jones, B. S..................County Surveyor and Farmer, Galva.
John H. Miles, B. S......................'...............Farmer, Bushnell.
Fannie M. Edwards, A. B., (Mrs. C. E. Brewster)...............
.....................1770 Emerson Ave., South, Minneapolis, Minn.
Lizzie E. Furniss, B. S., (Mrs. W. J. Moring)..............Kansas City, Mo.
Emma J. Livingston, L. A., (Mrs. A. T. Wing)...............Maryville, Mo.
Elma E. Williams, A. M...................................388 E. 57th St., Chicago.

1884.

Anna M. Brewster, M. S., (Mrs. E. H. West)................[Brewster.]
Gay M. Brunson, B. S., M. D., D. D. S....................Dentist, Joliet.
Lulu M. Burt, B. S., (Mrs. W. B. Cravens)..2401 E. 11th St., Kansas City, Mo.
Charles L. Edwards, B. S., Ph. D. (Leipsic)
                    Professor of Biology, Trinity College, Hartford, Conn.
Jay C. Edwards, M. S...............................522 50th St., Chicago.
Frank R. Jones, B. S.............Treasurer American Well Works, Aurora.

1885.

Jennie B. Conger, A. M., (Mrs. Conger)....1059 E. 34th St., Los Angeles, Cal.
Eugene. F. Carney, B. S., *1887...................................Galesburg.
Alma J. Devore, B. S., (Mrs. J. H. Miles).........................Bushnell.
Lizzie B. Hughes, B. L., (Mrs. D. Perry)........................Table Grove.
Ella Suiter, B. S., (Mrs. Geo. Pittard) *1894........................Alexis.
Hon. Lyman McCarl, M. S...............Attorney, 304 N. Sixth St., Quincy.
J. Douglas Welsh, B. S...........................County Judge, Galesburg.
George Crum, B. D.............................Clergyman, Athens, Penn.
Wallace F. Small, B. D..........................Clergyman, Everett, Wash.

1886.

Rainie Adamson, M. S., (Mrs. W. F. Small)................Everett, Wash.
L. Ward Brigham, M. S., M. D., B. D.   (Canton) Clergyman
                    578 Bedford Ave., Brooklyn, N. Y.
John M. Davies, M. S.....................Teacher, 612 Fifth St., Maywood.
Anna H. Ebberd, B. S., (Mrs. Cyrus Hannum)..............Campbell, Neb.
Alice L. Roberts, B. S., (Mrs. J. L. Andrew)..........[National City, Cal.]
Rachel A. Watkins, M. S., (Mrs. Billings), B. D., 1894..Siloam Springs, Ark.
August Dellgren, B. D.................................Clergyman, Chicago.
Hiram J. Orelup, B. D.................Clergyman, 221 Penn. Ave., Aurora.

1887.

Ella M. Grubb, A. M., (Mrs. James Simmons)................Owasso, Mich.
Henry C. Morris, A. M........Attorney, 188 Madison St., Suit 703, Chicago.
J. W. Crane, B. S......Attorney, 908 Guarantee Loan Bldg., Minneapolis, Minn.
Perry, B. Fuller, B. S..Clerk, Elgin.
Jay Welsh, M. S......................................Farmer, Williamsfield.
Alva T. Wing, B. S.........................Merchant, Maryville, Mo.
John R. Carpenter, B. D....................Clergyman, New Olmstead, O.
Osgood G. Colegrove, B. D.....................Clergyman, Woodstock, O.
Mary Garrard, B. D., (Mrs. I. Rollin Andrews)
                    35th St. and Hawthorne Ave., Omaha, Neb.

1888.

Peter T. Hawley, B. S...............................Merchant, Ralston, Ia.
Harry H. Jones, M. S............................Oil Wells, Texas.
Allen W. Lapham, M. S., M. D., *1894............................Victoria
Elmer E. Taylor, B. S., *1903......................College Mound, Mo.
Elfreda L. Shaffer, B. D., (Mrs. Newport)...........Clergyman, Wauponsee.

1889.

Elmer E. Taylor, B. S., A. B., *1903...................College Mound, Mo.
George E. Dutton, M. S...............L..............Banker, Sycamore.

Frank H. Fowler, B. S., Ph. D., (The University of Chicago)
Professor Lombard College, Galesburg.
Edward P. McConnell, M. S., *1902................................Chicago.
Allen F. Moore, B. S.............................Manufacturer, Monticello.
William T. Smith; M. S...Publisher Galesburg Gazette and Attorney, Galesburg.
Vanna R. Williams, B. L., (Mrs. W. W. Slaughter)...........Brookston, Ind.
Charles A. C. Garst, B. D., *1896...........................Riverside, Cal.
Carrie A. Rice, B. D...............Clergyman, 6019 Prairie Ave., Chicago.

1890.

Frank H. Fowler, B. S., A. B., Ph. D., (The University of Chicago)
...............Professor Lombard College, Galesburg.
Claude N. Anderson, B. S.......................Teacher, Tecumseh, Neb.
Bret H. Brigham, M. S........Insurance, 1819 Chestnut St., Milwaukee, Wis.
Elizabeth Gaile Durston, M. S., B. O., Columbus School of Oratory),
(Mrs. H. F. Simmons).................................Woodhull.
Fred Farlow, B. S..................................Stock Dealer, Camp Point.
Samuel D. Harsh, B. S., *1893...............................Creston, Iowa.
Anna E. Ross, M. S., (Mrs. A. Lapham), M. D., Physician
4256 Langley Ave., Chicago.
Richard L. Slater, B. S., *1894.....................................Wataga.
Loring Trott, M. S.........................Merchant, Junction City, Kan.
James J. Welsh, B. S..................................Attorney, Galesburg.
Lizzie Wigle, B. S., (Mrs. C. N. Anderson).................Tecumseh, Neb.
Burtrust T. Wilson, M. S........Professor Guadalupe College, Seguin, Texas.
Lillian J. Wiswell, B. L., (Mrs. E. P. McConnell) *1903·............Cameron.
Thomas E. Dotter, B. D...........................Clergyman, Sullivan, Mo.

1891.

Willard J. White, A. M., M. D......Professor of Medicine, Longmont, Colo.
M. McClelland Case, M. S..............Draughtsman, 215 63rd St., Chicago.
Villa A. Cole, B. S., (Mrs. M. M. Case)..............215 63rd St., Chicago.
S. Taylor Donohoe, M. S.......................................New Canton.
Jennie A. Grubb, B. S., (Mrs. F. H. Fowler)....................Galesburg.
Robert D. Hill, M. S.....................Principal of Schools, Colchester.
Della M. Rogers, B. L, (Mrs. Chas. Garber)...............Reardan, Wash.
William Franklin Smith, B. D., *1897...................Whitewater, Wis.

1892.

Frank N. Allen, B. S............Bookkeeper, 442 E. Forty-fifth St., Chicago.
Curtis P. Beale, M. S.................Principal of Schools, Farragut, Iowa.
Harry A. Blount, B. S..............................Merchant, Macomb.
Ben F. Brady, B. S...................................Attorney, Ottawa.
Alice C. Durston, A. M.......................................New Windsor.
Chas. W. Elliott, M. S...............................Jeweler, Williamsfield.
Grace S. Harsh, B. S...Creston, Iowa.
Lissie Seeley, B. S., (Mrs. Leonard Crew)......................Salem, Ia.
Daniel P. Wild, M. S..................................Banker, Sycamore.
Luther E. Wyman, B. S.............Broker, Board of Trade, Chicago.
Benjamin W. Jones, Jr., B. D., *1898..........................Barre, Vt.
Effie K. McCollum Jones, B. D., (Mrs. B. W. Jones) Clergyman, Waterloo, Ia.
George W. Skilling, B. D....................Clergyman, [Iowa Falls, Ia.]

1893.

Robert F. Anderson, A. B..............................
............Principal Columbia School, 517 W. Gift Ave., Peoria.
Carl C. Countryman, A. M............................
........Impersonator and Author, 801 N. Y. Life Bldg., Chicago.
Ethel M. Tompkins, A. M., (Mrs. W. S. Clayberg)..................Avon.
F. Louise Bradford, B. S.............................Teacher, Quincy.
Richard Brown, M. S.........................Attorney, Creston, Ia.
Kate A. Carlton, B. S., (Mrs. F. W. Smith)................DeLand, Fla.
J. Newton Conger, Jr., M. S........................Attorney, Galesburg.
States Dickson, B. S....................................Attorney, Kewanee.
S. Hepsey Fuller, M. S., (Mrs. J. M. Earhart)..................Wyoming.
Daisy D. Wiswell, M. S., (Mrs. G. A. Franklin)...........Carpintaria, Cal.
Guy A. Longbrake, B. L., M. D....................Physician, Galesburg.
Charles E. Varney, B. D...............................Clergyman, Clinton.

1894.

William Richard Tapper, A. B........................Attorney, Sycamore.
Guy Henry Bernard, B. S......................Bank Cashier, Glasco, Kan.
Lucy Minerva Conger, B. S., (Mrs. E. P. May)................
.................12 Gibbs St, Newton Center, Mass.
Joseph Amos Crum, B. S., M. D...........................Oshkosh, Wis.
Maude Alice Crum, B. L.................................Boone, Ia.
Adelphia Gould Durston, B. S., (Mrs. George Ohse)...........Yorkville, Ill.
Albert Prentice Smith, B. S........................Merchant, Denver, Colo.
Lucy Titus, B. S., (Mrs. R. F. Anderson)........517 W. Gift Ave., Peoria.
Eliza M. Drake Curtis, B. D., (Mrs. J. L. Everton)....Clergyman, Hoopeston.
Rachel C. Watkins Dellgren, B. D., (Mrs. Billings)....Siloam Springs, Ark.
Jasper Leroy Everton, B. D.........................Clergyman, Hoopeston.
Martha Dandridge Garner, B. D., (Mrs. L. P. Jones)............
.....................Clergyman, Blenheim, Ontario, Can.
Henry LaFayette Gillespie, B. D.................Clergyman, St. Louis, Mo.
Elijah Emmett Hamand, B. D............................
...........Clergyman, [1222 Lyden Ave., Kansas City, Mo.]
Rett E. Olmstead, B. D...........................Clergyman, Decorah, Ia.
Margaret Titus, B. D., (Mrs. R. E. Olmstead).......Clergyman, Decorah, Ia.
Albert Earnest Menke, Ph. D...................Chemist, Fayetteville, Ark.
Hans Schuler, Ph. D...........................Teacher, Flushing, N. Y.

1895.

John McDuffie, Ph. D.........................Teacher, Springfield, Mass.
Lucile Bragg, A. B...............................Clerk, Humboldt, Kan.
William Robert Chapin, B. S......................
........Buyer International Harvester Co., 7 Monroe St., Chicago.
Frank Loren Conger, A. B..........Cashier First National Bank, Galesburg.
Grace Winifred Conlee, A. B......................Postal Clerk, Galesburg.
Mabel Dow, A. B., (Mrs. F. L. Conger).......................Galesburg.
Robert Pinkney Higgins, B. S...............................Champaign.
John Richard Stanley, A. B......Agricultural Implement Dealer, Stronghurst.
Nellie Christine Tompkins, A. B, (Mrs. Giles M. Clayberg)...........Avon.
Albert Orin Wakefield, A. B...................Attorney, Sioux City, Ia.
Frances Elizabeth Cheney, B. D., *1902.......................Greenup.
Orrin Carlton Evans, B. D...................Clergyman, Rochester, Minn.
Charles Robert Jones, B. D.....................Clergyman, Nettleton, Mo.
Thomas Francis Rayon, B. D...............Clergyman, Rapid River, Mich.

1896.

Jessie Beatrice Brown, A. B., (Mrs. A. L. C. Clock)............
...................632 Indiana Ave., Winona, Minn.
Fred Leo Camp, A. B..........................Expressman, Galesburg.
Bertha Alice Cook, A. B., (Mrs. O. C. Evans).............Rochester, Minn.
Almira Lowrey Cheney, A. B................................Saybrook.
Elice Crissey, A. B.................................Teacher, Avon.
Homer Franklin Harsh, A. B.....................Stockman, Lowell, Neb.
Hamilton Lafayette Karr, Jr., A. B...................Attorney, Osceola, Ia.
Marion Alice Kendall, A. B..............................Ithaca, N. Y.
Harry McGee Lessig, A. B...........Clerk U. P. R. R. offices, Omaha, Neb.
Ralph Grierson Kimble, A. B........Professor Lombard College, Galesburg.
Iva Della Myers, A. B............................Bookkeeper, Galesburg.
Edward Leroy Shinn, A. B., Penn Collieries Co...147 Milk St., Boston, Mass.
Emma Genevra Van Liew, A. M., (Mrs. Guy Tuttle).............Bushnell.
Jean Gillette White, A. B., (Mrs. A. B. McGill)...................Peoria.
James Alvin Clark, B. D.................Clergyman, South Pasadena, Cal.
Charles William Edward Gossow, B. D............Clergyman, Wichita, Kan.
Maurice Gilbert Linton, B. D................Clergyman, Zanesville, Ohio.
Eugene Southwick, B. D......................Clergyman, [Corfu, N. Y.]
—————
Georgia Stanley, Diploma in Art, (Mrs. C. H. Wickham)......Anthony, Kan.

1897.

Frank Pierce Anderson, A. B........................Teacher, Yates City.
Loetta Frances Boyd, A. B............................Teacher, Oneida.
Flora May Cutter, A. B., (Mrs. Fred Boyer, Jr.)..............Camp Point.
Benjamin Downs, A. B............................Clerk, Winslow, Ariz.
Nina Alta Harris, A. B., (Mrs. C. E. Hunter)...................Galesburg.
Fred Louis Holcomb, A. B., M. D........................Zenda, Kan.
Theodore Lindquist, A. B............................
........Professor of Math., State Scientific School, Wahpeton, N. D.
Carrie Alice Stickney, A. B...............................
.......Teacher of Eng. and Eloc., Univ. of Chattanooga, Athens, Tenn.
Elmer Joseph Tapper, A. B..................Insurance Solicitor, Riverside.
.Claude Bryant Warner, A. B., A. M.......................Dentist, Avon.
Guy Henry Weeks, A. B..............................Teacher, Galesburg.
Frances Cora White, A. B...............................Galesburg.
Fred Minosuke Yamaguchi, A. B...Central Tabernacle, Honga, Tokio, Japan.
George Hilary Ashworth, B. D....................Clergyman, Bryan. O.
Edward Milton Minor, B. D..................Clergyman, Decatur, Mich.
George Burr Rogers, B. D......................Clergyman, Decatur, Mich.
William Willis Slaughter, B. D., *1901.....................Francis, Okla.
Simeon Lafayette Taylor, B. D.............Osteopath Physician, Hoopeston.

1898.

Mervin Wallace Allen, A. B............................Farmer, Maquon.
Alice Helen Bartlett, A. B.................................Galesburg.
Charles Reid Brown, A. B...........Lawyer, 100 Washington St., Chicago.
Joshua J. Bullman, A. B............................Farmer, Galesburg.
Ida Galbreath, A. B...................Teacher, Columbia City, Ind.
Charles Edward Piper, A. B..................6046 Princeton Ave., Chicago.
Simeon Lafayette Taylor, B. D., A. B........Osteopath Physician, Hoopeston.

Edna Madison McDonald, B. D., (Mrs Bonser)....Clergyman, Cheney, Wash.
John Willis Slaughter, B. D..................................
........Student Univ. of Mich. 311 S. Division St., Ann Arbor, Mich.
Benjamin Franklin Stacey, B. D., A. B.......................
.................Profesor Univ. of Arizona, Tucson, Arizona.
Oluf Tandberg, B. D........................Clergyman, Gardiner, Maine.

Isal Caldwell, Diploma in Vocal Music, (Mrs. Lewis)...........Knoxville.

1899.

Christen Martin Alsager, A. B............Principal City Schools, Winnebago.
Ella Berry Boston, A. B., (Mrs. J. L. Lieb)....................Springfield.
Henry William Dubee, A. B.........Instructor in German, Harvard College.
Howard Everett Foster, A. B., *1900...........................Galesburg.
Homer Edwin Garvin, A. B.......Merchant, 123 Union St., Memphis, Tenn.
Fannie Pauline Gingrich, A. B., (Mrs. Clarence Perrine)
326 Oakland Ave., Milwaukee, Wis.
George Runyan Longbrake, A. B.................;.........Clergyman, Seneca, Kan.
Helen Jessie Mackay, A. B........Society Reporter, *Evening Mail*, Galesburg.
Nellie Stuart Russell, A. B.............................Teacher, Woodhull.
Lora Adelle Townsend, A. B..................................Galesburg.
Lloyd Champlain, B. D., Mgr. Co-Operative League of Photo Art, Galesburg.

Edith C. Crissey, Diploma in Instrumental Music............Teacher, Avon.
Jennie Holmes, Diploma in Art....................N. Henderson.

1900.

Martha Belle Arnold, A. B.............................Teacher, Galesburg.
Fay Alexander Bullock, A. B...Business Department Evening Mail, Galesburg.
Gertrude Grace Kidder, A. B., (Mrs. Kerr)................Winona, Minn.
Edwin Julius McCullough, A. B.......................Aberdeen, S. Dak.
Carrie Ruth Nash, A. B., (Mrs. Donald P. McAlpine)........
......................118 N. Blackstone St., Jackson, Mich.
Charles Wait Orton, B. S........................Grocer, Sumner, Wash.
Burt G. Shields, B. S...........1420 Colorado Ave., Colorado Springs, Colo.
Iva May Steckel, A. B...Macomb.
Earl Wolcott Watson, A. B.....................Hardware Merchant, Barry.
Harry William Weeks, A. B.......Student, University of Illinois, Champaign.
William David Buchanan, B. D................Clergyman, Mt. Pleasant, Ia.

1901.

Martha Belle Arnold, A. M..........................Teacher, Galesburg.
Carrie Ruth Nash, A. M., (Mrs. Donald P. McAlpine)...............
......................118 N. Blackstone St., Jackson, Mich.
John Donington Bartlett, A. B......Student Rush Medical College, Chicago.
Nannie Mer Buck, B. S..............................Teacher, Galesburg.
Gertrude West Hartgrove, A. B...............................Galesburg.
Julia Evelyn Lombard, A. B...........................East Orange, N. J.
Jennie Eliza Marriott, A. B., (Mrs. W. D. Buchanan)....Mt. Pleasant, Iowa.
Donald Palmer McAlpine, A. B....:....................
...............Teacher, 118 N. Blackstone St., Jackson, Mich.
William J. Orton, A. B.......................Bank Clerk, Sumner, Wash.
Grace Olive Pingrey, A. B.............................Coon Rapids, Iowa.

Frederick Preston, A. B...................................Boston, Mass.
Grace Schnur, A. B.........................317 N. Thirteenth St., Quincy.
Francis Britton Bishop, B. D...................Clergyman, Marseilles.

Virginia Henney, Diploma in Music...................Mitchellville, Iowa.
Cyrena Weir, Diploma in Music.................501 Union Ave., Litchfield.

1902.

Charlotte Alspaugh, A. B..............................Washington, Kan.
John Andrew, Jr., A. B..Medical Student, Univ. of Colorado, Boulder, Colo.
Edna Mae Cranston, A. B., (Mrs. Mugg)................Indianapolis, Ind.
Charles Junius Efner, A. B..............Reporter, *Evening Mail*, Galesburg.
Edna Ethel Epperson, A. B...............................Teacher, Hanover.
Henry Ericson, A. B.................Teacher Todd's Seminary, Woodstock.
Augusta Eaton Hitchcock, A. B..............................Estherville, Ia.
Thaddeus Carey Kimble, A. B....................................
................Instructor of Biology, Lombard College, Galesburg.
Howard Walter Lauer, A. B..........With American Can Co., Melrose Park.
Emma Annette Muffler, A. B.......................................Serena.
Edward Milton Smith, A. B.................Principal High School, Maquon.
Alice Stokes, A. B...Galesburg.
Herbert Leonard Stoughton, A. B.....................
.............Law Student, 1323 4th St., S. E. Minneapolis, Minn.
Charles E. Varney, B. D., A. B........................Clergyman, Clinton.
Kiyoshi Satoh, B. D.............................Clergyman, Tokio, Japan.
George Francis Thompson, B. D....Ass't Supt. of Churches, Plain City, Ohio.
Mecca Varney, B. D., (Mrs. C. E. Varney).............Clergyman, Clinton.

1903.

Edwin Julius McCullough, A. M........................Aberdeen, S. Dak.
Mary Maud Andrew, A. B.................................New Salem.
Athol Ray Brown, A. B.......................Teacher, North Henderson.
Raymond R. Campbell, A. B.............................Bagdad, Florida.
Claude Dudley Fosher, A. B..........Student Lombard College, Galesburg.
Anna Moore Gillis, A. B., (Mrs. T. C. Kimble).................
.....................Instructor Lombard College, Galesburg.
Claude Webster Hartgrove, A. B.....................Fireman, Galesburg.
Willis Simon Kienholz, A. B..........Professor Lombard College, Galesburg.
Ralph Todd Miller, A. B.....................Insurance Agent, Galesburg.
Nellie Jeanette Needham, A. B..............................Racine, Wis.
Jenkins B. Rees, A. B...Oneida.
S. Martin Nieveen, B. D...................Clergyman, Vermilion, S. Dak.

Sarah Lucy Cook, Diploma in Music.........................Beecher City.
Grace Helen Elting, Diploma in Music.........................Sperry, Ia.
Faith Tenney Nash, Diploma in Music........................Galesburg.
Elsie Dorothy Sommers, Diploma in Music.................Burlington, Ia.
Leura Willis, Diploma in Music............................Table Grove.
Anne Marion Wrigley, Diploma in Music.........................Chicago.

HONORARY DEGREES.

The degree placed immediately after the name is the honoray degree conferred.by Lombard College.

An additional degree, followed by a date only, is one conferred by Lombard College.

An additional degree, without date, is one conferred by another institution, the name of which is given if known.

1858. *Rev. Otis A. Skinner, D. D........Ex-President Lombard University.
1859. Rev. George S. Weaver, A. M......................Canton, N. Y.
1860. *Ansel Streeter, A. M..................................Weston, Mo.
1862. *Rev. Ebenezer Fisher D. D...Prin. Theological School, Canton, N. Y.
1862. Rev. Joseph Selmon Dennis, A. M.........................Chicago.
1863. *Rev. William Henry Ryder, D. D.; A. M. (Harvard).......Chicago.
1864. *Rev. Holden R. Nye, A. M.........................Towanda, Pa.
1864. Rev. Charles Woodhouse, A. M.; M. D...............Rutland, Vt.
1865. Rev. A. G. Hibbard, A. M...............................Wheaton.
1865. *Rev. J. G. H. Hartzell, A. M.; D. D. (St. Lawrence)..Detroit, Mich.
1867. *Rev. William Ethan Manley, A. M...................Denver, Colo.
1867. Rev. Thomas B. St. John, A. M.................................
1868. *Rev Clement G. Lefevre, D. D...................Milwaukee, Wis.
1868. William B. Powell, A. M.......................Washington, D. C.
1868. Rev. James Harvey Tuttle, A. M.; D. D...38 W. 53rd St., N. Y. City.
1869. Rev. John Wesley Hanson, A. M.; D. D. (Buchtel)....Pasadena, Cal.
1869. Rev. William Wallace Curry, A. M...............Washington, D. C.
1869. *Rev. Daniel Parker Livermore, A. M................Melrose, Mass.
1869. Rev. Augusta J. Chapin, A. M..........459 W. 144th St., N. Y. City.
1870. Rev. John S. Cantwell, A. M........................Chicago.
1870. Daniel Lovejoy Hurd, A. M.; M. D..............................
1870. *Rev. George Truesdale Flanders, D. D.............Rockport, Mass.
1870. *Rev. Alfred Constantine Barry, D. D.................Lodi, Mass.
1872. *Rev. William Ethan Manley, D. D.; A. M., 1867.......Denver, Colo.
1872. *Rev. R. H. Pullman, A. M.........................Baltimore, Md.
1872. *Rev. Gamaliel Collins, A. M..............U. S. A., Chatham, Mass.
1872. *Rev. B. F. Rogers, A. M......................Fort Atkinson, Wis.
1875. *Rev. J. H. Chapin, Ph. D.; A. B., 1857; A. M., 1860..Meriden, Conn.
1876. Rev. George S. Weaver, D. D.; A. M., 1859......Canton, N. Y.
1876. Rev. John S. Cantwell, D. D.; A. M., 1870..............Chicago.
1877. Rev. O. Cone, D. D..................................Canton, N. Y.
1879. Elias Fraunfelter, Ph. D..........................Akron, Ohio.
1879. Milton L. Comstock, Ph. D......Professor Knox College, Galesburg.
1882. Rev. Charles W. Tomlinson, D. D...............Huntington, L. I.
1883. *Rev. Amos Crum, A. M.........................Webster City, Ia.
1884. Matthew Andrews, A. M...............................Monmouth.
1886. Rev. L. J. Dinsmore, A. M.; B. S., 1875 2155 N. Ashland Ave., Chicago.
1887. *Rev. Holden R. Nye, D. D.; A. M., 1864...........Towanda, Pa.
1887. *Rev. Charles Fluhrer, D. D.......................Albion, N. Y.

*Deceased.

1887. Hon. Lewis E. Payson, LL. D............................Pontiac.
1887. Hon. George W. Wakefield, A. M....................Sioux City, Ia.
1888. Rev. George H. Deere, D. D...,....................Riverside, Cal.
1888. Homer M. Thomas, A. M.; M. D........................Chicago.
1888. Rev. Charles A. Conklin, A. M......................Boston, Mass.
1888. Mary Hartman, A. M.; L. A., 1859........................Normal.
1890. Rev. Jacob Straub, D. D......'.................Columbia, Cuba.
1890. George B. Harrington, A. M...........................Princeton.
1890. Carl F. Kolbe, Ph. D....................................Akron, O.
1891. *Rev. A. G. Gaines, LL. D.; D. D...................Canton, N. Y.
1892. Rev. George Thompson Knight, D. D...........Tufts College, Mass.
1892. Charles Kelsey Gains, Ph. D............................
..................Professor St. Lawrence Univ., Canton, N. Y.
1892. Shirley C. Ransom, A. M.; B. S., 1878..................Abingdon.
1893. Rev. Augusta J. Chapin, D. D.; A. M., 1869..............
..............................459 W. 144th St., N. Y. City.
1893. *Rev. Amos Crum, D. D.; A. M., 1883.............Webster City, Ia.
1895. John Huston Finley, Ph. D..........................
...........President College of City of New York, New York City.
1893. Charles Loring Hutchinson, A. M........................Chicago.
1894. *Rev. Royal Henry Pullman, D. D.; A. M., 1872......Baltimore, Md.
1894. Rev. George B. Stocking, D. D.....................Lansing, Mich.
1895. Rev. Aaron Aldrich Thayer, D. D....................California.
1895. Rev. Andrew Jackson Canfield, Ph. D.; D. D........Worcester, Mass.
1897. Rev. Daniel Bragg Clayton, D. D.................Columbia, S. C.
1897. Rev. Thomas Sander Guthrie, D. D..................Muncie, Ind.
1898. Rev. Rodney F. Johonnot, D. D..........................Oak Park.
1898. Henry Priest, Ph. D.....Professor St. Lawrence Univ., Canton, N. Y.
1899. *John Wesley Hanson, Jr., A. M..........................Chicago.
1900. Rev. Alfred Howitzer Laing, D. D..........................Joliet.
1901. Edwin Hurd Conger, LL. D.........................Pekin, China.
1901. John Sharp Cook, D. D.............................Beecher City.
1902. Rev. Frederick Clarence Priest, D. D.............
......................691½ Washington Blvd., Chicago.

*Deceased.

ACKNOWLEDGMENT OF DONATION.

Twenty-six volumes for Library, Miss Belle Gibson, Chicago.

HARVARD UNIVERSITY SCHOLARSHIP.

Established by the Harvard Club of Chicago.

By request of the Harvard Club of Chicago we publish the following notice.

At its annual meeting, December 14, 1897, the Harvard Club of Chicago established a scholarship at Harvard University of the annual value of three hundred dollars. This scholarship is open to the graduates of the universities and colleges of Illinois who wish to follow a course of study at the Graduate School of Harvard University. Applications must be made before May 1st in each year, and senior students about to finish their undergraduate course are eligible as candidates. Communications from candidates for the year 1904-1905 should be addressed to Louis M. Greeley, 906 Tacoma Block, Chicago.

INDEX.

REV. LEWIS B. FISHER, D. D., President.

LOMBARD COLLEGE PUBLICATIONS—Series III., No. 2

[Issued Bi-Monthly by Lombard College.]

CATALOGUE

OF

LOMBARD COLLEGE

GALESBURG, ILLINOIS,

FOR THE YEAR ENDING JUNE 1, 1905.

GALESBURG, ILL.:
REPUBLICAN-REGISTER PRINT
1905

College Calendar.

1905

MARCH 7—Tuesday............................Registration. Third Term Begins.
MAY 6—Saturday.....................................Townsend Preliminary Contest.
MAY 13—Saturday.................   ....Senior Vacation Begins.
MAY 18—Thursday..Senior Theses Due.
MAY 25, 26—Thursday, Friday................................   ....Examinations.
MAY 28—Sunday.....................................   ....Baccalaureate Sermon.
MAY 29—Monday..   ....Field Day.
MAY 29—Monday, Evening.................. ....Townsend Prize Contest in Declamation.
MAY 30—Tuesday, Memorial Day   Annual Meeting of Association of Graduates.
MAY 30—Tuesday, Evening...Senior Class Play.
MAY 31—Wednesday.....................Annual Meeting of the Board of Trustees.
JUNE 1—Thursday ....Commencement Day.

Summer Vacation.

SEPT. 5—Tuesday...Entrance Examinations.
SEPT. 5—Tuesday.... ....Registration. College Year Begins.
NOV. 18—Saturday.................................... Orations for Swan Contest Due.
NOV. 27, 28—Monday, Tuesday.. .... Examinations.
NOV. 28—Tuesday........t............. ....First Term Ends.
NOV. 30—Thursday............................. ....Holiday. Thanksgiving Day.
DEC. 5—Tuesday.................................Registration. Second Term Begins.
DEC. 22—Friday.............. Last Day of ·Recitations preceding Christmas Recess.

Christmas Recess.

1906.

JAN. 3—Wednesday............................Recitations of Second Term Resumed.
JAN. 20—Saturday...... ....Swan Preliminary Contest.
FEB. 22—Thursday.............. ....Holiday. Washington's Birthday.
FEB. 23—Friday...................................... Swan Prize Contest in Oratory.
MARCH 7, 8—Wednesday, Thursday..Examinations.
MARCH 8—Thursday....................... ....Senior Syllabi Due. Second Term Ends.

Spring Vacation.

MARCH 13—Tuesday...........................:..........Registration. Third Term Begins.
MAY 5—Saturday......................................Townsend Preliminary Contest.
MAY 12—Saturday.....................................Senior Vacation Begins.
MAY 17—Thursday .... Senior Theses Due.
MAY 31, JUNE 1—Thursday, Friday.................................Examinations.
JUNE 3—Sunday......... ....Baccalaureate Sermon.
JUNE 4—Monday.................................Field Day. Gymnasium Exhibition.
JUNE 4.—Monday, Evening.................. ......Townsend Prize Contest in Declamation.
JUNE 5—Tuesday..................... ....Annual Meeting of Association of Graduates.
JUNE 5—Tuesday   ....Senior Class Play.
JUNE 6—Wednesday ....Annual Meeting of the Board of Trustees.
JUNE 7—Thursday.. ....Commencement Day.

BOARD OF TRUSTEES.

OFFICERS OF THE BOARD.

HON. J. B. HARSH, CRESTON, IOWA.
PRESIDENT.

CHARLES A. WEBSTER, HOLMES BUILDING, GALESBURG.
TREASURER.

PHILIP G. WRIGHT, 1443 EAST KNOX STREET, GALESBURG.
SECRETARY.

Executive Committee.

HOWARD KNOWLES, CHAIRMAN.

CHARLES A. WEBSTER, SECRETARY.

FREDERICK W. RICH.

ROBERT CHAPPELL.   J. DOUGLAS WELSH.

SCOPE AND IDEALS.

Between the high school or academy and the graduate, professional, or technical school, American educators are coming to recognize a distinct and imperative educational function which is discharged only by the college, properly so called. The broad results aimed at in character and in grasp of general principles, constitute the only adequate foundation in which to base the special training of the crafts and professions.

Owing to differing standards and degrees of efficiency the interval between the high school and the graduate school varies greatly. At Lombard College it has seemed wise to prescribe admission requirements which presume a four years' high school course.

Inasmuch as many applicants have not had access to a full four years' high school course, a considerable number of preparatory subjects are still offered at Lombard. Further, as there are some who desire to pursue certain subjects without claiming full college standing, provision is made for such special students upon equitable terms. The pure college ideal, however, enjoins us to regard these concessions as temporary, to be granted only so long as conditions necessitate them.

On the other hand, it is believed to be not inconsistent with the college idea to allow those students who intend to enter a graduate, professional, or technical school after graduation, to expedite the latter course and shorten the whole period of study by directly matching the college graduation requirements with the prospective entrance requirements of the technical school. Thus, by using his elective privilege in mapping out his college course, the Lombard A. B. may complete the subsequent Divinity course leading to the degree of B. D. in two additional years, and an Engineering course in three years.

The number of subjects offered at Lombard is largely in excess of graduation requirements. This allows exceptional opportunity for adapting the course to the individual student. The emphasis is laid upon quality rather than amount of work, upon principles more than upon mere facts. The cultivation of orderly, self-active mental life is the constant endeavor.

GENERAL STATEMENT.

HISTORY.

The Illinois Liberal Institute was chartered in 1851, opened for students in the autumn of 1852, invested with College powers in 1853, and took the name of Lombard University (in honor of Mr. Benjamin Lombard, at that time the largest donor to its properties) in 1855. It was one of the first Colleges in the country to admit women as students on the same terms with men, allowing them to graduate in the same class and with the same honors. The first class was graduated in 1856. The Ryder Divinity School was opened September 5, 1881. The official title of the institution was changed in 1899 to Lombard College.

THE COLLEGE CAMPUS.

The College Campus is situated in the southeastern part of the city, and may readily be reached by the electric cars. It is thirteen acres in extent and affords ample space for base-ball, foot-ball, tennis, and other athletic sports. A large part is planted with trees which have been growing many years and have attained noble size and graceful forms. Among them are pines, larches, hemlocks, cedars, maples, elms, ash-trees, tulip-trees, and others, embracing about forty species. The trees and lawns are well kept and cared for, and the beauty of the surround-ings thus created is a pleasing and attractive feature of the College.

THE COLLEGE YEAR.

The College year begins early in September and closes early in June. It is divided into three terms of approximately equal length. (See Calendar, page 2.)

Students should, if possible, enter at the beginning of the College year, since much of the work is arranged progressively from that date. They will, however, be allowed to enter at any time when there seems a prospect of their being able to do so profitably.

Commencement day occurs the first Thursday in June.

ADMISSION REQUIREMENTS.

The requirements for admission to the College of Liberal Arts for students who are candidates for a degree, are essentially the requirements recommended by the Committee of Thirteen of the National Educational Association. (See pages 18-24.)

Students not candidates for a degree may enter any class for which they are prepared, and at the end of their connection with the College they will be furnished a certificate, stating the amount and quality of the work accomplished while in the College.

GRADES OF SCHOLARSHIP.

From the courses of study offered, each student is expected to elect work to an amount sufficient to keep him profitably employed. In all full courses each recitation occupies one hour. Absence from a recitation will forfeit the mark in that study for the day.

At the end of every term the standing of a student in each of his courses will be expressed, according to his proficiency, by one of four grades, designated respectively by the letters, A, B, C, D.

The grade is determined by term work, estimated on the basis of attendance, quality of recitations or laboratory work, occasional tests, written exercises, etc., and by final examination at the end of the term, the term grade and the final examination being valued in the ratio of two to one.

Grade C is the lowest which will be accepted in any study as counting towards the fulfillment of the requirements of graduation.

Students who receive grade A in all their studies may pursue not more than four courses in the succeeding term.

Students whose lowest grade is B may pursue not more than three and one-half courses in the succeeding term.

Other students are not permitted to pursue more than three courses in any term.

CHAPEL EXERCISES.

Religious exercises are conducted daily in the College chapel.

With the view of imparting additional interest and value to these exercises, relieving them of mere formality, brief addresses by members of the faculty, or by invited speakers, upon practical life questions, or upon topics of the day, will be given from time to time.

LABORATORIES.

The department of Physics is equipped with apparatus for experimentation. Students have an opportunity to obtain a practical acquaintance with the principles of Physics, through a series of Laboratory experiments.

The extended courses in Chemistry, described elsewhere in this Catalogue, require a large amount of practical work on the part of the student. Each student in Chemistry has a desk provided with gas, water, re-agents and all necessary conveniences. The Laboratory is well equipped for work in General Chemistry, and in Qualitative and Quantitative Analysis.

A supply of superior microscopes, with other instruments and apparatus, affords a very satisfactory equipment for work in Biology.

LIBRARY AND READING ROOM.

The Library of the College contains about seven thousand volumes. It is located in the College building and is open daily. The books are systematically arranged and easy of access. They may be taken out by the students upon application to the librarian. A considerable fund has been raised, which will be expended as occasion arises, in the purchase of new books, thus assuring a substantial increment each year. The Reading Room is open daily, except Sundays, from 8:00 a. m. until 6:00 p. m.

GYMNASIUM.

The Gymnasium is a building 50x80 feet on the ground. On the ground floor, besides the Gymnasium proper, there is a large room, at the present used as a recitation room, which can be thrown into the main room by withdrawing the movable partitions. There is also a stage equipped with an adequate outfit of scenery, for the special use of the Department of Elocution. The apparatus, consisting of chest weights, dumb-bells, Indian clubs, parallel bars, horizontal bar, flying rings, travelling rings, rowing machine, etc., is of approved patterns. The basement contains bathrooms and lockers and other conveniences.

Regular exercises are held in the Gymnasiumn daily, except Saturdays and Sundays. The exercises will consist of class drill, under the charge of a director, or of special work on the apparatus in accordance with the prescription of the medical examiner. It is intended that the instruction shall be thoroughly scientific, aiming not so much at special muscular or athletic development as at a sound physical culture, which is the true basis of health and so of energy and endurance.

ATHLETICS..

The Athletic interests of the College are in charge of the Director of Physical Culture, assisted by a Board of Management, consisting of two members chosen from the student body, one from the faculty, and two from the alumni. The campus affords opportunity for foot-ball, base-ball, and track and field events. During the winter basket-ball is played in the Gymnasium. The Director of Physical Culture will take personal charge of the coaching of the foot-ball, basket-ball, base-ball, and track teams.

THE LADIES' HALL..

The new Ladies' Hall is a thoroughly modern building and complete in all its appointments. It is heated by steam, lighted by gas, fitted with sanitary plumbing, including porcelain baths, closets, lavatories, etc., and supplied with every convenience of a well equipped home. The Hall will accommodate forty.

Each room is finished with hard wood floor and furnished with bedstead, springs, mattress, chairs, desk, dresser, and rugs. The occupants are expected to provide bedding, pillows, towels, napkins, to pay for washing said articles, and to keep their own rooms in order.

Rates are stated on page 10.

Applications for rooms in the Hall should be made to the Dean.

LOMBARD COLLEGE PUBLICATIONS.

Lombard College Bulletin.

A series of papers is issued bi-monthly by the College, including the annual Catalogue, containing announcements, articles discussing educational questions, and other matter calculated to keep the College in touch with its friends, and to extend a knowledge of educational data, processes, and theories. Copies will be sent free upon application.

The Lombard Review.

A College paper called *The Lombard Review*, is published monthly by the students. It makes a record of College events, and serves as a medium of communication with the friends and alumni of the College. Subscription price $1.00.

SOCIETIES.

The Erosophian.

The Erosophian Society was organized January 29, 1860. Any male student connected with the College or Divinity school is eligible to membership, and is entitled to all the benefits of the society. Its regular meetings are held on Monday evenings of each week. The literary exercises consist of orations, debates, and essays.

The Zetecalian.

This society was organized in 1863 for the women of the College. Its exercises consist of debates, essays, historical narrations, and general discussions. Regular meetings are held fortnightly on Friday afternoons. The officers are elected quarterly.

Lombard Oratorical and Debating Association.

The Lombard Oratorical and Debating Association is the local branch of the Northern Illinois Intercollegiate Oratorical League. The League holds an annual prize contest in oratory on the last Friday in April. There are two prizes of twenty and ten dollars respectively. The local organization holds a preliminary contest to decide who shall represent the college in the contest of the League. All male students of the College are eligible for membership.

PRIZES.

1. The Swan Prizes.

Two prizes for excellence in Oratory are offered annually by Mrs. J. H. Swan, of Chicago. They consist of fifteen dollars and ten dollars respectively. The contest for these prizes is held in February.

2. The Townsend Prizes.

Two prizes for excellence in Declamation, established by the late Mrs. E. P. Townsend, are offered annually. They consist of fifteen dollars and ten dollars respectively. The contest for these prizes is held during Commencement week.

EXPENSES.

Board at College Commons.

Board, 37 weeks: Tuition, one year (without restriction of number of studies);

Incidentals, one year; payable annually or semi-annually in advance......$140.00

Board, one Term; Tuition, one term (without restriction of number of studies):

Incidentals, one term, payable in advance........................... 47.50

Board per week, payable in advance................................. 2.50

Meal tickets, 5 tickets.. 1.00

The yearly expenses may be estimated as follows.

Board at Commons, Tuition, Incidentals.............................$140.00

Room rent... 22.50

Washing... 15.00

Books... 15.00

$192.50

Students, however, are not required to board at the Commons; some board themselves, and some board in private families. Students who board themselves may possibly cut their expenses a trifle below the above rates. In private families rates of from $2.75 and upwards per week for board, may be obtained.

Board and Rooms in Ladies' Hall.

Board, per term, payable in advance, (not including Christmas recess).........$42.00

Room rent, (according to location of room)...................$9.00 to $18.00

Board to women students not rooming in Hall, per week.....................$3 25

Where one person occupies a double room from choice, an extra charge of fifty cents per week will be made, but the privilege of assigning two persons to such room is reserved.

Tuition and Incidentals.

Students in the College of Liberal Arts and Unclassified students will pay a tuition fee for each study pursued. The charge, except in theoretical music, is $4.00 per term for each full course, a course being a study taken for one term and counting as one credit toward graduation. The rate for each fractional course is in proportion to the credit allowed for such fractional course toward graduation. Thus, a half course is half rate; a third course, third rate, etc.

Students in Chemistry, Mineralogy, Histology, and Osteology, are required to deposit with the Registrar a sum sufficient to cover laboratory bills. Students in General Chemistry will deposit two dollars; students in Analytical Chemistry, five dollars; students in Mineralogy, three dollars; students in Histology, five dollars; students in Osteology, ten dollars each. At the close of the term there will be returned the balance remaining, after deducting cost of chemicals and broken apparatus.

Regular term fees are charged in each of the following laboratory courses: in Physics, one dollar; in Anatomy, five dollars; in Biology, two dollars; in Physiology, two dollars; in Zoology, two dollars; and in Botany, two dollars.

The charge for incidentals, to be paid by all students of the College, is $5.00 per term.

No students will be enrolled in any class until they present the Registrar's receipt for the payment of tuition and incidentals. The registration fee is one dollar. The payment of this fee will be remitted to all who register on the first day of the term. For any change in registration not advised by the faculty a fee of one dollar will be charged.

Tuition and incidentals will not be refunded. In case a student is absent a half term or more from sickness or other adequate cause, a certificate for a half term's tuition and incidentals will be given the student (at his request), said certificate good "to order" for its face value at any succeeding term.

Music and Art.

For information as to charges in Music and Art, see under these departments later in this Catalogue.

SCHOLARSHIPS.

High School Scholarships.

For the purpose of broadening the opportunities of young men and women for college training, Lombard College offers a limited number of scholarships to students graduating with high rank from High Schools and Academies. For further information apply to the Dean.

Endowed Scholarships.

Through the generosity of its friends the College is enabled to offer assistance to worthy students desiring to secure an education. The income of endowed scholarships is applied toward paying the tuition of a limited number.

Sixteen Endowed scholarships of $1,000 each have been founded by the following named persons:

The F. R. E. Cornell Scholarship, by Mrs. E. O. Cornell.
The George B. Wright Scholarship, by Mrs. C. A. Wright.
The George Power Scholarship, by George and James E. Power.
The Mrs. Emma Mulliken Scholarship, by Mrs. Emma Mulliken.
The Clement F. LeFevre Scholarship, by William LeFevre and Mrs. Ellen R. Coleman.
The Samuel Bowles Scholarship, by Samuel Bowles.
The Dollie B. Lewis Scholarship, by Mrs. Dollie B. Lewis.
The O. B. Ayres Scholarship, by O. B. Ayres.
The Mary Chapin Perry Scholarship, by T. T. Perry.

The C. A. Newcombe Scholarship, by C. A. Newcombe.

The Mary W. Conger Scholarship, by the children of Mrs. Mary W. Conger.

The Hattie A. Drowne Scholarship, by Rev. E. L. Conger, D. D.

The A. R. Wolcott Scholarship, by A. R. Wolcott.

The Women's Association Scholarship, by the Universalist Women's Association of Illinois.

The Calista Waldron Slade Scholarship, by E. D. Waldron and sisters.

The Mary L. Pingrey Scholarship, by Mrs. Mary L. Pingrey.

CATALOGUES.

Former students of the College, whether graduates or not, are requested to inform the Dean of any change of residence in order that the publications of the College may be sent them. Catalogues and circulars of information will promptly be sent to those who apply for them.

DISCIPLINE AND SOCIAL POLICY.

Aside from a few obvious regulations, designed to secure punctuality and regularity in attendance on College exercises, and to protect students and teachers from disturbance while at work, no formal rules are imposed upon the students.

It is expected that, as young men and women of somewhat mature years, they will observe the usual forms of good breeding, and enjoy the ordinary privileges of good society in so far as the latter do not conflict with the best interests of the institution or with their own health and intellectual advancement.

Should any student show a disposition to engage in conduct detrimental to his own best interests, or to those of his fellow students or of the College, the faculty will deal with the case in such manner as will protect the common welfare of all.

OFFICERS OF THE COLLEGE.

FREDERICK WILLIAM RICH, D. Sc., ACTING PRESIDENT.

DEAN OF THE COLLEGE OF LIBERAL ARTS.

*Conger Professor of Chemistry and Physics.

B. S., Cornell University, 1881; Graduate Student, Cornell University, 1881; D. Sc., St. Lawrence University, 1900; Instructor in Analytical Chemistry, Cornell University, 1882-84; Professor of Natural Science, Lombard College, 1884-1900; Professor of Chemistry and Physics, 1900—.

ISAAC AUGUSTUS PARKER, A. M., PH. D.

†Williamson Professor of the Greek Language and Literature.

A. B., Dartmouth College, 1853; A. M., ibid, 1856; Ph. D., Buchtel College, 1892; Principal Orleans Liberal Institute, Glover, Vt., 1853-58, Professor of Ancient Languages, Lombard University, 1858-68; Professor of Greek Language and Literature, Lombard College, 1868—.

NEHEMIAH WHITE, A. M., PH. D., S. T. D.

‡Hall Professor of Intellectual and Moral Philosophy.

In charge of the Ryder Divinity School, Professor of Biblical Languages and Exegesis.

A. B., Middlebury College, 1857; A. M., ibid, 1860; Ph. D., St. Lawrence University, 1876; S. T. D., Tufts College, 1889; Associate Principal Green Mt. Perkins Institute, 1857-58; Principal Clinton Liberal Institute, 1859-60; Principal Pulaski Academy, 1865; Professor of Mathematics and Natural Science, St. Lawrence University, 1865-71; Professor of Ancient Languages Buchtel College, 1872-75; President Lombard University, 1875-92; in charge of Ryder Divinity School, and Professor of Biblical Languages and Exegesis, 1892—.

JON WATSON GRUBB, M. S., REGISTRAR,

Assistant Professor of Mathematics.

B. S., Lombard University, 1879; M. S., Lombard University, 1882; Adjunct Professor of Mathematics, Lombard University, 1882-94; Registrar Lombard College, 1893—; Professor of Latin, Lombard College, 1894-1903; Assistant Professor of Mathematics, Lombard College, 1903—.

PHILIP GREEN WRIGHT, A. M.,

Professor of Mathematics, Astronomy, and Economics.

A. M. B., Tufts College, 1884; A. M., Harvard University, 1887; Teacher of Mathematics and Science, Goddard Seminary, Vt., 1883; Adjunct Professor of Mathematics, Buchtel College, 1884-86; Professor of Mathematics, Lombard College, 1892—.

---

*In honor of the late L. E. Conger, of Dexter, Iowa.
†In honor of the late I. D. Williamson, D. D., of Cincinnati.
‡In honor of the late E. G. Hall, of Chicago.

FRANK HAMILTON FOWLER, PH. D.,

Professor of Latin Language and Literature.

A. B., Lombard University, 1890: Ph. D., The University of Chicago, 1896; Graduate Student, Johns Hopkins University, 1890-91; Principal Peaster Academy, 1891-92; Fellow in the University of Chicago, 1892-96; Professor of English, Lombard College, 1897-1903; Professor Latin Language and Literature, Lombard College, 1903—.

RALPH GRIERSON KIMBLE, A. B.,

Professor of Sociology.

A. B., Lombard College, 1896; University Scholar in Sociology, University of Chicago, 1896-97; Senior Fellow in Sociology, ibid, 1897-1901; Special Lecturer in Sociology, Lombard College, Spring term, 1899; ibid, 1900: Special Lecturer in Sociological Theory, University of Wisconsin, Spring of 1902, Professor of Sociology, Lombard College, 1901—.

ALICE BERTHA CURTIS, B. DI., PH. D.

Professor of English and Public Speaking.

B. Di., Iowa State Normal School, 1896; Student University of Iowa, 1900; Student University of Wisconsin, 1902; Ph. B., University of Iowa, 1903; Graduate student and tutor in English, University of Iowa, 1903; Professor of English and Public Speaking, and Dean of Women, Lombard College, 1903—.

EDSON REIFSNIDER, B. D.,

Instructor in Homiletics and Pastoral Care.

B. D., Tufts College, 1898; Instructor in Homiletics and Pastoral Care, Lombard College, 1903—.

CHARLES ORVAL APPLEMAN, B. E., B. P., PH. B.

Physical Director and Professor of Biology.

B. E., Bloomsburg Literary Institute and State Normal School, 1897; B. P., ibid, 1898; Chautauqua School of Physical Culture, 1898; Department of Physical Training, Bloomsburg Literary Institute and State Normal School, 1898-99; Ph. B., Dickinson College, 1903; Director of Gymnastics Dickinson College, 1899-1903; Member of foot-ball, basket-ball, and track teams Dickinson College; Instructor in Biology and Physical Training, Swarthmore Preparatory School, 1903-1904; Student in Biology, University of Chicago, 1904; Physical Director and Professor of Biology, Lombard College, 1904—.

LOUISE MALLINCKRODT KUEFFNER, A. M.

Professor of German and French.

A. B., A. M., Washington University, 1896; Student at the University of Berlin, 1896-98; Student and Reader at the University of Chicago, 1901-03; Instructor of German in Mary Institute, St. Louis; Norwich Free Acadamy, Norwich, Conn; Professor of German and French at Oxford College, Oxford, Ohio; Instructor of German in the Correspondence Department of the University of Chicago; Prof. of German and French, Lombard College, 1904—.

M. AGNES HATHAWAY,

Instructor in History.

Graduate from Genesee Wesleyan Seminary, Lima, New York, 1888; Student at National Normal University, Lebanon, Ohio, 1895-96; Teacher in Public Schools of New York and Illinois; Dean of Women and Instructor in Preparatory School, Lombard College, 1900-03; Instructor in History, Lombard College, 1903—.

FRANCES ROSS,

Assistant in English.

ETHEL MARY CHAMBERLAIN,
Assistant in English.

LEVI BERL McDANIEL,
Assistant in Chemistry.

RALPH MARSHALL ATTERBERRY
Assistant in Chemistry.

EUGENE E. DAVIS,
Director of Conservatory of Music.
Graduate of the Imperial Conservatory of Vienna, Austria.

MRS. EUGENE E. DAVIS,
Voice Culture.
Pupil of Murio Celli.

W. H. CHEESMAN,
Instructor in Violin.

M. ISABELLE BLOOD,
Instructor in Drawing and Painting.
Studied with Dean Fletcher, N. Y; William Bertram, Chicago; at the Art Institute and with Nellie Davis, St. Louis; Instructor in Drawing and Painting, Lombard College, 1889—.

MRS. ADAH M. HALE,
Matron Ladies' Hall.

DR. GUY A. LONGBRAKE AND DR. DELIA M. RICE,
Medical Examiners

LAURA B. QUIGLEY,
Secretary to the President.

FRANK HAMILTON FOWLER, PH. D.,
Librarian.

JON WATSON GRUBB, M. S.,
Registrar.

CHARLES O. APPLEMAN,
Director of the Gymnasium.

ALLEN HARSHBARGER,
Janitor.

Standing Faculty Committees.

ADVISORY—
PROFESSORS WRIGHT AND CURTIS.

ACCREDITING—
PROFESSORS KIMBLE, WRIGHT, AND FOWLER.

HOMES AND EMPLOYMENT FOR STUDENTS—
PROFESSORS WRIGHT AND FOWLER

CATALOGUE—
PROFESSORS WRIGHT AND FOWLER.

ATHLETICS—
PROFESSORS KIMBLE AND APPLEMAN.

ORDER AND DISCIPLINE—
DEAN RICH AND PROFESSOR CURTIS.

Departments of the College.

Students at Lombard are divided primarily into Classified and Unclassified Students.

The Classified department includes all students who are candidates for a degree or diploma. It embraces the College of Liberal Arts, the Divinity School, and the Departments of Music and Art.

The Unclassified students include those who are pursuing studies at Lombard for a greater or less period, without any express intention of obtaining a degree or diploma.

THE GYMNASIUM.

COLLEGE OF LIBERAL ARTS.

Faculty of Liberal Arts.

FREDERICK WILLIAM RICH, D. Sc.
*Dean and Conger Professor of Chemistry and Physics.

ISAAC AUGUSTUS PARKER, A. M., Ph. D.,
†Williamson Professor of the Greek Language and Literature.

NEHEMIAH WHITE, A. M., Ph. D., S. T. D.,
‡Hall Professor of Intellectual and Moral Philosophy.

JON WATSON GRUBB, M. S.,
Assistant Professor of Mathematics.

PHILIP GREEN WRIGHT, A. M.,
Professor of Mathematics, Astronomy, and Economics.

FRANK HAMILTON FOWLER, Ph. D.,
Professor of the Latin Language and Literature.

RALPH GRIERSON KIMBLE, A. B.,
Professor of Sociology

ALICE BERTHA CURTIS, B. Di., Ph. B.,
Professor of English and Public Speaking.

CHARLES ORVAL APPLEMAN,
Physical Director and Professor of Biology.

LOUISE MALLINCKRODT KUEFFNER,
Professor of German and French.

---

*In honor of the late L. E. Conger, of Dexter, Iowa.
†In honor of the late I. D. Williamson, D. D., of Cincinnati.
‡In honor of the late E. G. Hall, of Chicago.

Requirements for Admission.

All applicants for admission to the College of Liberal Arts, except those from certain approved High Schools and Academies, are required to pass satisfactory examinations in Studies selected from the following list, to an aggregate of sixteen units:

STUDY.	UNITS.	STUDY.	UNITS.
English	3	Physics	1
Greek	3	Chemistry	1
Latin	3	Physiography	½ to 1
German	1	Physiology	½ to 1
French	1	Botany	½ to 1
Ancient History	1	Astronomy	1
English and American History	1	Meteorology	1
Algebra	1½	Political Economy	½ to 1
Plane Geometry	½ to 1	Zoology	½ to 1
Solid Geometry	½ to 1		

CONSTANTS.

The studies presented must include the following constants:

STUDIES.	UNITS.
English	3
One Foreign Language	3
History	1
Algebra	1½
Geometry	½
Science	2
	11

The two units in Science, one of which must include laboratory work, may be chosen from the following, viz: Physics, Chemistry, Physiography, Anatomy and Physiology, Botany, Zoology.

EXAMINATIONS.

Examinations in the above studies will be held during the first week in September, as follows:

HOUR.	TUESDAY, SEPT. 5.	WEDNESDAY, SEPT. 6.	THURS., SEPT. 7
7:30- 9:30	English.	French.	Plane Geometry
9:30-11:30	Greek—Astronomy.	Ancient History.	Physics.
11:30-12:30	Physiology.	Physiography.	Botany.
2:00- 4:00	Latin.	Algebra.	Chemistry.
4:00- 6:00	German—Solid Geom.	Eng. and Am. Hist.	Zoology—Pol. Ec.

ADMISSION BY CERTIFICATE.

Certificates from the principles or other authorized officers of certain approved High Schools and Academies will be accepted in lieu of examinations. *But these certificates must be presented during the term in which the student applies for admission in order to be accepted*, and no certificate will be valid for more than two years after the completion of the course of study to which the certificate refers. The credit allowed on them will be based upon the work accomplished; in general, one unit being equal to a year's work in a study reciting five hours a week in recitation periods of not less than forty minutes.

The detailed descriptions given below indicate more fully the amount of work required in each study to obtain the number of units given in the table. Students admitted by certificate enter classes on probation, and if it is found that their previous training is insufficient to render it advisable for them to continue in these classes, they will be assigned other work.

SCOPE OF PREPARATORY STUDIES.

The amount of work required in the several Preparatory studies to obtain the units assigned in the foregoing table, either by examination or certificate, is indicated by the following outline of examination requirements:

ENGLISH.

The examination will occupy two hours and will consist of two parts, which, however, cannot be taken separately:—

I. The candidate will be required to write a paragraph or two on each of several topics chosen by him from a considerable number—perhaps ten or fifteen—set before him on the examination paper.

In 1904, 1905, and 1906, the topics will be drawn from the following works:

Shakespeare's Merchant of Venice, and Julius Cæsar; The Sir Roger de Coverley Papers in the Spectator; Goldsmith's Vicar of Wakefield; Coleridge's Ancient Mariner; Scott's Ivanhoe; Carlyle's Essay on Burns; Tennyson's Princess; Lowell's Vision of Sir Launfal; George Eliot's Silas Marner.

The candidate is expected to read intelligently *all* the books prescribed. He should read them as he reads other books; he is expected, not to know them minutely, but to have freshly in mind their most important parts. In every case the examiner will regard knowledge of the book as less important than ability to write English.

II. A certain number of books are prescribed for careful study. This part of the examination will be upon subject-matter, literary form and logical structure, and will also test the candidate's ability to express his knowledge with clearness and accuracy.

The books prescribed for this part of the examination in 1904, 1905, and 1906, are: Shakespeare's Macbeth; Milton's Lycidas, Comus, L'Allegro, and Il Penseroso; Burke's speech on Conciliation with America; Macaulay's Essays on Milton and Addison.

No candidate will be accepted in English whose work is seriously defective in point of spelling, punctuation, grammar, or division into paragraphs.

In connection with the reading and the study of the prescribed books, parallel or subsidiary reading should be encouraged, and a considerable amount of English poetry should be committed to memory.   The essentials of English grammar should not be neglected in preparatory study.

The English written by a candidate in any of his examination-books may be regarded as part of his examination in English, in case the evidence afforded by the examination-book in English is insufficient.

As additional evidence of preparation the candidate may present an exercise book, properly certified by his instructor, containing compositions or other written work.

FRENCH.

(a) The translation at sight of ordinary Nineteenth Century prose.   (The passages set for translation must be rendered into simple and idiomatic English.)

(b) The translation into French of simple English sentences or of easy connected prose, to test the candidate's familiarity with elementary grammar.   Proficiency in grammar may also be tested by direct questions, based on the passages set for translation under *(a)*.

The passages set for translation into English will be suited to the proficiency of candidates who have read not less than four hundred pages (including reading at sight in class) from the works of at least three different authors.   It is desirable that a portion of the reading should be from works other than works of fiction.

Grammar should be studied concurrently with the reading as an indispensable means of insuring thoroughness and accuracy in the understanding of the language. The requirement in elementary grammar includes the conjugations of regular verbs, of the more frequent irregular verbs, such as *aller*, *envoyer*. *tenir*, *pouvoir*, *voir*, *vouloir*, *dire*, *savoir*. *faire*, and those belonging to the classes represented by *ouvrir*, *dormir*, *connaitre*, *conduire*, and *craindre;* the forms and positions of personal pronouns and of possessive, demonstrative, and interrogative adjectives; the inflection of nouns and adjectives for gender and number, except rare cases; the uses of articles, and the partitive constructions.

Pronunciation should be carefully taught, and pupils should have frequent opportunities to hear French spoken or read aloud.   The writing of French from dictation is recommended as a useful exercise.

GERMAN.

(a) The translation at sight of simple German prose. (The passages set for translation must be rendered into simple and idiomatic English.)

(b) The translation simple into German of English sentences, or of easy connected prose, to test the candidate's familiarity with elementary grammar.

The passages set for translation into English will be suited to the proficiency of candidates who have read not less than two hundred pages of easy German (including reading at sight in class.)

Grammar should be studied concurrently with the reading as an indispensable means of insuring thoroughness and accuracy in the understanding of the language. The requirement in elementary grammar includes the conjugation of the weak and the more usual strong verbs; the declension of articles, adjectives, pronouns and such nouns as are readily classified; the commoner prepositions; the simpler uses of the modal auxiliaries; the elements of syntax, especially the rules governing the order of words.

Pronunciation should be carefully taught, and the pupils should have frequent opportunities to hear German spoken or read aloud. The writing of German from dictation is recommended as a useful exercise.

LATIN.

The examination in Latin will consist of two parts.

I. Elementary Latin.

This examination will be designed to test the proficiency of those who have studied Latin in the high school for two years, and will count as two admission units. The student should have read at least four books of the Gallic War or an equivalent. The examination will include:—

(a) Translation at sight of Latin prose, with questions on ordinary forms, constructions, and idioms of the language.

(b) The translation into Latin of English sentences involving a knowledge of the more common words and constructions used by Cæsar.

II. Advanced Latin.

This examination will be designed to test the proficiency of those who have studied Latin in the high school for four years and together with I will count as four admission units. In preparation for this examination the candidate should have read, besides the four books of Cæsar mentioned under I, at least six orations of Cicero and six books of Vergil's Æneid, and should have had considerable practice in reading at sight and in Latin composition. The examination will include:—

(a) Translation at sight of passages of Latin prose and hexameter verse, with questions on ordinary forms, constructions, and idioms, and the principles of Latin verse.

(b) The translation into Latin prose of a passage of connected English narrative, limited in subject matter to the works usually read in preparation.

MATHEMATICS.

Algebra. The examination in Algebra will demand accuracy in the several processes of literal Arithmetic. Special emphasis will be laid on factoring, and the correct manipulation of negative and fractional exponents. It will include the solution of simple and quadratic equations (together with a knowledge of the theory of quadratic equations), elimination in the case of simultaneous equations of the first and second degrees, variation, and Arithmetical and Geometrical progression. . . . .

Plane Geometry. The examination in Plane Geometry will emphasize precision in the definition of Geometric terms, and accuracy in the demonstration of Geometric theorems. In scope it will demand a knowledge of all the propositions in Plane Geometry preceding Solid Geometry, included in such a standard text book in this subject as Phillips and Fisher's Elements.

Solid Geometry. As in Plane Geometry emphasis will be laid upon accuracy in definition and demonstration. In scope the examination will cover the propositions in Solid Geometry included in such a standard text book as Phillips and Fisher's Elements.

ASTRONOMY.

The examination in this subject will demand knowledge of descriptive rather than mathematical Astronomy. The student will be expected to undertand the theory of the celestial sphere, simple methods of computing latitude, time, and longitude; the astronomical features of the earth, the sun, and the moon; the principles of spectrum analysis; the motions and characteristics of the planets; the names and myths of the principal stars and constellations; the facts in regard to abberation, parallax, and proper motion of the stars; and the principles of a rational cosmogony as developed in LaPlace's nebular hypothesis. Young's Lessons in Astronomy is suggested as a text book embracing the matter with which students are expected to be acquainted who wish to prepare for this examination.

PHYSICS.

Students offering Physics for entrance credit must show an acquaintance with the more important phenomena and with the principles involved in the explanation of them. They must, in addition to the text book work, have completed a course of laboratory experiments and be able to work simple numerical problems, involving the laws of falling bodies; pendulum; properties of liquids and gases; thermometry and calorimetry; current strength, resistance, and electromotive force; properties of sound, refraction and reflection with the size and position of images.

CHEMISTRY.

The Elementary Course in Chemistry offered for entrance credit must include knowledge of the elements and compounds equivalent to that given in Remsen's Introduction to the study of Chemistry. In addition, students must have had a series of laboratory experiments illustrating the text book work and be able to write equations and solve simple chemical problems.

BOTANY.

Students presenting work in Botany for entrance credit should have a knowledge of the general laws and fundamental principles of plant nutrition, assimilation, growth, etc., as exemplified by plants chosen from the different groups, as well as the general comparative morphology and the broader relationships of plants. They should present an herbarium of at least twenty-five specimens, collected and mounted by themselves and certified to by their instructor.

ZOOLOGY.

Students desiring entrance credit for Zoology should have devoted the equivalent of five periods a week for at least one-half year to the study of general Zoology. A portion of this work must have been laboratory practice in the observation of living forms and dissection. Their laboratory notes and drawings, endorsed by the instructor, should be presented at the time of registration as evidence of the nature of this part of the work. This laboratory practice should include a study of at least twelve of the forms named in the following list: Amœba, paramœcium, sea-anemone, star-fish, sea-urchin, earth worm, cray-fish, lobster, spider, centipede, locust, (grasshopper), dragon-fly, squash-bug, bumblebee, clam, snail, a simple tunicate, shark, any soft rayed-fish, snake, turtle, frog, pigeon, rabbit, and cat.

PHYSIOLOGY.

Students presenting work in human Physiology for entrance credit should have a general knowledge of the human skeleton, muscular, circulatory, and nervous systems, the vital organs, viscera, and organs of special sense, and the processes of respiration and digestion.

The text-book used should cover the ground treated in such books as Martin's Human Body, or Huxley's Elementary Physiology (Lee's Revision.)

PHYSIOGRAPHY.

A course of study equivalent to Tarr's Elementary Physical Geography.

The examination will include a thorough test on all the leading subjects treated in Physical Geography, with maps to illustrate relief forms, currents, ocean beds, and the distribution of animal and plant life.

HISTORY (including Historical Geography).

Either of the two following groups, each including two fields of historical study:—

1. *Greek and Roman History.*—*(a)* Greek History to the death of Alexander, with due reference to Greek life, literature, and art. *(b)* Roman History to the downfall of the Western Roman Empire, with due reference to literature and government.

2. *English and American History.*—*(a)* English History, with due reference to social and political development. *(b)* American History, with the elements of Civil Government.

For preparation in each of the two historical fields presented, a course of study equivalent to at least five lessons a week for one year will be necessary.

The candidate will be expected to show on examination such general knowledge of each field as may be acquired from the study of an accurate text-book of not less than 300 pages, supplemented by suitable parallel readings amounting to not less than 500 pages. The examination will call for comparison of Historical characters, periods, and events, and in general for the exercise of judgment as well as memory. Geographical knowledge will be tested by means of an outline map.

It is desirable that Greek and Roman History be offered as a part of the preparation of every candidate.

POLITICAL ECONOMY.

The examination in Political Economy will demand a thorough knowledge of the fundamental economic laws relating to Production, Exchange, Distribution, and Consumption. The applicant will also be expected to discuss intelligently from an economic standpoint such questions as Free Trade, Socialism, Strikes, and Taxation. Bullock's Introduction to the study of Economics is suggested as a text covering the the ground required for the examination.

ADMISSION TO ADVANCED STANDING.

Students from other institutions, who present letters of honorable dismissal, may be admitted to such standing and upon such terms as the Faculty may deem equitable. Every such student is required to present, along with the catalogue of the institution in which he has studied, a full statement, duly certified, of the studies he has completed, including preparatory studies. Candidates for advanced standing who wish to receive credit for work accomplished in private study, are permitted to take examinations in such subjects upon payment of the regular term fee for the course in which the examination is taken.

Requirements for Graduation.

GROUP SYSTEM.

Having been admitted to the College of Liberal Arts, the student will elect one of the following groups as a course of study leading to his degree. These groups consist of certain required studies arranged logically with reference to some central subject, in addition to which, considerable option is allowed in the way of free electives. All the required studies, together with a sufficient number of electives to bring the total up to an aggregate of thirty-eight credits must be completed before the degree will be conferred. A credit is obtained by the satisfactory completion of one full course pursued for one term. Of the thirty-eight credits at least twenty-four must be above grade C. Two credits may be obtained by two full years' work in the Gymnasium classes.

THESIS.

In addition to the above requirements, every student who is a candidate for a degree, or a diploma, will present a graduation thesis upon some subject in which he or she has prosecuted original research or special study.

The subject of the thesis is to be approved by the professor under whose direction the work is to be done and by the advisory committee and is to be recorded as a part of the regular registration at the beginning of the fall term. The student will prepare monthly reports on the work done and these reports, approved by the professor, will be filed in the office of the President. At the end of the winter term the student will prepare a syllabus of the dissertation on the chosen subject, to be approved and filed as in the case of reports. Two weeks before commencement the student will present a dissertation embodying the results of his work, this dissertation to meet the approval of the faculty before recommendation for a degree is made.

For work done in preparing his thesis the student will receive college credits to such an extent as the professor in whose department the work is done shall deem him entitled. The number of credits received in this way, however, is not to exceed three.

RESIDENCE.

A minimum residence of the two terms next preceding the completion of the requirements for graduation, and a minimum of eight courses taken in this College, are required of all applicants for a baccalaureate degree.

ADVANCED DEGREE.

The degree of Master of Arts will be conferred upon graduates of this college or other institutions of equal rank, on the satisfactory completion of one year's residence work upon a course of study or research which shall have been submitted to and approved by the Faculty beyond the requirements for the baccalaureate degree.   The candidate must present a thesis showing original research in the special line of study pursued.

GROUPS.

On being admitted to the College of Liberal Arts, each student, who is a candidate for a degree, will elect one of these groups:

ENGLISH GROUP.

YEAR.	HOUR.	FALL TERM.	WINTER TERM.	SPRING TERM.
1st yr.	8:00 9:30 10:30	Germ. 1. Chem. 1. Eng. 5.	Germ. 2. Chem. 2. Eng. 6.	Germ. 3. Sociology. Eng. 7.
2nd yr.	8:00 10:30 1:45	Eng. 25 and 28. Germ. 4 or 5. Lat. 10.	Eng. 26 and 29. Germ. 6 or 7. Lat. 11.	Eng. 27 and 30. Germ. 8, or 9.. Lat. 12.
3rd yr.	8:00 10:30 11:30 1:45	Eng. 31 and 34. Math. 7. Hist. 8.	Eng. 32 and 35. Math. 8. Hist. 9.	Eng. 33 and 36. Psychology. Math. 9.
4th yr.	8:00	Eng. 19 and 22. Elective. Elective.	Eng. 20 and 23. Elective. Elective.	Eng. 21 and 24. Elective. Elective.

LATIN SCIENTIFIC.

YEAR.	HOUR.	FALL TERM.	WINTER TERM.	SPRING TERM.
1st yr.	9:30 10:30 1:45	{ Chem. 1 or { French 1 Eng. 5. Lat. 10.	{ Chem. 2 or { French 2. Eng. 6. Lat. 11.	{ Chem. 3 or { French 3. Lat. 12.
2nd. yr.	8:00 9:30 10:30 11:30	{ Germ. 1 or { Chem. 1. Math. 7.	{ Germ. 2 or { Chem. 2. Math. 8.	{ Germ. 3. or { Chem. 3. Psychology. Math. 9.
3rd yr.	8:00 9:30 10:30 11:30	Physics 1. Gen. Biol. 1. { Germ. 4 or 5, { or { French 4 or 5.	Physics 2. Biol. 2. { Germ. 6 or 7, { or { French 6 or 7.	Physics 3. Sociology. { Germ. 8 or 9, { or { French 8 or 9.
4th yr.	1:45	Elective. Elective. Hist. 8.	Elective. Elective. Hist. 9.	Elective. Elective.

MODERN LANGUAGE.

YEAR.	HOUR.	FALL TERM.	WINTER TERM.	SPRING TERM.
1st yr.	8:00 9:30 10:30	Germ. 1. Chem. 1. Eng. 5.	Germ. 2. Chem. 2. Eng. 6.	Germ. 3. Sociology.
2nd yr.	9:30 10:30 11:30	French 1. Germ. 4 or 5. Math. 7.	French 2. Germ. 6 or 7. Math. 8.	French 3. Germ. 8 or 9. Math. 9.
3rd yr.	9:30 10:30 11:30 1:45	Germ. 4 or 5. French 4 or 5. Hist. 8.	Germ. 6 or 7. French 6 or 7. Hist 9.	Psychology. Germ. 8 or 9. French 8 or 9.
4th yr.	11:30	French 4 or 5.	French 6 or 7.	French 8 or 9.

CLASSICAL GROUP.

YEAR.	HOUR	FALL TERM.	WINTER TERM.	SPRING TERM.
1st yr.	11:30 10:30 1:45	Greek 1. Eng. 5. Lat. 10.	Greek 2. Eng. 6. Lat. 11.	Greek 3. Psychology. Lat. 12.
2nd yr.	8:00 9:30 10:30	Germ. 1. Chem. 1. Greek 4.	Germ. 2. Chem. 2. Greek 5.	Germ. 3. Chem. 3. Greek 6
3rd yr.	8:00 10:30 1:45 9:30	Greek 7 or 10. Germ. 4, 5. Hist. 8.	Greek 8 or 11. Germ. 6, 7. Hist. 9.	Greek 9 or 12. Germ. 8, 9. Sociology.
4th yr.	8:00	Elective.	Elective.	Elective.

MATHEMATICS.

YEAR.	HOUR.	FALL TERM.	WINTER TERM.	SPRING TERM.
1st yr.	9:00 10:30 11:30	Chem. 1. Eng. 5. Math. 7.	Chem. 2. Eng. 6. Math. 8.	Chem. 3. Math. 9.
2nd yr.	8:00 9:30 10:30 1:45	Germ. 1 or French 1. Math. 10 or Ast. 1.	Germ. 2 or French 2. Math. 12 or 14.	Germ. 3 or French 3. Psychology 1. Math. 13 or 16.
3rd yr.	8:00 10:30 11:30 1:45	Physics 1. German 4 or 5. or French 4 or 5. Ast. 1 or Math. 10.	Physics 2. Ger. 6 or 7. or French 6 or 7. Math. 14 or 12.	Physics 3. Germ. 8 or 9 or French 8 or 9. Math. 16 or 13.
4th yr.	9:30 1:45	Hist. 8.	Hist. 9	Sociology.

CHEMISTRY AND PHYSICS.

YEAR.	HOUR.	FALL TERM.	WINTER TERM.	SPRING TERM.
1st yr.	8:00 9:30 10:30 11:30	Germ. 1 or French 1. Eng. 5. Math. 7.	Germ. 2 or French 2. Eng. 6. Math. 8.	Germ. 3 or French 3. Math. 9.
2nd yr.	9:30 10:30 11:30	Chem. 1. Germ. 4 or 5, or French 4 or 5.	Chem. 2. Germ. 6 or 7, or French 6 or 7.	Chem. 3 Germ. 8 or 9, or French 8 or 9.
3rd yr.	8:00 9:30 10:30 1:45	Astronomy. Biol. 1. Chem. 4.	Biol. 2. Geology. Chem. 5.	Sociology. Psychology. Chem. 6.
4th yr.	8:00 1:45	Physics 1. Chem. 7.	Physics 2. Chem. 8.	Physics 3.

SOCIAL SCIENCE.

YEAR.	HOUR.	FALL TERM.	WINTER TERM.	SPRING TERM.
1st yr.	9:30 10:30 11:30	Chem. 1. Eng. 5. Math. 7.	Chem. 2. Eng. Lit. Math. 8.	Sociology 1. Psychology 1. Math. 9.
2nd yr.	* 8:00 * 9:30 1:45	Germ. 1 or French 1. Hist. 8.	Germ. 2 or French 2. Hist. 9.	Germ. 3 or French 3. Hist. 10.
3d yr.	9:30 11:30	Economics 2.	Economics 3.	Economics 4. Sociology 2.
4th yr.	9:30 10:30		Gen. Biol. 1. Ethics.	Gen. Biol. 2.

Courses of Instruction.

RECITATIONS AND CREDITS.

The following studies are classed as full courses or fractional courses, according to the estimated amount of work in each, and its value in fulfilling the requirements for graduation. Unless otherwise stated, a course in any study consists of five hours of recitations or lectures, per week, for one term. Certain full courses, however, are given in three hours per week recitations. Laboratory courses require ten hours of work per week in the laboratory, in addition to a considerable amount of study outside. Certain other studies, as indicated in each case, count only as half courses, or less. It is intended to give each course during the year and term indicated. But the faculty reserves the right to make any change when it seems desirable to do so.

The general descriptions at the head of each department and the brief outline accompanying each course are designed to give in simple language the scope and purpose of the course to assist the student in making his elections.

The student is urged especially to notice the dependence of one course on another, so that in arranging his group, before electing any course, the prerequisite shall have been completed.

Regular recitations are held on Monday, Tuesday, Wednesday, Thursday and Friday of each week.

Courses in brackets will not be given in 1905-1906.

ENGLISH.

PROFESSOR ALICE B. CURTIS.

The study of English is considered of fundamental importance. For this reason thorough preparation in English is insisted on for admission to the College proper. The practical value of this study need hardly be mentioned. No matter what the occupation, there will be the necessity for expression, and this is to be obtained by the study of English. Closely related to this is the value attaching to the study as a preparation for other work of the College course. The ability to gather thought from the printed page rapidly and accurately, and the power of expression just mentioned, are prime requisites for the student. A peculiar value attaching to the study of English is that of correlating the studies of the curriculum, of making the college course more of a unit. History, Philosophy, Linguistics, Aesthetics, and Sociology may here find a common ground of meeting. As a corollary to this it may be said that English to an especial degree possesses the power of enlarging the student's mental horizon, of making a broader man of him. It is the aim of the department to utilize all these values of the study, and in order to do that to the full the endeavor is made so to foster a love of literature that the study will be pursued after the student has left college.

Primarily the object of the courses in English Composition, (5, 6, and 7,) is the acquiring on the part of the student the ability to write good English prose. It is believed, however, that the study properly pursued has a considerable disciplinary value. In these courses there is a minimum of theory and maximum of practice. The important principles are given in lectures; these principals are illustrated in the specimens of the writings of others; and the student is required to exemplify them in the preparation of daily and fortnightly themes. Courses 5 and 6 are required courses and, together with course 7, should be taken during the first year of college work.

In the courses in English Literature emphasis is laid on criticism rather than on the history. An introduction is made to the several forms of literature, special attention being given to the chief representative authors of each department. One course is given in Old English and one in the History of the English Language. The courses dealing with the Literature and Language are arranged in a cycle covering three years. The student is enabled to specialize in this study to such a degree that he may without further preparation, undertake graduate work in the Universities.

5. Rhetoric and Composition.

Mondays, Wednesdays, and Fridays. Fall term. Open to all college students.

6. The Forms of Discourse.

Mondays, Wednesdays, and Fridays. Winter term. Prerequisite, English 5.

7. The Forms of Discourse.

Mondays, Wednesdays, and Fridays. Spring term. Prerequisite, English 5.

[19. Middle English. (Two-fifths course.)]

Lectures on the life and times of Chaucer. Chaucer's shorter poems and "Canterbury Tales" will form the basis of the work. Tuesdays and Thursdays. Fall term. Prerequisite, English 5.

[20. English Essayists. (Two-fifths course.)]

A study of typical essays of Macaulay, DeQuincy, Carlyle, Burke, and Arnold, with special reference to style. Tuesdays and Thursdays. Winter term. Prerequisite, English 5.

[21. **The Novel.** (Two-fifths course.)]

This art form will be considered. Some of the great novels of the Victorian age will be read and criticised. Tuesdays and Thursdays. Spring term. Prerequisite, English 5.

[22. **Art of Shakespeare.** (Three-fifths course.)]

The elements of literary art as exemplified in Shakespeare. A detailed study of "Hamlet." Mondays, Wednesdays, and Fridays. Fall term. Prerequisite, English 5.

[23. **Art of Shakespeare.** (Three-fifths course.)]

Detailed study of "King Lear." Mondays, Wednesdays and Fridays. Winter term. Prerequisite, English 22.

[24. **Art of Shakespeare.** (Three-fifths course)]

"The Tempest," "As You Like It," "Antony and Cleopatra," "Julius Caesar." Mondays, Wednesdays, and Fridays. Spring term. Prerequisite, English 22 and 23.

[25. **History of English Literature to the time of Chaucer.**
(Two-fifths course.)]

Tuesdays and Thursdays. Fall term. Prerequisite, English 5.

[26. **History of English Literature from Chaucer to Shakespeare.**
(Two-fifths course.)]

Tuesdays and Thursdays. Winter term. Prerequisite, English 5.

[27. **History of English Literature from Shakespeare to Browning.**
(Two-fifths course.)]

Tuesdays and Thursdays. Spring term. Prerequisite, English 26.

[28. **Browning.** (Three-fifths course)]

Studies in the poems of Robert Browning. Mondays, Wednesdays, and Fridays. Fall term. Prerequisite, English 5.

[29. **Tennyson.** (Three-fifths course)]

Studies in the shorter poems and "Idylls of the King." Mondays, Wednesdays, and Fridays. Winter term. Prerequisite, English 5.

[30. **English and Scottish Ballads.** (Three-fifths course.)]

The nature of ballad poetry together with reading and interpretation of selected ballads. Mondays, Wednesdays, and Fridays. Spring term. Prerequisite, English 5.

31. American Literature. (Three-fifths course.)

A consideration of the representative prose writers of America. Mondays, Wednesdays, and Fridays. Fall term. Prerequisite, English 5.

32. American Literature. (Three-fifths course.)

A consideration of the representative poets of America. Mondays, Wednesdays, and Fridays. Winter term. Prerequisite, English 5.

33. Milton. (Three-fifths course.)

The shorter poems and "'Paradise Lost" will be studied. Mondays, Wednesdays, and Fridays. Spring term. Prerequisite, English 5.

34. Pre-Shakespearean Drama. (Two-fifths course.)

A history of the English drama before the time of Shakespeare. Tuesdays and Thursdays. Fall term. Prerequisite, English 5.

35. The Short Story. (Two-fifths course.)

Criticism of the best representative short stories of French, English, and American writers. The short story as an art form will be studied. Tuesdays and Thursdays. Winter term. Prerequisite, English 5, 6, and 7.

36. The Short Story. (Two-fifths course.)

Practice in advanced composition. Short stories will be written by members of the class. Tuesdays and Thursdays. Spring term. Prerequisite, English 35.

37. Old English. (Three-fifths course.)

A study of the grammar of Old English and the relations between Old and Modern English. Time to be arranged.

GERMAN.

PROF. LOUISE MALLINCKRODT KUEFFNER.

In all the courses, translation from German into English is dispensed with as far as possible, and "free reproduction" into German, is constantly cultivated. The Hœlzel charts are used as a basis for grammar, vocabulary, and elementary conversation. A further aid to direct apprehension of both the spoken and written word is given in the conversation club which meets socially at certain intervals. Collateral reading of German texts supplements the class work. The aim of the course in German is in general to prepare the student for a comprehension of German individuality and literature as a part of general culture.

1, 2, 3. First Year German.

Bierwirth's Abstract of Grammar, Newson's First German Book, Newson's German Reader, Wenkebach's Glueckauf. The Volksmaerchen is studied in connection with an outline of Teutonic Mythology; Grimm's Maerchen. The Kunstmaerchen: Fouqué's Undine, Baumbach's Sommermaerchen, Seidel's Wintermaerchen, Keller's Legenden. Fall, Winter, and Spring terms. Open to all college students.

4*, 5*. Modern Stories: the Village Story, the Story of Society, the Historic Story. (Three-fifths courses.)

The Village Story: Leben Jung-Stillings, Stifter's Haidedorf, Rosegger's Waldschulmeister, Keller's Romeo und Julie auf dem Dorfe. . *The Story of Society:* Storm's Immensee, Seidel's Leberecht Huenchen, and Der Lindenbaum, Freytag's Soll und Haben, Sudermann's Frau Sorge. *The Historic Story:* Meyer's Gustav Adolph's Page, Riehl's Das Spielmannskind, Keller's Dietegen, Sheffel's Ekkehard. As many as possible of these will be taken either in class or as collateral reading, and some literary analysis will be made. Mondays, Wednesdays, and Fridays. Fall and Winter term. Prerequisite, German 3.

6.* The Modern Drama. (Three-fifths course.)

Fulda's Talisman, Sudermann's Johannes, Hauptmann's Versunkene Glocke. Mondays, Wednesdays, and Fridays. Some literary analysis of the plays. Spring term. Prerequisite, German 5.

[7.* Goethe's Early Work. (Three-fifths course.)]

Faust, first part. Egmont or Goetz. Fall term. Prerequisite German 6.

[8.* Goethe's Later Work. (Three-fifths course)]

Iphigenie. Hermann and Dorothea. Study of Goethe's Lyrics in their connection with the Volkslied. White's collection of Volkslieder. Von Klenze's German Lyrics. Winter term. Prerequisite, German 7.

[9*. Schiller. (Three-fifths course.)]

Wilhelm Tell. Wallenstein. Shorter poems as given in Von Klenze's German Lyrics. Spring term. Prerequisite, German 8.

10.* The Romantic School. (Three-fifths course.)

Lectures and readings. Wilhelm Meister and the *romantic novel*. *The romantic tale:* Tiek, Fouqué, Eichendorff, Hoffmann, Kleist (Michael Kohlhaas.) *The romantic drama:* Tiek's Genoveva, Kleist's Prinz von Homburg. *The romantic lyric*, as given in Von Klenze's German Lyrics. Mondays, Wednesdays, and Fridays. Fall term. Prerequisite, German 6.

11.* German Literature since Kleist. (Three-fifths course.)

Grillparzer, Hebbel, Ludwig, and others. Later lyrics. Mondays, Wednesdays, and Fridays. Winter term. Prerequisite, German 7.

12.* Richard Wagner's Dramas. (Three-fifths course.)

Die Meistersaenger. Der Nibelungenring. Mondays, Wednesdays, and Fridays. Spring term. Prerequisite, German 8.

13. Grammar, Composition, and Conversation. (Two-fifths course each term.)

Review grammar, composition, conversation. Free reproduction. Newson's German Daily Life. Journalistic German. Tuesdays, throughout the year. Prerequisite, German 6.

14. Middle High German.

Some study is made of Middle High German and the history of the German language. Reading, grammar, and lectures. Once a week throughout the year.. Prerequisite, German 6.

15. German Literature in English.· (Two-fifths course each term.)

The social, artistic, and literary history of Germany. Knowledge of German not required. Lectures, and collateral reading from standard translations and from histories of German literature. This course is designed to meet the wants not only of students of German, but also of any students who are interested in the development of the world's thought and art. Those phases of German literature are studied that have had influence on English and American thought and literature, or have come to form a part of universal culture. The entire study will be conducted from the point of view of comparative literature.

In connection with the pagan period there will be a presentation of Teutonic mythology and such literary embodiments as the Edda; Morris' Sigurd, the Volsung; Matthew Arnold's Balder Dead. For the mediæval period Bryce's Holy Roman Empire, and such epics as the Nibelungenlied, Parzival, and Tristan and Isolde, with their background of Gothic art, will be studied. For the 16th century there will be a consideration of the Volkslied, and popular romances such as the legends of Faust and Till Eulenspiegel (with comparison of the English ballad and Marlowe's Faustus), and of the art of Duerer and Holbein. Goethe, the apostle of culture, called by Matthew Arnold, "the greatest poet, the clearest, the largest, the most helpful thinker," will be studied in detail, then Schiller, Heine, and others. For later times Wagner's Operas will be studied, and finally the modern· movement in such representatives as Hauptmann and Sudermann, including their master, the Norse Ibsen. Tuesdays and Thursdays, throughout the year. Open to all College students.

---

*These courses, which carry only three-fifths credit, are designed to be supplemented by German 13 or 15, which carry two-fifths credit. German 15 is required as part of the second year work in German.

FRENCH.

In all the courses, translation from French into English is dispensed with as far as possible, and "free reproduction" is constantly cultivated. The Hoelzel charts are used as a basis for grammar, vocabulary, and elementary conversation. The aim of the course is in general to prepare the student for a comprehension of French individuality and literature as a part of general culture.

1. Grammar.

Bevier's French Grammar, Part I ; Newson's First French Book; Guerber's Contes et Legendes. The fundamental forms of nouns, adjectives, and verbs, including irregular verbs, are presented early in the course. Fall term. Open to all college students.

2. Grammar: the Modern Comedy.

Bevier, Newson, continued. The modern comedy; Legouvé and Labiche's La Cigale chez les Fourmis ; Pailleron's Le Monde ou l'on s'ennuie. Augier's Le Gendre de M. Poirier; Rostand's Les Romanesques. Winter term. Prerequisite, French 1.

3. Grammar: The Modern Story.

Francois's Composition, The Modern Story; Daudet, Coppée, Maupassant, Loti. Prerequisite, French 2.

4, 5, 6. Review Grammar and Composition; The Classical Period.
(Three-fifths Course.)

Review Grammar and Composition; Newson's French Daily Life. A study is made of the social, literary, and artistic life of the 17th Century. Corneille's Le Cid, Cinna Theory of classicism in the drama. Crane's La Société francaise au dix-septième siècle Molière's Les Précieuses Ridicules, Le Bourgeois Gentilhomme, Le Misanthrope. Racine's Oreste, Britannicus, Athalie. Lafontaine's Fables. French Prose of the 17th Century. Prerequisite, French 3.

7. The 18th Century. (Three-fifths course.)

Beaumarchais' Le Barbier de Seville, Voltaire's Zaire, Le Sage's Gil Blas, Prévost's Manon Lescaut, St. Pierre's Paul et Virginie. Influences of Rousseau, Diderot, and Voltaire. Fall term. Prerequisite, French 3.

8. The Development of French Romanticism.
(Three-fifths course.)

Influences of George Sand, Chateaubriand, Lamartine. Crane's Le Romantisme francais, Hugo's Hernani, and Ruy Blas, De Musset's Trois Comédies. Winter term. Prerequisite, French 7.

9. Outline History of French Literature: The Mediaeval Period.
(Three-fifths course.)

Chanson de Roland, Aucassin and Nicolette, Lays of Marie de France, etc., studied in translation. The 19th Century in its movements of naturalism and new romanticism. Balzac's Le Curé de Tours, Zola, Daudet, Maupassant, Loti, Rostand, Maeterlink. Spring term. Prerequisite, French 8.

10. Mediaeval French Literature Read in the Original.

Bartsch's Chrestomathy. History of the French language. Once a week throughout the year. Prerequisite, French 6 or 8.

LATIN.
Professor Frank H. Fowler.

Of the courses enumerated below, Latin 5 to 8 inclusive are intended for those entering college with two units of credit in Latin. They may be taken with college credit or to secure additional credit for admission, two courses being necessary to secure one unit. Latin 9, given in the fall term, is intended as an introductory college course for those entering with four units of credit in Latin. Courses 13 to 21, inclusive, are arranged in a cycle of three years and, if taken, will enable the student to specialize in Latin, so that he may easily undertake graduate work in that subject in the Universities.

In courses 8 and following, the work for the most part will be literary; and even students taking Latin 5 should have previously obtained such proficiency in the art of reading Latin that they may be able to give the major portion of their attention to the study of the literature.

5. Cicero's Orations and Latin Prose Composition.
Winter term.

6. Cicero's Orations and Latin Prose Composition.
Spring term.

7. Vergil.
Fall term.

8. Vergil.
Winter term.

9. Livy.

One object of this course and of the two next following is to develop and increase the ability of the student to read Latin. Books XXI and XXII will be read in class and portions of Book I privately. Exercises in translating at sight and at hearing will be given. The relations existing between Rome and Carthage will be noticed. Fall term. Open to students who have completed Latin 8 or who have four units of credit for admission.

10. Cicero, De Senectute and De Amicitia.

Besides the reading of the above mentioned essays portions of the De Officiis will be assigned for private reading, a part of Wilkins' Primer will be studied, and the life and times of Cicero will be discussed. Spring term. Open to students who have completed Latin 8 or who have four units of credit for admission.

12. Horace, Odes and Epodes.

It is expected that students taking this course will be able to give nearly or quite all their attention to the study of literature. The odes will be read with due attention to the quantitative pronunciation in order that the true rhythmical character of Latin poetry may be appreciated and enjoyed. The Carmen Saeculare will be assigned as private reading. Winter term. Prerequisite, Latin 10.

13. Roman Comedy. (Three-fifths course.)

The Trinummus and the Captives of Plautus and the Phormio of Terence will be read; the sources and history of Latin Comedy will be studied and the peculiarities of early Latin will be noted. Fall term. Prerequisite, Latin 12.

14. Prose Literature of the Silver Age. (Three-fifths course.)

The Agricola of Tacitus and selected letters of Pliny will be read. The history of the Literature of the Silver Age will be studied. Winter term. Prerequisite, Latin 12.

[15. Catullus. (Three-fifths course.)]

The poems of Catullus will be read. The influences exerted upon him, the characteristics of his genius, and his relation to his times will be studied. Spring term. Prerequisite, Latin 12.

[16. Roman Satire. (Three-fifths course.)]

The Satires of Horace will be read, together with the extant fragments of the Satires of Ennius, Pacuvius, Lucilius, and Varro, and the history of Roman Satire will be studied. Fall term. Prerequisite, Latin 12.

[17. Roman Satire. (Three-fifths course.)]

The Satires of Juvenal with selections from Martial and Persius will be read. The private life of the Romans will be studied. Winter term. Prerequisite, Latin 12.

[18. Cicero; Brutus; and Quintilian, Book X. (Three-fifths course)].

The books will be read as a study in literary criticism among the Romans. Spring term. Prerequisite, Latin 12.

[19. Lucretius. (Three-fifths course.)]

A study of the De Rerum Natura from literary and philosophical standpoints. Fall term. Prerequisite, Latin 12.

[20. Roman History. (Three-fifths course.)]

Selections from the Annals and Histories of Tacitus will be read and the work of the more important Roman historians will be reviewed and compared. Winter term. Prerequisite, Latin 12.

21. Cicero. Selected Letters. (Three-fifths course.)

As many as possible of the letters will be read and studied with special reference to the light which they shed on Roman History and Roman political institutions. Spring term. Prerequisite, Latin 12.

22. Topography of Ancient Rome. (Two-fifths course.)

The topography and monuments of the ancient city will be studied. The subject will be illustrated by photographs of the existing monuments.

23. Roman Private Life. (Two-fifths course.)

The several topics will be illustrated by photographs of ancient art discovered in Pompeii, Herculaneum, and Rome.

24. Roman Political Institutions. (Two-fifths course.)

The course will deal with the magistracies and assemblies of ancient Rome.

GREEK.
PROFESSOR ISAAC A. PARKER.

It is the purpose in this department to give the student the ability to read understandingly the writings of the Greek authors and to enter into their spirit, and, also, to give him a general acquaintance with Greek literature. A correct translation gains no credit for a student, if upon questioning it is found that he has not a knowledge of words and constructions and has evidently obtained his translation from notes or some other source.

Approved English sentences are required in translation, and where the literal is not allowable in English, the student is expected to know the construction in the Greek, and to render into idiomatic English.

The student is required to present an essay on each work read, stating its scope and the peculiarities of its style, and giving a brief biography of its author.

Frequent reference is made to a dictionary of Classical Antiquities to elucidate allusions to the mythology and the manners and customs of the Ancient Greeks.

Much attention is paid to the derivation and composition of words, and English words derived from the Greek are noted.

Instruction is carefully given in the principles of accent, and from the beginning, in writing Greek exercises, students are required to be careful to accent correctly.

The student who meets the requirements in this department, not only learns to read with pleasure and profit the language which he is studying, but, what is more, he acquires a mental discipline and a habit of carefulness and accuracy which will aid him in the business of life. The discipline of mind and the knowledge which he gains will greatly assist him in other studies, especially those of the sciences and medicine, since the terms with which he will meet in these studies are to a great extent derived from the Greek.

1. Grammar and Lessons.

Boise and Pattengill's Greek Lessons.   Goodwin's Greek Grammar. Fall term.   Open to all college students.

2. Grammar and Lessons. (Continued.)

Winter term.   Prerequisite, Greek 1.

3. Anabasis.

Goodwin's Xenophon's Anabasis.   Collar and Daniell's Greek Composition.   Spring term.   Prerequisite, Greek 2.

4. Anabasis. (Continued.)

Collar and Daniell's Greek Composition.   Fall term.   Prerequisite, Greek 3.

5. Orations of Lysias.

Stevens's Edition.   Winter term.   Prerequisite, Greek 4.

6. Greek Historians.

Fernald's Selections.   Spring term.   Prerequisite, Greek 5.

7. Iliad.

Keep's Homer's Iliad.   Fall term.   Prerequisite, Greek 6.

[8. Plato's Apology of Socrates.]

Kitchel's Edition.   Winter term.   Prerequisite, Greek 6.

9. Prometheus of Aeschylus.

Wecklein's Edition.   Spring term.   Prerequisite, Greek 6.

[10. Odyssey.]

Merry's Homer's Odyssey. Fall term. Prerequisite, Greek 6.

11. Plato's Gorgias.

Lodge's Edition. Winter term. Prerequisite, Greek 6.

[12. Medea of Euripides.]

Allen's Edition. Spring term. Prerequisite, Greek 6.

13, 14, 15, 16. Greek New Testament.

The classes while primarily intended for theological students, are open also to College students who have the requisite preparation. A full description is given in the Divinity School Courses. Prerequisite, Greek 5.

BOOKS OF REFERENCE.

The following books are recommended for reference to those pursuing the study of Greek.

Liddell and Scott's Greek Lexicon; Autenrieth's Homeric Dictionary; Long's, or Ginn & Co.'s Classical Atlas; Anthon's, or Smith's Classical Dictionary; Harper's Dictionary of Classical Literature and Antiquities; Smith's History of Greece; Goodwin's Greek Grammar; Goodwin's Greek Modes and Tenses.

HEBREW.

PROFESSOR NEHEMIAH WHITE.

1, 2, 3. Grammar and Old Testament.

These are primarily courses in the Divinity School, but may be elected by students in the College of Liberal Arts whenever they are offered. Classes will be formed each year if a sufficient number of students apply.

It is the aim to give the students such a knowledge of the forms and structure of the Hebrew Language as shall enable them to use it efficiently in the criticism and literary analysis of the Old Testament Scriptures. The text-books used are H. G. Mitchell's Hebrew Lessons and the Hebrew Old Testament. Three terms—Fall, Winter, and Spring—each term counting as a course. Open to all students who, in the judgment of the instructor, are qualified by previous training to take the course.

MATHEMATICS.

PROFESSOR PHILIP G. WRIGHT.

The study of Mathematics is useful to the student in two ways: In the first place, it affords an admirable mental discipline, developing habits of precise thought and accurate statement. In the second place, as the necessary tool of the civil and electrical engineer, the architect, and all persons engaged in higher scientific work, it has a practical value to those intending to enter these professions.

It is the purpose of the department to keep these two objects steadily in view. Students are required to show their understanding of Mathematical principles and reasoning by rigid demonstrations, subject to the criticism of other members of the class. Problems are selected for solution which arise in the actual practice of surveying, engineering, physical research and the like.

Students who intend to enter any of the above mentioned professions may profitably take a large part of their work at Lombard, completing their courses in some technical school.

7. Solid Geometry.

This course is continuous with the courses in Plane Geometry ordinarily given in the High Schools and is open to all College students who have had such work. Fall term.

8. Higher Algebra.

This course assumes a thorough knowledge on the part of the student of Mathematics 4 and also some knowledge of Plane Geometry. It embraces the study of Permutations and Combinations, Probability, Determinants, and the Theory of Equations. Winter term. Prerequisites, Mathematics 4 and Mathematics 5.

9. Plane and Spherical Trigonometry.

This course includes the solution of trigonometric equations, the solution of plane and spherical triangles and problems involving an application of Trigonometry to Mensuration, Surveying, and Astronomy. Crockett's Plane and Spherical Trigonometry is used as a text book. Spring term. Prerequisite, Mathematics 8.

10. Analytic Geometry.

This course treats of the straight line, the conic sections, and higher plane curves. Fall term. Prerequisite, Mathematics 9.

11. Surveying and Leveling.

Field work and problems. Field work on Saturdays at the option of the instructor. Spring term. Prerequisite, Mathematics 9.

12. Differential Calculus.

Byerly's Differential Calculus is used. Winter term. Prerequisite, Mathematics 10.

13. Integral Calculus.

Spring term. Prerequisite, Mathematics 12.

In addition to the foregoing courses, classes will be formed, when there is a sufficient demand on the part of advanced students, to pursue work in Descriptive Geometry, Quaternions, the solution of original problems in the Calculus, and in the study of infinitesimals, probability, elliptic functions, life insurance, and other topics.

ASTRONOMY.
PROFESSOR PHILIP G. WRIGHT.

1. General Astronomy.

This course is largely descriptive in character, though some of the simpler mathematical problems connected with Astronomy are solved. It embraces a study of the imaginary lines of the celestial sphere; latitude, longitude, time; the sun, moon, and planets; comets, meteors, and the stars. Some attention is given to the constellations and the myths connected with them. The Nebular Hypothesis is presented and discussed. Young's General Astronomy is used. Fall term. Prerequisite, Mathematics 9.

PHYSICS.
PROFESSOR FREDERICK W. RICH.

The course in Physics extends through the year, four periods per week being devoted to lectures and recitations and four to laboratory work. The aim is to present the science of physics as a whole, that students may be led to note the general principles of mechanics that apply throughout, and which furnish the basis of explanation of all the various phenomena.

The work of this course consists of a careful consideration of the various laws treated under the six main divisions of the subject.

It is intended for the general student and no Mathematics higher than Plane Trigonometry is required. Numerous problems test the student's ability to think clearly and make a correct application of the principles involved.

The laboratory experiments are chiefly quantitative and give opportunity for the verification of fundamental laws and general formulæ. Each student is required to present carefully prepared notes which shall include the data obtained from observation and computed results.

1. Mechanics, Hydrostatics, Pneumatics.

Text-book, Ames's College Physics. Prerequisite, Mathematics 9.

2. Heat, Sound, and Light.

Winter term. Prerequisite, Mathematics 9.

3. Magnetism and Electricity.

Spring term. Prerequisite, Physics 2.

CHEMISTRY.

PROFESSOR FREDERICK W. RICH.

The courses in Chemistry have been arranged with several distinct objects in view: First—A clear understanding of the underlying principles of chemical changes. This involves a thorough knowledge of the theory of the structure of matter.

Second—The principles of Stoichiometry, or Chemical Arithmetic, are to be thoroughly mastered and applied in a large series of practical chemical problems.

Third—A study of the elements and their compounds with careful attention given to the writing of equations.

Fourth—A systematic course in the laboratory, designed to give the student practice in careful manipulation and also opportunity for verification of the laws of chemical combination. The experiments of this course include the preparation of common elements and compounds.

Fifth—A general course in Qualitative analysis in which the student becomes familiar with the methods of determining the composition of native and manufactured substances.

Sixth—A well graded course in Quantitative analysis which gives the student practice in the various gravimetric and volumetric methods.

This gives the student the basis for technical work and enables him, in the minimum time, to become familiar with special, practical methods in the arts, and in fact to take the position of chemist in many lines of trade or manufacture without further preparation.

The course includes the analysis of such substances as ores, soils, fertilizers, soaps, milk, butter, gas, air, water, etc.

1. Inorganic Chemistry.

Remsen's College Chemistry is used as the basis of courses 1 and 2. Fall term. Open to all students.

2. Inorganic Chemistry.

Winter term. Prerequisite, Chemistry 1.

3. Organic Chemistry.

This course consists of recitations, lectures with experimental demonstrations, and laboratory work. The consideration of food-stuffs is an important part of the work. Their composition, adulteration, and the new methods of preparation are carefully studied. Remsen's Organic Chemistry is used. Spring term. Prerequisite, Chemistry 2.

In each of the courses 1, 2, and 3, the work is profusely illustrated by experiments, and individual work by the student in the laboratory demonstrates the principles discussed. Four hours per week are devoted to recitations and lectures and four hours to laboratory work.

4. Analytical Chemistry.

Qualitative analysis, laboratory work, and recitations.   Fall term.
Prerequisite, Chemistry 2.

5. Analytical Chemistry.

Qualitative, and quantitative analysis, laboratory work.   Winter
term.   Prerequisite, Chemistry 4.

6. Analytical Chemistry.

Quantitative analysis. Laboratory work.   Spring term.   Prerequisite, Chemistry 5.

7. Physiological Chemistry.

A study of the organic compounds, and the chemical processes of
physiological change.   Specially useful in subsequent study of practical
medicine. Spring term.   Prerequisites, Chemistry 3 and 4.

GEOLOGY AND MINERALOGY.

PROF. FREDERICK W. RICH.

1. Geology.

The work in Geology is given by text-book recitations, supplemented
by lectures and excursions for field work.   The College has a valuable
collection of minerals, which serves for purposes of illustration and study.
Dana's work is used.   Spring term.   Prerequisites, Chemistry 1, Biology
3, and Biology 4.

2. Mineralogy.

The course consists of a qualitative determination of minerals by
means of the blow-pipe and a careful study of the principles of classification.   Winter term.   Prerequisite, Chemistry 2.

BIOLOGY.

PROF. CHARLES ORVAL APPLEMAN.

The courses offered in this department give the student a general
knowledge of life from its simplest to its most complex form.   The student
who faithfully does the work as outlined in these courses will be well prepared to teach them in secondary schools.   In this department the
student learns of life, of the structure and functions of the various organs
of which the organism is composed, and of their relations to each other.
He learns how to observe and appreciate the wonderful phenomena of
natnre. The numerous unsolved problems in this field offer many opportunities for investigation and advancement.

The Physiological and Anatomical laboratories have recently been equipped with the latest apparatus. An ample number of instruments. have been supplied. These include the apparatus necessary for experiments and demonstrations in blood pressure, heart-beat, muscle, nerve phenomena, respiration, digestion, phenomena of stimulation, etc., etc.

1. General Biology.

This course will furnish a sketch of the history of the science of Biology and discuss the aims and methods of biological research, composition of living substance, and fundamental vital phenomena, i. e. regeneration, cell division, irritability, spontaneity, etc. The course is intended to be largely introductory to the special branches which depend upon it. Lectures, recitations, and laboratory exercises. Eight hours. per week. Fall term.

2, 3. Botany.

The aim of these courses is to acquaint the student with the fundamentals of Physiology, Ecology, and Phylogeny and to present a more detailed study of Morphology and life History. Plant structure, function, and classification will be developed together in an attempt to trace the evolution of the plant kingdom. Some time is also devoted to teaching the use of ordinary taxonomic manuals. Lectures, recitations, and laboratory work. Eight hours per week. Winter and Spring terms.

4. Histology.

A course in Normal Histology, which will be divided into two parts. (*a*) The construction and use of the microscope, the methods of preparing microscopical sections, and work upon the fundamental mammalian tissues. (*b*) A study of the microscopic anatomy of mammalian organs, Eight hours per week. Fall term.

5, 6. Zoology.

These courses are devoted to a general consideration of the subject with special reference to important problems in animal ecology and to a careful and detailed study of the structure and life history of type forms, and to such comparison of these with related forms as to exemplify the modifications of structure which characterize the several branches of the animal kingdom. Eight hours per week. Winter and Spring terms.

[7. Physiology.]

Anatomy, Physiology and Hygiene, a general course extending throughout two terms. Lectures, laboratory and quizzes. Open to all college students.

HISTORY.

PROF. NEHEMIAH WHITE. MRS. CHARLES O. APPLEMAN.

5. History of the Christian Church.

A. The Ancient and Mediæval Eras [1-1517.]

This course in Church History is primarily intended for the members of the Divinity School, but is also open to College students. It will require the investigation of the early organization and extension of Christianity and the successive periods of the church down to the time of Charlemagne; followed by a careful inquiry into the causes of the rise of the Papacy, of the political relations of the Church, and of the Crusades. Fisher's History of the Church will be used as a hand book and topics will be assigned to each member of the class for special investigation and reports. Fall term.

6. History of the Christian Church.

B. The Modern Era [1517-1904.]

This course will begin with the study of the Reformation, and trace the history of the Church down to the present time. It will include the history of Christian missions, revivals, social reforms, and philanthropy. The same text-book will be used as in History 5. Winter term.

7. History of Christian Doctrines.

Fisher is used for text. Spring term.

11. History of Civilization.

Text, Guizot. Spring term.

12. Mediaeval History.

The topics especially dwelt upon are "The Decline of the Roman Empire," "The Fusion of the Teutonic Custom With Roman Law," "The New Empire of Charlemagne and its Dissolution," "Feudalism," "The Crusades," "The Contest Between the Pope and the Emperor for the Sovereignty of the World," and "The Emergence of National States from Feudal Anarchy. Fall term.

13. Modern History.

This course emphasizes the progress of constitutional government in England, the rise of Russia, the struggle between Prussia and Austria for the supremacy in Germany, and the triumph of republican principles in France. Winter term.

14. A Study of Epochs in American History.

A. Formation of the Union [*1750-1829.*]

In this epoch special attention is given to the development of the American Colonial and State Governments, the growth of the National Idea, the Constitutional Controversies of our National Life, and the History of Political Parties.

B. Division and Reunion [*1829-1889.*]

The facts especially dwelt upon in this epoch are the development of Parties, the Bank Question, Slavery, Secession, and Reconstruction. Spring term.

For courses dealing with certain topics in History of Rome, see Latin 22, 23, and 24. For certain other historical courses see also under the departments of German, Economics, and History of Art.

HISTORY OF ART.
Prof. Louise M. Kueffner.

The class meets several times a week, and, although the aim of the courses in History of Art is to make the student familiar with the famous buildings, statues, and paintings that embody some of man's highest conceptions, yet in method the work is not simple enumeration of pictures, or memorizing of artists' biographies, but, above all, a presentation of the great works, artists, and periods, as a development out of the physical, social, and religious conditions of each age and people, and as a part of "culture history." Full illustration by pictures. Lectures and collateral reading.

1. Egyptian, Assyrian, Greek, and Roman Art.

Greek art is studied very fully, inasmuch as it forms the basis of all European art in its presentation of the human form, and in its glorification of the perfect human animal. Fall term. Open to all college students.

2. Romanesque and Gothic Art.

The Renaissance in Italy. Winter term. Open to all college students.

3. Renaissance Art Outside of Italy.

Modern Art. Rise of the feeling for nature and its interpretation. Modern tendencies. Spring term. Open to all college students.

FINE ARTS.

Miss M. ISABELLE BLOOD.

2, 3, 4. Drawing.

This course includes perspective, drawing from casts in charcoal and crayon, still life studies in crayon, etc. It will count as one credit for the entire year. Open to all students,

ECONOMICS.

PROF. PHILIP G. WRIGHT.

2. Political Economy.

General Political Economy. Seager's Introduction to Economics is used. Fall term. Open to advanced college students.

3. Financial History of the United States.

This course embraces the finances of the Revolution; the financial administrations of Morris, Hamilton, and Gallatin; the bank struggle; tariff legislation; the financial measures of the Civil War, and the reconstruction period to the present time. Dewey's Financial History of the United States is used as a text, collateral reading is required, and frequent lectures are given. Winter term. Prerequisite, Economics 2.

4. Current Economic Problems.

It is the purpose in this course to investigate from a standpoint somewhat broader than that of purely economic considerations certain vital economic problems and reforms. Different topics will be discussed different years. The subject for 1905 is Schemes for Economic Improvement. Spring term. Prerequisite, Economics 2.

JURISPRUDENCE.

1. International Law.

The general principles which govern the relations of States, as historically developed in express agreements and by usage, are elucidated; and these principles are discussed from the standpoints of reason and justice. Special study is made of current international problems, and theses on these subjects are required. Particular attention is paid to terminology. Lawrence's International Law is used as a text book. Frequent reference is made to the works on International Law by Woolsey, Wheaton, Glenn, etc. Spring term.

SOCIOLOGY.
PROF. RALPH GRIERSON KIMBLE.

1, 2. General Sociology.

These courses are continuous and must be so taken in order to obtain credit. They constitute a study of the fundamental factors of human associate life. The work is specially designed to furnish a valuable basis for further work in branches dealing with the associate life of mankind. It will be of worth to students of History, Political Science, Economics, Jurisprudence, Law, and Religion. Open to all College students. Fall and Winter terms.

POLITICAL SCIENCE.
PROF. RALPH GRIERSON KIMBLE.

[1, 2. Political Science.]

These Courses are continuous and must be so taken in order to obtain credit. A study of the nature and functions of government and the state. Recitations, lectures, and assigned readings. Open to students who have completed General Sociology 1 and 2. Fall and Winter terms.

PSYCHOLOGY.
PROF. RALPH GRIERSON KIMBLE.

1, 2. Psychology.

A general study of the more accessible phenomena of the psychic life. Recitations, lectures, assigned readings, laboratory, and quizzes. In the latter part of the work great care is taken to make clear the relations of the course to other courses in the curriculum. Emphasis is laid upon the practical import of psychological knowledge. Open to all College students. Courses must be pursued continuously in order to obtain credit. Fall and Winter terms.

HISTORY OF PHILOSOPHY.
PROF. RALPH GRIERSON KIMBLE.

[1, 2. History of Philosophy.]

A study of the general course of philosophic thought. The work of the course presupposes that of Psychology 1 and 2. Lectures, recitations and assigned readings. Fall and Winter terms.

LOGIC.
PROF. RALPH GRIERSON KIMBLE.

[1. Logic.]

A study of the principles of inductive and deductive reasoning. The processes and laws of valid thinking are critically examined. Open to those who have completed Psychology 1 and 2.

METAPHYSIC.

PROF. NEHEMIAH WHITE.

This is primarily a course in the Divinity School, but it may be elected by students in the College of Liberal Arts whenever it is offered. Classes will be formed whenever a sufficient number of students apply. Lotze's Outline of Metaphysic is used as a text-book. Fall term.

ETHICS.

Ethics is treated from the standpoint of Philosophy, and the different systems are discussed. The nature and grounds of obligation are investigated and applied to the practical affairs of life. Open to students who, in the judgment of the instructor are qualified by previous training to take the course. Winter term.

PHILOSOPHY OF RELIGION.

PROF. NEHEMIAH WHITE.

Fairbairn's Philosophy of the Christian Religion is the text-book. Lotze, Sabatier, and Martineau are used as works of reference. The aim of the instructor is to acquaint the student with the proper offices of reason in the effort to find argumentative grounds for religious ideas. Most of the modern theories respecting the nature and scope of the religious feeling pass under review; and in such discussions free questioning on the part of the student is encouraged. Winter term. Open to students who, in the judgment of the instructor, are qualified by previous training to take the course.

ETHICAL THEORIES.

PROF. NEHEMIAH WHITE.

Martineau's Types of Ethical Theory is used as a text-book with frequent references to the works of Sidgwick, Green, Smyth, and others. Much attention is paid to the elucidation and criticism of the modern ethical theories. Spring term. Open to students who, in the judgment of the instructor, are qualified by previous training to take the course.

COMPARATIVE RELIGION.

PROF. NEHEMIAH WHITE.

The work consists of the examination and comparison of the authorities upon the great Non-Christian religions. Special topics are investigated and reports made by each member of the class. Spring term.

MUSIC.

PROF. EUGENE E. DAVIS.

1. Theory and Audition.

Pupils desiring to take up the study of Harmony and the subjects following will be expected to complete Music 1, 2, and 3. Rythm, Major, and Minor Dictation. Scale introduced. Fall term.

2. Theory and Audition.

Retardations, Anticipations, Cadences, Dictation, Arpeggios, introduced. Augmented and diminished intervals. Winter term.

3. Theory and Audition.

Suspensions, Resolutions, Dictations, Melody Writing, Melodic and Harmonic Scales, Chord Formation, Absolute Pitch.

4. Harmony.

Keys, scales and signatures, intervals, formation of the triad, chord connection, simple part writing begun. Normal and Foreign progressions. All common chords and the rules governing their treatment in part writing. Goetchin's "The Materials of Composition" is the text-book used. Two hours a week. Prerequisite, Music 3.

5. Harmony.

Part writing continued. The inversion of chords. Chords of the sixth and six-four, chords of the seventh and their inversions. Key-board work. Modulation begun. Two hours a week. Winter term. Prerequisite, Music 4.

6. Harmony.

Chords of the seventh continued. Altered and augmented chords explained and employed in harmonization. Modulation continued. Two hours a week. Spring term. Prerequisite, Music 5.

7. Single Counterpoint.

Writing from *canti fermi*. First species, note against note. Second species, two notes against one. Third species four notes against one. John Frederick Bridge's Counterpoint is the text-book used. Fall term. Prerequisite, Music 6.

8. Single Counterpoint.

Writing from *canti fermi* continued in fourth species. Syncopation, suspensions, retardations. Fifth species, florid counterpoint. Winter term. Prerequisite, Music 7.

9. Single and Double Counterpoint.

Florid counterpoint continued. Double counterpoint in all forms. Spring term. Prerequisite, Music 8.

10. Musical Form.

The section and phrase. The period. The small primary forms. The large primary forms. The motive and its development. The study (Etude), Dance forms, Rondo form. Vocal song. Sonata form. Musical form. Bussler-Cornell. Fall term. Prerequisite, Music 9.

11. Canon and Fugue.

Canon in two voices in all intervals. Fugue in two, three, and four voices. Text-books. Richter, double Counterpoint and Fugue; Higg's Fugue. Winter term. Prerequisite, Music 9.

12. Instrumentation.

Study of Berlioz on instrumentation, also Prout's work on same subject. Study of orchestral scores. Orchestral scoring of various musical passages, and of original work. Orchestral writing without recourse to piano scoring. Spring term. Prerequisite, Music 10 and 11.

13, 14, 15. History of Music.

These courses embrace a history of the development of music from the earliest times until today, with special reference to critical analysis of the works of the great masters. They also furnish an introduction to the lives of the great composers. One hour a week for the year.

PUBLIC SPEAKING.

PROF. ALICE B. CURTIS.

1. Expression. (Half Course.)

A consideration of the elements of Expression. Physical exercises are given for purposes of control and vocal development. The conversational tone and its acquirement are made a matter of special study. Fall term. Open to all students.

2. Expression. (Half course.)

Literary interpretation of masterpieces. Programs from various authors will be given throughout the term. Extemporaneous speaking forms a part of the work. Winter term. Prerequisite, Public Speaking 1.

3. Expression. (Half Course.)

Each student will be required to give a recital. The work will be criticised and special drill given by the instructor. Spring term. Prerequisite, Public Speaking 2.

4. **Oratory.** (Half Course.)

Study of the theory of oratory. Each student will be required to commit to memory and deliver various oratorical selections. Each student will prepare and deliver an oration under the supervision of the instructor. Fall term. Open to all students.

5. **Oratory.** (Half Course.)

The preparation and delivery of several orations. Winter term Prerequisite, Public Speaking 4.

6. **Argumentation.**

A study of the principles of argumentation. The handling of refutation, preparation of brief, writing of the forensic, and actual debate will form part of the work. Spring term. Open to all students.

GYMNASIUM WORK.

The system of physical education pursued at Lombard College does not aim to make athletes and gymnasts, ball players, prize fighters, or wrestlers. The idea that the gymnasium was solely for those already strong, or for the development of candidates for field honors, is not primarily considered. Incidentally the gymnasium affords ample facilities for indoor training of athletes, but this work is necessarily given a secondary place. Our system of physical education maintains that the development of mind and body go together and that one must not be sacrificed for the other. Its aim is not only to give a better and more useful physique, but to develop a will, a resolution of purpose, and to create a college spirit, which will bring with them loyalty and help to dignify American citizenship. When the student enters the gymnasium he is subjected to a rigid medical examination which is made the basis of all gymnasium work. It determines the condition of the heart and circulation, the lungs and respiration, the stomach and its appendages, vision, hearing, size and consistency of muscles, and the temperament of the nervous system. Deformities, or bodily defects, are carefully sought for. From this examination a scientific application of physical exercises as a means of development made. Occasionally in such examination organic heart trouble is revealed. Such persons are not permitted to take the usual gymnasium work, but are given special exercises of a milder nature which are helpful. Functional derangements of nutrition, circulation, respiration, etc., are often discovered. Here again special exercises are prescribed.

The greater part of the gymnasium work is conducted in classes which meet daily. Dumb-bell and club work are taken with a snap that puts life and vigor into every move. Class work is also done on the heavy apparatus, such as the buck and parallel bars. Individual work is done

with the chest weights and horizontal bars, traveling rings, climbing
poles, etc. During the winter term basket ball teams are organized, and
competitive games are held.

All students will provide themselves with regular gymnasium uniforms. The cost of the uniform is about $2.50 for the men, and $4.50
for the women.

PREPARATORY COURSES.

The following courses are designed chiefly for the benefit of those Unclassified Students who wish to complete the entrance requirements for admission to the College of Liberal Arts. They are. however, open to all students, *but if taken by students in the College of Liberal Arts they will not be counted on the thirty-eight credits required for graduation.*

ENGLISH.

MISS FRANCES ROSS. · MISS ETHEL CHAMBERLAIN.

The following courses are offered for the benefit of those wishing to pass the Engish Examination for admission as outlined on pages 23, 24. Courses, 2, 3 and 4 are full courses and will deal with composition and with the study of the books prescribed for careful study. Courses 2*b*, 3*b*, and 4*b* are half courses and will deal with the books prescribed for reading.

2. Macaulay's Essays on Milton and Addison, and Milton's L' Allegro and Il Penseroso.

Three days per week. Composition (Scott and Denney), one day per week. Fall term.

3. Milton's Comus and Lycidas, and Burke's Speech on Conciliation with America.

Three days per week. Composition (Scott and Denney), one day per week. Winter term.

4. Shakespeare's Macbeth.

Three days per week. Composition (Scott and Denney), one day per week. Spring term.

2. (b). Addison's Sir Roger de Coverly Papers in the Spectator, Goldsmith's Vicar of Wakefield, Lowell's Vision of Sir Launfal.
(Half Course.)
Three days per week. Fall term.

3. *(b)*. Scott's Ivanhoe, Coleridge's Ancient Mariner, Carlyle's
Essay on Burns, Shakespeare's Merchant of Venice.
(Half Course.)

Three days per week.　Winter term.

4. *(b)*. George Eliot's Silas Marner, Tennyson's Princess, Shakespeare's Julius Caesar. (Half Course.)

Three days per week.　Spring term.

LATIN.

1.　Latin Lessons.
Fall term.

2.　Latin Lessons.　(Continuation of 1.)
Winter term.

3.　Caesar and Latin Prose Composition.
Spring term.

4.　Caesar and Latin Prose Composition.
Fall term.

MATHEMATICS.
PROF. JON W. GRUBB.

1.　Elementary Algebra.

Wells's Essentials of Algebra is used.　Fall term.　Open to all
students.

2.　Elementary Algebra.　(Continued.)
Winter term.　Prerequisite, Mathematics 2.

3.　Elementary Algebra.　(Continued.)
Spring term.　Prerequisite, Mathematics 3.

4.　Algebra.

After a brief review of Quadratic Equations, with especial reference
to theory, the subjects of Simultaneous Equations of the second degree,
Indeterminate Equations, Ratio and Proportion, Arithmetical and
Geometrical progression will be considered.　Wells's College Algebra is
used.　Fall term.　Prerequisite, Mathematics 3.

5.　Plane Geometry.

This course is designed to give students thorough drill in the first
principles of Geometry.　Phillips and Fisher's Elements of Geometry is
used.　Winter Term.　Open to all students.

6. Plane Geometry.

This course consists of a review of Mathematics 5 together with the demonstration of a large number of original propositions.   Spring term. Prerequisite, Mathematics 5.

Mathematics 1, 2, 3, 4 and 5 are designed to meet the entrance requirements in Algebra and Plane Geometry.

HISTORY.

1. Greece.

History of Greece.   Fall term.   Open to all students.

3. Rome.

History of Rome.   Text book, Morey.   Winter term.   Open to all students.

4. England.

History of England.   Text-book, Higginson and Channing.   Spring term.   Open to all students.

PHYSICAL GEOGRAPHY.

1. Physical Geography.

Text-book, Tarr's Elementary Physical Geography.   Spring term. Open to all students.

UNCLASSIFIED STUDENTS.

Persons who wish to pursue studies at Lombard without becoming candidates for a degree will be admitted on probation to any class for which they are fitted by previous training.   In case the class in question demands a prerequisite, the applicant must bring a certificate in this prerequisite from an approved school, or pass an examination.

On severing their connection with the College, these students will receive, upon request, a certificate, signed by the President and their several instructors, stating the amount and quality of the work done.

If at any time such students wish to become candidates for a degree, they must fulfill all the requirements for admission to the department in which the degree is to be taken.

Among these also will be listed all students who have an ultimate purpose of taking a degree, but who need to pursue one or more of the preparatory courses to fulfill the requirements for admission to the College of Liberal Arts.

RYDER DIVINITY SCHOOL.

The Divinity School of Lombard College was opened for the admission of students on the 5th of September, 1881. The first class was graduated in 1885.

At the annual meeting of the Board of Trustees in 1890, it was voted to name the theological department of the College the RYDER DIVINITY SCHOOL, in honor of the late William Henry Ryder, D. D., whose munificent bequests to the College exceed fifty thousand dollars.

The largest benefaction to the Divinity School from any other source was received from the late Hon. A. G. Throop, founder of the Throop Polytechnic Institute at Pasadena, California. In 1890, Mr. Throop gave twenty thousand dollars toward the endowment of the Divinity School.

ADMISSION.

Applicants unknown to the faculty must bring satisfactory evidences of good moral and religious character. They should also bring certificates of their church membership.

Candidates for admission to the Divinity School must be prepared to sustain examination in the following subjects:

I. ENGLISH.

(a) **Grammar and Analysis.**

Reed and Kellogg's Higher Lessons in English, or an equivalent.

(b) **Composition.**

An extemporaneous composition on an assigned subject, correct as to spelling, paragraphing, grammar, and rhetorical form.

(c) **Literature.**

An equivalent of English 2, 2*b*, 3, 3*b*, 4, and 4*b* as described on page 71 of this catalogue.

II. HISTORY.

(a) **Bible History.**

A competent knowledge of the Bible as History, including the so-called Old Testament Apocrypha. The ground covered is given in the ten volume Historical Series for Bible Students, edited by Kent and Sanders, and published by Scribner's Sons.

(b) **Bible Geography and Archaeology.**

A general knowledge of localities, customs, manners., etc., of Bible times.

Rand and McNally's Manual of Biblical Geography and Jahn's Archeology or equivalents.

(c) **General History.**

Swinton's General History or an equivalent.

III. MATHEMATICS.

(a) **Arithmetic.**

Higher Arithmetic, including percentage, alligation, extraction of roots, mensuration, and the metric system.

(b) **Elementary Algebra.**

Wells's Academic Algebra or an equivalent.

IV. GEOGRAPHY.

Tarr's Elementary Geography or an equivalent.

V. SCIENCE.

(a) **Chemistry.**

The equivalent of Chemistry 1 and 2 as described on page 49. (Equivalent work in Physics and Botany may be accepted in lieu of Chemistry.)

(b) **Physiology.**

This calls for a general knowledge of the human skeleton, muscular, circulatory, and nervous systems, the vital organs, viscera, and organs of special sense, and the processes of respiration and digestion. The preparation required is covered in such text-books as Martin's Human Body, (advanced course), or Huxley's Elementary Physiology (Lee's Revision).

PRELIMINARY YEAR.

To accommodate those candidates for admission who are not fully prepared to satisfy the admission requirements an opportunity is given to complete their preparation in the school, and a preliminary year's work is mapped out (page 64), which, however, is susceptible of some modification to meet the special needs of the candidate.

As a further encouragement to candidates to avail themselves of this opportunity the Universalist General Convention will permit its grant of financial aid to be spread over five years, instead of four as hitherto. Thus the candidate who requires five years for the full course, including the Preliminary year, may receive, under the usual conditions, a maximum grant of $100 each year for the five years, or a maximum grant of $125 a year for four years as he may prefer.

ADMISSION BY CERTIFICATE.

Satisfactory grades from approved schools will be accepted in lieu of examination. Students thus admitted by certificate will be regarded as on probation during the first term of their course.

ADMISSION TO ADVANCED STANDING.

Students who bring satisfactory evidence of work done beyond the requirements of admission will be given credit for the same on the regular course, so far as the faculty may deem consistent with the special aims of that course.

The members of the Divinity School are admitted to the advantages presented by the other departments of the College.

REQUIREMENTS FOR GRADUATION.

(a) Class Work.

Candidates for the degree of B. D. will be required to complete the regular course of instruction scheduled on page 64.

(b) Thesis.

Candidates for the degree of B. D. will also be required to prepare a graduation thesis, the topic to be approved by one of the professors in the department and the work to be done under his supervision,

EXPENSES.

Tuition is free to all regular members of the Divinity School who are candidates for the ministry, on condition that the student maintains an average grade of at least 70 per cent.

The charge for incidentals is the same as in the College of Liberal Arts, $5 per term.

For board in Commons, see page 10.

Board in good families can be secured for from $2.50 to $3.25 per week. Students may somewhat reduce their expenses by forming clubs or boarding themselves.

PECUNIARY AID.

Students who are candidates for the ministry of the Universalist Church may, upon complying with the prescribed conditions and receiving the recommendation of the faculty, obtain assistance from the Universalist General Convention in the form of a gratuity, to an amount not exceeding $125 a year for four years. Applications will be granted by the Convention only when entirely satisfactory. The first installment of this gift will not be issued to entering students until January, the second will be issued in May. Students should therefore come with resources of their own sufficient to pay their expenses for at least one term.

Those who have not a definite purpose of entering the Universalist ministry are not eligible to the Convention gift.

Membership in some Universalist Church is also required as a condition of the gift.

The use of tobacco or other narcotic or stimulants is an absolute bar to the grant of the Convention aid.

The Convention aid may be withheld at any time, should the work or behavior of the candidate prove unsatisfactory.

After having had two terms in Homiletics, students who show due proficiency are permitted to secure appointments to preach, and thus add to their pecuniary resources.

COURSES OF INSTRUCTION.

1. Regular Course.

Candidates for the degree of B. D. will be expected to complete the course scheduled on page 64, and prepare a graduation thesis. This course, it will be observed, prescribes a certain amount of work in Greek, which is regarded as indispensible to the degree. In addition to the studies indicated in the schedule, a year's work in Hebrew will be offered to those who desire it, at some time during their residence. It is earnestly recommended that all students whose circumstances do not positively forbid their spending the requisite time, take the Regular Course.

2. Alternative Course.

It is, however, permitted to those who, after due deliberation, prefer to do so, omit the Greek and Hebrew, and to substitute therefor an equivalent amount of elective work in English, Modern Languages, Science, Mathematics, or Sociology, with the approval of the faculty. Those who complete such a course will be graduated at the Annual Commencement, and will be furnished a certificate showing what work they have done; but they will not be given the degree of B. D. or any other degree.

3. Special Work.

(a) Candidates for the ministry who cannot take either of the above described courses, will be permitted to elect particular studies, so far as their preparation warrants. Pastors already engaged in ministerial work, who can spare a period for further study, are particularly invited to avail themselves of this opportunity.

(b) The School is also open to persons who do not intend to enter the ministry. The pursuit of studies of a theological or religious character is an interesting and helpful means of personal culture. Such a course is especially recommended to those who desire to become better fitted for service in the Sunday School, the Church, the Young People's Christian Union and similar societies, or for charitable and philanthropic work. Upon those who come with these purposes, no denominational test will be imposed. Students of all denominations and beliefs will be welcome to the advantages of study and training in the Divinity School, as in other departments of the College.

Faculty of the Divinity School.

NEHEMIAH WHITE, A. M., PH. D., S. T. D.

*Hall Professor of Intellectual and Moral Philosophy.
In charge of the Ryder Divinity School, Professor of Biblical Languages and Exegesis.

†Hull Professor of Biblical Geography and Archæology.

ISAAC AUGUSTUS PARKER, A. M., PH. D.
Professor of Greek.

RALPH GRIERSON KIMBLE,
Professor of Sociology.

EDSON REIFSNIDER, B. D.
Instructor in Homiletics and Pastoral Care.

ALICE BERTHA CURTIS, B. DI., PH. B.,
Professor of English and Public Speaking.

NON RESIDENT LECTURER.

MARION D. SHUTTER, D. D.

*In honor of the late E. G. Hall, of Chicago.
†In honor of the Rev. Stephen Hull, of Kansas City, Mo.

Degree Conferred in 1904.

BACHELOR OF DIVINITY.

FRANKLIN GARDINER VARNEY.

Schedule.

1. Preliminary Year.

FALL TERM.	WINTER TERM.	SPRING TERM.
English 2, 2b.	English 3, 3b.	English 4, 4b.
Biblical History.	Biblical History.	Biblical Geography and
Chemistry.	Elementary Physiology.	Archæology.
		Elementary Botany.

2. Regular Course.

Leading to the degree of Bachelor of Divinity.

FIRST YEAR.

FALL TERM.	WINTER TERM.	SPRING TERM.
English 5.	English 6.	English 7.
Greek 1.	Greek 2.	Greek 3.
History 5.	History 6.	History 7.

SECOND YEAR.

Psychology 1.	Psychology 2.	Hermeneutics.
Greek 4.	Greek Testament.	Greek Testament.
Homiletics 1.	Homiletics 2.	Homiletics 3.
Elocution.	Elocution.	Elocution.

THIRD YEAR.

Homiletics 4.	Homiletics 5.	Homiletics 6.
Sociology 1.	Greek Testament.	Greek Testament.
Apologetics.	Dogmatic Theology.	Dogmatic Theology.
	Logic.	

FOURTH YEAR.

Charities and Corrections.	Charities and Corrections.	Pastoral Care.
Economics 2.	Ethics	O. T. Introduction (2 hrs.)
*Hebrew.	*Hebrew.	Ethical Theories, or
Preaching	Preaching	Philosophy of Religion, or
		Metaphysic, or
		Comparative Religions.

*Elective.

Description of Studies.

HEBREW.

PROF. NEHEMIAH WHITE.

1, 2, 3. Grammar and Old Testament.

These are primarily courses in the Divinity School, but may be elected by students in the College of Liberal Arts whenever they are offered. Classes will be formed each year if a sufficient number of students apply.

It is the aim to give the students such a knowledge of the forms and structure of the Hebrew Language as shall enable them to use it efficiently in the criticism and literary analysis of the Old Testament Scriptures. The text-books used are H. G. Mitchell's Hebrew Lessons and the Hebrew Old Testament. Three terms—Fall, Winter and Spring—each term counting as a course.

BIBLE STUDY.

1. Biblical History, A.

Kent's Studies in Biblical History and Literature is used. The aim is to present the contents of the Bible as they stand in our English version. Due account is made of contemporary history and the monumental data. In general the first term will be occupied with the material of the Old Testament; the second term with that of the New. Fall term.

2. Biblical History, B.

A continuation of the preceding. Winter term.

3. Biblical Geography and Archaeology.

A detailed study of the political and physical geography of the Bible countries, and a general study of the antiquities of the Bible peoples. Spring term.

4. Biblical Criticism.

Driver's Introduction to the Old Testament is used as a text-book, with reference to Frip, Ryle, Bacon, Robertson, and other works. A course of lectures is given on the Science of Documentary Analysis, the Principles and Methods of Historical Criticism, and the Religious aspects of the Higher Criticism. Winter term. PROFESSOR WHITE.

HERMENEUTICS.
PROFESSOR ISAAC A. PARKER.

It is the aim to set forth the principles of interpretation in connection with the translation and exposition of the portions of the Greek Testament to which attention is given.

Lectures intended to aid the student in interpreting the Greek Testament, and also on the History of Interpretation are given in the winter and spring terms.

PREPARATORY GREEK.
(Greek 1, 2, 3, 4, see pages 38, 39.)

THE GREEK TESTAMENT.
PROFESSOR ISAAC A. PARKER.

13. Translation and Exegesis of the Gospel of John.

Its date and genuineness. Portions of the Acts of the Apostles. Winter term.

14. Translation and Exegesis of Selections from the Gospel of Matthew and the Epistles of Paul.

Spring Term.

THEOLOGY.
PROFESSOR NEHEMIAH WHITE.

1. Christian Evidences.

The study of Christian Evidences will include an examination of the bases of Christian belief, Evolutionary theories and their relation to Philosophy, Ethics, and Religion, and the function and method of Apologetics. Comparison will be instituted between the modern methods in Apologetics and the methods of primitive Christianity. Instruction will be given mostly by lectures with frequent reference to Fisher, Schurman, Flint, Bruce, and others. Fall term.

2. Dogmatic Theology.

Martensen's Christian Dogmatics is used as a text-book. A thorough investigation is made of the several Christian doctrines, with an extended examination of associated questions and controversies. The widest liberty is given for questions and discussions on the various topics presented. Winter and spring terms.

3. Comparative Religions.

The work of the students consists in the examination and comparison of the authorities upon the great Non-Christian Religions. Special topics are investigated and reports made by each member of the class. Spring term.

APPLIED CHRISTIANITY.

The demand for a more thorough investigation of the bearings of Christian Doctrine upon the social, political, and industrial organisms, coupled with a demand for a more diversified and scientific administration of religion through the churches, is met at Lombard College by the establishment of a chair of Sociology. The course of study provided for will occupy four terms, three terms being devoted to Sociology, and one term to Pastoral Care.

SOCIOLOGY.
Prof. Ralph G. Kimble.

1. An Introduction to Sociological Theory.

A study of the characteristics of general sociological theory.

2. 3. Charities and Corrections.

Warner's American Charities, Wines' Punishment and Reform, and Devine's Principles of Relief, sufficiently indicate the scope and character of the work. Lectures, quizzes and field work. Open only to divinity students. Fall and winter terms.

PASTORAL CARE.
Prof. Edson Reifsnider.

A study of the spiritual, mental, and social qualifications of the minister for his work, and his administration of the special services of the church—baptism, confirmation, the Lord's Supper, marriage, and the burial of the dead. A liberal portion of the term will be devoted to an examination of various methods of church organization, for the purpose of giving the minister facility in adapting himself to parish needs, especially to those peculiar to the locality in which he may be settled. Also a study is made of the Manual of the Universalist General Convention. Spring term.

PSYCHOLOGY.
Prof. Ralph G. Kimble.

1. Introductory Psychology.

The purpose of the course is to guide the beginner in gaining the fundamentals of a thorough knowledge of psychology and of psychic life.

The course is organized about a careful study of the commoner characteristics of the more accessible mental processes. Emphasis is laid upon the ready and accurate use of the more important psychological terms. Some knowledge of the chief standpoints and methods of the science is gained. Collateral reading in connection with the text will be regularly assigned and a correct appreciation of the relation of this reading to the treatment presented in the text will be a requirement of the course. Experiments described in text and reading will be fully discussed; and, where circumstances will permit, the student will see performed by others or will himself perform in the laboratory certain type experiments. Fall term.

2. Introductory Psychology.
Continuation of Psychology 1. Winter term.

METAPHYSIC.
PROF. NEHEMIAH WHITE.

This is primarily a course in the Divinity School, but it may be elected by students in the College of Liberal Arts whenever it is offered. Lotze's Outlines of Metaphysic is used as a text-book. Spring term.

LOGIC.

Having first obtained a thorough grounding in the principles and methods of correct reasoning both deductive and inductive, at least one-half of the term is given to the detection and discrimination of fallacies in actual examples. Such examples the class is required to search out in current literature and bring in for discussion. Davis's Elements of Deductive Logic and Davis's Elements of Inductive Logic are used. Winter term.

ETHICS.
PROF. NEHEMIAH WHITE.

Ethics is treated from the standpoint of Philosophy, and the different systems are discussed. The nature and grounds of obligation are investigated and applied to the practical affairs of life. Winter term.

PHILOSOPHY OF RELIGION.
PROFESSOR NEHEMIAH WHITE.

Fairbairn's Philosophy of the Christian Religion is the text-book. Lotze, Sabatier, and Martineau are used as works of reference. The aim of the instructor is to acquaint the student with the proper office of reason in the effort to find argumentative grounds for religious ideas.

Most of the modern theories respecting the nature and scope of the religious feeling pass under review; and in such discussions free questioning on the part of the student is encouraged. Spring term.

ETHICAL THEORIES.
PROF. NEHEMIAH WHITE.

Martineau's Types of Ethical Theory is used as a text-book with frequent references to the works of Sidgwick, Green, Smyth, and others. Much attention is paid to the elucidation and criticism of the modern ethical theories. Spring term.

CHURCH HISTORY.
PROF. NEHEMIAH WHITE.

5. History of the Christian Church.

A. The Ancient and Mediæval Eras [1-1517.]

This course in Church History is primarily intended for the members of the Divinity School, but is also open to College students. It will require the investigation of the early organization and extention of Christianity and the successive periods of the Church down to the time of Charlmagne; followed by a careful inquiry into the causes of the rise of the Papacy, of the political relations of the Church, and of the Crusades. Fisher's History of the Church will be used as a hand book and topics will be assigned to each member of the class for special investigation and reports. Fall term.

6. History of the Christian Church.

B. The Modern Era [1517-1905.]

This course will begin with the study of the Reformation, and trace the history of the Church down to the present time. It will include the history of Christian missions, revivals, social reforms, and philanthropy. The same text-book will be used as in History 5. Winter term.

7. History of Christian Doctrine.

Special pains will be taken to make clear the aims of the History of Christian Doctrine and to indicate the process of its development.

HOMILETICS.
PROF. EDSON REIFSNIDER.

The course in Homiletics covers the second, third, and fourth years. The primary aim is practical. Upon a general but adequate groundwork of theory and history of preaching the effort is made to construct an art of effective pulpit oratory. Elaborate and exacting drill in the logical con-

ception and construction of the sermon plan, with constant application
of rhetorical principles, occupies the major part of the first year. Inspiration and direction are sought in the frequent analysis of the discourses
of great preachers of all styles, and in the study of their sources of
power. Individuality and originality are emphasized as desiderata. In
the second year the stress is laid upon flexibility and adaptability, upon
invention, upon the rationale of interesting preaching, and upon the
acquisition of freedom in extempore address. Throughout the course the
preparation and criticism of sermons by the class continues uninterruptedly.

PUBLIC SPEAKING.

PROF. ALICE B. CURTIS.

In view of the fact that a good delivery is of inestimable advantage
to the preacher, the students in the Divinity School are offered an extended course in Elocution and Physical Culture.

The students are not only admitted to all Elocution classes in the
College, but, also receive a large amount of individual training.

Courses 1, 2, 3, as outlined on page 52 of this catalogue, are required,
as well as regular drill and rehearsals for the preaching exercises.

ENGLISH.

For English 2, 3, 4, required for entrance to full standing in the
Divinity School, and taught in the Preliminary year, see page 55. For
English 5, 6, 7, which courses are required in the Divinity School, see
page 30 of this catalogue.

COLLEGE STUDIES AND THE A. B. DEGREE.

Divinity students are permitted, with the consent of the Faculty, to
pursue studies in the College of Liberal Arts. Graduates of the Divinity
School may receive the additional degree of Bachelor of Arts, upon the
satisfactory completion of an aggregate of twenty full courses taken in
the classes of the College of Liberal Arts, beyond the full requirements of
the Divinity School for the degree of Bachelor of Divinity.

In addition to the above twenty credits, the candidate must furnish
the full quota of sixteen units required for admission to the College of
Liberal Arts. Of these sixteen units, the courses required for admission
to the Divinity School (see pages 59 and 60) will count six.

DEPARTMENT OF MUSIC.

Instruction is provided in the various branches of Theoretical, Vocal, and Instrumental Music. These courses, except the courses in Theoretical Music and Musical History, are distinct from the work in the other departments of the College, and do not count toward a college degree. Students are classed and registered by the Director with whom all arrangements must be made, in order to secure certificates of standing from term to term and for all final examinations.

FACULTY.

EUGENE E. DAVIS,

DIRECTOR.

Instructor in Piano and Voice, all Theoretical Courses, and Organ.

MRS. EUGENE E. DAVIS,

Instructor in Voice.

W. H. CHEESMAN,

Instructor in Violin and other Stringed Instruments.

THEORETICAL COURSES.

1. Theory and Audition.

Pupils desiring to take up the study of Harmony and the subjects following will be expected to complete Music 1, 2, and 3. Rythm, Major, and Minor Dictation. Scale introduced. Fall term.

2. Theory and Audition.

Retardations, Anticipations, Cadences, Dictation, Arpeggios, introduced. Augmented and diminished intervals. Winter term.

3. Theory and Audition.

Suspensions, Resolutions, Dictations, Melody Writing, Melodic and Harmonic Scales, Chord Formation, Absolute Pitch.

4. Harmony.

Keys, scales and signatures, intervals, formation of the triad, chord connection, simple part writing begun, Normal and Foreign progressions. All common chords and the rules governing their treatment in part writing. Chadwick's Harmony is the text-book used. Two hours a week. Fall term.

5. Harmony.

Part writing continued. The inversion of chords. Chords of the sixth and six-four, chords of the seventh and their inversions. Key-board work. Modulation begun. Two hours a week. Winter term.

6. Harmony.

Chords of the seventh continued. Altered and augmented chords explained and employed in harmonization. Modulation continued. Two hours a week. Spring term.

7. Single Counterpoint.

Writing from *canti fermi*. First species, note against note. Second species, two notes against one. Third species four notes against one. John Frederick Bridge's Counterpoint is the text-book used. Fall term.

8. Single Counterpoint.

Writing from *canti fermi* continued in fourth species. Syncopation-suspensions, retardations. Fifth species florid counterpoint. Winter term.

9. Single and Double Counterpoint.

Florid counterpoint continued. Double counterpoint in all forms. Spring term.

(Students who expect to finish only the nine courses may substitute 10 for 9, with the advice and consent of the Director.)

10. Musical Form.

The section and phrase. The period. The small primary forms. The large primary forms. The motive and its development. The study (Etude), dance forms, Rondo form. Vocal song. Sonata form. Musical form. Bussler-Cornell. Fall term.

11. Canon and Fugue.

Canon in two voices in all intervals. Fugue in two, three, and four voices. Text books. Richter, Double Counterpoint and Fugue; Higgs, Fugue. Winter term.

12. Instrumentation.

Study of Berlioz on instrumentation, also Prout's work on same subject. Study of orchestral scores. Orchestral scoring of various musical passages, and of original work. Orchestral writing without recourse to piano scoring. Spring term.

13, 14, 15. History of Music.

These courses embrace a history of the development of music from the earliest time until today, with special reference to critical analysis of the works of the great masters. They also furnish an introduction to the lives of the great composers. One hour a week for the year.

PIANOFORTE COURSE.

1. Preparatory.

Stephen Emory's Foundation Studies; Herz's Scales or Handrock's Mechanical Studies; Enkhausen's Progressive Melodious Studies or Ehmant's Petite Ecole Melodique; Mathew's Graded Course first four books. The major and minor scales and major and minor chords must be played from memory.

The above fundamentals must be fully mastered before a pupil can be classified as a student in the Collegiate Musical Course. The mastery of these principles is of the greatest importance; as it is the only way to secure intelligent and sure progress in the advanced stages. No effort will be spared to induce the student to work with that personal relish so necessary to good work.

COLLEGE PIANOFORTE COURSE.

Some flexibility will and must be allowed in the course, to meet the peculiarities of the pupil; at the same time care will be taken not to graduate one-sided musicians.

1. First Year.

Mathew's Graded Course, Books 5 and 6; Daily Technical Exercises, Scales, Thirds and Sixths, Handstroke and Staccato, Arm Touch; Beren's New School of Velocity, Books 1 and 2; Selections from Clementi's and Kuhlau's Sonatinas; pieces by Bohm. Thome, Godard, Lebierre, Sapelnikoff and other suitable practice pieces.

2. Second Year.

Mathew's Graded Course, Book 7; Beren's New School of Velocity, Books 3 and 4; Low's Octave Studies; Selections from Haydn's and

Mozart's Sonatas; Bach's Inventions, Selections from Mendelssohn's Songs without Words; pieces by modern authors including Grieg, Chaminade, Rachmaninoff, Rubinstein.

3. Third Year.

Mathew's Graded Course 8 and 9; Hasert's Modern Finger Exercises, Books 1 and 2; Kullak's Octave Studies; Bach's Preludes and Fugues; Selections from Chopin and Schumann; Beethoven's Sonatas; Cramer's Etudes.

4. Fourth Year.

Chopin's Etudes; Bach's Advanced Works, Chromatic Fantasie and and Fugue in D minor, Bach-Tausig Toccata and Fugue D minor; Joseffy's Advanced School of Piano Playing; Beethoven's Sonatas continued; Selections from Chopin and Schumann; Selections from Liszt's Compositions. Liberal recognition is accorded the works of American composers in the entire course.

VOICE CULTURE.

1. Preparatory.

Elementary sight singing, Solfeggio practice and application of so-fa syllables to staff in simple music; breathing and voice placing exercises—sustained tones and scale work according to the Italian method as taught by Sims Reeves of London, Eng., (pupil of Mazzucato, an acknowledged descendant of the famous Porpora) also by Vannucini of Florence, Italy. Concone's Fifty Lessons; Panofka, Marchesi's Exercises, op. 1, First Part; Vaccai's Studies.

COLLEGE COURSE.

No student can be classified in the Collegiate Course in voice without passing examination in Solfeggio, or demonstrating to the satisfaction of the director the ability to read music of moderate difficulty at sight.

1. First Year.

Voice placing exercises, scales, sustained tones, and articulation exercises, Marchesi's Studies; Concone's Twenty-five Lessons; songs by American authors. Mendelssohn, Jensen, Grieg, Gastaldon, Denza, Cowen, and other good foreign authors.

2. Second Year.

Voice placing exercises, scales, etc. Marchesi's Studies; Concone's Fifteen Lessons; songs or solos by Schubert, Schumann, Mendelssohn, Grieg, Handel, Jensen and American authors.

3. Third Year.

Voice placing exercises; Marchesi's and Bordogni's exercises; solos from standard oratorios and operas, Sullivan, Mendelssohn, Handel, Mozart, and other authors.

4. Fourth Year.

Handelian Oratorio Solos, German Lieder, Wagnerian, and other opera solos.

PIPE ORGAN COURSE.

Students who wish to begin the study of the Organ should have completed the Second Grade of the Piano Course.

The chief aim of this department is the thorough preparation of church organists. Organ students should also make a conscientious study of Solo and Chorus Singing, with a view of becoming efficient chorus-masters and directors of church music.

The study of Harmony, Counterpoint, and History of Music is absolutely necessary to an intelligent study of the instrument.

1. First Grade.

Exercises in pedal playing. Ritter's Organ School. Hymns, Thayer's pedal studies. Elementary Registration.

2. Second Grade.

Studies in Pedal Phrasing by Buck, Volkmar, and Schneider. Polyphonic composition by Rink, Bach, Fisher. Easy pieces by Merkel, Dubois, Guilmant, Mendelssohn, and others. Registration, Structure of the Organ. Choir Accompaniment.

3. Third Grade.

Study of Sonatas and Fugues by Bach, Mendelssohn, Reinberger, and others. Modern compositions of German, English, and French masters. Choir Accompaniment.

VIOLIN COURSE.

1. Preparatory Grade.

Elementary exercises in position, bowing, etc. Easy exercises in major and minor keys in the first book from Wichtl's Violin School. Pleyel's Duets and twelve studies by H. E. Kayser, op. 20. Memorizing.

2. Intermediate Grade.

Studies by Kayer and Wohlfahrt. Systematic progress through the various positions, beginning with the second book of F. Hermann. Studies from Shradieck for the development of technic and pure tone qualities. Sections from compositions by Dancla, Mazas, Weiss, DeBeriot; also solos and fantasias based upon operetic themes.

3. Advanced Grade.

Technical studies from the works of Kreutzer, Fiorillo, Rode, together with duets, trios, and quartets, arranged for strings; overtures; sight reading: Sonatas and concertos by Bach, Haydn, Spohr, Beethoven, Mendelssohn, DeBeriot, Wieniawski, Grieg and others.

MANDOLIN AND GUITAR COURSES.

The study of these popular instruments has become a favorite recreation with those students of our colleges who may not have the time or inclination to pursue the study of music in its more serious forms.

At the conclusion of the first term of lessons (twelve weeks) a "Lombard Mandolin Club" will be organized, with rehearsals one evening a week. The Italian method is used entirely in the study of these instruments, thereby establishing the very best method of picking the strings and fingering, with special attention to the tone quality of the "tremolo," which relieves the mandolin of so much of its so-called monotony. Solos, duets, and quartets, will also be prepared in addition to the regular club work, with special numbers to be given by the lady members of the club.

SIGHT SINGING AND CHORUS CLASSES.

1. Elementary Sight Singing Class.

The rudiments of Music, the intervals of the Major Scale, exercises in one and two parts, and easy songs. Ear training. One college term.

2. Advanced Class.

Solfeggios in major and minor keys, three and four part songs. One college term.

3. Chorus Class.

Four part compositions, glees, sacred and secular choruses from our best classic and modern composers. Oratorios.

Only those students who have finished the work done in the advanced Sight-Singing Class will be admitted into the Chorus Class.

REQUIREMENT · FOR GRADUATION.

A diploma will be conferred upon any student who shall satisfactorily complete one of the following courses in instrumental or vocal music. In addition to the requirements enumerated below, the candidate will prepare a thesis, present an original musical composition, or perform other original work satisfactory to the instructor, and also appear in public at a graduating recital.

A. THE PIANOFORTE.

Musical Requirements.

The complete College Course; Nos. 1, 2, 3, 4, 5, 6, 10, 11, 12, 13, 14, and 15 of the Theoretical Courses; Acoustics; and one year's membership in the Chorus Class.

Literary Requirements.

English 2, 3, 4, 5, and two English electives; one year of French or German.

If the candidate upon entering brings satisfactory proof of proficiency in any of these courses he is advised to take one study each term from such electives in the College of Liberal Arts as the Advisory Committee may recommend.

B. THE PIPE ORGAN.

Musical Requirements.

The full Organ Course; Nos. 1, 2, 3, 4, 5, 6, 10, 11, 12, 13, 14, and 15 of the Theoretical Courses; and Acoustics.

Literary Requirements.

The same as for Piano students.

C. THE VOICE.

Musical Requirements.

All the prescribed studies for Voice Culture; 1 and 2 of the College Piano Courses, with special view to accompaniments; and Nos. 1, 2, 3, 10 and 11, of the Theoretical Courses.

Literary Requirements.

The same as for Piano students, except that Italian may be substituted for French or German.

D. THE VIOLIN.

Musical Requirements.

All the prescribed studies laid down in the Violin Courses; Nos. 1, 2, 3, 4, 5, 6, 10, and 11 of the Theoretical Courses; Acoustics; and proficiency in all kinds of ensemble playing.

Literary Requirements.

The same as for Piano students.

TUITION.

The following are the prices per term:

THEORETICAL COURSES—

Music 1 to 9, each, $5.00.
Music 10, 11, and 12, each, $3.00.

PIANOFORTE—

Private Lessons—one hour per week, $20.00.
Private Lessons—two half hours per week, $20.00.
Private Lessons—one half hour per week, $11.00.
Private Lessons—one forty-minute lesson per week, $15.00.

Class Lessons may be specially arranged for and when practical will be arranged for at the following rates:
Three pupils in two hour lessons per week, $15.00, each.
Three pupils in one hour lesson per week, $9.00, each.

VOICE CULTURE—

Charges same as for pianoforte.

RENT OF PIANO—

1 hour per day, per term, $2.75.
2 hours per day, per term. $5.00.
3 hours per day, per term, $6.75.
4 hours per day, per term, $8.00.

PIPE ORGAN—

Private Lessons—one hour per week, $24.00.
In classes of two one hour per week, each person, $13.00.

VIOLIN—

Private Lessons—one hour per week, $15.00.
Private Lessons—two half hours per week, $15.00.
Private Lessons—one forty-five minute lesson per week, $12.00.

CLASS LESSONS, one hour per week—

In classes of two each, $8.00.
In classes of three, each, $6.00.

Mandolin and Guitar—

Private Lessons—one hour per week, $12.00.
Private Lessons two half hours per week, $12.00.
Class Lessons—charges will be given on application to teacher.

(A weekly rehearsal for club practice without extra charge.)

Sight Singing Classes.

Each $1.00.

Chorus Class—

A charge of $1.00 per term, each, will be made for the use of music to be supplied by the department.

Rates for Children—

Students under 15 years of age and not having attained the 3rd grade may pursue either Instrumental or Vocal music at the term rate of $15.00.

HALL OF CONSERVATORY OF MUSIC.

DEPARTMENT OF ART.

Instructor,
M. ISABELLE BLOOD.

Course in Art.

The Art Department affords a practical course in Drawing and Painting to those who wish to become teachers, designers, illustrators, or portrait artists. Regular students in this department who wish to take the entire course in Art will be given careful training in the following branches: Perspective drawing; drawing from casts, in charcoal and crayon; still life studies in crayon, oil, water color, pastel; landscape from nature; and copying from good studies.

The entire course will occupy from two to three years, according to the ability of the student and the amount of time given to the work. A thorough knowledge of the elements of drawing being necessary to independent work, at least one year's work will be required in drawing in black and white from models of simple form, casts, still-life, and those studies which will best prepare the student for the special line of work preferred.

Students may enter the Art Department at any time; and, though they are advised to take a full course in order to obtain the best results, arrangements can be made for lessons in any line desired.

While portrait work, pen and ink drawing and china painting are not required in the regular course, credit will be given for good work in any of these branches if it is desired to substitute them in part for oil, water color, or pastel.

A course of study in the History of Art and a thesis upon some subject approved by the instructor will also be required of students wishing to graduate from this department.

Those who complete the work as outlined above will be entitled to a diploma.

For a description of courses in Free Hand Drawing, and for credit allowed for these courses in the College of Liberal Arts, see page 48.

THE LADIES' HALL.

TUITION.

The tuition fees will be as follows:

Drawing or Sketching—3-hour lesson, 35 cents.
Painting in Water Colors—3-hour lesson, 50 cents.
Oil Painting—3-hour lesson, 50 cents.
Portrait and China Painting—3-hour lesson, 50 cents.

For those who work six hours per week for the entire year, a rebate will be made at the end of the Spring term, so that the lessons in drawing will be less than 35 cents.

If pupils in Art desire four or more lessons per week, special rates are made.

STUDENTS IN ALL DEPARTMENTS.

Candidates for Degrees in 1905.

CANDIDATES FOR THE DEGREE OF BACHELOR OF ARTS IN 1905.

Andrew, William B.
Blout, Charles J.
Clark, Fred Andrew
Clay, Walter Timothy
Grimes, Lloyd O.

Grubb, Emma Welton
Hathaway, M. Agnes
Metcalf, Harold
Porter, Gail Quincy
Ross, Frances

CANDIDATES FOR THE DEGREE OF BACHELOR OF SCIENCE.

Rich, Willis Horton

Gillis, Hudson McBain

CANDIDATES FOR THE DEGREE OF BACHELOR OF DIVINITY IN 1905.

Adams, Frank D.
Bartholomew, Jennie L.
Fosher, Dudley C.

Manning, Stanley
Phillips, William

CANDIDATES FOR A DIPLOMA IN MUSIC IN 1905.

Nelson, Alvira
Rautenburg, Clare Marie

Rich, Willis Horton

Students in the Divinity School.

Adams, Frank D.
Bartholomew, Jennie L.
Fosher, Dudley. C.
Grimmer, J. W.
Hillstren, C. W.

Manning, Stanley
Martin, Marie Serena
Martin, Nellie Ruth
Phillips, William
Tanner, William R.

Students in the College of Liberal Arts.

Alvord, Francis M.
Andrew, William B.
Andrews, Euseba
Atterberry, Ralph M.
Austin, Ralph C.
Beatty, Dwight C.
Blout, Charles J.
Brown, Talent
Burnside, Roy
Carr, Fannie
Case, Schuyler
Case, Shelby
Chamberlain, Ethel
Clark, Fred A.
Clay, Walter T.
Conger, Delia
Cooper, Harry Mac
Cooper, Leona
Crocker, Edna
Dillow, Florence
Dillow, Ray
Edwards, Forrest
Eldridge, Jessie
Fosher, Cora M.
Foster, June
Gibbs, Minnie C.
Gillis, Hudson McBain
Golliday, Theo.
Grimes, Lloyd O.
Grubb, Emma W.
Hathaway, M. Agnes
Herlocker, Webb A.

Hobbs, Edith
Hoffman, Arthur C.
Hollister, Florence
Housh, Carter
Housh, Chester
Hughes, Walter J.
Huling, Grace
Justus, Ray W.
Linderholm, Ernest A.
Linderholm, Lillie C.
McDaniel, L. Berl
Martin, Vella
Metcalf, Harold
Pittman, Eskridge
Porter, Fannie
Porter, Gail Q.
Potter, Albert M.
Potter, Warren
Rich, Willis H.
Richards, Lucile
Richey, Frances
Robinson, LeRoy P.
Rockafellow, Will V.
Ross, Frances
· Ross, Louise
Shaffer, James C.
Stryker, E. Bell
Sykes, Katheryne
Tipton, Fred Lincoln
Titus, Murray T.
Wennstrom, Frank J.
Williamson, Bessie
Yoeman, Mahale

Students in the Department of Music.

Birmingham, Marie
Bishop, Rena May
Breece Amber L.
Brower, Mary L.
Byers, Frank
Byloff, Julia
Chambers, Oliver J.

Chapman, Janet
Conger, Ethelyn
Crocker, Edna
Currens, Elizabeth
Currens, Wayne
Ericson, Josephine L.
Foster, June

Garrett, Grace,.

Gast, Paul

Golliday, Theo.

Haffner, Mable

Hallene, Helen

Handley, Lulu

Hazzard, Lutheria

Hutchinson. Anna

Kornwebel, Augusta

Linderholm, Ernest

Linquist, Lillian

McLaughlin, Myrtle

Nelson, Alvira

Nelson, Edna

Olson, Amelia A.

Pittman, Eskridge

Rautenberg, Clare M.

Rich, Gertrude

Rich, Willis H.

Richards, Lucile

Rockafellow, Will

Snyder, Mrs. August

Swanson, George

Sweeney, Fannie

Templeton, Mabel

Tillia, Effie

Van Buren, Laura

Walline, Florence

Weber, Edna

Webster, Marion

Wright, Theodore P.

Wrigley, Marion

Zabriskie, Nelle

Students in the Department of Art.

Bishop, Rena May

Clark, Fred A.

Clark, Katherine

Clay, Walter T.

Coffman, Mrs. William

Curtis, Alice B.

Foster, May

Garrett, Grace

Harris, Mrs. William

Hopkins, Ida

James, Hazel

Legg, Grace

Nelson, Emma

Pittman, Eskridge

Planck, Marie

Swanson, Mrs. P. F

Taliaferro, Martha

White, Frances

Unclassified Students.

Bradshaw, George H.

Dunblazier, Locy E.

Field, Hattie E.

Gallup, Roscoe H.

Goad, Charles H.

Haffner, Grover,

Hartsook, Geo. S.

Hicks, Lee

Hutchinson, Anna

Jobe, Paris A.

Law, Fred W.

Moore, Aubrey C.

Myzner, C. Fred

Oberholtzer, E. E.

Quigley, Laura

Ray, Andrew

Rich, Gertrude

Richard, R. Ward

Satoh, Jinkuro

Standard, Harry A

Sumner, D. D.

Welcome, Eva Elgy

Wertman, Albert J.

Wilson, Harlan

Directory of Teachers and Students.

Adams, Frank D..................Div.... .... Avon
Alvord, Francis M................ Col...........Friendship, N. Y.
Andrew, William B...............Col ....New Salem
Andrew, Euseba............ ....Col...................Abingdon
Appleman, Prof. Charles O.....:...................711 Locust Street
Atterberry, Ralph M......... .... Col ....Atlanta, Mo.
Austin, Ralph C. ....Col ....Morrison
Bartholomew, Jennie L.............Div.... ....Table Grove
Beatty, Dwight C....... .... Col................... Fairview
Birmingham, Marie..............,... Mus............... . Galesburg
Bishop, Rena May................Mus-Art..........Warsaw, Wis.
Blood, M. Isabelle, Instructor in Art...............64 N. West Street
Blout, Charles J......:...:.........Col...............Ellisville
Bradshaw, George H................Unc. ....Blandinsville
Breece, Amber L...................Mus ....Gilson
Brower, Mary L.................Mus........... ... Fullerton, Neb.
Brown, Talent ....Col................... ... Rio
Burnside, Roy.....................Col .... Knoxville
Byers, Frank.....................Mus...................Galesburg
Byloff, Julia.....................Mus.................Galesburg
Carr, Fannie.................. ..... Col ....Avon
Case, Schuyler C. ....Col ....Avon
Case, Shelby C................,......... Col ....Avon
Chamberlain, Ethel..............,...Col...............Galesburg
Chambers, Oliver J.............., ... Mus ....Avon
Chapman, Janet.....................Mus.................Galesburg
Cheesman, Prof. W. H., Instructor in Violin....1198 N. Cherry Street
Clark, Fred A.....................Col ....Maquon
Clark, Katherine....................Art ....Maquon
Clay, Walter T.......... ....Col ....Galesburg
Coffman, Mrs. William ....:.Art................... Galesburg
Conger, Delia.....................Col..................Galesburg
Conger, Ethelyn...................Mus...................Galesburg
Cooper, Harry Mac................Col ....Oquawka
Cooper, Leona.................,......Col ....Oquawka
Crocker, Edna....................Col ....Knoxville
Currens, Elizabeth.................Mus...............Table Grove
Currens, Wayne...................Mus...............Table Grove
Curtis, Prof. Alice B...................................Ladies' Hall
Davis, Prof. Eugene, Director Conservatory of Music, 1115 E. Knox Street
Davis, Mrs. Eugene E., Instructor in Voice Culture, 1115 E. Knox Street
Dillow, Florence................. Col.............Creston, Iowa

Dillow, Ray......................... Col.............. Creston, Iowa
Dunblazier, Locy E............... Unc......... ......Table Grove
Edwards, Forrest.................. Col................. Princeville
Eldridge, Jessie.................. Col................. Dahinda
Ericson, Josephine L.............. Mus................. Galesburg
Field, Hattie E.... .... Unc................. Fairview
Fosher, Cora M....:............... Col................. Galesburg
Fosher, D. C...................... Div... .... Galesburg.
Foster, June...................... Col................. Bradford
Foster, May....................... Art................. Bradford
Fowler, Prof. Frank H............................ 1155 E. Knox Street
Gallup, Roscoe H................. Unc................. Edelstein
Garrett, Grace................... Mus............... Media
Gast, Paul....................... Mus............. Prospect, O.
Gibbs, Minnie C... .... Col............... Anoka, Minn.
Gillis, Hudson McBain............ Col.......... Mt. Pleasant, Iowa
Goad, Charles Howard............. Unc . ... Blandinsville
Golliday, Theo................... Col ....Galesburg
Grimes, Lloyd O.................. Col . ...Blue Hill, Neb.
Grimmer, J. W.................... Div .... Charlton, Ala.
Grubb, Emma W.................... Col .... Hamilton
Grubb, Prof. Jon Watson................... ...1427 E. Knox Street
Haffner, Grover.................. Unc............. Anderson, Ind.
Haffner, Mable.................. Mus....... .... Anderson, Ind.
Hale, Mrs. Adah M......................... Matron at Ladies' Hall
Hallene, Helen.................. Mus...:............. Galesburg
Handley, Lulu................... Mus... .... Pontiac
Harris, Mrs. William............. Art................. Galesburg
Hartsook, George S..... .... Unc................. Maquon
Hathaway, M. Agnes.. ....Col....
              ....The Blackmore Home, Tokyo, Japan
Hazzard, Lutheria................ Mus................. Galesburg
Herlocker, Webb A............. .....Col............... Table Grove
Hicks, Lee .... Unc............. Blandinsville
Hopkins, Ida.................... Art............. .....Galesburg
Hillstren, C. W.................. Div........ ....Galesburg
Hobbs, Edith.................... Col...... Benton Harbor, Mich.
Hoffman, Arthur C............... Col............. .....Knoxville
Hollister, Florence.............. Col................. Rockford
Housh, Carter................... Col....:............. Maquon
Housh, Chester.................. Col .... Maquon
Hughes, Walter J................ Col ....,........ Yates City
Huling, Grace................... Col .... Downer's Grove
Hutchinson, Anna................. Unc.... .... Oak Park

James, Hazel,.......................Art.................Good Hope.

Jobe, Paris A......................Unc..............Blandinsville

Justus; Ray W.....................Col..... ....Stockton

Kimble, Prof. Ralph G.........................427 Locust Street

Kornwebel, Augusta ....Mus ....Galesburg

Kueffner, Prof. Louise M............................. Ladies' Hall

Law, Fred W......................Unc..... ......Fountain Grove

Legg, Grace....:................Art...................Macomb

Linderholm, Ernest A.............Col ....Altona

Linderholm, Lillie C...............Col ....Galesburg

Linquist, Lillian..................Mus .... Galesburg

Longbrake, Dr. Guy A., Medical Examiner,..... .... 501 E. Losey St.

McDaniel, L. Berl................ Col.................Barry

McLaughlin, Myrtle..... .... Mus ....Galesburg

Manning, Stanley,.................Div...................Chicago

Martin, Marie Syrena..............Div....................Alexis

Martin, Nellie Ruth.... ....Div...................:..Alexis

Martin, Vella ....Col ....Galesburg

Metcalf, Harold................ ...:.. Col ....Blandinsville

Moore, Aubrey G...... ....Unc...............Table Grove

Myzner, C. Fred...............:..Unc ....Mt. Moriah, Mo.

Nelson, Alvira....................Mus ....Galesburg

Nelson, Edna.....................Mus ....:.Galesburg

Nelson, Emma ....Art..................Knoxville

Oberholtzer, E. E...................Unc ....Williamsfield

Olson, Amelia A...................Mus ....Galesburg

Parker, Prof. Isaac A..................... ....488 Lombard Street

Phillips, William..................Div...... ....Chicago

Pittman, Eskridge.................Col-Mus ....Prescott, Ark.

Planck Marie......................Art............ Red Oak, Iowa

Porter, Fannie....................Col...................DeLand

Porter, Gail Q....................Col...................DeLand

Potter, Albert M ....Col ...:...............Morrison

Potter, Warren.....................Col ....Morrison

Quigley, Laura....................Unc ....Princeton

Ray, Andrew...................... ......Unc ....`...Avon

Rautenberg, Clare ....Mus...........:... ......Lincoln

Reifsnider, Rev. Edson, Instructor in Homiletics and Pastoral Care

....257 North Street

Rice, Dr. Delia M., Medical Examiner...........486 N. Prairie Street

Rich, Dean Frederick William ....1379 E. Knox Street

Rich, Gertrude.......... ....Unc ....Galesburg

Rich, Willis H....................Col ....Galesburg

Richard, R. Ward.................Unc ....:.......Maquon

Richards, Lucile.............. .... Col............... Keswick, Va.
Richey, Frances.................. Col .... Galesburg
Robinson, LeRoy P... .... Col.........Mt. Pleasant, Iowa
Rockafellow, Will V................Col ....Fairview
Ross, Frances .... Col .... Avon
Ross, Louise.............. .... Col ....Avon
Satoh, Jinkuro............. .... Unc..........Miyagiken, Japan
Shaffer, James C.................... Col....... ....Williamsfield
Snyder, Mrs. August...............Mus.................Galesburg
Standard, Harry A................. Unc ....Vermont
Stryker, E. Bell.....................Col.....................Joliet
Sumner, D. D......................Unc .... Knoxville
Swanson, George.................... Mus ....Galesburg
Swanson, Mrs. P. F.............. . Art ....Galesburg
Sweeney, Fannie................. .. Mus ....Avon
Sykes, Katheryne A...................Col ....Galesburg
Taliaferro, Martha...................Art ....Roseville
Tanner, William R..................Div ....Minneapolis, Minn.
Templeton, Mabel...................Mus ....Galesburg
Tillia, Effie......................Mus ....Tiskilwa
Tipton, Fred Lincoln................ Mus.................Girard
Titus, Murray T...................Col............Batavia, Ohio
Van Buren, Laura F... ....Mus....... ....Marseilles
Walline, Florence.............. ...... Mus.................Galesburg
Weber, George C....................Unc ....Rochester, Minn.
Weber, Edna................... ....Mus..........Rochester, Minn.
Webster, Marion................ .... Mus.................Galesburg
Welcome, Eva Elgy.................Unc ....Galesburg
Wennstrom, Frank J.................Col ....Avon
Wertman, Albert J..................Unc . ...Villisca, Iowa
White, Frances.....................Art ....Galesburg
White, Prof. Nehemiah........................1473 E. Knox Street
Williamson, Bessie......:..........Col .... Galesburg
Wilson, Harlan................... Unc.................Knoxville
Wright, Prof. Philip G....... . ... 1443 E. Knox Street.
Wright, Theodore P................Mus ....Galesburg
Wrigley, Marion................... . Mus ....Chicago
Yeoman, Mahala....................Col .... Avon
Zabriskie, Nelle... ....Mus ....Fairview

GENERAL SUMMARY.

COLLEGE OF LIBERAL ARTS.

Candidates for Degrees in 1905

Bachelor of Arts...................................... 10
Bachelor of Science 2-12
Students in the College of Liberal Arts....................... 65

UNCLASSIFIED STUDENTS.

Unclassified Students 24

RYDER DIVINITY SCHOOL.

Candidates for degrees in 1905.

Bachelor of Divinity 5
Students in Divinity School................................. 10

MUSIC.

Candidates for Diploma in Music............................ 3
Students in Department of Music.... 47

ART.

Students in Art.. 18

184
Names entered twice................. 35

Total 149

ASSOCIATION OF GRADUATES.

1904-1905.

OFFICERS.

PRESIDENT,

FRANK H. FOWLER, GALESBURG.

VICE PRESIDENT,

HARRY A. BLOUNT, MACOMB.

SECRETARY,

MRS. C. E. HUNTER, GALESBURG.

TREASURER,

JON W. GRUBB, GALESBURG.

HISTORIAN,

GRACE S. HARSH, CRESTON, IOWA.

BOARD OF DIRECTORS.

FRANK H. FOWLER, EX-OFFICIO,   R. G. KIMBLE,

NINA HARRIS HUNTER, EX-OFFICIO,   W. T. SMITH,

ADAH HASBROOK HALE,   J. J. WELSH,

C. A. WEBSTER,   J. W. GRUBB,

JAMES CARNEY.

Graduates.

The degree of A. M. or M. S. placed immediately after a name, implies that the corresponding Bachelor's degree (A. B. or B. S.) was received on graduation.

The person to whose name a star is attached is deceased. The date following designates the year of his death.

Addresses known to be incorrect are bracketed.

1856.

Burson, William Worth, A. M...........Manufacturer, 3424 Sheridan Drive, Chicago.
Cole, William Ramey, A. M.....................Clergyman, Mt. Pleasant, Iowa.
Hurd, Addie, A. M. (Mrs. William Van Horn)......917 Sherbrook St. Montreal, Can.
McNeeley, Thompson W., A. M.....................Ex-M. C., Attorney, Petersburg.
Miles, Jennie, A. M., *1859..Decatur.
Simmons, Lewis Alden, A. M., *1889...............................Wellington, Kan.

1857.

Bond, Fielding B., A. B., *1862............ ....Greenbush
Brown, Floyd G., A. B,, *1868..... ....Mankato, Minn.
Chapin, James Henry, A. M., Ph. D., *1892...... ....Meriden, Conn.
Laning, Edward D., A. B.......................... ....Attorney, Petersburg.
Wike, Scott, B. S., *1901..Barry.

1858.

Clark, Anson L., A. M., M. D. President Bennett Eclectic Medical College,
    Chicago..Elgin.
Gorman, Thomas, A. B., *1891...Columbus, O.

1859.

Elwell, George W., B. S., *1869................ ....Chillicothe, Mo.
Fuller, Mary Jane, B. S................................. .... Tarpon Springs, Fla.
Hill, Eugene Beauharnais, B. S....................Manufacturer, Ottumwa, Iowa.
Kidder, Almon, A. M............... ....Attorney, Monmouth.
Miller, Ruth Waldron, M. S., (Mrs. F. F. Brower), *1892...................Chicago.

1860.

Brown, Jonathan Eden, A. B............... ....Farmer, Peabody, Kan.
Burr, Arick, B. S., *1860...... ....Charleston.
Frisbee, William Judah, A. M., *1903....................................Bushnell.
Lindsay, James Scott, A. B. *1860...Onarga.
Slater, Albert Sidney, M. S., M. D..Wataga.

1861.

Brower, Franklin Fayette, A M., *1869.....................................Ottawa.
Conger, Everett Lorentus, A. M., D. D..... ....Clergyman, Pasadena, Cal.
Miller, Mary Stewart, A. B., (Mrs. Catlin), *1867 ....Vinton, Ia.
Pollock, Henry George, A. M................... ..:........Clergyman, Madison, Ind.

1862.

Conger, Edwin Hurd, A. M...............U. S. Minister to Mexico, Mexico, Mexico.
Dow, Samuel Alvus, A. M., M. D...........Wyalong, New South Wales, Australia.
Dow, William Sampson, B. S., *1863..Galesburg.
Fuller, Eugenia Adaline, B. S., (Mrs. J. W. Ranstead)........................Elgin.
Holmes, Charles Allen, A. M ... .Attorney, New London, Wis.
Karr, Hamilton Lafayette, A. M................ .. ..Attorney, Osceola, Ia.
Livingston, Frederick Warren, M. S... ....Teacher, San Diego, Cal.
Rowell, Harvey, A. B...........................Solicitor of Patents, Columbus, Wis.
Sherwin, John Crocker, M. S., Ex-M. C.. .Attorney, [1234 Columbus St, Denver, Colo.]
Trego, Alfred Henry, A. M.......................Manufacturer, Hoopeston.
Turner, John George, A. M., M. D., *1899........ ....Oskaloosa, Ia.

1863.

Biddlecombe, Hanna Jane, M. S. Bookkeeper Glendale Furnace Co., Columbus, O.
Calhoun, Samuel Addison, A. B........Adv. Solicitor "German Demokiat," Peoria.
Crocker, Oricy Villa, L. A., (Mrs. Nead), *1880.................... ....Galesburg.
Miles, Sarah Jane, A. M., (Mrs. Bullman)......:...........................Galesburg.
Moore, Mary Addie, M. S., (Mrs. Sumner Ellis)..... .....2734 Prairie Ave., Chicago.
Pike, Sarah Jane, L. A., (Mrs. E. H. Conger)..........................Mexico, Mexico.
Ranstead, John W., B. S...Attorney, Elgin.

1864.

Chase, Elmore, B. S.......................................Teacher, Fair Oaks, Cal.
Greenwood, Leslie, A. M....... ..With Farmers' Loan and Trust Co., Sioux City, Ia.
Pike, Laura Lavinia, A. M., (Mrs. J. S. McConnell)..........4359 Lake Ave., Chicago.
Raymond, Josephine, A. M., (Antioch College), (Mrs. Maxwell)..........Champaign.
Raymond Sallie. L. A., (Mrs. J. B. Green)....................................Ramsey.

1865.

Chapin, Alice Caroline, B. S..............Teacher, 140 A. St., Salt Lake City, Utah.
Chase, Elmore, B. S., A. M................. ....Teacher, Fair Oaks, Cal.
McCormick, John Henry, B. S.......................................Caledonia, Mo.

1866.

Claycomb, Elwin Wallace, A. M...............................Farmer, Eureka, Kan.
Conger, Emma N. H., A. M., (Mrs. S. W. Conger)..................Villa Park, Cal.
McConnell, James Smith, B. S.......... ......Attorney, 84 Washington St., Chicago.
Shook, Geo. R., B. S..........................Teacher and Surveyor, Fruita, Colo.

1867.

Bingham, Helen Maria, L. A., M. D......................... .... Monroe, Wis.
Carlock, William Bryan, B. S..............................Attorney, Bloomington.
Woods, William Harvey, B. S....... ....Farmer, [Mendota.]

1868.

Beals, Almeda, L. A., (Mrs. Charles Wickwire), *1904....................Farmington.
Chase, Henry Moses, A. B., *1870..........:...: ....Concord, Vt.
Claycomb, Mary J., A. M., (Mrs. J. W. Grubb).................:.............Galesburg.
Edwards, Sarah Elvira, L. A., (Mrs. Otis Jones), *1899..............Los Angles, Cal.
Greenwood, Grace, L. A., (Mrs. E. E. Holroyd), *1898.............. ....Chicago.
Kirk, Emeline Elizabeth, L. A., *1881.........,.............................Rockford.
Kirk, Josephine Marian, A. M., (Mrs. Samuel Kerr). *1879...............:..Chicago.

O'Donnell, James, B. S., *1901...Cherokee, Ia.

Pike, Frances Elizabeth, L. A., (Mrs. J. Kirk Keller)....................
.............................Artist, 4509 Shenandoah Ave., St. Louis, Mo.

Smith, Wellington, B. S., *1870...Annawan.

Sparks, Mary Ann, L. A., (Mrs. Frank Milnor) ....Litchfield.

Tenney, Florence Adelaine, L. A., (Mrs. John Edwards), *1871..........Omaha, Neb.

Walbridge, Edward Keys, B. S............Loan and Real Estate Agent, Girard, Kan.

Weston, Mary Emeline, L. A., (Mrs. Woodman), *1888.................Portland, Me.

1869.

Cooper, Rause'don, B. S. *1903...Oquawka.

Dunton, Mary Emily, A. M., (Mrs. Samuel Kerr)......................... Oak Park.

Greenwood, Ella May, L. A., (Mrs. S. O. Snyder) 687 Third St., Salt Lake City, Utah.

Hartman, Mary, L. A., A. M...........Teacher in State Normal University, Normal.

Kerr, Samuel, A. M...................................Attorney, 189 LaSalle St., Chicago.

Knappenberger, Michael F., B. S., *1902.............................Jewel City, Kan.

Knowles, Howard, B. S..Galesburg.

Talent, Patrick, B. S ....Attorney, Hanford, Cal.

Wiley, John Ewalt, B. S.......................................Farmer, Elmwood.

1870.

Blood, Jared Perkins, A. B......................Attorney, Sioux City, Iowa.

Brown, Abraham Miller, A. M......................................Attorney, Galesburg.

Chapin, Mary Ann, L. A., (Mrs. T. T. Perry), *1883......................Girard, Kan.

Chase, Nathaniel Ray, A. M., M. D...............................Newport, R. I.

Crum, Mathias, M. S...Farmer City.

Edwards, Flora Amanda, L. A., (Mrs. J. F. Fargo)..................San Antonio, Cal.

Hasbrook, Charles Electus, A. M., LL. B., (Chicago University)........
...........................Publisher, Times Building, New York City.

Johnson, Elmer Clifford, B. S...........Manufacturer, 36 Main St., Evansville, Ind.

Jones, Otis, B. S. ... . Santa Anna, Cal.

Stockton, Israel Cyrus, M. S...
Clerk, Interior Dept., 1514 New Jersey Ave., N. W., Washington, D. C.

Walbridge, John Hill, B. S...............................Farmer, West Concord, Vt.

1871.

Brower, Martin Ireneus, A. M..............................Attorney, Fullerton, Neb.

Bullock, Ida, L. A., (Mrs. Thatcher), *1894 ....Attleboro, Mass.

Fuson, Willis Hardin, A. M., *1884..............................Wa Keeney, Kan.

Greenwood, Frank Tenney, A. B............................. Druggist, Seneca, Kan.

Haight, Hanna Laura, B. S..................................Teacher, Mendota.

Harris, Madison Reynolds, A. B..................Attorney, Reaper Block, Chicago.

Hasbrook, Adah May, A. M., (Mrs. Willis Hale).....................
.............Matron Ladies' Hall, Lombard College, Galesburg.

Knowles, Mary, L. A., (Mrs. J. S. Alspaugh) ....Washington, Kan.

McConnell, Samuel Parsons, A. B...
...........................Attorney, 135 Bond Street, New York, N. Y.

Prindle, Flora Adaline, L. A., (Mrs. A. G. Dow)............................Galesburg.

Stephenson, John DeBolt, B. S., *1872.............................Dexter, Ind.

1872.

Bingham, Alice M., L. A., (Mrs. Copeland, *1904)........................Monroe, Wis.

Burford, Mattie Wilburn, L. A., (Mrs. Bates)..............Merchant, [Wichita, Kan.]

Chase. Albert Elmore, B. S............Deputy U. S. Mining Surveyor, Boulder, Colo.

Gates, Joseph Albert, A. B......National Military Home, Box 97, Leavenworth, Kan.

1873.

Bingham, Ada D., L. A., M. D.. Monroe, Wis.
Brown, Ellen M., L. A., (Mrs. Salley,) *1883............................. Monroe, Wis.
Nelson, Anna L., L. A., (Mrs. W. H. Fuson)........... .... Emporia, Kan.
Richardson, Clara, L. A., (Mrs. G. F. Claycomb)............ ....
.................................3927 Woodlawn Park Ave., Seattle. Wash.
Richardson, Sarah A., A. M............................ .... Lawrence, Kan.
Stevens, Mary M., A. M............... ....871 East St., Lincoln, Neb.
Stevens, Theodore C., A. M., *1892.. Lincoln, Neb.

1874.

Albrecht, William, B. S., *1878........ .... Tiskilwa.
Brunson, Eugene E., B. S., M. D.....................................Ganges, Mich.
Clingingsmith, Daniel, B. S..Newton, Kan.
Conger, Irene A., L. A., (Mrs. Courtney) *1891.........................Chicago.
Day, William E., B. S.... ....Christian Science Healer, 4335 Lake Ave., Chicago.
Fletcher, Morris W., B. S., M. D....▪ ....Collierville, Tenn.
Sherman, Belle, B. S..Teacher, Ithaca, N. Y.

1875.

Brainard, Carrie W., A. M., B. D. (St. Lawrence)........Clergyman, Rome City, Ind.
Buck, Charles A., L. A.. Undertaker, Joliet.
Collins, Emma S., L. A., (Mrs. J. E. Buchanan)..............Teacher, Lake Forest.
Conger, Lillie E., L. A., *1877...Oneida.
Dinsmore, Lucien J., B. S., A. M..........Clergyman, 2155 N. Ashland Ave., Chicago.
Edwards, Genie R., L. A., (Mrs Richard Noteware), *1888........Minneapolis, Minn.
Nash, Charles Ellwood, A. M., S. T. D., (Tufts)...........................
......▪..Field Secretary Universalist Church, 36 West St., Boston, Mass.
Nelson, Jennie C., L. A., (Mrs. Nichols)......................St. Charles.
Pryne, Jose M., L. A...............................113 Hanover St., Mankato, Minn.
Warner, Luella R., B. S., (Mrs. Frank Hitchcock).....................
.... Teacher of Painting, Mosca, Colo.

1876.

Fuller, Charlotte, M. S., (Mrs. S. M. Risley)...........................Harvard, Neb.
Hale, Stella, L. A...Galesburg.
Hastings, J. L., B. S., *1894 ....Galesburg.
Leighton, Lottie E., B. S., (Mrs. L. J. Dinsmore)......2155 N. Ashland Ave., Chicago.
Parker, Izah T., A. M., *1891 ....Banning, Cal.

1877.

Baker, George F. S., A. M., *1891...................................... Goodenow.
Edwards, Clara Z., L. A., (Mrs. J. F. Calhoun)..... ....
.... 1900 Dupont Ave., South Minneapolis, Minn.
Fuller, Emily L., A. M............. .. ..Teacher, Galesburg.
Fuller, Eugenia, A. M.......... ....Principal High School, Riverside, Cal.
Humphrey, Lottie J., B. S., *1879............................ .... Tipton, Ia.
Maynard, Charles C., A. M..............Dentist, 97 South First St., San Jose, Cal.
McCullough, Ella, L. A., (Mrs. J. D. Welsh)...... ....Galesburg.

1878

Bostwick, Ozro P., A. B......................... .....Supt. City Schools. Clinton, Ia.
Chapin, Eben H., A. M., B. D., (Tufts) Clergyman......18 Maple St., Rockland, Me.
Mariner, Adah M., M. S., (Mrs. Stewart)..................................Bushnell.
Ransom, Shirley C., B. S., A. M., 1892.......................Insurance Agent, Abingdon.

1879.

Grubb, Jon W., M. S.................. ...... Professor, Lombard College, Galesburg.
Hale, Charles P.: A. M........ ....
.... Insurance and Real Estate Agt., 1087 Broadway, Denver, Col.
Myers, Douglas A., B. S...................... ....Real Estate Agent, Peoria.
Webster, Charles A., B. S......... .... Treasurer Lombard College, Galesburg.
Webster, J. Edwin, B. S............................ ... .Merchant, Galesburg.

1880.

Devendorf, Mollie B., B. S....... ....Stenographer, 682 N. California Ave., Chicago.
Livingston, Henry S., A. M., *1895............ ....:...Galesburg.
Livingston, William H., A. B......... ......Auditor Mercaptile Mutual
    Building and Loan Association, 301 New England Building, Kansas Lity, Mo.
Parker, William A., A. M..............Civil Engineer, U. P. R. R., Kansas City, Mo.
Swigart, Otto H., B. S..................., ...Farmer and Stockman, Champaign.
Townsend, Jennie B., B. S., (Mrs. C. A. Webster)........................Galesburg.

1881.

Bailey, Lura D., A. B., (Mrs. G. F. Hughes) ....Yates City.
Hughes, George F., A. B............................... ....Attorney, Yates City.
Summers, Milo C., M. S.............War Department Clerk, Surgeon
        ....General's Office, 314 Seventh St., Northeast, Washington, D. C.

1882.

Bower, Reuben D., B. S....................... ....Farmer, High River, Alberta, Canada.
Chase, Henry M., A. M.:.....................Loan and Real Estate Agent, Galesburg.
Swart. Lafayétte, B. S...................... ....Farmer, Christiana. Tenn.
West, Elmer H., M. S., *1894......................... ....Yates City.

1883.

Brewster, Chas. E., A. B. .. ..Loan and
        ..... Real Estate Agent, 1770 Emerson Ave., South, Minneapolis, Minn.
Carney, James Weston, B. S., B. D., (Tufts)...... ....Attorney, Galesburg.
Edwards, Fannie M., A. B., (Mrs. C. E. Brewster).....................
        ....1770 Emerson Ave., South, Minneapolis, Minn.
Furniss, Lizzie E., B. S., (Mrs. W. J. Moring).....................[Kansas City, Mo.]
Jones, Lloyd Z., B. S..........................County Surveyor and Farmer, Galva.
Livingston, Emma J., L. A., (Mrs. A. T. Wing)........................Portland, Ore.
Miles, John H., B. S..Farmer, Bushnell.
Williams, Elma E., A. M....................................338 E. 57th St. Chicago.

1884.

Brewster, Anna M., M. S., (Mrs. E. H. West')............................St. Louis, Mo.
Brunson, Gay M., B. S., M. D., D. D. S............. ....,.Dentist, Joliet.
Burt, Lulu M., B. S., (Mrs. W. B. Cravens).... ....2401 E. 11th St., Kansas City, Mo.
Edwards. Charles L., B. S., Ph. D., (Leipsic).... ....
        .... Professor of Biology, Trinity College, Hartford, Conn.
Edwards, Jay J., M. S...., ... Teacher, 522 50th St., Chicago.
Jones, Frank R., B. S,................ ....Manager Austin Mf'g. Co., Harvey, Ill.

1885.

Carney, Eugene F., B. S., *1887...Galesburg.
Conger, Jennie B., A. M., (Mrs. Conger)............1059 E. 34th St., Los Angeles, Cal.
Crum, George, B. D..................................... ....Clergyman, Logansport, Ind.
Devore, Alma J., B. S., (Mrs. J. H. Miles)....................................Bushnell.
Hughes, Lizzie B., B. L., (Mrs. D. Perry)........................... . Table Grove.
McCarl, Lyman, M. S. .. .. Attorney, 304 N. Sixth St., Quincy.
Small, Wallace F., B. D....: ....:Clergyman, Florence, Wash.
Suiter, Ella, B. S., (Mrs. George Pittard) *1894.................................Alexis.
Welsh, J. Douglas, B. S............................. .... County Judge, Galesburg.

1886.

Adamson, Rainie, M. S., (Mrs. W. F. Small)................... ......Florence, Wash.
Brigham, L. Ward, M. S., M. D., B. D., (Canton)......Clergyman
                                 578 Bedford Ave., Brooklyn, N. Y.
Davies, John M., M. S... ....Teacher, 612 Fifth Street, Maywood.
Dellgren, August, B. D., ...Clergyman, 1017 Sheffield Ave., Chicago.
Ebberd, Anna H., B. S., (Mrs. Cyrus Hannum)......................Campbell, Neb.
Orelup, Hiram J., B. D............................Clergyman, 221 Penn. Ave., Aurora
Roberts, Alice L., B. S., (Mrs. J. L. Andrew) . ...[National City, Cal.]
Watkins, Rachel A., M. S., (Mrs. Billings), B. D., 1894. ....Siloam Springs, Ark.

1887.

Carpenter, John R., B. D................... ....Clergyman, New Olmstead, O.
Colgrove, Osgood G., B. D.......... ....Clergyman, Woodstock, O.
Crane, J. W., B. S..........Attorney, 908 Guarantee Loan Bldg., Minneapolis, Minn.
Fuller, Perry B., B. S..................................... ....Clerk, Elgin.
Garrard, Mary, B. D. (Mrs. I. Rollin Andrews)
                              . 35th St. and Hawthorne Ave., Omaha, Neb.
Grubb, Ella M., A. M., (Mrs. James Simmons).... ....Owasso, Mich.
Morris, Henry C., A. M............Attorney, 100 Washington St., Suite 510, Chicago.
Welsh, Jay, M. S..Farmer, Williamsfield.
Wing, Alva T., B. S..... ....Advertiser, Portland, Ore.

1888.

Hawley, Peter T., B. S............ ....Merchant, Ralston, Iowa.
Jones, Harry H., M. S.................................Supt. Oil Wells, Jennings, La.
Lapham, Allen W., M. S., M. D., *1894............... .... Victoria.
Shaffer, Elfreda L., B. D., (Mrs. Newport).................Clergyman, Wauponsee.
Taylor, Elmer E., B. S., *1903...................................College Mound, Mo.

1889.

Dutton, George E., M. S....... ....:.............Banker, Sycamore.
Fowler, Frank H., B. S., Ph. D., (The University of Chicago)..........
                        ....Professor Lombard College, Galesburg.
Garst, Charles A. C., B. D., *1896......................................Riverside, Cal.
McConnell, Edware P., M. S., *1902..Chicago.
Moore, Allen F., B. S......................................Manufacturer, Monticello.
Rice, Carrie A., B. D....... ....Clergyman, 6019 Prairie Ave., Chicago.
Smith, William T., M. S..... Attorney and Publisher Galesburg Gazette, Galesburg.
Taylor, Elmer E., B. S., A. B., *1903...............................College Mound. Mo.
Williams, Vanna R., B. L., (Mrs. W. W. Slaughter)...................Brookston, Ind.

1890.

Anderson, Claude N., B. S............................... Teacher, Tecumseh, Neb.
Brigham, Bret H., M. S...............Insurance, 1819 Chestnut St., Milwaukee, Wis.
Dotter, Thomas E., B. D.............................. Clergyman, Sullivan, Mo.
Durston, Elizabeth Gaile, M. S., B. O , (Columbus School of Oratory)..
(Mrs. H. F. Simmons) .:.. Woodhull.
Farlow, Fred, B. S.................................... Stock Dealer, Camp Point.
Fowler, Frank H., B. S., A. B., Ph. D., (The University of Chicago).....
.... Professor Lombard College, Galesburg.
Harsh, Samuel D., B. S., *1893.............................. :......Creston, Iowa.
Ross, Anna E., M. S., M. D., (Mrs. A. Lapham), ...
.... :Physician 4256 Langley Ave., Chicago.
Slater, Richard L., B. S., *1894........................... :.............. Wataga.
Trott, Loring, M. S...................................Merchant, Junction City, Kan.
Welsh, James J., B. S...............................:................Attorney, Galesburg.
Wigle, Lizzie, B. S., (Mrs. C. N. Anderson)..................... Tecumseh, Neb.
Wilson, Burtust T., M. S..............Professor Guadalupe College, Segwin, Texas.
Wiswell, Lillian J., B. L., (Mrs. E. P. McConnell) *1903 .... Cameron.

1891.

Case, M. McClelland. M. S ....Draughtsman, 198 13th St., Milwaukee, Wis.
Cole, Villa A., B. S., (Mrs. M. M. Case)...............198 13th St., Milwaukee, Wis.
Donohoe, S. Taylor, M. S................................... Longmont, Colo.
Grubb, Jennie A., B. S., (Mrs. F. H. Fowler)........................ Galesburg.
Hill, Robert D., M. S............. ....Principal of Schools, Colchester.
Rogers, Della M., B. L., (Mrs. Charles Garber)..................... Reardan, Wash.
Smith, William Franklin, B. D., *1897.................. ...... Whitewater, Wis.
White, Willard J., A. M., M. D ....Lecturer on Hygiene
and Jurisprudence at University of Colorado, Longmont, Colorado.

1892.

Allen, Frank N., B. S ....Bookkeeper, 442 E. Forty-fifth St., Chicago.
Beale, Curtis P., M. S ....Principal of Schools, Farragut, Iowa.
Blount, Harry A., B. S..Merchant, Macomb.
Brady, Ben F., B. S... ....Attorney, Ottawa.
Durston, Alice C., A. M.................................. :....New Windsor.
Elliott, Chas. W., M. S...Jeweler, Galesburg.
Harsh, Grace S., B. S.. ....Creston, Iowa.
Jones, Benjamin W., Jr., B. D., *1898 .... Barre, Vt.
McCollum, Effie K., B. D., (Mrs. B. W. Jones)..............Clergyman, Waterloo, Ia.
Seeley, Lissie, B. S., (Mrs. Leonard Crew).............................. Salem, Ia.
Skilling, George W., B. D ....Photographer, Des Moines, Ia.
Wild, Daniel P., M. S........ .. ..,....................Banker, Sycamore.
Wyman, Luther E., B. S ....,...........Broker, Board of Trade, Chicago.

1893.

Anderson, Robert F., A. B.............................. .....Farmer, Philipsburg, Kan.
Bradford, F. Louise, B. S .... Teacher, Quincy.
Brown, Richard, M. S........ .... Attorney, Creston, Ia.
Carlton, Kate A., B. S., (Mrs. F. W. Smith) .... DeLand, Fla.
Conger, J. Newton, Jr., M. S........ .... Attorney, Galesburg.
Countryman, Carl C., A. M., Impersonator and Author, 801 N. Y. Life Bldg., Chicago.

Dickson, States, B. S........................ .... Attorney, Kewanee.
Fuller, S. Hepsey, M. S., (Mrs. J. M. Earhart).......................... Wyoming.
Longbrake, Guy A., B. L., M. D........................... ..Physician, Galesburg.
Tompkins, Ethel M., A. M., (Mrs. W. H. Clayberg) .... Avon.
Varney, Charles E., B. D .... Clergyman, Clinton.
Wiswell, Daisy D., M. S. (Mrs. G. A. Franklin) .... Carpentaria, Cal.

1894.

Bernard, Guy Henry, B. S........................ ....Bank Cashier, Glasco, Kan.
Conger, Lucy Minerva, B. S., (Mrs. E. P. May), Riverside Farm, Framingham, Mass.
Crum, Joseph Amos, B. S., M. D ....Oshkosh, Wis.
Crum, Maude Alice B. S..Boone, Ia.
Curtis, Eliza M. Drake, B. D., (Mrs. J. L. Everton).......... Clergyman, Hoopeston.
Dellgren, Rachel C. Watkins, B. D., (Mrs. Billings)............. Siloam Springs, Ark.
Durston, Adelphia Gould, B. S., (Mrs. George Ohse)........... ....Yorkville, Ill.
Everton, Jasper Leroy, B. D................................... Clergyman, Hoopeston.
Garner, Martha Dandridge, B. D., (Mrs. L. P. Jones)........ ......Clergyman, Marseilles.
Gillespie, Henry LaFayette, B. D...... .... Clergyman, St. Louis, Mo.
Hamand, Elijah Emmett, B. D......Clergyman, [1222 Lyden Ave., Kansas City, Mo.]
Menke, Albert Ernest, Ph. D.............................Chemist, Fayetteville, Ark.
Olmstead, Rett E., B. D.......... .... Clergyman, Decorah, Ia.
Schuler, Hans. Ph. D........................... .... Teacher, Flushing, N. Y.
Smith, Albert Prentice, B. S............................... ......Merchant, Denver, Colo.
Tapper, William Richard, A. B...............................Attorney, Sycamore.
Titus, Lucy, B. S., (Mrs. R. F. Anderson)..........................Philipsburg, Kas.
Titus, Margaret, B. D., (Mrs. R. E. Olmstead)............Clergyman, Decorah, Iowa.

1895.

Bragg, Lucile, A. B.......... ....Clerk, Humboldt, Kan.
Cheney, Frances Elizabeth, B. D., *1902..... ....Greenup.
Chapin, William Robert, B. S.................... . Planter, Pedro Sula, Honduras.
Conger, Frank Loren, A. B................Cashier, First National Bank, Galesburg.
Conley, Grace Winifred, A. B.............................Postal Clerk, Galesburg.
Dow, Mabel, A. B., (Mrs F. L. Conger)................. ....Galesburg.
Evans, Orrin Carlton, B. D.... ....Clergyman, Rochester, Minn.
Higgins, Robert Pinkney, B. S..................................... ....Champaign.
Jones, Charles Robert, B. D..............................Clergyman, Nettleton, Mo.
McDuffie, John, Ph. D................................Teacher, Springfield, Mass.
Rayon, Thomas Francis, B. D ....Clergyman, [Rapid River, Mich.]
Stanley, John Richard, A. B...............................Farmer, Roswell, N. M.
Tompkins, Nellie Christine, A. B., (Mrs. Giles M. Clayberg)...................Avon
Wakefield, Albert Orin, A. B..............................Attorney, Sioux City, Ia.

1896.

Brown, Jessie Beatrice, A. B., (Mrs. A. L. C. Clock).... ....
....632 Indiana Ave., Winona, Minn.
Camp, Fred Leo, A. B ....Galesburg.
Cheney, Almira Lowrey A. B.... ... .Saybrook.
Clark, James Alvin, B. D........ ....Clergyman, South Pasadena, Cal.
Cook, Bertha Alice, A. B., (Mrs. O. C. Evans)....................Rochester, Minn.
Crissy, Elice, A. B..Teacher, Avon.
Gossow, Charles William Edward, B. D .. .. Clergyman, Wichita, Kan.
Harsh, Homer Franklin, A. B.... ....Stockman, Lowell, Neb.
Karr, Hamilton Lafayette, Jr., A. B.................... ....Attorney, Murray, Iowa.

Kendall, Marion Alice, A. B.......... ....Ithaca, N. Y.
Kimble, Ralph Grierson, A. B....... ......Professor Lombard College. Galesburg.
Lessig, Harry McGee, A. B.................Clerk U. P. R. R. offices, Omaha, Neb.
Linton, Maurice Gilbert, B. D..........................Clergyman, Zanesville, Ohio.
Myers, Iva Della, A. B..Bookkeeper, Galesburg.
Shinn, Edward Leroy, A. B ....Merchants Coal Co., 131 State St., Boston, Mass.
Southwick. Eugene, B. D.............................Clergyman, [Corfu, N. Y.]
Stanley, Georgia, Diploma in Art, (Mrs. C. H. Wickham)..............Anthony, Kan.
Van Liew, Emma Genevra, A. M., (Mrs. Guy Tuttle)....................Bushnell.
White, Jean Gillette, A. B., (Mrs. A. B. McGill)...........................Peoria.

1897.

Anderson, Frank Pierce, A. B.................................Teacher. Yates City.
Ashworth, George Hilary, B. D............................Clergyman, Bryan, Ohio.
Boyd, Loetta Frances, A. B.................................Teacher, Oneida.
Cutter, Flora May, A. B., (Mrs. Fred Boger, Jr.)......................Camp Point.
Downs, Benjamin, A. B.....................State Senator, Winslow, Arizona.
Harris, Nina Alta, A. B., (Mrs. C. E. Hunter).... . ...:........ Galesburg.
Holcomb, Fred Louis, A. B., M. D.......................................Zenda, Kan.
Lindquist, Theodore, A. B.............. ....
        ....Professor of Math., State Scientific School, Walipeton, N. D.
Minor, Edward Milton, B. D............................Clergyman, Decatur, Mich.
Rogers, George Burr, B. D...............................Clergyman, Decatur, Mich.
Slaughter, William Willis, B. D., *1901...............................Francis, Okla.
Stickney. Carrie Alice, A. B...................................... .
        ...... Teacher of Eng. and Eloc., Univ. of Chattanooga, Athens, Tenn.
Tapper, Elmer Joseph, A. B..........................Insurance Solicitor, Riverside.
Taylor, Simeon Lafayette, B. D....................Osteopath Physician, Hoopeston.
Warner, Claude Bryant, A. B., A. M.................................Dentist, Avon.
Weeks, Guy Henry, A. B . ... Teacher, Galesburg.
White, Frances Cora, A. B...... . ...Galesburg.
Yamaguchi, Fred Minosuke, A. B   .. ..Central Tabernacle, Honga, Tokio, Japan.

1898.

Allen, Mervin Wallace, A. B.............................. ......Farmer, Maquon.
Bartlett, Alice Helen, A. B., (Mrs. Murray Bruner)..................... .. Aurora.
Brown, Charles Reid, A. B.......... ....Lawyer, 100 Washington St., Chicago.
Bullman, Joshua J., A. B...Farmer, Galesburg.
Caldwell, Isal, Diploma in Vocal Music, (Mrs. Lewis)....................Knoxville.
Galbreath, Ida, A. B.......... ....Teacher, Columbia City, Ind.
McDonald, Edna Madison, (Mrs. Bonser)..............Clergyman, Cheney, Wash.
Piper, Charles Edward, A. B....................... 6046 Princeton Ave., Chicago.
Slaughter, John Willis, B. D.................Docent, Clark Univ., Worcester, Mass.
Stacey, Benjamin Franklin, B. D., A. B. Professor Univ. of Arizona, Tucson, Arizona.
Tandberg, Oluf, B. D................................ .. Clergyman, Gardiner, Maine.
Taylor, Simeon Lafayette, B. D., A. B..............Osteopath Physician, Hoopeston.

1899.

Alsager, Christen Martin, A. B..................Principal City Schools, Winnebago.
Boston, Ella Berry, A. B., (Mrs. J. L. Lieb).......... . ...Springfield.
Champlain, Lloyd, B. D.......................................[Galesburg.]
Crissey, Edith C., Diploma in Instrumental Music....................Teacher, Avon.
Dubee, Henry William, A. B............. ....
        .... Professor of German, Univ. of Michigan, Ann Arbor, Mich

Foster, Howard Everett, A. B., *1900...Galesburg.
Garvin, Homer Edwin, A. B..............Merchant, 123 Union St., Memphis, Tenn.
Gingrich, Fannie Pauline, A. B., (Mrs. Clarence Perrine)...........Dexter, Kansas.
Holmes, Jennie, Diploma in Art...N. Henderson.
Longbrake, George Runyon, A. B....................Clergyman, Titusville, Penn.
MacKay, Helen Jessie, A. B.............Society Reporter, *Evening Mail*, Galesburg.
Russell, Nellie Stuart, A. B..................................Teacher, Woodhull.
Townsend, Lora Adelle, A. B...Galesburg.

1900.

Arnold, Martha Belle, A. B.................................Teacher, Galesburg.
Buchanan, William David, B. D.......................Clergyman, Tacoma, Wash.
Bullock, Fay Alexander, A. B............Advertising Manager, Siegel's Store, N. Y.
Kidder, Gertrude Grace, A. B., (Mrs. Kern).........................Winona, Minn.
McCullough, Edwin Julius, A. B.....................................Aberdeen, S. D.
Nash, Carrie Ruth, A. B., (Mrs. Donald P. McAlpine)...............Napoleon, Mich.
Orton, Charles Wait, B. S....................................Gardener, Sumner, Wash.
Shields, Burt G., B S....................Student, Univ. of Colorado, Boulder, Colo.
Steckel, Iva May, A. B...Denver, Colo.
Watson, Earl Wolcott, A. B ....Hardware Merchant, Barry.
Weeks, Harry William, A. B...Jackson, Mich.

1901.

Arnold, Martha Belle, A. M.....................................Teacher, Galesburg.
Bartlett, John Donnington, A. B.............Student, Rush Medical College, Chicago.
Bishop, Francis Britton, B. D.............................Clergyman, Blue Island.
Buck, Nannie Mer, B. S...Teacher, Joliet.
Hartgrove, Gertrude West, A. B................................Teacher, Galesburg.
Henney, Virginia, Diploma in Music...........................Mitchellville, Iowa.
Lombard, Julia Evelyn, A. B.....................................East Orange, N. J.
Marriot, Jennie Eliza, A. B., (Mrs. W. D. Buchanan)................Tacoma, Wash.
McAlpine, Donald Palmer, A. B......................Teacher, Napoleon, Mich.
Nash, Carrie Ruth, A. M., (Mrs. Donald P. McAlpine)..............Napoleon, Mich.
Orton, William J., A. B......................................Gardener, Sumner, Wash.
Pingrey, Grace Olive, A. B.....................................Coon Rapids, Iowa.
Preston, Frederick, A. B.......................................[Boston, Mass.]
Schnur, Grace, A. B.............................317 N. Thirteenth St., Quincy.
Weir, Cyrena, Diploma in Music. .... 501 Union Ave., Litchfield.

1902.

Alspaugh, Charlotte, A. B ....Washington, Kan.
Andrew, John, Jr., A. B. .... Medical Student, Univ. of Colorado, Boulder, Colo.
Cranston, Edna Mae, A. B., (Mrs. Mugg)........................Indianapolis, Ind.
Efner, Charles Junius, A. B...Galesburg.
Epperson, Edna Ethel, A. B.......................................Teacher, Hanover.
Ericson, Henry, A. B ....Teacher, Yale School, Los Angeles, Cal.
Hitchcock, Augusta Eaton, A. B....................................Estherville, Ia.
Kimble, Thaddeus Carey, A. B ....Physician, Abingdon.
Lauer, Howard Walter, A. B...Gulfport, Miss.
Muffler, Emma Annette, A. B...Serena.
Satoh, Kiyoshi, B. D.....................................Clergyman, Tokio, Japan.
Smith, Edward Milton, A. B..................... Principal High School, Maquon.
Stokes, Alice A. B...Galesburg.

Stoughton, Herbert Leonard, A. B....................................
...................Law Student, 1323 4th St., S. E. Minneapolis, Minn.
Thompson, George Francis, B. D...........................Clergyman, Eaton, Ohio.
Varney, Charles E., B. D., A. B...............................Clergyman, Clinton.
Varney, Mecca, B. D., (Mrs. C. E. Varney)...............Clergyman, Clinton.

1903.

Andrew, Mary Maud, A. B...New Salem.
Brown, Athol Ray, A. B ....Reporter, *Evening Mail*, Galesburg.
Campbell, Raymond R., B. D ....Florala, Ala.
Cook, Sarah Lucy, Diploma in Music.................................Beecher City.
Elting, Grace Helen, Diploma in Music..................................Sperry, Ia.
Fosher, Dudley Claude, A. B ....Student Lombard College, Galesburg.
Gillis, Anna Moore, A. B., (Mrs. T. C. Kimble)....................Abingdon.
Hartgrove, Claude Webster, A. B.......................Fireman, Galesburg.
Kienholz, Willis Simon, A. B...
..........,Director of Athletics, University of Colorado, Boulder, Colo.
McCullough, Edwin Julius, A. M.................................Aberdeen, S. Dak.
Miller, Ralph Todd, A. B., *1904 ....Galesburg.
Nash, Faith Tenney, Diploma in Music.........
..............Student in Boston Conservatory of Music, Boston, Mass.
Needham, Nellie Jeanette, A. B......................................Racine, Wis.
Nieveen, S. Martin, B. D..................................Clergyman, Vermilion, S. Dak.
Rees, Jenkins B., A. B...Oneida.
Sommers, Elsie Dorothy, Diploma in Music.........................Burlington, Ia.
Willis, Leura, Diploma in Music, *1904........ ....Table Grove.
Wrigley, Anne Marion, Diploma in Music ....Chicago.

1904.

Andreen, Frank G., A. B...............Student in Coll. of Phy. and Surg., Chicago.
Ayers, Frank Cope, A. B ....Reporter, *Sentinel*, Milwaukee, Wis.
Cease, Charles H., Diploma in Music.................................
....................Director of Music, Pike Coll., Bowling Green, Mo.
Cooper, Harry Mac, A. B........Collector, Central Union Telephone Co., Galesburg.
Grier, Ethelwyn Sophia, A. B...Racine, Wis.
Hopkins, Roy Victor, A. B..Teacher, Earlville.
Howell, Spencer Pritchard, A. B..............Government Employe, St. Louis.
Hurd, Jay Clinton, A. B.........................Grain Buyer, Maquon.
Jansen, Harry Albin, A. B....................With Sears Roebuck & Co., Chicago.
Kimble, Olin Arvin,, A. B., A. M........Student, Coll. Phy. and Surg., St. Louis, Mo.
Kober, Florence Leclerc, A. B................................Teacher, Table Grove.
Philbrook, Elizabeth Freeman, A. B.......................Teacher, Racine, Wis.
Sammons, Mabel Alta, A. B. ....Teacher, Joliet.
Scott, Preston Brown, A. B.................Student Chicago Vet. Coll., Chicago.
Varney, Franklin G., A. B., B. D............Clergyman, Decatur, Mich.

HONORARY DEGREES.

The degree placed immediately after the name is the honorary degree conferred by Lombard College.

An additional degree, followed by a date only, is one conferred by Lombard College.

An additional degree, without date, is one conferred by another institution, the name of which is given if known.

1858. *Rev. Otis A. Skinner, D. D..............Ex-President Lombard University.
1859. Rev. George S. Weaver, A. M................................Canton, N. Y.
1860. *Ansel Streeter, A. M.....................................Weston, Mo.
1862. *Rev. Ebenezer Fisher D. D........Prin. Theological School, Canton, N. Y.
1862. Rev. Joseph Selmon Dennis, A. M..........................Chicago.
1863. *Rev. William Henry Ryder, D. D.; A. M. (Harvard)......... Chicago.
1864. *Rev. Holden R. Nye, A. M...........:.....................Towanda, Pa.
1864. Rev. Charles Woodhouse, A. M., M. D.....................Rutland, Vt.
1865. Rev. A. G. Hibbard, A. M ....Wheaton.
1865. *Rev. J. G. H. Hartzell, A. M.; D. D. (St. Lawrence)..........Detroit, Mich.
1867. *Rev. William Ethan Manley, A. M.......................Denver, Colo.
1867. Rev. Thomas B. St. John, A. M..............................
1868. *Rev. Clement G. Lefevre, D. D...................'.........Milwaukee, Wis.
1868. William B. Powell, A. M.............................Washington, D. C.
1868. Rev. James Harvey Tuttle, A. M., D. D.... .. .... 38 W. 53rd St., N. Y. City.
1869. Rev. John Wesley Hanson, A. M., D. D., (Buchtel)........... Pasadena, Cal.
1869. Rev. William Wallace Curry, A. M ....Washington, D. C.
1869. *Rev. Daniel Parker Livermore, A. M........ .... Melrose, Mass.
1869. Rev. Augusta J. Chapin, A. M....................459 W. 144th St., N. Y. City.
1870. Rev. John S. Cantwell, A. M ....Chicago.
1870. Daniel Lovejoy Hurd, A. M.; M. D ......
1870. *Rev. George Truesdale Flanders, D. D....................Rockport, Mass.
1870. *Rev. Alfred Constantine Barry, D. D................ ......Lodi, Mass.
1872. *Rev. William Ethan Manley, D. D ; A. M., 1867............ ..Denver, Colo.
1872. *Rev. R. H. Pullman, A. M ....Baltimore, Md.
1872. *Rev. Gamaliel Collins, A. M.. ....U. S. A., Chatham, Mass.
1872. *Rev. B. F. Rogers, A. M .... Fort Atkinson, Wis.
1875. *Rev. J. H. Chapin, Ph. D.; A. B., 1857; A. M., 1860... .. ....Meriden, Conn.
1876. Rev. George S. Weaver, D. D.; A. M., 1859... ....Canton, N. Y.
1876. Rev. John S. Cantwell, D. D.; A. M., 1870.....................Chicago.
1877. Rev. O. Cone, D. D ....Canton, N. Y.
1879. Elias Fraunfelter, Ph. D........... .:...................Akron, Ohio.
1879. Milton L. Comstock, Ph. D..............Professor Knox College, Galesburg.
1882. Rev. Charles W. Tomlinson, D. D.......................Huntington, L. I.
1883. *Rev. Amos Crum, A. M... ....Webster City, Ia.
1884. Mathew Andrews, A. M..Monmouth.
1886. Rev. L. J. Dinsmore, A. M.; B. S., 1875........2155 N. Ashland Ave., Chicago.
1887. *Rev. Holden R. Nye, D. D.; A. M., 1864.....................Towanda, Pa.
1887. *Rev. Charles Fluhrer, D. D...............................Albion, N. Y.

*Deceased.

1887.   Hon. Lewis E. Payson, LL. D..Pontiac.
1887.   *Hon. George W. Wakefield, A. M ....Sioux City, Iowa.
1888.   Rev. George H. Deere, D. D.....................................Riverside, Cal.
1888.   Homer M Thomas, A. M., M. D.............................. .....Chicago.
1888.   Rev. Charles A. Conklin, A. M............................. ...Boston, Mass.
1888.   Mary Hartman, A. M., L. A., 1859...Normal.
1890.   Rev. Jacob Straub, D. D............,.... ....Columbia, Cuba.
1890.   George B. Harrington, A. M...Princeton.
1890.   Carl F. Kolbe, Ph. D ....Akron, O.
1891.   *Rev. A. G. Gaines, LL. D., D. D....... ....Canton, N. Y.
1892.   Rev. George Thompson Knight, D. D...................Tufts College, Mass.
1892.   Charles Kelsey Gains, Ph. D....Professor St. Lawrance Univ., Canton, N. Y.
1892.   Shirley C. Ransom, A. M., B. S., 1878..................... ....Abingdon.
1893.   Rev. Augusta J. Chapin, D. D., A. M., 1869.........459 W. 144th St., N. Y. City.
1893.   *Rev. Amos Crum, D. D., A. M., 1883.....................Webster City, Iowa.
1893.   John Huston Finley, Ph. D..President College of New York, New York, City.
1893.   , Charles Loring Hutchinson, A. M.....................................Chicago.
1894.   *Rev. Royal Henry Pullman, D. D., A. M., 1872................Baltimore, Md.
1894.   Rev. George B. Stocking, D. D.............................Lansing, Mich.
1895.   Rev. Aaron Aldrich Thayer, D. D.... . ...California.
1895.   Rev. Andrew Jackson Canfield, Ph. D., D. D..............:...Worcester, Mass.
1897.   Rev. Daniel Bragg Clayton, D. D............................Columbia, S. C.
1897.   Rev. Thomas Sander Guthrie, D. D..............................Muncie, Ind.
1898.   Rev. Rodney F. Johonnot, D. D.................................Oak Park.
1898.   Henry Priest, Ph. D............Professor St. Lawrance Univ., Canton, N. Y.
1899.   John Wesley Hanson, Jr., A. M............. ....Chicago.
1900.   Rev. Alfred Howitzer Laing, D. D............ ....Joliet.
1901.   Edwin Hurd Conger, LL. D......................... ....Mexico, Mexico.
1901.   John Sharp Cook, D. D...Beecher City.
1902.   Rev. Frederick Clarence Priest, D. D......691½ Washington Blvd., Chicago.

*Deceased.

HARVARD UNIVERSITY SCHOLARSHIP.

Established by the Harvard Club of Chicago.

By request of the Harvard Club of Chicago, we publish the following notice:

At its annual meeting, December 14, 1897, the Harvard Club of Chicago established a scholarship at Harvard University of the annual value of three hundred dollars. This Scholarship is open to the graduates of the universities and colleges of Illinois who wish to follow a course of study, at the graduate School of Harvard University. Applications must be made before May 1st in each year, and senior students about to finish their undergraduate course are eligible as candidates. Communications from candidates for the year 1905-1906 should be addressed to Frederick W. Burlingham, 108 LaSalle St., Chicago.

INDEX.

LOMBARD COLLEGE PUBLICATIONS—Series IV., No. 1
[Issued Bi-Monthly by Lombard College.]

CATALOGUE

OF

LOMBARD COLLEGE

GALESBURG, ILLINOIS,

FOR THE ACADEMIC YEAR 1905-1906
AND ANNOUNCEMENTS
FOR THE YEAR 1906-1907

❧ ❧ ❧

GALESBURG, ILL.:
MAIL PRINTING COMPANY
1906

College Calendar.

1906.

MARCH 13—Tuesday.....................Registration. Third Term Begins.
MAY 5—Saturday.........................Townsend Preliminary Contest.
MAY 12—Saturday...............................Senior Vacation Begins.
MAY 17—Thursday.....................................Senior Theses Due.
MAY 31, JUNE 1—Thursday, Friday.;.......................Examinations.
JUNE 3—Sunday.....................................Baccalaureate Sermon.
JUNE 4—Monday.............................._..........Students' Field Day.
JUNE 4—Monday, Evening...........Townsend Prize Contest in Declamation.
JUNE 5—Tuesday.;............Annual Meeting of Association of Graduates.
JUNE 5—Tuesday Evening........Concert, Glee Club and Music Department.
JUNE 6—Wednesday.............Annual Meeting of the Board of Trustees.
JUNE 6—Wednesday, Evening...........................President's Reception.
JUNE 7—Thursday......................................Commencement Day.

Summer Vacation.

SEPT. 4—Tuesday...............................Entrance Examinations.
SEPT. 4—Tuesday......................Registration. College Year Begins.
NOV. 26, 27—Monday, Tuesday...........................Examinations.
NOV. 27—Tuesday ....First Term Ends.
NOV. 29—Thursday........................Holiday. Thanksgiving Day.
DEC. 4—Tuesday...................Registration. Second Term Begins.
DEC. 21—Friday........Last Day of Recitations preceding Christmas Recess.

Christmas Recess.

1907.

JAN. 3—Thursday...................Recitations of Second Term Resumed.
JAN. 3—Thursday.......................Orations for Swan Contest Due.
JAN. 19—Saturday...........................Swan Preliminary Contest.
FEB. 22—Friday.....................Holiday, Washington's Birthday.
FEB. 22—Friday.....................Swan Prize Contest in Oratory.
MARCH 6, 7—Wednesday, Thursday...........................Examinations.
MARCH 7—Thursday...............Senior Syllabi Due. Second Term Ends.

Spring Vacation.

MARCH 12—Tuesday.....................Registration. Third Term Begins.
MAY 11—Saturday.........................Townsend Preliminary Contest.
MAY 18—Saturday...............................Senior Vacation Begins.
MAY 23—Thursday.....................................Senior Theses Due.
MAY 29, 31—Wednesday, Friday .... Examinations.
JUNE 2—Sunday.....................................Baccalaureate Sermon.
JUNE 3—Monday .... Field Day.
JUNE 3—Monday, Evening...........Townsend Prize Contest in Declamation.
JUNE 4—Tuesday............Annual Meeting of Association of Graduates.
JUNE 5—Wednesday.............Annual Meeting of the Board of Trustees.
JUNE 6—Thursday.....................................Commencement Day.

BOARD OF TRUSTEES.

OFFICERS OF THE BOARD.

HON. J. B. HARSH, Cʀᴇsᴛᴏɴ, Iᴏᴡᴀ.

PRESIDENT.

CHARLES A. WEBSTER, Hᴏʟᴍᴇs Bᴜɪʟᴅɪɴɢ, Gᴀʟᴇsʙᴜʀɢ.

TREASURER.

PHILIP G. WRIGHT, 1443 Eᴀsᴛ Kɴᴏx Sᴛʀᴇᴇᴛ, Gᴀʟᴇsʙᴜʀɢ.

SECRETARY.

Executive Committee.

HOWARD KNOWLES, Cʜᴀɪʀᴍᴀɴ.

CHARLES A. WEBSTER, Sᴇᴄʀᴇᴛᴀʀʏ.

LEWIS B. FISHER.

ROBERT CHAPPELL.   J. DOUGLAS WELSH.

SCOPE AND IDEALS.

Between the high school or academy and the graduate, professional, or technical school, American educators are coming to recognize a distinct and imperative educational function which is discharged only by the college, properly so called. The broad results aimed at in character and in grasp of general principles, constitute the only adequate foundation on which to base the special training of the crafts and professions.

Owing to differing standards and degrees of efficiency the interval between the high school and the graduate school varies greatly. At Lombard College it has seemed wise to prescribe admission requirements which presume a four years' high school course.

Inasmuch as many applicants have not had access to a full four years' high school course, a considerable number of preparatory subjects are still offered at Lombard. Further, as there are some who desire to pursue certain subjects without claiming full college standing, provision is made for such special students upon equitable terms. The pure college ideal, however, enjoins us to regard these concessions as temporary, to be granted only so long as conditions necessitate them.

On the other hand, it is believed to be not inconsistent with the college idea to allow those students who intend to enter a graduate, professional, or technical school after graduation, to expedite the latter course and shorten the whole period of study by directly matching the college graduation requirements with the prospective entrance requirements of the technical school. Thus, by using his elective privilege in mapping out his college course, the Lombard A. B. may complete the subsequent Divinity course leading to the degree of B. D. in two additional years, and an Engineering course in three years. See under Ryder Divinity School for further information.

The number of subjects offered at Lombard is largely in excess of graduation requirements. This allows exceptional opportunity for adapting the course to the individual student. The emphasis is laid upon quality rather than amount of work, upon principles more than upon mere facts. The cultivation of orderly, self-active mental life is the constant endeavor.

GENERAL STATEMENT.

HISTORY.

The Illinois Liberal Institute was chartered in 1851, opened for students in the autumn of 1852, invested with College powers in 1853, and took the name of Lombard University (in honor of Mr. Benjamin Lombard, at that time the largest donor to its properties) in 1855. It was one of the first Colleges in the country to admit women as students on the same terms with men, allowing them to graduate in the same class and with the same honors. The first class was graduated in 1856. The Ryder Divinity School was opened September 5, 1881. The official title of the institution was changed in 1899 to Lombard College.

THE COLLEGE CAMPUS.

The College Campus is situated in the southeastern part of the city, and may readily be reached by the electric cars. It is thirteen acres in extent and affords ample space for tennis, track, and other athletic sports. A large part is planted with trees which have been growing many years and have attained noble size and graceful forms. Among them are pines, larches, hemlocks, cedars, maples, elms, ash-trees, tulip-trees, and others, embracing about forty species. The trees and lawns are well kept and cared for, and the beauty of the surroundings thus created is a pleasing and attractive feature of the College.

THE COLLEGE YEAR.

The College year begins early in September and closes early in June. It is divided into three terms of approximately equal length. (See Calendar, page 2.)

Students should, if possible, enter at the beginning of the College year, since much of the work is arranged progressively from that date. They will, however, be allowed to enter at any time when there seems a prospect of their being able to do so profitably.

Commencement day occurs the first Thursday in June.

ADMISSION REQUIREMENTS.

The requirements for admission to the College of Liberal Arts for students who are candidates for a degree, are essentially the requirements recommended by the Committee of Thirteen of the National Educational Association. (See pages 19-26.)

Students not candidates for a degree may enter any class for which they are prepared, and at the end of their connection with the College they will be furnished a certificate, stating the amount and quality of the work accomplished while in the College.

GRADES OF SCHOLARSHIP.

From the courses of study offered, each student is expected to elect work to an amount sufficient to keep him profitably employed. In all full courses each recitation occupies one hour. Absence from a recitation will forfeit the mark in that study for the day.

At the end of every term the standing of a student in each of his courses will be expressed, according to his proficiency, by one of four grades, designated respectively by the letters, A, B, C, D.

The grade is determined by term work, estimated on the basis of attendance, quality of recitations or laboratory work, occasional tests, written exercises, etc., and by final examination at the end of the term, the term grade and the final examination being valued in the ratio of two to one.

Grade C is the lowest which will be accepted in any study as counting towards the fulfillment of the requirements of graduation.

Students who receive grade A in all their studies may pursue not more than four courses in the succeeding term.

Students whose lowest grade is B may pursue not more than three and one-half courses in the succeeding term

Other students are not permitted to pursue more than three courses in any term.

CHAPEL ASSEMBLY

Chapel Assembly is at 9 a. m. each Tuesday, Wednesday, Thursday, and Friday. This assembly is a combination of a brief devotional service and a mass meeting of the faculty and students, before which various phases of college life are considered.

Following the brief devotions anything ministering to mind, body, or spirit is considered in order. During the last year, Wednesday mornings have been occupied by a series of addresses by the professors, which have been very attractive to all.

The musical department will give frequent recitals.

The non-resident lecturers are heard at this assembly, and any speakers who are in the city from time to time.

This Chapel assembly is the center of college life, and the sentiments of comradeship, loyalty, and community of interests here fostered make it one of the chief agencies in maintaining the "Lombard Spirit" which is so characteristic of the College and of its sons and daughters scattered abroad.

LABORATORIES.

The department of Physics is· equipped with apparatus for experimentation. Students have an opportunity to obtain a practical acquaintance with the principles of Physics, through a series of Laboratory experiments.

The extended courses in Chemistry, described elsewhere in this Catalogue, require a large amount of practical work on the part of the student. Each student in Chemistry has a desk provided with gas, water, re-agents and all necessary conveniences. The Laboratory is well equipped for work in General Chemistry, and in Qualitative and Quantitative Analysis.

A supply of superior microscopes, with other instruments and apparatus, affords a very satisfactory equipment for work in Biology.

LIBRARY AND READING ROOM.

The Library of the College contains about seven thousand volumes. It is located in the College building and is open daily. The books are systematically arranged and easy of access. They may be taken out by the students upon application to the librarian. A considerable fund has been raised, which will be expended as occasion arises, in the purchase of new books, thus assuring a substantial increment each year. The Reading Room is open daily, except Sundays, from 8:00 a. m. until 6:00 p. m.

GYMNASIUM.

The Gymnasium is a building 50x80 feet on the ground. On the ground floor, besides the Gymnasium proper, there is a large room, at present used as a recitation room, which can be thrown into the main room by withdrawing the movable partitions There is also a stage equipped with an adequate outfit of scenery, for the special use of the Department of Elocution. The apparatus consisting of chest weights, dumb-bells, Indian clubs, parallel bars, horizontal bar, flying rings, travelling rings, rowing machine, etc., is of approved patterns. The basement contains bathrooms and lockers and other conveniences.

Regular exercises are held in the Gymnasium daily, except Saturdays and Sundays. The exercises will consist of class drill, under the charge of a director, or of special work on the apparatus in accordance with the prescription of the medical examiner. It is intended that the instruction shall be thoroughly scientific, aiming not so much at special muscular or athletic development as at a sound physical culture, which is the true basis of health and so of energy and endurance.

ATHLETICS.

The Athletic interests of the College are in charge of the Director of Physical culture, assisted by a Board of Management, consisting of two members chosen from the student body, one from the faculty, and two from the alumni. The campus affords opportunity for base-ball, and track and field events. During the winter basket-ball is played in the Gymnasium. The Director of Physical Culture will take personal charge of the coaching of the basket-ball, base-ball, and track teams.

COLLEGE COMMONS.

The Trustees of Lombard College have fitted up a kitchen and dining room on the sunny side of the basement floor.

These rooms are known as College Commons, and many of the students and often members of the faculty and others take meals here, rooming in the vicinity. Meals are furnished in Commons for $2.50 a week, payable in advance, or five meal tickets are sold for $1.00.

THE LADIES' HALL.

The Ladies' Hall is a thoroughly modern building and complete in all its appointments. It is heated by steam, lighted by gas, fitted with sanitary plumbing, including porcelain baths, closets, lavatories, etc., and supplied with every convenience of a well equipped home. The Hall will accommodate forty.

Each room is finished with hard wood floor and furnished with bed-stead, springs, mattress, chairs, desk, dresser, and rugs. The occupants are expected to provide bedding, pillows, towels, napkins, to pay for washing said articles, and to keep their own rooms in order.

Rates are stated on page 11.

Applications for rooms in the Hall should be made to the Dean.

LOMBARD COLLEGE PUBLICATIONS.

Lombard College Bulletin.

A series of papers is issued bi-monthly by the college, including the annual Catalogue, containing announcements, articles discussing educational questions, and other matter calculated to keep the College in touch with its friends, and to extend a knowledge of educational data, processes, and theories. Copies will be sent free upon application.

The Lombard Review.

A College paper called *The Lombard Review,* is published monthly by the students. It makes a record of College events, and serves as a medium of communication with the friends and alumni of the College. Subscription price, $1.00.

SOCIETIES.

The Erosophian.

The Erosophian Society was organized January 29, 1860. Any male student connected with the College or Divinity school is eligible to membership, and is entitled to all the benefits of the society. Its regular meetings are held on Monday evenings of each week. The literary exercises consist of orations, debates, and essays.

The Zetecalian.

This society was organized in 1863 for the women of the College. Its exercises consist of debates, essays, historical narrations, and general discussions. Regular meetings are held fortnightly on Friday afternoons. The officers are elected quarterly.

Lombard Oratorical and Debating Association.

The Lombard Oratorical and Debating Association is the local branch of the Northern Illinois Intercollegiate Oratorical League. The League holds an annual prize contest in oratory on the last Friday in April. There are two prizes of twenty and ten dollars respectively. The local organization holds a preliminary contest to decide who shall represent the college in the contest of the League. All male students of the College are eligible for membership.

Greek Letter Societies.

Lombard College admits several of the leading College Greek letter secret Societies and Sororities. But no student is permitted to join any of these, nor to be pledged to them until said student has attained acceptable standing in one of the regular College classes and expressed full determination to work for a College degree. These societies are for College men and women only. Students taking work only in the Preparatory, Music, Art, Domestic Science, or Commercial Departments are not eligible.

PRIZES.

1. The Swan Prizes.

Two prizes for excellence in Oratory are offered annually by Mrs. J. H. Swan, of Chicago. They consist of fifteen dollars and ten dollars respectively. The contest for these prizes is held in February.

2. The Townsend Prizes.

Two prizes for excellence in Declamation, established by the late Mrs. E. P. Townsend, are offered annually. They consist of fifteen dollars and ten dollars respectively. The contest for these prizes is held during Commencement week.

EXPENSES.

Board in College Commons, 37 weeks.............................$ 92.50	
Incidentals, three terms, at $5 per term............................	15.00
Tuition, one year, taking usual number of studies...................	36.00
Room rent, one year..	22.50
Washing, one year...	15.00
Books, one year...	15.00

$196.00

Students, however, are not required to board at the Commons; some board themselves, and some board in private families. Students who board themselves may possibly cut their expenses a trifle below the above rates. In private families rates of from $2.75 and upwards per week for board, may be obtained.

Board and Rooms in Ladies' Hall.

Board for 37 weeks at $3.50 per week.............................$129.50
Room rent, paid by each girl, two in a room, according to location of
room, per year...$27.00 to $54.00

Where one person occupies a double room from choice, an extra charge of fifty cents per week will be made, but the privilege of assigning two persons to such room is reserved.

Tuition and Incidentals.

Students in the College of Liberal Arts and Unclassified students will pay a tuition fee for each study pursued. The charge, except in theoretical music and art is $4.00 per term for each full course, a course being a study taken for one term and counting as one credit toward graduation. The rate for each fractional course is in proportion to the credit allowed for such fractional course toward graduation. Thus, a half course is half rate; a third course, third rate, etc.

Students in Chemistry, Mineralogy, and History, are required to deposit with the Registrar a sum sufficient to cover laboratory bills. Students in General Chemistry will deposit two dollars; students in Analytical Chemistry, five dollars; students in Mineralogy, three dollars; students in Histology, five dollars; students in Osteology, ten dollars each. At the close of the term there will be returned the balance remaining, after deducting cost of chemicals and broken apparatus.

Regular term fees are charged in each of the following laboratory courses: in Physics, two dollars; in Anatomy, five dollars; in Biology, two dollars; in Physiology, two dollars; in Zoology, two dollars; and in Botany, two dollars.

The charge for incidentals, to be paid by all students of the College, is $5.00 per term.

No students will be enrolled in any class until they present the Registrar's receipt for the payment of tuition and incidentals. The registration fee is one dollar. The payment of this fee will be remitted to all who register on the first day of the term. For any change in registration not advised by the faculty a fee of one dollar will be charged.

Tuition and incidentals will not be refunded. In case a student is absent a half term or more from sickness or other adequate cause, a certificate for a half term's tuition and incidentals will be given the student (at his request), said certificate good "to order" for its face value at any succeeding term.

Music and Art.

For information as to charges in Music and Art, see under these departments later in this Catalogue.

SCHOLARSHIPS.

High School Scholarships.

For the purpose of broadening the opportunities of young men and women for college training, Lombard College offers a limited number of scholarships to students graduating with high rank from High schools and Academies. For further information apply to the Dean.

Endowed Scholarships.

Through the generosity of its friends the College is enabled to offer assistance to worthy students desiring to secure an education. The income of endowed scholarships is applied toward paying the tuition of a limited number.

Sixteen Endowed scholarships of $1,000 each have been founded by the following named persons:

The F. R. E. Cornell Scholarship, by Mrs. E. O. Cornell.
The George B. Wright Scholarship, by Mrs. C. A. Wright.
The George Power Scholarship, by George and James E. Power.
The Mrs. Emma Mulliken Scholarship, by Mrs. Emma Mulliken.
The Clement F. LeFevre Scholarship, by William LeFevre and Mrs. Ellen R. Coleman.
The Samuel Bowles Scholarship, by Samuel Bowles.
The Dollie B. Lewis Scholarship, by Mrs. Dollie B. Lewis.
The O. B. Ayres Scholarship, by O. B. Ayres.
The Mary Chapin Perry Scholarship, by T. T. Perry.
The C. A. Newcombe Scholarship by C. A. Newcombe.
The Mary W. Conger Scholarship, by the children of Mrs. Mary W. Conger.

The Hattie A. Drowne Scholarship, by Rev. E. L. Conger, D. D.
The A. R. Wolcott Scholarship, by A. R. Wolcott.
The Women's Association Scholarship, by the Universalist Women's Association of Illinois.
The Calista Waldron Slade Scholarship, by E. D. Waldron and sisters.
The Mary L. Pingrey Scholarship, by Mrs. Mary L. Pingrey.

CATALOGUES.

Former students of the College, whether graduates or not, are requested to inform the Dean of any change of residence in order that the publications of the College may be sent them. Catalogues and circulars of information will promptly be sent to those who apply for them.

DISCIPLINE AND SOCIAL POLICY.

Aside from a few obvious regulations, designed to secure punctuality and regularity in attendance on College exercises, and to protect students and teachers from disturbance while at work, no formal rules are imposed upon the students.

It is expected that, as young men and women of somewhat mature years, they will observe the usual forms of good breeding, and enjoy the ordinary privileges of good society in so far as the latter do not conflict with the best interests of the institution or with their own health and intellectual advancement.

Should any student show a disposition to engage in conduct detrimental to his own best interests, or to those of his fellow students or of the College, the faculty will deal with the case in such manner as will protect the common welfare of all.

OFFICERS OF THE COLLEGE.

LEWIS BEALS FISHER, D. D., PRESIDENT.

Professor Canton Theological School, 1891-1905; D. D., St. Lawrence University, 1901; President Lombard College, 1905—.

FREDERICK WILLIAM RICH, D. Sc.

DEAN OF THE COLLEGE OF LIBERAL ARTS.

*Conger Professor of Chemistry and Physics.

B. S., Cornell University, 1881; Graduate Student, Cornell University, 1881; D. Sc., St. Lawrence University, 1900; Instructor in Analytical Chemistry, Cornell University, 1882-84; Professor of Natural Science, Lombard College, 1884-1900; Professor of Chemistry and Physics, 1900—.

ISAAC AUGUSTUS PARKER, A. M., PH. D.

†Williamson Professor of the Greek Language and Literature.

A. B., Dartmouth College, 1853; A. M., ibid, 1856; Ph. D., Buchtel College, 1892; Principal Orleans Liberal Institute, Glover, Vt., 1853-58; Professor of Ancient Languages, Lombard University, 1858-1868; Professor of Greek Language and Literture, Lombard College, 1868—.

‡Hall Professor of Intellectual and Moral Philosophy.

[At present unoccupied.]

PHILIP GREEN WRIGHT, A. M.,

Professor of Mathematics, Astronomy, and Economics.

A. M. B., Tufts College, 1884; A. M., Harvard University, 1887; Teacher of Mathematics and Science, Goddard Seminary, Vt., 1883; Adjunct Professor of Mathematics, Buchtel College, 1884-86, Professor of Mathematics, Lombard College, 1892—.

FRANK HAMILTON FOWLER, PH. D.,

Professor of Latin Language and Literature.

A. B., Lombard University, 1890: Ph. D., The University of Chicago, 1896; Graduate Student, Johns Hopkins University, 1890-91; Principal Peaster Academy, 1891-92; Fellow in the University of Chicago, 1892-96; Professor of English, Lombard College, 1897-1903; Professor Latin Language and Literature, Lombard College, 1903—.

RALPH GRIERSON KIMBLE, A. B.,

Professor of Social Science and Philosophy.

A.B., Lombard College, 1896; University Scholar in Sociology, University of Chicago, 1896-97; Senior Fellow in Sociology ibid., 1897-1901; Special Lecturer in Sociology, Lombard College, Spring term, 1899; ibid., 1900; Special Lecturer in Sociological Theory, University of Wisconsin, Spring of 1902, Professor of Sociology, Lombard College, 1901—.

---

*In honor of the late L. E. Conger, of Dexter, Iowa.
†In honor of the late I. D. Williamson, D. D., of Cincinnati.
‡In honor of the late E. G. Hall, of Chicago.

EDSON REIFSNIDER, B. D.,

Instructor in Homiletics and Pastoral Care.

B. D. Tufts College, 1898; Instructor in Homiletics and Pastoral Care, Lombard College, 1903—.

CHARLES ORVAL APPLEMAN, B. E., B. P., Ph. B.,

Physical Director and Professor of Biology.

B. E., Bloomsburg Literary Institute and State Normal School, 1897; B. P., ibid., 1898; Chautauqua School of Physical Culture, 1898; Department of Physical Training, Bloomsburg Literary Institute and State Normal School, 1898-99; Ph. B., Dickinson College, 1903; Director of Gymnastics Dickinson College, 1899-1903; Member of foot-ball, basket-ball, and track teams Dickinson College; Instructor in Biology and Physical Training, Swarthmore Preparatory School, 1903-1904; Student in Biology, University of Chicago, 1904; Physical Director and Professor of Biology, Lombard College, 1904—.

LOUISE MALLINCKRODT KUEFFNER, A. M.

Professor of German and French.

A. B., A. M., Washington University, 1896; Student at the University of Berlin, 1896-98; Student and Reader at the University of Chicago, 1901-03. Instructor of German in Mary Institute, St. Louis; Norwich Free Academy, Norwich, Conn.; Professor of German and French at Oxford College, Oxford, Ohio; Instructor of German in the Correspondence Department of the University of Chicago; Prof. of German and French, Lombard College, 1904—.

EMMA REEME APPLEMAN, Ph. B.

Instructor in History.

Ph. B., Dickinson, 1902; Instructor in History, Lombard College, 1905—.

FRANK A. POWER.

Director of Conservatory of Music.

INSTRUCTOR IN VOICE.

Studied at Moores Hill College, DePauw University, College of Music of Cincinnati, and in Berlin, Germany. Three years at Tiffin, Ohio; six years at Mansfield, Ohio, as Supervisor of Public School Music, Private teaching chorus and choir directing; Director of Power College of Music, Davenport, Iowa; Director Lombard Conservatory of Music, 1905—.

HATTIE R. HEIN, B. M.

Instructor in Piano and Violin.

Graduate Chicago Musical College, 1901; Post-graduate, 1902; Pupil of Arthur Freidheim, Rudolph Ganz, Wm. H. Sherwood, in piano; of Dr. Falk and Felix Borowski, in harmony, counterpoint, and composition; of Joseph T. Ohlheiser, and Leon Marx, in Violin; Instructor in Piano and Violin, Lombard College, 1905—.

MRS. HARRIET BEECHER DUDLEY,
In charge of Department of Domestic Science.

JOHN WEIGEL,
Assistant in Mathematics.

ETHEL MARY CHAMBERLAIN,
FLORENCE DILLOW,
Assistants in English.

THEO. GOLLIDAY,
Assistant in French.

RALPH MARSHALL ATTERBERRY,
Assistant in Chemistry.

MRS. ADAH M. HALE,
Matron Ladies' Hall.

Dr. GUY A. LONGBRAKE and Dr. DELIA M. RICE,
Medical Examiners.

NON-RESIDENT LECTURERS, 1906-1907.
Rev. W. H. McGlauflin, D. D.,
Rev. Effie K. McCollum Jones,
Rev. I. M. Atwood, D. D.,
Rev. George A. Sohlin,
Rev. T. B. Thayer Fisher,
Hon. W. C. Harris.

FRANK HAMILTON FOWLER, Ph. D.,
Librarian.

JON WATSON GRUBB, M. S.,
Registrar.

CHARLES O. APPLEMAN,
Director of the Gymnasium.

ALLEN HARSHBARGER,
Janitor.

Standing Faculty Committees.

ADVISORY—
PROFESSORS WRIGHT AND CURTIS.

ACCREDITING—
PROFESSORS KIMBLE, WRIGHT AND FOWLER.

HOMES AND EMPLOYMENT FOR STUDENTS—
PROFESSORS WRIGHT AND FOWLER.

CATALOGUE—
PROFESSORS WRIGHT AND FOWLER.

ATHLETICS—
PROFESSORS KIMBLE AND APPLEMAN.

ORDER AND DISCIPLINE—
DEAN RICH AND PROFESSOR CURTIS.

Departments of the College.

Students at Lombard are divided primarily into Classified and Unclassified students.

The Classified department includes all students who are candidates for a degree or diploma. It embraces the College of Liberal Arts, the Divinity School, and the Departments of Music and Art.

The Unclassified students include those who are pursuing studies at Lombard for a greater or less period, without any express intention of obtaining a degree or diploma.

COLLEGE OF LIBERAL ARTS.

Faculty of Liberal Arts.

LEWIS BEALS FISHER, D. D., PRESIDENT.

FREDERICK WILLIAM RICH, D. Sc.
*Dean and Conger Professor of Chemistry and Physics.

ISAAC AUGUSTUS PARKER, A. M., PH. D.,
Williamson Professor of the Greek Language and Literature.

PHILIP GREEN WRIGHT, A. M.,
Professor of Mathematics, Astronomy, and Economics.

FRANK HAMILTON FOWLER, PH. D.,
Professor of the Latin Language and Literature.

RALPH GRIERSON KIMBLE, A. B.,
Professor of Sociology.

ALICE BERTHA CURTIS, B. DI., PH. B.,
Professor of English and Public Speaking.

CHARLES ORVAL APPLEMAN, B. E., B. P., PH. B.,
Physical Director and Professor of Biology.

LOUISE MALLINCKRODT KUEFFNER, A. M.,
Professor of German and French.

EMMA REEME APPLEMAN, PH. B.,
Instructor in History.

honor of the late L. E. Conger, of Dexter, Iowa.
honor of the late I. D. Williamson, D. D., of Cincinnati.

Requirements for Admission.

All applicants for admission to the College of Liberal Arts are required to furnish evidence of proficiency in studies selected from the following list, to an aggregate of fifteen units:

The word unit as used in this catalogue means the equivalent of a year's work in an accredited high school in a study reciting five hours a week in recitation periods of not less than forty minutes.

STUDY	UNITS.	STUDY	UNITS.
English	3	Physics	1
Greek	3	Chemistry	1
Latin	3	Physiography	½ to 1
German	1	Physiology	½ to 1
French	1	Botany	½ to 1
Ancient History	1	Astronomy	1
English and American History	1	Meterology	1
Algebra	1½	Political Economy	½ to 1
Plane Geometry	½ to 1	Zoology	½ to 1
Solid Geometry	½ to 1		

CONSTANTS.

The studies presented must include the following constants:

STUDIES.	UNITS.
English	3
One Foreign Language	3
History	1
Algebra	1½
Geometry	½
Science	2

The two units in Science, one of which must include laboratory work, may be chosen from the following, viz: Physics, Chemistry, Physiography, Anatomy and Physiology, Botany, Zoology.

ADMISSION BY EXAMINATION.

For such applicants for admission to the College of Liberal Arts as do not present certificates from approved schools, examinations will be held in the above mentioned subjects, on Tuesday, September 4, 1906.

Applicants wishing to take these examinations should notify the Dean in advance, stating explicitly in what subjects examinations are desired.

ADMISSION BY CERTIFICATE.

Certificates from the principals or other authorized officers of certain approved High. Schools and Academies will be accepted in lieu of examinations. No certificate will be valid for more than two years after the completion of the course of study to which the certificate refers.

The number of units allowed upon such a certificate will be based upon the definition of a "unit" given on the preceding page, but the detailed descriptions given below. indicate more fully the amount of work required in each study to obtain the number of units given in the table. Students admitted by certificate enter classes on probation, and if it is found that their previous training is insufficient to render it advisable for them to continue in these classes, they will be assigned other work.

SCOPE OF PREPARATORY STUDIES.

The amount of work required in the several Preparatory studies to obtain the units assigned in the foregoing table, either by examination or certificate, is indicated by the following outline of examination requirements:

ENGLISH.

The examination will occupy two hours and will consist of two parts, which, however, cannot be taken separately:—

I. The candidate will be required to write a paragraph or two on each of several topics chosen by him from a considerable number —perhaps ten or fifteen—set before him on the examination paper.

In 1906, the topics will be drawn from the following works.

Shakespeare's Merchant of Venice, and Julius Caesar; The Sir Roger de Coverley Papers in the Spectator; Goldsmith's Vicar of Wakefield; Coleridge's Ancient Mariner; Scott's Ivanhoe; Carlyle's Essay on Burns; Tennyson's Princess; Lowell's Vision of Sir Launfal; George Eliot's Silas Marner.

The candidate is expected to read intelligently *all* the books prescribed. He should read them as he reads other books; he is expected, not to know them minutely, but to have freshly in mind their most important parts. In every case the examiner will regard knowledge of the book as less important than ability to write English.

II. A certain number of books are prescribed for careful study. This part of the examination will be upon subject-matter, literary form and logical structure, and will also test the candidate's ability to express his knowledge with clearness and accuracy.

The books prescribed for this part of the examination in 1906 are: Shakespeare's Macbeth; Milton's Lycidas, Comus, L'Allegro, and Il Penseroso; Burke's speech on Conciliation with America; Macaulay's Essays on Milton and Addison.

No candidate will be accepted in English whose work is seriously defective in point of spelling, punctuation, grammar, or division into paragraphs.

In connection with the reading and the study of the prescribed books, parallel or subsidiary reading should be encouraged, and a considerable amount of English poetry should be committed to memory. The essentials of English grammar should not be neglected in preparatory study.

The English written by a candidate in any of his examination-books may be regarded as part of his examination in English, in case the evidence afforded by the examination-book in English is insufficient.

As additional evidence of preparation the candidate may present an exercise book, properly certified by his instructor, containing compositions or other written work.

FRENCH.

(a) The translation at sight of ordinary Nineteenth Century prose. (The passages set for translation must be rendered into simple and idiomatic English.)

(b) The translation into French of simple English sentences or of easy connected prose, to test the candidate's familiarity with elementary grammar. Proficiency in grammar may also be tested by direct questions, based on the passages set for translation under *(a)*.

The passages set for translation into English will be suited to the proficiency of candidates who have read not less than four hundred pages (including reading at sight in class) from the works of at least three different authors. It is desirable that a portion of the reading should be from works other than works of fiction.

Grammar should be studied concurrently with the reading as an indispensable means of insuring thoroughness and accuracy in the understanding of the language. The requirement in elementary grammar includes the conjugations of regular verbs, of the more frequent irregular verbs, such as *aller, envoyer, tenir, pouvoir, voir, vouloir, dire, savior, faire,* and those belonging to the classes represented by *ouvrir, dormir, connaitre, conduire,* and *craindre;* the forms and positions of personal pronouns and of possessive, demonstrative, and interrogative adjectives; the inflection of nouns and adjectives for gender and number, except rare cases; the uses of articles, and the partitive constructions.

Pronunciation should be carefully taught, and pupils should have frequent opportunities to hear French spoken or read aloud. The writing of French from dictation is recommended as a useful exercise.

GERMAN.

(a) The translation at sight of simple German prose. (The passages set for translation must be rendered into simple and idiomatic English.)

(b) The translation into German of simple English sentences, or of easy connected prose, to test the candidate's familiarity with elementary grammar.

The passages set for translation into English will be suited to the proficiency of candidates who have read not less than two hundreu pages of easy German (including reading at sight in class.)

Grammar should be studied concurrently with the reading as an indispensible means of insuring thoroughness and accuracy in the understanding of the language. The requirement in elementary grammar includes the conjugation of the weak and the more usual strong verbs; the declension of articles, adjectives, pronouns and such nouns as are readily classified; the commoner prepositions; the simpler uses of the modal auxiliaries; the elements of syntax, especially the rules governing the order of words.

Pronunciation should be carefully taught, and the pupils should have frequent opportunities to hear German spoken or read aloud. The writing of German from dictation is recommended as a useful exercise.

LATIN.

The examination in Latin will consist of two parts.

I. Elementary Latin.

This examination will be designed to test the proficiency of those who have studied Latin in the high school for two years, and will count as two admission units. The student should have read at least four books of the Gallic War or an equivalent. The examination will include:—

(a) Translation at sight of Latin prose, with questions on ordinary forms, constructions, and idioms of the language.

(b) The translation into Latin of English sentences involving a knowledge of the more common words and constructions used by Cæsar.

II. Advanced Latin.

This examination will be designed to test the proficiency of those who have studied Latin in the high school for four years and together with (I) will count as four admission units. In preparation for this examination the candidate should have read, besides the four books of Cæsar mentioned under (I), at least six orations of Cicero and six books of Vergil's Æneid, and should have had considerable practice in reading at sight and in Latin composition. The examination will include:

(a) Translation at sight of passages of Latin prose and hexameter verse, with questions on ordinary forms, constructions, and idioms, and the principles of Latin verse.

(b) The translation into Latin prose of a passage of connected English narrative, limited in subject matter to the works usually read in preparation.

MATHEMATICS.

Algebra. The examination in Algebra will demand accuracy in the several processes of literal Arithmetic. Special emphasis will be laid on factoring, and the correct manipulation of negative and fractional exponents. It will include the solution of simple and quadratic equations (together with a knowledge of the theory of quadratic equations), elimination in the case of simultaneous equations of the first and second degrees, variation, and Arithmetical and Geometrical progression.

Plane Geometry. The examination in Plane Geometry will emphasize precision in the definition of Geometric terms, and accuracy in the demonstration of Geometric theorems. In scope it will demand a knowledge of all the propositions in Plane Geometry preceding Solid Geometry, included in such a standard text-book in this subject as Phillips and Fisher's Elements.

Solid Geometry. As in Plane Geometry emphasis will be laid upon accuracy in definition and demonstration. In scope the examination will cover the propositions in Solid Geometry included in such a standard text book as Phillips and Fisher's Elements.

ASTRONOMY.

The examination in this subject will demand knowledge of descriptive rather than mathematical Astronomy. The student will be expected to understand the theory of the celestial sphere, simple methods of computing latitude, time, and longitude; the astronomical features of the earth, the sun, and the moon; the principles of spectrum analysis; the motions and characteristics of the planets; the names and myths of the principal stars and constellations; the facts in regard to abberation, parallax, and proper motion of the stars; and the principles of a rational cosmogony as developed in LaPlace's nebular hypothesis. Young's Lessons in Astronomy is suggested as a text book embracing the matter with which students are expected to be acquainted who wish to prepare for this examination.

PHYSICS.

Students offering Physics for entrance credit must show an acquaintance with the more important phenomena and with the principles involved in the explanation of them. They must, in addition to the text book work, have completed a course of laboratory experiments and be able to work simple numerical problems, involving the laws of falling bodies; pendulum; properties of liquids and gases; thermometry and calorimetry; current strength, resistance, and electromotive force; properties of sound, refraction and reflection with the size and position of images.

CHEMISTRY.

The Elementary Course in Chemistry offered for entrance credit must include knowledge of the elements and compounds equivalent to that given in Remsen's Introduction to the study of Chemistry. In addition, students must have had a series of laboratory experiments illustrating the text book work and be able to write equations and solve simple chemical problems.

BOTANY.

Students presenting work in Botany for entrance credit should have a knowledge of the general laws and fundamental principles of plant nutrition, assimilation, growth, etc., as exemplified by plants chosen from the different groups, as well as the general comparative morphology and the broader relationships of plants. They should present an herbarium of at least twenty-five specimens, collected and mounted by themselves and certified to by their instructor.

ZOOLOGY.

Students desiring entrance credit for Zoology should have devoted the equivalent of five periods a week for at least one-half year to the study of general Zoology. A portion of this work must have been laboratory practice in the observation of living forms and dissection. Their laboratory notes and drawings, endorsed by the instructor, should be presented at the time of registration as evidence of the nature of this part of the work. This laboratory practice should include a study of at least twelve of the forms named in the following list: Amœba, paramœcium, sea-anemone, starfish, sea-urchin, earth worm, cray-fish, lobster, spider, centipede, locust, (grass-hopper), dragon-fly, squash-bug, bumblebee, clam, snail, a simple tunicate, shark, any soft rayed-fish, snake, turtle, frog, pigeon, rabbit, and cat.

PHYSIOLOGY.

Students presenting work in human Physiology for entrance credit should have a general knowledge of the human skeleton, muscular, circulatory, and nervous systems, the vital organs, viscera, and organs of special sense, and the processes of respiration and digestion.

The text-book used should cover the ground treated in such books as Martin's Human body, or Huxley's Elementary Physiology (Lee's Revision).

PHYSIOGRAPHY.

A course of study equivalent to Tarr's Elementary Physical Geography.

The examination will include a thorough test on all the leading subjects treated in Physical Geography, with maps to illustrate relief forms, currents, ocean beds, and the distribution of animal and plant life.

HISTORY (including Historical Geography).

Either of the two following groups each including two fields of historical study:—

1. *Greek and Roman History.*—*(a)* Greek History to the death of Alexander, with due reference to Greek life, literature, and art. *(b)* Roman History to the downfall of the Western Roman Empire, with due reference to literature and government.

2. *English and American History.*—*(a)* English History, with due reference to social and political development. *(b)* American History, with the elements of Civil Government.

For preparation in each of the two historical fields presented, a course of study equivalent to at least five lessons a week for one year will be necessary.

The candidate will be expected to show on examination such general knowledge of each field as may be acquired from the study of an accurate text-book of not less than 300 pages, supplemented by suitable parallel readings amounting to not less than 500 pages. The examination will call for comparison of Historical characters, periods, and events, and in general for the exercise of judgment as well as memory. Geographical knowledge will be tested by means of an outline map.

It is desirable that Greek and Roman be offered as a part of the preparation of every candidate.

POLITICAL ECONOMY.

The examination in Political Economy will demand a thorough knowledge of the fundamental economic laws relating to Production, Exchange, Distribution, and Consumption. The applicant will also be expected to discuss intelligently from an economic standpoint such questions as Free Trade, Socialism, Strikes, and Taxation. Bullock's Introduction to the study of Economics is suggested as a text covering the ground required for the examination.

ADMISSION TO ADVANCED STANDING.

Students from other institutions, who present letters of honorable dismissal, may be admitted to such standing and upon such terms as the Faculty may deem equitable. Every such student is required to present, along with the catalogue of the institution in which he has studied, a full statement, duly certified, of the studies he has completed, including preparatory studies. Candidates for advanced standing who wish to receive credit for work accomplished in private study, are permitted to take examinations in such subjects upon payment of the regular term fee for the course in which the examination is taken.

Requirements for Graduation.

GROUP SYSTEM.

Having been admitted to the College of Liberal Arts, the student will elect one of the following groups as a course of study leading to his degree. It is the purpose of these groups so to arrange the course of study that every graduate of Lombard College will at least have come in contact with all the great divisions into which human knowledge is divided. Language, Science, Philosophy, and Mathematics. To effect this end all of the groups are made nearly the same the first year, diverging from this point and permitting the student to specialize to some extent in that direction which represents the peculiar bent of his mind. All the required studies, together with a sufficient number of electives to bring the total up to an aggregate of thirty-eight credits must be completed before the degree will be conferred. A credit is obtained by the satisfactory completion of one full course pursued for one term. Of the thirty-eight credits at least twenty-four must be above grade C. Two credits may be obtained by two full years' work in the Gymnasium classes.

THESIS.

In addition to the above requirements, every student who is a candidate for a degree, or a diploma, will present a graduation thesis upon some subject in which he or she has prosecuted original research or special study.

The subject of the thesis is to be approved by the professor under whose direction the work is to be done and by the advisory committee and is to be recorded as a part of the regular registration at the beginning of the fall term. The student will prepare monthly reports on the work done and these reports, approved by the professor, will be filed in the office of the President. At the end of the winter term the student will prepare a syllabus of the dissertation on the chosen subject, to be approved and filed as in the case of reports. Two weeks before commencement the student will present a dissertation embodying the results of his work, this dissertation to meet the approval of the faculty before recommendation for a degree is made.

For work done in preparing his thesis the student will receive college credits to such an extent as the professor in whose department the work is done shall deem him entitled. The number of credits received in this way, however, is not to exceed three.

RESIDENCE.

A minimum residence of the two terms next preceding the completion of the requirements for graduation, and a minimum of eight courses taken in this College, are required of all applicants for a baccalaureate degree.

ADVANCED DEGREE.

The degree of Master of Arts will be conferred upon graduates of his college or other institutions of equal rank, on the satisfactory completion of one year's residence work upon a course of study or research which shall have been submitted to and approved by the Faculty beyond the requirements for the baccalaureate degree. The candidate must present a thesis showing original research in the special line of study pursued.

GROUPS.

On being admitted to the College of Liberal Arts, each student who is a candidate for a degree, will elect one of these groups. The courses printed are those required in the group. Others sufficient to bring the student's aggregate of credits up to thirty-eight must be elected by the student with the advice and consent of the professors in charge of the group before the degree will be conferred.

I. Literary Group (Classical). Leading to **A**. B. degree.

Advisers in charge of the group, Prof. Parker and Prof. Fowler.

YEAR.	HOUR.	FALL TERM.	WINTER TERM.	SPRING TERM.
1st yr.	9:30 10:30 10:30 11:30 3:00	(5) Greek 1. (3) Latin 9. (2) English 5. (4) Math. 7. (2) Gymnasium.	(5) Greek 2. (3) Latin 11. (2) English 6. (4) Math. 8. (2) Gymnasium.	(5) Greek 3. (3) Latin 12. (2) English 7. (4) Math. 9. (2) Gymnasium.
2nd yr.	8:00 8:00 9:30 10:30 11:30 1:45	{ (5) German 1 or { (5) French 1. } (5) Chem. 1 or { (5) Astronomy. (3) Latin 13. (5) Greek 4.	{ (5) German 2 or { (5) French 2. } Chemistry 2 or { Biology. (3) Latin 14. (5) Greek 5.	{ (5) German 3 or { (5) French 3. { Chemistry 3 or { Biology. (3) Latin 15. (5) Greek 6.
3rd yr. and 4th yr.	Elective. except that the student must take one year of History, one year of Philosophy or Social Science, one additional year of Greek, unless Greek is presented for admission; and one additional year of German, if German is taken the second year.			

II. Literary Group (Modern). Leading to A. B degree.

Advisers in charge of the group, Prof. Curtis and Prof. Kueffner.

YEAR.	HOUR.	FALL TERM.	WINTER TERM.	SPRING TERM.
1st yr.	8:00 10:30 10:30 11:30 3:00	(5) German 1. (3) Latin 9 (2) English 5. (4) Math. 7. (2) Gymnasium.	(5) German 2. (3) Latin 11. (2) English 6. (4) Math. 8. (2) Gymnasium.	(5) German 3. (3) Latin 12. (2) English 7. (4) Math. 9. (2) Gymnasium.
2nd yr.	8:00 9:30 10:30	(5) English Lit. (5) Chemistry 1. (5) German 4, 19.	(5) English Lit. (5) Chemistry 2. (5) German 5, 20.	(5) English Lit. (5) Chemistry 3. (5) German 6, 21.
3rd and 4th years		Elective, except that the student must take one year of history, one year of Philosophy or Social Science, and is advised to take one year of French. A year in Astronomy and Biology may also be taken instead of the year's work in Chemistry prescribed in the second year		

III. Social Science and Philosophy Group. Leading to A. B. degree.

Advisers in charge of the group, Prof. Wright and Prof. Kimble.

YEAR.	HOUR.	FALL TERM.	WINTER TERM.	SPRING TERM.
1st yr.	9:30 10:30 10:30 11:30 3:00	(5) History 12. (2) English 5. (3) Latin 9. (4) Math. 7. (2) Gymnasium.	(5) History 13. (2) English 6. (5) Latin 11. (4) Math. 8. (2) Gymnasium.	(5) History 14. (2) English 7. (3) Latin 12. (4) Math. 8. (2) Gymnasium.
2nd yr.	9:30 11:30 10:30	(5) Sociology 1. (5) Psychology 1. (5) Astronomy 1.	(5) Sociology 2. (5) Psychology 2. (5) Biology.	(5) Sociology 3. (5) Psychology 3. (5) Biology.
3rd and 4th years		Elective except that the student must take two years of German or one year of French, and one year of Economics. A year in Chemistry may also be taken instead of the Astronomy and Biology prescribed for the second year.		

IV. Science Group. Leading to B. S. degree.

Advisers in charge of the group, Prof Rich and Prof. Appleman.

YEAR.	HOUR.	FALL TERM.	WINTER TERM.	SPRING TERM.
1st yr.	9:30 10:30 10:30 11:30 3:00	(5) Chemistry 1. (3) Latin 9. (2) English 5. (4) Math. 7. Gymnasium.	(5) Chemistry 2. (3) Latin 11. (2) English 6. (4) Math. 8. Gymnasium.	(5) Chemistry 3. (3) Latin 12. (2) English 7. (4) Math. 9. Gymnasium.
2nd yr.	8:00 10:30 1:45	(5) German 1. (5) Astronomy 1. (5) Chemistry 4.	(5) German 2. (5) Biology (5) Chemistry 5.	(5) German 3. (5) Biology (5) Chemistry 6.
3rd yr. ·and 4th yr.		Elective, except that student must take one additional year of German, one year of History, and one year of Social Science or Philosophy.		

NOTES: The figures in parentheses prefixed to teach of the studies indicate the number of recitations per week. In the case of English 5, 6, and 7, there are, as indicated, two recitations, but the theme work to be done outside makes the course equivalent to a four hour course. The Laboratory courses in chemistry (4, 5, and 6) meet five times a week but each recitation period is two hours long.

In addition to the courses enumerated, a thesis is required during the Senior year from students in all the groups.

Courses of Instruction.

RECITATIONS AND CREDITS.

The following studies are classed as full courses or fractional courses, according to the estimated amount of work in each, and its value in fulfilling the requirements for graduation. Unless otherwise stated, a course.in any study consists of five hours of recitations or lectures, per week, for one term. Certain full courses, however, are given in three hours per week recitations. Laboratory courses require ten hours of work per week in the laboratory, in addition to a considerable amount of study outside. Certain other studies, as indicated in each case, count only as half courses, or less. It is intended to give each course during the year and term indicated. But the faculty reserves the right to make any change when it seems desirable to do so.

The general descriptions at the head of each department and the brief outline accompanying each course are designed to give in simple language the scope and purpose of the course to assist the student in making his elections.

The student is urged especially to notice the dependence of one course on another, so that in arranging his group, before electing any course, the prerequisite shall have been completed.

Regular recitations are held on Monday, Tuesday, Wednesday, Thursday and Friday of each week.

Courses in brackets will not be given in 1906-1907.

ENGLISH.

PROFESSOR ALICE B. CURTIS.

The study of English is considered of fundamental importance. For this reason thorough preparation in English is insisted on for admission to the College proper. The practical value of this study need hardly be mentioned. No matter what the occupation, there will be the necessity for expression, and this is to be obtained by the study of English. Closely related to this is the value attaching to the study as a preparation for other work of the College course. The ability to gather thought from the printed page rapidly and accurately, and the power of expression just mentioned, are prime requisites for the student. A peculiar value attaching to the study of English is that of correlating the studies of the curriculum, of making the college course more of a unit. History, Philosophy, Linguistics, Aesthetics, and Sociology may here find a common ground of meeting. As a corollary to this it may be said that English to an especial degree possesses the power of enlarging the student's mental horizon, of making a broader man of him. It is the aim of the department to utilize all these values of the study, and in order to do that to the full the endeavor is made so to foster a love of literature that the study will be pursued after the student has left college.

Primarily the object of the courses in English Composition, (5, 6, and 7,) is the acquiring on the part of the student the ability to write good English prose. It is believed, however, that the study properly pursued has a considerable disciplinary value. In these courses there is a minimum of theory and maximum of practice. The important principles are given in lectures; these principles are illustrated in the specimens of the writings of others; and the student is required to exemplify them in the preparation of daily and fortnightly themes. Courses 5 and 6 are required courses and, together with course 7' should be taken during the first year of college work.

· In the courses in English Literature emphasis is laid on criticism rather than on the history. An introduction is made to the several forms of literature, special attention being given to the chief representative authors of each department. One course is given in Old English and one in the History of the English Language. The courses dealing with the Literature and Language are arranged in a cycle covering three years. The student is enabled to specialize in this study to such a degree that he may without further preparation, undertake graduate work in the Universities.

5. Rhetoric and Composition.

Mondays, Wednesdays, and Fridays. Fall term Open to all college students.

6. The Forms of Discourse.

Mondays, Wednesdays, and Fridays. Winter term. Prerequisite, English 5.

7. The Forms of Discourse.

Mondays, Wednesdays, and Fridays. Spring term. Prerequisite, English 5.

19. Middle English.   (Two-fifths course.)

Lectures on the life and times of Chaucer. Chaucer's shorter poems and "Canterbury Tales" will form the basis of the work. Tuesdays and Thursdays. Fall term. Prerequisite, English 5.

20. English Essayists.   (Two-fifths course.)

A study of typical essays of Macaulay, DeQuincy, Carlyle, Burke, and Arnold, with special reference to style. Tuesdays and Thursdays. Winter term. Prerequisite, English 5.

21. The Novel.   (Two-fifths course.)

This art form will be considered. Some of the great novels of the Victorian age will be read and criticised. Tuesdays and Thursdays. Spring term. Prerequisite, English 5.

22. Art of Shakespeare.   (Three-fifths course.)

The elements of literary art as exemplified in Shakespeare. A detailed study of "Hamlet." Mondays, Wednesdays, and Fridays. Fall term. Prerequisite, English 5.

23. Art of Shakespeare.   (Three-fifths course.)

Detailed study of "King Lear." Mondays, Wednesdays, and Fridays. Winter term. Prerequisite, English 22.

24. Art of Shakespeare.   (Three-fifths course.)

"The Tempest," "As You Like It," "Antony and Cleopatra," "Julius Cæsar." Mondays, Wednesdays, and Fridays. Spring term. Prerequisite, English 22 and 23.

[25. History of English Literature to the time of Chaucer.]
(Two-fifths course.)
Tuesdays and Thursdays. Fall term. Prerequisite, English 5.

[26. History of English Literature from Chaucer to Shakespeare.]
(Two-fifths course.)
Tuesdays and Thursdays. Winter term. Prerequisite, English 5.

[27. History of English Literature from Shakespeare to Browning.]
(Two-fifths course.)
Tuesdays and Thursdays. Spring term. Prerequisite, English 26.

[28. Browning. (Three-fifths course.)]

Studies in the poems of Robert Browning. Mondays, Wednesdays, and Fridays. Fall term. Prerequisite, English 5.

[29. Tennyson. (Three-fifths course.)]

Studies in the shorter poems and "Idylls of the King." Mondays, Wednesdays, and Fridays. Winter term. Prerequisite, English 5.

[30. English and Scottish Ballads. (Three-fifths course.)]

The nature of ballad poetry together with reading and interpretation of selected ballads. Mondays, Wednesdays, and Fridays. Spring term. Prerequisite, English 5.

[31. American Literature. (Three-fifths course.)

A consideration of the representative prose writers of America. Mondays, Wednesdays, and Fridays. Fall term. Prerequisite, English 5.

[32. American Literature. (Three-fifths course.) !

A consideration of the representative poets of America. Mondays, Wednesdays, and Fridays. Winter term. Prerequisite, English 5.

[33. Milton · (Three-fifths course.)]

The shorter poems and "Paradise Lost," will be studied, Mondays, Wednesdays, and Fridays. Spring term. Prerequisite, English 5.

[34. Pre-Shakespearean Drama. (Two-fifths course.)]

A history of the English drama before the time of Shakespeare. Tuesdays and Thursdays. Fall term. Prerequisite, English 5.

[35. The Short Story. (Two-fifths course.]

Criticism of the best representative short stories of French, English, and American writers. The short story as an art form will be studied. Tuesdays and Thursdays. Winter term. Prerequisite, English 5, 6, and 7.

6. The Short Story. (Two-fifths course.)]

Practice in advanced composition. Short stories will be written by members of the class. Tuesdays and Thursdays. Spring term. Prerequisite, English 35.

[37. **Old English·** (Three-fifths course.)]

A study of the grammar of Old English and the relations between Old and Modern English. Time to be arranged.

GERMAN.

PROF. LOUISE MALLINCKRODT KUEFFNER.

In all the courses, translation from German into English is dispensed with as far as possible, and "free reproduction" into German, is constantly cultivated. The Hoelzel charts are used as a basis for grammar, vocabulary, and elementary conversation. A further aid to direct apprehension of both the spoken and written word is given in the conversation club which meets socially at certain intervals. Collateral reading of German texts supplements the class work. The aim of the course in German is in general to prepare the student for a comprehension of German individuality and literature as a part of general culture. It is aimed also to organize a German conversation club which meets at certain intervals·

1, 2, 3. First Year German·

Bierwirth's Abstract of Grammar; Newson's First German Book and German Reader; Wenkebach's Glueckauf. Talks on German geography, history, customs. The Volksmaerchen is studied in connection with an outline of Teutonic Mythology, Grimm's Maerchen. The Nibelungenlied read in translation. The Kunstmaerchen: Fouqué's Undine, Baumbach's Sommermaerchen, Seidel's Wintermaerchen, Keller's Legenden. Tales by Tieck and Hoffmann read in translation. Fall, Winter, and Spring terms. Open to all college students.

4*, 5* Modern Stories.

The Village Story, the Story of Society, the Historic Story. (Three-fifths courses).

The Village Story.: Stifter's Hardedorf, Rosegger's Waldschulmeister, Keller's Romeo and Julie auf dem Dorfe, etc. *The Story of Society:* Ludwig's Himmel und Erde, Freytag's Soll und Haben, Sudermann's Frau Sorge, Seidel's Leberecht Huehnchen, etc. *The Historic Story:* Meyer's Gustav Adolphs Page, Keller's Dietegen, Riehl's Fluch der Schoenheit, etc. Class and collateral

---

*These courses, which carry only three-fifths credit, are designed to be supplemented by German 13, 14, 15 and 19, 20, 21, which carry two-fifths credit. German 19, 20, 21 are required as part of the second year work in German in the modern literature course and are a prerequisite for German 7.

reading. Some literary analysis will be made. Mondays, Wednesdays and Fridays. Fall and Winter terms. Prerequisite, German 3.

6*. The Modern Drama. (Three-fifths course.)

Hauptmann's Versunkene Glocke, Hauptmann's Die Weber, Sundermann's Teja, etc. Class and collateral reading. Some literary analysis of the plays. Mondays, Wednesdays, and Fridays. Prerequisite, German 6.

7*. Goethe's Early Work. (Three-fifths course.)

Tendencies of the Storm and Stress. Goetz, Werther, Egmont, Faust I. Fall term. Mondays, Wednesdays, and Fridays. Prerequisite, German 6.

8*. Goethe's Later Work and His Lyrics. (Three-fifths course.)

Iphigenie. Tasso. Hermann and Dorothea. Study of Goethe's Lyrics in connection with the Volkslied. White's collection of Volkslieder. VonKlenze's German Lyrics. Selections from Faust II, and Wilhelm Meister. Winter term. Prerequisite, German 7.

9*. Schiller. (Three-fifths course.)

Wallenstein. Brant Von Messina. Wilhelm Tell. Shorter poems as given in Von Klenze's German Lyrics. Schiller's philosophical and aesthetic ideas. Spring term. Mondays, Wednesdays, and Fridays. Prerequisite, German 6.

[10*, 11. The Romantic School. (Three-fifths course.)]

Lectures and readings. Tieck, Novalis, Kleist, Werner, Brentano, Hoffmann, Fouqué, Eichendorff, Chamisso, Heine, Uhland. Mondays, Wednesdays, and Fridays. Fall and Winter terms. Prerequisite, German 6.

[12*. Later German Literature.]

Grillparzer, Hebbel, Ludwig, Auzengruber, etc. Wagner's Die Meistersaenger, Der Nibelungenring, studied in connection with his socialism, philosophy, and aesthetic theory. Modern Lyrics. Spring term. Prerequisite, German 6.

13, 14, 15. Review Grammar, Composition, Conversation. (Two-fifths courses.)

Free reproduction of tales and legends. Journalistic German. Newson's German Daily Life. Paskowsky's Lesebuch. Synonyms. Fall, Winter, and Spring terms. Prerequisite, German 6.

16, 17, 18. Middle High German.

Some study is made of Middle High German and the history of the German language. . Reading, grammar, and lectures. Once a week throughout the year. ·Prerequisite, German 6.

19, 20, 21. German Literature in English.

(Two-fifths course each term.)

The social, artistic, and literary history of Germany. Knowledge of German not required. Lectures, and collateral reading from standard translations and from histories of German literature. This course is designed to meet the wants not only of students of German, but also of any students who are interested in the development of the world's thought and art. Those phases of German literature are studied that have had influence on English and American thought and literature, or have come to form a part of universal culture. The entire study will be conducted from the point of-view of comparative literature.

In connection with the pagan period there will be a presentation of Teutonic mythology and such literary embodiments as the Edda.; Morris' Sigurd, the Volsung; Matthew Arnold's Balder Dead. For the mediæval period .Bryce's Holy Roman Empire, and such epics as the Nibelungenlied, Parzival, and Tristan and Isolde, with their background of Gothic art, will be studied. For the 16th century there will be a consideration of the Volkslied, and popular romances such as the legends of Faust and Till Eulenspiegel (with comparison of the English ballad and Marlowe's Faustus), and of the art of Duerer and Holbein.

Lessing's importance as critic, dramatist, and thinker will be considered. Goethe, the apostle of culture, called by Matthew Arnold, "The greatest poet, the clearest, the largest, the most helpful thinker," will be studied in detail, then Schiller, Heine, and others For later times Wagner's Operas will be studied, and finally the modern movement in such representatives as Hauptmann and Sudermann, including their master, the Norse Ibsen. Tuesdays and Thursdays, throughout the year. Open to all College students.

FRENCH.

In all the courses, translation from French into English is dispensed with as far as possible, and "free reproduction" is constantly cultivated. The Hoelzel charts are used as a basis for grammar, vocabulary, and elementary conversation. The aim of the course is in general to prepare the student for a comprehension of French individuality and literature as a part of general culture.

1. Grammar.

Bevier's French Grammar, Part I; Newson's First French Book; Guerber's Contes et Legendes. The fundamental forms of nouns, adjectives, and verbs, including irregular verbs, are presented early in the course. Fall term. Open to all College students.

2. Grammar: the Modern Comedy.

Bevier, Newson, continued. The modern comedy; Legouvé and Labiche's La Cigale chez les Fourmis; Pailleron's Le Monde ou l'on s'ennuie. Augier's Le Gendre de M. Poirier; Rostand's Les Romanesques. Winter term. Prerequisite, French 1.

3. Grammar: the Modern Story.

François's Composition,. The Modern Story; Daudet, Coppée, Maupassant Loti. Spring term. Prerequisite, French 2. .

[4, 5, 6. Review Grammar and Composition: The Classical Period.]
(Three-fifths Course.)

Review Grammar and Composition; Newson's French Daily Life. A study is made of the social, literary, and artistic life of the 17th Century. Corneille's Le Cid, Cinna. Theory of Classicism in the drama. Crane's La Société francaise au dix-septième siecle. Molière's Les Précieuses Ridicules, Le Bourgeois Gentilhomme, Le Misanthrope. Racine's Oreste, Britannicus, Athalie. Lafontaine's Fables. French Prose of the 17th Century. Prerequisite, French 3.

[7. The 18th Century. (Three-fifths course.)]

Beaumarchais Le Barbier de Seville, Voltaire's Zaire, Le Sage's Gil Blas, Prevost's Manon Lescaut, St. Pierre's Paul et Virginie. Influences of Rousseau, Diderot, and Voltaire. Fall term. Prerequisite, French 3. .

[8. The Development of French Romanticism.]
(Three-fifths Course.)

Influences of George Sand, Chateaubriand, Lamartine; Crane's Le Romantisme français, Hugo's Hernani, and Ruy Blas, De Musset's Trois Comédies. Winter term. Prerequisite, French 7.

[9. Outline History of French Literature. The Mediaeval Period.]
(Three-fifths course.

Chanson de Roland, Aucassin and Nicolette, Lays of Marie de France, etc., studied in translation. The 19th Century in its movements of naturalism and new romanticism. Balzac's Le Cure de Tours, Zola, Daudet, Maupassant, Loti, Rostand, Maeterlink. Spring term. Prerequisite, French 8.

[10, 11, 12. Mediaeval French Literature Read in the Original.]

Bartsch's Chrestomathy. History of the French language. Once a week throughout the year. Prerequisite, French 6.

LATIN.

PROF. FRANK H. FOWLER.

In general it will be expected that students taking the courses in Latin have obtained a fair degree of proficiency in reading the language. The work will, in the main, be literary. The object of the study will be acquaintance with Roman Literature, the influences that shaped it and its effects upon English Literature

(For courses 5 to 8 inclusive, which may be taken with College credit, see p. 57.)

9, 10, 12. Introduction to the Study of Roman Literature.

(Three-fifths course each term.)

The study will be both historical and critical. The student will become acquainted with the main outlines of the history and development of Roman Literature, the influences that went to make it what it was and is, and the relations between the literature and other departments of Roman life and civilization. Especially will be noted the influence of the literature of the Romans upon our own. The principles of literary criticism will be stated and illustrated in the specimens read. In translation care will be taken to improve the student's literary style. So far as possible the study will be illustrated by photographs and prints of Greek and Roman Art and Antiquities. Such selections from the writings of the more important Latin authors will be read as will furnish the best basis for the study outlined. The student will also be called upon to read certain specimens of English Literature as illustrations of the classical impulse. Lectures, recitations, and reports. Fall, winter, and spring terms. Open to students who have a fair reading knowledge of Latin.

13. Roman Comedy. (Three-fifths course.)

Several plays of Plautus and Terence will be read; the sources and history of Latin Comedy will be studied and the peculiarities of early Latin will be noted. Winter term. Prerequisite, Latin 12.

14. Prose Literature of the Silver Age. (Three-fifths course.)

The Agricola of Tacitus and selected letters of Pliny will be read. The history of the Literature of the Silver Age will be studied. Spring term. Prerequisite, Latin 12.

15. Roman Lyric Poetry. (Three-fifths course.)

The poems of Horace, Catullus, and others will be read. The influences exerted upon those authors, the characteristics of their genius, and their relation to their times will be studied. Fall term. Prerequisite, Latin 12.

[**16. Roman Satire.** (Three-fifths course.)]

The Satires of Horace will be read, together with the extant fragments of the Satires of Ennius, Pacuvius, Lucilius, and Varro, and the history of Roman Satire will be studied. Fall term. Prerequisite, Latin 12.

[**17. Roman Satire.** (Three-fifths course.)]

The Satires of Juvenal with selections from Martial and Persius will be read. The private life of the Romans will be studied. Winter term. Prerequisite, Latin 12.

[**18. Cicero, Brutus, Quintilian, Book X.** (Three-fifths course.)]

The books will be read as a study in literary criticism among the Romans. Spring term. Prerequisite, Latin 12.

[**19. Lucretius.** (Three-fifths course.)]

A study of the De Rerum Natura from literary and philosophical standpoints. Fall term. Prerequisite, Latin 12.

[**20. Roman History.** (Three-fifths course.)]

Selections from the Annals and Histories of Tacitus will be read and the work of the more important Roman historians will be reviewed and compared. Winter term. Prerequisite, Latin 12.

[**21. Cicero. Selected Letters.** (Three-fifths course.)]

As many as possible of the letters will be read and studied with special reference to the light which they shed on Roman History and Roman political institutions. Spring term. Prerequisite, Latin 12.

GREEK.

PROFESSOR ISAAC A. PARKER.

It is the purpose in this department to give the student the ability to read understandingly the writings of the Greek authors and to enter into their spirit, and, also, to give him a general acquaintance with Greek literature. A correct translation gains no credit for a student, if upon questioning it is found that he has not a knowledge of words and constructions and has evidently obtained his translation from notes or some other source.

Approved English sentences are required in translation, and where the literal is not allowable in English, the student is expected to know the construction in the Greek, and to render into idiomatic English.

The student is required to present an essay on each work read, stating its scope and the peculiarities of its style, and giving a brief biography of its author.

Frequent reference is made to a dictionary of Classical Antiquities to elucidate allusions to the mythology and the manners and customs of the Ancient Greeks.

Much attention is paid to the derivation and composition of words, and English words derived from the Greek are noted.

Instruction is carefully given in the principles of accent, and from the beginning, in writing Greek exercises, students are required to be careful to accent correctly.

The student who meets the requirements in this department, not only learns to read with pleasure and profit the language which he is studying, but, what is more, he acquires a mental discipline and a habit of carefulness and accuracy which will aid him in the business of life. The discipline of mind and the knowledge which he gains will greatly assist him in other studies, especially those of the sciences and medicine, since the terms with which he will meet in these studies are to a great extent derived from the Greek.

1. Grammar and Lessons.

Boise and Pattengill's Greek Lessons. Goodwin's Greek Grammar. Fall term. Open to all college students.

2. Grammar and Lessons. (Continued.)

Winter term. Prerequisite, Greek 1.

3. Anabasis.

Goodwin's Xenophon's Anabasis. Collar and Daniell's Greek Composition. Spring term. Prerequisite, Greek 2.

4. Anabasis. (Continued.)

Collar and Daniell's Greek Composition. Fall term. Prerequisite, Greek 3.

5. Iliad.

Seymour's Edition. Winter term. Prerequisite, Greek 4.

6. Iliad.

Seymour's Edition. Spring term. Prerequisite, Greek 5.

7. Orations of Lysias.

Stevens's Edition. Fall term. Prerequisite, Greek 6.

[8. Plato's Apology to Socrates.]

Kitchell's Edition. Winter term. Prerequisite, Greek 6.

9. Prometheus of Aeschylus.

Wecklein's Edition. Spring term. Prerequisite, Greek 6.

[10. Odyssey.]

Merry's Homer's Odyssey. Fall term. Prerequisite, Greek 6.

11. Plato's Gorgias.

Lodge's Edition. Winter term. Prerequisite, Greek 6.

[12. Medea of Euripides.]

Allen's Edition. Spring term. Prerequisite, Greek 6.

13, 14, 15, 16. Greek New Testament.

These classes while primarily intended for theological students, are also open to College students who have the requisite preparation. A full description is given in the Divinity School Courses Prerequisite, Greek 4.

BOOKS OF REFERENCE.

The following books are recommended for reference to those pursuing the study of Greek.

Liddell and Scott's Greek Lexicon; Autenrieth's Homeric Dictionary; Long's, or Ginn & Co's. Classical Atlas; Anthon's or Smith's Classical Dictionary; Harper's Dictionary of Classical Literature and Antiquities; Smith's History of Greece; Goodwin's Greek Grammar; Goodwin's Greek Modes and Tenses.

MATHEMATICS.

PROFESSOR PHILIP G. WRIGHT.

The study of Mathematics is useful to the student in two ways: In the first place, it affords an admirable mental discipline, developing habits of precise thought and accurate statement. In the second place, as the necessary tool of the civil and electrical engineer, the architect, and all persons engaged in higher scientific work, it has a practical value to those intending to enter these professions.

It is the purpose of the department to keep these two objects steadily in view. Students are required to show their understanding of Mathematical principles and reasoning by rigid demonstrations, subject to the criticism of other members of the class. Problems are selected for solution which arise in the actual practice of surveying, engineering, physical research and the like.

Students who intend to enter any of the above mentioned professions may profitably take a large part of their work at Lombard, completing their courses in some technical school.

7. Solid Geometry.

This course is continuous with the courses in Plane Geometry ordinarily given in the High Schools and is open to all College students who have had such work. Fall term.

8. Higher Algebra.

This course assumes a thorough knowledge on the part of the student of Mathematics 4 and also some knowledge of Plane Geometry. It embraces the study of Series, Permutations and Combinations, Probability, and the Theory of Equations. Winter term. Prerequisites, Mathematics 4 and Mathematics 5.

9. Plane and Spherical Trigonometry.

This course includes the solution of trigonometric equations, the solution of plane and spherical triangles and problems involving an application of Trigonometry to Mensuration, Surveying, and Astronomy. Crockett's Plane and Spherical Trigonometry is used as a text book. Spring term. Prerequisite, Mathematics 8.

10. Analytic Geometry.

This course treats of the straight line, the conic sections, and higher plane curves. Fall term. Prerequisite, Mathematics 9.

11. Surveying and Leveling.

Field work and problems. Field work on Saturdays at the option of the instructor. Spring term. Prerequisite, Mathematics 9.

12. Differential Calculus.

Osborne's Differential Calcucus is used. Winter term. Prerequisite, Mathematics 10.

13. Integral Calculus.

Spring term. Prerequisite, Mathematics 12.

In addition to the foregoing courses, classes will be formed, when there is a sufficient demand on the part of advanced students, to pursue work in Descriptive Geometry, Quaternions, the solution of original problems in the Calculus, and in the study of infinitesimals, probability, elliptic functions, life insurance, and other topics.

ASTRONOMY.

PROFESSOR PHILIP G. WRIGHT.

1. General Astronomy.

This course is largely descriptive in character, though some of the simpler mathematical problems connected with Astronomy are solved. It embraces a study of the imaginary lines of the celestial sphere; latitude, longitude, time; the sun, moon and planets; comets, meteors, and the stars. Some attention is given to the constellations and the myths connected with them. The Nebular Hypothesis is presented and discussed. Young,s General Astronomy is` used. Fall term. Prerequisite, Mathematics 9.

PHYSICS.

PROFESSOR FREDRICK W. RICH.

The course in Physics extends through the year, four periods per week being devoted to lectures and recitations and four to laboratory work. The aim is to present the science of physics as a whole, that students may be led to note the general principles of mechanics that apply throughout, and which furnish the basis of explanation of all the various phenomena and laws.

It is intended for the general student and no Mathematics higher then Plane Trigonometry is required. Numerous problem test the student's ability to think clearly and make a correct application of the principles involved.

The laboratory experiments are chiefly quantitative and give opportunity for the verification of fundamental laws and general formulæ. Each student is required to present carefully prepared notes which shall include the data obtained from observation and computed results.

1. Mechanics, Hydrostatics, Pneumatics.

Text-book, Ames's College Physics. Prerequisite, Mathematics 9.

2. Heat, Sound, and Light.

Winter term. Prerequisite, Physics 1.

3. Magnetism and Electricity.

Spring term. Prerequisite, Physics 2.

CHEMISTRY.

PROFESSOR FREDERICK W. RICH.

The courses in Chemistery have been arranged with several distinct objects in view: First—A clear understanding of the underlying principles of chemical changes. This involves a thorough knowledge of the theory of the structure of matter.

Second—The principles of Stoichiometry are to be thoroughly mastered and applied in a large series of practical chemical problems.

Third—A study of the elements and their compounds with careful attention given to the writing of equations.

Fourth—A systematic course in the laboratory, designed to give the student practice in careful manipulation and also opportunity for verification of the laws of chemical combination. The experiments of this course include the preparation of common elements and compounds.

Fifth—A general course in Qualitative analysis in which the student becomes familiar with the methods of determining the composition of native and manfactured substances.

Sixth—A well graded course in Quantitative analysis which gives the student practice in the various gravimetric and volumetric methods.

This gives the student basis for technical work and enables him, in the minimum time, to become familiar with special, practical methods in the arts, and in fact to take the position of chemist in many lines of trade or manufacture without further preparation.

The course includes the analysis of such substances as ores, soils, fertilizers, soaps, milk, butter, gas, air, water, etc.

1. Inorganic Chemistry.

Remsen's College Chemistry is used as the basis of courses 1 and 2. Fall term. Open to all students.

2. Inorganic Chemistry.

Winter term. Prerequisite, Chemistry 1.

3. Organic Chemistry.

This course consists of recitations, lectures with experimental demonstrations, and laboratory work. The consideration of food-stuffs is an important part of the work. Their composition, adulteration, and the new methods of preparation are carefully studied. Remsen's Organic Chemistery is used. Spring term. Prerequisite, Chemistry 2.

In each of the courses 1, 2, and 3, the work is profusely illus-trated by experiments, and individual work by the student in the laboratory demonstrates the principles discussed. Four hours per week are devoted to recitations and lectures and four hours to laboratory work.

4. Analytical Chemistry.

Qualitative analysis, laboratory work, and recitations. Fall term. Prerequisite, Chemistry 2.

5. Analytical Chemistry.

Qualitative, and quantitative analysis, laboratory work. Winter term. Prerequisite, Chemistry 4.

6. Analytical Chemistry.

Quantitative analysis. Laboratory work. Spring term. Prerequisite, Chemistry 5.

GEOLOGY AND MINERALOGY.

PROF. FREDERICK W. RICH.

1. Geology.

The work in Geology is given by text-book recitations, supplemented by lectures and excursions for field work. The College has a valuable collection of minerals, which serves for purposes of illustration and study. Spring term. Prerequisites, Chemistry 1, Biology 2, and Biology 3.

2. Mineralogy.

The course consists of a qualitative determination of minerals by means of the blow-pipe and a careful study of the principles of classification. Winter term. Prerequisite, Chemistry 2.

BIOLOGY.

Prof. Charles Orval Appleman.

The courses offered in this department give the student a general knowledge of life from its simplest to its most complex form. The student who faithfully does the work as outlined in these courses will be well prepared to teach them in secondary schools. In this department the student learns of life, of the structure and functions of the various organs of which the organism is composed, and of their relations to each other. He learns how to observe and appreciate the wonderful phenomena of nature. The numerous unsolved problems in this field offer many opportunities for investigation and advancement.

The Physiological and Anatomical laboratories have recently been equipped with the latest apparatus. An ample number of instruments have been supplied. These include the apparatus necessary for experiments and demonstrations in blood pressure, heart-beat, muscle, nerve phenomena, respiration, digestion, phenomena of stimulation, etc., etc.

1, 2. Botany.

The aim of these courses is to acquaint the student with the fundamentals of Physiology, Ecology, and Phylogeny and to present a more detailed study of Morphology and life History. Plant structure, function, and classification will be developed together in an attempt to trace the evolution of the plant kingdom. Some time is also devoted to teaching the use of ordinary taxonomic manuals. Lectures, recitations, and laboratory work. Eight hours per week. Winter and Spring terms.

6. Histology.

A course in Normal Histology, which will be divided into two parts. (a) The construction and use of the microscope, the methods of preparing microscopical sections, and work upon the fundamental mammalian tissues. (*b*) A study of the microscopic anatomy of mammalian organs. Eight hours per week. Fall term. Biology 6, alternates with Biology 5.

3, 4, 5. Zoology.

These courses are devoted to a general consideration of the subject with special reference to important problems in animal ecology and to a careful and detailed study of the structure and life history of type forms, and to such comparison of these with related forms as to exemplify the modifications of structure which characterize the several branches of the animal kingdom.

Courses 3, 4, Invertebrates. Winter and Spring terms.

Course 5, Vertebrates. Winter term. Prerequisite, Biology 3, 4. (Alternates with Biology 6).·

[7. Physiology.]

Anatomy, Physiology and Hygiene, a general course extending throughout two terms. Lectures, laboratory and quizzes. Open to all college students.

HISTORY.

PRES. LEWIS B. FISHER. MRS. CHARLES O. APPLEMAN.

1. Hebrew History.

The United and the Divided Kingdoms. Fall term.

2. Jewish History.

The Babylonian, Persian, Greek, Maccabean and Roman Periods. Winter term.

3. The Life of Jesus in its Historical Settings.

Spring term.

4. History of the Christian Church, Ancient, and Mediaeval Periods, 1-1517.

Fall term.

5. History of the Christian Church, Modern Period, 1571 1906.

Winter term.

6. History of Christian Doctrines.

Spring term.

These courses in History are primarily intended for the members of the Divinity School, but are also open to College students.

The text and reference books used are Kent, Riggs, Cornill, Fisher, McGiffert, Allen, and Smith.

12. Mediaeval History.

The topics especially dwelt upon are "The Decline of the Roman Empire," "The Fusion of the Teutonic Custom with Roman Law," "The New Empire of Charlemagne and its Dissolution," "Feudalism," "The Crusades," "The Contest Between the Pope and the Emperor for the Sovereignty of the World," and "The Emergence of National States from Feudal Anarchy. Fall term.

13. Modern History.

This course emphasizes the progress of constitutional government in England, the rise of Russia, the struggle between Prussia and Austria for the supremacy in Germany, and the triumph of republican principles in France. Winter term.

14. A Study of Epochs in American History.

A. Formation of the Union [1750-1829.]

In this epoch special attention is given to the development of the American Colonial and State Governments, the growth of the National Idea, the Constitutional controversies of our National Life, and the History of Political Parties.

B. Division and Reunion [1829-1889.]

The facts especially dwelt upon in this epoch are the development of Parties, the Bank Question, Slavery, Secession, and Reconstruction. Spring term.

For courses dealing with certain topics in History, see under the departments of German, Economics, and History of Art.

HISTORY OF ART.

PROF. LOUISE M. KUEFFNER.

Although the aim of the courses in History of Art is to make the student familiar with the famous buildings, statues, and paintings that embody some of man's highest conceptions, yet in method the work is not simple enumeration of pictures, or memorizing of artists' biographies, but, above all, a presentation of the great works, artists, and periods, as a development out of the physical, social, and religious conditions of each age and people, and as a part of "culture history." Full illustration by pictures. Lectures and collateral reading.

1. Egyptian, Assyrian, Greek, and Roman Art.

Greek art is studied very fully, inasmuch as it forms the basis of all European art in its presentation of the human form, and in its glorification of the perfect human animal. Fall term. Open to all College students.

2. Romanesque and Gothic Art; the Renaissance in Italy.

Winter term. Open to all College students. Two-fifths course.

3. Renaissance Art Outside of Italy; Modern Art.

Rise of the feeling for nature and its interpretation. Modern tendencies. Spring term. Open to all College students. Two-fifths course.

ECONOMICS.

PROF. PHILIP G. WRIGHT.

2. Political Economy.

General Political Economy. Seager's Introduction to Economics is used. Fall term. Open to advanced college students.

3. Financial History of the United States.

This course embraces the finances of the Revolution; the financial administrations of Morris, Hamilton, and Gallatin; the bank struggle; tariff legislation; the financial measures of the Civil War, and the reconstruction period to the present time. Dewey's Financial History of the United States is used as a text, collateral reading is required, and frequent lectures are given. Winter term. Prerequisite, Economics 2.

4. Current Economic Problems.

It is the purpose in this course to investigate from a standpoint somewhat broader than that of purely economic considerations certain vital economic problems and reforms. Different topics will be discussed different years. Spring term. Prerequisite, Economics 2.

SOCIAL SCIENCE.*

PROF. RALPH GRIERSON KIMBLE.

1, 2, 3. General Sociology.

It is the purpose of these courses to study the elementary and fundamental factors, forms, and laws of human associate life. The

*An important part of the work in all the courses of this department is a serious study of history. Probably two-fifths of the time of the courses are spent in this way.

work is designed especially to answer the needs of the general college student who wishes to gain in a comparatively brief time the knowledge of social phenomena which will be of most value to him in the further pursuit of his college work and in after life. The course is an introductory and orienting course in the entire field of social phenomena and is calculated to be of such importance as to be strictly essential to every student. Open to all students. Fall, Winter, and Spring. The course must be taken throughout the year in order to gain credit.

[4, 5, 6. Political Science.]

These courses are continuous and must be so taken in order to obtain credit. A study of the nature and functions of government and the state. Recitations, lectures, and supplementary work in History. Open to all students. Fall, Winter, and Spring terms.

PSYCHOLOGY.

PROF. RALPH GRIERSON KIMBLE.

1, 2, 3. Psychology.

A general study of the more accessible phenomena of the psychic life. Recitations, lectures, assigned readings, laboratory, and quizzes. In the latter part of the work great care is taken to make clear the relations of the course to other courses in the curriculum. Emphasis is laid upon the practical import of psycho logical knowledge. Open to all College students. Courses must be pursued continuously in order to obtain credit. Fall, Winter and Spring terms.

HISTORY OF PHILOSOPHY

PROF. RALPH GRIERSON KIMBLE.

[1, 2, 3. History of Philosophy.]

A study of the general course of philosophic thought. Open to all college students. Lectures, recitations, and assigned readings. Fall, Winter, and Spring terms.

LOGIC.

PROF. RALPH GRIERSON KIMBLE.

A study of the principles of inductive and deductive reasoning. The processes and laws of valid thinking are critically examined. Open to those who have completed Psychology. Fall and first half of Winter terms.

ETHICS.

PROF. RALPH GRIERSON KIMBLE.

A study of the moral life—of the nature and end of conduct. Students can pursue this course to best advantage who have had previous work in psychology and sociology. Studied without these backgrounds, ethics must always remain an arbitrary and largely incomprehensible body of knowledge. Those who would elect this work are definitely advised first to seek preliminary training in the fields mentioned. Last half of Winter term and entire Spring term.

PHILOSOPHY OF RELIGION

Fairbairn's Philosophy of the Christian Religion is the text-book. Lotze, Sabatier, and Martineau are used as works of reference. The aim of the instructor is to acquaint the student with the proper offices of reason in the effort to find argumentative grounds for religious ideas. Most of the modern theories respecting the nature and scope of the religious feeling pass under review; and in such discussions free questioning on the part of the student is encouraged. Winter term. Open to students who, in the judgment of the instructor, are qualified by previous training to take the course.

MUSIC.

PROF. FRANK A. POWER.

1. Theory and Audition.

Pupils desiring to take up the study of Harmony and the subjects following will be expected to complete Music 1, 2, and 3 Rythm, Major and Minor Dictation. Scale introduced. One term.

2. Theory and Audition.

Retardations, Anticipations, Cadences, Dictation, Arpeggios, introduced. Augmented and diminished intervals. One term.

3. Theory and Audition.

Suspensions, Resolutions, Dictations, Melody Writing, Melodic and Harmonic Scales, Chord Formation, Absolute Pitch. One term.

4. Harmony.

Keys, scales and signatures, intervals, formation of the triad, chord connection, simple part writing begun. Normal and Foreign progressions. All common chords and the rules governing their treatment in part writing. Broekhoven's Harmony is the text-book used. Two hours a week. One term. Prerequisite, Music 3.

5. Harmony.

Part writing continued. The inversion of. chords. Chords of the sixth and six-four, chords of the seventh and their inversions. Key-board work. Modulation begun. Two hours a week. One term. Prerequisite, Music 4.

6. Harmony.

Chords of the seventh continued. Altered and Augmented chords explained and employed. in harmonization. Modulation continued. Two hours a week. One term. Prerequisite, Music 5.

7. Single Counterpoint.

Writing from *canti fermi*. First species, note against note. Second species, two notes against one Third species, four notes against one. John Frederick's Counterpoint is the text-book used. One term. Prerequisite, Music 6.

8. Single Counterpoint.

Writing from *canti fermi* continued in fourth species. Syncopation, suspensions, retardations. Fifth species, florid counterpoint. One term. Prerequisite, Music 7.

9. Single and Double Counterpoint.

Florid counterpoint continued. Double counterpoint in all forms. One term. Prerequisite, Music 8.

10. Musical Form.

The section and phrase. The period. . The small primary forms. The large primary forms. The motive and its development. The study (Etude), Dance forms, Rondo form. Vocal song. Sonata form. Musical form. Bussler-Cornell. One term. Prerequisite, Music 9.

11. Canon and Fugue.

Canon in two voices in all intervals. Fugue in two, three, and four voices. Text-books; Richter, double Counterpoint and Fugue; Higg's Fugue. One term. Prerequisite, Music 9.

12. Instrumentation.

Study of Berlioz on instrumentation, also Prout's work on same subject. Study of orchestral scores. Orchestral scoring of various musical passages, and of original work. Orchestral writing without recourse to piano scoring. One term. Prerequisite, Music 10 and 11.

13. History of Music.

This course embraces a history of the development of music from the earliest times until to-day, with special reference to critical analysis of the works of the great masters. It also furnishes an introduction to the lives of the great composers.

PUBLIC SPEAKING.

PROF. ALICE B. CURTIS, MISS VICTORIA D. MARRIOTT.

1. Expression. (Half Course.)

A consideration of the elements of Expression. Physical exercises are given for purposes of control and vocal development. The conversational tone and its acquirement are made a matter of special study. Fall term. Open to all students.

2. Expression. (Half Course.)

Literary interpretation of masterpieces. Programs from various authors will be given throughout the term. Extemporaneous speaking forms a part of the work. Winter term. Prerequisite, Public Speaking 1.

3. Expression. (Half Course.)

Each student will be required to give a recital. The work will be criticized and special drill given by the instructor. Spring term. Prerequisite, Public Speaking 2.

4. Oratory. (Half Course.)

Study of the theory of oratory. Each student will be required to commit to memory and deliver various oratorical selections. Each student will prepare and deliver an oration under the supervision of the instructor. Fall term. Open to all students.

5. Oratory. (Half Course.)

The preparation and delivery of several orations. Winter term. Prerequisite, Public Speaking 4.

6. Argumentation.

A study of the principles of argumentation. The handling of refutation, preparation of brief, writing of the forensic, and actual debate will form part of the work. Spring term. Open to all students.

THE GYMNASIUM.

DOMESTIC SCIENCE.
MRS. HARRIET B. DUDLEY.

This course includes one three-hour lesson per week in practical cooking, supplemented by lectures in Chemistry and Economics. Fall, Winter, and Spring terms. Open to all students.

GYMNASIUM WORK.
PROF. CHARLES O. APPLEMAN.

The system of physical education pursued at Lombard College does not aim to make athletes and gymnasts, ball players, prize fighters, or wrestlers. The idea that the gymnasium was solely for those already strong, or for the development of candidates for field honors, is not primarily considered. Incidentally the gymnasium affords ample facilities for indoor training of athletes, but this work is necessarily given a secondary place. Our system of physical education maintains that the development of the mind and body go together and that one must not be sacrificed for the other. Its aim is not only to give a better and more useful physique, but to develop a will, a resolution of purpose, and to create a college spirit, which will bring with them loyalty and help to dignify American citizenship. When the student enters the gymnasium he is subjected to a rigid medical examination which is made the basis of all gymnasium work. It determines the condition of the heart and circulation, the lungs and respiration, the stomach and its appendages, vision, hearing, size and consistency of muscles, and the temperament of the nervous system. Deformities, or bodily defects, are carefully sought for. From this examination a scientific application of physical exercises as a means of development is made. Occasionally in such examination organic heart trouble is revealed. Such persons are not permitted to take the usual gymnasium work, but are given special exercises of a milder nature which are helpful. Functional derangements of nutrition, circulation, respiration, etc., are often discovered. Here again special exercises are prescribed.

The greater part of the gymnasium work is conducted in classes which meet daily. Dumb-bell and club work are taken with a snap that puts life and vigor into every move. Class work is also done on the heavy apparatus, such as the buck and parallel bars. Individual work is done with the chest weights and horizontal bars, traveling rings, climbing poles, etc. During the winter term basket ball teams are organized, and competitive games are held.

All students will provide themselves with regular gymnasium uniforms. The cost of the uniform is about $2.50 for the men, and $4.50 for the women.

PREPARATORY COURSES.

The following courses are designed chiefly for the benefit of those Unclassified Students who wish to complete the entrance requirements for admission to the College of Liberal Arts. They are, however, open to all students, *but if taken by students in the College of Liberal Arts they will be counted on the thirty-eight credits required for graduation.*

ENGLISH.

MISS FLORENCE DILLOW.

The following courses are offered for the benefit of those wishing to pass the English Examination for admission as outlined on pages 20, 21. Courses 2, 3 and 4 are full courses and will deal with composition and with the study of the books prescribed for careful study. Courses 2b, 3b, and 4b are half courses and will deal with the books prescribed for reading.

2. Macaulay's Essays on Milton and Addison, and Milton's L' Allegro and Il Penseroso.

Three days per week. Composition (Scott and Denny), one day per week. Fall term.

3. Milton's Comus and Lycidas, and Burke's Speech on Conciliation with America.

Three days per week. Composition (Scott and Denny) one day per week. Winter term.

4. Shakespeare's Macbeth.

Three days per week. Composition (Scott and Denny), one day per week. Spring term.

2. (b) Addison's Sir Roger de Coverly Papers in the Spectator, Goldsmith's Vicar of Wakefield, Lowell's Vision of Sir Launfal.

(Half Course)

Three days per week. Fall term.

3. (*b*). **Scott's Ivanhoe, Coleridge's Ancient Mariner, Carlyle's Essay on Burns, Shakespeare's Merchant of Venice.**

(Half Course.)

Three days per week. Winter term.

4. (*b*). **George Eliot's Silas Marner, Tennyson's Princess, Shakespeare's Julius Caesar.** (Half Course.)

Three days per week. Spring term.

LATIN.
PROF. FRANK H. FOWLER.

1. **Latin Lessons.**

Fall term.

2. **Latin Lessons.** (Continuation of 1.)

Winter term.

3. **Caesar and Latin Prose Composition.**

Spring term.

4. **Caesar and Latin Prose Composition.**

Fall term.

5. **Cicero's Orations and Latin Prose Composition.**

Winter term.

6. **Cicero's Orations and Latin Prose Composition.**

Spring term.

7. **Vergil.**

Fall term.

8. **Vergil.**

Winter term.

MATHEMATICS.
JOHN C. WEIGEL.

1. **Elementary Algebra.**

Wells's Essentials of Algebra is used. Fall term. Open to all students.

2. **Elementary Algebra.** (Continued.)

Winter term. Prerequisite, Mathematics 2.

3. Elementary Algebra. (Continued.)

Spring term. Prerequisite, Mathematics 3.

4. Algebra.

After a brief review of Quadratic Equations, with especial reference to theory, the subjects Simultaneous Equations of the second degree, Intermediate Equations, Ratio and Proportion, Arithmetical and Geometrical progression will be considered. Wells's College Algebra is used. Fall term. Prerequisite, Mathematics 3.

5. Plane Geometry.

This course is designed to give students thorough drill in the first principles of Geometry. Phillips and Fisher's Elements of Geometry is used. Winter term. Open to all students.

6. Plane Geometry.

This course consists of a review of Mathematics 5 together with the demonstration of a large number of original propositions. Spring term. Prerequisite, Mathematics 5.

Mathematics 1, 2, 3, 4 and 5 are designated to meet the entrance requirements in Algebra and Plane Geometry.

HISTORY.

2. Greece.

History of Greece. Fall term. Open to all students.

3. Rome.

History of Rome. Text book, Morey. Winter term. Open to all students.

4. England.

History of England. Text-book, Higginson and Channing. Spring term. Open to all students.

PHYSICAL GEOGRAPHY.

1. Physical Geography.

Text-book, Tarr's Elementary Physical Geography. Spring term. Open to all students.

UNCLASSIFIED STUDENTS.

Persons who wish to pursue studies at Lombard without becoming candidates for a degree will be admitted on probation to any class for which they are fitted by previous training. In case the class in question demands a prerequisite, the applicant must bring a certificate in this prerequisite from an approved school, or pass an examination.

On severing their connection with the College, these students will receive, upon request, a certificate, signed by the President and their several instructors, stating the amount and quality of the work done.

If at any time such students wish to become candidates for a degree, they must fulfill all the requirements for admission to the department in which the degree is to be taken.

Among these also will be listed all students who have an ultimate purpose of taking a degree, but who need to pursue one or more of the preparatory courses to fulfill the requirements for admission to the College of Liberal Arts.

RYDER DIVINITY SCHOOL.

The Divinity School of Lombard College was open for the admission of students on the 5th of September, 1881. The first class was graduated in 1885.

At the annual meeting of the Board of Trustees in 1890, it was voted to name the theological department of the College the RYDER DIVINITY SCHOOL, in honor of the late William Henry Ryder, D. D., whose munificent bequests to the College exceed fifty thousand dollars.

The largest benefaction to the Divinity School from any other source was received from the late Hon. A. G. Throop, founder of the Throop Polytechnic Institute at Passadena, California. In 1890 Mr. Throop gave twenty thousand dollars toward the endowment of the Divinity School.

ADMISSION.

Applicants unknown to the faculty must bring satisfactory evidences of good moral and religious character. They should also bring certificates of their church membership.

Candidates for admission to the Divinity School must be prepared to sustain examination, in the following subjects:

I. ENGLISH.

(a) **Grammar and Analysis.**

Reed and Kellogg's Higher Lessons in English, or an equivalent.

(b) **Composition.**

An extemporaneous composition on an assigned subject, correct as to spelling, paragraphing, grammar, and rhetorical form.

(c) **Literature.**

An equivalent of English 2, 2b, 3, 3b, 4, and 4b as described on pages 56, 57 of this catalogue.

(e) **Bible Geography and Archaeology.**

A general knowledge of localities, customs, manners, etc., of Bible times.

Rand and McNally's Manuel of Bibical Geography 'and Jahn's Archeology or equivalents.

(*f*) **General History.**

Swinton's General History or an equivalent.

III. MATHEMATICS.

(*a*) **Arithmetic.**

Higher Arithmetic, including percentage, alligation, extraction of roots, mensuration, and the metric system.

(*b*) **Elementary Algebra.**

Wells's Academic Algebra or an equivalent.

IV. GEOGRAPHY.

Wells's Academic Algebra or an equivalent.

V. SCIENCE.

(*a*) **Chemistry.**

The equivalent of Chemistry 1 and 2 as described on page 46. (Equivalent work in Physics and Botany may be accepted in lieu of Chemistry.)

(*b*) **Physiology.**

This calls for a general knowledge of the human skeleton, muscular, circulatory, and nervous systems, the vital organs, viscera, and organs of special sense, and the processes of respiration and digestion. The preparation required is covered in such text-books as Martin's Human Body, (advanced course), or Huxley's Elementary Physiology (Lee's Revision.)

PRELIMINARY YEAR.

To accommodate those candidates for admission who are not fully prepared to satisfy the admission requirements an opportunity is given to complete their preparation in the school, and a preliminary year's work is mapped out (page 66), which, however, is susceptible of some modification to meet the special needs of the candidate.

As a further encouragement to candidates to avail themselves of this opportunity the Universalist General Convention will permit its grant of financial aid to be spread over five years, instead of four as hitherto. Thus the candidate who requires five years for the full course, including the Preliminary year, may receive, under the usual conditions, a maximum grant of $100 each year for the five years, or the maximum grant of $125 a year for four years as he may prefer.

ADMISSION BY CERTIFICATE.

Satisfactory grades from approved schools will be accepted in lieu of examination. .Students thus admitted by certificate will be regarded as on probation during the first term of their course.

ADMISSION TO ADVANCED STANDING.

Students who bring satisfactory evidence of work done beyond the requirements of admission will be given credit for the same on the regular course, so far as the faculty may deem consistent with the special aims of that course.

The members of the Divinity School are admitted to the advantages presented by the other departments of the College.

REQUIREMENTS FOR GRADUATION.

(a) **Class Work.**

Candidates for the degree of B. D. will be required to complete the regular course of instruction scheduled on page 66

(b) **Thesis.**

Candidates for the degree of B. D. will also be required to prepare a graduation thesis, the topic to be approved by one of the professors in the department and the work to be done under his supervision.

EXPENSES.

Tuition is free to all regular members of the Divinity School who are candidates for the ministry, on condition that the student maintains an average grade of at least 70 per cent.

The charge for incidentals is the same as in the College of Liberal Arts, $5 per term.

For board in Commons, see page 11.

Board in good families can be secured for from $2.50 to $3.25 per week. Students may somewhat reduce their expenses by forming clubs or boarding themselves.

PECUNIARY AID.

Students who are candidates for the ministry of the Universalist Church may, upon complying with the prescribed conditions and receiving the recommendation of the faculty, obtain assistance from the Universalist General Convention in the form of a gratuity, to an amount not exceeding $125 a year for four years. Applications will be granted by the Convention only when entirely satisfactory. The first installment of this gift will not be issued to entering students until January, the second will be issued in May. Students should therefore come with resources of their own sufficient to pay their expenses for at least one term.

Those who have not a definite purpose of entering the Universalist ministry are not eligible to the Convention gift.

Membership in some Universalist Church is also required as a condition of the gift.

The use of tobacco or other narcotic or stimulants is an absolute bar to the grant of the Convention aid.

The Convention aid may be withheld at any time, should the work or behavior of the candidate prove unsatisfactory.

After having had two terms in Homiletics, students who show due proficiency are permitted to secure appointments to preach, and thus add to their pecuniary resources.

COURSES OF INSTRUCTION.

1. Regular Course.

Candidates for the degree of B. D. will be expected to complete the course scheduled on page 66 and prepare a graduation thesis. This course, it will be observed, prescribes a certain amount of work in Greek, which is regarded as indispensible to the degree. It is earnestly recommended that all students whose circumstances do not forbid their spending the requisite time, take the Regular Course.

2. Alternative Course.

It is, however, permitted to those who, after due deliberation, prefer to do so, to omit the Greek and Hebrew, and to substitute therefor for an equivalent amount of elective work in English, Modern Languages, Science, Mathematics, or Sociology, with the approval of the faculty. Those who complete such a course will be graduated at the Annual Commencement, and will be furnished a certificate showing what work they have done; but they will not be given the degree of B. D. or any other degree.

3. Special Work.

(a) Candidates for the ministry who cannot take either of the above described courses, will be permitted to elect particular studies, so far as their preparation warrants. Pastors already engaged in ministerial work, who can spare a period for further study, are particularly invited to avail themselves of this opportunity.

(b) The School is also open to persons who do not intend to enter the ministry. The pursuit of studies of a theological or religious character is an interesting and helpful means of personal culture. Such a course is especially recommended to those who desire to become better fitted for service in the Sunday School, the church, the Young People's Christian Union and similar societies, or for charitable and philanthropic work. Upon those who come with these purposes, no denominational test will be imposed. Students of all denominations and beliefs will be welcome to the advantages of study and training in the Divinity School, as in other departments of the College.

Faculty of the Divinity School.

LEWIS B. FISHER, D. D., PRESIDENT.

*Hall Professor of Intellectual and Moral Philosophy.
(At present unoccupied.)

†Hull Professor of Biblical Geography and Archæology.
(At present unoccupied.)

ISAAC AUGUSTUS PARKER, A. M., PH. D.
Professor of Greek.

RALPH GRIERSON KIMBLE, A. B.,
Professor of Social Science and Philosophy.

EDSON REIFSNIDER, B. D.,
Instructor in Homiletics and Pastoral Care

ALICE BERTHA CURTIS, B. Dr.; PH. B.,
Professor of English and Public Speaking.

NON-RESIDENT LECTURERS.

REV. W. H. McGLAUFLIN, D. D.,

REV. I. M. ATWOOD, D. D.,

REV. EFFIE McCOLLUM JONES,

REV. J. B. THAYER FISHER,

REV. GEORGE H. SAHLIN.

*In honor of the late E. G. Hall, of Chicago.
†In honor of the Rev. Stephen Hull, of Kansas City, Mo.

Degrees Conferred in 1905.

FRANK D. ADAMS.   JENNIE BARTHOLOMEW.
STANLEY MANNING.   WILLIAM PHILLIPS.

Schedule.

1. Preliminary Year.

FALL TERM.	WINTER TERM.	SPRING TERM.
English 2, 2b.	English 3, 3b.	English 4, 4b.
Biblical History.	Biblical History.	Biblical Geography and Archæology.
Chemistry.	Elementary Physiology.	Elementary Botany.

2. Regular Course.

Leading to the degree of Bachelor of Divinity.

FIRST YEAR.

FALL TERM.	WINTER TERM.	SPRING TERM.
English 5.	English 6.	English 7.
Greek 1.	Greek 2.	Greek 3.
History 5.	History 6.	History 7.

SECOND YEAR.

Psychology 1.	Psychology 2.	Hermeneutics.
Greek 4.	Greek Testament.	Greek Testament.
Homiletics 1.	Homiletics 2.	Homiletics 3.
Elocution.	Elocution.	Elocution.

THIRD YEAR.

Homiletics 4.	Homiletics 5.	Homiletics 6.
Sociology 1.	Greek Testament.	Greek Testament.
Apologetics.	Dogmatic Theology.	Dogmatic Theology.
	Logic.	

FOURTH YEAR.

Charities and Corrections.	Charities and Corrections.	Pastoral Care.
Economics 2.	Ethics.	O. T. Introduction (2 hrs.)
Preaching.	Preaching.	Ethical Theories, or
		Philosophy of Religion, or
		History of Religion

Description of Studies.

BIBLICAL CRITICISM.

Driver's Introduction to the Old Testament is used as a text-book, with reference to Frip, Ryle, Bacon, Robertson, and other works. A course of lectures is given on the Science of Documentary Analysis, the Principles and Methods of Historical Criticism, and the Religious aspects of the Higher Criticism. Winter term.

HERMENEUTICS.

PROFESSOR ISAAC A. PARKER.

It is the aim to set forth the principles of interpretation in connection with the translation and exposition of the portions of the Greek Testament to which attention is given.

Lectures intended to aid the student in interpreting the Greek Testament, and also on the History of Interpretation are given in the winter and spring terms.

PREPARATORY GREEK.

(Greek 1, 2, 3, 4, see pages 41, 42.)

THE GREEK TESTAMENT.

PROFESSOR ISAAC A. PARKER.

13. Translation and Exegesis of the Gospel of John.

Its date and genuineness. Portions of the Acts of the Apostles. Winter term.

14. Translation and Exegesis of Selections from the Gospel of Matthew and the Epistles of Paul.

Spring term.

THEOLOGY.

1. Christian Evidences.

The study of Christian Evidences will include an examination of the bases of Christian belief, Evolutionary theories and their relation to Philosophy, Ethics, and Religion, and the function and method of Apologetics. Comparison will be instituted between the modern methods in Apologetics and the methods of primitive Christianity. Instruction will be given mostly by lectures with frequent reference to Fisher, Flint, Bruce, and others. Fall term.

2. Dogmatic Theology.

A thorough investigation is made of the several Christian doctrines, with an extended examination of associated questions and controversies. The widest liberty is given for questions and discussions on the various topics presented. Winter and spring terms.

3. History of Religion.

The work of the students consists in the examination and comparison of the authorities upon the great Non-Christian Religions. Special topics are investigated and reports made by each member of the class. Spring term.

SOCIOLOGY.
PROF. RALPH GRIERSON KIMBLE.

1, 2, 3. General Sociology.

It is the purpose of these courses to study the elementary and fundamental factors, forms, and laws of human associate life. The work is designed especially to answer the needs of the general college student who wishes to gain in a comparatively brief time the knowledge of social phenomena which will be of most value to him in the further pursuit of his college work and in after life. The course is an introductory and orienting course in the entire field of social phenomena and is calculated to be of such importance as to be strictly essential to every student. Open to all students. Fall, Winter, and Spring. The course must be taken throughout the year in order to gain credit.

4, 5. Charities and Corrections.

Warner's American Charities, Wines' Punishment and Reform, and Devine's Principles of Relief, sufficiently indicate the scope and character of the work. Lectures, quizzes and field work. Open only to divinity students. Fall and winter terms.

PASTORAL CARE.
REV. EDSON REIFSNIDER.

A study of the spiritual, mental, and social qualifications of the minister for his work, and his administration of the special services of the church—baptism, confirmation, the Lord's Supper, marriage, and the burial of the dead. A liberal portion of the term will be devoted to an examination of various methods of church organization, for the purpose of giving the minister facility in adapting himself to parish needs, especially to those peculiar to the locality in which he may be settled. Also a study is made of the Manual of the Universalist General Convention. Spring term.

PSYCHOLOGY.

PROF. RALPH GRIERSON KIMBLE.

1, 2, 3. Psychology.

A general study of the more accessible phenomena of the psychic life. Recitations, lectures, assigned readings, laboratory, and quizzes. In the latter part of the work great care is taken to make clear the relations of the course to other courses in the curriculum. Emphasis is laid upon the practical import of psychological knowledge. Open to all College students. Courses must be pursued continuously in order to obtain credit. Fall, Winter and Spring terms.

LOGIC.

PROF. RALPH GRIERSON KIMBLE.

A study of the principles of inductive and deductive reasoning. The processes and laws of valid thinking are critically examined. Open to those who have completed Psychology. Fall and first half of Winter terms.

ETHICS.

PROF. RALPH GRIERSON KIMBLE.

A study of the moral life—of the nature and end of conduct. Students can best pursue this course to advantage who have had previous work in psychology and sociology. Studied without these backgrounds, ethics must always remain an arbitrary and largely incomprehensible body of knowledge. Those who would elect this work are definitely advised first to seek preliminary training in the fields mentioned. Last half of Winter term and entire Spring term.

PHILOSOPHY OF RELIGION.

Fairbairn's Philosophy of the Christian Religion is the textbook. Lotze, Sabatier, and Martineau are used as works of reference. The aim of the instructor is to acquaint the student with the proper offices of reason in the effort to find argumentative grounds for religious ideas. Most of the modern theories respecting the nature and scope of the religious feeling pass under review; and in such discussions free questioning on the part of the student is

encouraged. Winter term. Open to students who, in the judgment of the instructor, are qualified by previous training to take
the course.

HISTORY.

PRES. LEWIS B. FISHER.

1. Hebrew History.

The United and the Divided Kingdoms. Fall. term.

2. Jewish History.

The Babylonian, Persian, Greek, Maccabean and Roman Periods. Winter term.

3. The Life of Jesus in its Historical Settings.

Spring term.

4. History of the Christian Church, Ancient and Mediaeval Periods, 1-1517.

Fall term.

5. History of the Christian Church, Modern Period, 1571-1906.

Winter term.

6. History of Christian Doctrines.

Spring term.

These courses in History are primarily intended for the mem-
bers of the Divinity School, but are also open to College students.
The text and reference books used are Kent, Riggs, Cornill, Fisher,
McGiffert, Allen, and Smith.

HOMILETICS.

REV. EDSON REIFSNIDER.

The course in Homiletics covers the second, third, and fourth
years. The primary aim is practical. Upon a general but adequate
groundwork of theory and history of preaching the effort is made
to construct an art of effective pulpit oratory. Elaborate and exacting drill in the logical conception and construction of the sermon plan, with constant application of rhetorical principles, occupies the major part of the first year. Inspiration and direction
are sought in the frequent analysis of the discourses of great
preachers of all styles, and in the study of their sources of power.
Individuality and originality are emphasized as desiderata. In the

second year the stress is laid upon flexibility and adaptability, upon invention, upon the rationale of interesting preaching, and upon the acquisition of freedom in extempore address. Throughout the course the preparation and criticism of sermons by the class continues uninterruptedly.

PUBLIC SPEAKING.

PROF. ALICE B. CURTIS.

In view of the fact that a good delivery is of inestimable advantage to the preacher, the students in the Divinity School are offered an extended course in Elocution and Physical Culture.

The students are not only admitted to all Elocution classes in the College, but, also receive a large amount of individual training.

Courses 1, 2, 3, as outlined on page 54 of this catalogue, are required, as well as regular drill and rehearsals for the preaching exercises.

ENGLISH.

For English 2, 3, 4, required for entrance to full standing in the Divinity School, and taught in the Preliminary year, see page 56. For English 5, 6, 7, which courses are required in the Divinity School, see page 32 of this catalogue.

COLLEGE STUDIES AND THE A. B. DEGREE.

Divinity students are permitted, with the consent of the faculty, to pursue studies in the College of Liberal Arts. Graduates of the Divinity School may receive the additional degree of Bachelor of Arts, upon the satisfactory completion of an aggregate of twenty full courses taken in the classes of the College of Liberal Arts, beyond the full requirements of the Divinity School for the degree of Bachelor of Divinity.

In addition to the above twenty credits, the candidate must furnish the full quota of sixteen units required for admission to the College of Liberal Arts. Of these sixteen units, the courses required for admission to the Divinity School (see pages 60 and 61) will count six.

CANDIDATES FOR THE A. B. and B. D. DEGREE.

The College of Liberal Arts has decided that certain studies usually pursued in the Theological Schools only, are properly regarded as culture studies, and therefore offers them to all its students.

Taking advantage of this fact, the student who enters College with Greek and other good preparation, may so shape his course as to obtain the degree of Bachelor of Arts in four years and that of Bachelor of Divinity in one more year.

He may receive A. B. at the end of four years, or with B. D. at the end of his course as he may choose.

In order to do this work in five years the student must begin it in his Freshman year, and must manifest ability to carry with profit so heavy a program. The synopsis of this five year course is as follows: the term "a credit" meaning a study carried five hours a week for one term of twelve weeks.

CREDITS

```
Language (Latin, Greek, German)..................................  7
Science (Mathematics, Chemistry, Astronomy, Biology.................  5
History (Civil and Religious)......................................  8
Bible (Language, History)  .......................................10
Philosophy (Psychology, Logic, Ethics, Theology)...................10
Sociology (Economics Applied Christianity)......................... 9
English (Rhetoric, Literature, Oratory, Homiletics)................11
                                                                   ——
          Total...................................................60
Deduct (counted twice)  ................  ......................... 5
                                                                   ——
                                                                   55
```

DEPARTMENT OF MUSIC.

Instruction is provided in the various branches of Theoretical, Vocal, and Instrumental Music. These courses, except the courses in Theoretical Music and Musical History, are distinct from the work in the other departments of the College, and do not count toward a college degree. Students are classed and registered by the Director with whom all arrangements must be made, in order to secure certificates of standing from term to ·term and for all final examinations.

FACULTY.

FRANK A. POWER, DIRECTOR,
Instructor in Voice and Theoretical Courses.

HATTIE R. HEIN,
Instructor in Piano and Violin.

COURSE OF STUDY.

It is impossible to lay out a definite course in any branch of music study, except the theoretical branches. One pupil may have more natural talent than another, and some will have certain deficiences that others have not, therefore requiring work along certain lines that another will not need. The aim of the course laid out here is to develop broad, well-rounded musicians, not to develop *technique* and leave the *soul* dwarfed, neither to attempt to develop a musician without sufficient technique. The course is not to be followed strictly but other work will be substituted for studies in the course whenever the teacher may see the advisability of so doing.

The work in the entire department has been divided into two general grades. The first comprising from two to three years work leading to a teacher's certificate; the second grade comprising one to two year work and leading to a diploma. The advantage to the pupil is apparent. Many find it necessary to drop out of school before the course is completed and they have this certificate as a testimonial of actual work done and recommending them as fitted to teach such branches. Students working for a certificate in any branch of music study will be required to complete theoretical courses 1 to 6 and 13. Those working for a diploma will be required to take in addition theoretical courses 7, 8, 9, and 10.

Any pupil working for teacher's certificate must be able to play simple piano accompaniments at sight.

THEORETICAL COURSES.

1. Theory and Audition.

Pupils desiring to take up the study of Harmony and the subjects following will be expected to complete Music 1, 2, and 3. Rythm, Major, and Minor Dictation. Scale introduced. One term.

2. Theory and Audition.

Retardations, Anticipations, Cadences, Dictation, Arpeggios, introduced. Augmented and diminished intervals. One term.

3. Theory and Audition.

Suspensions, Resolutions, Dictations, Melody Writing, Melodic and Harmonic Scales, Chord Formation, Absolute Pitch. One term.

4. Harmony.

Keys, scales and signatures, intervals, formation of the triad, chord connection, simple part writing begun, Normal and Foreign Progressions. All common chords and the rules governing their treatment in part writing. Broekhoven's Harmony is the textbook used. Two hours a week. One term.

5. Harmony.

Part writing continued. The inversion of chords. Chords of the sixth and six-four, chords of the seventh and their inversions. Key-board work. Modulation begun. Two hours a week. One term.

6. Harmony.

Chords of the seventh continued. Altered and augmented chords explained and employed in harmonization. Modulation continued. Two hours a week. One term.

7. Single Counterpoint.

Writing from *canti fermi*. First species, note against note. Second species, two notes against one. Third species four notes against one. John Frederick Bridge's Counterpoint is the textbook used. One term.

8. Single Counterpoint.

Writing from *canti fermi* continued in fourth species. Syncopation-suspensions, retardations. Fifth species, florid counterpoint. One term.

9. Single and Double Counterpoint.

Florid counterpoint continued. Double counterpoint in all forms. One term.

(Students who expect to finish only the nine courses may substitute 10 for 9, with the advice and consent of the Director.)

10. Musical Form.

The section and phrase. The period. The small primary forms. The large primary forms. The motive and its development. The study (Etude), dance forms, Rondo form. Vocal song. Sonata form. Musical form. Bussler-Cornell. One term.

11. Canon and Fugue.

Canon in two voices in all intervals Fugue in two, three, and four voices. Text-books, Richter, Double Counterpoint and Fugue; Higgs, Fugue. One term.

12. Instrumentation.

Study of Berlioz on instrumentation, also Prout's work on same subject. Study of orchestral scores. Orchestral scoring of various musical passages, and of original work. Orchestral writing without recourse to piano scoring. One term.

13. History of Music.

These courses embrace a history of the development of music from the earliest time until to-day, with special reference to critical analysis of the works of the great masters. They also furnish an introduction to the lives of the great composers.

VOICE.

Grade I.

Voice placing and breath control. Exercises by the teacher to suit the individual. Concones fifty lessons, Lütgen's Studies in Execution, Paureron, Vaccai Marchesi and Concone's twenty-five and fifteen exercises.

In the meantime songs will be studied both of the modern and classical school, selected according to the individual needs of the pupil. Particularly songs of Schubert, Schumann, Franz, etc., and some of the oratorio and opera songs.

Grade II.

Lamperti, Marchesi, and Lablache studies, English, French, German and Italian songs and oratorio and operas. All voice pupils are required to attend the sight singing and chorus classes and must have a knowledge of the great vocal works for all voices.

PIANO.

Preparatory.

Rudiments of Music, studies in melody, rhythm, elementary harmony, études of technical and musical value by representative composers, wrist studies, scales four octaves (various accents) broken chords, diminished 7th, arpeggio; sonatinas by Clementi, Kuhlan, Gurlitt, Reinecke and others, Kunz 200 two-part canons (transposed to all keys), Etudes by Haberbier, Heller, Czerny, Kullak preparatory octave studies, left hand studies, selections from the easier works of Schubert, Schumann, Mendelssohn and others, also lighter pieces; pedal studies.

Teachers' Certificate.

Tausig, daily studies. Kullak, octave studies, op. 48 (part 2), Sherwood-Hatch Ed. Bach, two part inventions. Cramer, Etudes, Scales, Major and Minor. Dom. 7th and Dim. 7th chords in Arpeggio form (with various accents). Left hand studies, Arthur Foote. Arpeggio Studies, op. 144. Gurlitt, Bk. I and II. Haydn, Mozart, and Beethoven, easier Sonatas. Chopin Preludes (selected, Mazurkas, March Funèbre, Schumann Album. Lighter pieces, Grieg, Chaminade, Moszkwoski, Godard and others. Harmony, Musical History, Musical Terms, Ensemble Work.

Graduate Diploma.

Clementi, Gradus ad Parnassum. Etudes, Moscheles, Czerny Op. 740. Bach, three part Inventions. Beethoven, Sonatas. Scales in double thirds. Selections from Handel, Schumann, Chopin, Liszt, Raff, Rubinstein, Mendelssohn, Grieg and others. Ensemble work.

Harmony, Counterpoint, Canon, Fugue, Analysis, Musical Forms.

VIOLIN.
Preparatory.

Elementary exercises in position, bowing, ear training. Wohlfahrt, Rosenkranz, book for beginners. Sevick, Op. I, Kayser, Bk. I and II. Wohlfahrt, Op. 45. Sitt, Studies, Op. 32. Bk. I. 1st, pos., Bk. 2, 2-5 pos., Bk. III changing positions. Dont Op. 37 and 38. Scale studies Schradieck arpeggio. Wrist studies by Gustav Hille. Bowings, Consorti. Easy solos by Dancla, Sitt, Bohm, Viotti, de Beriot and others.

Teachers' Certificate.

Etudes by Dont, Schradieck, Fiorillo, Kreutzer, etc. Concertos, Viotti, deBeriot, Rode, Kreutzer. Selections by modern composers. Scales in three octaves. Must be able to play at sight and have a knowledge of the piano.

Harmony, History of Music, Analysis.

Graduate Diploma.

Technical Studies from the works of Kreutzer, Fiorillo, Rode, Gavini, Leonard. Double stops, scales, thirds, sixths, octaves. Selections from Ries, Wieniawski, Beethoven, Tartini and others.

Must be able to play well at sight and have a knowledge of the piano.

Counterpoint, Musical Form, Theory. (Same as piano.)

PUBLIC SCHOOL MUSIC FOR SUPERVISORS.
Contents of Public School Course.

This course will be completed in one year and will include all subjects necessary to be taught in a twelve or thirteen year public school course. Such as development of the scale, tone by tone, by the use of the scale ladder; exercises in reading, using numerals; principles involved in composing such exercises; introducing the staff, notes, rote singing; what constitutes a good rote song; the long note, marking time, the rest, different measures; how to produce good, pure tones; the three beat note, etc., etc., through all the rudiments.

Other Subjects Required.

Principles of composition; writing rote songs, words and music; writing two part exercises; Harmony, up to and including modulation; normal work in which each pupil takes charge of the class and presents a given subject. Also study of musical terms, biographies, etc. The boys' changing voice. Talks on how to get boys to sing; which parts for boys, which for girls.

Chorus.

The College Chorus affords practice in ensemble singing and is free to students. Voice pupils are required to take that work.

Sight Singing Class.

The Sight Singing class affords practice in studying the rudiments of Music, and in note reading, ear training, etc. All music pupils are urged to take this work.

Glee Club.

A College Glee Club has been organized under the direct supervision of Prof. Power. Arrangements will be made for a tour each year for the Club.

TUITION.

The following are the prices per term:

THEORETICAL COURSES—

> Music 1 to 9, each, $5.00.
> Music 10, 11, and 12, each, $3.00.

PIANOFORTE—

> Private Lessons—one hour per week, $20.00.
> Private Lessons—two half hours per week, $20.00.
> Private Lessons—one half hour per week, $11.00.
> Private Lessons—one forty-minute lesson per week, $15.00. •

Class Lessons may be specially arranged for and when practical will be arranged for at the following rates:

> Three pupils in two hour lessons per week, $15.00 each.
> Three pupils in one hour lesson per week, $9.00 each.

VOICE CULTURE—

> Charges same as for pianoforte.

RENT OF PIANO—

> 1 hour per day, per term, $2.75.
> 2 hours per day, per term, $5.00.
> 3 hours per day, per term, $6.75.
> 4 hours per day, per term, $8.00.

VIOLIN—

> Private Lessons—one hour per week, $15.00.
> Private Lessons—two half hours per week, $15.00.
> Private Lessons—one forty-five minute lesson per week, $12.00.

CLASS LESSONS, one hour per week—

> In classes of two, each, $8.00.
> In classes of three, each, $6.00.

SIGHT SINGING CLASSES—

> Each $1.00.

CHORUS CLASS—

> A charge of $1.00 per term, each, will be made for the use of music to be supplied by the department.

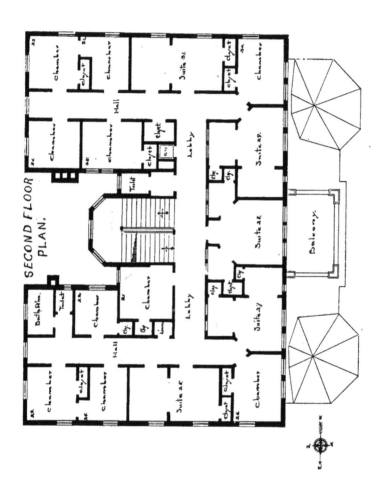

SECOND FLOOR
PLAN.

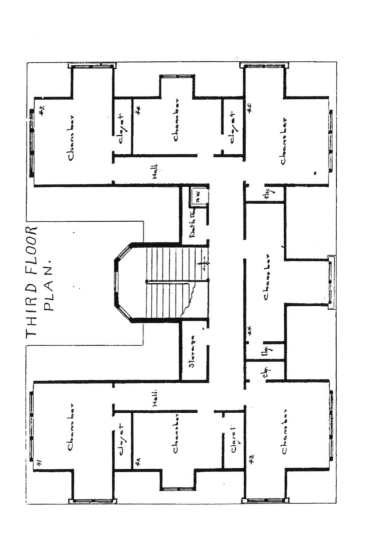

THIRD FLOOR PLAN.

LADIES' HALL

Floor Plans

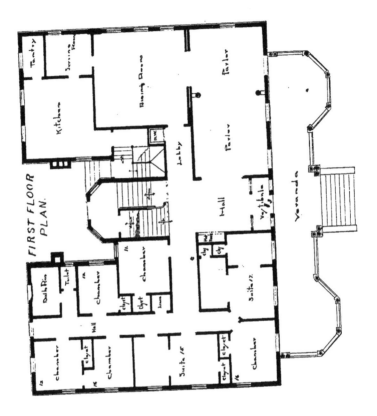

DEPARTMENT OF ART.

PROFESSOR STANSBURY NORSE.
Director.

The college has made arrangements with the well known teacher, artist, author, and lecturer, Stansbury Norse, to have charge of the Department of Art.

He will receive classes and private pupils in free-hand and mechanical drawing, oil painting, and water color painting.

A special normal and training class to fit pupils for teachers in the public schools has been established also.

For further particulars, including terms, send for a circular of the department to Prof. Stansbury Norse, Galesburg, Ill.

DEPARTMENT OF DOMESTIC SCIENCE.

This course is a tentative effórt to teach the student how to directly and practically apply to the problems of the maintenance of the institutions of the home and the family the knowledge acquired in college.

The attempt will be made to present the principles of Sociology, Eugencics, Ethics, Psychology and Economics and kindred sciences in their bearing on the modern Christian home and family.

The sciences of Biology, Botany, Histology, Bacteriology, Physiology, Chemistry and Physics will be related to the construction and hygiene of the house and home.

An effort will be made to hold the courses to a strictly college grade, and if experience warrants they will be added to from time to time, and more definitely co-ordinated until a fully formulated course of study of first importance to future home makers can be offered. It is believed that this department of college work can be made of immense value to our modern world.

Students who desire to take this course will do the prescribed Freshman and Sophomore work belonging practically to all groups of studies.

Elective work belonging specifically to this Department will be under the advice and direction of the teachers of the sciences named above, and will mostly belong to the Junior and Senior years.

At present we are able to offer a year's work of three hours a week in instruction in buying of foods in the market, their preparation and the cooking of all common foods in the best ways.

Instruction will be given in table service, the preparation of a variety of menus, and cooking of food for the sick.

New apparatus has been purchased for this work and an earnest effort will be made to build up a strong department.

STUDENTS IN ALL DEPARTMENTS.

Candidates for Degrees in 1906.

CANDIDATES FOR THE DEGREE OF BACHELOR OF ARTS IN '1906·

Chamberlain, Ethel M.
Conger, Delia C.

Linderholm, Ernest A.

CANDIDATE FOR THE DEGREE OF BACHELOR OF DIVINITY IN 1906.

Hillstren, Charles W.

CANDIDATE FOR A DIPLOMA IN MUSIC IN 1906.

Kough, Evangeline

Students in the Divinity School.

Grimmer, J. Wyatt
Hillstren, Charles W.
Martin, Nelle Ruth

Reel, J. S.
Tanner, William R.

Students in the College of Liberal Arts.

S✚ Adams, Robert I.
Atterberry, Ralph M.
Austin, Ralph C.
Beatty, Dwight C.
Belcher, Roy Swan
Bignall, Roy E.
✚.S Bilsland, Guy Willis
Brown, Talent
Buck, Hiram H.
Burnside, Pearle
Burnside, R. Roy
Chamberlain, Ethel M.
Chamberlain, Ruth

Conger, Delia C.
✚ Cook, Grace
Crellin, Robert R.
Crocker, Edna
Dillow, Florence
Dillow, Ray
✚ Edwards, Forest Glen
Eldridge, Jessie
Evans, Julia
Fay, Irene Margaret
✝ Fennessy, Ethel C.
Fisher, Carolyn S.
Fosher, Cora M.

Gibbs, Minnie C.
Gibbs, Florence E.
Golliday, Theo
Grier, Theo C.
Hagerty, Thomas W.
Harter, William E.
Hoffman, Arthur H.
Hollister, Florence G.
Housh, Carter F.
Housh, Chester C.
Hughes, Walter J.
Justus, Ray W.
Linderholm, Ernest A.
Mabee, Helen M.
Martin, Vella

McDaniel, Levi Berl
Moffitt, Hazel
Newman, Winna Louise
Porter, Fanny
Richey, Frances
Robinson, LeRoy P.
Ross, George L.
Ross, Louise
Ruland, Maude
Stryker, E. Bell
Titus, Murray
Vandenberg, Nellie
Webster, Marion
Weigel, John C.
Williamson, Bessie

Students in the Department of Music.

Adams, Rober
Atterberry, Be
Atterberry, Eula
Atterberry, Ralph
Austin, Ralph C.
Bilsland, Guy W.
Buck, Hiram H.
Bye, Della
Claycomb, Louise
Conger, Ethelin W.
Courtney, Lilian C.
Crellin, Robert R.
Crocker, Edna
Dillow, Ray
Fay, Irene M.
Fisher, Carolyn S.
Goettler, Theophilus
Grimmer, J. Wyatt
Grubb, Ray A.

Harter, William E.
Hazzard, Luthera
Hurd, Caroline F.
Irwin, Mabel J.
Kough, Evangeline
Linderholm, Ernest A.
Newman, Winna Louise
O'Frell, Blenda
Porter, Fanny
Reel, Mrs. Birdie
Reel, J. S.
Rich, Gertrude M.
Robinson, LeRoy P.
Sandburg, Esther
Silver, Vora
Snow, Grace Lewis
Thompson, Aleen
Webster, Marion
Wright, Theodore P.

Students in the Department of Art.

Chalmers, Mrs. G. S.
Chapman, Mrs. Ada
Courtney, Lilian C.
Elder, Alta
Eldridge, Jessie

Fisher, Carolyn S.
Ross, Louise
Ryan, Mabel
Terry, Ruth

Free Art Class.

(Established by Prof. Norse for the benefit of teachers an working women.)

Armstrong, Anna
Armstrong, Henrietta
Armstrong, Nellie
Brainard, Ruth
Branham, Eva
Burkhalter, Euphemia
Chapin, Carrie L.
Davis, Teresa
Estes, Carrie A.
Frey, Clara
Fuller, Cora
Fuller, Emily
Fuller, Mary Edith
Gillespie, Edna F.
Goldquist, L.
Guenther, Caroline
Guenther, Rosa B.
Gustafson, Bertha
Hague, F.
Hammond, E. May
Harris, Eleanor
Hemstreet, Cora G.
Johnson, Linda
Kennedy, Edna
Lapham, Gail
Lewis, Mrs. D.

Lind, Johanna
Lufkin, Mary C.
McLernon, Bernardine
McLernon, Mary
Maley, Adele
Maley, Mary E.
Marble, Mrs. R.
Morse, May Betle
Mathis, S. E.
Munson, Dorothy
Munson, Rosa
Olson, Louise
Peck, Lilian
Phillips, Margaret
Rhodes, Helen G.
Risley, Inez M.
Rowe, Annie
Rusk, Luella
Russell, Grace
Stewart, Maud M.
Stromberg, Mrs. W. M.
Swartwout, Claribel
Ward, Flora A.
Wenquist, Anna C.
Wilbur, Ida E.

Unclassified Students.

Atterberry, Eunice
Claycomb, Louise
Conger, Ethelin W.
Courtney, Lilian C.
Cunningham, Edwin B.
Davidson, George E.
Gallup, Roscoe H.
Gilmore, Harold
Goad, Charles Howard
Golliday, Gail H.

Grubb, Ray A.
Hendel, Mabel I.
Hillstren, Mrs. Augusta S.
Hurd, Caroline F.
✝ Irwin, Mabel J.
MacHale, Lilian E.
Marriott, Victoria D.
Martin, John H.
Metcalf, Roscoe F.
North, Harold E.

Oberholtzer, Ernest E.   Root, Douglas
Reel, Mrs. Birdie   *Seeney, Joe Ellen
Rich, Gertrude M.   .   Thompson, Alleen

*Deceased.

Directory of Teachers and Students.

Adams, Robert I..................Col .... Earlville
Appleman, Prof. Charles O.....................711 Locust Street
Appleman, Mrs. Emma Reeme..................711 Locust Street
Armstrong, Anna ....Art .... Galesburg
Armstrong, Henrietta ....Art .... Galesburg
Armstrong, Nellie .... Art .... Galesburg
Atterberry, Bernice M.............Mus ....Atlanta, Mo.
Atterberrv, Eula Claire ....Mus ....Atlanta, Mo.
Atterberry, Eunice ....Unc ....Atlanta, Mo.
Atterberry, Ralph M...............Col .... Atlanta, Mo.
Austin, Ralph C....:.............Col .... Morrison
Beatty, Dwight C.................Col .... Fairview
Belcher, Roy Swan ....Col .... Galesburg
Bignall, Roy E..................Col .... Marseilles
Bilsland, Guy Willis..............Col .... Cook, Neb.
Brainard, Ruth ....Art .... Galesburg
Branham, Eva ....Art .... Galesburg
Brown, Talent ....Col .... Galesburg
Buck, Hiram H..................Col .... Joliet
Burkhalter, Euphemia ....Art .... Galesburg
Burnside, Pearle ....Col .... Knoxville
Burnside, R. Roy ....Col .... Knoxville
Bye, Della ....Mus .... Kansas City, Mo.
Chalmers, Mrs. G. S..............Art .... Galesburg
Chamberlain, Ethel M.............Col .... Galesburg
Chamberlain, Ruth ....Col .... Galesburg
Chapin, Carrie L..................Art .... Galesburg
Chapman, Mrs. Ada ....Art .... Galesburg
Claycomb, Louise ....Unc .... Sycamore
Conger, Delia C..................Col .... Galesburg
Conger, Etheline W...............Unc .... Galesburg
Cook, Grace ....Col .... Indianapolis, Ind.
Courtney, Lilian C................Unc .... Chicago
Crellin, Robert R.................Col .... Joliet
Crocker, Edna ....Col .... Knoxville
Cunningham, Edwin B.............Unc .... LaPlatte, Mo.

Curtis, Prof. Alice B. ....Ladies' Hall
Davidson, George E. ....Unc .... Bushnell
Davis, Teresa ....Art .... Galesburg
Dillow, Florence ....Col ....Creston, Iowa
Dillow, Ray ....Col ....Creston, Iowa
Dudley, Mrs. H. B. ....66 Division St.
Edwards, Forrest Glen ....Col .... Princeville
Elder, Alta ....Art .... Galesburg
Eldridge, Jessie ....Col .... Knoxville
Estes, Carrie A. ....Art .... Galesburg
Evans, Julia ....Col .... Knoxville
Fay, Irene Margaret ....Col .... Peoria
Fennessey, Ethel C. ....Col .... Avon
Fisher, Carolyn S. ....Col .... Galesburg
Fisher, Pres. Lewis B. ....,......1115 E Knox Street
Fosher, Cora M. ....Col .... Galesburg
Fowler, Prof. Frank H. ....1155 E. Knox Street
Frey, Clara ....Art .... Galesburg
Fuller, Cora ....Art .... Galesburg
Fuller, Emily ....Art .... Galesburg
Fuller, Mary Edith ....Art .... Galesburg
Gallup, Roscoe. H. ....Unc .... Edelstein
Gibbs, Florence E. ....Col .... Danvers, Mass.
Gibbs, Minnie C. ....Col ....Anoka, Minn.
Gillespie, Edna F. ....Art .... Galesburg
Gilmore, Harold ....Unc .... Fairview
Goad, Charles Howard ....Unc .... Blandinsville
Goettler, Theophilus C. ....Mus .... Galesburg
Goldquist, L. ....Art .... Galesburg
Golliday, Gail H. ....Unc .... Galesburg
Golliday, Theo ....Col .... Galesburg
Grier, Theo. C. ....Col .... Racine, Wis.
Grimmer, J. Wyatt ....Div .... Charlton, Ala.
Grubb, Prof. J. W. ....1427 E. Knox Street
Grubb, Ray A. ....Unc .... Hamilton
Guenther, Caroline ....Art .... Galesburg
Guenther, Rosa B. ....Art .... Galesburg
Gustafson, Bertha ....Art .... Galesburg
Hagerty, Thomas W. ....Col .... Wyoming
Hague, F. ....Art .... Galesburg
Hale, Mrs. Adah M. ....Matron Ladies' Hall
Hammond, E. May ....Art .... Galesburg
Harris, Eleanor ....Art .... Galesburg

Harter, William E..................Col .... Racine, Wis.
Hazzard, Luthera ....Mus .... Galesburg
Hein, Hattie R. ....1247 E. Knox Street
Hemstreet, Cora G.................Art .... Galesburg
Hendel, Mabel I.....................Unc .... Colchester
Hillstren, Mrs. Augusa S...........Unc .... Galesburg
Hilstren, Charles W.................Div .... Galesburg
Hoffman, Arthur H................Col .... Knoxville
Hollister, Florence G..............Col .... Rockford
Housh, Carter F....................Col .... Maquon
Housh, Chester C ....Col .... Maquon
Hughes, Walter J..................Col .... Yates City
Hurd, Caroline F..................Unc .... Maquon
Irwin, Mabel J.....................Unc .... Little Rock, Ark.
Johnson, Linda ....Art .... Galesburg
Justus, Ray W.....................Col .... Stockton
Kennedy, Edna ....Art .... Galesburg
Kimble, Prof. Ralph G.........................427 Locust Street
Kough, Evangeline .... Mus .... Davenport, Ia.
Kueffner, Prof. Louise M..........................Ladies' Hall
Lapham, Gail ....Art .... Galesburg
Lewis, Mrs. D.....................Art .... Galesburg
Lind, Johanna ....Art .... Galesburg
Linderholm, Ernest A..............Col .... Altona
Longbrake, Dr. Guy H. (Medical Examiner)...501 E. Losey Street
Lufkin, Mary C.....................Art .... Galesburg
Mabee, Helen M....................Col .... Galesburg
McDaniel, L. B.....................Col .... Barry
MacHale, Lilian E.................Unc .... Galesburg
McLernon, Bernardine ....Art .... Galesburg
McLernon, Mary ....Art .... Galesburg
Maley, Adele ....Art .... Galesburg
Maley, Mary E.....................Art .... Galesburg
Marble, Mrs. R.....................Art .... Galesburg
Marriott, Victoria D..............Unc .... Lamoille
Martin, John H....................Unc .... Leroy
Martin, Nelle Ruth ....Div .... Alexis
Martin, Vella ....Col .... Galesburg
Metcalf, Roscoe F................Unc .... Blandinsville
Moffitt, Hazel ....Col .... Wyoming
Morse, May Belle ....Art .... Galesburg
Mathis, S. E.....................Art .... Galesburg
Munson, Dorothy ....Art .... Galesburg

Munson, Rosa ....Art .... Galesburg
Newman, Winna Louise ....Col .... Elgin
Norse, Prof. Stansbury....................926 Beecher Avenue
North, Harold E.................Unc .... Yates City
Oberholtzer, Ernest E..............Unc .... Williamsfield
O'Frell, Blenda ....Mus .... Galesburg
Olson, Louise ....Art · .... Galesburg
Parker, Prof. Isaac A.....................488 Lombard Street
Peck, Lilian ....Art .... Galesburg
Phillips, Margaret ....Art .... Galesburg
Porter, Fanny ....Col ....De Land
Power, Prof. Frank A........................ Arlington Hotel
Reel, Mrs. Birdie ....Unc .... Galesburg·
Reel, J. S.........................Div .... Galesburg
Reifsnider, Rev. Eds·n........................257 North Street
Rhodes, Helen G................Art .... Galesburg
Rice, Dr. Delia (Medical Examiner).........486 N. Prairie Street
Rich, Dean Frederick W.....................1379 E. Knox Street
Rich, Gertrude M..·...............Unc .... Galesburg
Richey, Frances ....Col .... Galesburg
Risley, Inez M....................Art .... Galesburg
Robinson, LeRoy P...............Col ....Mt. Pleasant, Ia.
Root, Douglas ....Unc .... Chicago
Ross, George L....................Col ....:............ Avon
Ross, Louise ....Col .... Avon
Rowe, Annie ....Art .... Galesburg
Ruland, Maude ....Col .... Knoxville
Russel, Grace ....Art .... Galesburg
Ryan, Mabel ....Art .... Galesburg
Sandburg, Esther ....Mus .... Galesburg
*Seeney, Joe Ellen ....Unc .... Atlanta, Mo.
Silver, Vora ....Mus .... Pendleton, Ind.
Snow, Grace Lewis ....Mus .... Atlanta, Mo.
Stewart, Maude M................Art .... Galesburg
Stromberg, Mrs. W. M............Art .... Galesburg
Stryker, E. Bell...................Col .... Joliet
Swartwout, Claribel .....·.......Art .... Galesburg
Tanner, William R................Div ...... Minneapolis, Minn.
Terry Ruth ....Art ...·......... Galesburg
Thompson, Alleen ....Unc ·............ Colchester
Titus, Murray ....Col .... Batavia, Ohio
Vanderberg, Nellie ....Col .... Kansas City, Mo.
Ward, Flora A....................Art .... Galesburg

Webster, Marion ....Col .... Galesburg
Weigel, John C...................Col .... Joliet
Wenquist, Anna C................Art .... Galesburg
Wilbur, Ida E....................Art ....'. Galesburg
Williamson, Bessie ....Col .... Galesburg
Wright, Prof. Philip G.....................1443 E. Knox Street
Wright, Theodore P.............. Mus .... Galesburg

*Deceased.

GENERAL SUMMARY.

COLLEGE OF LIBERAL ARTS.

Candidates for degrees in 1906
    Bachelor of Arts 3
Students in the College of Liberal Arts.......... 56

UNCLASSIFIED STUDENTS.

Unclassified Students 26

RYDER DIVINITY SCHOOL.

Candidates for degrees in 1906
    Bachelor of Divinity............................. 1
Students in Divinity School............................. 5

MUSIC.

Candidates for Diploma in Music....................... 1
Students in Department of Music....................... 38

ART.

Students in Art... 60

                                          190
Names entered twice..................................... 36
      Total... 154

ASSOCIATION OF GRADUATES.

1905-1906.

OFFICERS.

PRESIDENT,
FRANK H. FOWLER, GALESBURG.

VICE PRESIDENT,
FRANK L. CONGER, GALESBURG.

SECRETARY,
MRS. C. E. HUNTER, GALESBURG.

TREASURER,
JON W. GRUBB, GALESBURG.

HISTORIAN,
GRACE S. HARSH, CRESTON, IOWA.

BOARD OF DIRECTORS.

FRANK H. FOWLER, EX-OFFICIO, R. G. KIMBLE,
NINA HARRIS HUNTER, SEC. W. T. SMITH,
ADAH HASBROOK HALE, J. J. WELSH,
C. A. WEBSTER, J .W. GRUBB,
J. E. WEBSTER.

Graduates.

The degree of A. M. or M. S. placeed immediately after a name, implies that the corresponding Bachelor's degree (A. B. or B. S.) was received on graduation.

The person to whose name a star is attached is deceased. The date following designates the year of his death.

Addresses known to be incorrect are bracketed

1856.

Burson, William Worth, A. M...Manufacturer, 3424 Sheridan Drive, Chicago.
Cole, William Ramey, A. M..............Clergyman, Mt. Pleasant, Iowa.
Hurd, Addie, A. M. (Mrs. W. Van Horn)..917 Sherbrook St., Montreal, Can.
McNeeley, Thompson W., A. M.............Ex-M. C., Attorney, Petersburg.
Miles, Jennie, A. M., *1859................................... Decatur.
Simmons, Lewis Alden, A. M., *1889..................Wellington, Kan.

1857.

Bond, Fielding B., A. B., *1862..............................Greenbush
Brown, Floyd G., A. B., *1868.........................Mankato, Minn.
Chapin, James Henry, A. M., Ph. D., *1892...............Meriden, Conn.
Laning, Edward D., A. B.........................Attorney, Petersburg.
Wike, Scott, B. S., *1901...Barry.

1858.

Clark, Anson L., A. M., M. D. President Bennett Eclectic Medical College
     Chicago.. Elgin.
Gorman, Thomas, A. B., *1891..........................Columbus, Ohio.

1859.

Elwell, George W., B. S., *1869.........................Chillicothe, Mo.
Fuller, Mary Jane, B. S........................Tarpon Springs, Fla.
Hill, Eugene Beauharnais, B. S..............Manufacturer, Ottumwa, Iowa.
Kidder, Almon, A. M........................Attorney, Monmouth.
Miller, Ruth Waldron, M. S., (Mrs. F. F. Brower), *1892..........Wataga.

1860.

Brown, Jonathan Eden, A. B....................Farmer, Peabody, Kan.
Burr, Arick, B. S., 1860......................................Charleston.
Frisbee, William Judah, A. M., *1903..........................Bushnell.
Lindsay, James Scott, A. B., *1860.............................Onarga.
Slater, Albert Sidney, M. S., M. D..............................Wataga.

1861.

Brower, Franklin Fayette, A. M., *1869.........................Ottawa.
Conger, Everett Lorentus, A. M., D. D...........Clergyman, Pasadena, Cal.
Miller, Mary Stewart, A. B., (Mrs. Catlin), *1867.............Vinton, Ia.
Pollock, Henry George, A. M..................Clergyman, Madison, Ind.

1862.

Conger, Edwin Hurd, A. M.............................Pasadena, Cal.
Dow, Samuel Alvus, A. M., M. D......Wyalong, New South Wales, Australia.
Dow, William Sampson, B: S., *1863......................Galesburg.
Fuller, Eugenia Adaline, B. S., (Mrs. J. W. Ranstead) *1905.......Elgin.
Holmes, Charles Allen, A. M..................Attorney, New London, Wis.
Karr, Hamilton Lafayette, A. M.....................Attorney, Osceola, Ia.
Livingston, Frederick Warren, M. S................Teacher, San Diego, Cal.
Rowell, Harvey, A. B.................Solicitor of Patents, Columbus, Wis.
Sherwin, John Crocker, M. S., Ex-M. C., Att'y, [1234 Columbus St., Denver,Col.]
Trego, Alfred Henry, A. M.....................Manufacturer, Hoopeston.
Turner, John George, A. M., M. D., *1899...................Oskaloosa, Ia.

1863.

Biddlecombe, Hanna Jane, M. S.   Bookkeeper Glendale Furnace Co.,
     Columbus, O.
Calhoun, Samuel Addison, A. B..Adv. Solicitor "German Demokrat," Peoria.
Crocker, Oricy Villa, L. A., (Mrs. Nead), *1880.................Galesburg.
Miles, Sarah Jane, A. M., (Mrs. Bullman)...................Galesburg.
Moore, Mary Addie, M. S., (Mrs. Sumner Ellis)...2734 Prairie Ave., Chicago.
Pike, Sarah Jane, L. A., (Mrs. E. H. Conger).............Pasadena, Cal.
Ranstead, John W., B. S.................................Attorney, Elgin.

1864.

Chase, Elmore, B. S............................Teacher, Fair Oaks, Cal.
Greenwood, Leslie, A. M...Auditor Farmers' Loan & Trust Co., Sioux City, Ia.
Pike, Laura Lavina, A. M., (Mrs. J. S. McConnell)..4359 Lake Ave., Chicago.
Raymond, Josephine, A. M., (Antioch College), (Mrs. Maxwell)..Champaign.
Raymond, Sallie, L. A., (Mrs. J. B. Green)....................Ramsey.

1865.

Chapin, Alice Caroline, B. S......Teacher, 140 A. St., Salt Lake City, Utah.
Chase, Elmore, B. S., A. M....................Teacher, Fair Oaks, Cal.
McCormick, John Henry, B. S..........................Caledonia, Mo.

1866.

Claycomb, Elwin Wallace, A. M...................Farmer, Eureka, Kan.
Conger, Emma N. H., A. M., (Mrs. S. W. Conger).......Villa Park, Cal.
McConnell, James Smith, B. S.........Attorney, 84 Washington St., Chicago.
Shook, Geo. R, B. S.................Teacher and Surveyor, Fruita, Colo.

1867.

Bingham, Helen Maria, L. A., M. D.......................Monroe, Wis.
Carlock, William Bryan, B. S.....................Attorney, Bloomington.
Woods, William Harvey, B. S.........................Farmer, [Mendota.]

1868.

Beals, Almeda, L. A., (Mrs. Charles Wickwire), *1904..........Farmington.
Chase, Henry Moses, A. B., *1870...........................Concord, Vt.
Claycomb, Mary J., A. M., (Mrs. J. W. Grubb).................Galesburg.

Edwards, Sarah Elvira, L. A., (Mrs. Otis Jones), *1899..Los Angeles, Cal.
Greenwood, Grace, L. A., (Mrs. E. E. Holroyd), *1898............Chicago.
Kirk, Emeline Elizabeth, L. A., *1881.........................Rockford.
Kirk, Josephine Marian, A. M., (Mrs. Samuel Kerr)) *1879......Chicago.
O'Donnell, James, B. S., *1901..............................Cherokee, Ia.
Pike, Frances Elizabeth, L. A., (Mrs. J. Kirk Keller)..Artist, Paris, France.
Smith, Wellington, B. S., *1870....................................Annawan.
Sparks, Mary Ann, L. A., (Mrs. Frank Milnor).................Litchfield.
Tenney, Florence Adelaine, L. A., (Mrs. John Edwards), *1871..Omaha, Neb.
Walbridge, Edward Keys, B. S.....Loan and Real Estate Agent, Girard, Kan.
Weston, Mary Emeline, L. A., (Mrs. Woodman), *1888......Portland, Me.

1869.

Cooper, Rauseldon, B. S., *1903·.............................Oquawka.
Dunton, Mary Emily, A. M., (Mrs. Samuel Kerr)...............Oak Park.
Greenwood, Ella May, L. A., (Mrs. S. O. Snyder)..............
.........................687 Third St., Salt Lake City, Utah.
Hartman, Mary, L. A., A. M....Teacher in State Normal University, Normal.
Kerr, Samuel, A. M...................Attorney, 189 LaSalle St., Chicago.
Knappenberger, Michael F., B. S., *1902.................Jewel City, Kan.
Knowles, Howard, B. S ....Galesburg.
Talent, Patrick, B. S.....................·...Attorney, Hanford, Cal.
Wiley, John Ewalt, B. S.............................Farmer, Elmwood.

1870

Blood, Jared Perkins, A. B.....................Attorney, Sioux City, Iowa.
Brown, Abraham Miller, A. M.......................Attorney, Galesburg.
Chapin, Mary Ann, L. A., (Mrs. T. T. Perry), *1883.......Girard, Kan.
Chase, Nathaniel Ray, A. M., M. D.......................Newport, R. I.
Crum, Mathias, M. S.......................................Farmer City.
Edwards, Flora Amanda, L. A., (Mrs. J. F. Fargo)......San Antonio, Cal.
Hasbrook, Charles Electus, A. M., LL. B., (Chicago University)....
.................Publisher, Times Building, New York City.
Johnson, Elmer Clifford, B. S....Manufacturer, 36 Main St., Evansville, Ind.
Jones, Otis, B. S.......................................Santa Anna, Cal.
Stockton, Israel Cyrus, M. S..............................·...·.
Clerk, Interior Dept., 1514 New Jersey Ave., N. W., Washington.
Walbridge, John Hill, B. S.................Farmer, West Concord, Vt.

1871.

Brower, Martin Ireneus, A. M.................Attorney, Fullerton, Neb.
Bullock, Ida, L. A., (Mrs. Thatcher)' *1894................Attleboro, Mass.
Fuson, Willis Hardin, A. M., *1884.....................Wa Keeney, Kan.
Greenwood, Frank Tenny, A. B................:...Druggist, Seneca, Kan.
Haight, Hanna Laura, B. S.......................Teacher, Mendota.
Harris, Madison Reynolds, A. B.........Attorney, Reaper Block, Chicago.
Hasbrook,, Adah May, A. M., (Mrs. Willis Hale)............
.............Matron Ladies Hall, Lombard College, Galesburg.
Knowles, Mary, L. A., (Mrs. J. S. Alspaugh)............Washington, Kan.
McConnell, Samuel Parsons, A. B............................
.................Attorney, 135 Bond St., New York, N. Y.
Prindle, Flora Adaline, L. A., (Mrs. A. G. Dow)...............Galesburg.
Stephenson, John DeBolt, B. S., *1872.....................Dexter, Ind.

1872.

Bingham, Alice M., L. A., (Mrs. Copeland. *1904)............Monroe, Wis.
Burford, Mattie Wilburn, L. A., (Mrs. Bates)....Merchant, [Wichita, Kan.]
Chase, Albert Elmore, B. S.....Deputy U. S. Mining Surveyor, Boulder, Col.
Gates, Joseph Albert, A. B., National Military Home, Box 97, Levenworth, Kan.

1873.

Bingham, Ada D., L. A., M. D.............................Monroe, Wis.
Brown, Ellen M., L. A..(Mrs. Salley,) *1883·................Monroe, Wis.
Nelson, Anna L., L. A., (Mrs. W. H. Fuson)................Emporia, Kan.
Richardson, Clara, L. A., (Mrs. G. F. Claycomb)..............
..................·....3927 Woodlawn Park Ave., Seattle, Wash.
Richardson, Sarah A., A. M.........................Lawrence, Kan.
Stevens, Mary M., A. M......................871 East St., Lincoln, Neb.
Stevens, Theodore C., A. M., *1878.......................Lincoln, Neb.

1874.

Albrecht, William, B. S., *1878.......................Tiskilwa.
Brunson, Eugene E., B. S., M. D......................Ganges, Mich.
Clingingsmith, Daniel, B. S.............................Newtown, Kan.
Conger, Irene A., L. A., (Mrs. Courtney) *1891.................Chicago.
Day, William E., B. S., *1905...........................Chicago.
Fletcher, Morris W., B. S., M. D.....................Collierville, Tenn.
Sherman, Belle, B. S...........................Teacher, Ithaca, N. Y.

1875.

Brainard, Carrie W., A. M., B. D., (St. Lawrence)............
....Supt. Knox Co. Free Kindergarten and Children's Home, Galesburg.
Buck, Charles A., L. A..............................Undertaker, Joliet.
Collins, Emma S., L. A., (Mrs. J. E. Buchanan)....Teacher [Lake Forest.]
Conger, Lillie E., L. A., *1870......................................Oneida.
Dinsmore, Lucien J., B. S., A. M..Clergyman, 2155 N. Ashland Ave., Chicago.
Edwards, Genie R., L. A., (Mrs Richard Noteware), *1888..Minneapolis, Minn.
Nash, Charles Edward, A. M., S. T. D., (Tufts)................
......Field Secretary Universalist Church, 30 West St., Boston, Mass.
Nelson, Jennie C., L. A., (Mrs. Nichols)....................St. Charles.
Pryne, Josephine M. J., L. A..............113 Hanover St., Mankato, Minn.
Warner, Luella R., B. S., (Mrs. Frank Hitchcock)..............
..........................Teacher of Painting, Mosca, Colo.

1876.

Fuller, Charlotte M. S.,. (Mrs. S. M. Risley)................Harvard, Neb.
Hale, Stella, L. A..Galesburg.
Hastings, J. L., B. S., *1894.................................Galesburg.
Leighton, Lottie E., B. S., (Mrs. L. J. Dinsmore).............·..
..........................2155 N. Ashland Ave., Chicago.
Parker, Izah T., A. M., *1891............................Banning, Cal.

1877.

Baker, George F. S., A. M., *1891.................⁻..........Goodenow.
Edwards, Clara Z., L. A., (Mrs. J. F. Calhoun)...............
..................1900 Dupont Ave. South, Minneapolis, Minn.

Fuller, Eugenia, A. M.................Principal High School, Riverside, Cal.
Humphrey, Lottie J., B. S., *1879..............................Tipton, Ia.
Maynard, Charles C., A. M......Dentist, 97 South First St., San Jose, Cal.
McCullough, Ella, L. A., (Mrs. J. D. Welsh)...................Galesburg.

1878.

Bostwick, Ozro P., A. B...................Supt. City Schools, Clinton, Ia.
Chapin, Eben H., A. M., B. D., (Tufts) Clergyman...............
..............................18 Maple St., Rockland, Me.
Mariner, Adah M., M. S., (Mrs. Stewart)......................Bushnell.
Ransom, Shirley C., B. S., A. M., 1892...................
..............Supt. of Grounds, Ill. School for Deaf, Jacksonville.

1879.

Grubb, Jon W., M. S...............Professor, Lombard College, Galesburg.
Hale, Charles P., A. M..
......Insurance and Real Estate Agt., 1087 Broadway, Denver, Col.
Myers, Douglas A., B. S........................Real Estate Agent, Peoria.
Webster, Charles A., B. S..........Treasurer, Lombard College, Galesburg.
Webster, J. Edwin, B. S...........................Merchant, Galesburg.

1880.

Devendorf, Mollie B., B. S...Stenographer, 682 N. California Ave., Chicago.
Livingston, Henry S., A. M., *1895...........................Galesburg.
Livingston, William H., A. B.......Real Estate, Insurance and Loans
301 New England Bldg., Kansas City, Mo.
Parker, William A., A. M.....Civil Engineer, U. P. R. R., Kansas City, Mo.
Swigart, Otto H., B. S...............Farmer and Stockman, White Heath.
Townsend, Jennie B., B. S., (Mrs. C. A. Webster).............Galesburg.

1881.

Bailey, Lura D., A. B., (Mrs. G. F. Hughes)...................Yates City.
Hughes, George F., A. B...........................Attorney, Yates City.
Summers, Milo C., M. S........War Department Clerk, Surgeon
....General's Office, 314 Seventh St., Northeast, Washington, D. C.

1882.

Bower, Reuben D., B. S..............Farmer, High River, Alberta, Canada.
Chase, Henry M., A. M.............Loan and Real Estate Agent, Galesburg.
Swart, Lafayette, B. S.......................Farmer, Christiana, Tenn.
West, Elmer H., M. S., *1894.................................Yates City.

1883.

Brewster, Chas. E., A. B............Loan and Real Estate Agent,
......................717 Kenwood Blvd., Minneapolis, Minn.
Carney, James Weston, B. S., B. D. (Tufts)..........Attorney, Galesburg.
Edwards, Fannie M., A. B., (Mrs. C. E. Brewster)......................
....................1770 Emerson Ave., South, Minneapolis, Minn.
Furniss, Lizzie E., B. S., (Mrs. W. J. Moring)............McGehee, Kan.
Jones, Lloyd Z., B. S.............County Surveyor and Farmer, Galva.
Livingston Emma J., L. A., (Mrs. A. T. Wing)............Springfield, Mo.
Miles, John H., B. S............................Manufacturer, Bushnell.
Williams, Elma E., A. M....................5211 Jefferson Ave., Chicago.

1884.

Brewster, Anna M., M. S., (Mrs. E. H. West)...........New. Canton, Mo.
Brunson, Gay M., B. S., M. D., D. D. S..................Dentist, Joliet.
Burt, Lulu M., B. S., (Mrs. W. B. Cravens).................
...............................2401 E. 11th St., Kansas City, Mo.
Edwards, Charles L., B. S., Ph. D., (Leipsic).............. ..
.............Professor of Biology, Trinity College, Hartford, Conn.
Edwards, Jay J., M. S.................Teacher, 118 S. Park Ave., Chicago.
Jones, Frank R., B. S..............Manager Austin Mf'g. Co., Harvey, Ill.

1885.

Carney, Eugene F., B. S., *1887.............................Galesburg.
Conger, Jennie B., A. M., (Mrs. Conger)..1059 E. 34th St., Los Angeles, Cal.
Crum, George B. D.............................Clergyman, Logansport, Ind.
Devore, Alma J., B. S., (Mrs. J. H. Miles)...:...................Bushnell.
Hughes, Lizzie B., B. L., (Mrs. D. Perry)....................Table Grove.
McCarl, Lyman, M. S...... ....Attorney, 304 N. Sixth St., Quincy.
Small, Wallace F., B. D.......................Teacher, Florence, Wash.
Suiter, Ella, B. S., (Mrs. George Pittard) *1894....................Alexis.
Welsh, J. Douglas, B. S.......................County Judge, Galesburg.

1886.

Adamson, Rainie, M. S., (Mrs. W. F. Small).............Florence, Wash.
Brigham, L. Ward, M. S., M. D., B. D., (Canton)....Clergyman
........................578 Bedford Ave., Brooklyn, N. Y.
Davies, John M., M. S.................Teacher, 612 Fifth Street, Maywood.
Dellgren, August, B. D...........Clergyman, 1017 Sheffield Ave., Chicago.
Ebberd, Anna H., B. S., (Mrs. Cyrus Hannum).............Campbell, Neb.
Orelup, Hiram J., B. D.............Clergyman, 1017 Sheffield Ave., Chicago.
Roberts, Alice L., B. S., (Mrs. J. L. Andrew).........[National City, Cal.]
Watkins, Rachel A., M. S., (Mrs. Billings), B. D., 1894.........Diggs, Ark.

1887.

Carpenter, John R., B. D....................Clergyman, Mount Gilead, O.
Colgrove, Osgood G., B. D.......State Supt. of Universalist Church
....Woodstock, O.
Crane, J. W., B. S..Attorney, 908 Guarantee Loan Bldg., Minneapolis, Minn.
Fuller, Perry B., B.........................Real Estate and Loans, Elgin.
Garard, Mary, B. D., (Mrs. I. Rollin Andrews)..................
.....................35th St. and Hawthorne Ave., Omaha, Neb.
Grubb, Ella M., A. M., (Mrs. James Simmons)................Owasso, Mich.
Morris, Henry C., A. M....Attorney, 100 Washington St., Suite 510, Chicago.
Welsh, Jay, M. S..................................Farmer, Williamsfield.
Wing, Alva T., B. S..........................Advertiser, Springfield, Mo.

1888.

Hawley, Peter T., B. S...............................Merchant, Ralston, Iowa.
Jones, Harry H., M. S...................... ....Supt. Oil Wells, Jennings, La.
Lapham, Allen W., M. S., M. D., *1894..........................Victoria.
Shaffer, Elfreda L., B. D., (Mrs. Newport).........Clergyman, Wauponsee.
Taylor, Elmer E., B. S., *1903.......................College Mound, Mo.

1889.

Dutton, George E., M. S..............................Capitalist, Sycamore.
Fowler, Frank H., B. S., Ph. D., (The University of Chicago)......
.........................Professor Lombard College, Galesburg.
Garst, Charles A. C., B. D., *1896·.......................Riverside, Cal.
McConnell, Edward P.. M. S., *1902............................Chicago.
Moore, Allen F., B. S.........................Manufacturer, Monticello.
Rice, Carrie A., B. D...............Clergyman, 6019 Prairie Ave., Chicago.
Smith, William T., M. S.............................Attorney, Galesburg.
Taylor, Elmer E., B. S., A. B., *1903..................College Mound, Mo.
Williams, Vanna R., B. L., (Mrs. W. W. Slaughter)........Brookston, Ind.

1890.

Anderson, Claude N., B. S..........Teacher, State Normal, Kearney, Neb.
Brigham, Bret H., M. S......Insurance, 1819 Chestnut St., Milwaukee, Wis.
Dotter, Thomas E., B. D...............Newspaper publisher, Sullivan, Mo.
Durston, Elizabeth Gaile, M. S., B. O., (Columbus School of Oratory)....
(Mrs. H. F. Simmons).............................Woodhull.
Farlow, Fred, B. S,...........................Stock Dealer, Camp Point.
Fowler, Frank H., B. S., A. B., Ph. D., (The University of Chicago)....
.........................Professor Lombard College, Galesburg.
Harsh, Samuel D., B. S., *1893............................Creston, Iowa.
Ross, Anna E., M. S., M. D., (Mrs. A. Lapham)..................
.............Physician 4256 Langley Ave., Chicago.
Slater, Richard L., B. S., *1894................................Wataga.
Trott, Loring, M. S......................Merchant, Junction City, Kan.
Welsh, James J., B. S.............................Attorney, Galesburg.
Wigle, Lizzie, B. S., (Mrs. C. N. Anderson).................Kearney, Neb.
Wilson, Burtrust T., M. S.......Professor Guadalupe College, Seguin, Texas.
Wiswell, Lillian J., B. L., (Mrs. E. P. McConnell) *1903.........Cameron.

1891.

Case, M. McClelland, M. S......Draughtsman, 198 13th St., Milwaukee, Wis.
Cole, Villa A., B. S., Mrs. M. M. Case)........198 13th St., Milwaukee, Wis.
Donohoe, S. Taylor, M. S....................................Longmont, Colo.
Grubb, Jennie A., B. S., (Mrs. F. H. Fowler)..................Galesburg.
Hill, Robert D., M. S....................Principal of Schools, Colchester.
Rogers, Della M., B. L., (Mrs. Charles Garber)...........Reardan, Wash.
Smith, William Franklin, B. D., *1897..................Whitewater, Wis.
White, Willard J., A. M., M. D...........................Longmont, Colo.

1892.

Allen, Frank N., B. S..........Bookkeeper, 442 E. Forty-fifth St., Chicago.
Beale, Curtis P., M. S.................Principal of Schools, Farragut, Iowa.
Blount, Harry A., B. S.............................Merchant, Macomb.
Brady, Ben F., B. S..................Attorney, 159 LaSalle St., Chicago.
Durston, Alice C., A. M...................................New Windsor.
Elliott, Chas. W., M. S...............................Jeweler, Galesburg.
Marsh, Grace S., B. S...................................Creston, Iowa.
Jones, Benjamin W., Jr., B. D., *1898........................Barre, Vt.
McCollum, Effie K., B. D., (Mrs. B. W. Jones).....Clergyman, Waterloo, Iowa.

Seeley, Lissie, B. S., (Mrs. Leonard Crew)......................Salem, Ia.
Skilling, George W., B. D..................Photographer, Des Moines, Ia.
Wild, Daniel P., M. S.................................Banker, Sycamore.
Wyman, Luther E., B. S...............Broker, 68 Van Buren St., Chicago.

1893.

Anderson, Robert F., A. B......................Farmer, Philipsburg, Kan.
Bradford, F. Louise, B. S...............................Teacher, Quincy.
Brown, Richard, M. S.............................Attorney, Creston, Ia.
Carlton, Kate A., B. S., (Mrs. F. W. Smith).................DeLand, Fla.
Conger, J. Newton, Jr., M. S......................Attorney, Galesburg.
Countryman, Carl C., A. M...................................
........Impersonator and Author, 801 N. Y. Life Bldg., Chicago.
Dickson, States, B. S.............................Attorney, Kewanee.
Fuller, S. Hepsey, M. S., (Mrs. J. M. Earhart..................Wyoming.
Longbrake, Guy A., B. L., M. D....................Physician, Galesburg.
Tompkins, Ethel M., M. A., (Mrs. W. H. Clayberg).................Avon.
Varney, Charles E., B. D.............................Clergyman, Clinton.
Wiswell, Daisy D., M. S., (Mrs. G. A. Franklin)..........Carpentaria, Cal.

1894.

Bernard, Guy Henry, B. S......................Bank Cashier, Glasco, Kan.
Conger, Lucy Minerva, B. S., (Mrs. E. P. May),.............
..................................Riverside Farm, Framingham, Mass.
Crum, Joseph Amos, B. S., M. D............................Oshkosh, Wis.
Crum, Maude Alice, B. S.................................Manchester, Ia.
Curtis, Eliza M., Drake, B. D., (Mrs. J. L. Everton)..Clergyman, Hoopeston.
Dellgren, Rachel C. Watkins, B. D., (Mrs. Billings)............Driggs, Ark.
Durston, Adelphia Gould, B. S., (Mrs. George Ohse)..........Yorkville, Ill.
Everton, Jasper Leroy, B. D.......................Clergyman, Hoopeston.
Garner, Martha Dandridge, (Mrs. L. P. Jones).....Clergyman, Fulton, N. Y.
Gillespie, Henry LaFayette, B. D................Clergyman [St. Louis, Mo.]
Hamand, Elijah Emmett, B. D..............................
..............Clergyman, [1222 Lyden Ave., Kansas City, Mo.]
Menke, Albert Ernest, Ph. D.....................Chemist, Fayetteville, Ark.
Olmstead, Rett E., B. D........................Clergyman, Decorah, Ia.
Schuler, Hans, Ph. D..........................Teacher, Flushing, N. Y.
Smith Albert Prentice, B. S......................Merchant, Denver, Colo.
Tapper, William Richard, A. B........................Attorney, Sycamore.
Titus, Lucy, B. S., (Mrs. R. F. Anderson)...............Philipsburg, Kas.
Titus, Margaret, B. D., (Mrs. R. E. Olmstead)....Clergyman, Decorah, Iowa.

1895.

Bragg, Lucile, A. B...............................Clerk, Humboldt, Kan.
Cheney, Frances Elizabeth, B. D., *1902.........................Greenup.
Chapin, William Robert, B. S., *1905.............Pedro Sula, Honduras.
Conger, Frank Loren, A. B........Cashier, First National Bank, Galesburg.
Conley, Grace Winifred, A. B......................Postal Clerk, Galesburg.
Dow, Mabel, A. B., (Mrs. F. L. Conger)......................Galesburg.
Evans, Orrin Carlton, B. D.......................Clergyman, Litchfield.
Higgins, Robert Pinkney, B. S...............................Champaign.
Jones, Charles Robert, B. D....................Clergyman, Nettleton, Mo.

McDuffie, John, Ph. D....................Teacher, Springfield, Mass.
Rayon, Thomas Francis, B. D.............Clergyman, [Rapid River, Mich.]
Stanley, John Richard, A. B.....................Farmer, Roswell, N. M.
Tompkins, Nellie Christine, A. B., (Mrs. Giles M. Clayberg).........Avon.
Wakefield, Albert Orin, A. B...................Attorney, Sioux City, Iowa.

1896.

Brown, Jessie Beatrice, A. B., (Mrs. A. L. C. Clock),...............
..............................632 Indiana Ave., Winona, Minn.
Camp, Fred Leo, A. B...Galesburg.
Cheney, Almira Lowrey, A. B...................................Saybrook.
Clark, James Alvin, B. D.................Contractor, South Pasadena, Cal.
Cook, Bertha Alice, A. B., (Mrs. O. C. Evans)..............Litchfield, Minn.
Crissey, Elice, A. B..Teacher, Avon.
Gossow, Charles William Edward, B. D............Clergyman, Topeka, Kan.
Harsh, Homer Franklin, A. B.....................Stockman, Lowell, Neb.
Karr, Hamilton Lafayette, Jr., A. B...............Attorney, Murray, Iowa.
Kendall, Marion Alice, A. B...............................Ithaca, N. Y.
Kimble, Ralph Grierson, A. B..........Professor Lombard College, Galesburg.
Lessig, Harry McGee, A. B..........Clerk U. P. R. R. offices, Omaha, Neb.
Linton, Maurice Gilbert, B. D..................Clergyman, Charlotte, Mich.
Myers, Iva Della, A. B...........................Bookkeeper, Galesburg.
Shinn, Edward Leroy, B. D...Merchants Coal Co., 131 State St., Boston, Mass.
Southwick, Eugene, B. D.......................Clergyman, [Corfu, N. Y.]
Stanley, Georgia, Diploma in Art, (Mrs. C. H. Wickham)....Anthony, Kan.
Van Liew, Emma Genevra, A. M. (Mrs. Guy Tuttle)..............Bushnell.
White, Jean Gillette, A. B., (Mrs. A. B. McGill)..................Peoria.

1897.

Anderson, Frank Pierce, A. B........................Teacher, Yates City.
Ashworth, George Hilary, B. D................Clergyman, Hightown, N. J.
Boyd, Loetta Frances, A. B...............................Teacher, Oneida.
Cutter, Flora May, A. B., (Mrs. Arthur C. Boger, Jr.).........Camp Point.
Downs, Benjamin, A. B..................State Senator, Winslow, Arizona.
Harris, Nina Alta, A. B., (Mrs. C. E. Hunter).................Galesburg.
Holcomb, Fred Louis, A. B., M. D......................Caldwaller, Kan.
Lindquist, Theodore, A. B., Professor of Mathematics...............
.......................State Scientific School, Wahpeton, N. D.
Minor, Edward Milton, B. D....................Clergyman, Norwalk, O.
Rogers, George Burr, B. D.........................Banker, Decatur, Mich.
Slaughter, William Willis, B. D., *1901....................Francis, Okla.
Stickney, Carrie Alice, A. B...1006 Washabeh Ave., Colorado Springs, Colo.
Tapper, Elmer Joseph, A. B.................Insurance Solicitor, Riverside.
Taylor, Simeon Lafayette, B. D........Osteopath Physician, Des Moines, Ia.
Warner, Claude Bryant, A. B., A. M......................Dentist, Avon.
Weeks, Guy Henry, A. B.............................Teacher, Galesburg
White, Frances Cora, A. B..............................Longmont, Colo.
Yamaguchi, Fred Minosuke, A. B...Central Tabernacle, Honga, Tokio, Japan.

1898.

Allen, Mervin Wallace, A. B.........................Farmer, Maquon.
Bartlett, Alice Helen, A. B., (Mrs. Murray Bruner)................Aurora.
Brown, Charles Reid, A. B..............Lawyer, 79 Dearborn St., Chicago.
Bullman, Joshua J., A. B...........................Farmer, Galesburg.
Caldwell, Isal, Diploma in Vocal Music, (Mrs. Lewis)...........Knoxville.
Galbreath, Ida, A. B.......................Teacher, Columbia City, Ind.
McDonald, Edna Madison, (Mrs. Bonser), B. D....Clergyman, Cheney, Wash.
Piper, Charles Edward, A. B.............:........6046 Princeton Ave., Chicago.
Slaughter, John Willis, B. D.........Docent, Clark Univ., Worcester, Mass.
Stacey, Benjamin F., B. D., A. B..............................
................Professor Univ. of Arizona, Tuscon, Arizona.
Tandberg, Oluf, B. D.......................Clergyman, Gardiner, Maine.
Taylor, Simeon Lafayette, B. D., A. B..Osteopath Physician, Des Moines, Ia.

1899.

Alsager, Christen Martin, A. B..........Principal City Schools, Winnebago.
Boston, Ella Berry, A. B., (Mrs. J. R. Leib)......................
................1271 West Washington St., Springfield.
Champlain, Lloyd, B. D......................................[Galesburg.]
Crissey, Edith C., Diploma in Instrumental Music...........Teacher, Avon.
Dubee, Henry William, A. B., Professor of German,..............
......................Univ. of Michigan, Ann Arbor, Mich.
Foster, Howard Everett, A. B., *1900..........................Galesburg.
Garvin, Homer Edwin, A. B......Merchant, 123 Union St., Memphis, Tenn.
Gingrich, Fannie Pauline, A. B., (Mrs. Clarence Perrine).......Dexter, Kan.
Holmes, Jennie, Diploma in Art, (Mrs. Frank Overstreet)..........Woodhull.
Longbrake, George Runyon, A. B...................Clergyman, Bryan, O.
MacKay, Helen Jessie, A. B......Society Reporter, *Evening Mail*, Galesburg.
Russell, Nellie Stuart, A. B...........................Teacher, Woodhull.
Townsend, Lora Adelle, A. B.................................Galesburg.

1900.

Arnold, Martha Belle, A. B..........................Teacher, Galesburg.
Buchanan, William David, B. D................Clergyman, Tacoma, Wash.
Bullock, Fay Alexander, A. B.....Advertising Manager, Siegel's Store, N. Y.
Kidder, Gertrude Grace, A. B., (Mrs. Kern)....................Galesburg.
McCullough, Edwin Julius, A. B......................Aberdeen, S. D.
Nash, Carrie Ruth, A. B., (Mrs. Donald P. McAlpine..)....Brooklyn, Mich.
Orton, Charles Wait, B. S......................Gardener, Sumner, Wash.
Shields, Burt G., B. S.......................In U. S. Mint, Denver, Colo.
Steckel, Iva May, A. B.................................Denver, Colo.
Watson, Earl Wolcott, A. B...................Hardware Merchant, Barry.
Weeks, Harry William, A. B........With Geological Survey, St. Louis, Mo.

1901.

Arnold, Martha Belle, A. M...........................Teacher, Galesburg.
Bartlett, John Donnington, A. B......Interne, St. Joseph's Hospital, Chicago.
Bishop, Francis Britton, B. D....................Clergyman, Blue Island.
Buck, Nannie Mer, B. S...............................Teacher, Joliet.
Hartgrove, Gertrude West, A. B.......................Teacher, Galesburg.
Henney, Virginia, Diploma in Music....................Mitchellville, Iowa.

Lombard, Julia Evelyn, A. B..........................East Orange, N. J.
Marriot, Jennie Eliza, A. B., (Mrs. W. D. Buchanan)........Tacoma, Wash.
McAlpine, Donald Palmer, A. B..................Teacher, Brooklyn, Mich.
Nash, Carrie Ruth, A. M., (Mrs. Donald P. McAlpine)......Brooklyn, Mich.
Orton, William J., A. B.........................Gardener, Sumner, Wash.
Pingrey, Grace Olive, A. B...........................Coon Rapids, Iowa.
Preston, Frederick, A. B...............................*.[Boston, Mass.]
Schnur, Grace, A. B......................................,............Adams, Ill.
Weir, Cyrena, Diploma in Music.................501 Union Ave, Litchfield.

1902.

Alspaugh, Charlotte, A. B..............................Washington, Kan.
Andrew, John Jr., A. B .. Med. Student, Univ. of Colorado, Boulder, Colo.
Cranston, Edna Mae, A. B., (Mrs. Mugg)...............Indianapolis, Ind.
Efner, Charles Junius, A. B...................................Galesburg.
Epperson, Edna Ethel, A. B.............................Teacher, Hanover.
Ericson, Henry, A. B..........Graduate student, Univ. of Chicago, Chicago.
Hitchcock, Augusta Eaton, A. B............................Estherville, Ia.
Kimble, Thaddeus Carey, A. B.. ....Physician, Abingdon.
Lauer, Howard Walter, A. B...............................Gulfport, Miss.
Muffler, Emma Annette, A. B.....................................Serena.
Satoh, Kiyoshi, B. D.............................Clergyman, Tokio, Japan.
Smith, Edward Milton, A. B..........................Farmer, Edinburgh.
Stokes, Alice, A. B..Galesburg.
Stoughton, Herbert Leonard, A. B..................Attorney, Osage, Iowa.
Thompson, George Francis, B. D....................Clergyman, Eaton, Ohio.
Varney, Charles E., B. D., A. B.........................Clergyman, Clinton.
Varney, Mecca, B. D., (Mrs. C. E. Varney)...........Clergyman, Clinton.

1903.

Andrew, Mary Maud, A. B................................Teacher, Rio.
Brown, Athol Ray, A. B.............City Editor, *Evening Mail,* Galesburg.
Campbell, Raymond R, B. D..................................Florala, Ala.
Cook, Sarah Lucy, Diploma in Music....................Indianapolis, Ind.
Elting, Grace Helen, Diploma in Music......................Sperry, Ia.
Losher, Dudley Claude, A. B...................Clergyman, Unionville, Mo.
Gillis, Anna Moore, A. B., (Mrs. T. C. Kimble)..................Abingdon.
Hartgrove, Claude Webster, A. B.....................Fireman, Galesburg.
Kienholz, Willis Simon, A. B................................
..........Director of Athletics, Univ. of Colorado, Boulder, Colo.
McCullough, Edwin Julius, A. M.....................[Aberdeen, S. Dak.]
Miller, Ralph Todd, A. B., *1904...............................Galesburg.
Nash, Faith Tenney, Diploma in Music......................
..........Student in Boston Conservatory of Music, Boston, Mass.
Needham, Nellie Jeanette, A. B.....................,..Teacher, Racine, Wis.
Nieveen, S. Martin, B. D.......................Clergyman, Seneca, Kan.
Rees, Jenkins B., A. B...Oneida.
Sommers, Elsie Dorothy, Diploma in Music.................Burlington, Ia.
Willis, Leura, Diploma in Music, *1904......................Table Grove.
Wrigley, Anne Marion, Diploma in Music.......................
..............Teacher of Music, Hanover College, Hanover, O.

1904.

Andreen, Frank G., A. B........Student in Coll. of Phy. and Surg., Chicago.
Ayers, Frank Cope, A. B...............Reporter, *Sentinel*, Milwaukee, Wis.
Cease, Charles H., Diploma in Music....................
................Director of Music, Pike Coll., Bowling Green, Mo.
Cooper, Harry Mae, A. B..............Manager Telephone Exchange, Galva.
Grier, Ethelwyn Sophia, A. B...................Teacher, New London, Wis.
Hopkins, Roy Victor, A. B.............................Teacher, Earlville.
Howell, Spencer Pritchard, A. B......With Geological Survey
.....................5969 Von Versen Ave., St. Louis, Mo.
Hurd, Jay Clinton, A. B................................Farmer, Maquon.
Jansen, Harry Albin, A. B..............With Sears Roebuck & Co., Chicago.
Kimble, Olin Arvin., A. B., A. M..............................
..............Medical Student, Univ. of Mich., Ann Arbor, Mich.
Kober, Florence Leclerc, A. B........................Teacher, Table Grove.
Philbrook, Elizabeth Freeman, A. B.....................Teacher, Sycamore.
Sammons, Mabel Alta, A. B...............................Teacher, Joliet.
Scott, Preston Brown, A. B...................Veterinary Surgeon, Chicago.
Varney, Franklin G., A. B., B. D.....·...........Clergyman, Decatur, Mich.

1905.

Adams, Frank D., B. D................................Clergyman, Avon.
Andrew, William B., B. D............With Telephone Co., Longmont, Colo.
Bartholmew, Jennie L., B. D.....................Clergyman, Table Grove.
Blout, Charles J., A. B................................Teacher, Wataga.
Clark, Fred Andrew, A. B.............With Simpson Lumber Co., Galesburg.
Clay, Walter Timothy, A. B...........................Teacher, Etherley.
Gillis, Hudson McBain, B. S...Student, Coll. Phy. and Surg., St. Louis, Mo.
Grimes, Lloyd O., A. B......................................Omaha, Neb.
Grubb, Emma Welton, A. B...........................Teacher, Hamilton.
Hathaway, M. Agnes, A. B.......................Missionary, Tokio, Japan.
Manning, Stanley, B. D......................Clergyman, Americus, Ga.
Metcalf, Harold, A. B...........Graduate Student, Harvard Univ., Boston.
Nelson Alvira, Diploma in Music, *1905.......................Galesburg.
Phillips, William, B. D.......................Clergyman, Markesan, Wis.
Porter, Gail Quincy, A. B.................Lumber Merchant, Florala, Ala.
Rautenberg, Clare Marie, Diploma in Music.....................
.....................Teacher of Music, Hanover Coll., Hanover, O.
Rich, Willis Horton, B. S....With Marshall Field Wholesale House, Chicago.
Ross, Frances, A. B......................................Teacher, Avon.

HONORARY DEGREES.

The degree placed immediately after the name is the honorary degree conferred by Lombard College.

An additional degree, followed by a date only, is one conferred by Lombard College.

An additional degree, without date, is one conferred by another institution, the name of which is given if known.

1858. *Rev. Otis A. Skinner, D. D........Ex-President Lombard University.
1859. Rev. George S. Weaver, A. M......................Canton, N. Y.
1860. *Ansel Streeter, A. M...............................Weston, Mo.
1862. *Rev. Ebenezer Fisher, D. ....Prin. Theological School, Canton, N. Y.
1862. Rev. Joseph Selmon Dennis, A. M.......................Chicago.
1863. *Rev. William Henry Ryder, D. D.; A. M., (Harvard).......Chicago.
1864. *Rev. Holden R. Nye, A. M..........................Towanda, Pa.
1864. Rev. Charles Woodhouse, A. M., M. D................Rutland, Vt.
1865. Rev. A. G. Hibbard, A. M................................Wheaton.
1865. *Rev. J. G. H. Hartzell, A. M.; D. D. (St. Lawrence)..Detroit, Mich.
1867. *Rev. William Ethan Manley, A. M..................Denver, Colo.
1867. Rev. Thomas B. St. John, A. M.....................................
1868. *Rev. Clement G. Lefevre, D. D...................Milwaukee, Wis.
1868. William B. Powell, A. M......................Washington, D. C.
1868. Rev. James Harvey Tuttle, A. M., D. D..38 W. 53rd St., N. Y. City.
1869. Rev. John Wesley Hanson, A. M., D. D., (Buchtel)....Pasadena, Cal.
1869. Rev. William Wallace Curry, A. M..............Washington, D. C.
1869. *Rev. Daniel Parker Livermore, A. M...............Melrose, Mass.
1869. Rev. Augusta J. Chapin, A. M..........459 W. 144th St., N. Y. City.
1870. Daniel Lovejoy Hurd, A. M.; M. D.................................
1870. *Rev. George Truesdale Flanders, D. D...........Rockport, Mass.
1870. *Rev. Alfred Constantine Barry, D. D................Lodi, Mass.
1872. *Rev. Ethan William Manley, D. D.; A. M.; 1867......Denver, Colo.
1872. *Rev. R. H. Pullman, A. M......................Baltimore, Md.
1872. *Rev. Gamaliel Collins, A. M..............U. S. A., Chatham, Mass.
1872. Rev. B. F. Rogers, A. M......................Fort Atkinson, Wis.
1875. *Rev. J. H. Champin, Ph. D.; A. B., 1857; A. M., 1860..Meriden, Conn.
1876. Rev. George S. Weaver, D. D.; A. M., 1859...........Canton, N. Y.
1876. Rev. John S. Cantwell, D. D.; A. M., 1870...............Chicago.
1877. Rev. O. Cone, D. D..................................Canton, N. Y.
1879. Elias Fraunfelter, Ph. D................................Akron, O.
1879. Milton L. Comstock, Ph. D.......Professor Knox College, Galesburg.
1882. Rev. Charls W. Tomlinson, D. D.................Huntington, L. I.
1883. *Rev. Amos Crum, A. M.........................Webster City, Ia.
1884. *Mathew Andrew, A. M...............................Monmouth.
1886. Rev. L. J. Dinsmore, A. M.; B. S., 1875..2155 N. Ashland Ave., Chicago.
1887. *Rev. Holden R. Nye, D. D.; A. M., 1864..............Towanda, Pa.

*Deceased.

1887. *Rev. Charles Fluhrer, D. D....................Albion, N. Y.
1887. Hon. Lewis E. Payson, LL. D.......................Pontiac.
1887. *Hon George W. Wakefield, A. M................Sioux City, Ia.
1888. Rev. George H. Deere, D. D..................Riverside, Cal.
1888. Homer M. Thomas, A. M., M. D......................Chicago.
1888. Rev. Charles A. Conklin, A. M..................Boston, Mass.
1888. Mary Hartman, A. M., L. A., 1869.....................Normal.
1890. Rev. Jacob Straub, D. D...................Columbia, Cuba.
1890. George B. Harrington, A. M.........................Princeton.
1890. Carl F. Kolbe, Ph. D..............................Akron, O.
1891. *Rev. A. G. Gaines, LL.D., D. D...............Canton, N. Y.
1892. Rev. George Thompson Knight, D. D...........Tufts College, Mass.
1892. Charles Kelsey Gaines, Ph. D..Prof. St. Lawrence Univ., Canton, N. Y.
1802. Shirley C. Ransom, A. M., B. S., 1878...................Abingdon.
1893. Rev. Augusta Chapin, D. D., A. M., 1869..459 W. 144th St., N. Y. City.
1893. *Rev. Amos Crum, D. D., A. M., 1883..........Webster City, Iowa.
1893. John Huston Finley, Ph. D...Pres. Coll. of New York, New York City.
1893. Charles Loring Hutchinson, A. M.......................Chicago.
1894. *Rev. Royal Henry Pullman, D. D., A. M. 1872......Baltimore, Md.
1894. Rev. George B. Stocking, D. D..................Lansing, Mich.
1895. Rev. Aaron Aldrich Thayer, D. D....................California.
1895. Rev. Andrew Jackson Canfield, Ph. D., D. D........Worcester, Mass.
1897. Rev. Daniel Bragg Clayton, D. D.................Columbia, S. C.
1897. Rev. Thomas Sander Gutnrie, D. D...................Muncie, Ind.
1898. Rev. Rodney F. Johonnot, D. D.....................Oak Park.
1898. Henry Priest, Ph. D........Prof. St. Lawrence Univ., Canton, N. Y.
1899. John Wesley Hanson, Jr., A. M......................Chicago.
1900. Rev. Alfred Howitzer Laing, D. D.......................Joliet.
1901. Edwin Hurd Conger, LL. D....................Pasadena, Cal.
1901. John Sharp Cook, D. D...................... Indianapolis, Ind.
1902. Rev. Frederick Clarence Priest, D. D..69½ Washington Blvd., Chicago.

*Deceased.

TIME SCHEDULE.

Figurés in parentheses indicate the number of Recitations per week.

HOUR	FALL TERM	WINTER TERM	SPRING TERM
8:00	(2) English 19 (3) English 22 (5) French 1 (5) German 1 (5) Latin 4 (5) Mathematics 10 (5) Physics 1	(2) English 20 (3) English 23 (5) French 2 (5) German 2 (5) Latin 5 (5) Mathematics 12 (5) Physics 2	(2) English 21 (3) English 24 (5) French 3 (5) German 3 (5) Latin 6 (5) Mathematics 13 (5) Physics 3
9:00	Chapel Assembly	Chapel Assembly	Chapel Assembly
9:30	(5) Chemistry 1 (5) Economics 1 (5) Greek 1 (5) History 12 (5) Latin 1 (5) Sociology 1	(5) Biology 1 (5) Chemistry 2 (5) Economics 2 (5) Greek 2 (5) History 13 (5) Latin 2 (5) Sociology 2	(5) Biology 2 (5) Chemistry 3 (5) Economics 3 (5) Greek 3 (5) History 14 (5) Latin 3 (5) Sociology 3
10:30	(5) Astronomy (2) Elocution 1 (2) English 5 (5) Logic (3) German 7 (1) German 13 (1) German 16 (1) History of Art (3) Latin 9	(5) Biology 3 (5) Biology 6 (2) Elocution 2 (2) English 6 (5) Logic—Ethics (3) German 8 (1) German 14 (1) German 17 (1) History of Art (3) Latin 10	(5) Biology 4 (2) Elocution 3 (2) English 7 (5) Ethics (3) German 9 (1) German 15 (1) German 18 (1) History of Art (3) Latin 12
11:30	(3) German 4 (2) German 19 (3) Greek 7 (3) Latin 13 (4) Mathematics 7 (5) Psychology 1	(3) German 5 (2) German 20 (3) Greek 9 (3) Latin 14 (4) Mathematics 8 (5) Psychology 2	(5) Geology (3) German 6 (2) German 21 (3) Greek 11 (3) Latin 15 (4) Mathematics 9 (5) Psychology 3
1:45	(5) Chemistry 4 (2) Elocution 4 (5) Greek 4	(5) Chemistry 5 (2) Elocution 5 (5) Greek 5 (5) Gk. Exegesis (5) Mineralogy	(5) Chemistry 6 (2) Elocution 6 (5) Greek 6 (5) Gk. Exegesis (5) Mathematics
3:15	Gymnasium Work	Gymnasium Work	Gymnasium Work

INDEX